Technical Writing

Principles, Strategies, and Readings

THIRD EDITION

Diana C. Reep
The University of Akron

Allyn and Bacon
Boston London Toronto Sydney Tokyo Singapore

Vice President, Humanities: Joseph Opiela
Editorial Assistant: Kate Tolini
Marketing Manager: Lisa Kimball
Editorial Production Service: Chestnut Hill Enterprises, Inc.
Composition Buyer: Linda Cox
Manufacturing Buyer: Megan Cochran
Cover Administrator: Linda Knowles

Library of Congress Cataloging-in-Publication Data

Reep, Diana C.
    Technical writing : principles, strategies, and readings / Diana
C. Reep — 3rd ed.
      p.   cm.
    Includes bibliographical references and index.
    ISBN 0–205–26077–2 (pbk.)
    1. English language—Technical English. 2. English language–
–Rhetoric. 3. Technical writing. 4. College readers. I. Title.
PE1475.R44   1996
808′.0666—dc20   96–12470
                                          CIP

Credits

Pages 51–54. "Arthritis (brochure)." Reprinted with permission of the American Academy of Orthopaedic Surgeons, Rosemont, IL.

Page 56. From "Installation Instructions," *Maintenance and Troubleshooting Manual ACS:180.* Reprinted with permission of Ciba Corning Diagnostics Corp.

Credits continue on page 602, which constitutes an extension of the copyright page.

Printed in the United States of America

10 9 8 7 6 5 4   01 00 99 98

For Kim and Trisha

Contents

3   Organization   61

4   Document Design   90

10   Short and Long Reports   269

11   Types of Reports   306

12   Letters and Memos   357

13   Oral Presentations   414

Appendix   Guidelines for Grammar, Punctuation, and Mechanics   428

PART 2: Technical Writing Advice from the Workplace   447

Thematic Contents for Part 2 Readings

Lists

Manuals

Oral Presentations: Audience

Oral Presentations: Delivery

Oral Presentations: Graphic Aids

Oral Presentations: Organization

Oral Presentations: Conferences and Workshops

Proofreading

Revising and Editing

Style

Preface

I have been gratified by the enthusiastic response from instructors and students using *Technical Writing: Principles, Strategies, and Readings.* This textbook is a unique combination of instructional chapters covering standard topics in technical communication; models illustrating a variety of documents and purposes; exercises providing challenging in-class and out-of-class writing assignments; and articles offering advice from professional technical writers for a variety of on-the-job communicating situations. This third edition retains the flexible organization that instructors using this textbook said they prefer, and it can readily be used in conjunction with an instructor's personal teaching materials. *Technical Writing: Principles, Strategies and Readings* is designed for students who study technical writing as part of their career preparation in science, business, engineering, social services, and technical fields.

INSTRUCTIONAL CHAPTERS

The textbook contains 13 chapters of instruction covering the writing process, audience analysis, revision, graphics, organization, definitions, description, instructions and process explanations, correspondence, formal report elements, report types, and oral presentations. For this new edition, the chapters have been revised to reflect changing contemporary technical writing practices:

- In Chapter 1, "Technical Writing on the Job," the description of the writing process now reflects how computers serve on-the-job writers in organizing documents.
- Chapters 2, "Audience," and 13, "Oral Presentations," have been expanded to include discussion about factors that affect clear communication with an international audience.
- Chapter 12, "Letters and Memos," has been revised and expanded to include guidelines for sending documents by e-mail and fax. Also, the coverage of résumé writing now includes guidelines for a résumé format

that accommodates electronic scanning by employers. More sample résumés have been added, including one for someone returning to the workplace after an absence.

- Chapter 9, "Formal Report Elements," has been completely revised to reflect recent changes in APA documentation style, including sample entries for films, television programs, computer software, CD-ROM sources, and on-line data bases.

Chapters include (1) checklists to guide students in planning, drafting, and revising documents; (2) sample outlines for specific document types; (3) models of technical documents; (4) exercises for practice and for developing full original documents; and (5) chapter summaries that highlight major points for students.

MODELS

This third edition includes new model documents representing the variety of technical writing tasks on the job. The numbering system has been revised so that all models in a chapter are numbered sequentially whether they appear within the chapter or at the end.

Several models show successive drafts of a document, so students can analyze changes made during the drafting process. Student models are also included, some in response to exercises in the chapters. All models include commentary that explains the purpose of the document and rhetorical strategies used by the writer. The models are not presented as "perfect" samples; students are encouraged to critique and revise them. Every model is accompanied by discussion questions, and, usually, writing tasks specific to the model or to the type of document under discussion. The writing exercises can be used as in-class practice or for out-of-class assignments.

WRITING ASSIGNMENTS

New writing assignments appear in every chapter. The assignments vary in difficulty and may require students to (1) revise a sample of poor writing; (2) develop a full, original document; (3) read one or more articles in Part 2 and use them in a writing task; (4) prepare an oral presentation; (5) collaborate with other students in drafting a document or making an oral presentation.

APPENDIX

The appendix offers a convenient reference for the fundamentals of grammar, punctuation, and mechanics of style.

READINGS

Part 2 contains 27 short articles by specialists in technical communication subjects. The articles most popular with instructors have been retained, while new readings have been added on the following topics:

- *International Communication*—Two new articles, "Editing for an International Audience," and " 'Big Emerging Markets' Have Diverse Cultures, but Common Attributes," discuss how differences in cultures affect communication.
- *Electronic Communication*—Four new articles, "Voicemail," "Electronic Conferencing," "Teleconferencing," and "Electronic Mail," discuss the technology that is changing communication methods.
- *Collaboration*—A new article, "Ideology and Collaboration in the Classroom and in the Corporation," discusses the ethical problems that can develop as a result of inadequate collaboration within a company.
- *Business Etiquette*—"Business Manners from the '90s" offers tips on handling typical business situations.
- *Document Design*—A new article, "Color: The Newest Tool for Technical Communicators," discusses how color can emphasize information and guide readers through a document.
- *Job Search*—"Preparing Students for the Behavioral Job Interview," discusses a new approach to employment interviews.

The thematic table of contents for Part 2 provides easy access to topics of interest. Also, each chapter includes a list of readings in Part 2 that complement the topics covered in the chapter.

INSTRUCTOR'S MANUAL

The instructor's manual available with this textbook offers suggestions to those instructors who wish to try new approaches with familiar topics and to new instructors who are teaching technical communication for the first time. The manual includes suggestions for course policies, sample syllabi, a directory of document types that appear in the book, chapter-by-chapter teaching suggestions, reading quizzes for each chapter, a list of additional readings, and a list of academic journals that cover research in professional communication.

ACKNOWLEDGMENTS

Many people contributed in various ways to the development of this book. I am grateful for the assistance of people who provided technical writing models and information about on-the-job writing practices: Maggie R. Kohls, Holabird & Root, LLP, Chicago, Illinois; Trisha L. Kohls, The Walt Disney Company, Burbank, California; Sidney Dambrot, Ford Motor Company, Brook Park, Ohio; Jacquelyn Biel, Kompas/Biel Associates, Milwaukee, Wisconsin; Debra Canale, Roadway Express, Inc., Akron, Ohio; Michele A. Oziomek, Lewis Research Center, Cleveland, Ohio; Mary H. Bailey, Construction Specifications Institute, Alexandria, Virginia; Ellen Heib, Reinhart, Boerner, Van Dueren, Norris & Rieselbach, Attorneys at Law, Milwaukee, Wisconsin; Michelle Merritt, Ciba Corning Diagnostics, Oberlin, Ohio; Kristen Sutton, Ciba Corning Diagnostics, Medfield, Massachusetts; Brain S. Fedor, LTV Steel, Cleveland, Ohio; and Michael J. Novachek, Akron, Ohio. Colleagues who offered support and advice include Gerald J. Alred, Thomas Dukes, Patricia Harkin, and Janet Marting. Special thanks to Faye H. Dambrot for all her help and encouragement.

At Allyn and Bacon, Joseph Opiela led this project from the initial idea through this third edition. I want to thank my reviewers, John W. Ferstel, University of Southwestern Louisiana; Michael DiRaimo, Manchester Community College; Anthony J. Cotterell, University of Nevada-Reno; Judith Q. McMullen, Iowa State University; and Carol Franks, Portland State University. My thanks to research assistants Marie Toth-Patten and William Hamilton for library work. Finally, my intense gratitude to Sonia Dial who cheerfully typed, retyped, sorted, and copied multiple drafts of every page.

I am interested in hearing from instructors and students who use this third edition. Please contact me with ideas or comments.

Diana C. Reep
Rldcr@DAX.cc.uakron.edu

PART 1

Technical Writing: Ways of Writing

CHAPTER 1

Technical Writing on the Job

WRITING IN ORGANIZATIONS
Reader/Purpose/Situation
Diversity in Technical Writing

WRITING AS A PROCESS
One Writer's Process
Stages of Writing
    Planning
    Multiple Drafting
    Revising and Editing

WRITING WITH OTHERS
Writing with a Partner
Writing on a Team
    Team Planning
    Team Drafting
    Team Revising and Editing
    Handling Conflict among Writers

Writing for Management Review
Writing with a Technical Editor

WRITING ETHICALLY

CHAPTER SUMMARY

SUPPLEMENTAL READINGS IN PART 2

ENDNOTES

MODELS

EXERCISES

WRITING IN ORGANIZATIONS

No matter what your job is, writing will be important to your work because you will have to communicate your technical knowledge to others, both inside and outside the organization. Consider these situations. An engineer writes an article for a professional engineering journal, describing a project to restructure a city's sewer pipelines. A police officer writes a report for every arrest and incident that occurs on a shift. An artist writes a grant application asking for funds to create a large, postmodern, steel sculpture. A dietitian writes a brochure about choosing foods low in cholesterol for distribution to participants in a weight-control seminar. Anyone who writes about job-related information prepares technical documents that supply information to readers who need it for a specific purpose.

Surveys of people on the job indicate that writing consumes a significant portion of their working time. One study reported that engineers spend 25% of their job-related time writing technical documents and 23% reading technical and business materials.[1] Another study reported that 62.8% of the upper-level managers, 39.3% of the mid-level managers, and 43.5% of the low-level managers surveyed said that written communication was "extremely important" as a management tool.[2] And a survey of people in four different career areas reported that 39.4% in management positions, 22.2% in technical fields, 20.8% in clerical positions, and 31% in social-service occupations said they spend 21% to 40% of their job-related time writing.[3]

Employers want to hire people with communication skills. A survey of personnel directors indicated that written and oral communication skills were two of the top four skills college graduates need to get employment. For successful job performance, the personnel directors ranked written and oral communication in the top three factors, and for entry-level management, written communication skill was ranked number one.[4] Another survey of personnel directors at companies that hire large numbers of new college graduates revealed that 43% were dissatisfied with the writing ability of recent college graduates.[5] It is understandable, therefore, that job advertisements often list communication skills as requirements. A review of one issue of *National Business Employment Weekly* found communication skills required in 85 of 120 job listings. Employers asked for such skills as "ability to write proposals," "able to conduct reviews of company operations and procedures and report findings," and "able to write quality procedures."[6] All these studies indicate that writing is an important element in most careers.

Reader/Purpose/Situation

Three elements to consider in writing any technical documents are reader, purpose, and writing situation. The reader of a technical document seeks information for a specific purpose, and the writer's goal is to design a document that will serve the reader's needs and help the reader understand and use the information efficiently. The writing situation consists of both reader and purpose, as well as such factors as the sponsoring organization's size, budget, ethics, deadlines, policies, competition, and priorities. Consider this example of a writing situation.

Lori Vereen, an occupational therapist, must write a short article about the new Toddler Therapy Program, which she directs, at Children's Hospital. Her article will be in the hospital's monthly newsletter, which is sent to people who have donated funds in the past ten years. Newsletter readers are interested in learning about hospital programs and new medical technology, and many of the readers will donate funds for specific programs. Reading the articles in the newsletter helps them decide how to allocate their donations.

Lori understands her readers' purpose in using the newsletter. She also knows that the hospital's management wants to encourage readers to donate to specific programs (writer's purpose). Although she could include in her article much specialized information about new therapy techniques for children with cerebral palsy, she decides that her readers will be more interested in learning how the children progress through the program and develop the ability to catch a ball or draw a circle. Scientific details about techniques to enhance motor skills will not interest these readers as much, or inspire as many donations, as stories about children needing help will. Lori's writing situation is restricted further by hospital policy (she cannot use patients' names), space (she is limited to 700 words), and time (she has one day to write her article).

Like Lori, you should consider reader, purpose, and situation for every on-the-job writing task you have. These three elements will influence all your decisions about the document's content, organization, and format.

Diversity in Technical Writing

Science and engineering were once considered the only subjects of technical writing, but that limitation no longer applies. All professional fields require technical documents that help readers perform tasks and understand specific tasks. These sentences are from technical documents that provide readers with guidelines for properly completing a specific procedure:

- "Retired employees who permanently change their state of residence must file Form 176-B with the Human Resources Office within 90 days of moving to transfer medical coverage to the regional plant serving their area." (This sentence is from a manufacturing company's employee handbook. Readers are employees who need directions for keeping their company benefit records up to date.)

- "Be sure your coffeemaker is turned OFF and unplugged from the electrical outlet." (This sentence is from a set of instructions packed with a new product. Readers are consumers who want to know how to use and care for their new coffeemaker properly.)

- "The diver must perform a reverse three-and-a-half somersault tuck with a 3.4 degree of difficulty from a 33-ft platform." (This sentence is from the official regulations for a college diving competition. The readers are coaches who need to train their divers to perform the specific dives required for the meet.)

- "For recover installations, pressure-relieving metal vents should be installed at the rate of 1 for every 900 square feet of roof area." (This sentence is from a catalog for roofing products and systems. The readers are architects and engineers who may use these products in a construction project. If they do, they will include the manufacturer's specifications for the products in their own construction design documents.)

Although these sentences involve very different topics, they all represent technical writing because they provide specific information to clearly identified readers who will use the information for a specific purpose.

WRITING AS A PROCESS

The process of writing a technical document includes three general stages—planning, multiple drafting, and revising—but remember, this process is not strictly linear. If you are like most writers, you will revise your decisions about the document many times as you write. You may get an entirely new idea about format or organization while you are drafting, or you may change your mind about appropriate content while you are revising. You probably will also develop a personal writing process that suits your working conditions and preferences. Some writers compose a full draft before tailoring the document to their readers' specific needs; others analyze their readers carefully before gathering any information for the document. No one writing system is appropriate for all writers, and even experienced writers continue to develop new habits and ways of thinking about writing.

One Writer's Process

Margo Keaton is a mechanical engineer who works for a large construction firm in Chicago. Presently, her major project is constructing a retirement community in a Chicago suburb. As the project manager, she meets frequently with the general contractor, subcontractors, and construction foremen. At one meeting with the general contractor and six subcontractors, confusion arises concerning each subcontractor's responsibility for specific construction jobs, including wiring on control motors and fire-safing the wall and floor openings. Because no one appears willing to take the responsibility for the jobs or to accept statements at the meeting as binding, Margo realizes that, as project manager, she will have to determine each subcontractor's precise responsibility.

When she returns to the office she shares with five other engineers, she considers the problem. Responsibility became confused because some subcontractors were having trouble keeping their costs within their initial bids for the construction project. Eliminating some work would ease their financial burden. Then too, no one, including the general contractor, is certain about who has definite responsibilities for the wiring system and for fire-safing the openings. Margo's task is to sort out the information and write a report that will delegate responsibility to the appropriate subcontractors. As Margo thinks about the problem, she realizes that her audience for this report consists of several readers who will each use the report differently. The general contractor needs the information to understand the chain of responsibility, and the subcontractors need the report as an assignment of duties. All the readers will have to accept Margo's report as the final word on the subject.

While analyzing the situation, Margo makes some notes on the problem, the objectives of her report, and the information that should be included. She decides that she needs the original specifications for the project, previous reports, and the original bids. When she calls the design engineer, he offers to send her the original specifications via e-mail. After looking at her notes again, Margo decides that she also needs to find correspondence with the subcontractors to check for records of any changes in the original agreements. She next lists the people she regards as her readers at this point.

The next morning, Margo checks her e-mail and finds the specifications sent by the design engineer. She then calls up her computer files for the project and locates the correspondence with the subcontractors. She finds several progress reports and the minutes of past meetings, but they do not mention the specific responsibilities under dispute. After she checks all her material, she decides to enlarge her list of readers to include the design engineer, whose specifications she intends to quote, and the owner's representative, who attended all the construction meetings and heard the arguments over responsibilities. Although the design engineer and the owner's representative are not directly involved in the argument over construction responsibilities, Margo knows they want to keep up to date on all project matters.

Margo needs to compile and organize relevant information, so she opens two new files—FIRESAFE and WIRING. As she reads through the specifications and her own correspondence files, she selects relevant paragraphs and data and saves them to her clipboard. She then sorts and enters these items in either the FIRESAFE file or the WIRING file.

Margo makes her first decision about organization because she knows that some of her readers will resent any conclusions in her report that assign them more responsibility. The opening summary she usually uses in short reports will not suit this situation. Some of her readers might become angry and stop reading before they reach the explanation based on the specifications. Instead, Margo decides to structure the report so that the documentation and explanation come first, followed by the assignment of responsibilities. She plans to quote extensively from the specifications.

In her opening she will review the misunderstanding and remind her readers why this report is needed. Because the general contractor ultimately has the task of enforcing assignment of responsibilities, she decides to address the report to him and send copies of it to all other parties.

The information in the FIRESAFE and WIRING files is not in any particular order, so Margo prints a hard copy of each file and makes notes about organization in the margins. She groups her information according to specific task, such as wiring the control motors, and puts a code in the margin. All the information about wiring the control motors is coded "B". She also notes in the margins the name of the subcontractor responsible for each task.

Because the original design specification indicated which subcontractor was to do what and yet everyone seems confused, she decides that she should not only quote from the documents, but also paraphrase the quotations to ensure that her readers understand. By the end of the report, she will have assigned responsibility for each task in the project.

When she is fairly confident about her organizational decisions, she reorders the material in the FIRESAFE and WIRING files, adds her marginal notes, such as "put definition here," and prints another hard copy of both files. After making a few more notes in the margins, Margo opens a new file on her computer and begins a full draft of her report, using the information she has gathered but rewriting completely for her readers and purpose. As she writes her draft, she also chooses words carefully because her readers will resent any tone that implies they have been trying to avoid their responsibilities or that they are not intelligent enough to figure out the chain of responsibility for themselves. She writes somewhat quickly because she has already made her major organizational decisions. The report turns out to be longer than she expected because of the need to quote and paraphrase so extensively, but she is convinced that such explanations are crucial to her purpose and her readers' understanding. Looking at her first draft again, she changes her mind about the order of the sections and decides to discuss the least controversial task first to keep her readers as calm as possible for as long as possible.

Her second draft reflects the organization she thinks her readers will find most helpful. Margo's revision at this stage focuses on three major considerations: (1) Is all the quoted material adequately explained? (2) Are there enough quotations to cover every issue and clearly establish who is to do what? (3) Is her language neutral, so no one will think she is biased or dictatorial? She decides that she does have enough quoted material to document each task and that her explanations are clear. Finally, she runs her spell-check and grammar-check programs. The spell-check stops at every proper name, and she reviews her records to ensure she has the correct spelling. The grammar-check stops at the use of passive voice, but Margo wants passive voice in some places to avoid an accusatory tone when she talks about tasks that have not been completed.

Because the situation is controversial, she takes the report to her supervisor and asks him whether he thinks it will settle the issue of job responsibilities. When Margo writes a bid for a construction project, her supervisor always reads the document carefully to be sure that special conditions and costs applying to the project are covered thoroughly. For this report, he assumes Margo has included all the pertinent data. He suggests adding a chart showing division of responsibilities.

Margo agrees and creates a chart to attach to her report. Knowing her spell-check and grammar-check cannot find all errors, she then edits for *surface accuracy*—clear sentence structure and correct grammar and punctuation. She reads the report aloud, so she can hear any problems in sentence structure or word choice. Her edit reveals a dangling modifier and three places where she inadvertently wrote "assign" instead of "assigned." She makes all the corrections, prints a final draft, and gives her report to Kimberly, the secretary, who will make copies and distribute them.

Stages of Writing

Margo Keaton's personal writing process enables her to control her writing tasks even while working at a busy construction company where interruptions occur every few minutes. She relies on notes and lists to keep track of both information and her decisions about a document because she often has to leave the office in the middle of a writing task. Her notes and lists enable her to pick up where she left off when she returns.

Aside from using personal devices for handling the writing process, most writers go through the same three general stages as they develop a document. Remember that all writers do not go through these stages in exactly the same order, and writers often repeat stages as they make new decisions about the content and format of a document.

Planning

In the planning stage, a writer analyzes reader, purpose, and the writing situation; gathers information; and tentatively organizes the document. All these activities may recur many times during the writing.

Analyzing Readers.   No two readers are exactly alike. They differ in knowledge, needs, abilities, attitudes, relation to the situation, their purpose in using the document. All readers are alike, however, in that they need documents that provide information they can understand and use. As a writer, your task is to create a document that will fit the precise needs of your readers. Margo Keaton's readers were all technical people, so she was free to use technical terms without defining them. Because she knew some readers would be upset by her report, she made her first organizational decision—she would not use an opening summary. Detailed strategies for thinking about readers are discussed in Chapter 2. In general, however, consider these questions whenever you analyze readers and your readers' needs:

- Who are my specific readers?
- Why do they need this document?
- How will they use it?
- Do they have a hostile, friendly, or neutral attitude toward the subject?
- What is the level of their technical knowledge about the subject?
- How much do they already know about the subject?
- Do they have preferences for some elements, such as tables, headings, or summaries?

Analyzing Purpose.   A document should accomplish something. Remember that a document actually has two purposes: (1) what the writer wants the reader to know or do and (2) what the reader wants to know or do. The writer of instructions, for example, wants to explain a procedure so that readers can perform it. Readers of instructions want to follow the steps to achieve a specific result. The two purposes obviously are closely related, but they are not identical. Margo Keaton wrote her report to assign responsibilities (writer's purpose), as well as to enable her readers to understand the situation and plan their actions accordingly (reader's purpose). A writer should consider both in planning a document. Furthermore, different readers may have different purposes in using the same document, as Margo Keaton's readers did. In analyzing your document's purpose, you may find it helpful to think first of these general purposes:

> *To instruct*—The writer tells the reader how to do a task and why it should be done. Documents that primarily instruct include training and operator manuals, policy and procedure statements, and consumer instructions. Such documents deal with
> - The purpose of the procedure
> - Steps in performing the procedure
> - Special conditions that affect the procedure
>
> *To record*—The writer sets down the details of an action, decision, plan, or agreement. The primary purpose of minutes, file reports, and laboratory reports is to record events both for those currently interested and for others who may be interested in the future. Such documents deal with
> - Tests or research performed and results
> - Decisions made and responsibilities assigned
> - Actions and their consequences

To inform (for decision making)—The writer supplies information and analyzes data to enable the reader to make a decision. For decision making a reader may use progress reports, performance evaluations, or investigative reports. Such documents deal with

- Specific facts that materially affect the situation
- The influence the facts have on the organization and its goals
- Significant parts of the overall situation

To inform (without decision making)—The writer provides information to readers who need to understand data but do not intend to take any action or make a decision. Technical writing that informs without expectation of action by the reader includes information bulletins, literature reviews, product descriptions, and process explanations. Such documents deal with

- The specific who, what, where, when, why, and how of the subject
- A sequence of events showing cause and effect
- The relationship of the information to the company's interests

To recommend—The writer presents information and suggests a specific action. Documents with recommendation as their purpose include simple proposals, feasibility studies, and recommendation reports. Such documents deal with

- Reasons for the recommendation
- Expected benefits
- Why the recommendation is preferable to another alternative

To persuade—The writer urges the reader to take a specific action or to reach a specific conclusion about an issue. To persuade, the writer must convince the reader that the situation requires action and that the information in the report is relevant and adequate for effective decision making. A report recommending purchase of a specific piece of equipment, for instance, may present a simple cost comparison between two models. However, a report that argues the need to close a plant in one state and open a new one in another state must persuade readers about the practicality of such a move. The writer will have to (1) explain why the facts are relevant to the problem, (2) describe how they were obtained, and (3) answer potential objections to the plan. Documents with a strong persuasive purpose include construction bids, grant applications, technical advertisements, technical news releases, and reports dealing with sensitive topics, such as production changes to reduce acid rain. Such documents emphasize

- The importance or urgency of the situation
- The consequences to the reader or others if a specific action is not taken or a specific position is not supported

- The benefits to the reader and others if a specific action is taken or a specific position is supported

To *interest*—The writer describes information to satisfy a reader's intellectual curiosity. Although all technical writing should satisfy readers' curiosity, writing that has interest as its main purpose includes science articles in popular magazines, brochures, and pamphlets. Such documents deal with

- How the subject affects daily life
- Amusing, startling, or significant events connected to the subject
- Complex information in simplified form for general readers

The general purpose of Margo Keaton's report was to inform her readers about construction responsibilities. Her specific purpose was to delegate responsibilities so that the subcontractors could work efficiently. The readers' specific purpose was to understand their duties. Remember that technical documents have both a general purpose and a specific purpose relative to the writing situation. Remember also that documents generally have multiple purposes because of the specific needs of the readers. For instance, a report that recommends purchasing a particular computer model also must provide enough information about capability and costs so that the reader can make a decision. Such a report also may include information about the equipment's design to interest the reader and may act as a record of costs and capability as of a specific date.

Strategies for analyzing readers' purpose are included in Chapter 2. Consider these questions in determining purpose:

- What action (or decision) do I want my reader to take (or make)?
- How does the reader intend to use this document?
- What effect will this document have on the reader's work?
- Is the reader's primary use of this document to be decision making, performing a task, or understanding information?
- If there are multiple readers, do they all have the same goals? Will they all use the document in the same way?
- Do my purpose and my reader's purpose conflict in any way?

Analyzing the Writing Situation.   No writer on the job works completely alone or with complete freedom. The organization's environment may help or hinder your writing and certainly will influence both your document and your writing process. The organizational environment in which you write includes (1) the roles and authority both you and your readers have in the organization and in the writing situation, (2) the communication atmosphere, that is, whether information is readily available to employees or only to a few top-level managers, (3) preferences for specific documents, formats, or types of information, (4) the organization's relationship with the community, customers, competitors, unions, and government agencies, (5) government regulations controlling both actions and communication about those actions, and (6) trade or professional associations with standards or ethical codes the organization follows. You can fully understand an organization's environment only by working in it, because each is a unique combination of individuals, systems, relationships, goals, and values.

When Margo Keaton analyzed her writing situation, she realized that (1) her readers were hostile to the information she was providing, (2) work on the retirement community could not continue until the subcontractors understood and accepted her information about construction responsibilities, and (3) the delay caused by the dispute among subcontractors jeopardized her own position because she was responsible for finishing the project on time and within budget. Margo's writing situation, therefore, included pressures from readers' attitudes and time constraints. In analyzing your writing situation, consider these questions:

- Is this subject controversial within the organization?

- What authority do my readers have relative to this subject?

- What events created the need for this document?

- What continuing events depend on this document?

- Given the deadline for this document, how much information can be included?

- What influence will this document have on company operations or goals?

- Is this subject under the control of a government agency or specific regulations?

- What external groups are involved in this subject, and why?

- Does custom indicate a specific document for this subject or a particular organization and format for this kind of document?

Gathering Information. Generally, you will have some information when you begin a writing project. Some writers prefer to analyze reader, purpose, and situation and then gather information; others prefer to gather as much information as possible early in the writing process and then decide which items are needed for the readers and purpose. Information in documents should be (1) accurate, (2) relevant to the readers and purpose, and (3) up to date or timely. Margo Keaton's information gathering was focused on existing internal documents because she had to verify past decisions. Many sources of information are available beyond your own knowledge and company documents. Chapter 10 discusses how to find information from outside sources.

Organizing the Information.   As you gather information, you will probably think about how best to organize your document so that your readers can use the information efficiently. As Margo Keaton gathered information for her report, she separated it into major topics in two computer files. She then grouped the information according to specific tasks and made notes about additions. She printed a hard copy of her reordered notes for easy reference before starting her first full draft. General strategies for organizing documents are discussed in Chapter 3. In organizing information, a writer begins with two major considerations: (1) how to group the information into specific topics and (2) how to arrange the information within each topic.

Grouping Information into Topics.   Arranging information into groups requires looking at the subject as a whole and recognizing its parts. Sometimes you know the main topics from the outset because the subject of the document is usually organized in a specific way. In a report of a research experiment, for example, the information would probably group easily into topics, such as research purpose, procedure, specific results, and conclusions. Always consider what groupings will help the reader use the information most effectively. In a report comparing two pieces of equipment, you might group information by such topics as cost, capability, and repair costs to help your reader decide which model to purchase. If you were writing the report for technicians who will maintain the equipment, you might group information by such topics as safety factors, downtime, typical repairs, and maintenance schedules. Consider these questions when grouping information:

- Does the subject matter have obvious segments? For example, a process explanation usually describes a series of distinct stages.

- Do some pieces of information share one major focus? For example, data about equipment purchase price, installation fees, and repair costs might be grouped under the major topic "cost," with subtopics covering initial cost, installation costs, and maintenance costs.

- Does the reader prefer that the same topics appear in a specific type of document? For example, some readers may want "benefits" as a separate section in any report involving recommendations.

Arranging Information within a Topic.   After grouping the information into major topics and subtopics, organize it effectively within each group. Consider these questions:

- Which order will enable the reader to understand the material easily? For example, product descriptions often describe a product from top to bottom or from bottom to top so that readers can visualize the connecting parts.

- Which order will enable the reader to use this document? For example, instructions should present the steps in the order in which the reader will perform them. Many managers involved in decision making want information in descending order of importance so that they can concentrate on major issues first.

- Which order will help the reader accept this document? For example, when Margo Keaton organized her sections, she held back information her readers were not eager to have until the end of the report.

By making a master list of your topics in order or by reorganizing your notes in computer files as Margo Keaton did, you will be able to visualize your document's structure. The master list of facts in order is an *outline*. Although few writers on the job take the time to make a formal outline with Roman numerals or decimal numbering, they usually make some kind of informal outline because the information involved in most documents is too lengthy or complicated to be organized coherently without using a guide. Some writers use lists of the major topics; others prefer more detailed outlines and list every major and minor item. Outlines do not represent final organization decisions. You may reorganize as you write a draft or as you revise, but an outline will help you control a writing task in the midst of on-the-job interruptions. After a break in the writing process, you can continue writing more easily if you have an outline.

Multiple Drafting

Once you have tentatively planned your document, a rough draft is the next step. At this stage, focus on thoroughly developing the information you have gathered, and do not worry about grammar, punctuation, spelling, and fine points of style. Thinking about such matters during drafting will interfere with your decisions about content and organization. Follow your initial plan of organization, and write quickly. When you have a completed draft, then think about revision strategies. A long, complicated document may require many drafts, and most documents except the simplest usually require several drafts. Margo Keaton wrote her first rough draft from beginning to end using the notes she had organized; other writers may compose sections of the document out of order and then put them in order for a full draft. Keep your reader and purpose firmly in mind while you write, because ideas for new information to include or new ways to organize often occur during drafting.

Revising and Editing

Revision takes place throughout the writing process, but particularly after you have begun drafting. Read your draft and rethink these elements:

- *Content*—Do you need more facts? Are your facts relevant for the readers and purpose?

- *Organization*—Have you grouped the information into topics appropriate for your readers? Have you put the details in an order that your readers will find easy to understand and use? Can your readers find the data easily?

- *Headings*—Have you written descriptive headings that will guide your readers to specific information?

- *Openings and closings*—Does your opening establish the document's purpose and introduce the readers to the main topic? Does your closing provide a summary, offer recommendations, or suggest actions appropriate to your readers and purpose?

- *Graphic aids*—Do you have enough graphic aids to help your readers understand the data? Are the graphic aids appropriate for the technical knowledge of your readers?

- *Language*—Have you used language appropriate for your readers? Do you have too much technical jargon? Have you defined terms your readers may not know?

- *Reader usability*—Can your readers understand and use the information effectively? Does the document format help your readers find specific information?

After you are satisfied that you have revised sufficiently for your readers and purpose, edit the document for correct grammar, punctuation, spelling, and company editorial style. For Margo Keaton, revision centered on checking the report's content to be sure that every detail relative to assigning construction responsibilities was included. She also asked her supervisor to read the report to check that the information was clear and that the tone was appropriate for the sensitive issue. Her final editing focused on grammar and punctuation. Remember that no one writes a perfect first draft. Revising and editing are essential for producing effective technical documents.

WRITING WITH OTHERS

Writing on the job usually means collaborating with others. A survey of members of six professional associations, such as the American Institute of Chemists and the American Consulting Engineers Council, found that 87% of those responding said they sometimes wrote in collaboration with others, and 98% said that effective writing was "very important" or "important" to successfully doing their work.[7]

You may informally ask others for advice when you write, or you may write a document with a partner or a team of writers. When writers work together to produce a document, problems often arise beyond the usual questions about content, organization, style, and clarity. Overly harsh criticism of another's work can result in a damaged ego; moreover, frustration can develop among writers when their writing styles and paces clash. In addition to other writers, you may also collaborate with a manager who must approve the final document, or you may work with a technical editor who must prepare the document for publication.

Writing with a Partner

Writing a document with a partner often occurs when two people report research or laboratory tests they have conducted jointly. In other situations, two people may be assigned to a feasibility study or field investigation, and both must write the final report. Sometimes one partner will write the document and the other will read, approve, and sign it. More often, however, the partners will collaborate on the written document, contributing separate sections or writing the sections together. Here is a checklist for writing with a partner:

- Plan the document together so that you both clearly understand the document's reader and purpose.

- Divide the task of gathering information so that neither partner feels overworked.

- Decide who will draft which sections of the document. One partner may be strong in certain topics and may prefer to write those sections.

- Consult informally to clarify points or to change organization and content during the drafting stage.

- Draft the full document together so that you both have the opportunity to suggest major organizational and content changes.

- Edit individually for correctness of grammar, punctuation, usage, and spelling, and then combine results for the final draft. Or if one partner is particularly strong in these matters, that person may handle the final editing alone.

Writing on a Team

In addition to writing alone or with a partner, writers frequently work on technical documents with a group. An advantage to writing with a team is that several people, who may be specialists in different areas, are working on the same problem, and the final document will reflect their combined knowledge and creativity—several heads are better than one. A disadvantage of writing with a group is that conflicts arise among ideas, styles, and working methods—too many cooks in the kitchen. An effective writing team must become a cohesive problem-solving group in which conflict is used productively.

Team Planning

The initial meetings of the writing team are important for creating commitment to the project as well as mutual support. All team writers should feel equally involved in planning the document. Here is a checklist for team planning:

- Select someone to act as a supervisor of the team, call meetings, and organize the agenda. The supervisor also can act as a discussion leader, seeking consensus and making sure that all questions are covered.

- At meetings, select someone to take notes on decisions and assignments. These notes should be distributed to team members as soon as possible.

- Clarify the writing problem so that each team member shares the same understanding of reader and purpose.

- Generate ideas about strategy, format, and content without evaluating them until all possible ideas seem to be on the table. This brainstorming should be freewheeling and noncritical so that members feel confident about offering ideas.

- Discuss and evaluate the various ideas; then narrow the suggestions to those that seem most suitable.

- Arrive at a group agreement on overall strategy, format, and content for the document.

- Organize a tentative outline for the major sections of the document so that individual writers understand the shape and boundaries of the sections they will write.

- Divide the tasks of collecting information and drafting sections among individual writers.

- Schedule meetings for checking progress, discussing content, and evaluating rough drafts. Frequent meetings help team members stay committed to the goals of the project and the efforts of each individual.

- Schedule deadlines for completing rough drafts.

Team Drafting

Meetings to work on the full document generally focus on the drafts from individual writers. Team members can critique the drafts and offer revision suggestions. At these meetings, the group also may decide to revise the outline, add or omit content, and further refine the format. Here is a checklist for team drafting:

- Be open to suggestions for changes in any area. No previous decision is carved in stone; the drafting meetings should be sessions that accommodate revision.

- Encourage each team member to offer revision suggestions at these meetings. Major changes in organization and content are easier to incorporate in the drafting stage than in the final editing stage.

- Ask questions to clarify any points that seem murky.

- Assign someone (usually the supervisor) to coordinate the full draft and, if needed, send it for review to people not on the team, such as technicians, marketing planners, lawyers, and upper-level management.

- Schedule meetings for revising and editing the full draft.

Team Revising and Editing

The meetings for revising and editing should focus on whether the document achieves its purpose. This stage includes final changes in organization or content as well as editing for accuracy. Here is a checklist for revising and editing:

- Evaluate comments from outside reviewers and incorporate their suggestions or demands.

- Assign any needed revisions to individual writers.

- Assign one person to evaluate how well the format, organization, and content fit the document's reader and purpose.

- Check that the technical level of content and language is appropriate for the audience.

- Decide how to handle checking grammar, punctuation, and spelling in the final draft. One writer who is strong in these areas might volunteer to take on this editing.

Handling Conflict among Writers

Even when writers work well together, some conflict during a project is inevitable; however, conflict can stimulate effort and creativity. Remember these strategies for turning conflict into productive problem solving:

- Discuss all disagreements in person rather than through memos or third parties.

- Assume that others are acting in good faith and are as interested as you in the success of the project.

- Avoid feeling that all conflict is a personal challenge to your skills and judgment.

- Listen carefully to what others say; do not interrupt them before they make their points.

- Paraphrase the comments of other people to make sure you understand their meaning.

- Solicit ideas for resolving conflicts from all team members.

- Acknowledge points on which you can agree.

- Discuss issues as if a solution or compromise is possible instead of trying to prove other people wrong.

By keeping the communication channels open, you can eliminate conflict and develop a document that satisfies the goals of the writing team.

Writing for Management Review

The procedure called *management review*—in which a writer composes a document that must be approved and perhaps signed by a manager—holds special problems. First, management review almost inevitably involves criticism from a writer's superior. Second, the difference in company rank between manager and writer makes it difficult for the two to think of themselves as partners. Finally, the writer often feels responsible for the real work of producing the document, while the manager is free to cast slings and arrows at it without having struggled through the writing process. Management review works best when writers feel that they share in making the decisions instead of merely taking orders as they draft and redraft a document. Here are guidelines for both writers and managers who want a productive management review:

- Hold meetings in a quiet workplace where the manager will not be interrupted with administrative problems.

- Discuss the writing project from the beginning so that you both agree on purpose, reader, and expected content.

- Review the outline together before the first draft. Changes made at this point are less frustrating than changes made after sections are in draft.

- As the project progresses, meet periodically to review draft sections and discuss needed changes.

- Be certain that meetings do not end before you both agree on the goals of the next revision and the strategies for changes.

The manager involved in a management review of a document is ultimately responsible for guiding the project. In some cases, the manager is the person who decides what to write and to whom. In other situations, the manager's primary aim is to direct the writer in developing the final document's content, organization, and format. Here are guidelines for a manager who wants a successful management review:

- Criticize the problem, not the person.

- Avoid criticism without specifics. To say, "This report isn't any good," without pinpointing specific problems will not help the writer revise.

- Criticize the project in private meetings with the writer; do not discuss the review process publicly.

- Analyze the situation with the writer rather than dictate solutions or do all the critiquing yourself.

- Project an objective, calm frame of mind for review meetings.

- Concentrate on problem solving rather than on the writer's "failure."

- Have clear-cut reasons for requesting changes, and explain them to the writer. Avoid changes made for the sake of change.

- If the standard company format does not fit the specific document very well, encourage the writer to explore new formats.

- Seek outside reviewers for technical content or document design before a final draft.

- Listen to the writer's ideas and be flexible in discussing writing problems.

- Begin the review meetings by going over the successful parts of the document.

Most managers dislike having to give criticism, but subordinates dislike even more having to accept it. Dwelling on the criticism itself will interfere with the writing process. Here are guidelines for a writer involved in a management review:

- Concentrate on the issues that need to be solved, not on your personal attachment to the document.

- Accept the manager's criticism as guidance toward creating an improved document rather than as an attack on you.

- Remember that every document can be improved; keep your ego out of the review process.

- Ask questions to clarify your understanding of the criticism. Until you know exactly what is needed, you cannot adequately revise.

Writing with a Technical Editor

A writer of technical documents may also work with a technical editor during the review. Documents with a large and diverse audience, such as policy and procedures manuals or consumer booklets, usually require a technical editor. The editor may work with the writer in the development stage to (1) help plan the content and organization, (2) clarify the purpose and audience, and (3) anticipate difficulties in format and production or spot potential legal problems. In some cases, the editor may not see the document until it has gone through several drafts and technical reviews. If the schedule permits, the editor should begin work before the final technical review to avoid last-minute conflicts between necessary changes and pending deadlines.

The writer should present a draft that is accurate and free of errors in grammar, punctuation, and spelling. The editor will review several areas. First, the editor will review the document's structure, ensure that graphic aids are placed appropriately, and check for consistent terminology throughout the sections. Second, the editor will mark the draft for clarity; revise sentences that seem overly long, garbled, ambiguous, or awkward; and review word choice. Third, the editor will check punctuation, grammar, mechanics, and spelling. Last, the editor will mark for standard company style. Both the editor and writer need to think of themselves as a team rather than as adversaries. Here are some guidelines for writers and editors working together:

- Prepare for editorial conferences. The writer should receive the editor's marked copy before a scheduled conference, so the writer can review changes and comments and prepare for the meeting.

- Discuss how editorial changes clarify the document's meaning or serve the reader's purpose rather than focusing on personal preferences in style or format.

- Do not try to cover all editorial matters for a long document in one editorial conference. Schedule separate meetings for format, content, grammar and mechanics, organization, and consistency.

- Check to ensure that editorial changes do not alter the document's meaning or appropriate tone.

- Be open-minded and flexible. Listen to each other's ideas and ask each other questions about purpose, audience, strategy, and content.

After each editorial conference, the writer incorporates the agreed-upon changes. The editor will review the production checklist to be sure the final draft is complete, correct, and properly formatted. The editor is responsible for overseeing the production process. Remember, the editor and writer have a common goal—to produce a document that serves its readers efficiently.

WRITING ETHICALLY

Ethics is a broad term that refers to a set of moral principles. These principles vary according to someone's culture, religion, and personal values. Many companies now have a written corporate code of ethics that includes statements outlining the company's goals and its responsibilities to customers, employees, dealers, stockholders, and others.

In producing technical documents, writers who want to behave ethically should consider how their communication choices affect readers, the company, and other writers on the project. Review the following when writing a document:

- Have you included enough information to avoid harming the reader or damaging equipment?

- Have you warned readers of all possible hazards in specific terms?

- Have you presented comparable facts (e.g., sales figures) similarly to avoid manipulating the reader's understanding?

- Are your facts accurate and do your graphics present data without distortion or bias?

- Have you differentiated clearly between fact and opinion?

- Have you checked for potentially misleading word choice, such as "minor leak," referring to a flow that could cause serious damage if left unchecked?

- Are your research sources reliable and appropriate for an unbiased presentation of data?

- Is your information presented in a context that helps readers understand the implications of the facts?

- Have you tested the document for usability, or, if no interaction with the reader is possible, have you anticipated the reader's needs?

- Have you included any potentially libelous statements or misrepresentations that could cause the company to lose its reputation or that could result in lawsuits?

- Have you used confidential or classified company information inappropriately in the document?

- Have you been receptive to other writers' suggestions for the document and worked with them in a cooperative spirit?

As a writer, consider the ethical aspects of a document from the perspectives of both those who provide information and those who use it.

CHAPTER SUMMARY

This chapter discusses the importance of writing on the job, the writing process, and writing with others. Remember:

- Writing is important in most jobs and often takes a significant portion of job-related time.

- Technical writing covers many subjects in diverse fields, and every writing task involves analyzing reader, purpose, and writing situation.

- Each writer develops a personal writing process that includes the general stages of planning, multiple drafting, and revising and editing.

- The planning stage of the writing process includes analyzing reader, purpose, and writing situation; gathering information; and organizing the document.

- The multiple drafting stage of the writing process involves developing a full document and redrafting as writers rethink their original planning.

- The revising and editing stage of the writing process includes revising the document's content and organization, and editing for grammar, punctuation, spelling, and company style.

- Writing on the job often requires collaborating with others by writing with a partner, writing on a team, writing for management review, or writing with a technical editor.

- Conflict among writers working together can be productive if writers concentrate on the project and exchange ideas freely.

- A writer should consider the ethical implications in the content and format of every technical document.

SUPPLEMENTAL READINGS IN PART 2

Buehler, M. F. "Defining Terms in Technical Editing: The Levels of Edit as a Model," *Technical Communication*, p. 486.

Kirtz, M. K., and Reep, D. C. "A Survey of the Frequency, Types and Importance of Writing Tasks in Four Career Areas," *The Bulletin of the Association for Business Communication*, p. 522.

Porter, J. E. "Ideology and Collaboration in the Classroom and in the Corporation," *The Bulletin of the Association for Business Communication*, p. 543.

Wicclair, M. R. and Farkas, D. K. "Ethical Reasoning in Technical Communication: A Practical Framework," *Technical Communication*, p. 581.

ENDNOTES

1. Charlene M. Spretnak, "A Survey of the Frequency and Importance of Technical Communication in an Engineering Career," *The Technical Writing Teacher* 9.3 (Spring 1982): 133–136.

2. Marie E. Flatley, "A Comparative Analysis of the Written Communication of Managers at Various Organizational Levels in the Private Business Sector," *Journal of Business Communication* 19.3 (Summer 1982):35–49.

3. Mary K. Kirtz and Diana C. Reep, "A Survey of the Frequency, Types and Importance of Writing Tasks in Four Career Areas," *The Bulletin of the Association for Business Communication* 53.4 (December 1990):3–4.

4. Dan B. Curtis, Jerry L. Winsor, and Ronald D. Stephens, "National Preferences in Business and Communication Education," *Communication Education* 38.1 (January 1989): 6–14.

5. Leslie J. Davison, James M. Brown, and Mark L. Davison, "Employer Satisfaction Ratings of Recent Business Graduates," *Human Resource Development Quarterly* 4.4 (Winter 1993):391–399.

6. Vanessa Dean Arnold, "The Communication Competencies Listed in Job Descriptions," *The Bulletin of the Association for Business Communication* 55.2 (June 1992):15–17.

7. Andrea Lunsford and Lisa Ede, "Why Write . . . Together: A Research Update," *Rhetoric Review* 5.1 (Fall 1986):71–81.

This model shows a writer's first two outlines for an administrative bulletin at a manufacturing company. Because the company has defense contracts, many written and visual materials include classified information that must be coded according to Department of Defense regulations. The company administrative bulletin will describe the correct procedures for marking classified materials. Readers are the six clerks who work in the Security Department and are responsible for marking the materials correctly. The clerks are accustomed to following company guidelines in administrative bulletins.

The writer begins planning the document by scanning the Department of Defense regulations and noting those that apply to his company. He then lists these items and makes his first outline.

After talking to several Security Department clerks about the kinds of classified materials they handle and their preferences for written guidelines in the company bulletins, the writer expands and rearranges his first list.

In his second list, he adds specific detail to each item. Based on his discussions with the clerks, he now lists the most common classified materials first and the least common last, He also records two special items that he must explain in the bulletin—materials that cannot be classified in the usual manner and documents that include paragraphs classified at different levels.

Discussion

1. Assume you are the writer in this situation. Discuss what kinds of information you would want to have about your readers and about how they intend to use the bulletin.

2. In his second list, the writer includes more detail under each item. Identify the types of information he added to his list. Discuss why he probably chose to draft a second list at this stage rather than write his first full draft of the bulletin.

3. After talking to the clerks, the writer rearranged items in his second list according to how frequently they appear. Discuss what other principle he appears to be using in grouping his items.

MARKING CLASSIFIED INFORMATION
- BOOKS, PAMPHLETS, BOUND DOCS
- CORRESPONDENCE + NONBOUND DOCS
- ARTWORK
- PHOTOS, FILM, MICROFILM
- LETTERS OF TRANSMITTAL
- SOUND TAPES
- MESSAGES
- UNMARKABLE MATERIAL
- CHARTS, TRACINGS, DRAWINGS

AUTHORITY FOR CLASSIFYING
- CONTRACTING AGENCY

CLASSIFIED - ALL INFO CONNECTED TO PROJECT

OTHER INFO - COMPANY MAY CLASSIFY -
REGIONAL OFFICE REVIEWS

MARKING PARAGRAPHS FOR DIFFERENT CLAS-
SIFICATIONS
- PREFERRED
- OR STATEMENT ON FRONT
- OR ATTACH CLASSIFICATION GUIDE FOR
CONTENT

NOTE: MATERIAL IN PRODUCTION
- EMPLOYEES NOTIFIED OF CLASSIFI-
CATION

First Outline

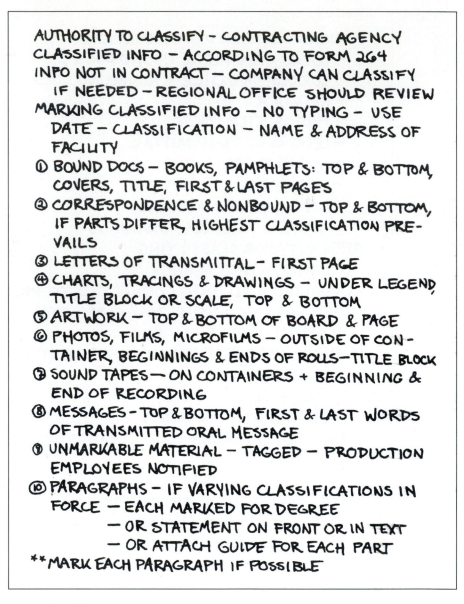

AUTHORITY TO CLASSIFY – CONTRACTING AGENCY
CLASSIFIED INFO – ACCORDING TO FORM 264
INFO NOT IN CONTRACT – COMPANY CAN CLASSIFY
   IF NEEDED – REGIONAL OFFICE SHOULD REVIEW
MARKING CLASSIFIED INFO – NO TYPING – USE
   DATE – CLASSIFICATION – NAME & ADDRESS OF
   FACILITY
① BOUND DOCS – BOOKS, PAMPHLETS: TOP & BOTTOM,
   COVERS, TITLE, FIRST & LAST PAGES
② CORRESPONDENCE & NONBOUND – TOP & BOTTOM,
   IF PARTS DIFFER, HIGHEST CLASSIFICATION PRE-
   VAILS
③ LETTERS OF TRANSMITTAL – FIRST PAGE
④ CHARTS, TRACINGS & DRAWINGS – UNDER LEGEND,
   TITLE BLOCK OR SCALE, TOP & BOTTOM
⑤ ARTWORK – TOP & BOTTOM OF BOARD & PAGE
⑥ PHOTOS, FILMS, MICROFILMS – OUTSIDE OF CON-
   TAINER, BEGINNINGS & ENDS OF ROLLS – TITLE BLOCK
⑦ SOUND TAPES – ON CONTAINERS + BEGINNING &
   END OF RECORDING
⑧ MESSAGES – TOP & BOTTOM, FIRST & LAST WORDS
   OF TRANSMITTED ORAL MESSAGE
⑨ UNMARKABLE MATERIAL – TAGGED – PRODUCTION
   EMPLOYEES NOTIFIED
⑩ PARAGRAPHS – IF VARYING CLASSIFICATIONS IN
   FORCE – EACH MARKED FOR DEGREE
           – OR STATEMENT ON FRONT OR IN TEXT
           – OR ATTACH GUIDE FOR EACH PART
 **MARK EACH PARAGRAPH IF POSSIBLE

Second Outline

This model shows the first two drafts of the administrative bulletin. The writer's first draft is based on his expanded outline, and he follows company style guidelines by numbering items and giving the bulletin a title and number. He also capitalizes "company" wherever it appears. He develops each point from his second outline into full, detailed sentences, including instructions for each item and special considerations for specific items.

Before writing his second draft, the writer asks the senior clerk to read his first version and suggest changes. The writer then revises based on her comments.

In the second draft, the writer uses a headline that clarifies the purpose of the bulletin and includes headings in the document to separate groups of information. In addition to numbering the classified materials, the writer underlines key words that identify each item.

Item 10 in the first draft becomes a separate section in the second draft because the senior clerk noticed that the information about marking paragraphs applies to all written material.

Discussion

1. Discuss the changes in format and headings the writer made from his first to his second draft. Why will these changes be helpful to the readers?

2. In his discussion with the clerks, the writer learned that they prefer to divide their work so that each handles only specific types of classified materials. Discuss further changes in format and organization that might help the clerks use the bulletin efficiently For instance, what changes would help a clerk who worked only with items 1, 2, and 3?

3. Compare the first draft and second draft as if you were a clerk who must mark a 20-page booklet in which the sections have different classifications. Discuss how the organization changes will help you find the information you need.

Military Security Guide—Bulletin 62A

The contracting federal agency shall have the authority for classifying any information generated by the Company. All information developed or generated by the Company while performing a classified contract will be classified in accordance with the specifications on the "Contract Security Classification Specification," Form 264. Information generated by the Company shall not be classified unless it is related to work on classified contracts; however, the facility management can classify any information if it is believed necessary to safeguard that information in the national interest. Moreover, the information classified by Company management should be immediately reviewed by the regional security office.

MARKING CLASSIFIED INFORMATION AND MATERIAL

All classified information and material must be marked (not typed) with the proper classification, date of origin, and the name and address of the facility responsible for its preparation.

1. Bound Documents, Books, and Pamphlets shall be marked with the assigned classification at the top and bottom on the front and back covers, the title page, and first and last pages.

2. Correspondence and Documents Not Bound shall be marked on the top and bottom of each page. When the separate components of a document, such as sections, etc., have different classifications, the overall classification is the highest one for any section. Mark sections individually also.

3. Letters of Transmittal shall be marked on the first page according to the highest classification of any component. A notation may be made that, upon removal of classified material, the letter of transmittal may be downgraded or declassified.

4. Charts, Drawings, and Tracings shall be marked under the legend, title block, or scale and at the top and bottom of each page.

5. Artwork shall be marked on the top and bottom margins of the mounting board and on all overlays and cover sheets.

6. Photographs, Films, and Microfilms shall be marked on the outside of the container. In addition, motion picture films shall be marked at the beginning and end of each roll and in the title block.

First Draft

7. Sound tapes shall be marked on their containers and an announcement made at the beginning and end of the recording.

8. Messages, such as telegrams, sent electronically shall have the classification marking at the top and bottom of each page. In addition, the first and last word of the message shall be the classification.

9. Classified Material that cannot be marked shall be tagged with the classification and other markings. Material still in production that cannot be tagged requires that all employees be notified of the proper classification.

10. Paragraphs in documents, bound or nonbound, which are of different classifications, shall be marked to show the degree of classification, if any, of the information contained therein. Or a statement on the front of the document or in the text shall identify the parts of the document that are classified and to what degree. Or an appropriate classification guide shall be attached to cover the classified contents of the document. Marking paragraphs individually is the preferred method. Neither of the other two alternatives may be used until it is determined that paragraph marking is not possible.

Military Security Guide—Bulletin 62A

MARKING CLASSIFIED INFORMATION AND MATERIAL

Authority

The contracting federal agency shall have the authority for classifying any information generated by the Company. All information developed or generated by the Company while performing a classified contract will be classified in accordance with the specifications on the "Contract Security Classification Specification," Form 264. Information generated by the Company shall not be classified unless it is related to work on classified contracts; however, management can classify any information that may affect the national interest. The information classified by Company management should be immediately reviewed by the regional security office.

Required Marking

All classified information and material must be marked (not typed) with (1) the proper classification, (2) date of origin, and (3) the name and address of the facility responsible for its preparation.

Types of Information and Material

1. Bound Documents, Books, and Pamphlets shall be marked with the assigned classification at the top and bottom on the front and back covers, the title page, and first and last pages.

2. Correspondence and Documents Not Bound shall be marked on the top and bottom of each page. If the components of a document, such as sections or chapters, have different classifications, the overall classification is the highest one for any section. Individual sections shall be marked also.

3. Letters of Transmittal shall be marked on the first page according to the highest classification of any component. A notation may be made that, upon removal of classified material, the letter of transmittal may be downgraded or declassified.

4. Charts, Drawings, and Tracings shall be marked under the legend, title block, or scale and at the top and bottom of each page.

Second Draft

5. Artwork shall be marked on the top and bottom margins of the mounting board and on all overlays and cover sheets.

6. Photographs, Films, and Microfilms shall be marked on the outside of the container. In addition, motion picture films shall be marked at the beginning and end of each roll and in the title block.

7. Sound Tapes shall be marked on their containers and an announcement made at the beginning and end of the recording.

8. Electronic Messages, such as telegrams, shall have the classification marking at the top and bottom of each page. In addition, the first and last word of the message shall be the classification.

9. Classified Material that cannot be marked shall be tagged with the classification and other markings. All employees shall be notified of the proper classification for material still in production that cannot be tagged.

Individual Paragraphs

Paragraphs of documents, bound or nonbound, which are of different classifications, shall be marked to show the degree of classification. Material shall be marked in one of three ways:

- Individual paragraphs shall be marked separately.

- A statement on the front of the document or in the text shall identify the parts of the document that are classified and to what degree.

- An appropriate classification guide shall be attached to provide the classifications of each part of the document.

Marking paragraphs individually is the preferred method. Neither of the other two alternatives may be used until facility management determines that paragraph marking is not possible.

Chapter 1   Exercises

1. Read "Ethical Reasoning in Technical Communication: A Practical Framework" by Wicclair and Farkas in Part 2. In groups, discuss Case 3 described in the article. Assume your group represents the technical writer's friend at another government agency, and draft a memo advising the writer how to handle the ethical dilemma. Compare your group's draft with the drafts of other groups. *Next,* discuss your group's collaborative process. For example, (1) Which group member led the discussion or had the most influence? (2) How were decisions made? (3) How was the drafting process handled? (4) How was conflict resolved? Compare your group's collaborative process with that of other groups.

2. Find a sales letter or an advertisement for a product and identify the reader and purpose. Using the checklist included under "Writing Ethically" in this chapter, analyze the document and decide whether the writer has made ethical choices in language and content.

3. Interview someone you know who has a job that requires some writing. Ask the person about his or her personal writing process. What kinds of documents and for whom does the person write? How do company requirements affect the writing process? Is team writing or management review usually involved? What activity in the writing process does the person find most difficult? How much rewriting does the person do for a typical writing task? What part of the person's writing process would he or she like to change or strengthen? Write a memo to your instructor describing how this person handles a typical writing task. Use the memo format shown in Chapter 12.

4. Your task is to write a description of another student's job—either a current job or a recent vacation job. The description you write will be included in *Ways to Earn Money for College,* a booklet for incoming freshmen who want to work part time during the school year or full time during vacations. In class, discuss what kinds of information would be most helpful to these freshmen. Then interview a student and determine his or her job duties, salary, hours, and so on. Next, organize the job information you collected by topics and put the details in the order you decide is appropriate under each topic. Then write a draft of the job description.

Next, in pairs in class, each assume the role of a manager who will review the other's writing. Read each other's drafts and make suggestions for revision. Then revise your rough draft according to the suggestions you received from your "manager." Submit to your instructor (a) your first draft with the notes from your "management review" and (b) your revised draft.

CHAPTER 2

Audience

ANALYZING READERS

Each reader represents a unique combination of characteristics and purpose that will affect your decisions about document content and format. To prepare an effective technical document, therefore, analyze your readers during the planning stage of the writing process. Consider your readers in terms of these questions:

- How much technical knowledge about the subject do they already have?

- What positions do they have in the organization?

- What are their attitudes about the subject or the writing situation?

- How will they read the document?

- What purpose do they have in using the document?

If you have multiple readers for a document, you also need to consider the differences among your readers.

Subject Knowledge

Consider how much information your readers already have about the main subject and subtopics in the document. In general, you can think of readers as having one of these levels of knowledge about any subject:

- *Expert level*—Readers with expert knowledge of a subject understand the theory and practical applications as well as most of the specialized terms related to the subject. Expert knowledge implies years of experience and/or advanced training in the subject. A scientist involved in research to find a cure for emphysema will read another scientist's report on that subject as an expert, understanding the testing procedures and the discussion of results. A marketing manager may be an expert reader for a report explaining possible strategies for selling a home appliance in selected regions of the country.

    Expert readers generally need fewer explanations of principles and fewer definitions than other readers, but the amount of appropriate detail in a document for an expert reader depends on purpose. The expert reader who wants to duplicate a new genetic test, for instance, will want precise information about every step in the test. The expert reader who is interested primarily in the results obtained will need only a summary of the test procedure.

- *Semiexpert level*—Readers with semiexpert knowledge of a subject may vary a great deal in how much they know and why they want information. A manager may understand some engineering principles in a report but probably is more interested in information about how the project affects company planning and budgets, subjects in which the manager is an expert. An equipment operator may know a little about the scientific basis of a piece of machinery but is more interested in information about handling the equipment properly. Other readers with semiexpert knowledge may be in similar fields with overlapping knowledge. A financial analyst may specialize in utility stocks but also have semiexpert knowledge of other financial areas. Semiexpert readers, then, may be expert in some topics covered in a document and semiexpert in other topics. To effectively use all the information, the semiexpert reader needs more definitions and explanations of general principles than the expert reader does.

- *Nonexpert level*—Nonexpert readers have no specialized training or experience in a subject. These people read because (1) they want to use new technology or perform new tasks or (2) they are interested in learning about a new subject. Nonexperts using technology for the first time or beginning a new activity are such readers as the person using a stationary exercise bike, learning how to play golf, or installing a heat lamp in the bathroom. These readers need information that will help them use equipment or perform an action. They are less interested in the theory of the subject than in its practical application. Nonexperts who read to learn more about a subject, however, are often interested in some theory. For instance, someone who reads an article in a general science magazine about the disappearance of the dinosaurs from the Earth will probably want information about scientific theories on the cause of the dinosaurs' disappearance. If the reader becomes highly interested in the topic and reads widely, he or she then becomes a semiexpert in the subject, familiar with technical terms, theories, and the physical qualities of dinosaurs.

All readers, whatever their knowledge level, have a specific reason for using a technical document, and they need information tailored to their level of knowledge. Remember that one person may have different knowledge levels and objectives for different documents. A physician may read (1) a report on heart surgery as an expert, seeking more information about research, (2) a report recommending new equipment for a clinic as a semiexpert who must decide whether to purchase the equipment, (3) an article about space travel as a nonexpert who enjoys learning about space, and (4) an owner's manual for a new camera as a consumer who needs instructions for operating the camera.

Position in the Organization

Your reader's hierarchical position in the company and relationship with you are also important characteristics to consider. Readers are either external (outside the company) or internal (inside the company). Those outside the company include customers, vendors, stockholders, employees of government agencies or industry associations, competitors, and the general public. The interests of all these groups center on how a document relates to their own activities. Within all companies, the hierarchy of authority creates three groups of readers:

- *Superiors*—Readers who rank higher in authority than the writer are superiors. They may be executives who make decisions based on information in a document. Superiors may be experts in some aspects of a subject, such as how cost projections will affect company operations, and they may be semiexperts in the production systems. If you are writing a report to superiors about a new company computer system, your readers would be interested in overall costs, the effect of the system on company operations, expected benefits company wide, and projections of future computer uses and needs.

- *Subordinates*—Readers who rank lower in authority than the writer are subordinates. They may be interested primarily in how a document affects their own jobs, but they also may be involved in some decision making, especially for their own units. If your report on the new computer system is for subordinates, you will probably emphasize information about specific models and programs, locations for the new computers, how these computers support specific tasks and systems, and how the readers will use the computers in their jobs.

- *Peers*—Those readers on the same authority level as the writer are peers, although they may not be in the same technical field as the writer. Their interests could involve decision making, coordinating related projects, following procedures, or keeping current with company activities. Your report on the new computer system, if written for peers, might focus on how the system will link departments and functions, change current procedures, and support company or department goals.

Personal Attitudes

Readers' personal responses to a document or a writing situation often influence the document's design. As you analyze your writing situation, assess these considerations for your readers:

- *Emotions*—Readers can have positive, negative, or neutral feelings about the subject, the purpose of the document, or the writer. Even when readers try to read objectively, these emotions can interfere. If your readers have a negative attitude about a subject, organizing the information to move from generally accepted data to less accepted data or starting with shared goals may help them accept the information.

- *Motivation*—Readers may be eager for information and eager to act. On the other hand, they may be reluctant to act. Make it easy for your readers to use the information by including items that will help them. Use lists, tables, headings, indexes, and other design features to make the text more useful. Most important, tell readers why they should act in this situation.

- *Preferences*—Readers sometimes have strong personal preferences about documents they must use. Readers may demand features such as lists or charts, or they may refuse to read a document that exceeds a specified length or does not follow a set format. If you discover such preferences in your readers, adjust your documents to suit them.

Reading Style

Technical documents usually are not read, nor are they meant to be read, from beginning to end like a mystery novel. Readers read documents in various ways, determined partly by their need for specific information and partly by personal habit. These reading styles reflect specific readers' needs:

- *Readers use only the summary or abstract.* Some readers want only general information about the subject, and the abstract or opening summary will serve this purpose. An executive who is not directly involved in a production change may read only the abstract of a report that describes the change in detail. This executive needs up-to-date information about the change, but only in general form. A psychologist who is looking for research studies about abused children may read the abstract of an article in order to decide whether or not the article contains the kind of information needed. Relying on the abstract for an overview or using the abstract to decide whether to read the full document saves time for busy readers.

- *Readers check for specific sections of information.* A reader may be interested only in some topics covered in a lengthy document. A machine operator may read a technical manual to find the correct operating procedures for a piece of equipment, but a design engineer may look for a description of the machine, and a service technician will turn to the section on maintenance. Long reports and manuals often have multiple readers who are interested only in the information relevant to their jobs or departments. Use descriptive headlines to direct these readers to the information they need.

- *Readers scan the document, pausing at key words and phrases.* Sometimes readers quickly read a document for a survey of the subject, but they concentrate only on information directly pertaining to topics that affect them. The manager of an insurance company annuity department may scan a forecasting report to learn about company planning and expected insurance trends over the next ten years. The same manager, however, will read carefully all information that in any way affects the annuity department. Such information may be scattered throughout the report so that the manager will look for key words. To help such a reader, use consistent terms throughout.

- *Readers study the document from beginning to end.*   Readers who need all the information in order to make a decision are likely to read carefully from beginning to end. A reader who is trying to decide what automobile to buy may read the manufacturers' brochures from beginning to end, looking for information to aid in the decision. Someone who needs to change an automobile tire will read the instructions carefully from beginning to end in order to perform the steps correctly. For these readers, highlight particularly important information in lists or boxes, direct their attention to information through headings, and summarize main points to refresh their memories.

- *Readers evaluate the document critically.*   Someone who opposes a project or the writer's participation in it may read a document looking for information that can be used as negative evidence. The multiple readers of a report recommending a company merger, for instance, may include those opposed to such a plan. Such readers will focus on specific facts they believe are inadequate to support the recommendation. If you know that some of your readers are opposed to the general purpose of your report, anticipate criticisms of the plan or of your data and include information that will respond to these criticisms.

Multiple Readers

Technical documents usually have multiple readers. Sometimes the person who receives a report will pass it on informally to others. Manuals may be used by dozens of employees, and documents outlining policies and procedures may apply to employees in all departments of an organization. Readers inside and outside a company study annual reports. Consumer instruction manuals are read by millions. This diversity among readers presents extra problems in document design. In addition to analyzing readers based on technical knowledge, positions in the organization, attitudes, and reading styles, you should consider whether readers are primary or secondary.

Primary Readers

Primary readers will take action or make decisions based on the document. An executive who decides whether to accept a recommendation to change suppliers and purchase equipment is a primary reader. A consumer who buys a blender and follows the enclosed instructions for making drinks is a primary reader. The technical knowledge, relationship to the organization and to the writer, and personal preferences of these two primary readers are very different, but each is the person who will use the document most directly.

Secondary Readers

Secondary readers do not make decisions or take direct action because of the document, but they are affected or influenced by it. A technician may be asked to read a report about changing suppliers and to offer an opinion. If the change takes place, the technician will have to set up maintenance procedures for the new equipment. A report suggesting new promotion policies will have one or more primary readers who are authorized to make decisions. All the employees who have access to the report, however, will be secondary readers with a keen interest in the effect of any changes on their own chances for promotion. Remember that secondary readers are not necessarily secondary in their interest in a subject, but only in their power or authority to act on the information.

After deciding which readers are primary and which are secondary, plan adjustments in the document according to the readers' characteristics discussed earlier. Your primary readers are the first priority, but adjustments for secondary readers are necessary too.

Content.   Include the technical detail that is appropriate for the primary audience. If the secondary readers are more technically knowledgeable than the primary ones, you can add statistical appendixes, detailed illustrations, or supplementary technical materials for them. If the secondary readers are less technically knowledgeable than the primary ones, you can add appendixes that illustrate the information more simply, include glossaries of technical terms, or provide summaries that highlight important points.

Structure.   Divide the document into sections that will serve both primary and secondary audiences. Headings, such as "Recommendations," "Objectives," or "Cost Analysis," will guide specific readers to the information they need. Use graphics and appendixes to clarify information for readers with different technical knowledge and interests. You can also develop specific parts of the document for different readers. Include an abstract for nonexpert readers or a summary of main points for decision makers.

Style.   Use language appropriate for your primary readers. If they are nonexperts in the subject, include definitions of technical terms and provide checklists of important points. If your primary readers are experts, use the appropriate technical terms and include glossaries for secondary readers, if needed.

If your document has multiple primary readers, plan for those who need the most help in understanding the subject and the technical language. For instance, when preparing a bulletin for dozens of regional sales representatives, some of whom have been with the company many years and some of whom are newly hired, include the amount of detail and the language most appropriate for the least experienced in the group. New sales representatives need full explanations, but experienced people can skim through the bulletin and read the sections they have a specific interest in if you include descriptive headings.

In some situations, the differences among primary readers or between primary and secondary readers may be so great that you decide to write separate documents. For example, one report of a medical research program cannot serve both the general public and experts. The two groups of readers have entirely different interests and abilities for dealing with the specialized medical information. Even within a company, if the amount of technical information needed by one group will shut out other readers, separate documents may be the easiest way to serve the whole audience.

International Readers

Growing international trade, company branch offices in foreign markets, and booming immigration into the United States have created new challenges for writers. Many documents you write may be used by people for whom English is a second language or who must rely on translations. If you have international readers, you must research their specific communication customs and expectations in order to write an effective document. Even if your international readers use English to conduct business, you need to find out about cultural customs, so you can avoid offending or confusing people who rely on the documents you write. Here are only a few areas you should consider when developing documents for use by international readers:

- *Graphics.*   In the United States, we expect readers to scan pictures or drawings from left to right, but some cultures scan graphics in a circular direction or up and down. "Universal" symbols are not necessarily universal. One computer company discovered that the trash-can icon was not useful in foreign markets because people put their trash in different types of containers.[1]

- *Colors.*   Cultures attach different meanings to colors. In the United States, a blue ribbon is first prize, but in England first prize is a red ribbon. Red, however, represents witchcraft and death in some African countries. In Japan, white flowers symbolize death, but in Mexico purple flowers symbolize death.[2]

- *Shapes.*   The meaning of shapes and gestures differs among countries. The OK sign we make in the United States by putting thumb and forefinger together is a symbol for money in Japan and is considered vulgar in Brazil.[3]

- *Numbers.*   Some countries do not use an alphabet with the telephone system. Therefore, telephone numbers or fax numbers should be given only in figures even if the company uses a word in its telephone number for advertising in the United States.[4]

- *Names and rank.*   Countries differ widely on the correct use of names and titles. First names are seldom used in Germany during business transactions, but in Thailand, first names are used except on the most formal occasions. In Belgium, French-speaking people are addressed differently than Dutch-speaking people are.[5]

- *Format.*   Acceptable document format varies by country. Dates are often given in a different style from that in the United States. Correspondence salutations and closings differ from country to country. You must also adopt the appropriate formality or informality that your readers expect in correspondence.

There are thousands of variations in communication style among the world's cultures. Taking the time to research the customs of your international readers shows respect, but it is also the only way to ensure that your document fulfills its purpose. Because there are so many cultural variables, you may have to design different documents for different countries.

FINDING OUT ABOUT READERS

Sometimes you will write for readers whom you know well. But how do you find out about readers whom you do not know well or whom you will never meet? Gathering information about your readers and how they plan to use a document can be time-consuming, but it is essential at the planning stage of the writing process. Use both informal inquiries and formal interviews to identify readers' characteristics and purposes.

Informal Checking

When you are writing for people inside your organization, you often can find out about them and their purposes by checking informally in these ways:

- Talk in person or by telephone with the readers themselves or with those who know them, such as the project director, the person who assigned you the writing task, and people who have written similar documents. If you are writing to a high-level executive, you may not feel comfortable calling the executive, but you can talk with others who are familiar with the project, the purpose of the document, and the reader's characteristics.

- Check the readers' reactions to your drafts. You can find out how your readers will use the information in your document by sharing drafts during the writing process. If you are writing a procedures manual, sharing drafts with the employees who will have to follow the procedures will help you clarify how they intend to use the document and what their preferences are.

- Analyze your organization's chain of responsibility relative to the document you are writing. For example, the marketing director may supervise 7 regional managers, who, in turn, supervise 21 district managers, who, in turn, supervise the sales representatives. Perhaps all are interested in some aspects of your document. By analyzing such organizational networks, you can often identify secondary readers and adjust your document accordingly.

- Brainstorm to identify readers' characteristics for groups. If you are writing a document for a group of readers, such as all registered nurses at St. Luke's Hospital, list the characteristics that you know the readers have in common. You may know, for example, that the average nurse at St. Luke's has been with the hospital for 4.5 years, has a B.S. degree, grew up in the area, and attends an average of two professional training seminars a year. Knowing these facts about your readers will help you tailor your document to their needs.

Interviewing

Writers on the job use interviews as part of the writing process in two ways: (1) to gather information about the subject from experts and technicians and (2) to find out readers' purposes and intended uses of a document. Whether you are interviewing experts for information about the subject or potential readers to decide how to design the document, a few guiding principles will help you control the interview and use the time effectively.

Preparing for the Interview

Interviewers who are thoroughly prepared get the most useful information while using the least amount of time.

- *Make an appointment for the interview.*   Making an appointment shows consideration for the other person's schedule and indicates that the interview is a business task, not a casual chat. Be on time, and keep the interview within the estimated length.

- *Do your background research before the interview.*   Interview time should be as productive as possible. Do not try to discuss the document before having at least a general sense of the kinds of information and overall structure required. You are then in a position to ask more specific questions about content or ask for and use opinions about document design.

- *Prepare your questions ahead of time.* Write out specific questions you intend to ask. Ask the expert for details that you need to include in the document. Project yourself into your readers' minds and imagine how the document might serve their purposes; then frame your questions to pinpoint exactly how your readers will respond to specific sections, headings, graphic aids, and other document features.

- *Draft questions that require more than yes or no answers.* Interview time will be more productive if each question requires a detailed answer. Notice the following ineffective questions and their more effective revisions:

    Ineffective: Do you expect to use the manual daily for repair procedures?

    Effective: For which repair and maintenance procedures do you need to consult the manual?

This revision will get more specific answers than the first version.

    Ineffective: What do you think operators need in a manual like this one?

    Effective: Which of the following features are essential in an operator's manual for this equipment? (List all that you can think of and then ask if there are others.)

The first version may get a specific answer, but it will not necessarily be comprehensive. Check all possibilities during an interview to avoid repeating questions later.

Conducting the Interview

Think of the interview as a meeting that you are leading. You should guide the flow of questioning, keep the discussion on the subjects, and cover all necessary topics.

- *Explain the purpose of the interview.* Tell the person why you want to ask questions and how you think the interview will affect the final document.

- *Break the ice if necessary.* If you have never met the person before, spend a few minutes discussing the subject in general terms so that the two of you can feel comfortable with each other.

- *Listen attentively.* Avoid concentrating on your questions so much that you miss what the other person is saying. Sometimes in the rush to cover all the topics, an interviewer is more preoccupied with checking off the questions than with listening carefully to answers.

- *Take notes.*   Take written notes so that you can remember what the reader told you about special preferences or needs. If you want to tape the interview, ask permission before arriving. Remember, however, that some people are intimidated by recording devices.

- *Group your questions by topic.*   Do not ask questions in random order. Thoroughly cover each topic, such as financial information, before moving on to other subjects.

- *Ask follow-up questions.*   Do not stick to your list of questions so rigidly that you miss asking obvious follow-up questions. Be flexible, and follow a new angle if it arises.

- *Ask for clarification.*   If you do not understand an answer, ask the person for more detail immediately. It is easier to clarify meaning on the spot than days later.

- *Maintain a sense of teamwork.*   Although you need to control the interview, think of the meeting as a partnership to solve specific questions of content and format.

- *Keep your opinions out of the interview.*   What you think about the project or the purpose of the document is not as relevant during an interview as what the other person thinks about these topics. Concentrate on gathering information rather than on debating issues.

- *Ask permission to follow up.*   End the interview by requesting a chance to call with follow-up questions if needed.

- *Thank the interviewee.*   Express your appreciation for the person's help and cooperation.

Immediately after the interview, write up your notes in a rough draft so that you can remember the details.

TESTING READER-ORIENTED DOCUMENTS

Along with analyzing and interviewing readers, writers sometimes evaluate audience needs through user tests of a document while it is still in draft. Manuals and instructions are particularly good candidates for user tests because their primary purpose is to guide readers in performing certain functions and because they are meant for groups of readers. When potential readers test a document's usefulness before the final draft stage, a writer can make needed changes in design and content based on actual experience with the document. There are three types of user tests.

Readers Answering Questions

Asking readers to answer questions after reading a document helps a writer decide whether the content will be easily understood by the audience. A utility company may want to distribute a brochure that explains to consumers how electricity use is computed and how they can reduce their energy consumption. Through a user test, the writer can determine if the brochure answers consumers' questions. Several versions of the same brochure also can be tested to determine which version readers find most useful. The test involves these steps:

1. A group of typical consumers reads the draft or drafts of the brochure.

2. The consumers then answer a series of questions on the content and perhaps try to compute an energy-consumption problem based on the information in the brochure.

3. The consumers also complete a demographic questionnaire, which asks for age, sex, job title, education level, length of time it took to complete the questions, and their opinions as to the readability of the brochure.

4. The writer then analyzes the results to see how correctly and how fast the consumers answered the questions and what the demographic information reveals about ease of use for different consumer groups.

5. Finally, the writer revises any portions of the brochure that proved difficult for readers and then retests the document.

Readers Performing a Task

In another situation, a writer may be most concerned about whether readers will be able to follow instructions and perform a task correctly. A manual may be tested in draft by operators and technicians who will use the final version. This user test follows the same general pattern as the preceding one, but the emphasis is on performing a task.

1. Selected operators follow the written instructions to perform the steps of a procedure.

2. The length of time to complete the task is recorded, as well as how smoothly the operators proceeded through the steps of the procedure.

3. The operators next complete a demographic questionnaire, comment on how effective they found the instructions, and point out areas that were unclear.

4. Analysis of the results focuses on correctness in completing the task, the length of time required, and the portions of the document that received most criticism from the readers.

5. The writer revises the sections that were not clear to the readers and retests the document.

Readers Thinking Aloud

Another type of user test requires readers to think aloud as they read through a document. This method (called *protocol analysis*) allows the writer or design-review team to record readers' responses everywhere in the document, analyze readers' comments, and revise content, structure, and style accordingly. Readers may be puzzled by the terminology, the sequence of items, too much or too little detail, the graphics, or sentence clarity. The writer can then revise these areas before the final draft.

User tests have become increasingly important for audience analysis, especially in large corporations. The Document Design Center of the American Institutes for Research in Washington, D.C., established a Usability Test Laboratory in 1985 to assist businesses in testing documents and evaluating readers' responses to written materials.

CHAPTER SUMMARY

This chapter discusses analyzing readers and testing reader use of documents. Remember:

- Writers analyze readers according to the level of their readers' technical knowledge, positions in the organization, attitudes, reading styles, and positions as primary or secondary readers.

- Readers generally have one of three levels of technical knowledge— expert, semiexpert, and nonexpert.

- A reader's position in the organization may be as the writer's superior, subordinate, or peer.

- A reader's response to a document may be influenced by emotions, motivation, and preferences.

- Readers may differ in their reading styles. Some read only the abstract or introduction; others look for specific sections or topics; others read from beginning to end; and some may read in order to criticize the information or project.

- When a document has multiple readers, the writer must develop content, organization, and style to serve both primary and secondary readers.

- When writing for international readers, a writer must research cultural differences in communication style.

- Writers find out about their readers through informal checking and formal interviewing.

- Writers test document effectiveness by asking readers to (1) read the document and answer questions about content, (2) read the document and then perform the task explained in the document, and (3) talk about their reactions to the document.

SUPPLEMENTAL READINGS IN PART 2

" 'Big Emerging Markets' Have Diverse Cultures, but Common Attributes," *Business America,* p. 466.

Bowman, J. P., and Okuda, T. "Japanese-American Communication: Mysteries, Enigmas, and Possibilities," *The Bulletin of the Association for Business Communication,* p. 480.

Ridgway, L. "The Writer as Market Researcher," *Technical Communication,* p. 550.

Tarutz, J. H. "Editing for an International Audience," *Technical Editing,* p. 572.

ENDNOTES

1. Emily A. Thrush, "Bridging the Gaps: Technical Communication in an International and Multicultural Society," *Technical Communication Quarterly* 2.3 (Summer 1993): 271–283.

2. "Recognizing and Heeding Cultural Differences Can Be Key to International Business Success," *Business America* 115.10 (October 1994): 8–11.

3. "Recognizing and Heeding."

4. Ernest Plock, "Understanding Cultural Traditions Is Critical When Doing Business with the Newly Independent States," *Business America* 115.10 (October 1994): 14.

5. "Recognizing and Heeding."

MODEL 2-1   Commentary

This brochure is designed to help arthritis patients understand their disease. Other readers might be family members or friends of the patients. The brochure begins by defining the disease and the types of arthritis that typically occur. The drawing shows readers the differences between a normal hip and an arthritic one. The brochure concludes with an explanation of the kinds of treatment available and offers the assurance that the disease is treatable if not curable.

Discussion

1. Discuss the section headings. Why are they appropriate for the readers of the brochure?

2. Discuss the purpose of the photo in the brochure. Is it worth the space it uses or should more information about the disease be included?

3. This brochure is written for multiple readers—all nonexperts in the subject. In groups, decide what information you would include in a 500-word summary to be read by the spouses of arthritis patients. What information would you omit? Draft the 500-word summary, and compare your draft with those written by other groups.

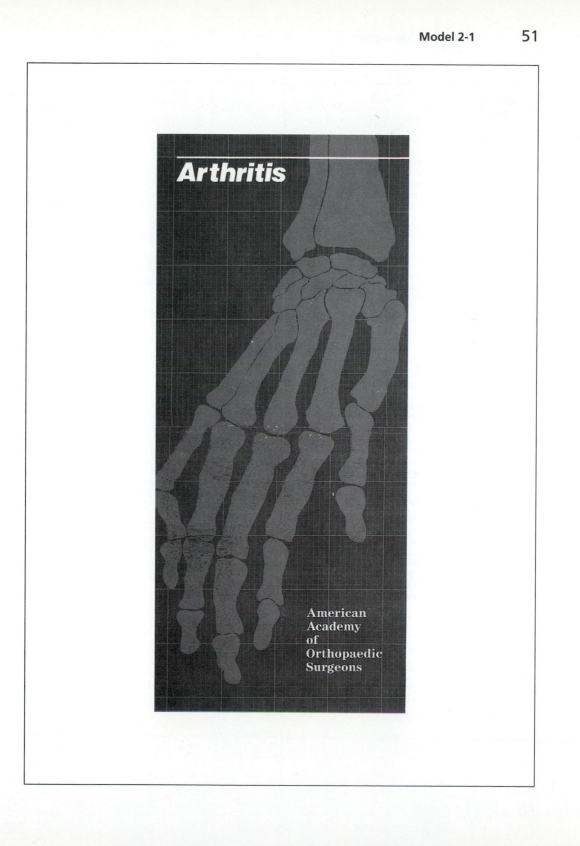

What is arthritis?

The word "arthritis" means joint inflammation (*arthr* = joint; *itis* = inflammation). As many as 36 million people in the United States have some form of arthritis. It is a major cause of lost work time and causes serious disability in many persons. Although arthritis is mainly a disease of adults, children may also have it.

What is a joint?

A joint is a special structure in the body where the ends of two or more bones meet. For example, a bone of the lower leg called the tibia and the thigh bone, which is called the femur, meet to form the knee joint. The hip is a simple ball and socket joint. The upper end of the femur is the ball. It fits into the socket, a part of the pelvis called the acetabulum.

The bone ends of a joint are covered with a smooth, glistening material called hyaline cartilage. This material cushions the underlying bone from excessive force or pressure and allows the joint to move easily without pain. The joint is enclosed in a capsule with a smooth lining called the synovium. The synovium produces a lubricant, synovial fluid, which helps to reduce friction and wear in a joint. Connecting the bones are ligaments, which keep the joint stable. Crossing the joint are muscles and tendons, which also help to keep the joint stable and enable it to move.

What is inflammation?

Inflammation is one of the body's normal reactions to injury or disease. When a part of the body is injured, infected, or diseased, the body's natural defenses work to repair the problem. In an injured or diseased joint, this results in swelling, pain, and stiffness. Inflammation is usually temporary, but in arthritic joints, it may cause long-lasting or permanent disability.

Normal hip

Arthritic hip

Types of arthritis

What is osteoarthritis?

There are more than 100 different types of arthritis. One major type is osteoarthritis, which is sometimes called degenerative joint disease. It occurs to some extent in most people as they age. Osteoarthritis can begin earlier as a result of a joint injury or overuse. Often, weightbearing joints such as the knee, hip, and spine, are involved. The wrists, elbows, and shoulders are usually not affected by osteoarthritis. These joints may be affected if they are used extensively in either work or recreational activities, or if they have been damaged from fractures or other injuries.

In osteoarthritis, the cartilage surface covering the bone ends becomes rough and eventually wears away. In some cases, an abnormal bone growth called a "spur" can develop. Pain and swelling result from joint inflammation. Continued use of the joint produces more pain. It may be relieved somewhat by rest.

What is rheumatoid arthritis?

Rheumatoid arthritis is a chronic, or long-lasting disease that can affect many parts of the body, including the joints. In rheumatoid arthritis, the joint fluid contains chemical substances that attack the joint surface and damage it. Inflammation occurs in response to the disease. The joints most commonly involved are those in the hands, wrists, feet, and ankles, but large joints such as hips, knees, and elbows may also be involved. Swelling, pain, and stiffness are usually present even when the joint is not used. These are the main signs of rheumatoid arthritis and its related diseases. Rheumatoid arthritis can affect persons of all ages, even children, although more than 70% of persons with this disease are over thirty. Many joints of the body may be involved at the same time.

How is arthritis diagnosed?

Diagnosing arthritis includes noting the patient's symptoms, performing a physical examination, and taking x-rays, which are important in showing the extent of damage to the joint. Blood tests and other laboratory tests, such as examination of the joint fluid, may help to determine the type of arthritis the patient has. Once the diagnosis has been made, treatment can begin.

In most cases, people with arthritis can continue to perform the activities of daily living.

How is arthritis treated?

The goals of treatment are to provide pain relief and also to maintain or restore function to the arthritic joint. There are several kinds of treatment:

Medication–Many medications, including aspirin and other anti-inflammatory drugs, may be used to control pain and inflammation in arthritis. The physician chooses a particular medication by taking into account the type of arthritis, its severity, and the patient's general physical health. At times, injections of a substance called cortisone directly into the joint may help to relieve pain and swelling. It is important to know, however, that repeated frequent injections into the same joint can have undesirable side effects.

Joint protection–Canes, crutches, walkers, or splints may help relieve the stress and strain on arthritic joints. Protection of the joint also includes learning methods of performing daily activities that are the least stressful to painful joints. In addition, certain exercises and other forms of physical therapy, such as heat treatments, are used to treat arthritis. They can help to relieve stiffness and to strengthen the weakened muscles around the joint. The type of physical therapy depends on the type and severity of the arthritis and the particular joints involved.

Surgery–In general, an orthopaedist will perform surgery for arthritis when other methods of non-surgical treatment have failed to give the patient sufficient relief. The physician and patient will choose the type of surgery by taking into account the type of arthritis, its severity, and the patient's physical condition. Surgical procedures include
- removal of the diseased or damaged joint lining;
- realignment of the joints;
- total joint replacement; and
- fusion, which permanently places the bone ends of a joint together to prevent joint motion.

Is there a cure for arthritis?

At present, most types of arthritis cannot be cured. Researchers continue to make progress in finding the underlying causes for the major types of arthritis. Often, when a cause is found for a disease, preventive measures can be undertaken. In the meantime, orthopaedists, working with other physicians and scientists, have developed effective treatments for arthritis.

In most cases, persons with arthritis can continue to perform the activities of daily living. Weight reduction for obese persons with osteoarthritis, physical therapy, and anti-inflammatory drugs are measures that can be taken to reduce pain and stiffness.

In persons with severe cases of arthritis, orthopaedic surgery can provide dramatic pain relief and restore lost joint function. A total joint replacement, for example, can enable a person with severe arthritis in the hip or the knee to walk without pain or stiffness.

Some types of arthritis, especially the rheumatoid form, are best treated by a team of health care professionals with special abilities. These professionals include rheumatologists (nonsurgeons who are arthritis specialists), physical and occupational therapists, social workers, as well as orthopaedic surgeons.

MODEL 2-2   Commentary

This page is the first in a set of instructions from a company service manual. The instructions cover one stage of the complicated procedure of installing a hard disk drive. The opening paragraph identifies the intended reader and states the purpose of the instructions. The writer also refers the reader to other manuals that will be needed to complete the installation. A list of parts appears before the instruction steps.

Discussion

1. The parts for this procedure are packaged in a kit. Discuss why the writer decided to list the parts separately.

2. Discuss the format. What is the purpose of the detailed heading at the top right? Compare the format to that in Model 2-1. How does format aid the reader of each model?

3. Compare the language of Models 2-1 and 2-2. Discuss whether the reader of Model 2-2 is probably a nonexpert, semiexpert, or expert in the subject.

CIBA·CORNING

ACS: *180° PLUS*

ACS: *180°*

Express® Plus

Hard Disk Drive Kit
Part No. 1458x390

Installation Instructions

These instructions are intended for Field Service Engineers trained by Ciba Corning to service ACS:180® and Express® Plus systems. Use these instructions to install the hard disk drive on the ACS:180 or the Express Plus systems.

NOTE: This procedure requires you to format the new hard disk drive, load the software, restore the calibrations, and restore the customer parameters. Refer to the current version of the *ACS:180 Software Installation Instructions* or the *Express Plus Software Installation Instructions*.

Hard Disk Drive Kit:

Item	Part Number	Quantity
Quantum LPS 170S or 270S Hard Disk Drive	27307	1
LED Cable	1458x328	1

For the ACS:180 Systems

1. Turn the system off and disconnect the power cord.
2. Remove the CRT module:
   a. Disconnect the cable from position J36 on the Backplane board.
   b. Remove the top two screws and the bottom right screw from the front of the bracket that holds the CRT module.
   c. Slide the CRT module forward.

 CAUTION: The hard disk data cable is not keyed; therefore, if this cable is incorrectly connected to the hard disk drive, the system will not operate properly and could cause damage to the hard disk drive.

3. Remove the following cables from the hard disk drive:
   • Hard disk data cable
   • Power cable
   • LED cable assembly
4. Remove the floppy disk drive from the system.
5. Remove the hard disk drive from the bracket, as shown in Figure 1. Set the screws and washers aside.

This model shows the opening page of a report by research chemists for the U.S. Bureau of Mines. The report is an investigative study of the thermodynamics of certain chemical compounds. Readers are other research scientists interested in this experiment and the results that might influence their own research. The abstract is written for expert readers and does not provide a summary for nonexpert readers. You probably cannot understand the language or the content of this document.

The report language is highly specialized. None of the technical terms or chemical symbols is defined because the writer expects only experts to read the report.

Discussion

Compare the language, kinds of information, and formats of Models 2-1, 2-2, and 2-3, and discuss how each document is appropriate for its readers.

Enthalpy of Formation of 2CdO • CdSO$_4$

by H. C. Ko[1] and R. R. Brown[1]

ABSTRACT

The Bureau of Mines maintains an active program in thermochemistry to provide thermodynamic data for the advancement of mineral science and technology. As part of this effort, the standard enthalpy of formation at 298.15 K, $\Delta Hf°$, for 2CdO · CdSO$_4$ was determined by HCl acid solution calorimetry to be −345.69 ±0.61 kcal/mol.

INTRODUCTION

Cadmium oxysulfate (2CdO · CdSO$_4$) is known as an intermediate compound in the decomposition process of cadmium sulfate (CdSO$_4$). There is only one reported value ([4])[2] for the enthalpy of formation at 2CdO · CdSO$_4$, and that value was determined by a static manometric method. The objective of this investigation was to establish the standard enthalpy of formation for this compound by HCl solution calorimetry, which is inherently a more accurate method. This investigation was conducted as part of the Bureau of Mines effort to provide thermodynamic data for the advancement of mineral technology.

MATERIALS

Cadmium oxide: Baker[3] analyzed reagent-grade CdO was dried at 500°C for 2 hr. X-ray diffraction analysis indicated that the pattern matched the one given by PDF card 5–640 ([2]). Spectrographic analysis indicated 0.05 pct Pb to be present as the only significant impurity.

Cadmium oxysulfate: 2CdO · CdSO$_4$ was prepared by reacting stoichiometric quantities of anhydrous CdSO$_4$ and CdO in a sealed, evacuated Vycor tube according to the following procedure. The materials were blended and transferred to a Vycor reaction tube. The reaction tube was evacuated and heated to 330°C for 17 hr to remove traces of water that may have been introduced during blending and transferring. The tube was then sealed and heated to 600°C for 19 hr. The temperature was. . . .

[1]Research chemist, Albany Research Center, Bureau of Mines, Albany, Oreg.
[2]Underlined numbers in parentheses refer to items in the list of references at the end of this report.
[3]Reference to specific trade names does not imply endorsement by the Bureau of Mines.

1. Assume that your school is completing construction of a new, full-service athletic club to serve (for a membership fee) students, faculty, and staff. You are on the communication team assigned to write a brochure that will attract potential users to join the athletic club. In groups, or as a class, develop a list of questions to ask potential users, so you know what information about the club they are most interested in. Consider such points as types of activities, types of equipment, need for parking, lockers, dressings rooms, childcare, and anything else appropriate for your campus. As a group, define two specific kinds of potential users, e.g., married students over age 25, faculty with children under age 12, or first-year students. Each group member will then interview five of these potential users. Group members will then pool the results and decide what kinds of information should be included in the brochure to interest these specific readers. *Or,* your instructor may prefer that each group interview one specific type of potential users and then groups will compare the results.

2. The following is the form letter sent to newly admitted freshmen at Spring County Community and Technical College. Students have been complaining that they are wasting time and becoming frustrated because of this letter. Identify the problems in the letter for a freshman reader, and, in groups, revise the letter for a more effective and helpful message. Add any information you wish.

> Dear Student:
> Welcome to Spring County Community and Technical College. To assist you in your educational experience, your advisor is Teresa Rios. You have been designated as Med Tech-RAD. If you have any questions about graduation requirements, please contact your advisor. Registration begins at the end of August, and late registration results in a fee penalty. Register promptly.
> Enclosed is the form to obtain your student identification card. Fill the form out and submit it to the Learning Center. Also enclosed is a brochure on alcohol abuse and drug counseling. You must submit a proposed schedule of classes to obtain your student identification card and registration materials. Please see Philip Whitman to sign up for Freshman Orientation.

3. Select either (1) a document used by most students on campus (e.g., parking regulations, instructions for library use) or (2) a consumer document (e.g., leaflet from a utility company, instructions packed with a product) and interview an international student about what changes in language or graphics would be necessary in that student's country. Discuss the results of your interview with the class.

4. Discuss the following situation and decide what kinds of information the readers will need in the document.

> The end of the year is approaching, and, traditionally, the offices at the Madison County Social Services Agency will be decorated with various displays. Last year, a small fire broke out in the Children's Services Division. The fire was quickly extinguished, but as Director of Support Services, you believe a memo should go to all employees this year reminding them of proper procedures for arranging and maintaining displays.

5. Find a user manual for a word-processing program. Rewrite one page of the introductory material for an eighth-grade student who is going to start using the program.

6. Individually, or in groups if your instructor prefers, develop a reader test as discussed in this chapter under "Testing Reader-oriented Documents." Bring to class a short brochure intended for general readers and distributed by a utility company, a charitable organization, or a consumer-products company. Develop five questions designed to test a reader's understanding of the information in the brochure. Follow the testing procedure described under "Readers Answering Questions." Analyze the results and identify any sections of the brochure that could be improved. Rewrite one section of the brochure based on your reader test. Submit both the original brochure and your revision of one section to your instructor.

7. Read the article by Ridgway entitled "The Writer as Market Researcher" in Part 2. Bring to class a copy of the official directions issued on your campus to guide students in registering for classes each semester or quarter. In groups, develop a set of interview questions to test student understanding and use of these directions. Each group member will then interview three students outside the class, using these questions. The group members will pool their results and come to some conclusions about the usefulness of the registration directions. Report your group results to the rest of the class, and discuss how the registration directions might be revised to better serve the students on your campus.

CHAPTER 3

Organization

SORTING INFORMATION

The organization of a document has a strong influence on how well the reader understands and is able to use the information. If a document is well organized with headings, lists, and key words that trigger a reader's memory of prior knowledge of the subject, a reader can learn and use new information effectively. Reading studies show that if adults are given poorly organized information, they tend to reorganize it themselves and to omit information that does not clearly fit into their prior knowledge.[1] As a writer you must organize documents to help readers learn and remember new information.

In some writing situations, documents have predetermined organizational patterns. Social workers at a child welfare agency may be directed to present information in all case reports under the major topics of living conditions, parental attitudes, previous agency contact, and suspected child abuse. Because these major topics appear in all the agency case reports, readers who use them regularly, such as attorneys and judges, know where to look for the specific details they need. Such consistency is useful to readers if the documents have a standard format—only the details change from situation to situation.

If you are writing a document that does not have standard categories for information, however, your first step will be to organize the information into major topics and identify appropriate subtopics.

Select Major Topics

Begin organizing your document by sorting the information into major topics. Select the topics based on your analysis of your readers' interest in and need for information. If you are writing a report about columns or pillars, you should group your information into major topics that represent what your readers want to know about the subject. If your readers are interested in Greek and Roman column design, you can group your information according to classic column type—Doric, Ionic, and Corinthian. Readers interested in learning about column construction may prefer an organization based on construction materials, such as brick, marble, wood, stone, and metal. Readers interested in the architectural history of columns may prefer an organization based on time period, such as Ancient, Medieval, and Renaissance. Readers interested in the cultural differences in column design may prefer the information grouped according to geographic region, such as Asian, Mediterranean, and North American.

As you sort your information into major topics, remember that the topics should be similar in type and relatively equal in importance. You should not have one major topic based on column design and one based on time period. Such a mix of topics would confuse your readers. You should also be certain that the major topics you select are distinct. You would not want to use time periods that overlap, such as the Renaissance and the fifteenth century, or column designs that overlap, such as Doric and Tuscan. Consider carefully which major topics represent appropriate groups of information for your readers.

Identify Subtopics

After you determine your major topics, consider how to sort the information into appropriate subtopics. Do not simply lump facts together. Instead, think about what specific information you have that will support each major topic. If your major topics are based on classic column types, your readers may be interested in such subtopics as Greek design, Roman design, changes in design over time, and how the Greeks and Romans used the columns. These subtopics, or specific pieces of information, should appear under each of the major topics because your readers want to know how these details relate to each column type. When you have identified your major topics and have selected appropriate subtopics, you are ready to begin outlining.

CONSTRUCTING OUTLINES

Think of an outline as a map that identifies the major topics and shows their location in a document. Outlines provide three advantages to a writer:

1. A writer can "see" the structure of a document before beginning a rough draft in the same way that a traveler can follow the route of a journey on a road map before getting into a car.

2. Having a tentative organizational plan helps a writer concentrate on presenting and explaining the information in the rough draft rather than on writing and organizing at the same time.

3. A writer can keep track of organizational decisions no matter how many interruptions occur in the writing process.

An outline usually begins as a short, informal list of topics and grows into a detailed list that includes all major topics and subtopics and groups them into chunks of information most appropriate for the reader. Consider this situation: Al Martinez's first project as a summer intern in the Personnel Department of Tri-Tech Chemical Company is to write a bulletin explaining the company rules on travel and business expenses. Al's readers will be both the managers who travel and the secretaries who handle the paperwork. At present, the pertinent information is scattered through more than a dozen memos written over the last three years. After reading all these memos and noting appropriate items, Al begins to organize his information. He begins with an informal outline.

Informal Outlines

An *informal outline* is a list of main topics in the order the writer expects to present them in the rough draft. Computers have made outlining faster and easier than it used to be. With word processing, a writer can quickly (1) add or delete items and rearrange them without recopying sections that do not change and (2) keep the outline up to date by changing it to match revisions in rough drafts. In developing an informal outline, remember these guidelines:

1. List all the relevant topics in any order at first. Al listed the main topics for his bulletin in the order in which he found them discussed in previous memos in company files.

2. Identify the major groups of related information from your list. Looking at his list of items, Al saw immediately that most of his information centered around types of expenses and reimbursement and approval procedures. Al therefore clustered his information into groups representing these topics.

3. Arrange the information groups in an order that will best serve the readers' need to know. Al decided to present reimbursement procedures first because readers would need to know about those before traveling. He then organized groups representing types of expenses from most common to least common so that the majority of readers could find the information they needed as quickly as possible.

Model 3-1 shows Al's informal outline for his bulletin. Writers usually use informal outlines to group and order information in the planning stage. Often, an informal outline is all that a writer needs. For some documents, such as a manual, however, a writer must prepare a formal outline that will be part of the document. Also, some writers prefer to work with formal outlines in the planning stage.

Formal Outlines

A *formal outline* uses a special numbering system and includes subtopics under each major section. A formal outline is a more detailed map of the organization plan for a document. Writers usually use one of two numbering

1. Travel Authorization and Reimbursement Rules
2. Meals
3. Hotels
4. Transportation
5. Daily Incidental Expenses
6. Spouse's Travel
7. Entertainment
8. Gifts
9. Loss or Damage
10. Nonreimbursed Items

MODEL 3-1   Al's Informal Outline

systems for outlines: (1) Roman and Arabic numerals or (2) decimals (also called the *military numbering system*). Choose whichever numbering system you prefer unless your outline will be part of the final document. In that case, use the numbering system most familiar to your readers or the one your company prefers. Model 3-2 shows a set of topics organized by both numbering systems.

Al Martinez decided to develop his informal outline into a formal one because he wanted a detailed plan before he began his rough draft.

Topic Outlines

A *topic outline* lists all the major topics and all the subtopics in a document by key words. Like the major topics, all subtopics should be in an order that the readers will find useful. Al developed his formal topic outline by adding the items he knew he had to explain under each major topic and using the Roman-Arabic numbering system. Model 3-3 shows Al's formal topic outline.

In drafting his formal topic outline, Al knew that he wanted to begin his bulletin by explaining the process of applying for and receiving reimbursement for travel expenses because his readers needed to understand that system before they began collecting travel-expense information and preparing expense reports. He organized expense topics in the order in which they appeared on the forms his readers would have to submit and then listed specific items under each main topic. While redrafting his outline, Al revised some of his earlier organizational decisions. First, he decided that the topic "Spouse's Travel" was not really a separate item and ought to be covered under each travel expense item, such as "Hotels." He also decided that the topic "Gifts" was really a form

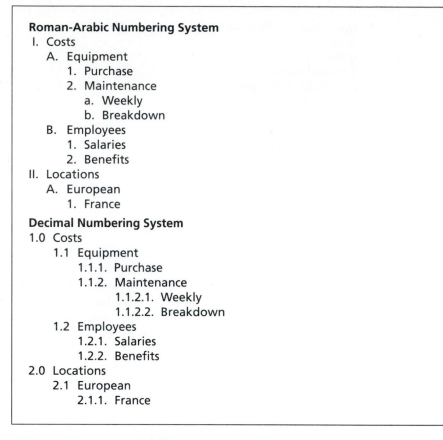

MODEL 3-2   Formal Outline Numbering Systems

of entertainment for clients, so he listed gifts under "Entertainment" in his formal topic outline.

Sentence Outlines

A *sentence outline* develops a topic outline by stating each point in a full sentence. When a project is long and complicated or the writer is not confident about the subject, a sentence outline helps clarify content and organization before drafting begins. Some writers prefer sentence outlines because they can use the sentences in their first drafts, thereby speeding up the initial drafting. Al Martinez also decided to expand his topic outline into a sentence outline as a way of moving closer to his first draft. Model 3-4 shows a portion of Al's sentence outline.

I. Travel Authorization and Reimbursement
  A. Approval
  B. Forms
      1. Form 881
      2. Form 669
      3. Form 40-A
      4. Form 1389
  C. Submission
II. Meals
  A. Breakfast
  B. Lunch
  C. Dinner
III. Hotels
  A. Chain Guaranteed Rates
  B. Suites
IV. Transportation
  A. Automobile
      1. Personal Cars
          a. Mileage
          b. Maintenance
      2. Rental Cars
          a. Approved Companies
          b. Actual Costs Only
  B. Airplane
      1. Tri-Tech Aircraft
      2. Other Companies' Aircraft
      3. Commercial Aircraft
  C. Railroad
  D. Taxi, Limousine, Bus
V. Daily Incidental Expenses
  A. Parking and Tolls
  B. Tips
  C. Laundry and Telephone
VI. Entertainment
  A. Parties
      1. Home
      2. Commercial
  B. Meals
  C. Gifts
      1. Tickets
      2. Objects
VII. Loss or Damage
VIII. Nonreimbursed Items
  A. Personal Items
  B. Legal, Insurance Expenses

MODEL 3-3   Al's Formal Topic Outline

I. Travel Authorization and Reimbursement. Tri-Tech will pay travel expenses directly or reimburse an employee for costs of traveling on company business.
   A. All official travel for Tri-Tech must be approved in advance by supervisors.
   B. Several company forms must be completed and approved.
      1. Form 881, "Travel Authorization," is used for trip approval if travel reservations are needed.
      2. Form 669, "Petty Cash Requisition," is used if no travel reservations are needed.
      3. Form 40-A, "Domestic Travel Expenses," is used to report reimbursable expenses in the United States.
      4. Form 1389, "Foreign Expense Payment," is used to report reimbursable expenses outside the United States.
   C. Travel authorization forms should be submitted to the employee's supervisor, but posttravel forms should be sent directly to the Travel Coordinator in the Personnel Department.
II. Meals. Tri-Tech will reimburse employees for three meals a day while traveling.
   A. Breakfast expenses are reimbursed if the employee is away overnight or leaves home before 6:00 a.m.

MODEL 3-4   A Portion of Al's Formal Sentence Outline

DEVELOPING EFFECTIVE PARAGRAPHS

Each paragraph in a document is a unit of sentences that focuses on one idea and acts as a visual element to break up the text into manageable chunks of information. Effective paragraphs guide readers by

- Introducing individually distinct but related topics
- Emphasizing key points
- Showing relationships between major points
- Providing visual breaks in pages to ease reading

For effective paragraphs, writers should consider unity, coherence, development, and an organizational pattern for presenting information.

Unity

Unity in a paragraph means concentration on a single topic. One sentence in the paragraph is the *summary sentence* (also called the *topic sentence*), and it establishes the main point. The other sentences explain or expand the main point. If a writer introduces several major points into one paragraph without developing them fully, the mix of ideas violates the unity of the paragraph and leaves readers confused. Here is a paragraph that lacks unity:

> Many factors influence the selection of roofing material. Only project managers and engineers have the authority to change the recommendations, and the changes should be in writing. The proper installation of roofing material is important, and contractors should be trained carefully. Roof incline, roof deck construction, and climatic conditions must be considered in selecting roofing material.

The first sentence appears to be a topic sentence, indicating that the paragraph will focus on factors in selecting roofing. Readers therefore would expect to find individual factors enumerated and explained. However, the second and third sentences are unrelated to the opening and instead introduce two new topics: authority to select roofing and the training of contractors. The fourth sentence returns to the topic of selecting roofing material. Thus the paragraph actually introduces three topics, none of which is explained. The paragraph fails to fulfill the expectations of the reader. Here is a revision to achieve unity:

> Three factors influence the selection of roofing material. One factor is roof incline. A minimum of ¼ in. per foot incline is recommended by all suppliers. A second factor is roof deck construction. Before installing roofing material, a contractor must cover a metal deck with rigid installation, prime a concrete deck to level depressions, or cover a wooden deck with a base sheet. Finally, climatic conditions also affect roofing selection. Roofing in very wet climates must be combined with an all-weather aluminum roof coating.

In this version, the paragraph is unified under the topic of which factors influence the selection of roofing materials. The opening sentence establishes this main topic; then the sentences that follow identify the three factors and describe how contractors should handle them. Remember, readers are better able to process information if they are presented one major point at a time.

Coherence

A paragraph is *coherent* when the sentences proceed in a sequence that supports one point at a time. Transitional, or connecting, words and phrases help coherence by showing the relationships between ideas and by creating a smooth flow of sentences. Here are the most common ways writers achieve transition:

- Repeat key words from sentence to sentence.
- Use a pronoun for a preceding key term.

- Use a synonym for a preceding key term.

- Use demonstrative adjectives (*this* report, *that* plan, *these* systems, *those* experiments).

- Use connecting words (*however, therefore, also, nevertheless, before, after, consequently, moreover, likewise, meanwhile*) or connecting phrases (*for example, as a result, in other words, in addition, in the same manner*).

- Use simple enumeration (*first, second, finally, next*).

Here is a paragraph that lacks clear transitions, and the sentences are not in the best sequence to explain the two taxes under discussion:

> Married couples should think about two taxes. When a person dies, an estate tax is levied against the value of the assets that pass on to the heirs by will or automatic transfer. Income tax on capital gains is affected by whatever form of ownership of property is chosen. Under current law, property that one spouse inherits from the other is exempt from estate tax. Married couples who remain together until death do not need to consider estate taxes in ownership of their homes. The basic rule for capital gains tax is that when property is inherited by one person from another, the financial basis of the property begins anew. For future capital gains computations, it is treated as though it were purchased at the market value at the time of inheritance. When the property is sold, tax is due on the appreciation in value since the time it was inherited. No tax is due on the increase in value from actual purchase to time of inheritance. If the property is owned jointly, one-half gets the financial new start.[2]

This paragraph attempts to describe the impact of two federal taxes on married couples who own their homes jointly. The writer begins with the topic of estate tax, but he or she quickly jumps to the capital gains tax, then returns to the estate tax, and finally concludes with the capital gains tax. Since readers expect information to be grouped according to topic, they must sort out the sentences for themselves in order to use the information efficiently. The lack of transition also forces readers to move from point to point without any clear indication of the relationships between ideas. Here is a revision of the paragraph:

> For financial planning, married couples must think about two taxes. First is the estate tax. When an individual dies, this tax is levied against the value of the assets that pass on to the heirs by will or automatic transfer. Under current law, any amount of property that one spouse inherits from the other is exempt from estate tax. Therefore, married couples who remain together until death do not need to consider estate taxes in planning ownership of their home. The second relevant tax is capital gains tax. Unlike estate tax, capital gains tax is affected by what form of ownership of property a couple chooses. The basic rule for capital gains tax is that when property is inherited by one person from another, it begins anew for tax purposes. That is, for future capital gains computation, the property is treated as though it were purchased at the

market value at the time of inheritance. When the property is sold, tax is due on the appreciation in value since the time it was inherited. No tax, however, is due on the increase in value from actual purchase to time of inheritance. If the property is owned jointly, one-half begins anew for tax purposes.

In this revision, the sentences are rearranged so that the writer gives information first about the estate tax and then about the capital gains tax. Transitions come from repetition of key words, pronouns, demonstrative adjectives, and connecting words or phrases.

Coherence in paragraphs is essential if readers are to use a document effectively. When a reader stumbles through a paragraph trying to sort out the information or decide the relationships between items, the reader's understanding and patience diminish rapidly.

Development

Develop your paragraphs by including enough details so that your reader understands the main point. Generally, one- and two-sentence paragraphs are not fully developed, unless they are used for purposes of transition or emphasis or are quotations. Except in these circumstances, a paragraph should contain a summary or topic sentence and details that support the topic.

Here is a poorly developed paragraph from a brochure that explains diabetes to patients who must learn new eating habits.

> People with insulin-dependent diabetes need to plan meals for consistency. Insulin reactions can occur if meals are not balanced.

This sample paragraph is inadequately developed for a new patient who knows very little about the disease. The opening sentence suggests that the paragraph will describe meal planning for diabetics. Instead, the second sentence tells what will happen without meal planning. Either sentence could be the true topic sentence, and neither point is developed. The reader is left, therefore, with an incomplete understanding of the subject and no way to begin meal planning. Here is a revision:

> People with insulin-dependent diabetes need to plan meals for consistency. To control blood sugar levels, schedule meals for the same time every day. In addition, eat about the same amounts of carbohydrates, protein, and fat every day in the same combinations and at the same times. Your doctor will tell you the exact amounts appropriate for you. This consistency in eating is important because your insulin dose is based on a set food intake. If your meal plan is not balanced, an insulin reaction may occur.

In this revision, the writer develops the summary sentence by giving examples of what consistency means. The paragraph is developed further by an explanation of the consequences if patients do not plan balanced meals. The point about an insulin reaction is now connected to the main topic of the paragraph—meal planning.

In developing paragraphs, think first about the main idea and then determine what information the reader needs to understand that idea. Here are some ways to develop your paragraphs:

- Provide examples of the topic.

- Include facts, statistics, evidence, details, or precedents that confirm the topic.

- Quote, paraphrase, or summarize the evidence of other people on the topic.

- Describe an event that has some influence on the topic.

- Define terms connected with the topic.

- Explain how equipment operates.

- Describe the physical appearance of an object, area, or person.

In developing your paragraphs, remember that long, unbroken sections of detailed information may overwhelm readers, especially those without expert knowledge of the subject, and may interfere with the ability of readers to use the information.

Patterns for Presenting Information

The following patterns for presenting information can be effective ways to organize paragraphs or entire sections of a document. Several organizational patterns may appear in a single document. A writer preparing a manual may use one pattern to give instructions, another to explain a new concept, and a third to help readers visualize the differences between two procedures. Select the pattern that will best help your readers understand and use the information.

Ascending or Descending Order of Importance Pattern

To discuss information in order of importance to the reader, use the ascending (lowest-to-highest) or descending (highest-to-lowest) pattern. If you are describing the degrees of hazard of several procedures or the seriousness of several production problems, you may want to use the descending pattern to alert your readers to the matter most in need of attention. In technical writing, the descending order usually is preferred by busy executives because they want to know the most important facts about a subject first and may even stop reading once they understand the main points. However, the ascending order can be effective if you are building a persuasive case on why, for example, a distribution system should be changed.

This excerpt from an advertisement for a mutual fund illustrates the descending order of importance in a list of benefits for potential investors in the fund:

> Experienced and successful investors select the Davies-Meredith Equity Fund because
>
> 1. The Fund has outperformed 98% of all mutual funds in its category for the past 18 months.
> 2. The Fund charges no investment fees or commissions.
> 3. A 24-hour toll-free number is available for transfers, withdrawals, or account information.
> 4. Each investor receives the free monthly newsletter, "Investing for Your Future."

Although a reader may be persuaded to invest in the fund by any of these reasons, most potential investors would agree that the first item is most important and the last item least important. The writer uses the descending order of importance to attract the reader's attention.

The writer, however, uses the ascending order of importance to illustrate the gains in an investment over time:

> Long-term investment brings the greatest gains. An initial investment of $1000 in 1990 would have nearly doubled in six years:
>
> | | |
> |---|---|
> | 1 year | $1045 |
> | 2 years | $1211 |
> | 4 years | $1571 |
> | 6 years | $1987 |

The ascending order pattern here emphasizes to the investor the benefits of keeping money in the fund for several years.

Cause-and-Effect Pattern

The cause-and-effect pattern is useful when a writer wants to show readers the relationship between specific events. If you are writing a report about equipment problems, the cause-and-effect pattern can help readers see how one breakdown led to another and interrupted production. Be sure to present a clear relationship between cause and effect and give readers evidence of that relationship. If you are merely speculating about causes, make this clear:

> The probable cause of the gas leak was a blown gasket in the transformer.

Writers sometimes choose to describe events from effects back to cause. Lengthy research reports often establish the results first and then explain the causes of those results.

This excerpt from a pamphlet for dental patients uses cause-and-effect to explain how periodontal disease develops:

> Improper brushing or lack of flossing and regular professional tooth cleaning allows the normal bacteria present in the mouth to form a bacterial plaque. This plaque creates spaces or pockets between the gums and roots of the teeth. Chronic inflammation of the gums then develops. Left untreated, the inflammation erodes the bone in which the teeth are anchored, causing the teeth to loosen or migrate. Advanced periodontal disease requires surgery to reconstruct the supporting structures of the teeth.

Chronological Pattern

The chronological pattern is used to present material in stages or steps from first to last when readers need to understand a sequence of events or follow specific steps to perform a task. This excerpt from consumer instructions for a popcorn maker illustrates the chronological pattern:

1. Before using, wash cover, butter-measuring cup, and popping chamber in hot water. Rinse and dry. *Do not immerse housing in water.*
2. Place popcorn container under chute.
3. Preheat the unit for 3 minutes.
4. Using the butter-measuring cup, pour ½ cup kernels into popping chamber.

Instructions should always be written in the chronological pattern. This pattern is also appropriate when the writer needs to describe a test or a process so the reader can visualize it, as in this description of the test method from a media research report:

> The television viewers ($N = 923$) first completed a demographic questionnaire. They then watched a 2- to 3-minute clip of the television program they were rating. After seeing the clip, viewers used the Personal Attributes Questionnaire to rate the male and female characters for stereotypical traits. Finally, viewers rated themselves on the Personal Attributes Questionnaire for comparison purposes.

Classification Pattern

The classification pattern involves grouping items in terms of certain characteristics and showing your readers the similarities within each group. The basis for classification should be the one most useful for your purpose and your readers.

You might classify foods as protein, carbohydrate, or fat for a report to dietitians. In a report on foods for a culinary society, however, you might classify them as beverages, appetizers, and desserts. Classification is useful when you have many items to discuss, but if your categories are too broad, your readers will have trouble understanding the distinctiveness of each class. Classifying all edibles under "food" for either of the two reports just mentioned would not be useful because you would have no basis for distinguishing the individual items.

This excerpt from an article for managers of low-power television stations uses classification to explain types of antennas appropriate for those stations:

> Today, there are several antenna types in general use for LPTV. Among these are the pylon, the panel, the zigzag, and—more recently for UHF LPTV—the turnstile or super turnstile antennas. . . .
>
> Pylon antennas are basically slot antennas and consist of a cylinder ranging from 8 to 50 feet in length. . . .
>
> Panel antennas are made up of yagi (herringbone) receiving antennas enclosed within a fiberglass radome. . . .
>
> The zigzag antenna has a fiberglass panel casing, inside which is a vertical zigzag radiator that, in effect, is a vertical series of dipoles and reflectors. . . .
>
> The turnstile or super turnstile (a modern version of the very early batwing antenna) resembles the turnstiles found in public entrances . . . it is contained within a fiberglass cylinder for protection. . . .[3]

Partition Pattern

The partition pattern, in contrast to the classification pattern, involves separating a topic or system into its individual features. This division allows readers to master information about one aspect of the topic before going on to the next. Instructions are always divided into steps so that readers can perform one step at a time. The readers' purpose in needing the information should guide selection of the basis for partition. For example, a skier on the World Cup circuit would be interested in a discussion of skis based on their use in certain types of races, such as downhill or slalom. A manufacturer interested in producing skis might want the same discussion based on materials used in production. A sales representative might want the discussion based on costs of the different types of skis.

This excerpt from a NASA pamphlet for the general public uses partition to explain the major sections of the Space Shuttle:

> *The Parts of the Space Shuttle*
>
> The flight components of the Space Shuttle are two solid rocket boosters, an external tank, and a winged orbiter. . . .
>
> The two solid rocket boosters are each 149.1 feet (45.4 meters) high and 12.2 feet (3.7 meters) in diameter. Each weighs 1,300,000 pounds (589.670 kilograms). Their solid propellant consists of a mixture of. . . .

The huge external tank is 154 feet (47 meters) long and 28.6 feet (8.7 meters) in diameter. It weighs a total of 7.3 million pounds (756,441 kilograms) at liftoff. . . .

The orbiter carries the crew and payload. It is 122 feet (37 meters) long and 57 feet (17 meters) high, has a wingspan of 78 feet (24 meters), and weighs from 168,000 to 175,000 pounds (76,000 to 79,000 kilograms) empty. . . .[4]

Comparison and Contrast Pattern

The comparison and contrast pattern focuses on the similarities (comparison) or differences (contrast) between subjects. Writers often find this pattern useful because they can explain a complex topic by comparing or contrasting it with another familiar topic. For this pattern, the writer has to set up the basis for comparison according to what readers want to know. In evaluating the suitability of two locations for a new restaurant, a writer could compare the two sites according to accessibility, neighborhood competition, and costs. There are two ways to organize the comparison and contrast pattern for this situation. In one method (topical), the writer could compare and contrast location A with location B under specific topics, such as

---

Accessibility
1. Location A
2. Location B

Neighborhood competition
1. Location A
2. Location B

Costs
1. Location A
2. Location B

In the other method (complete subject), the writer could present an overall comparison by discussing all the features of location A and then all the features of location B, keeping the discussion in parallel order, such as

---

Location A
1. Accessibility
2. Neighborhood competition
3. Costs

Location B
1. Accessibility
2. Neighborhood competition
3. Costs

In choosing one method over another, consider the readers' needs. For the report on two potential restaurant locations, readers might prefer a topical comparison to judge the suitability of each location in terms of the three vital factors. The topical method does not force readers to move back and forth between major sections looking for one particular item as the complete subject method does. In comparing two computers, however, a writer may decide that readers need an overall description of the two in order to determine which seems to satisfy more office requirements. In this case, the writer would present all the features of computer A and then all those of computer B.

This excerpt showing comparison is taken from a report written by a swimming coach to a university director of athletics who needs to know about coaching techniques used on campus:

> This year the swim team has been using a nontraditional training regimen. As you may know, the traditional training method relies on swimmers developing a good aerobic base by swimming between 10,000 and 20,000 yards a day at a steady pace for two months before the meet season. The new training method we are using involves lower yardage but higher swimming pace. This new method calls for 4000 yards of swimming daily, but all swimming is to be at race pace. The two methods both develop an aerobic base, but the second emphasizes race conditions.

Definition Pattern

The purpose of definition is to explain the meaning of a term that refers to a concept, process, or object. Chapter 6 discusses writing definitions for objects or processes. Definition also can be part of any other organizational pattern when a writer decides that a particular term will not be clear to readers. An *informal definition* is a simple statement using familiar terms:

> A drizzle is a light rainfall.

A *formal definition* places the term into a group and then explains the term's special features that distinguish it from the group:

term   group   special features

A pronator is a muscle in the forearm that turns the palm downward.

Writers use *expanded definitions* to identify terms and explain individual features when they believe readers need more than a sentence definition. Definitions can be expanded by adding examples, using an analogy, or employing one of the organization patterns, such as comparison and contrast or partition.

This excerpt from a student's biology report uses the cause-and-effect pattern to expand the definition of arteriosclerosis:

> Arteriosclerosis is a disease of the arteries, commonly known as hardening of the arteries. As we age, plaques of fatty deposits, called atheromas, form in the blood and cling to the walls of the arteries. These deposits build up and narrow the artery passage, interfering with the flow of blood. Fragments of the plaque, called emboli, may break away and block the arteries, causing a sudden blockage and a stroke. Even if no plaque fragments break away, eventually the artery will lose elasticity, blood pressure will rise, and blood flow will be sufficiently reduced to cause a stroke or a heart attack.

Spatial Pattern

In the spatial pattern, information is grouped according to the physical arrangement of the subject. A writer may describe a machine part by part from top to bottom so that readers can visualize how the parts fit together. The spatial pattern creates a path for readers to follow. Features can be described from top to bottom, side to side, inside to outside, north to south, or in any order that fits the way readers need to "see" the topic.

This excerpt is from an architect's report to a civic restoration committee about an old theater scheduled to be restored:

> The inside of the main doorway is surrounded by a Castilian castle facade and includes a red-tiled parapet at the top of the castle roof. A series of parallel brass railings just beyond the doorway creates corridors for arriving movie patrons. Along the side walls are ornamented white marble columns behind which the walls are covered with 12-ft-high mirrors. The white marble floor sweeps across the lobby to the wall opposite the entrance, where a broad split staircase curves up from both sides of the lobby to the triple doors at the mezzanine level. The top of the staircase at the mezzanine level is decorated with a life-size black marble lion on each side.

▬ *CHAPTER SUMMARY*

This chapter discusses organizing information by sorting it into major topics and subtopics, constructing outlines, and developing effective paragraphs. Remember:

- Information should be grouped into major topics and subtopics based on the way the readers want to learn about the subject.

- An informal outline is a list of major topics.

- A formal outline uses a special numbering system, usually Roman and Arabic numerals or decimals, and lists all major topics and subtopics.

- A topic outline lists all the major topics and subtopics by key words.

- A sentence outline states each main topic and subtopic in a full sentence.

- Effective paragraphs need to be unified, coherent, and fully developed.

- Organizational patterns for effective paragraphs include ascending or descending order of importance, cause and effect, chronological, classification, partition, comparison and contrast, definition, and spatial.

SUPPLEMENTAL READINGS IN PART 2

Benson, P. J. "Writing Visually: Design Considerations in Technical Publications," *Technical Communication,* p. 451.

Buehler, M. F. "Defining Terms in Technical Editing: The Levels of Edit as a Model," *Technical Communication,* p. 486.

Marra, J. L. "For Writers: Understanding the Art of Layout," *Technical Communication,* p. 525.

Plunka, G. A. "The Editor's Nightmare: Formatting Lists within the Text," *Technical Communication,* p. 536.

"Six Graphics Guidelines," *Simply Stated,* p. 562.

ENDNOTES

1. Duin, Ann Hill. "Factors That Influence How Readers Learn from Text: Guidelines for Structuring Technical Documents," *Technical Communication* 36.1 (February 1989): 97–101.

2. Adapted from Allen Bernstein, *1988 Tax Guide for College Teachers* (College Park, MD: Academic Information Service, 1987).

3. From Battison, John H. "The Last Link," *LPTV Report* (April 1992), pp. 4–6. Reprinted with permission of *LPTV Report.*

4. From *Space Shuttle,* NASA, PMS 013-B (KSC), December 1991.

This model shows a memo written by a human resources director to the managers of a large manufacturing company. The readers already know the company is launching an alcohol and drug treatment program. The memo's purpose is to announce a seminar designed to show the readers appropriate methods for handling employees with such problems. The writer includes general information about the rise of health care costs, the reasons for starting a company treatment program, and specific information about the seminar itself.

Discussion

1. Attendance at this seminar is mandatory. Discuss why the writer lists the topics covered in the seminar and the names of the leaders—all information that readers would find out when they attend the seminar.

2. Discuss the headings used in this memo. How helpful are they to the reader? Are there any changes you would suggest?

3. Discuss the opening sections on background and rationale. What is the purpose of these sections, and how useful are they to the reader?

4. The writer states the date of the seminar in three places. Is this a case of careless repetition? Discuss the final paragraph and why the writer includes all these pieces of information in this paragraph.

To: All Department Supervisors and Unit Managers

From: Alicia Dumaine
             Director, Human Resources

Date: November 2, 1995

Re: New Employee Assistance Program for Drug and Alcohol Abuse

As you already know, on January 1, 1996, Winslow Manufacturing
Company is launching a new program for the prevention and treatment
of drug and alcohol abuse. As part of the preparation stage, a
management seminar on awareness and intervention skills is scheduled
for Friday, December 8, 1995. This all-day seminar will provide training
in appropriate procedures for managers and supervisors.

Background

All employers today are concerned with the rising costs in health
benefits for workers. Since the 1950s, most employers pay for or
provide some access to health coverage for workers and their families.
Winslow Manufacturing has always taken pride in the full coverage
offered employees. With the rise in health care costs in the 1970s and
1980s, however, Winslow has had to develop specific strategies to aid
employees in avoiding health problems. The Winslow Health Club
established in 1986 was one way to foster employee wellness. Drug and
alcohol abuse treatment plans are another way Winslow can aid its
employees and help control the costs of health coverage.

Rationale for Program

Research studies (available in the Human Resources Office) indicate that
attitudes and behaviors can be changed by programs in the workplace.
Most treatment programs have a high rate of relapse, up to 60 percent,
especially if the drugs involved are cocaine or heroin. Intensive initial
treatment plans have been ineffective if the person returns to the
original environment without a program for aftercare. Regular
counseling sessions and group therapy can help keep a person stable
after initial treatment. Research also indicates that women tend to use
different drugs than men do, and, therefore, women may need different
treatment plans. Individual treatment plans are most effective.

Winslow Manufacturing Program

The new health plan for substance abuse includes both in-house
counseling and referral to community treatment centers. Crisis

Department supervisors and unit managers   page 2
November 2, 1995

intervention will also be available as needed. The coordinating efforts
will be in the Human Resources Office in consultation with the Falls
Valley Treatment Center.

Management Training Seminar

The seminar leaders on Friday, December 8, will be Dr. Henry Rios and
Dr. Cynthia Banning, both of the ChemHealth Clinic in Tucson, Arizona.
The seminar will include sessions on the following:

- nature and extent of substance abuse in the workplace

- special problems of substance abuse in manufacturing

- special problems of multiple addiction

- detection of impaired performance or behavior

- documentation of impaired performance or behavior

- reduced job stress for employees returning from in-patient
  treatment

The seminar leaders also will conduct a role-playing session to illustrate
the principles of supervisory interviews with employees who may have
substance abuse problems. Finally, you will all receive a Manager's
Assessment Kit that contains fact sheets on alcohol and drug abuse,
checklists of management procedures, and copies of the company's
policy on alcohol and drug abuse.

Please mark your calendars for Friday, December 8, 1995. The seminar
will be in the Training Center, third floor. A continental breakfast will be
available, so the first session can begin promptly at 8:00 a.m. Sessions
will end at 4:45 p.m. Mr. Winslow will make opening remarks.

MODEL 3-6   Commentary

This letter report was written by an engineer to a client who had requested an analysis of suitable roadway improvement processes and a recommendation for future work. The engineer reviews the current conditions of the city's roads, then describes the two available types of recycled asphalt processes, and concludes with the firm's recommendation. The writer also offers to discuss the subject further and to provide copies of reports he mentions in his letter.

Discussion

1. Discuss the headings the writer uses in his letter report. How helpful are they to the reader? Are there any revisions you would make in the headings?

2. In his "Recommendation" section, the writer mentions environmental concerns. How much impact does this mention of the environment have in this section? What revisions in content or organization would you make to increase the emphasis on environmental reasons for using recycled asphalt?

3. Identify the organizational strategies the writer uses throughout his report.

MANNING-HORNSBY ENGINEERING CONSULTANTS
3200 Farmington Drive
Kansas City, Missouri 64132
(816) 555–7070

November 23, 1996

Mr. Marvin O. Thompson
City Manager
Municipal Building, Suite 360
Ridgewood, MO 64062

Dear Mr. Thompson:

This report covers the Manning-Hornsby review of the current roadway conditions in Ridgewood, Missouri, analysis of the available recycled asphalt processes, and our recommendation for the appropriate process for future Ridgewood roadway improvement projects.

Current Ridgewood Maintenance Program

The City of Ridgewood has 216 miles of roadways. Half of these have curbs and gutters, while the other half have bermed shoulders with drainage ditches. About 95 percent of the roadways are of asphalt composition. The remaining 5 percent are of reinforced concrete construction or are unimproved.

Condition: Over the last five years, 40 miles of existing roadways have been improved. Improvements generally consist of crack sealing and removal and replacement of minor sections of pavement followed by a resurfacing overlay. Roadways with curbs and gutters are typically overlayed with 3–4 inch layers of hot-mix asphalt. Roadways with berms and drainage ditches are typically overlayed with 3–4 inch layers of cold-mix asphalt, also known as "chip and seal." No form of recycled asphalt has ever been used on these roadways.

Both these processes are appropriate for Ridgewood roadways. Hot-mix asphalt is a bituminous pavement, mixed hot at an asphalt plant, delivered hot to the site, and rolled to a smooth compacted state. The cold-mix asphalt is mixed and placed at lower temperatures with higher asphalt contents. Cold-mix asphalt is usually covered with bitumen and stone chips. Generally, the hot mix provides a smoother surface than the cold mix but is more susceptible to future cracking. The cold mix is more resilient than the hot mix and will reform itself in the summer heat and high temperatures.

Mr. Marvin O. Thompson   -2-   November 23, 1996

Problem: One of the problems associated with the current maintenance process is that roadways are being overlayed without the removal of existing asphalt. Therefore, the roadway grades are increasing. In some cases, the curbs are starting to disappear. Drainage problems are occurring due to the flattening road surface, permanent cross slopes, and grade changes. These conditions cause low spots that do not drain to existing catchbasins.

So that the curb and drainage problems noted above are eliminated, future projects should include the removal of existing layers of asphalt before resurfacing begins. Plans should call for milling off a depth of existing asphalt that is equal to or greater than the proposed overlay thickness. The milling process will make it possible to achieve curb heights, pavement cross slopes, and pavement grades that are similar to the originally constructed roadway. The City must then decide what it wants to do with the milled asphalt.

Recycled Asphalt

Recycling products has become a popular operation in today's environmentally conscious world. One waste material already being used extensively is asphalt. Most experts agree that using recycled asphalt in roadways does not detract from performance. Using recycled asphalt becomes advantageous specifically in cases where existing asphalt removal is necessary on projects because past overlays are affecting curb heights and creating drainage problems. In these cases, using recycled asphalt creates two main benefits. First, by reusing existing asphalt, the municipality takes another step toward solving its environmental problems by reducing solid waste in landfills. Second, using recycled asphalt reduces project costs as noted below. There are two types of recycled asphalt appropriate for roadways such as those in Ridgewood.

Hot In-Place Recycled Asphalt: Hot in-place asphalt recycling has been used throughout the United States with satisfactory results. Hot in-place recycling consists of milling off existing asphalt to a specified depth, mixing the recycled asphalt with virgin asphalt at high temperatures, laying the hot asphalt, and rolling it to a highly compacted density. Mixing is performed either at the asphalt plant or in a mixing vehicle that follows directly behind the milling equipment and directly in front of the paver. Reports from other municipalities and states indicate using hot in-place recycled asphalt can save 10 to 30 percent in road costs.

Mr. Marvin O. Thompson   -3-   November 23, 1996

<u>Cold In-Place Recycled Asphalt:</u> Cold in-place asphalt recycling usually consists of milling off existing asphalt to a specified depth, mixing that asphalt with virgin materials and/or rejuvenating liquids, then laying it back in place. The mixing is done either at the plant or in a paving machine directly behind the milling machine. The advantage of this procedure is the ability to use existing material to correct road profile problems. During in-place recycling, a new roadway crown can be established. The cold mix is commonly used for base or intermediate layers on low volume roads. The main benefit here is the cold mix's ability to prevent old cracks from reflecting through the overlay. The majority of users of recycled cold mix top it with virgin asphalt or chip and seal. The latest reports indicate that using cold in-place recycled asphalt can save local governments from 6 to 67 percent in road costs.

Recommendation

The existing roadways in Ridgewood have undergone years of overlays in road maintenance. The future improvement projects will have to reestablish road grades for proper drainage and for standard curb heights. Increasing evidence shows that cost savings can be achieved by using both hot and cold in-place recycled asphalt. In addition, these processes provide an environmentally sound alternative to wasting asphalt in land fills. Manning-Hornsby recommends that the City of Ridgewood adopt this recycled asphalt process in future roadway improvement projects.

I would be happy to discuss this recommendation with you in more detail, and I can provide copies of the reports from other areas about the use of recycled asphalt. I will call your office next week to set up a time convenient to you. In the meantime, please do not hesitate to contact me with any questions.

Sincerely,

Joseph F. Lennetti

Joseph F. Lennetti
Senior Engineer
MANNING-HORNSBY ENGINEERING CONSULTANTS

Chapter 3 Exercises

1. The following memo was sent to the staff of a large medical clinic. The purpose of the memo was to announce the installation of a new computer network and the resulting required overtime. Revise the memo for a more effective organization, so readers can use the information easily. Before revising, read "The Editor's Nightmare: Formatting Lists within the Text" by Plunka in Part 2.

Effective July 10–12, 1995, the computer system will be installed at our new offices. During the period of installing the computer system and moving to the new offices, we will need to work overtime every Friday and Saturday. Excuses cannot be accepted during this period. Charts will have to be transferred between the offices as needed. Every staff member is required to be available to transport the charts for the training sessions on the new computer system.

Training will begin on Friday, July 12. Patient data will be entered during the training sessions in order to combine training with regular duties. We should complete the move by August 10, and new office hours will be in effect during the transition period. Time off during this transition period must be approved by Dr. Jared.

Charts must be pulled on Thursdays, based on assigned letters of the alphabet. Monday through Thursday work hours are 8 a.m. to 5 p.m., as always. At the new offices, we will work on Fridays 9 a.m. to 6 p.m. On Saturdays, the hours are 8 a.m. to 5 p.m. Since no patients are scheduled on Fridays, all office staff will report to the new offices with the assigned charts for the training sessions.

On Saturdays, report to the new offices on time. The last three hours on Saturdays will be spent transporting charts back to the current offices. No charts can remain overnight at the new offices. Also, on Saturdays, we will file and prepare Monday morning charts. Feel free to dress in comfortable clothes during the training sessions.

2. The following bulletin is addressed to home owners and provides information about radon hazards in the home. Organize this information into a useful document for interested readers who know very little about the subject.

The health risk associated with prolonged inhalation of radon gas is an increased risk of developing lung cancer. There are also indications that risk increases as the level of radon concentration and duration of exposure increases. Radon is a colorless, odorless, tasteless gas that occurs worldwide in the environment as a byproduct in the environment of natural decay of uranium present in the earth. Radon is present in varying quantities in the atmosphere and in soils around the globe. The only way to know if a home has a radon problem is to test it. Radon levels vary from home to home, depending on the structure of the house and the surrounding soil. The U.S. Environmental Protection Agency has determined that short-term exposure to a high concentration of radon is not as severe a risk as long-term exposure to a lower level of the gas. Radon from surrounding soil enters a house through small spaces, such as cracks in concrete, floor drains, sump pump openings, wall/floor joints in basements, and the pores in hollow block walls. There are several ways to make a preliminary screening test for radon. Kits are available over the counter in hardware, grocery, and convenience stores. Tests that measure the amount of radon in water normally require you to send a sample of tap water to a laboratory for analysis. Radon generally concentrates most in the areas of a home closest to the ground. Radon levels generally decrease in upper stories. Radon can also seep into underground water and remain trapped there. If a home has a ground water supply source (such as a well), there is a greater potential for radon problems. Follow directions carefully when doing testing. Short-term testing is one way to determine if radon exists, but long-term testing is a more accurate way to determine if radon is present consistently. Both kinds of testing kits are easy to use. If radon is present in the water supply, it can be removed altogether or reduced by special filter systems. Houses with water supplied by a municipal water supply have fewer problems with radon in the water. Radon gas breaks down into radioactive particles that remain in the air. As these particles are breathed in, they break down and release bursts of radiation that damage lung tissue. Out of doors, radon gas diffuses into the atmosphere and is not a health hazard. The costs for radon removal will depend on the number of radon sources, the amount of radon in the land or water supply, and the kind of construction in the house. No level of radon is considered safe. It is always prudent to use trained personnel in removal of radon. The cost of installing radon reduction equipment ranges from several hundred to several thousand dollars.

3. You are on a student committee that is preparing an information brochure for incoming freshmen. Your assignment is to write a section of the brochure that will explain one of the following:

Fraternity and sorority activities on campus

Library facilities

Sports activities on campus

Placement and advising services on campus

Effective study habits

Counseling and health services on campus

In writing your section, consider carefully how to organize the information to make the section appealing to the freshman readers. Read the article entitled "Six Graphics Guidelines" in Part 2 before organizing your section. Prepare an outline of your section for your instructor before you submit your written section.

4. Select an article from Part 2 and create an outline of the organization the writer used. The articles in Part 2 primarily offer advice to people already on the job. If you were to revise the article you selected for students not yet in full-time careers, what changes would you make in the organization? Would you add, delete, or rearrange topics? Revise the outline for a student audience and submit it and the original outline to your instructor.

CHAPTER 4

Document Design

UNDERSTANDING DESIGN FEATURES

Document design refers to the physical appearance of a document. Because the written text and its presentation work together to provide readers with the information they need, think about the design of your documents during the planning stage—even before you select appropriate information and organize it.

Readers do not read only the printed words on a page; they also "read" the visual presentation of the text, just as a television viewer pays attention not only to the main actor and the words he or she speaks, but also to the background action, noises, music, and other actors' movements. In an effective document, as in an effective television scene, the words and visuals support each other.

Desktop publishing has expanded the writer's role in producing technical documents. A writer with sophisticated computer equipment and design software packages can create finished documents with most of the design features discussed in this chapter. Desktop publishing makes it easy to produce newsletters, catalogs, press releases, brochures, training materials, reports, and proposals—all with graphic aids, columns, headlines, mastheads, bullets, and any design feature needed by readers.

Rapidly developing computer technology increases the capabilities of desktop publishing with each new scanner, printer, and software package. It is not an exaggeration to say that desktop publishing has launched a printing revolution as more companies produce more of their own documents. No matter whether a document is produced on centuries-old movable type or on the latest computer technology, however, the writer's goal is the same—to provide readers with the information they need in a form they can use.

Purpose of Design Features

Some documents, such as business letters, have well-known, conventional formats, but letters and other documents also benefit from additional design features—graphic aids and the format elements of written cues, white space, and typographic devices. These design features increase the usefulness of documents in several ways.

1. They guide readers through the text by directing attention to individual topics and increasing the ability of readers to remember the important, highlighted sections.

2. They increase reader interest in the document. Unbroken blocks of type have a numbing effect on most readers, but eye-catching graphic aids and attention-getting format devices keep readers focused on the information they need.

3. They create a document that reflects the image you wish readers to have. A conservative law firm may want to project a solid, traditional,

no-nonsense image with its documents, whereas a video equipment company may prefer to project a trendy, dramatic image. Both images can be enhanced by specific design features.

Design Principles

The principles of design are qualities important to any visual presentation regardless of topic or audience. Experienced designers use the principles of design to create the "look" they want for a document. The general principles most designers consider in all documents are balance, proportion, sequence, and consistency.

Balance

Page balance refers to having comparable visual "weight" on both sides of a page or on opposing pages in a longer document. A page in a manual filled with text and photographs followed by a page with only a single paragraph in the center would probably jar the reader. If this unsettling effect is not your intent, avoid such imbalance in page design.

Think of page balance as similar to the scales held by the figure of Justice you have seen so often. Formal balance on a page would be the same as two evenly filled scales hanging at the same level. Informal balance, which is used more often by experienced page designers, would be represented by a heavily weighted scale on one side balanced by two smaller scales equal to the total weight of the larger scale on the other side.

One large section of a page, then, can be balanced by two smaller sections. Every time an element is added to or removed from a page, however, the balance shifts. A photograph that is dominant on one page may not be dominant on another page. Remember these points about visual "weight":

- Big weighs more than small.
- Dark weighs more than light.
- Color weighs more than black and white.
- Unusual shapes weigh more than simple circles or squares.

Proportion

Proportion in page design refers to size and placement of text, graphic aids, and format elements on the page. Experienced designers rarely use an equal amount of space for text and graphics page after page. Not only would this be monotonous for readers, but it would interfere with the readers' ability to use the document. Reserving the same amount of space for one heading called "Labor" and another called "Budgetary Considerations" would result in the long heading looking cramped and the short heading looking lost in the space available. In a similar fashion, you would not want every drawing in a parts manual to be the same size regardless of the object it depicts. Each design feature should be the size that is helpful to the readers and appropriate for the subject.

Sequence

Sequence refers to the arrangement of design features so that readers see them in the best order for their use of the document. Readers usually begin reading a page at the top left corner and end at the bottom right corner. In between these two points, readers tend to scan from left to right and up to down. Readers also tend to notice the features with the most "weight" first. Effective design draws readers through the page from important point to important point.

Consistency

Consistency refers to presenting similar features in a similar style. Keep these elements consistent throughout a document:

- *Margins.* Keep uniform margins on all pages of a document.
- *Typeface.* Use the same size and style of type for similar headings and similar kinds of information.
- *Indentations.* Keep uniform indentations for such items as paragraphs, quotations, and lists.

Do not mistake consistent format for boring format. Consistency helps readers by emphasizing similar types of information and their similar importance. A brochure published by the Ohio Department of Health to alert college students to the dangers of AIDS is designed as a series of questions. Each question (e.g., "What is AIDS?" and "How Do You Get AIDS?") is printed in all capital letters in light blue. The answers are printed in black. This consistency in design helps the readers quickly find the answers to their questions.

CREATING GRAPHIC AIDS

Graphic aids, called *figures* and *tables,* are not merely decorative additions to documents or oral presentations. Often graphic aids are essential in helping readers understand and use the information in a document. Instructions may be easier to use when they have graphics that illustrate some steps, such as directions for gripping a tennis racquet properly or for performing artificial respiration.

Purpose of Graphic Aids

Think about which graphic aids would be appropriate for your document during the planning stage. Graphic aids are important in technical documents in these ways:

- Graphic aids provide quick access to complicated information, especially numerical data. For example, a reader can more quickly see the highs and lows of a production trend from a line graph than from a long narrative explanation.

- Graphic aids isolate the main topics in complex data and appeal particularly to general and nonexpert readers. Newspapers, for instance, usually report government statistics with graphic aids so that their readers can easily see the scope of the information.

- Graphic aids help readers see relationships among several sets of data. Two pie graphs side by side will illustrate more easily than a narrative can the differences between how the federal government spent a tax dollar in 1932 and in 1992.

- Graphic aids, such as detailed statistical tables, can offer expert readers quick access to complicated data that would take pages to explain in written text.

Readers of some documents expect graphic aids. Scientists reading a research report expect to see tables and formulas that show the experimental method and results. Do not, however, rely solely on graphic aids to explain important data. Some readers are more comfortable with written text than with graphics, and for these readers, your text should thoroughly analyze the facts, their impact on the situation or on the future, their relevance for decision making or for direct action, and their relation to other data. For consistency and reader convenience, follow these guidelines for all graphic aids.

1. Identify each graphic aid with a specific title, such as "1987–1993 Crime Rates" or "Differences in Patient Response to Analgesics."

2. Number each graphic aid. All graphics that are not tables with words or numbers in columns are called figures. Number each table or figure consecutively throughout the document, and refer to it by number in the text:

    The results shown in Table 1 are from the first survey. The second survey is illustrated in Figure 2.

3. Place each graphic aid in the text as near after the first reference to it as possible. If, however, the document has many tables and charts or only some of the readers are interested in them, you may decide to put them all in an appendix to avoid breaking up the text too frequently.

The guidelines in this chapter for creating various types of graphic aids provide general advice for such illustrations. Effective graphic aids, however, can violate standard guidelines and still be useful to the readers who need them. The daily newspaper *USA Today* contains many innovative illustrations of data for its readers who are interested in a quick understanding of the latest statistical or technical information. The key to creating effective graphic aids is to analyze purpose and reader before selecting graphic formats. While an industrial psychologist may prefer a detailed statistical table of the results of a survey of construction workers, a general reader may want—and need—a simple pie chart showing the key points.

Tables

A table shows numerical or topical data in rows and columns, thus providing readers with quick access to quantitative information and allowing readers to make comparisons among items easily. Model 4-1 shows a table that presents a comparison of data from company service centers over a 2-year period.

Here are general guidelines for setting up tables:

1. Provide a heading for each column that identifies the items in the column.

2. Use footnotes to explain specific items in columns. Footnotes for specific numbers or columns require lowercase superscript letters (e.g., [a], [b], [c]). If the footnote is for a specific number, place the letter directly after the number (e.g., 432[a]). If the footnote applies to an entire column, place the letter directly after the column heading (e.g., Payroll[b]). List all footnotes at the left margin of the table, directly below the data.

3. Space columns sufficiently so that the data do not run together.

4. Give the source of your data below the table. If you have multiple sources and have compiled the information into a table, explain this in the text, if necessary.

5. Use decimals and round off figures to the nearest whole number.

6. Indicate in the column heading if you are using a particular measure for units, such as "millions of dollars" or "per 5000 barrels."

TABLE 1   Shipments from Service Centers

	1994	1995	% Change
Liberty, MO	4,167	4,012	− 3.72
Saukville, WI	4,857	4,118	− 15.22
Franklin, TN[a]	623	5,106	+719.58
Medina, OH	3,624	3,598	− 0.72
Salem, OR	3,432	3,768	+ 9.79
Lafayette, LA	2,740	3,231	+ 17.92
Tucson, AZ	5,024	5,630	+ 12.06
Sweetbriar, KY[b]	2,616	3,967	+ 51.64
TOTALS	27,083	33,430	+ 23.44

[a]Opened in June 1994.
[b]Opened in March 1994.

MODEL 4-1   A Sample Table

Figures

All graphic aids that are not tables are considered figures. Information in tables can often be presented effectively in figures as well, and sometimes readers can use figures more readily than tables. A geologist seeking information about groundwater levels may want a table giving specific quantities in specific geologic locations. Someone reading a report in the morning newspaper on groundwater levels across the United States, however, may be better served by a set of bars of varying lengths representing groundwater levels in regions of the country, such as the Pacific Northwest. Before selecting graphic aids for your document, consider your readers and their ability to interpret quantitative information and, particularly, their need for specific or general data. The most common types of graphic aids are bar graphs, pictographs, line graphs, pie graphs, organization charts, flowcharts, line drawings, cutaway drawings, exploded drawings, maps, and photographs.

Bar Graphs

A *bar graph* uses bars of equal width in varying lengths to represent (1) a comparison of items at one particular time, (2) a comparison of items over time, (3) changes in one item over time, or (4) a comparison of portions of a single item. The horizontal and vertical axes represent the two elements being

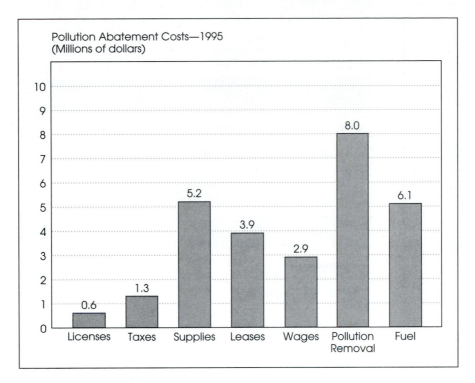

MODEL 4-2   A Typical Vertical Bar Graph

illustrated, such as time and quantity. Model 4-2 is a typical vertical bar graph in which bars represent different types of pollution-reduction costs incurred by a company.

Bars can extend in either a vertical direction, as in Model 4-2, or in a horizontal direction, as in Model 4-3. In Model 4-3, the bars emphasize the increasing sales over the 5-year period. Notice that, in both Models 4-2 and 4-3, a specific figure indicating a dollar amount is printed at the top or the end of the bar.

Bars can also appear on both sides of the axis to indicate positive and negative quantities. Model 4-4 uses bars on both sides of the horizontal axis, indicating positive and negative quantities. Notice that the zero point in the vertical axis is about one-third above the horizontal axis and that the quantities are labeled positive above the zero point and negative below it.

Bar graphs cannot represent exact quantities or provide comparisons of quantities as precisely as tables can, but bar graphs are generally useful for readers who want to understand overall trends and comparisons.

Depending on the size of the graph and the shading or color distinctions, up to four bars can represent different items at any point on an axis. Label

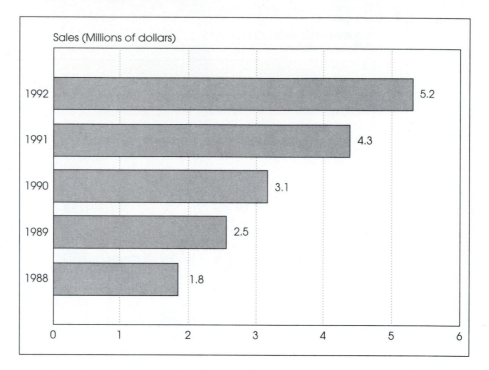

MODEL 4-3   A Typical Horizontal Bar Graph Showing Sales Growth

each bar or provide a key to distinguish among shadings or colors. Model 4-5 shows a bar graph with multiple bars representing three different kinds of fish.

Pictographs

A *pictograph* is a variation of a bar graph that uses symbols instead of bars to illustrate specific quantities of items. The symbols should realistically correspond to the items, such as, for example, a cow representing milk production. Pictographs provide novelty and eye-catching appeal, particularly in documents intended for consumers. Pictographs are limited, however, because symbols cannot adequately represent exact figures of fractions. When using a pictograph, (1) make all symbols the same size, (2) space the symbols equally on the axis, (3) show increased quantity by increasing the number of symbols rather than the size of the symbol, (4) round off the quantities represented instead of using a portion of a symbol to represent a portion of a unit, and (5) include a key indicating the quantity represented by a symbol. Model 4-6 uses houses to represent the trend in housing sales during a 6-month period.

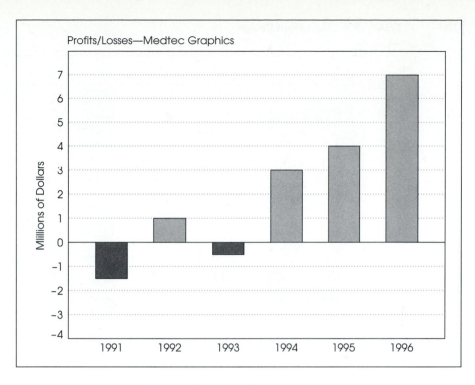

MODEL 4-4   Bars Used on Both Sides of Horizontal Axis

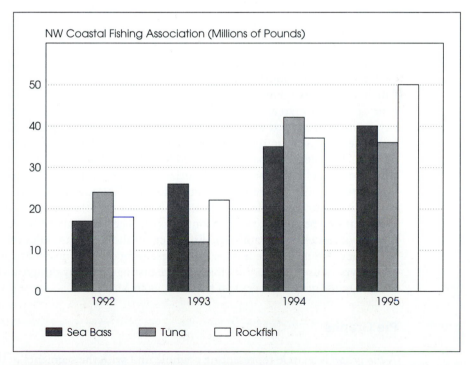

MODEL 4-5   Example of Use of Multiple Bars

MODEL 4-6   A Typical Pictograph

Line Graphs

A *line graph* uses a line between the horizontal and vertical axes to show changes in the relationship between the elements represented by the two axes. The line connects points on the graph that represent a quantity at a particular time or in relation to a specific topic. Line graphs usually plot changes in quantity or in position and are particularly useful for illustrating trends. Three or four lines representing different items can appear on the same graph for comparison. The lines must be distinguished by color or design, and a key must identify them. Label both vertical and horizontal axes, and be sure that the value segments on the axes are equidistant. Model 4-7 uses three lines, each representing sales for a specific corporation. The lines plot changes in sales (vertical axis) during specific years (horizontal axis). The amounts indicated are not exact, but readers can readily see differences in the corporate sales over time.

Model 4-8 uses three lines, each representing energy consumption by a different type of user. Notice that the lines are distinguished by design and they are labeled in the graph rather than by a key, as in Model 4-7.

Pie Graphs

A *pie graph* is a circle representing a whole unit with the segments of the circle, or pie, representing portions of the whole. Pie graphs are useful if the whole

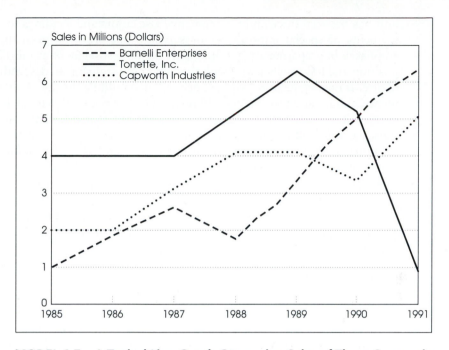

MODEL 4-7   A Typical Line Graph Comparing Sales of Three Companies

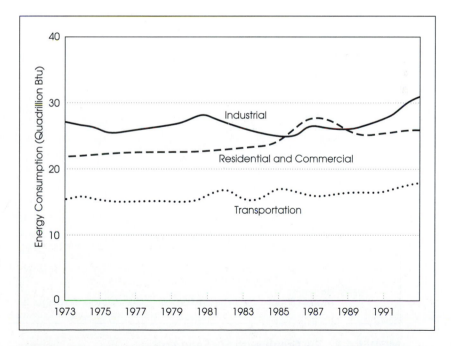

MODEL 4-8   A Typical Line Graph Comparing Energy Consumption by Three Types of Users

unit has between three and ten segments. Use colors and shadings to highlight segments of special importance, or separate one segment from the pie for emphasis. In preparing a pie graph, start the largest segment at the 12 o'clock position and follow clockwise with the remaining segments in descending order of size. If one segment is "Miscellaneous," it should be the last. Label the segments, and be sure their values add up to 100% of the total. Model 4-9 is a pie graph with six segments. The segments represent four different companies—those heating and cooling contractors with the largest share of the Chicago area business. The segment representing Wisconsin-based contractors appears ahead of the "Other" segment because it is the more specific group. One section of a pie chart may be separated from the pie to emphasize the item or quantity represented by that section, as in Model 4-10. In this case, the writer wants to emphasize the percentage spent on computers. Notice that the computer section of the pie is also distinguished by stripes to further highlight it for the reader.

Pie charts and other figures often have call-outs to identify specific parts of the illustration. Call-outs consist of lines leading from a specific part of the illustration to a number, often circled, which corresponds to an item in a separate list. The call-out line may also lead to a written term. Notice that the call-outs in Model 4-9 are small arrows that connect a specific section of the pie to the identification of the contractors and percentages represented. The call-out lines in

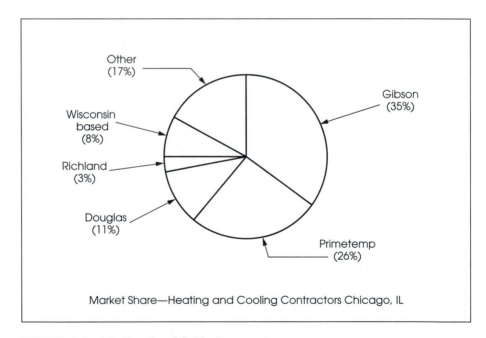

MODEL 4-9   Pie Graph with Six Segments

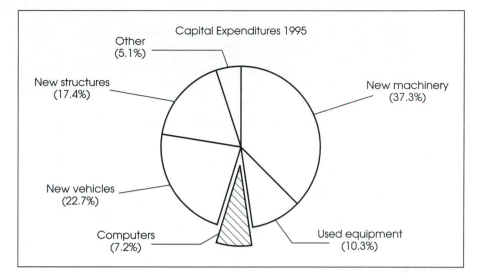

MODEL 4-10   A Pie Graph that Emphasizes One Segment

Model 4-10 lead to the type of expenditure and the percentage. Call-out lines should always touch the edge of the section or part being identified.

Organization Charts

An *organization chart* illustrates the individual units in a company or any group and their relationships to each other. Organization charts are most often used to illustrate the chain of authority—the position with the most authority at the top and all other positions leading to it in some way. Organization charts also indicate the lines of authority between units or positions and which positions are on the same level of authority. Rectangles or ovals usually represent the positions in an organizational chart. Label each clearly. Model 4-11 is an organization chart showing the committees at a charitable foundation.

Flowcharts

A *flowchart* illustrates the sequence of steps in a process. A flowchart can represent an entire process or only a specific portion of it. As a supplement to a written description of a process, a flowchart is useful in enabling readers to

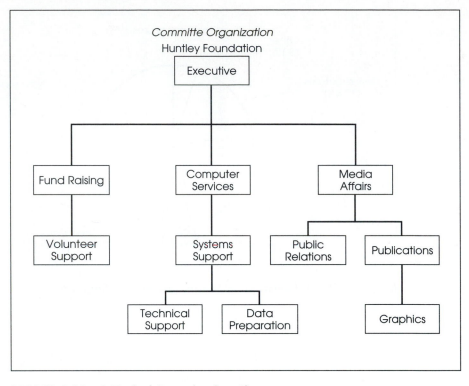

MODEL 4-11   A Typical Organization Chart

visualize the progression of steps. An open-system flowchart shows a process that begins at one point and ends at another. A closed-system flowchart shows a circular process that ends where it began. Use rectangles, circles, or symbols to represent the steps of the process, and label each clearly. Model 4-12 uses simple rectangles to represent each step in the production cycle of copper. Model 4-13 uses drawings to illustrate the stages in the process of converting offshore ore deposits to refined minerals.

Line Drawings

A *line drawing* is a simple illustration of the structure of an object or the position of a person involved in some action. The drawing may not show all the details but, instead, highlight certain areas or positions that are important to the discussion. If details of the interior of an object are important, a cutaway drawing is more appropriate. If the relationship of all the components is important, an exploded drawing is more appropriate. Model 4-14 is a line

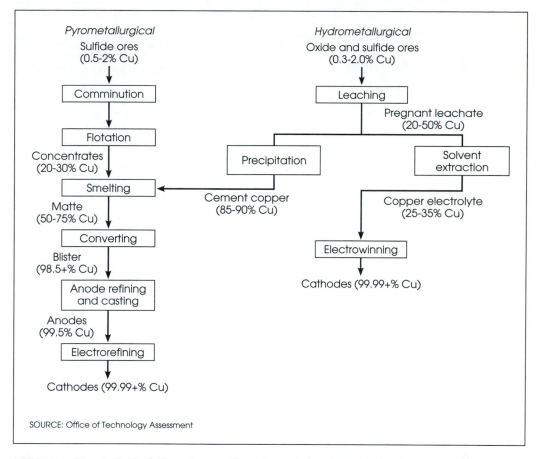

MODEL 4-12   A Typical Flowchart—Flowchart for Copper Production
SOURCE: U.S. Congress, Office of Technology Assessment, *Copper: Technology and Competitiveness,*
OTA-E-367 (Washington, DC: U.S. Government Printing Office, September 1988).

drawing of a police officer conducting a driver sobriety test. The drawing shows customary positions of the driver and police officer as the driver tries to walk a straight line.

Cutaway Drawings

A *cutaway drawing* shows an interior section of an object or an object relative to a location and other objects so that readers can see a cross section below the surface. Cutaway drawings show the location, relative size, and relationships of interior components. Use both horizontal and vertical cutaway views if your

MODEL 4-13   A Typical Flowchart Employing Drawings—To Illustrate Technologies for Processing Offshore Mineral Ores
SOURCE: U.S. Congress, Office of Technology Assessment, *Marine Minerals: Exploring Our New Ocean Frontier*, OTA-0-342 (Washington, DC: U.S. Government Printing Office, July 1987).

readers need a complete perspective of an interior. Model 4-15 is a cutaway drawing of a suction dredge revealing its parts and its position in the water.

Model 4-16 shows another cutaway drawing, this time showing the interior of a specialized furnace used in testing transmission qualities of nonsilicon-based glass.

MODEL 4-14   A Line Drawing of a Police Officer Conducting a Driver Sobriety Test
SOURCE: "One-Leg-Stand Test," from U.S. Department of Transportation, National Highway Traffic Safety Administration, *Improved Sobriety Testing,* 1984 (Washington, DC: U.S. Government Printing Office, 1984).

Exploded Drawings

An *exploded drawing* shows that individual components of an object as separate but in the sequence and location they have when put together. Most often used in manuals and instruction booklets, exploded drawings help readers visualize how exterior and interior parts fit together. Model 4-17 is an exploded drawing of a cart used to illustrate assembly instructions for a consumer.

Maps

A *map* shows (1) geographic data, such as the location of rivers and highways, or (2) demographic and topical data, such as density and distribution of population or production. If demographic or topical data are featured, eliminate unnecessary geographic elements and use dots, shadings, or symbols to show

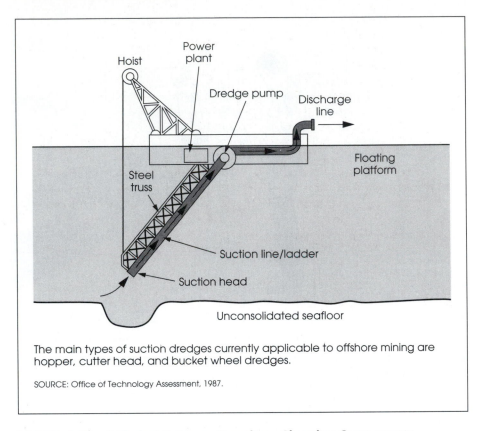

The main types of suction dredges currently applicable to offshore mining are hopper, cutter head, and bucket wheel dredges.

SOURCE: Office of Technology Assessment, 1987.

MODEL 4-15   A Typical Cutaway Drawing—Showing Components of a Suction Dredge
SOURCE: U.S. Congress, Office of Technology Assessment, *Marine Minerals: Exploring Our New Ocean Frontier,* OTA-0-342 (Washington, DC: U.S. Government Printing Office, July 1987).

distribution or density. Include (1) a key if more than one topical or demographic item is illustrated, (2) a scale of miles if distance is important, and (3) significant boundaries separating regions. Model 4-18 uses shading to distinguish differences in rental vacancies. Notice also that the map is exploded to emphasize the geographic divisions named.

Photographs

A *photograph* provides a surface view of an object or event. To be effective, photographs must be clear and focus on the pertinent item. Eliminate distracting backgrounds or other objects from the photograph. If the size of an object is important, include a person or well-known item in the photograph to illustrate the comparative size of the object. Model 4-19 is a typical product photograph.

MODEL 4-16   A Cutaway Drawing—Showing an Acoustic Levitation Furnace

SOURCE: From *Spacelab J, Microgravity and Life Sciences,* NASA, Marshall Space Flight Center, n.d.

MODEL 4-17   An Exploded Drawing of a Cart

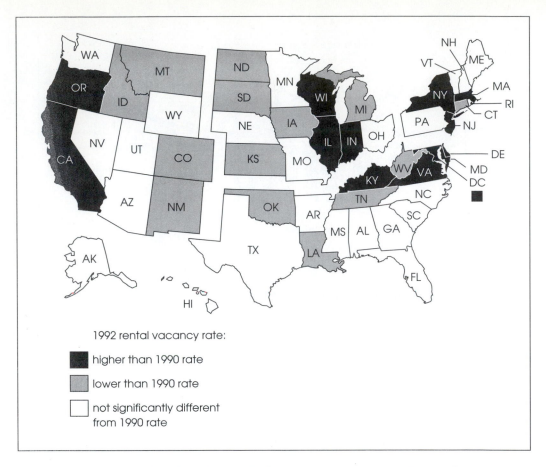

MODEL 4-18   A Map Showing Changes in Rental Vacancy Rates by State, 1990 and 1992

MODEL 4-19   Typical Product Photograph

USING FORMAT ELEMENTS

For many internal documents, such as reports, company procedures, and bulletins, the writer is responsible for determining the most effective format elements. Just as you use graphic aids to provide readers with easy access to complicated data, use format elements to help readers move through the document, finding and retaining important information. For printed documents, the writer often does not have the final word on which format elements to use. However, always consider these elements, and be prepared to consult with and offer suggestions to the technical editor and art director about document design. The following guidelines cover three types of format elements: (1) written cues, (2) white space, and (3) typographic devices.

Written Cues

Written cues help readers find specific information quickly. The most frequently used written cues are headings, headers and footers, jumplines, and company logos.

Headings

Headings are organizational cues that alert readers to the sequence of information in a document. Use headings

- To help readers find specific data
- To provide an outline that helps readers see the hierarchical relationship of sections
- To call attention to specific topics
- To show where changes in topics occur
- To break up a page so that readers are not confronted with line after line of unbroken text.

Include headings for major sections and for topics within the sections. If one heading is followed by several pages of text, divide that section into subsections with more headings. If, on the other hand, every heading is followed by only two or three sentences, regroup your information into fewer topics. Headings are distinguished by level and style according to their placement and use of format typographic devices.

Levels.   First-level headings represent major sections or full chapters of a document. Center such headings on the page and type them in all capital letters:

STATIC ELECTRICITY

Static electricity, a well-known byproduct of. . . .

Second-level headings represent major units of a chapter or of a long section in a document. Center such headings, type them both capital and lowercase letters, and underline them:

Flash Floods

Flash floods are the leading weather-related cause. . . .

Type third-level headings flush with the left margin in capital and lowercase letters and underline them:

Increase in Rheumatic Fever

The average number of children who contracted rheumatic. . . .

The text following any of the first three levels of headings begins two lines below the heading. Type fourth-level headings in capital and lowercase letters, flush with the left margin, underlined, and with a period following them. The text for fourth-level headings begins on the same line:

Changing Your Beneficiary. Use Form RBE/26 to change the beneficiary on your. . . .

Computers make it easy to use boldface type as another distinguishing characteristic of headings. Some writers use boldface for first-level headings; others make all headings boldface and use placement to distinguish them. Some organizations have specific guidelines for headings in documents, and professional journals often have guidelines for headings in technical articles. Check appropriate style guides.

Style.   Use nouns, phrases, or sentences for headings. All headings of the same level, however, should be the same part of speech. If you want to use a noun for a heading, all headings of that level should be nouns. If one heading is a phrase, all headings of that level should be phrases. Here are three types of headings:

Nouns:	Protein
	Fat
	Carbohydrate
Phrases:	Use of Tests
	Development of Standards
	Rise in Cost
Sentences:	Accidents Are Rising.
	Support Is Not Available.
	Reductions Are Planned.

Nouns and phrases are the most commonly used headings. Be sure also that your headings clearly indicate the topic of the section they head so that readers do not waste time reading through unneeded information. Keep sentence headings short. Headings such as "Miscellaneous" or "General Principles" provide no guide to the information covered in the section. Write headings with specific terms and informative phrases so that readers can scan the document for the sections of most interest.

Headers and Footers

A *header* or *footer* is a notation on each page of a document that identifies it for the reader and includes one or more of the following: (1) document date, (2) title, (3) document number, (4) topic, (5) author, or (6) title of the larger publication the document is part of. Place headers at the tops of pages and footers at the bottoms flush with either the right or left margin. Here is an example:

```
Interactive Systems Check, No. 24-X,
May 1, 1996.
```

Jumplines

A *jumpline* is a notation indicating that a section is continued in another part of a document. Place a jumpline below the last line of text on the page. Here is an example:

```
Continued on page 39
```

Logos

A *company logo* is a specific design used as a symbol of a company. It may be a written cue or a visual one or a combination. Examples include the red cross of the American Red Cross, the golden arches of McDonald's, and the line drawing of a bell for the regional telephone companies. A logo identifies an organization for readers, and it also may unify the document by appearing at the beginning of major sections or on each page.

White Space

White space is the term for areas on a page that have no text or graphics. Far from being just a wasted spot on a page, white space helps readers process the text efficiently. In documents with complicated data and lots of detail, white space rests readers' eyes and directs them to important information. Think of white space as having a definite shape on the page, and use it to create balance and proportion in your documents. White space commonly appears in margins, heading areas, columns, and indentations.

Margins

Margins of white space provide a frame for the text and graphics (called the "live area") on a page. To avoid monotony, experienced designers usually vary the size of margins in printed documents. The bottom margin of a page is generally the widest, and the top margin is slightly smaller. If a document, such as a manual, is bound with facing pages, the inside margin is usually the narrowest, and the outside margin is slightly wider than the top margin.

Heading Areas

White space provides the background and surrounding area to set off headings. Readers need sufficient white space around headings to be able to separate them from the rest of the text.

Columns

In documents with columns of text, the white space between the columns both frames and separates the columns. Too much or too little space here will upset the balance and proportion of the page. Generally, the wider the columns, the more space that is needed between columns to help readers see them as separate sections of text.

Indentations

The white space at the beginning of an indented sentence and after the last word of a paragraph sets off a unit of text for readers, as does the white space between lines, words, and single-spaced paragraphs. Add extra space between paragraphs to increase readability. Youhaveonlytotrytoreadalinewithout whitespacebetweenwordstoseehowimportantthistinywhitespaceis.

White space is actually the most important format element, because without it most readers would quickly give up trying to get information from a document.

Typographic Devices

Typographic devices are used to highlight specific details or specific sections of a document. Highlighting involves selecting different typefaces or using boldface type, lists, and boxes.

Typefaces

Type is either *serif* or *sans serif*. Serif type has small projections at the top or bottom of the major vertical strokes of a letter. Sans serif type does not have these little projections.

This sentence is printed in serif type.

This sentence is printed in sans serif type.

A *typeface* is a particular design for the type on a page. Typeface should be appropriate to readers and purpose. An ornate, script typeface suitable for a holiday greeting card would be out of place in a technical manual.

Poor: *Feasibility Tests in Mining Ventures*

Better: **Feasibility Tests in Mining Ventures**

Follow these general guidelines if you are involved in selecting the typeface for a printed document:

1. Stay in one typeface group, such as Times New Roman, throughout each document. Most typefaces have enough variety in size and weight to suit the requirements of one document.

2. Use the fewest possible sizes and weights of typeface in one document. A multitude of type sizes and weights, even from the same typeface, distracts readers.

3. Avoid type smaller than 10 points because readers over age 40 will have trouble reading it.

4. Use both capital and lowercase letters for text. This combination is more readable than all capitals or all lowercase letters.

5. Use italics sparingly. The Appendix in this book explains the conventional use of italics. Avoid using them for emphasis because they are harder to read than regular type.

Here are some samples of common typefaces:

Times New Roman   Bembo

Bodoni   Baskerville

Optima   Caledonia

Boldface

Boldface refers to type with extra weight or darkness. Use boldface type to add emphasis to (1) headings, (2) specific words, such as warnings, or (3) significant topics. This example shows how boldface type sets off a word from a sentence:

> Depending on the type of incinerator, **gas temperatures** could vary more than 2000 degrees.

Lists

Lists highlight information and guide readers to what facts they specifically need. In general, lists are distinguished by numbers, bullets, and squares.

Numbers.   Traditionally, lists in which items are numbered imply either that the items are in descending order of importance or that the items are sequential stages in a procedure. Here is a sample from an operator's manual:

1. Clean accumulated dust and debris from the surface.

2. Run the engine and check for abnormal noises and vibrations.

3. Observe three operating cycles.

4. Check operation of the brake.

Because numbered lists set off information so distinctly from the text, they are often used even when the items have only minor differences in importance. If a list has no chronology, you may use bullets to set off the items.

Bullets.   *Bullets* are small black circles that appear before each item in a list just as a number would. On a typewriter or word processor without a bullet symbol, use the small o and fill it in with black ink. Use bullets where there is no distinction in importance among items and where no sequential steps are involved. Here is an example from a company safety bulletin:

> A periodic survey is needed to check for the following:
>
> • Gasoline and paint vapors
> • Alkaline and acid mists
> • Dust
> • Smoke

Squares.   Squares are used with checklists if readers are supposed to respond to questions or select items on the page itself. A small square precedes each item in the same position as a number or a bullet would appear. Here is an example from a magazine subscription form:

> ☐ Please bill me for the total cost.

☐ Please bill me in three separate installments.

☐ Please charge to my credit card.

Boxes

A box is a frame that separates specific information from the rest of the text. In addition to the box itself, designers often use a light color or shading to further set off a box. Here is an example of boxed information:

Boxes are used

- to add supplemental information that is related to the main subject but not part of the document's specific content.
- to call reader attention to special items such as telephone numbers, dates, prices, and return coupons.
- to highlight important terms or facts.

Boxes are effective typographic devices, but overuse of them will result in a cluttered, unbalanced page. Use restraint in boxing information in your text.

CHAPTER SUMMARY

- This chapter discusses document design features—graphic aids and format elements. Remember:

- Design features guide readers through the text, increase reader interest, and contribute to a document "image."

- Basic page design principles include balance, proportion, sequence, and consistency.

- Graphic aids (1) provide readers with quick access to information, (2) isolate main topics, (3) help readers see relationships among sets of data, and (4) offer expert readers quick access to complicated data.

- All graphic aids should be identified with a descriptive heading and a number and should be placed as near as possible to the reference in the text.

- The most frequently used graphic aids are tables, bar graphs, pictographs, line graphs, pie graphs, organization charts, flowcharts, line drawings, cutaway drawings, exploded drawings, maps, and photographs.

- Written format elements such as headings, headers and footers, jumplines, and logos help readers find special information.

- White space, the area without text or graphics, directs readers to information sections.

- Typographic devices such as typefaces, boldface type, lists, and boxes highlight specific sections or specific details.

SUPPLEMENTAL READINGS IN PART 2

Benson, P. J. "Writing Visually: Design Considerations in Technical Publications," *Technical Communication,* p. 451.

Holcombe, M. W. and Stein, J. K. "How to Deliver Dynamic Presentations: Use Visuals for Impact," *Business Marketing,* p. 509.

Marra, J. L. "For Writers: Understanding the Art of Layout," *Technical Communication,* p. 525.

Plunka, G. A. "The Editor's Nightmare: Formatting Lists within the Text," *Technical Communication,* p. 536.

"Six Graphics Guidelines," *Simply Stated,* p. 562.

White, J. V. "Color: The Newest Tool for Technical Communicators," *Technical Communication,* p. 576.

Model 4-20   Commentary

This article appeared in an employee magazine published by Children's Hospital Medical Center of Akron (Autumn 1989). Employees take the magazine home to show friends and family, and the magazine is also distributed to hospital donors and others in the community. The article describes the activities of the Sports Medicine Center at the hospital and includes statements from the director about common injuries and therapeutic equipment used at the center.

Discussion

1. Identify and discuss the design features in this article. What other features might be useful?

2. Discuss how effectively the photographs support the text. What image of the Sports Medicine Center do the photographs help to create?

3. The information about steroids is not part of the main story and is not set off in a box. How effectively does the information catch the reader's attention? What other design features could you use to draw attention to this section?

4. Bring a company newsletter or magazine to class. Select one page and identify its format and graphics features. Discuss their usefulness for the reader.

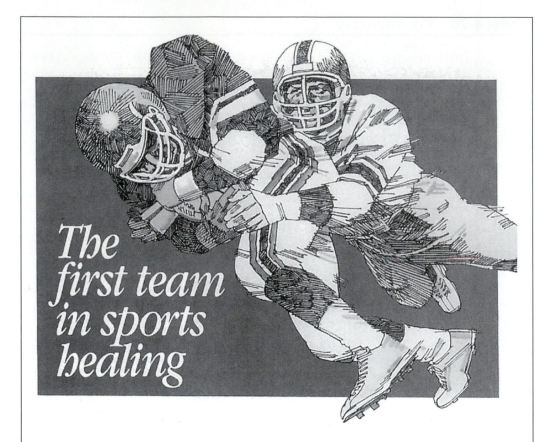

The first team in sports healing

*I*t's third down and ten. The quarterback drops back to pass. Around the ends come two bulky 200-pound linemen rushing to sack the quarterback. The boy sees them coming towards his thin body and tries to escape, but to no avail. He is sacked as the game ends. As the opponents celebrate, the quarterback slowly rises, holding his right arm.

He says his arm hurts and has trouble moving it. The team doctor confirms his injury, saying that he has pulled some ligaments in his arm. For this senior's season, there will be no more football this year.

Injuries occur in football games as well as other sports almost every day. As a result, there is an increasing need for specialized medical care for sports related injuries. For these athletes, there is the Sports Medicine Center at Children's Hospital Medical Center of Akron.

The Sports Medicine Center, which opened in 1984, is a full-service diagnosis, treatment and prevention facility. From Little Leaguers to high school football players and weekend joggers, the Center's staff is trained to treat athletes of all ages.

"Our goal is to provide good medical care to all athletes," said Joseph Congeni, M.D., Medical Director of the Center. "Our job is to help athletes return to their sport as fast as possible, and to return safely."

The staff not only treats the injuries of the athletes, but also educates them on how they injured themselves and

Continued on next page

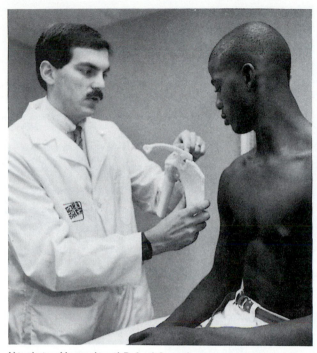

Using plastic model as a teaching aid, Dr. Joseph Congeni demonstrates to a high school football player how he sustained a shoulder injury.

continued from previous page

how to prevent the injury from happening again. With the help of plastic models, the staff shows the athletes exactly what happened to their bodies as a result of their injuries.

"Patient education and understanding is vitally important," said Dr. Congeni. "If the patients don't know what they did to their bodies, or how to prevent injuries in the future, they'll likely hurt themselves again, maybe even worse than before.

"To help the athelete understand his or her injury, we use plastic models of their particular injury as a visual aid device. The model helps reinforce what we say, as it allows us to actually show the part of their body they injured. It can often be as important to explain what injury they don't have as well as what they do have."

In addition to its healing mission, the Center is a powerful advocate for children's safety in sporting events. The Center supports changes in rules and regulations that would bring greater safety in youth sports. The staff serves as lecturers and advisors at coaches' clinics and seminars, youth leagues, CYO's and at junior and senior high schools.

"We also speak to PTA's and other organizations that deal with kids," said Dr. Congeni. "We talk with doctor groups as well trying to get the word

"Our job is to help athletes return to their sport as fast as possible, and to return safely."

— Dr. Joseph Congeni

out — *all* doctors who deal with kids should be advocates of child safety."

Dr. Congeni points out that the message of promoting children's safety and prevention is not yet fully appreciated by the community. Statistics show that the majority of injuries happening to athletes occur when they are under 18 years of age.

"With children, we see an increasing number of injuries that used to occur only in older athletes," explained Dr. Congeni. "For example, we see children with overuse injuries. This type of injury is wear and tear of the same muscle tendon group over and over again. This used to happen almost exclusively with high school or college age patients. But in the recent past, this type of injury has increased dramatically in the 5 to 10 year old age group. In this very young age group, we now find such overuse injuries as swimmer's shoulder, runner's knee and stress fractures."

The Center's approach to healing involves state-of-the-art medical and exercise equipment. This approach is both therapeutic and rehabilitative to the injured athlete. It involves stretching, strengthening and increasing flexibility of the injured area. To help achieve the best treatment possible, the Center uses ultrasound equipment, muscle stimulation and cold and heat therapy on the injury to help the athlete recover faster.

"We use a computerized testing device called the Cybex Machine," explained Dr. Congeni, "to accurately access strength and stamina of the patient. We use it as a guide to indicate when the patient can resume sports activity. We also use some Nautilus machines, life cycles and treadmills."

The Center's staff includes: Dr. Congeni, Donald Marshall, Coordinator; Michael Huth and Michael Krutel, Physical Therapists; Aaron Galpert, Athletic Trainer; Anita Kapelewski, Assistant Athletic Trainer; Laura Moore, Patient Services Coordinator; and Nita Parke, Secretary.

"We work with other departments within Children's Hospital," said Dr. Congeni, "to develop a uniform approach to treatment and rehabilitation of injuries. We work with dietitians in our Nutrition Department, with people in Pulmonary Medicine and in the Emergency Room."

Using all their talents together, as a team, the Center's staff is able to diagnose, treat and prevent injuries to all athletes young and old. With their starting lineup of professionals, the Sports Medicine Center's staff is the "First Team" in sports healing. ▣

Safety Zones

The Sports Medicine Center issues a free seasonal newsletter entitled *Safety Zones* for coaches, parents, athletic trainers, sports medicine professionals and others interested in sports medicine, safety and prevention. All of the articles are written by the Sports Medicine's staff on a variety of topics.

To recieve *Safety Zones*, send your name and address to Laura Moore, Coordinator, Sports Medicine Center, 300 Locust Street, Suite #100, Akron, Ohio 44308.

Physical Therapist Michael Huth helps patient use Cybex equipment to regain leg muscle strength.

Athletic Trainer Aaron Galpert assists patient with foot injury.

Steroids: a dangerous choice

"I get calls every day from other physicians asking about steroids," said Joseph Congeni, M.D., Medical Director, Sports Medicine Center, "and I always tell them that there is *no* proper place for steroids in a sports medicine program."

Steroids, or anabolic steroids, are a group of chemicals made by modifying the male hormone testosterone to reduce hormonal side effects and make the medication stay longer in the system.

Athletes are the most frequent, and most celebrated, abusers of the drug. Specifically football players, weight lifters and wrestlers find steroids attractive because the drugs increase their muscle mass faster than normal.

"It (steroids) improves the inital thrust of strength," said Dr. Congeni, "but it's not for the long term. The problem is the long term side effects.

"For men, shrinking of the testicles, impotence, sterility, premature balding and acne are some early warning signs.

"For women, early warning signs include masculinizing (secondary male sex characteristics), such as deepening of the voice, facial hair growth, loss of regular menstrual cycle and formation of a male muscle pattern."

Steroids have also been found to cause cancer of the liver, heart disease, high blood pressure and heart rhythm disturbances.

"The risks far outweigh any benefits," concludes Dr. Congeni. "It's not worth the immediate gratification. You pay the price for serious problems later!"

Steroids do work... BUT!

HOTLINE

Do you have a sports related injury needing immediate treatment? Call the Sports Medicine 24-hour Emergency Hotline:

(216) 379-8930

MODEL 4-21   Commentary

This model is a page from a 91-page catalog published by the Hunter Fan Company. The catalog, written for consumers, explains the advantages of using fans for energy conservation and cost savings, describes the principles of fan construction, and features photographs and descriptions of dozens of fan designs. This page shows a cutaway view of the fan mechanism and lists the special features of the company fans.

Discussion

1. Discuss why the company would want to feature this illustration ahead of all photographs of decorative fans suitable for various rooms and purposes.

2. Discuss balance, proportion, sequence, and consistency in this page design.

3. Discuss the text. Why might the writer have listed features in this particular order? What is the advantage of using a list here?

4. Discuss the use of white space and how it helps or hinders the reader of this page.

5. Bring a consumer catalog to class. In groups, analyze the design of a single page from each catalog. As a group, select which one of these pages is most effective for a consumer, and explain your choice to the rest of the class.

THE HUNTER ORIGINAL®

For the Customer Demanding the Very Best . . . The Original.
Made for a Lifetime – Tested for a Lifetime – Backed for a Lifetime!

- Made in USA
- Lifetime Warranty
- 15° Blade Pitch for Maximum Air Movement
- Indestructible Cast Iron Housing
- Maintenance Free Oil Bath Design
- Unique Motor Design Accommodates 4 or 5 Blades
- 3 Speeds, Electrically Reversible
- No Rubber Flywheel to Replace
- Swivel Mount Canopy for Angled Ceiling Mount (2nd Century Models)
- Hardwood Veneer Blades

THE ORIGINAL®

MODEL 4-22   Commentary

This page is from the consumer instructions for a Panasonic VCR.

Discussion

1. Identify the graphic aids and format elements used in this page. Discuss why the designer probably chose to use them. How would photographs instead of line drawings help or hinder readers trying to set up a new VCR?

2. Discuss the use of white space here and how it helps or hinders readers.

3. Bring in a page of consumer instructions for a home appliance or piece of electronic equipment that you believe needs improvement. Identify the format and graphic features, and discuss the features that need to be improved.

4. Look at Models 2-1 and 2-2 and identify the graphic aids and format elements. Discuss how effectively these features help readers use the information. Would you make any format changes in these models or in the models in this chapter?

TO GET STARTED

Taking the steps shown on this page will prepare your VCR, so you can start a playback to watch a tape. Steps 1 and 2 are one time system setup steps.

VCR TO TV SYSTEM CONNECTION

1 Connect the supplied VHF Connecting Cable from the VCR to the TV as shown here.

Follow illustration A or B depending on the type of terminals available on the back of your TV.

A

Back of VCR

VHF OUT

VHF IN

VHF Connecting Cable (supplied)

Back of TV

(Example)

B

Back of VCR

VHF OUT

VHF IN

TV

VHF Connecting Cable (supplied)

SELECT VCR CHANNEL (CHANNEL 3 OR 4)

2 Your VCR must control one TV channel permanently just as a TV broadcast station does. To decide which channel to use, select either channel 3 or 4 with the Channel 3/4 switch on the back of the VCR.
To avoid local interference, the channel 3/4 switch position you choose should match the number of the TV channel that is not normally broadcast in your area.

Now, tune your TV to the same channel that you selected for the channel 3 or 4 switch.

(VCR Monitor Channel)
CHANNEL 3/4 Switch

CH3

CH4

Back of VCR

SELECT YOUR VCR OR TV FOR VIEWING

2 Set the VCR/TV Selector to "VCR"

VCR/TV Selector

Press

REMOTE CONTROL

once

or

twice

VCR Indicator ──────

VCR Front Panel

ON: TO WATCH A VIDEO PLAYBACK OR TUNE CHANNELS AT VCR WITH THE CHANNEL UP/DOWN KEYS.

OFF: TO WATCH AND TUNE CHANNELS AT THE TV.

Refer to the separate <u>Basic Guide For VCR Connections</u> and select the section with details on the particular hookup you want to use.

Chapter 4   Exercises

1. As a new employee at the National Marine Fisheries Service, you have been assigned to write a brochure reporting current statistics about the size, scope, and world position of U.S. fisheries and the U.S. supply and consumption of fishery products. The brochure is intended for the general public. After sorting through the data, you decide to create graphic aids that will help readers understand the information. Following are the areas you decide to illustrate:

   a. The United States used 79% of its domestic catch for human food in 1994 compared with 74% in 1993. Industrial (nonfood) use increased to 12% compared with 6% in 1993. Fish used for canned bait and pet food declined to 9% compared with 20% in 1993.

   b. Total fishery imports in 1994 were $9.9 billion compared with $8.9 billion in 1993, $10.1 billion in 1992, $8.5 billion in 1991, and $9.6 billion in 1990. Exports have been increasing to $10.4 billion in 1994, compared with $7.8 billion in 1993, $6.7 billion in 1992, $5.8 billion in 1991, and $4.3 billion in 1990.

   c. The United States ranks sixth among major fishing nations with a 1994 catch at 5.6 metric tons. Other countries are Japan at 9.8 metric tons, China at 13.6 metric tons, Peru at 6.8 metric tons, Russia at 9.8 metric tons, and Chile at 6.2 metric tons.

   d. In terms of volume, the top five species caught by U.S. commercial fishers in 1994 were Alaska pollock (30.8%), salmon (7.4%), flounder (6.7%), menhaden (17.1%), crab (6.5%), and other species at 31.5%. The total volume was 9.6 billion lb.

After completing the graphics, write a brief explanation of the significance of the statistics in each case to explain trends for the readers.

2. In groups, assume you are members of a volunteer committee of citizens advising the Social Services Center of Drayton, North Carolina. The committee is preparing a report concerning housing needs of the elderly citizens in the community. As a group, create graphic aids to illustrate the following areas:

   a. There is little difference between elderly renters and home owners who have central heating. Among home owners with central heating, 83% of those over 85 years have it; 85% of those between 75 and 84 have it; and 87% of those 65 to 74 have it. Among renters 85 years or older, 91% have central heat; 88% of those 75 to 84 years have it, and 86% of those 65 to 74 to have it.

   b. In Drayton, the elderly population is 63% ages 65 to 74, 24% ages 74 to 84, and 13% over age 85. Of the total, 77% of the men and 42% of the women are married; 14% of the men and 48% of the women are widowed; 4% of both men and women were never married; and 5% of the men and 6% of the women are divorced.

    c. The typical elderly person's annual income came from the following sources: Social Security (40%), pensions (19%), earnings (18%), and family assistance (23%).

    d. The most frequently occurring health problems in 100 elderly persons surveyed were arthritis (48), cataracts (17), diabetes (11), hypertension (36), heart disease (32), visual impairment (9), hearing impairments (32), sinusitis (16), and orthopedic impairments (19). Some surveyed reported more than one health problem.

After completing the graphic aids, write a brief analysis of the significance of these facts for planning elderly housing.

3. Collect two different documents used on your campus. Such items as student information brochures from the career planning office or student health services, annual reports, announcements of events or degree programs, newsletters, or official registration procedures would be appropriate. Assume the Director of Communications has hired you as an assistant. The director is planning to reprint the documents you have collected and asks you to evaluate their design features and recommend changes. In your short report to the director, identify and evaluate the audience and purpose of each document, overall organization, design and placement of tables and figures, and use of typographic devices. Include your opinion as to the effectiveness of each document and recommend specific changes. *Note:* Short reports are discussed in Chapter 10. *Or,* if your instructor prefers, redesign one of the documents and submit the original and your revision to your instructor.

4. Find a technical document from a company and make enough copies for the other students in class. Prepare an oral critique of the document relative to the design guidelines given in this chapter. Explain how you would revise the document for a more effective format.

CHAPTER 5

Revision

CREATING A FINAL DRAFT

As you plan and draft a document, you probably will change your mind many times about content, organization, and style. In addition to these changes, however, you should consider revision as a separate stage in producing your final document. During drafting, you should concentrate primarily on developing your document from your initial outline. During revision, concentrate on making changes in content, organization, and style that will best serve your readers and their purpose. These final changes should result in a polished document that your readers can use efficiently.

Thinking about revision immediately after finishing a draft is difficult. Your own writing looks "perfect" to you, and every sentence seems to be the only way to state the information. Experienced writers allow some time between drafting and revising whenever possible. The longer the document, the more important it is to let your writing rest before final revisions so that you can look at the text and graphic aids with a fresh attitude and read as if you were the intended reader and had never seen the material before. Most writers divide revision into two separate stages—global, or overall document revision, and fine-tuning, or style and surface-accuracy revision.

Global Revision

The process of *global revision* involves evaluating your document for effective content and organization. At this level of revision, you may add or delete information; reorganize paragraphs, sections, or the total document; and redraft sections.

Fine-tuning Revision

The process of *fine-tuning revision* involves the changes in sentence structure and language choice that writers make to ensure clarity and appropriate tone. This level also involves checking for surface accuracy, such as correct grammar, punctuation, spelling, and mechanics of technical style. Many organizations have internal style guides that include special conventions writers must check for during fine-tuning revision.

With word processing, both global and fine-tuning revisions can be fast and easy. Depending on the type of word-processing program you have, you can make revisions using these capabilities:

1. *Delete and insert.*   You can omit or add words, sentences, and paragraphs anywhere in the text.

2. *Search for specific words.*   You can search through the full text for specific words or phrases that you want to change. If you want to

change the word *torpid* to *inactive* throughout the document, the computer will locate every place *torpid* appears so that you can delete it and insert *inactive*.

3. *Moving and rearranging text.*   You can take your text apart as if you were cutting up typed pages and arranging the pieces in a new order. You can move whole sections of text from one place to another and reorder paragraphs within sections. You also may decide that revised sentences should be reorganized within a paragraph.

4. *Re-format.*   You can easily change margins, headlines, indentations, spacing, and other format elements.

5. *Check spelling and word choice.*   Many software programs have spelling checkers that scan a text and flag misspelled words that are in the checker's dictionary. Spelling checkers, however, cannot find usage errors, such as *affect* for *effect,* or spelling errors in proper names and unusual terms. The checkers also will not flag correctly spelled words that you have used incorrectly, such as *personal* for *personnel.* A thesaurus program will suggest synonyms for specific words. You can select a synonym and substitute it wherever the original word appears in the text.

6. *Check grammar and punctuation.*   Many grammar checkers are now available, and they can find such problems as fragments, comma splices, and agreement errors. The checkers can also flag wordy phrases, passive voice, and jargon. However, do not accept the grammar checkers as "always right." They cannot substitute for a solid understanding of grammar and punctuation on your part. Dangling modifiers and verb tense problems, for example, usually slip past the grammar checkers. As a careful writer, you should reread your document slowly and make appropriate decisions about corrections and style.

Revision on a computer is so convenient that some people cannot stop making changes in drafts. Do not change words or rearrange sentences simply for the sake of change. Revise until your document fulfills your readers' needs, and then stop.

MAKING GLOBAL REVISIONS

For global revisions, rethink your reader and purpose, and then review the content and organizational decisions you made in the planning and drafting stages. Consider changes that will help your readers use the information in the document efficiently.

Content

Evaluate the content of your document and consider whether you have enough information or too little. Review details, definitions, and emphasis.

Details.   Have you included enough details for your readers to understand the general principles, theories, situations, or actions? Have you included details that do not fit your readers' purpose and that they do not need? Do the details serve both primary and secondary readers? Are all the facts, such as dates, amounts, names, and places, correct? Are your graphic aids appropriate for your readers? Do you need more? Have you included examples to help your readers visualize the situation or action?

Definitions.   Have you included definitions of terms that your readers may not know? If your primary readers are experts and your secondary readers are not, have you included a glossary for secondary readers?

Emphasis.   Do the major sections stress information suitable for the readers' main purpose? Do the conclusions logically result from the information provided? Is the urgency of the situation clear to readers? Are deadlines explained? Do headings highlight major topics of interest to readers? Can readers easily find specific topics?

After evaluating how well the document serves your readers and their need for information, you may discover that you need to gather more information or that you must omit information you have included in the document. Reaching the revision stage and finding that you need to gather more information can be frustrating, but remember, readers can only work with the information they are given. The writer's job is to provide everything readers need to use the document efficiently for a specific purpose.

Organization

Evaluate the overall organization of your document as well as the organization of individual sections and paragraphs. Review these elements:

Overall Organization.   Is the information grouped into major topics that are helpful and relevant to your readers? Are the major topics presented in a logical order that will help readers understand the subject? Are the major sections divided into subsections that will help readers understand the information and highlight important subtopics? Do some topics need to be combined or further divided to highlight information or to make the information easier to understand? Do readers of this document expect or prefer a specific organization, and is that organization in place?

Introductions and Conclusions.   Consider the introductions and conclusions both for the total document and for major sections. Does the introduction to the full document orient readers to the purpose and major topics covered? Do the section introductions establish the topics covered in each section? Does the conclusion to the full document summarize major facts, results, recommendations, future actions, or the overall situation? Do the section conclusions summarize the major points and show why these are important to readers and purpose?

Paragraphs.   Do paragraphs focus on one major point? Are paragraphs sufficiently developed to support that major point with details, examples, and explanations? Is each paragraph organized according to a pattern that will help readers understand the information, such as chronological or ascending order of importance?

Headings.   Are the individual topics marked with major headings and sub-headings? Do the headings identify the key topics? Are there several pages in a row without headings, or is there a heading for every sentence, and therefore, do headings need to be added or omitted?

Format.   Are there enough highlighting devices, such is headings, lists, boxes, white space, and boldface type, to lead readers through the information and help them see relationships among topics? Can readers quickly scan a page for key information?

After evaluating the organization of the document and of individual sections, make necessary changes. You may find that you need to write more introductory or concluding material or reorder sections and paragraphs. Remember that content alone is not enough to help readers if they have to hunt through a document for relevant facts. Effective organization is a key element in helping readers use a document quickly and efficiently.

MAKING FINE-TUNING REVISIONS

When you are satisfied that your global revisions have produced a complete and well-organized draft, you should go on to the fine-tuning revision stage, checking for sentence structure, word choice, grammar, punctuation, spelling, and mechanics of technical style. This level of revision can be difficult because by this time you probably have the document or sections of it memorized. As a result, you may read the words that should be on the page rather than the words that are on the page. For fine-tuning revisions you need to slow your reading pace so that you do not overlook problems in the text. You also should stop thinking about content and organization, and think instead about individual sentences and words. Experienced writers sometimes use these techniques to help them find trouble spots:

- *Read aloud.*   Reading a text aloud will help you notice awkward or overly long sentences, insufficient transitions between sentences or paragraphs, and inappropriate language. Reading aloud slows the reading pace and helps you hear problems in the text that your eye could easily skip over.

- *Focus on one point at a time.*   You cannot effectively check for sentence structure, word choice, correctness, and mechanical style all at the same time, particularly in a long document. Experienced writers usually revise in steps, checking for one or two items at a time. If you check for every problem at once, you are likely to overlook items.

- *Use a ruler.*   By placing a ruler under each line as you read it and moving the ruler from line to line, you will focus on the words rather than on the content of the document. Using a ruler also slows your reading pace, and you are more likely to notice problems in correctness and technical style.

- *Read backward.*   Some writers read a text from the bottom of the page up in order to concentrate only on the typed lines. Reading from the bottom up will help you focus on words and find typographic errors, but it will not help you find problems in sentence structure or grammar because sentence meaning will not be clear as you move backward through the text.

You may find a combination of these methods useful. You may use a ruler, for example, and focus on one point at a time as you look for sentence structure, word choice, and grammar problems. As a final check when you proofread, you may read backward to look for typographic errors.

The following items are those most writers check for during fine-tuning revision. For a discussion of grammar, punctuation, and mechanical style, see the Appendix.

Overloaded Sentences

An overloaded sentence includes so much information that readers cannot easily understand it. This sentence is from an announcement to all residents in a city district:

You are hereby notified, in accordance with Section 107–27 of the Corinth City Code, that a public hearing will be held by a committee of the Common Council on the date and time, and at the place listed below, to determine whether or not to designate a residential permit parking district in the area bounded by E. Edgewood Avenue on the north, E. Belleview Place on the south, the Corinth River on the west, and Lake McCormick on the east, except the area south of E. Riverside Place and west of the north/south alley between N. Oakland Avenue and N. Bartlett Avenue and the properties fronting N. Downer Avenue south of E. Park Place.

No reader could understand and remember all the information packed into this sentence. Here is a revision:

> As provided in City Code Section 101–27, a committee of the Common Council of Corinth will meet at the time and place shown below. The purpose of the meeting is to designate a residential permit parking district for one area between the Corinth River on the west and Lake McCormick on the east. The area is also bounded by E. Edgewood Avenue on the north and E. Belleview Place on the south. Not included is the area south of E. Riverside Place and west of the north/south alley between N. Oakland Avenue and N. Bartlett Avenue and the properties fronting N. Downer Avenue south of E. Park Place.

To revise the original overloaded sentence, the writer separated the pieces of information and emphasized the individual points in shorter sentences. The first sentence in the revision announces the meeting. The next two sentences identify the meeting purpose and the streets included in the parking regulations. A separate sentence then identifies streets not included. Readers will find the shorter sentences easier to understand and, therefore, the information easier to remember. Because so many streets are involved, readers will also need a graphic aid—a map with shading that shows the area in question. Avoid writing sentences that contain so many pieces of information that readers must mentally separate and sort the information as they read. Even short sentences can contain too much information for some readers. Here is a much shorter sentence than the preceding one, yet if the reader were a nonexpert interested in learning about cameras, the sentence holds more technical detail than he or she could remember easily:

> The WY–30X camera is housed in a compact but rugged diecast aluminum body, including a 14X zoom lens and 1.5-in. viewfinder, and has a signal-to-noise ratio of 56 dB, resolution of more than 620 lines on all channels, and registration of 0.6% in all zones.

In drafting sentences, consider carefully how much information your readers are likely to understand and remember at one time.

Clipped Sentences

Sometimes when writers revise overloaded sentences, the resulting sentences become so short they sound like the clipped phrases used in telegrams. Do not cut these items from your sentences just to make them shorter: (1) articles (*a, an, the*), (2) pronouns (*I, you, that, which*), (3) prepositions (*of, at, on, by*), and (4) linking verbs (*is, seems, has*). Here are some clipped sentences and their revisions:

Clipped:	Attached material for insertion in Administration Manual.
Revised:	The attached material is for insertion in the Administration Manual.
Clipped:	Questioned Mr. Hill about compensated injuries full-time employees.
Revised:	I questioned Mr. Hill about the compensated injuries of the full-time employees.
Clipped:	Investigator disturbed individual merits of case.
Revised:	The investigator seems disturbed by the individual merits of the case.

Do not eliminate important words to shorten sentences. The reader will try to supply the missing words and may not do it correctly, resulting in ambiguity and confusion.

Lengthy Sentences

Longer sentences demand that readers process more information, whereas shorter sentences give readers time to pause and absorb facts. A series of short sentences, however, can be monotonous, and too many long sentences in a row can overwhelm readers, especially those with nonexpert knowledge of the subject. Usually, short sentences emphasize a particular fact, and long sentences show relationships among several facts. With varying sentence lengths you can avoid the tiresome reading pace that results when writers repeat sentence style over and over. This paragraph from a letter to bank customers uses both long and short sentences effectively:

> Your accounts will be automatically transferred to the Smith Road office at the close of business on December 16, 1996. You do not need to open new accounts or order new checks. If for some reason another Federal location is more convenient, please stop by 2900 W. Manchester Road and pick up a special customer courtesy card to introduce you to the office of your choice. The Smith Road office is a full-service banking facility. Ample lobby teller stations, auto teller service, 24-hour automated banking, night depository, as well as a complete line of consumer and commercial loans are all available from your new Federal office. You will continue to enjoy the same fine banking service at the Smith Road office, and we look

forward to serving you. If you have questions, please call me at
555–8876.

In this paragraph the writer uses short sentences to emphasize the fact that customers do not have to take action, as well as that the new bank office is a full-service branch. Longer sentences explain the services and how to use them. The offer of help is also in a short sentence for emphasis.

Passive Voice

Active voice and passive voice indicate whether the subject of a sentence performs the main action or receives it. Here are two sentences illustrating the differences:

Active: The bridge operators noticed severe rusting at the stone abutments.

Passive: Severe rusting at the stone abutments was noticed by the bridge operators.

The active-voice sentence has a subject (*bridge operators*) that performs the main action (*noticed*). The passive-voice sentence has a subject (*rusting*) that receives the main action (*was noticed*). Passive voice is also characterized by a form of the verb *to be* and a prepositional phrase beginning with *by* that identifies the performer of the main action—usually quite late in the sentence. Readers generally prefer active voice because it creates a faster pace and is more direct. Passive voice also may create several problems for readers:

1. Passive voice requires more words than active voice because it includes the extra verb (*is, are, was, were, will be*) and the prepositional phrase that introduces the performer of the action. The preceding passive-voice sentence has two more words than the active-voice sentence. This may not seem excessive, but if every sentence in a 10-page report has two extra words, the document will be unnecessarily long.

2. Writers often omit the *by* phrase in passive voice, decreasing the number of words in the sentence but also possibly concealing valuable information from readers. Notice how these sentences offer incomplete information without the *by* phrase:

Incomplete: At least $10,000 was invested in custom software.
Complete: At least $10,000 was invested in custom software by the vice president for sales.

Incomplete: The effect of welded defects must be addressed.
Complete: The effect of welded defects must be addressed by the consulting engineer.

3. Writers often create dangling modifiers when using passive voice. In the active-voice sentence below, the subject of the sentence (*financial analyst*) is also the subject of the introductory phrase.

Active: Checking the overseas reports, the company financial analyst estimated tanker capacity at 2% over the previous year.

Passive: Checking the overseas reports, tanker capacity was estimated at 2% over the previous year.

In the second sentence, the opening phrase (*Checking . . .*) cannot modify *tanker capacity* and is a dangling modifier.

4. Passive voice is confusing in instructions because readers cannot tell *who* is to perform the action. Always write instructions and direct orders in active voice.

Unclear: The cement should be applied to both surfaces.
Revised: Apply the cement to both surfaces.

Unclear: The telephone should be answered within three rings.
Revised: Please answer the telephone within three rings.

In technical writing, passive voice is sometimes necessary. Use passive voice when

1. You do not know who or what performed the action:

The fire was reported at 6:05 A.M.

2. Your readers are not interested in who or what performed the action:

Ethan McClosky was elected district attorney.

3. You are describing a process performed by one person, and naming that person in every sentence would be monotonous. Identify the performer in the opening and then use passive voice:

The carpenter began assembling the base by gluing each long apron to two legs. The alignment strips were then cut for the tray bottoms to finished dimensions. The tabletop was turned upside down and. . . .

4. For some reason, perhaps courtesy, you do not want to identify the person responsible for an action:

The copy machine jammed because a large sheaf of papers was inserted upside down.

Jargon

Jargon refers to the technical language and abbreviated terms used by people in one particular field, one company, or one department or unit. People in every workplace and every occupation use some jargon. A waitress may refer to "watering the tables" (putting water glasses on the tables), a public relations executive may ask a secretary to get "the glossies" (glossy photographs), or a psychologist may remark to another psychologist that the average woman has a "24F on the PAQ" (a femininity score of 24 on the Personal Attributes Questionnaire). In some cases, jargon may be so narrow that employees in one department cannot understand the jargon used in another department. Use jargon in professional communications only when you are certain your readers understand it.

Here is a sentence from a memo sent by a purchase coordinator to his supervisor:

> Guttenhausen (Deutsche) big R price is list less 40 to Inventory versus rest to Corporate.

When the supervisor included this information in a memo he prepared for the division head about the weekly orders, he revised it as follows:

> Guttenhausen Industries (Bonn) will pay our standard price less 40% (in deutsche marks) for the Model RR–28 transformer, charged to the Inventory account. The difference between this price and our usual cost plus 15% will be charged to the Corporate account.

The supervisor cut the original jargon and clarified the message by fully identifying the company, the transformer model, and the prices and by explaining how the costs would be charged. The revision required two sentences. Jargon allows employees to exchange briefer messages, but only if the readers understand every term and the abbreviated references. When in doubt, cut out jargon and clarify your terms.

Sexist Language

Sexist language refers to words or phrases that indicate a bias against women in terms of importance or competence. Most people would never use biased language to refer to ethnic, religious, or racial groups, but sexist language often goes unnoticed because many common terms and phrases that are sexist in nature have been part of our casual language for decades. People now realize that sexist language influences our expectations about what women can accomplish and also relegates women to an inferior status. Using such language is not acceptable any longer. In revising documents, check for these slips into sexist language:

1. Demeaning or condescending terms. Avoid using casual or slang terms for women.

   Sexist: The girls in the Records Department will prepare the reports.
   Revised: The clerks in the Records Department will prepare the reports.

Sexist: The annual division picnic will be June 12. Bring the little woman.

Revised: The annual division picnic will be June 12. Please bring your spouse.

2. Descriptions for women based on standards different from those for men. Avoid referring to women in one way and men in another.

Sexist: The consultants were Dr. Dennis Tonelli, Mr. Robert Lavery, and Debbie Roberts.

Revised: The consultants were Dr. Dennis Tonelli, Mr. Robert Lavery, and Ms. Debra Roberts.

Sexist: There were three doctors and two lady lawyers at the meeting.

Revised: There were three doctors and two lawyers at the meeting.

Sexist: The new mechanical engineers are Douglas Ranson, a graduate of MIT and a Rhodes scholar, and Marcia Kane, an attractive redhead with a B.S. from the University of Michigan and an M.S. from the University of Wisconsin.

Revised: The new mechanical engineers are Douglas Ranson, a graduate of MIT and a Rhodes scholar, and Marcia Kane, with a B.S. from the University of Michigan and an M.S. from the University of Wisconsin.

3. Occupational stereotypes. Do not imply that all employees in a particular job are the same sex.

Sexist: An experienced pilot is needed. He must. . . .

Revised: An experienced pilot is needed. This person must. . . .

Sexist: The new tax laws affect all businessmen.

Revised: The new tax laws affect all businesspeople.

Although some gender-specific occupational terms remain common, such as *actor/actress, waiter/waitress,* and *host/hostess,* most such terms have been changed to neutral job titles.

Sexist: The policeman should fill out a damage report.

Revised: The police officer should fill out a damage report.

Sexist: The stewardess reported the safety problem.

Revised: The flight attendant reported the safety problem.

4. Generic *he* to refer to all people. Using the pronoun *he* to refer to unnamed people or to stand for a group of people is correct grammatically in English, but it might be offensive to some people. Avoid the generic *he* whenever possible, particularly in job descriptions that could apply to either sex. Change a singular pronoun to a plural:

Sexist: Each technical writer has his own office at Tower Industries.

Revised: All technical writers have their own offices at Tower Industries.

Eliminate the pronoun completely:

Sexist: The average real estate developer plans to start his construction projects in April.

Revised: The average real estate developer plans to start construction projects in April.

Use *he* or *she* or *his* or *hers* very sparingly:

Sexist: The x-ray technician must log his hours daily.

Revised: The x-ray technician must log his or her hours daily.

Better: All x-ray technicians must log their hours daily.

Concrete versus Abstract Words

Concrete words refer to specific items, such as objects, statistics, locations, dimensions, and actions that can be observed by some means. Here is a sentence using concrete words:

> The 48M printer has a maximum continuous speed of 4000 lines per minute, with burst speeds up to 5500 lines per minute.

Abstract words refer generally to ideas, conditions, and qualities. Here is a sentence from a quarterly report to stockholders that uses abstract words:

> The sales position of Collins, Inc., was favorable as a result of our attention to products and our response to customers.

This sentence contains little information for readers who want to know about the company activities. Here is a revision using more concrete language:

> The 6% rise in domestic sales in the third quarter of 1992 resulted from our addition of a safety catch on the Collins Washer in response to over 10,000 requests by our customers.

This revision in concrete language clarifies exactly what the company did and what the result was. Using concrete or abstract words, as always, depends on what you believe your readers need. However, in most professional situations, readers want and need the precise information provided by concrete words.

The paragraphs that follow are from two reports submitted by management trainees in a large bank after a visit to the retail division of the main branch. The trainees wrote reports to their supervisors, describing their responses to the procedures they observed. The paragraph from the first report uses primarily abstract, nonspecific language:

> The first department I visited was very interesting. The way in which the men buy and investigate the paper was very interesting and informative. This area, along with the other areas, helped me where I am right now—doing loans. Again, the ways in which the men deal with the dealers was quite informative. They were friendly, but stern, and did not let the dealers control the transaction.

The paragraph from the second report uses more concrete language:

> The manual system of entering sales draft data on the charge system seems inefficient. It is clear that seasonal surges in charge activity (for example, Christmas) or an employee illness would create a serious bottleneck in processing. My talk with Eva Lockridge confirmed my impression that this operation is outdated and needs to be redesigned.

The first writer did not identify any specific item of interest or explain exactly what was informative about the visit. The second writer identified both the system that seemed outdated and the person with whom she talked. The second writer is providing her reader with concrete information rather than generalities.

Gobbledygook

Gobbledygook is writing that is indirect, vague, pompous, or longer and more difficult to read than necessary. Writers of gobbledygook do not care if their readers can use their documents because they are interested only in demonstrating how many large words they can cram into convoluted sentences. Such writers are primarily concerned with impressing or intimidating readers rather than helping them use information efficiently. Gobbledygook is characterized by these elements:

1. Using jargon the readers cannot understand.

2. Making words longer than necessary by adding suffixes or prefixes to short, well-known words (e.g., *finalization, marginalization*). Another way to produce gobbledygook is to use a longer synonym for a short, well-known word. A good example is the word *utilize* and its variations to substitute for *use*. *Utilize* is an unnecessary word because *use* can be

substituted in any sentence and mean the same thing. Notice the revisions that follow these sentences:

Gobbledygook:	The project will utilize the Acme trucks.
Revision:	The project will use the Acme trucks.
Gobbledygook:	By utilizing the gravel already on the site, we can save up to $5000.
Revision:	By using the gravel already on the site, we can save up to $5000.
Gobbledygook:	Through the utilization of this high-speed press, we can meet the deadline.
Revision:	Through the use of this high-speed press, we can meet the deadline.

The English language has many short, precise words. Use them.

3. Writing more elaborate words than are necessary for document purpose and readers. The writer who says "deciduous perennial, genus *Ulmus*" instead of "elm tree" is probably engaged in gobbledygook unless his or her readers are biologists.

This paragraph from a memo sent by a unit supervisor to a division manager is supposed to explain why the unit needs more architects:

> In the absence of available adequate applied man-hours, and/or elapsed calendar time, the quality of the architectural result (as delineated by the drawings) has been and will continue to be put ahead of the graphic quality or detailed completeness of the documents. In order to be efficient, work should be consecutive not simultaneous, and a schedule must show design and design development as scheduled separately from working drawings on each project, so that a tighter but realistic schedule can be maintained, optimizing the productive efforts of each person.

You will not be surprised to learn that the division manager routinely threw away any memos he received from this employee without reading them.

Fad Words

Fad words are words that arise from a particular field and then are used to apply to situations not in the original context of the word. The words become popular and drift into general use. The expression *bottom line,* for example, is from accounting, where it means the final figure showing profit or loss. Now people often use the expression to mean any final determination, deadline, or result:

> The bottom line is that shipments have to begin Monday, or the company will close three refineries.

In some cases, the fad word is not connected to any field, but instead is a common word that people begin using in a new way. Frequently, the word is a noun that people have converted to a verb by adding verb endings to it. Here are examples of current fad words:

1. *Access* is a noun meaning the ability to approach something or someone:

   > He has access to important people in the White House.

   The computer industry uses *access* as a verb meaning to retrieve files from a database:

   > The secretary accessed the medical records.

2. *Impact* is a noun meaning the force with which one object strikes another or the influence of one thing on another:

   > The impact of the boulder demolished the automobile.

   Many people in business now use *impact* as a verb meaning to affect or to influence:

   > October's sales drop will impact our dealers.

   Impact used as a verb probably results from the uncertainty many people have about the difference between *affect,* meaning to influence, and *effect,* meaning result.

3. *Reference* is a noun meaning the mention of something or someone:

   > The quality-control engineer included a reference to last year's test in his report.

   Reference is a particularly confusing fad word because it is used as a substitute for a variety of words. Here are some samples:

Fad word:	The two chemists *referenced* six previous studies in their article.
Revision:	The two chemists cited six previous studies in their article.
Fad word:	*Reference* your request for. . . .
Revision:	Referring to your request for. . . .
Fad word:	The vice president *referenced* the dam project in his speech.
Revision:	The vice president mentioned the dam project in his speech.

Fad word:	My assistant is *referencing* the manual before printing.
Revision:	My assistant is editing the manual before printing.
Fad word:	Clear *referencing* of load sources and allowable stress is required in each calculation.
Revision:	Clear statements of load sources and allowable stress are required in each calculation.

Fad words can be as confusing as jargon if readers are not familiar with the meaning of the words in a particular context. Avoid using the latest fad words whenever a clearer, more standard word is available.

Wordiness

Wordiness refers to writing that includes superfluous words that add no information to a document. Wordiness stems from several causes:

1. *Doubling terms.* Using two or more similar terms to make one point creates wordiness. These doubled phrases can be reduced to one of the words:

   final ultimate result (result)

   the month of July (July)

   finished and completed (finished or completed)

   unique innovation (innovation)

2. *Long phrases for short words.* Wordiness results when writers use long phrases instead of one simple word:

   at this point in time (now)

   in the near future (soon)

   due to the fact that (because)

   in the event that (if)

3. *Unneeded repetition.* Repeating words or phrases too often increases wordiness and disturbs sentence clarity:

   The Marshman employees will follow the scheduled established hours established by their supervisors, who will establish the times required to support production.

   This sentence is difficult to read because *established* appears three times, once as an adjective and twice as a verb. Here is a revision:

   The Marshman employees will follow the schedule established by their supervisors, who will set times required to support production.

4. *Empty sentence openings.* These sentences are correct grammatically but their structure contributes to wordiness:

It was determined that the home office sent income statements to all pension clients.

It is necessary that the loader valves (No. 3C126) be scrapped because of damage.

It might be possible to open two runways within an hour.

There will be times when the videotapes are not available.

There are three new checking account options available from Southwest National Bank.

There is a full kitchenette with microwave and wet bar in every resort condo.

These sentences have empty openings because the first words (*There is* / *There are* / *It is* / *It was* / *It might be*) offer the reader no information, and the reader must reach the last half of the sentence to find the subject. Here are revisions that eliminate the empty openings:

The home office sent income statements to all pension clients.

The loader valves (No. 3C126) must be scrapped because of damage.

Two runways might open within an hour.

Sometimes the videotapes will not be available.

Southwest National Bank is offering three new checking account options.

Every resort condo has a full kitchenette with microwave and wet bar.

Remember that wordiness does not refer to the length of a document, but to excessive words in the text. A 40-page manual containing none of the constructions discussed here is not wordy, but a half-page memo full of them is.

CHAPTER SUMMARY

This chapter discusses two stages of revision—global revision and fine-tuning revision. Remember:

- Revision consists of two distinct stages—global revision, which focuses on content and organization, and fine-tuning revision, which focuses on sentence structure, word choice, correctness, and the mechanics of technical style.

- For global revision, writers check content to see if there are enough details, definitions, and emphasis on the major points.

- For global revision, writers also check organization of the full document and of individual sections for (1) overall organization, (2) introductions and conclusions, (3) paragraphs, (4) headings, and (5) format.

- For fine-tuning revision, writers check sentence structure for overloaded sentences, clipped sentences, overly long sentences, and overuse of passive voice.

- For fine-tuning revision, writers also check word choice for unnecessary jargon, sexist language, overly abstract words, gobbledygook, fad words, and general wordiness.

SUPPLEMENTAL READINGS IN PART 2

Bagin, C. B. and Van Doren, J. "How to Avoid Costly Proofreading Errors," *Simply Stated*, p. 448.

Buehler, M. F. "Defining Terms in Technical Editing: The Levels of Edit as a Model," *Technical Communication*, p. 486.

"The Practical Writer," *The Royal Bank of Canada*, p. 545.

Tarutz, J. H. "Editing for an International Audience," *Technical Editing*, p. 572.

MODEL 5-1   Commentary

This model shows three drafts of a company bulletin outlining procedures for security guards who discover a fire while on patrol. The bulletin will be included in the company's "Security Procedures Manual," which contains general procedures for potential security problems such as fire, theft, physical fights, and trespassing. The bulletins are not instructions to be used on the job. Rather, the guards are expected to read the bulletins, become familiar with the procedures, and follow them if a security situation arises.

Discussion

1. In the first draft, identify the major topics the writer covers, and discuss how well the general organization fits the purpose of the readers.

2. Compare the first and second drafts, and discuss the changes the writer made in organization, sentence structure, and detail. How will these changes help the readers understand the information?

3. Compare the third draft with the first two, and discuss how the specific changes will improve the usefulness of the bulletin.

4. In groups, draft a fourth version of this bulletin, making further organization changes to increase clarity. Or, if your instructor prefers, rewrite one section of the third draft, and make further fine-tuning revisions according to the guidelines in this chapter.

5. Follow the guidelines for fine-tuning revisions in this chapter, and revise one section of any of the models in the first three chapters of this textbook.

BULLETIN 46-RC   FIRE EMERGENCIES—PLANT SECURITY PATROLS

Following are procedures for fire emergencies discovered during routine security patrols. All security personnel should be familiar with these procedures.

General Inspection

Perimeter fence lines, parking lots, and yard areas should be observed by security personnel at least twice per shift. Special attention should be given to outside areas during the dark hours and nonoperating periods. It is preferable that the inspection of the yard area and parking lots be made in a security patrol car equipped with a spot light and two-way radio communications. Special attention should be given to the condition of fencing and gates and to yard lighting to assure that all necessary lights are turned on during the dark hours and that the system is fully operative. Where yard lights are noted as burned out, the guard should report these problems immediately to the Plant Engineer for corrective action and maintain follow-up until the yard lighting is in full service. Occasional roof spot checks should be made by security patrols to observe for improper use of roof areas and fire hazards, particularly around ventilating equipment.

Discovery

When a guard discovers a fire during an in-plant security patrol, he should immediately turn in an alarm. This should be done before any attempt is made to fight the fire because all too frequently guards think they can put out the fire with the equipment at hand, and large losses have resulted.

Whenever possible, the guard should turn in the alarm by using the alarm box nearest the scene of the fire. If it is necessary to report the fire on the plant telephone, he should identify the location accurately so that he may give this information to the plant fire department or to the guard on duty at the Security Office, who will summon the employee fire brigade and possibly the city fire department.

Once he has turned in the alarm, the guard should decide whether he can effectively use the available fire protection equipment to fight the fire. If the fire is beyond his control, he should proceed to the main aisle of approach where he can make contact with the fire brigade or firemen and direct them to the scene of the fire. If automatic sprinklers have been engaged, the men in charge of the fire fighting crew will make the decision to turn off the system.

First Draft

BULLETIN 46-RC   FIRE EMERGENCIES—PLANT SECURITY PATROLS

All security guards should be familiar with the following procedures for fire emergencies that occur during routine security patrols.

Inspection Areas

Inspection of the yard area and parking lots should be made in a security patrol car equipped with a spot light and two-way radio communications. At least twice per shift, the guard should inspect (1) fence lines, (2) parking lots, and (3) yard areas. These outside areas require special attention during the dark hours and nonoperating periods. The guard should inspect carefully the condition of the fencing and gate closures. The yard lighting should be checked to ensure that all necessary lights are turned on during the dark hours and that the system is fully operative. If the guard notes that yard lights are burned out, he should report these problems to the Plant Engineer for corrective action and maintain follow-up until the yard lighting is in full service.

Roof Checks

Occasional roof spot checks should be made by the guard to observe improper use of roof areas and any fire hazards, particularly around ventilating equipment.

Fires

When a guard discovers a fire during an in-plant security patrol, he should immediately turn in an alarm before he makes any attempt to fight the fire. In the past, attempts to fight the fire without sounding an alarm have resulted in costly damage and larger fires than necessary.

Whenever possible, the guard should turn in the alarm at the alarm box nearest the scene of the fire. If he must use a plant telephone, he should identify the location accurately. This information helps the plant fire department or the guard on duty at the Security Office, who must summon the employee fire brigade or the city fire department.

Once he has turned in the alarm, the guard should decide whether he can fight the fire with the available equipment. If the fire is beyond his control, he should go to the main entrance of the area so that he can direct the fire fighters to the scene of the fire. If the automatic sprinklers are on, the supervisor of the fire fighting crew will decide when to turn off the system.

Second Draft

BULLETIN 46-RC   FIRES—PLANT SECURITY PATROLS

All security guards should be familiar with the following procedures for fires that occur during routine security patrols.

Inspection Areas

The guard should inspect the outside areas in a security patrol car equipped with a spot light and two-way radio. The outside areas require special attention after dark and during nonoperating hours. At least twice per shift, the following should be inspected:

Fence Lines—The guard should check fences for gaps or breaks in the chain and gate closures for tight links and hinges.

Parking Lots and Yards—The guard should monitor the lighting in all parking lots and open yards to ensure that all necessary lights are on after dark and that the system is fully operative. If any lights are burned out, the guard should report the locations to the Plant Engineer and maintain follow-up until the lighting is repaired.

Occasional spot checks during a shift should be made of the following:

Roofs—The guard should check for improper use of the roof areas and any fire hazards, particularly around ventilating equipment.

Fires

Discovery—Upon discovering a fire during an in-plant security patrol, the guard must turn in an alarm before attempting to fight the fire. In the past, attempts to fight the fire before turning in an alarm have resulted in costly damage and larger fires than necessary.

Alarms—Whenever possible, the guard should turn in the alarm at the alarm box nearest the scene of the fire. If a plant telephone is more convenient or safer, the guard should be sure to identify the fire location accurately. This information is needed by the plant fire department and the guard at the Security Office, who must summon the employee fire brigade or the city fire department.

Fire Fighting—Once the alarm is in, the guard should decide whether to fight the fire with the available equipment. If the fire is beyond control, the guard should go to the main entrance to the fire area and direct the fire brigade or city fire fighters to the scene of the fire. If the automatic sprinklers are on, the supervisor of the fire brigade or of the fire department crew will decide when to turn off the system.

Third Draft

1. The following memo was written by the office manager of a real estate company. Within a day, several employees complained to the company owner. Identify the problems in the memo and revise it for a more effective message.

> As a result of our merger with Markling Reality Company, we are adding several necessary and badly needed consultants from companies that provide management consultants to assist in mergers. First to join us on Monday, October 2, will be Gina Ashton, an experienced consultant with Winkler Management Associates. Gina will be working with Peggy and Ellen to consolidate and combine our records and data from the various clients we have had over the thirty years at Ludlow Realty. Now that we are merging with Markling, we need to combine and merge our records to avoid duplicating and repeating actions already taken. Also joining our staff, but not until October 10, will be Mr. Anthony Berenger, a consultant with ten years' experience at Hunt Associates. Mr. Berenger will be advising Mr. Shental and Mr. Borkoi on the many ramifications of merging two real estate firms, particularly regarding financial records. Mr. Berenger comes to us with high qualifications, including a management degree from the University of Texas at Austin. Let's all make an effort to cooperate and assist Gina and Mr. Berenger in their work. I've asked Patty and Jinny to take Gina to lunch on her first day. Mr. Markling will take Mr. Berenger to lunch on his first day with us.

2. The following bulletin was posted in the admissions office of a psychiatric hospital, and clerks quickly complained the directions were hard to understand. Revise the bulletin for a clearer message. Add any information you wish in order to clarify the meaning.

PSYCHIATRIC ADMISSIONS

> It has come to our attention that the recent difficulties and confusion surrounding the attempts to admit new patients is causing extreme hardship for the patients and for the admitting clerks who are trying to utilize the most efficient methods recently referenced. Here are some guidelines to facilitate the interactions with new patients. Clients under 18 years old cannot be pink slipped, but must be REG under our old guidelines. They must be directly admitted under the green mode to the regular psychiatric unit. In the case of dealing with a client under 18 years old, it should be determined whether the parents or one of the parents or other relatives are available. In the case of a client under 18 years old, a doctor on call

may coordinate and consult with other doctors, and a final determination should be developed as to which doctor will be the doctor of record. If a psychologist or police officer has signed the admission form, it must be determined whether the client needs emergency room service. Full utilization of the emergency room facilities may be necessary, but avoidance should be the goal of the admitting clerks, particularly since CISCS security is understaffed at this time and will be in the near future.

3. A manager, trying to impress the new vice president, sent the following memo. After glancing at it, the vice president sent it back with a note—"Write it so I can read it." Revise the memo for a clearer message.

Pursuant to our recent informal conversation concerning the implementation of the Order Processing software to be supplied by Office Technology, my preliminary feasibility study has been completed. While it is anticipated that the order processing software may require considerable effort in modification in order to be utilized fully by the gals in Systems Processing, a complete implementation by the previously agreed date seems feasible. While the implementation of the order processing software is certainly an important part of our overall computer update, its early implementation should not be allowed to jeopardize the timely implementation of those software applications most crucial to utilizing our full capacities expected. There are additional considerations and constraints to this early implementation project that also need to be discussed and/or resolved. I will await your feedback on this implementation matter.

4. Find a "real-world" letter, memo, bulletin, pamphlet, or report. Analyze the writing style according to the guidelines in this chapter. Write a brief evaluation of the writing style and identify specific places in the document where revision would make the writing easier to understand. *Or,* if your instructor prefers, rewrite the original document to improve the style according to the guidelines in this chapter. Hand in both your revision and the original document.

CHAPTER **6**

Definition

UNDERSTANDING DEFINITIONS

Definition is essential in good technical writing because of the specialized vocabulary in many documents. All definitions are meant to distinguish one object or procedure from any that are similar and to clarify them for readers by setting precise limits on each expression. In writing definitions, use vocabulary understandable to your readers. Defining one word with others that are equally specialized will frustrate your readers; no one wants to consult a dictionary in order to understand an explanation that was supposed to make referring to a dictionary unnecessary.

Certain circumstances always call for definitions:

1. When technical information originally written for expert readers is revised for nonexpert readers, the writer must include definitions for all terms that are not common knowledge.

2. A document with readers from many disciplines or varied backgrounds must include definitions enabling readers with the lowest level of knowledge to understand the document.

3. All new or rare terms should be defined even for readers who are experts in the subject. Change is so rapid in science and technology that no one can easily keep up with every new development.

4. When a term has multiple meanings, a writer must be clear about which meaning is being used in the document. The word *slate,* for example, can refer to a kind of rock, a color, a handheld chalkboard, or a list of candidates for election.

As discussed in Chapter 3, writers frequently use definitions in reports addressed to multiple readers because some of the readers may not be familiar with the technical terminology used. Definitions in reports may range from a simple phrase in a sentence to a complete appendix at the end of the report. In all cases, the writer decides just how much definition the reader needs to be able to use the report effectively. Definitions also may be complete documents in themselves; for example, entries in technical handbooks or science dictionaries are expanded definitions. Furthermore, individual sections of manuals, technical sales literature, and information pamphlets are often expanded definitions for readers who lack expert knowledge of the field but need to understand the subject.

The three types of definitions are (1) informal, (2) formal sentence, and (3) expanded. All three can appear in the same document, and your use of one or another depends on your analysis of the needs of your readers and your purpose in using a specific item of information.

WRITING INFORMAL DEFINITIONS

Informal definitions explain a term with a word or a phrase that has the same general meaning. Here are some examples of informal definitions:

> Contrast is the difference between dark and light in a photograph.
>
> Terra cotta—a hard, fired clay—is used for pottery and ornamental architectural detail.
>
> Viscous (sticky) substances are used in manufacturing rayon.
>
> Leucine, an amino acid, is essential for human nutrition.

The first definition is a complete sentence; the other definitions are words or phrases used to define a term within a sentence. Notice that you can set off the definition with dashes, parentheses, or commas. Place the definition immediately after the first reference to the term. Informal definitions are most helpful for nonexpert readers who need an introduction to an unfamiliar term. Be sure to use a well-known word or phrase to define a difficult term.

The advantage of informal definitions is that they do not significantly interrupt the flow of a sentence or the information. Readers do not have to stop thinking about the main idea in order to understand the term. The limitation of informal definitions is that they do not thoroughly explain the term and, in fact, are really identifications rather than definitions. If a reader needs more information than that provided by a simple identification, use a formal sentence definition or an expanded definition.

WRITING FORMAL SENTENCE DEFINITIONS

A *formal sentence definition* is more detailed and rigidly structured than an informal definition. The formal definition has three specific parts.

Term		*Group*	*Distinguishing features*
An *ace*	is	a tennis serve	that is successful because the opponent cannot reach the ball to return it.

The first part is the specific term you want to define, followed by the verb *is* or *are, was* or *were*. The second part is the group of objects or actions to which the term belongs. The third part consists of the distinguishing features that set this term off from others in the same group. In this example, the group part *a tennis serve* establishes both the sport and the type of action the term refers to. The distinguishing features part explains the specific quality that separates this tennis serve from others—the opponent cannot reach it.

These formal definitions illustrate how the group and the distinguishing features become more restrictive as a term becomes more specific:

Term		Group	Distinguishing features
A *firearm*	is	a weapon	from which a bullet or shell is discharged by gunpowder.
A *rifle*	is	a firearm	with spiral grooves in the inner surface of the gun barrel to give the bullet a rotary motion and increase its accuracy.
A *Winchester*	is	a rifle	first made about 1866, with a tubular magazine under the barrel that allows the user to fire a number of bullets without reloading.

In writing a formal sentence definition, be sure to place the term in as specific a group as possible. In the preceding samples, a rifle could be placed in the group *weapon,* but that group also includes clubs, swords, and nuclear missiles. Placing the rifle in the group *firearm* eliminates all weapons that are not also firearms. The distinguishing features part then concentrates on the characteristics that are special to rifles and not to other firearms. The distinguishing features part, however, cannot include every characteristic detail of a term. You will have to decide which features most effectively separate the term from others in the same group and which will best help your readers understand and use the information.

When writing formal sentence definitions, remember these tips:

1. Do not use the same key word in the distinguishing features part that you used in one or both of the other two units.

   Poor: A blender is an electric kitchen appliance that blends liquids or solid foods with propellerlike blades.

   Better: A blender is an electric kitchen appliance that mixes, chops, grinds, or purees liquids or solid foods with a single set of propellerlike blades at the base of the single food container.

   Poor: An odometer is a measuring instrument that measures the distance traveled by a vehicle.

   Better: An odometer is a measuring instrument that records the distance traveled by a vehicle.

In the first example, the distinguishing features part includes the verb *blend,* which is also part of the term being defined. In the second example, the distinguishing features part includes the verb *measures,* which is used in the group part. In both cases, the writer must revise to avoid repetition that will send readers in a circle. Sometimes you can assume that your readers know what a general term means. If you are certain your readers understand the term *horse* and your purpose is to clarify the term *racehorse,* you may write, "A racehorse is a horse that is bred or trained to run in competition with other horses."

2. Do not use distinguishing features that are too general to adequately specify the meaning of the term.

Poor: Rugby is a sport that involves rough contact among players as they try to send a ball over the opponent's goal lines.

Better: Rugby is a team sport that involves 13 to 15 players on each side who try to send a ball across the opponent's goal line during two 40-minute halves.

Poor: A staple is a short piece of wire that is bent so as to hold papers together.

Better: A staple is a short piece of wire that is bent so both ends pierce several papers and fold inward, binding the papers together.

In both examples, the distinguishing features are not restrictive enough. Many sports, such as football and soccer, involve rough contact between players who try to send a ball over the opponent's goal line. The revision focuses on the number of players and the minutes played, features which distinguish rugby from similar team sports. Notice also that the group has been narrowed to *team sport* to further restrict the definition and help the reader understand it. In the second poor example, the distinguishing features could apply to a paper clip as well as a staple. Remember to restrict the group as much as possible and provide distinguishing features that isolate the term from its group.

3. Do not use distinguishing features that are too restrictive.

Poor: A tent is a portable shelter made of beige canvas in the shape of a pyramid, supported by poles.

Better: A tent is a portable shelter made of animal skins or a sturdy fabric and supported by poles.

Poor: A videotape is a recording device made of a magnetic ribbon of material ¾ in. wide and coated plastic that registers both audio and visual signals for reproduction.

Better: A videotape is a recording device made of a magnetic ribbon of material, usually coated plastic, that registers both audio and visual signals for reproduction.

In the first example, the distinguishing features are too restrictive because not all tents are pyramid-shaped or made of beige canvas. The second example establishes only one size for a videotape, but videotapes come in several sizes, so size is not an appropriate distinguishing feature. Do not restrict your definition to only one brand or one model if your term is meant to cover all models and brands of that particular object.

4. Do not use *is when, is where,* or *is what* in place of the group part in a formal definition.

Poor: A tongue depressor is what medical personnel use to hold down a patient's tongue during a throat examination.

Better: A tongue depressor is a flat, thin, wooden stick used by medical personnel to hold down a patient's tongue during a throat examination.

Poor: Genetic engineering is when scientists change the hereditary code on an organism's DNA.

Better: Genetic engineering is the set of biochemical techniques used by scientists to move fragments from the genes of one organism to the chromosomes of another to change the hereditary code on the DNA of the second organism.

In both examples, the writer initially neglects to place the term in a group before adding the distinguishing features. The group part is the first level of restriction, and it helps readers by eliminating other groups that may share some of the distinguishing features. The first example, for instance, could apply to any object shoved down a patient's throat. The poor definition of genetic engineering refers only to the result and does not clarify the term as applying to specific techniques that will produce that result.

WRITING EXPANDED DEFINITIONS

Expanded definitions can range from one paragraph in a report or manual to an entry several pages long in a technical dictionary. Writers use expanded definitions in these circumstances:

1. When a reader must fully understand a term to successfully use the document. A patient who has just been diagnosed with hypoglycemia probably will want a more detailed definition in the patient information booklet than just a formal sentence definition. Similarly, a decision maker who is reading a feasibility study about bridge reconstruction will want expanded definitions of such terms as *cathodic protection* or *distributed anode system* in order to make an informed decision about the most appropriate method for the company project.

2. When specific terms, such as *economically disadvantaged* or *physical therapy,* refer to broad concepts and readers other than experts need to understand the scope and application of the terms.

3. When the purpose of the document, such as a technical handbook or a science dictionary, is to provide expanded definitions to readers who need to understand the terms for a variety of reasons.

A careful writer usually begins an expanded definition with a formal sentence definition and then uses one or more of the following strategies to enlarge the definition with more detail and explanation.

Cause and Effect

Writers use the cause-and-effect (or effect-and-cause) strategy to illustrate relationships among several events. This strategy is effective in expanded definitions of terms that refer to a process or a system. The following paragraph is from a student report about various types of exercises used in athletic training. The definition explains the effect aerobic exercise has on the body.

> Aerobic exercise is a sustained physical activity that increases the body's ability to obtain oxygen, thereby strengthening the heart and lungs. Aerobic effect begins when an exercise is vigorous enough to produce a sustained heart rate of at least 150 beats a minute. This exercise, if continued for at least 20 minutes, produces a change in a person's body. The lungs begin processing more air with less effort, while the heart grows stronger, pumping more blood with fewer strokes. Overall, the body's total blood volume increases and the blood supply to the muscles improves.

Classification

Classification is used in expanded definitions when a writer needs to break a term into types or categories and discuss the similarities and differences among the categories. The following expanded definition is from a report written by a public television station manager to a donors group, soliciting funds for equipment purchases. The writer uses classification to define videotape machines. Note that the writer does not begin with a formal sentence definition and that the distinguishing features actually appear in the second sentence.

> The videotape recorder/player is an electronic device that is one of the most important components of television station operation. The videotape recorder creates distinct video and audio tracks during recording; then, during playback, the videotape player "reads" the images and sound information from the recorded tracks. Videotape machines fall into three categories—production, editing, and playback. A production recorder preserves images on tape for later editing. The editing recorder plays back an image on one machine and records it on a second machine. The playback machine must reproduce the best signal possible from a recorded tape so that the edit recorder can capture the best possible image and record it on another tape. The requirements for each of these VCRs vary because each is expected to do a different job.

Comparison or Contrast

Writers use comparison to show readers the similarities or differences between the term being defined and another commonly understood term. When using this strategy, be sure the term you are using for comparison or contrast is familiar to your readers. The following definition is from a book about Civil War military equipment written for general readers. The writer compares a specific style of tent to a hoop skirt and a teepee, objects most readers have seen in films or books. A third comparison occurs when the writer explains how the men arranged themselves to sleep, further illustrating the shape and size of the tent and creating an image that general readers will understand easily.

> Much more popular and efficient was the Sibley tent, named for its inventory, Henry H. Sibley, now a brigadier general in the Confederate service. One Reb likened it to a "large hoop skirt standing by itself on the ground." Indeed, it resembled nothing so much as an Indian teepee, a tall cone of canvas supported by a center pole. Flaps on the sides could be opened for ventilation, and an iron replica of the tent cone called a Sibley stove heated the interior—sort of. Often more than twenty men inhabited a single tent, spread out like the spokes of a wheel, their heads at the outer rim and their feet at the center pole.[1]

Description

A detailed description of a term being defined will expand the definition. Reading about the physical properties of a term often helps readers to visualize the concept or object and remember it more readily. Chapter 7 provides a detailed discussion of developing physical descriptions. This excerpt from an encyclopedia illustrates the use of physical description as part of an expanded definition of *bison*:

> Head and body length is 2100 to 3500 mm, tail length is 500 to 600 mm, shoulder height is 1500 to 2000 mm, and weight is 350 to 1000 kg. Males average larger than females. The pelage of the head, neck, shoulders, and forelegs is long, shaggy, and brownish black. There is usually a beard on the chin. The remainder of the body is covered with short hairs of a lighter color. Young calves are reddish brown. The forehead is short and broad, the head is heavy, the neck is short, and the shoulders have a high hump. The horns, borne by both sexes, are short, upcurving, and sharp. Females have smaller humps, thinner necks, and thinner horns than males.[2]

Development or History

Writers may expand definitions by describing how the subject has changed from its original form or purpose over time. When using development or history to expand a definition, you may include (1) discovery or invention of the concept or object, (2) changes in the components or design of the concept or object, or (3) changes in the use or function of the concept or object. The following excerpt from a science pamphlet for general readers expands the definition of the telegraph by briefly explaining some of its history:

> Although the term *telegraph* means a system or apparatus for sending messages over a long distance and, therefore, could include smoke and drum signals, the term now generally refers to the electric telegraph developed in the nineteenth century. In the late eighteenth century, Frenchman Claude Clappe designed a system of signals that relied on a vertical pole and moveable crossbar with indicators. Using a telescope, operators in towers three miles apart read the signals and then passed the messages from tower to tower between principal French cities. The success of this system encouraged experimentation. In the early nineteenth century, researchers discovered that electric current through a wire could cause a needle to turn. The development of the electromagnet then allowed Samuel F. B. Morse to devise a practical system of transmitting and receiving electric signals over long distances, and he invented a message code of dots, dashes, and spaces. By mid-nineteenth century, telegraph systems spread across the United States and Europe.

Etymology

Etymology is the study of the history of individual words. The term derives from the Greek *etymon* (true meaning) and *logos* (word). Writers rarely use etymology as the only strategy in an expanded definition, but they often include it with other strategies. The following definition of *ligament* is from a brochure for orthopedic patients:

> In anatomy, a ligament is a band of white fibrous tissue that connects bones and supports organs. The word *ligament* comes from the Latin *ligare* (to tie or bind). Although a ligament is strong, it does not stretch, so if the bones are pulled apart, the ligament connecting them will tear.

Examples

Another way to expand a definition is to provide examples of the term. This strategy is particularly effective in expanding definitions for nonexpert readers who need to understand the variety included in one term. This definition of a combat medal is taken from a student examination on military history:

> A combat medal is a military award given to commemorate an individual's bravery under fire. Medals are awarded by all branches of the armed forces and by civilian legislative bodies. The Congressional Medal of Honor, for instance, is awarded by the President in the name of Congress to military personnel who have distinguished themselves in combat beyond the call of duty. The Purple Heart is awarded by the branches of the armed services to all military personnel

who sustain wounds during combat. The Navy Cross is awarded to naval personnel for outstanding heroism against an enemy.

Method of Operation or Process

Another effective strategy for expanding a definition is to explain how the object represented by the term works, such as how a scanner reads images, stores them on disks, and prints them. Also, a writer may expand a definition of a system or natural process by describing the steps in the process, such as how a drug is produced or how a hurricane occurs. Chapter 8 covers developing process explanations.

This excerpt, from a pamphlet about first aid procedures, expands the definition of mouth-to-mouth artificial respiration by explaining the process:

> The purpose of mouth-to-mouth artificial respiration is to maintain an open air passage to the lungs. The rescuer first places the patient on his back and clears the mouth of any foreign objects. Then the patient's head is tilted back until the chin juts upward, thus opening the air passage. The rescuer next places his mouth over the patient's, holds the patient's nostrils shut, and blows a deep breath into the patient's mouth. The patient's mouth is then uncovered to allow exhalation. This cycle is repeated 12 times a minute for an adult victim. If the victim is a child, the rescuer blows shallow breaths 15–20 times a minute.

Negation

Writers occasionally expand a definition by explaining what a term *does not* include. This definition of the ocean from a book about oceanography uses negation as part of the definition of the ocean and its extent:

> The *ocean* is the big blue area on a globe that covers 72 percent of the earth and has a volume of 1.37 billion cubic kilometers. It does *not* include rivers, lakes, or shallow, mostly landlocked bays and estuaries whose volume is insignificant by comparison.[3]

Partition

Separating a term into its parts and explaining each part individually can effectively expand a definition and help the reader visualize the object. In a biology report on blood circulation in humans, a student uses partition to expand her definition of artery:

> An artery is a blood vessel that carries blood from the heart to other parts of the body. All arteries have three main layers: the intima, the media, and the adventitia. The intima is the innermost layer and consists primarily of connective tissue and elastic fibers. The media,

or middle layer, consists of smooth muscle fibers and connective tissue. The outermost layer is the adventitia, which is mainly connective tissue. Each of these layers consists of sublayers of muscle and elastic fibers. The thickness of all the layers depends on the size of the artery.

Stipulation

In some circumstances, writers need to restrict the general meaning of a term in order to use it in a particular context. Such stipulative definitions are often necessary in research reports when the reader needs to understand the limitations of the term as used by the writer. Without the stipulative definition, the reader probably would assume a broader meaning than the writer intends. The following is a stipulative definition from a sociologist's report of interviews with women in homeless shelters in a large city:

> For this report, the term *homeless women* applies to females over the age of 20 who, at the time of the study, had been in a recognized homeless shelter for at least one week. In addition, the women were unemployed when they were interviewed and had been on welfare assistance at least once before going to the shelter.

PLACING DEFINITIONS IN DOCUMENTS

If a definition is part of a longer document, you need to place it so that readers will find it useful and nondisruptive. Include definitions (1) within the text, (2) in an appendix, (3) in footnotes, and/or (4) in a glossary.

Within the Text

Informal definitions or formal sentence definitions can be incorporated easily into the text of a document. If an expanded definition is crucial to the success of a document, it can also be included in the text. However, expanded definitions may interrupt a reader's concentration on the main topic. If the expanded definitions are not crucial to the main topic, consider placing them in an appendix or glossary.

In an Appendix

In a document intended for multiple readers, lengthy expanded definitions for nonexpert readers may be necessary. Rather than interrupt the text, place such expanded definitions in an appendix at the end of the document. Readers who do not need the definitions can ignore them, but readers who do need them can easily find them. Expanded definitions longer than one paragraph usually should be in an appendix unless they are essential to helping readers understand the information in the document.

In Footnotes

Writers often put expanded definitions in footnotes at the bottoms of pages or in endnotes listed at the conclusion of a long document. Such notes do not interrupt the text and are convenient for readers because they appear on the same page or within a few pages of the first reference to the term. If a definition is longer than one paragraph, however, it is best placed in an appendix.

In a Glossary

If your document requires both formal sentence definitions and expanded definitions, a glossary or list of definitions may be the most appropriate way to present them. Glossaries are convenient for readers because the terms are listed alphabetically and all definitions appear in the same location. Chapter 9 discusses preparation of glossaries.

▬▬▬ *CHAPTER SUMMARY*

This chapter discusses how to write definitions of technical terms that readers need to understand. Remember:

- Definitions distinguish an object or concept from similar objects or concepts and clarify for readers the limits of the term.

- Definitions are necessary when (1) technical information for expert readers must be rewritten for nonexpert readers, (2) not all readers will understand the technical terms used in a document, (3) rare or new technical terms are used, and (4) a term has more than one meaning.

- Informal definitions explain a term with another word or a phrase that has the same general meaning.

- Formal sentence definitions explain a term by placing it in a group and identifying the features that distinguish it from other members of the same group.

- Expanded definitions explain the meaning of a term in a full paragraph or longer.

- Writers expand definitions by using one or more of these strategies: cause and effect, classification, comparison or contrast, description, development or history, etymology, examples, method of operation or process, negation, partition, and stipulation.

- Definitions may be placed within the text, in an appendix, in footnotes, or in a glossary, depending on the needs of readers.

SUPPLEMENTAL READINGS IN PART 2

Benson, P. J. "Writing Visually: Design Considerations in Technical Publications," *Technical Communication*, p. 451.

"Six Graphics Guidelines," *Simply Stated*, p. 562.

White, J. V. "Color: The Newest Tool for Technical Communicators," *Technical Communication*, p. 576.

ENDNOTES

1. From W. C. Davis, *Rebels & Yankees: Fighting Men of the Civil War* (New York: Gallery Books, 1989), p. 132.

2. From *Walker's Mammals of the World*, 4th ed. (Baltimore, MD: Johns Hopkins University Press, 1983), p. 1254.

3. From W. Bascom, *The Crest of the Wave: Adventures in Oceanography* (New York: Doubleday, 1988), p. 294.

MODEL 6-1   Commentary

This model is a brochure published by the American Diabetes Association for people who have been diagnosed with diabetes and their families. The information is presented as answers to a series of questions that readers who do not know much about the disease might ask.

The opening section provides a sentence definition and explains other terms that refer to the same disease. The writer expands the definition by explaining the symptoms of the disease, the treatment plan, and possible complications of the disease. Throughout this expanded definition, the writer also uses informal definitions for various terms.

Discussion

1. Locate the informal definitions and discuss why the writer chose to provide them.

2. Discuss why the writer probably decided to organize this brochure around specific questions. Discuss the advantages and disadvantages of such an organization.

3. In groups, draft an expanded definition of one of the conditions that affect students—writer's block, oral presentation panic, or text anxiety. Assume you are writing the definition for a brochure to be distributed to incoming freshmen at orientation.

WHAT IS INSULIN-DEPENDENT DIABETES?

Insulin-dependent diabetes is a disease that affects the way your body uses food. Insulin-dependent diabetes is also called type I diabetes or insulin-dependent diabetes mellitus (IDDM, for short).

Type I diabetes starts when your body stops making insulin or makes only a tiny amount. Your body needs insulin to use food for energy. Without insulin, your body cannot control blood levels of sugar. And without insulin, you would die. So people with type I diabetes give themselves at least one shot of insulin every day.

Type I diabetes usually strikes children and young adults, but it can occur at any age. It used to be called juvenile-onset diabetes. More than 300,000 Americans have this type of diabetes. That is about 10 percent of all Americans diagnosed with diabetes.

WHY INSULIN SHOTS?

You must inject insulin under the skin—in the fat—for it to work. You cannot take insulin in a pill. The juices in your stomach would destroy the insulin before it could work. Scientists are looking for new ways to give insulin. But today, shots are the only method.

WHAT ARE THE SIGNS AND SYMPTOMS OF TYPE I DIABETES?

Type I diabetes often appears suddenly. Signs and symptoms are:

- high levels of sugar in the blood
- high levels of sugar in the urine
- frequent urination (and/or bed-wetting in children)
- extreme hunger
- extreme thirst
- extreme weight loss
- weakness and tiredness
- feeling edgy and having mood changes
- feeling sick to your stomach and vomiting

WHAT CAUSES TYPE I DIABETES?

We do not know exactly what causes diabetes. We do know that people inherit a tendency to get diabetes, but not all people who have this tendency will get the disease. Other things such as illnesses must also come into play for diabetes to begin.

Diabetes is not like a cold. Your friends and family cannot catch it from you.

WHAT DOES LIVING WITH DIABETES MEAN?

People with type I diabetes can live happy, healthy lives. The key is to follow your diabetes treatment plan. The goal of this plan is to keep your blood-sugar level as close to normal as possible (good blood-sugar control). Your treatment plan will probably include:

1. *Insulin,* which lowers blood sugar. Your health-care practitioner will pre-scribe how much and when to take insulin and what kinds.

2. *Food,* which raises blood sugar. Most people with type I diabetes have a meal plan. A registered dietitian makes a plan for you. It tells you how much food you can eat and when to eat it. Most people have three meals and at least two snacks every day. Your meal plan can have foods you enjoy.

3. *Exercise,* which lowers blood sugar. Like insulin, exercise also helps your body to use blood sugar. So exercise will probably be prescribed for you. Your health-care practitioner can help you fit exercise safely into your daily routine.

4. *Blood and urine testing.* Testing your blood lets you know if your blood-sugar level is high, low, or near normal. The tests are simple. You prick your finger to get a drop of blood. A nurse-educator can teach you how to do this test and use the test results.

You may need to test your urine for ketones. Ketones in the urine may mean that your diabetes is not under good control. A nurse-educator can teach you how to test ketones.

PROBLEMS YOU MAY HAVE

Type I diabetes can cause problems that you should be prepared for. There are three key problems:

- *Hypoglycemia,* or low blood sugar; sometimes called an insulin reaction. This occurs when your blood sugar drops too low. You correct this problem by eating some sugar—such as 3 glucose tablets, 6 ounces of regular soda, or 5 or 6 Lifesavers.™ Your health-care practitioner will teach you the signs of hypoglycemia and show you how to treat it.

- *Hyperglycemia,* or high blood sugar. This occurs when your blood sugar is too high. It can be a sign that diabetes is not well controlled. Your health-care practitioner will explain the signs and symptoms and the best way to treat hyperglycemia.

- *Ketoacidosis,* or diabetic coma. This is very serious. Discuss its signs with your health-care practitioner.

This expanded definition of solid and hazardous wastes is taken from a 667-page set of guidelines issued by the Department of Housing and Urban Development (September 1990). The guidelines cover dozens of topics, all connected to the identification and removal of lead-based paint as part of the department's public and Indian housing program. The readers include anyone involved with maintenance and renovation of public housing projects that may contain lead-based paint.

The definition begins with a reference to legislation regarding solid wastes. The writer first defines the term informally and then cites the official definition in the 1976 Resource Conservation and Recovery Act. A definition for hazardous wastes, a subcategory, follows. The writer uses a variety of expansion strategies and format devices in this appendix.

Discussion

1. Identify the strategies the writer uses to expand this definition of solid and hazardous wastes. How helpful is this definition to readers who must be able to recognize hazardous wastes?

2. Discuss how useful the format of this appendix would be to the readers.

3. Discuss changes you might make in content, organization, or format to increase the document's usefulness to readers.

4. In groups, draft an expanded definition of the computer term *hacking*. Include at least one example of the term to illustrate how a hacker operates. Identify a specific audience before you begin drafting.

Appendix 6: Waste Disposal: Solid and Hazardous Wastes

6.0   THE RESOURCE CONSERVATION AND RECOVERY ACT (RCRA)

The *Resource Conservation and Recovery Act* of 1976, what we commonly refer to as RCRA, is an amendment to the first piece of Federal solid waste legislation called the Solid Waste Disposal Act of 1965. RCRA was amended in 1980 and most recently on November 8,1984, by HSWA.

6.1   DEFINING SOLID AND HAZARDOUS WASTES

Solid wastes include such diverse wastes as household trash, sewage sludge, and discarded industrial materials. Solid wastes are not, however, necessarily solid.

They may be liquid, semisolid, or gaseous. The term "solid waste" is further defined in Section 1004(27) of RCRA as follows:

> The term "solid waste" means any garbage, refuse, sludge, from a waste treatment plant, water supply treatment plant, or air pollution control facility and other discarded material, including solid, liquid, semisolid, or contained gaseous material resulting from industrial, commercial, mining, and agricultural operations, and from community activities, but does not include solid or dissolved material in domestic sewage, or solid or dissolved materials in irrigation return flows or industrial discharges which are point sources subject to permits under Section 402 of the Federal Water Pollution Control Act, as amended (86 Stat. 880), or source, special nuclear, or byproduct material as defined by the Atomic Energy Act of 1954, as amended (68 Stat. 923).

Hazardous wastes are a sub-category of solid wastes. They can be solid, liquids, or gases. They may appear in a variety of forms:

- In barrels or drums.
- In pits, ponds, or lagoons.
- In sludges.
- As part of contaminated soil.
- In bottles or other fragile or nondurable containers.
- In aboveground or underground storage tanks.
- As part of building materials (e.g., asbestos).

In general, a waste is considered hazardous if it can endanger human health or damage the environment. Congress defined the term "hazardous waste" in Section 1004(5) of the Resource Conservation and Recovery Act (RCRA) of 1976 (42 U.S.C. S6901 *et seq.*) as follows:

> The term "hazardous waste" means a solid waste, or combination of solid wastes, which because of its quantity, concentration, or physical, chemical or infectious characteristics may:
>
> A) cause, or significantly contribute to an increase in mortality or an increase in serious irreversible, or incapacitating reversible, illness; or,
>
> B) pose a substantial present or potential hazard to human health or the environment when improperly treated, stored, transported, or disposed of, or otherwise managed.

In issuing regulations under RCRA, EPA has defined a hazardous waste to mean a solid waste that meets one of four conditions:

- It shows by observation or testing to have any of the four characteristics of hazardous waste (ignitable, reactive, corrosive, or toxic).
- It has been named and listed (see below) as a hazardous waste.
- It is a mixture containing a listed hazardous waste and a non-hazardous waste solid (unless the mixture is explicitly excluded).
- It is not excluded from regulation as a hazardous waste.

6.2   LISTING OF HAZARDOUS WASTES

The U.S. Environmental Protection Agency (EPA) has determined that certain wastes are hazardous. These wastes are incorporated into lists published by EPA. Wastes on these lists must always be handled as hazardous wastes regardless of their concentrations. The lists expand and change as new research and testing are performed; therefore, it is important to consult the lists periodically.

The lists are organized into three categories: 1) specific-source wastes (wastes from specific industries); 2) generic wastes (wastes from common manufacturing and industrial process, such as solvents); and 3) discarded commercial chemical products (such as creosote and some pesticides). The hazardous wastes associated with lead-based paint are generic wastes and discarded commercial chemical products.

Any mixture containing one or more listed hazardous wastes, or a mixture of solid waste and listed hazardous waste, is also considered a hazardous waste. This applies regardless of the percentage of the mixture that is listed as hazardous waste. There are several exemptions to this mixture rule.

If the solid waste is *not* included in the EPA list of hazardous wastes, or is *not* a mixture that contains one of these wastes, it may still be a hazardous waste if it exhibits the characteristic of **ignitability, corrosivity, reactivity,** or **toxicity.** EPA's definition of these characteristics is contained in 40 CFR, Sections 261.20 to 261.24. The standard measures specified by EPA to test for these properties are summarized in Table A-6.1.

The Resource Conservation and Recovery Act (RCRA) was passed in 1976 to address the problems posed by the improper disposal of municipal and industrial wastes. RCRA was amended in 1980 and again in 1984. The goals of RCRA are to protect human health and the environment, reduce waste and conserve energy and natural resources, and reduce or eliminate the generation of hazardous waste as expeditiously as possible. Two programs developed under RCRA affect disposal of wastes generated during lead-based paint abatement:

- *Subtitle D* governs the management of solid wastes, primarily nonhazardous wastes.
- *Subtitle C* controls hazardous waste from the time it is generated until its ultimate disposal.

1. The following formal sentence definitions are poorly written. Identify the writer's error and rewrite each into an effective formal sentence definition.

   a. A landslide is when a mass of earth and rock slips downward.

   b. A kidnapper is a person who detains another person.

   c. A veil is a piece of fabric used to veil the face.

   d. A window is an opening in a building that lets in light.

   e. A fingerprint is a means of identification.

   f. A caster is a small wheel.

   g. A camera is what a photographer uses to record images.

   h. A table is a piece of furniture with four legs and a flat surface.

   i. A scalpel is what a surgeon uses.

   j. A dune results when the wind piles up a ridge of sand.

2. In groups, write a formal sentence definition of all these sports terms. Share your completed definitions with the class.

free throw	back hand
bunt	drop kick
putt	dribble
drop shot	slam-dunk
fly ball	camel spin

3. In groups, write one formal sentence definition for each of the following terms. Compare your definitions with those written by other groups in class and discuss how many definitions are possible for each term.

driver	drum
scalp	tip
trap	shift
chest	tie
cup	bar

4. Write an expanded definition of one of the following terms. Identify a specific audience and purpose for your definition. List the specific expansion strategies you use at the end of your definition.

any video or audio equipment	tricycle
any sports equipment	theater
any hobby equipment	comic strip
any room in a campus building	cookies

any computer equipment	television game show
any public building	science fiction film
any automotive equipment	heavy metal music

5. Find a technical article about a subject in your field. Assume you are going to rewrite it for a general reader. Identify the terms you will have to define in such a revision. Then write formal sentence definitions for each term, *or,* if your instructor prefers, write an expanded definition of one term.

6. Read the articles "Ideology and Collaboration in the Classroom and in the Corporation" by Porter and "Ethical Reasoning in Technical Communication: A Practical Framework" by Wicclair and Farkas in Part 2. Write an expanded definition of what you regard as ethical writing practices, based on your reading.

7. Identify a problem on campus, such as "inadequate parking," "unsafe hallway lighting," or "inconvenient library hours." Write an expanded definition of the problem. Assume this definition is for the president of your school who is unaware of the problem.

8. Write a memo to your boss at your present job to request a new piece of equipment or new supplies. You know that your boss is reluctant to spend money on equipment right now, but you think this equipment is necessary. Include a formal sentence definition of the item you are requesting and an expanded definition using two of the expansion strategies discussed in this chapter. *Note:* Memo format is explained in Chapter 12.

9. Write a memo to the appropriate administrator on your campus to request a piece of equipment for use in one of your classes or for a campus activity. Assume that you are the chair of a student committee that has the task of making such requests on behalf of the student body. Include a formal sentence definition of the object you are requesting and an expanded definition using two or three of the expansion strategies discussed in this chapter. *Note:* Memo format is explained in Chapter 12.

CHAPTER 7

Description

UNDERSTANDING DESCRIPTION

Technical description provides readers with precise details about the physical features, appearance, or composition of a subject. A technical description may be a complete document in itself, such as an entry in an encyclopedia or a technical handbook. Manufacturing companies also need complete technical descriptions of each product model as an official record. Frequently, too, technical descriptions are separate sections in longer documents, such as these:

1. *Proposals and other reports.* Readers usually need descriptions of equipment and locations in a report before they can make decisions. A report discussing the environmental impact of a solid-waste landfill at a particular site, for example, would probably include a description of the location to help readers visualize the site and the potential changes.

2. *Sales literature.* Both dealers and consumers need descriptions of products—dealers so that they can advise customers and answer questions and consumers so that they can make purchase decisions. A consumer examining a new automobile in a showroom is likely to overlook certain features. A brochure containing a description of the automobile features ensures that the consumer will have enough information for decision making.

3. *Manuals.* Descriptions of equipment help operators understand the principles behind running a piece of machinery. Technicians need a record of every part of a machine and its function in order to effectively assess problems and make repairs. Consumer instruction manuals often include descriptions to help readers locate important parts of the product.

4. *Magazine articles and brochures for general readers.* Articles and brochures about science and technology often include descriptions of mechanisms, geologic sites, or natural phenomena to help readers understand the subject. An article for general readers about a new wing design on military aircraft may include a description of the wings and their position relative to the body of the aircraft to help readers visualize the design. A brochure written for visitors at a science institute describing the development of a solar heat collector may include several descriptions of the mechanism in development so that readers can understand how the design changed over time.

Plan and draft a technical description with the same attention to readers and their need for the information that you apply to other writing tasks.

PLANNING DESCRIPTIONS

In deciding whether to include descriptions in your document, consider your readers' knowledge of the subject and why they need your information. A student in an introductory botany class has little expert knowledge about the basic parts of a flower. Such a student needs a description of these parts to understand the variations in structure of different flowers and how seeds are formed. A research report to botanists about a new hybrid flower, however, would probably not include a description of these basic parts because botanists already know them well. The botanists, on the other hand, do need a description of the hybrid flower because they are not familiar with this new variety, and they need the description to understand the research results in the report. Both types of readers, then, need descriptions, but they differ in (1) the subjects they need described, (2) the kinds of information they need, (3) the appropriate language and detail, and (4) the appropriate graphic aids.

Subjects

As you analyze your readers' level of knowledge about a subject and their need for information, consider a variety of subjects that, if described in detail, might help your readers understand and use the information in your document. Here are some general subjects to consider as you decide what to describe for readers:

1. *Mechanism*—any machine or device with moving parts, such as a steam turbine, camera, automobile, or bicycle.

2. *Location*—any site or specific geologic area, such as the Braidwood Nuclear Power Plant, the Lake Michigan shoreline at Milwaukee, or the Moon surface.

3. *Organism*—any form or part of plant or animal life, such as an oak tree, a camel, bacteria, a kidney, or a hyacinth bulb.

4. *Substance*—any physical matter or material, such as cocaine, lard, gold, or milk.

5. *Object*—any implement without moving parts, such as a paper cup, a shoe, a photograph, or a floppy disk.

6. *Condition*—the physical state of a mechanism, location, organism, substance, or object at a specific time, such as a plane after an accident, a tumor before radiation, or a forest area after a fire.

Whenever your readers are not likely to know exactly what these subjects look like and need to know this in order to understand the information in your document, provide descriptions.

Kinds of Information

To be useful, a technical description must provide readers with a clear image of the subject. Include precise details about the following whenever such information will help your readers understand your subject better:

- Purpose or function

- Weight, shape, measurements, materials

- Major and minor parts, their locations, and how they are connected

- Texture, sound, odor, color

- Model numbers and names

- Operating cycle

- Special conditions for appropriate use, such as time, temperature, frequency

The writer of this excerpt from an architectural book about the development of greenhouses uses specific details about measurements, materials, and shapes to describe a particular building:

> The wooden tie beams in the Great Conservatory at Chatsworth represent a building innovation in the application of not only cast-iron but also wrought-iron semicircular ribs, in arches and in frameworks. In this building the creation of space and the various forms of iron rib were further developed structurally. This free-standing building, 124 feet wide and 68 feet high, was created by the construction of two glass vaults, built in the ridge-and-furrow system, with a basilicalike cross-section. Rows of cast-iron columns joined by cast-iron girders carried the semicircular wooden ribs of the Paxton gutters to form a high nave with a span of 70 feet. The glass vaults of the aisles, reaching down to the low masonry base, abutted from both sides onto the main iron frame at a height of 40 feet. The aisle had the same profile, but it had quadrant-shaped ribs. The ribs of the surrounding aisles also functioned as buttresses to support the lateral thrust of the main ribs of the nave.[1]

To determine the amount and kinds of details appropriate for a technical description, assess your reader's level of knowledge about the subject and purpose in reading. The reader of this description is probably familiar with architectural terms, such as trusses and vaults. The description focuses on the components of the building's supporting structure and provides measurements—all details relevant to readers who are interested in architecture. If the readers were horticulturists, a description of the interior design and arrangement of plants and flowers would probably be of more interest.

The following description of the effects of lead poisoning in children is from a report to Congress by the Department of Housing and Urban development.

The emphasis is on the typical physical condition of a child suffering from lead poisoning:

> Very severe childhood lead poisoning—involving such symptoms as kidney failure, gastrointestinal problems, comas, convulsions, seizures, and pronounced mental retardation—can occur at blood lead levels as low as 80 ug/dl. At or above 40 ug/dl, children may experience reduced hemoglobin (the oxygen-carrying substance in blood), the accumulation of a potential neurotoxicant known as ALA, and mild anemia. Near 30 ug/dl, studies have found slowed nerve conduction velocity. And between 10–15 and 25 ug/dl, researchers have documented slower reaction time, reductions in intelligence and short-term memory, other neurobehavioral deficits, and adverse effects on heme biosynthesis and vitamin D and calcium metabolism.[2]

In this description, the writer begins by naming potential diseases in general terms and then shifts to specific technical details about blood factors. Notice the informal definition included for the primary (nonexpert) readers.

This description of a location centers on the area around the site of a sunken Spanish galleon:

> The anchor has been found in 25 feet of water on the southern edge of an area known as the "Quicksands." The name didn't mean the area swallowed divers, but that the bottom was covered with a sand composed of loose shell fragments that are constantly shifted by the waves and tides. The result is a series of sinuous "dune" formations on the bottom. Tidal channels cross these dunes, running from northeast to southwest. Around the anchor, the sand is nearly 15 feet deep. Below it is a bed of limestone, the surface of which is rippled and pocked with small hollows and crevices. The sand piled on top of the limestone gradually thins out until it disappears about a quarter of a mile from the anchor. Southeast of the Quicksands, the water depth increases gradually to about 40 feet, and the sand covering the bedrock thins out to a veneer just two and a half inches thick. Small sponges and sea fans grow in this area, which we called the Coral Plateau. Continuing to the southeast, away from the anchor, the Coral Plateau slopes downward into the "Mud Deep." Here, the bedrock dips sharply, possibly following the channel of a river that may have flowed through the area when it was above sea level thousands of years ago. This channel is filled with muddy silt.[3]

In this description, the writer includes a few measurements, but he emphasizes the natural formations of sand and rock present in the area. Notice that the writer organizes spatially—the area around the anchor first and then progressively farther away, moving southeast.

Remember that descriptions may cover either (1) a particular mechanism, location, organism, substance, object, or condition, or (2) the general type. The description of the typical child with lead poisoning is a general one. Individual cases may differ, but most children with lead poisoning will fit this description in some way. The descriptions of the conservatory and the sea area, however, are specific to that building and that location. In the same manner, a product description of Model XX must be specific to that model alone and, therefore, different from a description of Model YY. Be sure to clarify for the reader whether you are describing a general type or a specific item.

Detail and Language

All readers of technical descriptions need accurate detail. However, some readers need more detail and can understand more highly technical language than others. Here is a brief description from a book about the solar system written for general readers interested in science:

> The Galaxy is flattened by its rotating motion into the shape of a disk, whose thickness is roughly one-fiftieth of its diameter. Most of the stars in the Galaxy are in this small disk, although some are located outside it. A relatively small, spherical cluster of stars, called the nucleus of the Galaxy, bulges out of the disk at the center. The entire structure resembles a double sombrero with the galactic nucleus as the crown and the disk as the brim. The Sun is located in the brim of the sombrero about three-fifths of the way out from the center to the edge. When we look into the sky in the direction of the disk we see so many stars that they are not visible as separate points of light, but blend together into a luminous band stretching across the sky. This band is called the Milky Way.[4]

In this description, the writer compares the galaxy to a sombrero, something most general readers are familiar with, and then locates the various parts of the galaxy on areas of the sombrero, thus creating an image that general readers will find easy to use. The writer also uses an informal tone, drawing readers into the description by saying, "When we look into the sky. . . ." This informal tone is appropriate for general readers but not for expert readers who need less assistance in visualizing the subject.

Here is a description of television station equipment that appeared in a magazine written for owners and technical staff of low-power television stations. The product description is used by technical staff in making decisions about future equipment purchases.

> Microdyne Corporation manufactures a complete line of fixed and motorized satellite receiving antennas, ranging in size from 1.2 meters to 7 meters and suitable for both C-band or Ku-band applications. The 3.66-meter (12-foot) antenna is specially designed for broadcast quality reception. It is a 10-piece parabolic antenna made from exceptionally strong space age fiber and polyester materials. It features a prime focus feed, superb side lobe characteristics, and high gains. The dish can view 100° of the geostationary arc and satellites within 69° west to 139° west. This feature means easy alignment with any line of sight satellite in the geostationary orbit. An optional motorized actuator is available.[5]

Clearly, the expected readers for this technical description have expert knowledge because the specialized terms, such as *geostationary arc,* are not defined, and the description stresses features of this antenna and how it will function at a television station, details that expert readers need to aid their decision making. Because this description is intended to encourage readers to purchase the equipment, the features are described in persuasive language—"specially designed," "exceptionally strong," "superb side lobe," "easy alignment." A nonexpert reader interested in learning about antennas would not find this description particularly useful. Such a reader would want an overall description of antennas in general and fewer details specific to one model. The reader would want to know, for example, what is the usual appearance of a satellite-receiving antenna? Where is it mounted? What are the major parts and their functions? What is the difference between a fixed and motorized antenna? Your readers' purpose must guide your decisions about how many details and which details to include.

Follow these guidelines for using appropriate language in technical descriptions:

1. Use specific rather than general terms. Notice these examples:

General terms	*Specific terms*
short	1 in. tall
curved	S-shaped
thin	$\frac{1}{8}$ in. thick
light	cream-colored
nearby	4 in. from the base
fast	400 rpm
large	7 ft high
light	1.5 oz
heavy	16 tons
noise	high-pitched shriek

2. Indicate a range in size if the description is of a general type that varies, or give an example.

    Poor: Bowling balls for adults usually weigh 12 lbs.

    Better: Bowling balls for adults vary in weight from 10 to 16 lbs.

3. Use precise language but not language too technical for your readers. Do not write "a combination of ferric hydroxide and ferric oxide" if "rust" will do.

4. If you must use highly technical terms or jargon and some of your readers are nonexperts, define those terms:

    The patient's lipoma (fatty tumor) had not grown since the previous examination.

5. Compare the subject to simple, well-known items and situations to help general readers visualize it:

The difference in size between the Sun and the Earth is similar to the difference between a baseball and a grape seed.

Be specific and accurate, but do not overwhelm your readers with details they cannot use. Consider carefully the language your readers need and the number of details they can use appropriately.

Graphic Aids

Graphic aids are an essential element in descriptions because readers must develop a mental picture of the subject and words alone may not be adequate to paint that picture successfully. Chapter 4 discusses graphic aids in detail along with format devices to highlight certain facts. These graphic aids are usually effective ways to illustrate details in descriptions:

1. *Photographs.*   Photographs supply a realistic view of the subject and its size, color, and structure, but they may not properly display all features or show locations clearly. Photographs are most useful for general readers who want to know the overall appearance of a subject. A guide to house plants for general readers should include photographs, for instance, so readers can differentiate among plants. A research article for botanists, however, would probably include line drawings showing stems, leaves, whorls, and other distinctive features of the plants being discussed.

2. *Line drawings.*   Line drawings provide an exterior view showing key features of mechanisms, organisms, objects, or locations and special conditions, as well as how these features are connected. Line drawings are useful when readers need to be familiar with each part or area.

3. *Cutaway and exploded drawings.*   Cutaway drawings illustrate interior views, including layers of materials that cannot be seen from photographs or line drawings of the exterior. Exploded drawings emphasize the separate parts of a subject, especially those which might be concealed if the object is in one piece. Often readers need both line drawings of the exterior and interior and exploded drawings to fully understand a subject.

4. *Maps, floor plans, and architects' renderings.*   Maps show geographic locations, and floor plans and architects' renderings show placement of objects within a specified area. Features that may be obscured in a photograph from any angle can be marked clearly on these illustrations,

giving readers a better sense of the composition of the area than any photograph could.

Use as many graphic aids as you believe your readers need to get a clear picture of your subject. Also, be sure to direct your readers' attention to the graphic aids by references in the text, and always use the same terms in the text and in your graphic aids for specific parts or areas.

WRITING DESCRIPTIONS

After identifying your expected readers and the kinds of information they need, consider how to organize your descriptions.

Organization

In some cases, company policy or institution requirements dictate the organization of a description.

An example of a predetermined description format appears in Model 7-6, a portion of a police report. Although police report formats may vary from city to city, most departments require a narrative section describing the incident that led to police intervention. The writer must follow the department's established format because readers—police, attorneys, judges, and social-service workers—handle hundreds of similar reports and rely on seeing all reports in the same format with similar information in the same place.

If you are not locked into a specific description format for the document you are writing, select an organizational pattern that will best serve your readers, usually one of these:

Spatial.   The spatial pattern is most often used for descriptions of mechanisms, objects, and locations because it is a logical way to explain how a subject looks. Remember that you must select a specific direction and follow it throughout the description, such as from base to shade for a lamp, from outside to inside for a television set, and from one end to the other for a football field. Writers often also explain the function of a subject and its main parts. This additional information is particularly important if readers are not likely to know the purpose of the subject or it will not be apparent from the description of parts or composition. Thus a description of a stomach pump may include an explanation of the function of each valve and tube so that readers can understand how the parts work together.

Chronological.   The chronological pattern describes features of a subject in the order they were produced or put together. This information may be central to a description of, for example, a Gothic church that took two centuries to build or an anthropological dig where layers of sediments containing primitive tools have been deposited over two million years.

In all cases, consider your readers' knowledge of the subject and the organization that will most help them use the information effectively. A general reader of a description of a Gothic church may want a chronological description that focuses on the historical changes in exterior and interior design. A structural engineer, however, may want a chronological description that focuses on changes in materials and construction techniques.

Sections of a Technical Description

Model 7-1 presents a typical outline for a technical description of an object or mechanism. As this outline illustrates, a technical description has three main sections: an introduction, a description of the parts, and a description of the cycle of operations.

  I. Introduction
    A. Definition of the object
    B. Purpose of the object
    C. Overall description of the object—size, color, weight, etc.
    D. List of main parts
  II. Description of Main Parts
    A. Main part 1
      1. Definition of main part 1
      2. Purpose of main part 1
      3. Details of main part 1—color, shape, measurements, etc.
      4. Connection to main part 2 or list of minor parts of main part 1
      5. Minor part 1 (if relevant)
        (a) Definition of minor part 1
        (b) Purpose of minor part 1
        (c) Details of minor part 1—color, shape, measurements, etc.
      6. Minor part 2 (if relevant)
        ⋮
    B. Main part 2
      ⋮
 III. Cycle of Operation
    A. How parts work together
    B. How object operates
    C. Limitations

MODEL 7-1   Model Outline of Technical Description

Introduction

The introduction to a technical description orients readers to the subject and gives them general information that will help them understand the details in the body of the description. Follow these guidelines:

1. Write a formal sentence definition of the complete mechanism or object to ensure that your readers understand the subject. If the item is a very common one, however, you may omit the formal definition unless company policy calls for it.

2. Clarify the purpose if it is not obvious from the definition. In some cases, how the object or mechanism functions may be most significant to your readers, so explain this in the introduction.

3. Describe the overall appearance so that readers have a sense of size, shape, and color. For general readers, include extra details that may be helpful, such as a comparison with an ordinary object. Also include, if possible, a graphic illustration of the object or mechanism.

4. List the main parts in the order you plan to describe them.

Description of Parts

The body of a technical description includes a formal definition and the physical details of each major and minor part presented in a specific organizational pattern, such as spatial or chronological. Include as many details as your readers need to understand what the parts look like and how they are connected. If your readers plan to construct the object or mechanism, they will need to know every bolt and clamp. General readers, on the other band, are usually interested only in major parts and important minor parts. Graphic illustrations of the individual parts or exploded drawings are helpful to readers in this section.

Cycle of Operation

Technical descriptions for in-house use or for expert readers seldom have conclusions. General readers, however, may need conclusions that explain how the parts work together and what a typical cycle of operation is like. If the description will be included in sales literature, the conclusion often stresses the special features or advantages of the product.

Sample Technical Descriptions

Model 7-2 shows one section in a 469-page reference manual written for clinical biology technicians who run tests on fluid samples, screening for medical

Reagent Probes Subsystem

This section describes the reagent probes subsystem and its components.

Figure 2 – 10. Reagent Probes Subsystem

Table 2 – 4. Reagent Probes Subsystem Components

Component Name	Description
Reagent probe syringes	Components that set the volume and speed of the fluid that each reagent probe aspirates and dispenses. There is one reagent probe syringe for each of the three reagent probes.
Reagent probes	Three components, connected to the reagent probe carriage, that aspirate reagents from the reagent tray and dispense them into a cuvette in the cuvette track.
Reagent probe carriage	Component that extends the reagent probes over the reagent tray, then retracts the reagent probes when they are not in use.
Reagent probe cover	Clear cover that fits around the three reagent probes.
Probe cover sensors	Sensing devices that detect if the reagent probe cover is installed. The system will not operate unless the probe cover is installed.
Reagent probe wash stations	Small wells where the outside and inside of the reagent probes are washed with deionized water. Each reagent probe has its own wash station.
Heating bath	A long chamber located on the upper left side of the system that contains oil for heating the reagents. The assay reagents aspirated by the reagent probes travel through insulated tubing to the heating bath, which warms them to 37°C. The reagent probes then dispense the warmed reagents into a cuvette. The heating bath is a closed system; you do not need to change or replenish the oil that heats the reagents.

conditions and for therapeutic drug monitoring. This description focuses on one of the seven subsystems in a complex automated testing device that includes the testing mechanism and computer software and hardware with which the technician runs the test and reviews data. The description here covers the specific parts of the subsystem, and the line drawing that accompanies the description shows only the subsystem, not the entire testing device. The text is in columns, the specific part listed on the left and the corresponding description on the right. Not all the components listed are included in the drawing. In the full system, the reagent probe syringes and the heating bath are located above the reagent probe cover. The probe cover sensors are part of the computer program to alert the technicians. However, because the components function as part of the reagent probe subsystem, they are included in this section. In each component description, the focus is on the purpose of the part and how it fits into the subsystem. Notice that the last description for the heating bath includes instructions to the technicians who will be reading this manual.

Model 7-3 is a technical description of a specific model of a toaster written by a student as a section of a consumer manual that includes a description, operating instructions, and maintenance guidelines. Because this description is of a particular model, the writer describes the parts and their locations in detail. The organization is spatial, moving from the lowest part, the base, to the cord, which enters the housing above the base, and then to the housing. Because the housing is so large, the writer partitions it, describing the outer casing first, the heating wells second, and then the control levers. The writer ends with a brief description of the operating cycle. Notice that this description contains (1) formal sentence definitions of the toaster and each main part, (2) headings to direct readers to specific topics, and (3) specific measurements for each part.

Model 7-4 is a technical description of the planet Mercury based on data obtained from the Mariner 10 spacecraft on its first approach to the planet. The writer begins by explaining the purpose and necessity of the Mariner 10 flight. The organization is topical according to the source of the data. First, the writer describes the details of surface appearance revealed by the photographs radioed back to Earth and then reports the details about atmosphere, temperature, and surface composition recorded by instruments aboard the Mariner 10. The conclusion focuses on other Mariner 10 passes near the planet and emphasizes that information is still incomplete. Notice that measurements are given in both metric and English units for the convenience of the nonexpert reader.

I. Introduction

The Kitchen King toaster, Model 49D, is an electric appliance that browns bread between electric coils inside a metal body. The toaster also heats and browns frozen and packaged foods designed especially to fit in the vertical heating wells of a toaster. The Kitchen King Model 49D is $6\frac{3}{4}$ in. high, $4\frac{1}{2}$ in. wide, $8\frac{3}{4}$ in. long, and weighs 2 lbs. There are three main parts: the base, the cord, and the housing.

II. Main Parts

The Base

The base is a flat stainless steel plate, $4\frac{1}{2}$ in. wide and $8\frac{3}{4}$ in. long. It supports the housing of the toaster and is nailed to it at all four corners. The base rests on four round, black, plastic feet, each $\frac{1}{2}$ in. high and $\frac{3}{4}$ in. in diameter. The feet are attached to the base $\frac{1}{2}$ in. inside the four corners. The front and back of the base ($2\frac{1}{2}$ in. wide) are edged in black plastic strips that protrude $\frac{3}{4}$ in. past the base. A removable stainless steel plate, $3\frac{1}{2}$ in. wide and $5\frac{1}{4}$ in. long, called the crumb tray, is centered in the base. One of the shorter sides of the crumb tray is hinged. The opposite side has a catch that allows the hinged plate to swing open for removal of trapped crumbs.

The Cord

The cord is an insulated cable that conducts electric current to the heating mechanism inside the body of the toaster. It is 32 in. long and $\frac{1}{8}$ in. in diameter. Attached to the base of the toaster at the back, it enters the housing through an opening just large enough for the cable. At the other end of the cord is a two-terminal plug, measuring 1 in. long, $\frac{3}{4}$ in. wide, and $\frac{1}{2}$ in. thick. The two prongs are $\frac{1}{2}$ in. apart and are each $\frac{5}{8}$ in. long, $\frac{1}{4}$ in. wide, and $\frac{1}{16}$ in. thick. The plug must be attached to an electrical outlet before the toaster is operable.

Housing

The housing is a stainless steel boxlike cover that contains the electric heating mechanism and in which the toasting process takes

MODEL 7-3   Technical Description: Kitchen King Toaster, Model 49D

place. The housing is $8\frac{3}{4}$ in. long, $6\frac{1}{4}$ in. high, and $4\frac{1}{2}$ in. wide. The front and back are edged at the top with black plastic strips that protrude past the housing $\frac{3}{4}$ in. The housing also contains two heating wells and two control levers.

Heating Wells.   The heating wells are vertical compartments, $5\frac{1}{2}$ in. long, $1\frac{1}{4}$ in. wide, $5\frac{3}{4}$ in. deep. The wells are lined with electric coils that brown the bread or toaster food when the mechanism is activated. Inside each heating well is a platform on which the toast rests and which moves up and down the vertical length of the well.

Control Levers.   The control levers are square pieces of black plastic attached to springs that regulate the heating and the degree of browning. The levers are $6\frac{1}{2}$ in. square and are on the front of the toaster.

Heat Control Lever.   The heat control lever is centered 1 in. from the top of the housing and is attached to the platforms inside both heating wells. When the lever is pushed down, it moves along a vertical slot to the base of the toaster, lowering the platforms inside the heating wells. This movement also triggers the heating coils.

Browning Lever.   The browning lever is located in the lower right corner on the front of the toaster. The browning lever moves horizontally along a 2-in. slot. The slot is marked with three positions: dark, medium, and light. This lever controls the length of time the heating mechanism is in operation and, therefore, the degree of brownness that will result.

III. Conclusion

The user must insert the cord into a 120-volt ac electrical outlet to begin the operating cycle. Next, the user inserts one or two pieces of bread or toaster food into the heating wells, moves the browning lever to the desired setting, and lowers the heat control lever until it catches and activates the heating mechanism. The toaster will turn off automatically when the heating cycle is complete, and the platforms in the heating wells will automatically raise the bread or toasted food so the user can remove it easily.

MODEL 7-3   *continued*

MERCURY

Obtaining the first close-up views of Mercury was the primary objective of the Mariner 10 spacecraft, launched on November 3, 1973, from Kennedy Space Center in Florida. After a journey of nearly five months, including a flyby of Venus, the spacecraft passed within 703 kilometers (437 miles) of the solar system's innermost planet on March 29, 1974.

Until Mariner 10, little was known about Mercury. Even the best telescopic views from Earth showed Mercury as an indistinct object lacking any surface detail. The planet is so close to the Sun that it is usually lost in solar glare. When the planet is visible on Earth's horizon just after sunset or before dawn, it is obscured by the haze and dust in our atmosphere. Only radar telescopes gave any hint of Mercury's surface conditions prior to the voyage of Mariner 10.

The photographs Mariner 10 radioed back to Earth revealed an ancient, heavily cratered surface, closely resembling our own Moon. The pictures also showed huge cliffs crisscrossing the planet. These apparently were created when Mercury's interior cooled and shrank, buckling the planet's crust. The cliffs are as high as 3 kilometers (2 miles) and as long as 500 kilometers (310 miles).

Instruments on Mariner 10 discovered that Mercury has a weak magnetic field and a trace of atmosphere—a trillionth the density of Earth's atmosphere and composed chiefly of argon, neon, and helium. When the planet's orbit takes it closest to the Sun, surface temperatures range from 467 degrees Celsius (872 degrees Fahrenheit) on Mercury's sunlit side to –183 degrees Celsius (–298 degrees Fahrenheit) on the dark side. This range in surface temperature—650 degrees Celsius (1,170 degrees Fahrenheit)—is the largest for a single body in the solar system. Mercury literally bakes and freezes at the same time.

Days and nights are long on Mercury. The combination of a slow rotation relative to the stars (59 Earth days) and a rapid revolution around the Sun (88 Earth days) means that one Mercury solar day takes 176 Earth days or two Mercury years—the time it takes the innermost planet to complete two orbits around the Sun!

Mercury appears to have a crust of light silicate rock like that of Earth. Scientists believe Mercury has a heavy iron-rich core making up slightly less than half of its volume. That would make Mercury's core larger, proportionally, than the Moon's core or those of any of the planets.

After the initial Mercury encounter, Mariner 10 made two additional flybys—on September 21, 1974, and March 16, 1975—before control gas used to orient the spacecraft was exhausted and the mission was concluded. Each flyby took place at the same local Mercury time when the identical half of the planet was illuminated; as a result, we still have not seen one-half of the planet's surface.

MODEL 7-4   Technical Description of the Planet Mercury

CHAPTER SUMMARY

This chapter discusses writing technical descriptions. Remember:

- Descriptions provide readers with precise details about the physical features, appearance, or composition of a subject.

- In planning a description, writers consider what subjects readers need described, the kinds of information readers need, appropriate detail and language, and helpful graphic aids.

- Subjects for descriptions may include mechanisms, locations, organisms, substances, objects, and conditions.

- Descriptions should include precise details about purpose, measurements, parts, textures, model numbers, operation cycles, and special conditions when appropriate for readers.

- The amount of detail and degree of technical language in a description depends on the readers' purpose and their technical knowledge.

- Graphic aids are essential in descriptions to help readers develop a mental picture of the subject.

- Most descriptions are organized spatially or chronologically.

- Descriptions generally have three main sections: an introduction, a description of each major and minor part, and a description of the cycle of operation.

SUPPLEMENTAL READINGS IN PART 2

Benson, P. J. "Writing Visually: Design Considerations in Technical Publications," *Technical Communication*, p. 451.

"Six Graphics Guidelines," *Simply Stated*, p. 562.

White, J. V. "Color: The Newest Tool for Technical Communicators," *Technical Communication*, p. 576.

ENDNOTES

1. From G. Kohlmaier and B. von Sartory, *Houses of Glass, A Nineteenth-Century Building Type* (Cambridge, MA: The MIT Press, 1991), pp. 87–88.

2. From U.S. Department of Housing and Urban Development, *Comprehensive and Workable Plan for the Abatement of Lead-Based Paint in Privately Owned Housing* (Washington, DC: U.S. Government Printing Office, December 7, 1990), pp. 2–3.

3. From R. D. Mathewson, III, *Treasure of the Atocha* (New York: E. P. Dutton, 1986), p. 67.

4. From R. Jastrow, *Red Giants and White Dwarfs* (New York: W. W. Norton, 1979), p. 27.

5. From *The LPTV Report* 4 (October 1989), p. 42.

These pages are from a 52-page product description manual written by a professional technical writer at Diebold, Inc. The manual describes the structure and function of a specific series of automatic teller machines (ATMS) and includes line drawings of the entire machines and of specific parts of the machines. This detailed description serves as a record of the product features and as a guide to bank administrators who are interested in installing the ATMS. This manual took nearly nine months to complete, as the writer drafted and redrafted in response to reviews by engineers, technicians, and managers.

Discussion

1. Discuss how the organization and format elements help the reader understand the information easily.

2. Review the description and discuss whether the language is strictly objective or contains some sales appeal. Cite specific places in the text to support your opinion.

3. Compare this model with Model 4–21. Both documents are intended for potential customers. Discuss the differences in format and amount of detail provided. In what ways is each model appropriate for its readers?

2.2 CONSUMER INTERFACE PANEL

The Consumer Interface Panel guides the consumer through transactions and allows the consumer to request transactions and enter data. Also, the Consumer Interface Panel can perform important consumer education and advertising functions.

CONSUMER DISPLAY

OPERATION KEYS

CONSUMER KEYPAD

E-5153-1

Figure 2-2 Consumer Interface Panel Components (Secure Interior ATM)

Consumer Display

Besides welcoming consumers and showing the instructions that permit transaction processing, the Consumer Display performs two important functions: it can attract new consumers to the ATM, and it can communicate with the user through pictures, words, or both. Pictorial icons or programmable non-English character sets allow the terminal to communicate with people of any nationality.

Two Consumer Displays are available: monochrome and color

Monochrome Monitor

The enhanced brightness, monochrome Consumer Display adjusts for surrounding lighting conditions. This enhances readability (even in direct sunlight), reduces the chance of CRT burn-in, and prolongs the CRT's operational life. This monitor is standard on the *is* terminals.

Color Monitor (ATP only)

The nine-inch (22.9 cm), high-resolution color monitor supports graphics in 16 colors). The color monitor has a resolution of 640 × 240 pixels (horizontal × vertical). The color monitor can show a series of still color images in rapid succession to give the impression of screen animation (see Appendix B).

Both monitors are capable of displaying 20 lines of 40 characters. Additionally, they can show the same 32 × 16 right-justified grid used by the TABS 9000 terminals, a 32 × 16 left-justified grid, or a 32 × 16 center-justified grid.

The Consumer Display has the following additional capabilities:

- Backspacing
- Blinking characters
- Inverse video (40 × 20 grid only)
- Delayed character display
- Graphics

Both Consumer Displays can show the 5 × 9, dot matrix standard and alternate character sets in Appendix A.

Privacy Screen

An optional Privacy Screen attaches to the Consumer Display. Louvers embedded in the Privacy Screen create a Venetian blind effect, so that only a consumer positioned directly in front of the Consumer Display can read the screen.

Consumer Keypad

The Consumer Keypad allows the consumer to enter data into the terminal. On all terminals except the Drive-up and the Island, the Consumer Keypad is recessed for consumer privacy.

Two Consumer Keypads are available; an 11-key keypad and a 16-key keypad. The 11-key keypad has ten numeric keys (0 through 9) and a CANCEL key. The 16-key keypad has ten numeric keys (0 through 9), a CANCEL key, and five additional operational keys. Each keypad provides audible and tactile response to each keystroke and, in the U.S., is equipped with braille key caps.

Operation Keys

To initiate transactions, the consumer evaluates the choices shown on the Consumer Display and presses the appropriate operation key.

Each *i* Series terminal, except the CCD and CTT, is equipped with eight operation keys. These operation keys are installed on both sides of the Consumer Display.

2.3 DISPLAY GRAPHICS

The *i* Series terminals support two kinds of software-driven graphics options for the Consumer Display.

- The Enhanced Monochrome Graphics (EMG) allows fonts and icons to be shown on a monochrome monitor.

- The Color Graphics Feature (CGF) allows 16-color, high-resolution graphics to be shown on a color monitor.

Enhanced Monochrome Graphics (EMG)

The EMG feature allows you to use the prepackaged fonts, icons, and character sets; or you can create your own.

The standard EMG PROM stores the prepackaged library of default fonts and icons (Appendix B) on STP-equipped terminals. On ATP-equipped terminals, these default fonts and icons are stored on disk. You can use these fonts and icons without changing them, or you can customize them for your purposes.

In addition, you can create monochrome graphics on a personal computer using the Diebold Design Utility (DDU). After creating the graphics, you install them at the controller or host for down-line loading to the *i* Series terminal.

Color Graphics Feature (CGF)

Using a PC graphics package, you can create color icons. Or instead of creating new graphics, you can use a hand scanner to electronically scan existing graphics.

The output of the file you create or scan must be in the industry-standard PCX format. Next, you run the Diebold Design Utility (DDU) on a personal computer to convert the PCX file to a format compatible with the *i* Series terminal. The resulting DDU files are stored on the hard drive on an ATP.

The Color Graphics Feature (CGF) offers the same default library of fonts and icons as EMG (Appendix B). However, unlike the EMG where the graphic library is stored on PROM, the default CGF graphics library is stored on disk. For more details on the Color Graphics Feature, refer to the *Color Graphics Feature Programming Manual,* TP-799344-000A and the *MDS Enhanced Graphics Product Description,* TP-799345-000A.

2.4 CONSUMER PRINTERS

All *i* Series terminals provide the consumer with a printed verification of transactions. Two types of Consumer Printers are available:

- A 35-column Consumer Printer
- An 80-column Consumer Printer

35-column Consumer Printer

InterBold's 35-column, dot matrix Consumer Printer is recommended for most general printing applications. This printer incorporates the latest printer technology such as an automated self-loading feature. Operators can change ink ribbon cartridges without removing the paper.

The printer uses 2.75-inch paper (either blank, rolled stock or rolled stock with pre-printed top-of-form marks). A ten-inch supply roll (1,900 linear feet) yields 7,600 three-inch forms or 3,800 six-inch forms.

Control characters in the network-supplied printer text activate special features like selectable horizontal and vertical pitch and graphics printing. At the standard horizontal pitch of 12 characters per inch (CPI), the Consumer Printer prints 25 columns. You can also select a 16 CPI horizontal pitch and print 35 columns. The printer has the following features:

- Bi-directional
- Print rate: 4.3 lines per second
- Character sets: Standard and alternate (Appendix A)
- Form length: 3 to 6 inches
- Horizontal pitch: 10, 12, or 16 CPI
- Vertical pitch: 6 to 8 lines per inch
- Double-width printing
- Double-density printing
- Graphics printing

Figure 2-3 35-column Consumer Printer

This portion of a police accident report is the required narrative after routine identifications, license numbers, date, and times have been recorded. The readers of police reports include district attorneys, defense lawyers, police, social workers, judges, insurance investigators, and anyone who may have a legal involvement in the case. For consistency, the sections in all such reports are always in the same order.

Each section provides specific details about locations, conditions, and physical damage. The officer includes estimates of distances and notes the paths of the vehicles so that skid marks can be checked later for vehicle speed and direction. In addition, the officer identifies the ambulance service, hospital, and paramedics and lists other police reports that relate to the same case. This information will help readers who need to see all the documents in the case or who may need to interview medical personnel about injuries.

Discussion

1. Discuss the kinds of information included in each section of this report. How would this information help the district attorney prosecuting the case?

2. Assume that an accident has occurred at an intersection you know well. Write a description of the intersection that would be appropriate for the "Description of Scene" section of this type of police report.

3. In groups, assume that an accident has taken place in the classroom you are in. Your group members are witnesses and must write a description of the classroom for the insurance investigator. Compare your description with the ones written by other groups.

SUPPLEMENTAL COLLISION NARRATIVE	Date of Incident: 1/7/96
Location: Newbury Blvd. and Downer Ave. Shorewood, WI	Citation: MM36-T40
Subject: Coronal Primary Collision Report 96-07-42	Officer ID: 455
	Time: 19:25

Description of Scene: Newbury Boulevard is an east-west roadway of asphalt construction with two lanes of traffic in either direction and divided by a grassy median 10 ft wide. All lanes are 14 ft wide. A curb approximately 6 in. high is on the periphery of the East 2 and West 2 lanes. This is a residential street with no business district. Downer Avenue is a north-south roadway of asphalt construction with two lanes of traffic in either direction separated by a broken yellow line. All lanes are 12 ft wide. A curb approximately 6 in. high is on the periphery of the North 2 and South 2 lanes. At the intersection with Newbury Boulevard, Downer Avenue is a residential street. A business district exists four blocks south. The speed on both streets is posted at 30 mph. The roadways are unobstructed at the intersection. Both roadways are straight at this point, and the intersection is perpendicular. At the time of the accident, weather was clear, temperature about 12°F, and the pavements were dry, without ice. Ice was present along the curb lanes extending about 4 in. from the curbs into the East 2, West 2 lanes of Newbury Boulevard.

Description of Vehicle: The Chevrolet Nova was found at rest in a westerly direction on Newbury Boulevard. The midrear of the vehicle was jammed into the street light pole at the curb of lane West 2 of Newbury Boulevard. Pole number is S-456-03. The vehicle was upright, all four wheels inflated, brakes functional, speedometer on zero, and bucket front seats pressed forward against the dashboard. The front of the vehicle showed heavy damage from rollover. The grillwork was pushed back into the radiator, which, in turn, was pushed into the fan and block. The driver's door was open, but the passenger door was wedged closed. The vehicle rear wheels were on the curb, the front wheels in lane West 2 of Newbury. The windshield was shattered, but still within the frame. Oil and radiator coolant were evident on the roadway from the curb to approximately 6 ft into lane West 2 of Newbury, directly in front of the vehicle.

<u>Driver:</u> Driver Coronal was standing on the curb upon my arrival. After detecting the distant odor of alcohol on his breath and clothes and noting his red, watery eyes and general unsteadiness, I administered a field sobriety test, which Coronal failed. (See Arrest Report 96-07-16.)

<u>Passenger:</u>   Passenger Throckmorton was in the passenger seat of the vehicle, pinned between the bucket seat and the dashboard. He was in obvious pain and complained of numbness in his right leg. Passenger was removed from the vehicle and stabilized at the scene by paramedics from Station 104 and transported to Columbia Hospital by Lakeside Ambulance Service.

<u>Physical Evidence:</u> A skid mark approximately 432 ft long began at the center line of Downer Avenue and traveled westerly in an arc into lane West 2 of Newbury Boulevard, ending at the vehicle position on the curb. Gouge marks began in the grassy devil's strip between the curb and the sidewalk. The gouge marks ended at the light pole under the rear wheels of the vehicle. A radio antenna was located 29 ft from the curb, lying on the grassy median of Newbury Boulevard. The antenna fits the antenna base stub on the Chevrolet Nova.

Other reports: Arrest 96-07-16
                 Blood Alcohol Test 96-07-28
                 Coefficient of Friction Test 96-O7-16
                 Hospital Report on Throckmorton

1. In groups, assume you are on a student committee that is preparing a detailed request for funding to renovate campus buildings. The request will be submitted to the Pratt Foundation, headed by Mr. Bradley Pratt, who graduated from your school in 1958 with high honors as both an outstanding athlete and an outstanding scholar. Your group has been told to select a building and prepare the description to be included in the request. Before you begin, discuss what factors besides the physical details of the building might be important in your description in this situation.

2. The following description of a desk-top tape dispenser was written by a student in response to Exercise 3. The student identified the reader as a consumer and the purpose as a section in a product catalog available at a large office supply store. In groups, discuss this description and evaluate its appropriateness for the reader and purpose. Consider how well it follows the guidelines in this chapter. Then rewrite the description (using a desk-top tape dispenser as a model) for the same reader and purpose. *Or,* if your instructor prefers, write a description of a small object available in the classroom, such as a pencil, chalkboard eraser, pencil sharpener, ballpoint pen. Identify a reader and purpose before you begin.

TAPE DISPENSER

A desk-top tape dispenser is a piece of office equipment that allows the user to roll out and cut off a piece of cellophane adhesive tape. The major parts of the dispenser are the base and the reel. The base rests on the work surface and holds the reel and the cutting edge. The base is a contoured piece of black plastic with a nonskid $\frac{1}{16}$-in. thick foam pad on the bottom. Dimensions of the oval-shaped bottom of the base are $7\frac{1}{2}$ in. long and $2\frac{3}{4}$ in. wide at its widest point. The base slopes up to a height of $3\frac{1}{4}$ in. at its highest point at the end opposite the cutting edge. The cutting edge side is $2\frac{3}{4}$ in. high.

The base has a well in which the reel rests. The well is $3\frac{3}{16}$ in. long at the top and runs lengthwise in the base. The well is 1 in. wide and $1\frac{3}{4}$ in. long at the deepest point. Each side of the well has an L-shaped recess which is $\frac{3}{8}$ in. high and $\frac{1}{4}$ in. wide. The recess holds the reel of tape. The cutting edge is serrated, 1 in. long, and $\frac{1}{4}$ in. wide.

The reel is black plastic with a diameter of 1 in. The reel has an axle which projects $\frac{5}{16}$ in. on each side and rests in the well. The roll of tape fits tightly over the reel.

To use the desk-top tape dispenser, the user mounts a roll of tape and pulls the edge off the tape across the cutting edge, cutting off a selected length of tape.

3. Write a description of one of the following. Assume your description will be included in a consumer booklet the company is planning to produce for customers who are interested in details about the products they buy.

    a. any piece of sports equipment

    b. any piece of gardening equipment

    c. any piece of computer equipment

    d. any piece of audio or video equipment

    e. any piece of personal grooming equipment

    f. any piece of office equipment

Include a graphic aid to help the reader understand your description.

4. Assume that you are the consulting architect for the local historical society. The director, Felicia Southworth, has asked you to prepare a memo report recommending a building in the community as the society's next restoration project. You will need to include a description of the exterior of this building in your report. (The description of interiors will be handled by Gregory Chang, interior design specialist, if the society decides to pursue your recommendation.) For this assignment, select a building with some historical value—a building on campus, an old theater, an old Victorian-style or frontier-style home, a railroad station, or a civic building—and then write a description of its exterior that could be included in your report to the historical society. *Or,* if your instructor prefers and you have already covered short report style (explained in Chapter 10), write the complete memo report to Southworth. For a memo report, include the historical background of the building itself or of the era it represents so that Southworth can readily understand why this building should be preserved.

5. Assume that you have just taken out a special insurance policy on your room against destruction of the contents and the interior. The insurance company has asked you to prepare a full description of the room and its contents to keep on file as a record of what was insured in case of loss and claim for damages. Write such a description.

6. In groups, write a description of a movable classroom desk chair with attached writing surface. Identify your specific audience and purpose before you write. Begin the description with a formal sentence definition. Compare your group's draft with the drafts of other groups. Discuss how the descriptions differ and how each draft is appropriate for the specific reader and purpose.

7. Locate a description of a specialized topic in your field or of one of the following topics in an encyclopedia or handbook directed to readers with some knowledge of the topic and the terminology used in that field. Rewrite the description for a nonexpert reader who is interested in learning about the subject but who does not know much about its function or use.

    a. Specific structural form, e.g., escalator

    b. Specific flower or plant, e.g., Tetratheca

   c. Human body part, e.g., skin

   d. Specific wild animal, e.g., eland

   e. Specific geologic site, e.g., Olduvai Gorge, Tanzania

Attach a copy of the original description to your revision, and submit both to your instructor.

CHAPTER 8

Instructions, Procedures, and Process Explanations

UNDERSTANDING INSTRUCTIONS, PROCEDURES, AND PROCESS EXPLANATIONS

This chapter discusses three related but distinct strategies for explaining the stages or steps in a specific course of action. Instructions, procedures, and process explanations all inform readers about the correct sequence of steps in an action or how to handle certain materials, but readers and purpose differ.

Instructions

Instructions provide a set of steps that readers can follow to perform a specific action, such as operate a fork lift or build a sundeck. Readers of instructions are concerned with performing each step themselves to complete the action successfully.

Procedures

Procedures in business and industry provide guidelines for three possible situations: (1) steps in a system to be followed by one employee, (2) steps in a system to be followed by several employees, and (3) standards and rules for handling specific equipment or work systems. Readers of procedures include (1) those who must perform the actions, (2) those who supervise employees performing the actions, and (3) people, such as upper management, legal staff, and government inspectors, who need to understand the procedures in order to make decisions and perform their own jobs.

Process Explanations

Process explanations describe the stages of an action or system either in general (how photosynthesis occurs) or in a specific situation (how an experiment was conducted). Readers of a process explanation do not intend to perform the action themselves, but they need to understand it for a variety of reasons.

In some situations, these three methods of presenting information about systems may overlap, but in order to adequately serve your readers, consider each strategy separately when writing a document. Because so many people rely on instructions and procedures and companies may be liable legally for injuries or damage that results from unclear documents, directions of any sort are among the most important a company produces.

Graphic Aids

Instructions, procedures, and process explanations all benefit greatly from graphic aids illustrating significant aspects of the subject or those aspects that readers find difficult to visualize. Readers need such graphic aids as (1) line drawings showing where parts are located, (2) exploded drawings showing how parts fit together, (3) flowcharts illustrating the stages of a process, and (4) drawings or photographs showing how actions should be performed or how a finished product should look.

Do not, however, rely on graphic aids alone to guide readers. Companies have been liable for damages because instructions or procedures did not contain enough written text to adequately guide readers through the steps. Visual perceptions vary, and all readers may not view a drawing or diagram the same way. Written text, therefore, must cover every step and every necessary detail.

WRITING INSTRUCTIONS

To write effective instructions, consider (1) your readers and their knowledge of the subject, (2) an organizational pattern that helps readers perform the action, and (3) appropriate details and language. In addition to the initial instructions, readers may need troubleshooting instructions that tell them what to do if, after performing the action, the mechanism fails to work properly or the expected results do not appear.

Readers

As you do before writing anything, consider who your readers will be. People read instructions in one of three ways. Some, but only a few, read instructions all the way through before beginning to follow any of the steps. Others read and perform each step without looking ahead to the next. And still others begin a task without reading any instructions and turn to them only when difficulties arise. Since you have no way to control this third group, assume that you are writing for readers who will read and perform each step without looking ahead. Therefore, all instructions must be in strict chronological order.

Everyone is a reader of instructions at some point, whether on the job or in private. Generally, readers fall into one of two categories:

1. *People on the job who use instructions to perform a work-related task.* Employees have various specialties and levels of technical knowledge, but all employees use instructions at some time to guide them in doing a job. Design your instructions for on-the-job tasks for the specific groups that will use them. Research chemists in the laboratory, crane operators, maintenance workers, and clerks all need instructions that match their needs and capabilities.

2. *Consumers.* Consumers frequently use instructions when they (a) install a new product in their homes, such as a VCR or a light fixture, (b) put

an object together, such as a toy or a piece of furniture, and (c) perform an activity, such as cook a meal or refinish a table.

Consumers, unlike employees assigned to a particular task, represent a diverse audience in capabilities and situations.

Varied Capabilities.   A consumer audience usually includes people of different ages, education, knowledge, and skills. Readers of a pamphlet about how to operate a new gasoline lawn mower may be 12 years old or 80, may have elementary education only or postgraduate degrees, may be skilled amateur gardeners, or may have no experience with a lawn mower. When writing for such a large audience, aim your instructions at the level of those with the least education and experience, because they need your help most. Include what may seem like overly obvious directions, such as, "Make sure you plug in the television set," or obvious warnings, such as, "Do not put your fingers in the turning blades."

Varied Situations.   Consider the circumstances under which consumers are likely to use your instructions. A person building a bookcase in the basement is probably relaxed, has time to study the steps, and may appreciate additional information about options and variations. In contrast, someone in a coffee shop trying to follow the instructions on the wall for the Heimlich maneuver to rescue a choking victim is probably nervous and has time only for a quick glance at the instructions.

In all cases, assume that your readers do not know how to perform the action in question and that they need guidance for every step in the sequence.

Organization

Readers have come to expect consistency in all instructions they use—strict chronological order and numbered steps. Model 8-1 presents a typical outline for a set of instructions for either consumers or employees. As the outline illustrates, instructions generally have a descriptive title and three main sections.

Title

Use a specific title that accurately names the action covered in the instructions.

Poor:	Snow Removal
Better:	Using Your Acme Snow Blower
Poor:	Good Practices
Better:	Welding on Pipelines

I. Introduction
   A. Purpose of instructions
   B. Audience
   C. List of parts
   D. List of materials/tools/conditions needed
   E. Overview of the chronological steps
   F. Description of the mechanism or object, if needed
   G. Definitions of terms, if needed
   H. Warnings, cautions, notes, if needed
II. Sequential Steps
   A. Step 1
      1. Purpose
      2. Warning or caution, if needed
      3. Instruction in imperative mood
      4. Note on condition or result
   B. Step 2
      ⋮
III. Conclusion
   A. Expected result
   B. When or how to use

MODEL 8-1   Model Outline for Instructions

Introduction

Depending on how much information your readers need to get started, your introduction may be as brief as a sentence or as long as a page or more. If appropriate for your readers, include these elements:

Purpose and Audience.   Explain the purpose of the instructions unless it is obvious. The purpose of a coffee maker, for instance, is evident from the name of the product. In other cases, a statement of purpose and audience might be helpful to readers:

> This manual provides instructions for mechanics who install Birkins finewire spark plugs.

> These instructions are for nurses who must inject dye into a vein through a balloon-tipped catheter.

> This safe practices booklet is for employees who operate cranes, riggers, and hookers.

Lists of Parts, Materials, Tools, and Conditions.   If readers need to gather items in order to follow the instructions, put lists of those items in the introduction. *Parts* are the components needed, for example, to assemble and finish a table, such as legs, screws, and frame. *Materials* are the items needed to perform the task, such as sandpaper, shellac, and glue. *Tools* are the implements needed, such as a screwdriver, pliers, and a small paintbrush. Do not combine these items into one list unless the items are simple and the list is very short. If the lists are long, you may place them after the introduction for emphasis. *Conditions* are special circumstances that are important for completing the task successfully, such as using a dry, well-ventilated room. Be specific in listing items, such as

- One $\frac{3}{4}$-in. videotape
- One Phillips screwdriver
- Three pieces of fine sandpaper
- Five 9-volt batteries
- Maintain a 70°F to 80°F temperature

Overview of Steps.   If the instructions are complicated and involve many steps, summarize them for the reader:

> The following sections cover installation, operation, start-up and adjustment, maintenance, and overhaul of the Trendometer DR-33 motors.

Description of the Mechanism.   A complete operating manual often includes a technical description of the equipment so that readers can locate specific parts and understand their function. Chapter 7 explains how to prepare technical descriptions.

Definitions.   If you use any terms your readers may not understand, define them. Chapter 6 explains how to prepare formal and informal definitions.

Warnings, Cautions, and Notes.   Readers must be alerted to potential danger or damage before they begin following instructions. If the potential danger or damage pertains to the whole set of instructions, place these in the introduction. When only one particular step is involved, place the warning or caution *before* the step.

Both *Danger* and *Warning* refer to potential injury of a person. *Danger* means that a serious injury or death *will definitely* occur if a hazard is not avoided:

> DANGER: The compressed gas will EXPLODE if the valve is unsealed. DO NOT open the valve.

A *Warning* means that a serious injury or death *may* occur if a hazard is not avoided:

WARNING: To prevent electrical shock, do not use this unit in water.

Caution refers to possible damage to equipment:

CAUTION: Failure to latch servicing tray completely may damage the printer.

Notes give readers extra information about choices or conditions:

Note: A 12-in. cord is included with your automatic slicer. An extension cord may be used if it is 120 volt, 10 amp.

In addition to these written alerts, use an appropriate symbol or graphic aid to give the reader a clear understanding of the hazard or condition. Use capital letters or boldface type to highlight key words.

Sequential Steps

Explain the steps in the exact sequence readers must perform them, and number each step. Explain only one step per number. If two steps must be performed simultaneously, explain the proper sequence:

While pushing the button, release the lever slowly.

Include the reason for a particular action if you believe readers need it for more efficient use of the instructions:

Tighten the belt. *Note:* A taut belt will prevent a shift in balance.

Use headings to separate the steps into categories. Identify the primary stages, if appropriate:

- Separating
- Mixing
- Applying

Identify the primary areas, if appropriate:

- Top drawer
- Side panel
- Third level

Refer readers to other steps when necessary:

> If the valve sticks, go to Step 12.

Then tell readers whether to go on from Step 12 or go back to a previous step:

> When the valve is clear, go back to Step 6.

For regular maintenance instructions, indicate the suggested frequency of performing certain steps:

Once a month:	• Check tire pressure
	• Check lights
	• Check hoses
Once a year:	• Inspect brakes
	• Change fuel filter
	• Clean choke

Conclusion

If you include a conclusion, tell readers what to expect after following the instructions and suggest other uses and options if appropriate:

> Your food will be hot, but not as brown as if heated in the oven rather than in the microwave. A few minutes of standing time will complete the cooking cycle and distribute the heat uniformly.

Model 8-2 shows a typical set of consumer instructions for changing a typewriter ribbon. These instructions have a descriptive title that names the action readers want to do. The step-by-step instructions are numbered and include references to line drawings that show readers how to insert the new ribbon. Notice that Step 1 has an extra note telling readers what will happen after performing this step. Without this note, readers might think that the typewriter had broken and be afraid to continue with the instructions. Steps 1 and 6 might seem rather elementary, but for widely used products, you must always assume that consumers do not know anything about the proper action. Therefore, include every necessary step.

Details and Language

Whether you are writing for consumers or for highly trained technicians, follow these guidelines:

1. Keep parallel structure in lists. Be sure that each item in a list is in the same grammatical form.

Changing the Ribbon Cassette

1. Raise the typewriter cover.
   • When this cover is raised, the typewriter is deactivated.
2. Remove the ribbon cassette by lifting it upward (Figure A).
3. Before inserting the new cassette, tighten the ribbon by turning the drive gear in the direction of the arrow (Figure B).
   Important: Be careful not to crease the ribbon while rolling it into the cassette.
4. While inserting the cassette, hold it tilted toward the keyboard, inserting the two guides on the ribbon cassette into the mounting slots (Figure C).
5. Press the cassette down (Figure D).
6. Close the cover.

MODEL 8-2   Instructions for Changing a Typewriter Ribbon
Source: Reprinted by permission from Actionwriter 1 Typewriter Operator Guide, copyright © 1985 by International Business Machines Corporation.

Nonparallel: This warranty does not cover:
a. Brakes
b. Battery
c. Using too much oil

This list is not parallel because the first two items are names of things (nouns) and the last item is an action (verbal phrase). Rewrite so that all items fit the same pattern.

Parallel: This warranty does not cover:
a. Brakes
b. Battery
c. Excess oil consumption

In this revision, all items are things—brakes, battery, and consumption. Lists also can confuse readers if the listed items do not all fit the same category. Here is an example:

Poor: Parts Included for Assembly:
End frames
Caster inserts
Casters
Screwdriver
Sleeve screws
Detachable side handles

The screwdriver is not a part included in the assembly package, but the consumer might think it is and waste time looking for it. List the screwdriver in a different category, such as "Tools Needed."

2. Maintain the same terminology for each part throughout the instructions, and be sure the part is labeled similarly in illustrations. Do not refer to "Control Button," "Program Button," and "On/Off Button" when you mean the same control.

3. Use headings to help readers find specific information. Identify sections of the instructions with descriptive headings:

Assembly Kit Contents
Materials Needed
Preparation
Removing the Cover
Checking the Fuel Filter

4. Use the imperative mood for sequential steps. Readers understand instruction steps better when each is a command:

Adjust the lever.
Turn the handle.
Clean the seal.

5. Never use passive voice in instructions. The passive voice does not make clear who is to perform the action in the step.

Poor: The shellac should be applied.

Better: Apply the shellac.

6. State specific details. Use precise language in all sections.

Poor: Turn the lever to the right.

Better: Turn the lever clockwise one full revolution.

Poor: Keep the mixture relatively cool.

Better: Keep the mixture at 50°F or less.

Poor: Place the pan near the tube.

Better: Place the pan 1 in. from the bottom of the tube.

Poor: Attach the wire to the terminal.

Better: Attach the green wire to the AUDIO OUT terminal.

7. Write complete sentences. Long sentences in instructions can be confusing, but do not write fragments or clip out articles and write "telegrams."

Poor: Repairs excluded.

Better: The warranty does not cover repairs to the electronic engine controls.

Poor: Adjust time filter PS.

Better: Adjust the time filter to the PS position.

8. Do not use *should* and *would* to mean *must* and *is*.

Poor: The gauge should be on empty.

Better: The gauge must be on empty.

Poor: The seal would be unbroken.

Better: The seal is unbroken.

Both *should* and *would* are less direct than *must* and *is* and may be interpreted as representing possible conditions rather than absolute situations. A reader may interpret the first sentence as saying, "The gauge should be on empty, although it might not be." Always state facts definitely.

Troubleshooting Instructions

Troubleshooting instructions tell readers what to do if the mechanism fails to work properly or results do not match expectations. Model 8-3 shows a typical three-part table for troubleshooting instructions. These troubleshooting instructions (1) describe the problem, (2) suggest a cause, and (3) offer a solution. Readers find the problem in the left column and then read across to the suggested solution. Troubleshooting instructions are most helpful when simple adjustments can solve problems.

Problem	Possible Cause	Solution
Snow in picture	Antenna Interference	Check antenna connection Turn off dishwasher, microwave, nearby appliances
Fuzzy picture	Focus pilot	Adjust Sharpness Control clockwise
Multiple images	Antenna Lead-in wire	Check antenna connection Check wire condition
Too much color	Color saturation	Adjust Color Control counterclockwise
Too little color	Color saturation	Adjust Color Control clockwise
Too much one color	Tint level	Adjust Tint Control clockwise

MODEL 8-3   Troubleshooting Guide for a Television Set

WRITING PROCEDURES

Procedures often appear similar to instructions, and people sometimes assume that the terms mean the same thing. However, the term *procedures* most often and most accurately refers to official company guidelines covering three situations: (1) a system with sequential steps that must be completed by one employee, (2) a system with sequential steps that involves several employees interacting and supporting each other, and (3) the standards and methods for handling equipment or events with or without sequential steps.

Because these documents contain the rules and appropriate methods for the proper completion of tasks, they have multiple readers, including (1) employees who perform the procedures, (2) supervisors who must understand the system and oversee employees working within it, (3) company lawyers concerned about liability protection through the use of appropriate warnings, cautions, and guidelines, (4) government inspectors from such agencies as the Occupational Safety and Health Administration who check procedures to see if they comply with government standards, and (5) company management who must be aware of and understand all company policies and guidelines. Although the primary readers of procedures are those who follow them, remember that other readers inside and outside the company also use them as part of their work.

Procedures for One Employee

Procedures for a task that one employee will complete are similar to basic instructions. These procedures are organized, like instructions, in numbered steps following the general outline in Model 8-1. Include the same items in the introduction: purpose, lists of parts and materials, warnings and cautions, and any information that will help readers perform the task more efficiently. Most company procedures include a description of the principles behind the system, such as a company policy or government regulation, research results, or technologic advances. When procedures involve equipment, they often include a technical description in the introduction.

Procedures for one employee also share some basic style elements with instructions:

- Descriptive title
- Precise details
- Complete sentences
- Parallel structure in lists
- Consistent terms for parts
- Headings to guide readers

The steps in the procedure are always in chronological order. Steps may be written as commands, in passive voice, or in indicative mood:

To prevent movement of highway trucks and trailers while loading or unloading, set brakes and block wheels. (*Command*)

The brakes should be set and the wheels should be blocked to prevent movement of highway trucks and trailers during loading and unloading. (*Passive voice*)

To prevent movement of highway trucks and trailers while loading or unloading, the driver sets brakes and blocks wheels. (*Indicative mood*)

The indicative mood can become monotonous quickly if each step begins with the same words, such as "The driver places, . . ." or "The driver then sets. . . ." Commands and passive voice are less repetitious. Do not use the past tense for procedures because readers may interpret this to mean that the procedures are no longer in effect.

Procedures for Several Employees

When procedures involve several employees performing separate but related steps in a sequential system, the *playscript organization* is most effective. This organization is similar to a television script that shows the dialogue in the order the actors speak it. Playscript procedures show the steps in the system and indicate which employee performs each step. The usual pattern is to place the job title on the left and the action on the same line on the right:

Operator:	1. Open flow switch to full setting.
	2. Set remote switch to temperature sensor.
Inspector:	3. Check for water flow to both chiller and boiler.
Operator:	4. Change flow switch to half setting.
	5. Tighten mounting bolt.
Inspector:	6. Check for water flow to both boiler and chiller.
Operator:	7. Shut off chiller flow.
Inspector:	8. Test boiler flow for volume per second.
	9. Complete test records.
Operator:	10. Return flow switch to appropriate setting.

Generally, the steps are numbered sequentially no matter how many employees are involved. One employee may perform several steps in a row before another employee participates in the sequence. The playscript organization ensures that all employees understand how they fit into the system and how they support other employees also participating in the system. Use job titles to identify employee roles because individuals may come and go, but the tasks remain linked to specific jobs.

Include the same information in the introduction to playscript procedures as you do in step-by-step procedures for a single employee, such as warnings, lists of materials, overview of the procedure, and the principles behind the system. The steps in playscript organization usually are commands, although the indicative mood and passive voice are sometimes used.

Procedures for Handling Equipment and Systems

Procedures for handling equipment and systems include guidelines for (1) repairs, (2) installations, (3) maintenance, (4) assembly, (5) safety practices, and (6) systems for conducting business, such as processing a bank loan or fingerprinting suspected criminals. These procedures include lists of tools, definitions, warnings and cautions, statements of purpose, and the basic principles. They differ from other procedures in an important way: The steps are not always sequential. Often the individual steps may be performed in any order, and they are usually grouped by topic rather than by sequence.

Model 8-4 shows a typical organization for company procedures about safe practices on a construction site. The introduction establishes the purpose

---

PROCEDURES FOR SAFE EXCAVATIONS

This safety bulletin specifies correct procedures for all excavation operations. In addition, all Clinton Engineering standards for materials and methods should be strictly observed. Failure to do so could result in injury to workers and to passersby.

PERSONAL PROTECTION:

- Wear safety hard hat at all times.
- Keep away from overhead digging equipment.
- Keep ladders in trenches at all times.

EXCAVATION PROTECTION:

- Protect all sites by substantial board railing or fence at least 48 in. high or standard horse-style barriers.
- Place warning lights at night.

EXCAVATED MATERIALS:

- Do not place excavated materials within 2 ft of a trench or excavation.
- Use toe boards if excavated materials could fall back into a trench.

DIGGING EQUIPMENT:

- Use mats or heavy planking to support digging equipment on soft ground.
- If a shovel or crane is placed on the excavation bank, install shoring and bracing to prevent a cave-in.

MODEL 8-4   A Typical Company Procedures Bulletin Outlining Safe Practices on a Construction Site

of the procedures and warns readers about possible injury if these and other company guidelines are not followed. The individual items are grouped under topic headings. Notice that the items are not numbered because they are not meant to be sequential. In this sample, the items are written as commands, but like other procedures, they may be in the passive voice or indicative mood as well.

WRITING PROCESS EXPLANATIONS

A *process explanation* is a description of how a series of actions leads to a specific result. Process explanations differ from instructions and procedures in that they are not intended to guide readers in performing actions but only in understanding them. As a result, a process explanation is written as a narrative, without listed steps or commands, describing four possible types of actions:

- Actions that occur in nature, such as how diamonds form, how the liver functions, or how a typhoon develops.

- Actions that produce a product, such as how steel, light bulbs, or baseballs are made.

- Actions that make up a particular task, such as how gold is mined, how blood is tested for cholesterol levels, or how a highway is paved.

- Actions in the past, such as how the Romans built their aqueducts or how the Grand Canyon was formed.

Readers

A process explanation may be a separate document, such as a science pamphlet, or a section in a manual or report. Although readers of process explanations do not intend to perform the steps themselves, they do need the information for specific purposes, and one process explanation will not serve all readers.

A general reader reading an explanation in a newspaper of how police officers test drivers for intoxication wants to know the main stages of the process and how a police officer determines if a driver is indeed intoxicated. A student in a criminology class needs more details in order to understand each major and minor stage of the process and to pass a test about those details. An official from the National Highway Traffic Safety Administration may read the narrative to see how closely it matches the agency's official guidelines, while a judge may want to be sure that a driver's rights are not violated by the process. Process explanations for these readers must serve their specific needs as well as describe the sequential stages of the process. Model 8-5 shows how process explanations of sobriety testing may differ for general readers and for students. Notice that the version for students includes more details about what constitutes imbalance and

For a general reader:

THE WALK-AND-TURN TEST

The police officer begins the test by asking the suspect to place the left foot on a straight line and the right foot in front of it. The suspect then takes nine heel-to-toe steps down the line, turns around, and takes nine heel-to-toe steps back. The suspect is given one point each for eight possible behaviors showing imbalance, such as stepping off the line and losing balance while turning. A score of two or more indicates the suspect is probably legally intoxicated.

For a student reader:

The Walk-and-Turn Test

The test is administered on a level, dry surface. People who are over 60 years old, more than 50 pounds overweight, or have physical impairments that interfere with walking are not given this test.

The police officer begins the test by asking the suspect to place the left foot on a straight line and the right foot in front of it. The suspect must maintain balance while listening to the officer's directions for the test and must not begin until the officer so indicates. The suspect then takes nine heel-to-toe steps down the line, keeping hands at the sides, eyes on the feet, and counting aloud. After nine steps, the suspect turns and takes nine heel-to-toe steps back in the same manner. The officer scores one point for each of the following behaviors: failing to keep balance while listening to directions, starting before told to, stopping to regain balance, not touching heel to toe, stepping off the line, using arms to balance, losing balance while turning, and taking more or less than nine steps each way. If the suspect falls or cannot perform the test at all, the officer scores nine points. A suspect who receives two or more points is probably legally intoxicated.

MODEL 8-5   Two Process Explanations of Sobriety Testing

more explanation about the conditions under which the test should or should not be given.

For all process explanations, analyze the intended reader's technical knowledge of the subject and why the reader needs to know about the process. Then decide the number of details, which details, and the appropriate technical terms to include in your narrative.

Organization

Model 8-6 presents a model outline for a process explanation. As the outline illustrates, process explanations have three main sections: an introduction, the stages in the process, and a conclusion.

I. Introduction
   A. Definition
   B. Theory behind process
   C. Purpose
   D. Historical background, if appropriate
   E. Equipment, materials, special natural conditions
   F. Major stages
II. Stages in the Process
   A. Major stage 1
      1. Definition
      2. Purpose
      3. Special materials or conditions
      4. Description of major stage 1
      5. Minor stage 1
         a. Definition
         b. Purpose
         c. Special materials or conditions
         d. Description of minor stage 1
      6. Minor stage 2
            ⋮
   B. Major stage 2
         ⋮
III. Conclusion
   A. Summary of major stages and results
   B. Significance of process

Model 8-6   Model Outline for a Process Explanation

Introduction

The introduction should include enough details about the process so that readers understand the principles underlying it and the conditions under which it takes place. Depending on your readers' technical expertise and how they intend to use the process explanation, include these elements:

- *Definition.*   If the subject is highly technical or readers are not likely to recognize it, provide a formal definition.

- *Theory behind the process.*   Explain the scientific principles behind the process, particularly if you are describing a research process.

- *Purpose.*   Explain the purpose unless it is obvious from the title or the readers already know it.

- *Historical background.*   Readers may need to know the history of a process and how it has changed in order to understand its current form.

- *Equipment, materials, and tools.*   Explain what types of equipment, materials, and tools are essential for proper completion of the process.

- *Major stages.*   Name the major stages of the process so that readers know what to expect.

Stages of the Process

Explain the stages of the process in the exact sequence in which they normally occur. In some cases, one sentence may adequately explain a stage. In other cases, each stage may actually be a separate process that contributes to the whole. In describing each stage, (1) define it, (2) explain how it fits the overall process, (3) note any dangers or special conditions, (4) describe exactly how it occurs, including who or what does the action, and (5) state the results at the end of that particular stage. If a major stage is made up of several minor actions, explain each of these and how they contribute to the major stage. Include the reasons for the actions in each stage:

> The valve is closed before takeoff because. . . .
> The technician uses stainless steel implements because. . . .

Conclusion

The conclusion of a process explanation should explain the expected results, what they mean, and how this process influences or interacts with others, if it does.

Model 8-7 on the facing page briefly describes the process of takeoff, flight, and landing of a NASA shuttle mission. Notice that this process explanation does not refer to a specific mission, so when the writer describes such details as landing speed, a range of miles per hour is included.

Details and Language

Process explanations, like instructions, can include these elements:

- Descriptive title
- Precise details
- Complete sentences
- Consistent terms for actions or parts
- Headings in long narratives to guide readers
- Simple comparisons for general readers

TYPICAL SHUTTLE MISSION

The rotation of the Earth has a significant bearing on the payload capabilities of the Space Shuttle. A due east launch from the Kennedy Space Center in Florida uses the earth's rotation as a launch assist, since the ground is turning to the east at that point at a speed of 915 miles (1,473 kilometers) per hour.

Spacecraft and other items of payload arrive at the Kennedy Space Center and are assembled and checked out in special buildings before being loaded into the orbiter. Each Shuttle arrives as a set of component parts. The solid rocket booster propellant segments are received and checked out in a special facility, then taken to the Vehicle Assembly Building (VAB) and stacked on a mobile launcher platform to form two complete rockets. The external tank is received and prepared for flight in the VAB, then mated to the solid rockets. An orbiter is checked out in the Orbiter Processing Facility, then moved to the VAB and attached to the external tank. A giant crawler-transporter picks up the mobile launcher platform and the assembled Shuttle and takes them to the pad. The Shuttle remains on the platform until liftoff.

The orbiter's main engines ignite first and build to full power before the huge solid rockets ignite and liftoff occurs. The solid rockets burn out after about two minutes, are separated from the tank, and parachute into the ocean about 160 miles (258 kilometers) from the launch site. Two special recovery ships pull the parachutes out of the water and tow the rocket casings to land, where they are refurbished and sent back to the manufacturer to be refilled with propellant.

The orbiter continues on into space—a total of over eight minutes of burn-time on the three main engines—and then separates from the external tank. The latter breaks up as it reenters the atmosphere over an uninhabited area of the Indian Ocean.

On most missions the orbiter enters an elliptical orbit, then coasts around the Earth to the opposite side. The OMS engines then fire long enough to stabilize and circularize the orbit. On some missions the OMS engines are also fired soon after the tank separates, to place the orbiter at a desired altitude for the second burn that circularizes the orbit. Later OMS burns can raise or adjust this orbit, if required by the needs of the mission. A typical Shuttle flight lasts from two to ten days, but modifications now being performed will enable some orbiters to stay in space for experiments lasting several weeks.

After deploying the payload spacecraft, operating the onboard scientific instruments, taking observations, etc., the orbiter re-enters the atmosphere and lands, normally at either the Kennedy Space Center or Edwards AFB in California. Unlike prior manned spacecraft, which followed a ballistic trajectory, the orbiter has a crossrange capability (can move to the right or left off the straight line of its entry path) of about 1,270 miles (2,045 kilometers). The landing speed is from about 212 to 226 miles (341 to 364 kilometers) per hour. The orbiter is immediately "safed" by a ground crew with special equipment, the first step in the process which will result in another launch of this particular orbiter.

MODEL 8-7   Process Explanation

In addition, remember these style guidelines:

- Do not use commands. Because readers do not intend to perform the actions, commands are not appropriate.

- Use either passive voice or the indicative mood. Passive voice is usually preferred for process explanations that involve the same person performing each action in order to eliminate the monotony of repeating "The technician" over and over. However, natural processes or processes involving several people are easier to read if they are in the indicative mood (see Model 8-5).

- If you are writing a narrative about a process you were involved in, such as an incident report or a research report, use of the first person is appropriate:

  I arrested the suspect. . . .

  I called for medical attention. . . .

  I spliced both genes. . . .

- Use transition words and phrases to indicate shifts in time, location, or situation in individual stages of the process:

Shifts in time:	then, next, first, second, before
Shifts in location:	above, below, adjacent, top
Shifts in situation:	however, because, in spite of, as a result, therefore

CHAPTER SUMMARY

This chapter discusses writing effective instructions, procedures, and process explanations. Remember:

- Instructions, procedures, and process explanations are related but distinct strategies for explaining the steps in a specific action.

- Instructions provide the steps in an action for readers who intend to perform it, either for a work-related task or for a private-interest task.

- Instructions typically have an introduction that includes purpose; lists of parts, materials, tools, and conditions; overview of the steps; description of a mechanism (if appropriate); and warnings, cautions, and notes.

- The steps in instructions should be in the exact sequence in which a reader will perform them.

- The conclusion in instructions, if included, explains the expected results.

- Instructions should be in the imperative mood and include precise details.

- Troubleshooting instructions explain what to do if problems arise after readers have performed all the steps in an action.

- Procedures are company guidelines for (1) a system with sequential steps that must be completed by one employee, (2) a system with sequential steps that involves several employees, and (3) handling equipment or events with or without sequential steps.

- Procedures for a task that one employee will perform are similar to instructions with numbered steps.

- Procedures for several employees are best written in playscript organization.

- Procedures for handling equipment and systems are often organized topically rather than sequentially because the steps do not have to be performed in a specific order.

- Process explanations describe how a series of actions leads to a specific result.

- The stages of the process are explained in sequence in process explanations, but because readers do not intend to perform the process, the steps are not written as commands.

SUPPLEMENTAL READINGS IN PART 2

Marra, J. L. "For Writers: Understanding the Art of Layout," *Technical Communication*, p. 525.

Plunka, G. A. "The Editor's Nightmare: Formatting Lists within the Text," *Technical Communication*, p. 536.

White, J. V. "Color: The Newest Tool for Technical Communicators," *Technical Communication*, p. 576.

MODEL 8-8 Commentary

These instructions are part of a Ciba Corning reference manual that includes operating instructions for technicians running a computer-operated testing system. The instructions shown here cover filling water bottles and emptying waste bottles—essential procedures. The technical writer who prepared these instructions uses the internationally recognized caution symbol—an exclamation point inside a triangle. The biohazard symbol tells the reader to read an appendix containing precautions for working with biohazardous materials.

Notice that the first step in the instructions is a major one, followed by the six steps necessary to perform the major step. Also notice that the writer directs the reader to other sections in the manual in steps two and five.

Discussion

1. Identify the design elements in these instructions. Discuss how effectively the format serves the reader who must follow the instructions.

2. In groups, write a process explanation for "Preparing the ACS Bottles." Assume your reader is a supervisor who has never performed the process but needs to understand it before attending a meeting with the clinical biology technicians who perform the process daily.

3. Write instructions for cleaning a piece of equipment in your field *or* for cleaning and adjusting a piece of classroom equipment, such as an overly full pencil sharpener or an out-of-focus overhead projector. Identify a specific reader before you begin.

Preparing the ACS Bottles

Use this procedure to fill the ACS water bottle and empty the ACS waste bottle, if required.

If the Extended Operation Module (EOM) is connected to the ACS:180, complete this procedure when you prepare the EOM bottles at the start of each day or shift. Ensure that the EOM is inactive when you prepare the ACS bottles by pressing the EOM button and checking to see that the LED next to the EOM is off. Press the EOM button to activate the EOM when you complete the procedure.

 BIOHAZARD: Refer to Appendix B, *Protecting Yourself from Biohazards,* for recommended precautions when working with biohazardous materials.

 CAUTION: Do not perform this procedure while the system is assaying samples. The system stops the run and the tests in process are not completed.

NOTE: For optimum assay and system performance, fill the ACS water bottle with fresh deionized water at the start of each day or shift.

1. Remove the ACS water bottle and the ACS waste bottle.

   a. Lift the lid above the water bottle until the tubing clears the mouth of the bottle.

   b. Grasp the handle of the water bottle and lift the bottle up and out, and set it aside.

   c. Lift the waste bottle lid until the tubing clears the mouth of the waste bottle.

   d. If the EOM is connected to the ACS:180, disconnect the ACS waste bottle from the waste tubing by pressing the metal latch on the tubing fitting.

   e. Grasp the handle of the waste bottle and lift the bottle up and out.

   f. Gently lower the lid.

2. Empty the contents of the waste bottle into a container or drain approved for biohazardous waste.

   If required, clean the waste bottle as described in Section 2, *Cleaning the ACS Water and the Waste Bottles,* in your *ACS:180 Maintenance and Troubleshooting Manual.*

3. Fill the water bottle with fresh deionized water.

(Continued)

Preparing the ACS Bottles

4. Install the bottles on the system, as shown in Figure 6 – 2.

   a. Lift the waste bottle lid and return the waste bottle to its location.

   b. If the EOM is connected to the ACS:180, connect the waste tubing to the waste bottle by pressing the tubing into the fitting on the bottle, if required.

   c. Lower the waste bottle lid.

   d. Install the water bottle, insert the tubing into the bottle, and lower the water bottle lid.

5. Proceed to Replenishing Supplies, Page 6 – 13.

Figure 6 – 2. Installing the ACS Water and Waste Bottles

MODEL 8-8   *continued*

This sample from a long troubleshooting guide identifies the computer system error messages that appear on the monitor when the system detects a problem. The messages are listed in alphabetical order in the left-hand column. The instructions for solving the problem appear in the right-hand column. Notice that for some problems the reader is directed to other sections of the manual. If the technician cannot clear up the system error, the last step of the instructions directs him or her to the company's Technical Assistance Center.

Discussion

1. Identify the format elements used here and discuss how helpful they are in guiding the reader through the steps.

2. In groups, select a piece of sports equipment or a household appliance and write a set of troubleshooting instructions to guide someone who has never used the object.

System Error Messages

Message (Alphabetic Order)	Probable Cause and Solution
Dark read data return error: error code **	1. At the Schedule Tests/Review Contents screen, delete the worklist. 2. At the Main Menu, press **F6 Diagnostics and Maintenance.** 3. Press **F4 System Performance Tests.** 4. Press **F5 PMT Test,** then press **START.** 5. Refer to Section 3, *Using the SPTs to Troubleshoot the ACS:180,* Page 3 – 21, to review the test results and take the appropriate action. 6. If the error message appears again, call the Ciba Corning Technical Assistance Center.
Dark read error: error code **	1. At the Schedule Tests/Review Contents screen, delete the worklist. 2. At the Main Menu, press **F6 Diagnostics and Maintenance.** 3. Press **F4 System Performance Tests.** 4. Press **F5 PMT Test,** then press **START.** 5. After the PMT test is finished, schedule and perform the Backgrnd

(Continued)

System Error Messages

Message (Alphabetic Order)	Probable Cause and Solution
	profile as described in Section 3, *Verifying System Performance.*
	6. Refer to Section 3, *Using the SPTs to Troubleshoot the ACS:180,* Page 3 – 21, to review the test results and take the appropriate action.
	7. If error message appears again, call the Ciba Corning Technical Assistance Center.
Diskette was removed during operation.	Removing the diskette while the system is reading or writing to the diskette causes the operation to stop and may also damage the diskette. Format the diskette again before using it.
	⚠ **CAUTION:** Formatting erases all current files on the diskette.
	1. At the System Management/Result Database Operations/Archive Results screen, press **F4 Format Diskette.**
	2. Insert a diskette in the diskette drive and press **Y.**
	3. If it is a high-density diskette, press **Y**; if not, press **N.**
Due to excessive errors, cuvettes cannot be dispensed.	This message may indicate a jam in the cuvette loading bin.
	1. At the Main Menu, press **F6 Diagnostics and Maintenance.**
	2. Press **F1 Manual Operations.**
	3. Press **F1 Home System.**
	4. If needed, home the system again.
	5. If needed, clear cuvette jams and track problems at the cuvette loading bin and the cuvette preheater, as described in *Clearing the Cuvette Track,* Page 4–33.
	6. If the problem persists, call the Ciba Corning Technical Assistance Center.
Due to excessive errors, reagent probe 1, 2, or 3 has been taken off-line.	1. At the Main Menu, press **F6 Diagnostics and Maintenance.**
	2. Press **F1 Manual Operations.**
	3. Press **F1 Home System.**
	4. If needed, home the system again.
	5. Press **STATUS.**
	6. Review the errors for reagent probe 1, 2, or 3 at the System Status/Probe Status: Reagent Probe screen, and take the appropriate action.
	7. If the problem persists, call the Ciba Corning Technical Assistance Center.

(Continued)

System Error Messages

Message (Alphabetic Order)	Probable Cause and Solution
Due to excessive errors, the reagent transport has been taken off-line	1. At the Main Menu, press **F6 Diagnostics and Maintenance.** 2. Press **F1 Manual Operations.** 3. Press **F1 Home System.** 4. If needed, home the system again. 5. Press **STATUS.** 6. Review the errors for the reagent transport at the System Status/Sample and Reagent Transport Status screen, and take the appropriate action. 7. If the problem persists, call the Ciba Corning Technical Assistance Center.

** indicates an error code displayed with message

Model 8–10 Commentary

These procedures were written by a student in response to Exercise 6 in this chapter. The student uses the playscript organization to present the system for handling the company tuition-refund program.

Headings call the readers' attention to the sequence of actions. Each step is a command, and the steps are numbered sequentially from beginning to end, no matter which employee is performing the step.

Discussion

1. Assume that you are an employee interested in the company's tuition-refund program. Is there any point in these procedures where you might be uncertain what to do next? If so, discuss how to revise.

2. The introduction discusses the company policy on tuition refunds and includes some additional information about eligibility. Is there any information in the numbered steps that you believe should be included in the introduction? If so, rewrite the introduction and incorporate all the information you believe readers should know about the procedures before starting the process of applying for a tuition refund.

PROCEDURES FOR EMPLOYEE TUITION-REFUND PROGRAM

The Whitstone Corporation offers an employee tuition-refund program to encourage employees to continue their technical training or complete advanced degrees. All full-time employees who have worked at Whitstone for one year may receive full reimbursement for courses taken for academic credit at fully accredited technical schools, colleges, or universities according to the following procedures:

Before Registration

Supervisor:

1. Send a memo to all employees on August 1, December 1, and May 1, informing them of the company tuition program and inviting them to discuss education plans with you.

Employee:

2. See your supervisor at least two weeks before the start of classes to allow time to approve your courses for the tuition-refund program.

Supervisor:

3. Discuss employee's education plans and explain the application form.

Employee:

4. Complete the application form.

5. Submit the application form to supervisor.

Supervisor:

6. Review the application form for completeness and send it to Human Resources Clerk.

Human Resources Clerk:

7. Check the application for compliance with company regulations.

8. Approve or deny the application and return it to supervisor with comments.

Supervisor:

9. Inform employee of the decision.

10. If the decision is favorable, sign the Tuition-refund Contract with employee and send it to Human Resources Clerk.

11. Be sure employee knows the required grade and employment status for a full refund.

<u>After Registration</u>

Employee:

12. Submit fee invoice form to your supervisor after paying tuition, so your record is in order for reimbursement.

Supervisor:

13. Send employee's fee invoice to Human Resources Clerk with Form 26A.

Human Resources Clerk:

14. Record the fee invoice as a potential tuition refund in employee's file.

Supervisor:

15. Meet informally with employee once a month to ascertain progress in the course.

16. If the employee is having difficulty with the course, suggest a meeting with the Training Director to discuss study approaches.

<u>After Completion</u>

Employee:

17. Upon completion of the course, with a grade of at least B–, submit your final grade report to your supervisor.

Supervisor:

18. Send employee's final grade report with Form 26B to Human Resources Clerk.

Human Resources Clerk:

19. Check course identification and status and prepare a reimbursement check for the full course fee.

Supervisor:

20. Present the check to the employee and offer company congratulations.

This process explanation is a pamphlet published by the American Diabetes Association for people who have just been diagnosed with diabetes. The pamphlet begins by defining the disease and explaining the purpose of blood testing. The third section is the process explanation for testing blood and includes both standard methods. Notice that the process explanation includes the reader in the process by using such phrases as, "you place the test strip."

Discussion

1. Discuss why the writer probably decided to begin this process explanation with a definition of the disease. What are the advantages of defining both types of diabetes and both blood testing methods?

2. Review the headings used in the pamphlet. Discuss possible revisions and why they might help guide the reader through the information. Discuss the effect of using "you" throughout the text.

3. In groups, select a typical campus activity, such as voting for student government. Write a definition of the activity and a process explanation for it aimed at a new student on campus.

WHAT IS BLOOD TESTING?

Blood testing is one of the main tools you have to keep your diabetes in control. Blood testing is what this pamphlet is about. But, to help you understand the reasons behind testing your blood, we first need to discuss what diabetes is.

Diabetes is a disease in which the body does not make or respond to insulin. Insulin is a hormone produced by your pancreas. Without insulin, your body is unable to change food into energy. You need energy to live, work, and play. Your body gets energy from glucose. Glucose is a form of sugar that your body makes from the foods you eat. Glucose enters body cells with the help of insulin. Insulin acts as a key that unlocks the door to the cells to let glucose in.

There are two main types of diabetes: insulin-dependent (type I) and non-insulin-dependent (type II). In type I diabetes, the pancreas makes little or no insulin—there is no key to unlock the door. In type II diabetes, either the pancreas does not make enough insulin or the body does not respond properly to the insulin—the key fits the lock but can't open the door.

The goal of people with diabetes is to keep blood-glucose levels (the amount of glucose in your blood) as near to normal (nondiabetic levels) as possible. This is known as good diabetes control. Good control doesn't happen by itself. You must work at it. You can aim for good control by properly balancing diet (what and how much you eat), exercise (how much activity you get), and insulin or oral medication (prescription medicines). Taking control of your diabetes also includes testing your blood to know your blood-glucose level.

WHY DO I NEED TO TEST?

Blood testing lets you know what your blood-glucose level is at any one time. This information will help you decide what adjustments to make in your diabetes control plan. For example: After exercising, you feel shaky and sweaty. Do you feel this way because you've exercised, or because your blood glucose is low? If your blood test shows that your glucose is low, then you know you need to eat a fast-acting sugar. If your blood test shows normal, then you know you are shaky and sweaty because you exercised. Then you won't eat anything extra, which could cause your blood glucose to be high later.

HOW DO I TEST MY BLOOD?

There are two ways you can test your blood. In both tests, you first need to prick your finger with a special needle called a lancet to get a drop of blood. You then place the drop of blood on a test strip. The steps you follow to do your blood test will depend on what brand of test strip you use or what brand of meter you use. Ask your doctor or nurse educator to walk through the testing process *you* need to follow. In one method, you wait for the test strip to change colors. (The glucose in your blood causes the change.) You then match the color of the strip to a color chart, which is usually on the test strip container. The colors represent ranges of glucose levels, such as 60–90. If your test-strip color matches 60, then your blood glucose is 60. If it falls between the 60 and 90 color, then it is recorded as 75.

In the second method, you place the test strip in a blood-glucose meter. A meter is a small computerized machine that 'reads' your test strip. Your blood-glucose level is printed on a digital screen (like those on a pocket calculator).

Meters may provide more accurate blood-glucose readings than matching the test-strip colors to a chart. This is because the meter gives you an exact number so you don't have to guess at the number. It is important that you follow the test directions exactly. Not following the test directions may give you false results.

RECORD THE RESULTS

Be sure to write down your blood-test results. These records will help you and your doctor make adjustments in your diabetes control plan. If your blood-glucose levels are frequently higher or lower than normal, you should contact your doctor.

Getting in the habit of testing may be hard at first. But as you get used to it, you'll find that blood testing makes keeping your diabetes in control a lot easier.

1. Write a set of instructions for one of the following activities. Identify your reader and purpose before you begin. Include appropriate warnings and cautions and develop at least one graphic aid, illustrating some aspect of your instructions.

- driving from campus to two points of interest in your community and then driving back to campus
- correctly handling a specific piece of sports equipment
- performing routine maintenance on an automobile, bicycle, or other vehicle
- performing an outdoor household chore
- performing an indoor household chore
- cooking and serving a specific food
- performing a specific laboratory test or activity in your field
- safely handling a specific piece of equipment at your job
- performing a hobby

2. Write a set of troubleshooting instructions that supplement the instructions you wrote for Exercise 1.

3. Write a set of safety tips to supplement the instructions you wrote for Exercise 1. Include appropriate graphic aids.

4. Using the process explanations of the "Walk-and-Turn Test" in Model 8-5, write a set of instructions for a rookie police officer who is administering the test for the first time.

5. The following are some Quinn Manufacturing Company safety rules for proper operation of cranes. The rules are intended for crane operators and employees working with the operators. Using this list, write a formal set of procedures for safe crane operation and develop an appropriate graphic aid. *Note:* These rules are not sequential steps.

- The crane operator must be sure the hoist brake will hold a heavy load. If in doubt, test it after the load has been lifted a few inches.
- Do not carry loads over railroad equipment during a switching operation.
- A load shall be set only in a safe place.
- When approaching bridge or trolley bumpers, it is necessary to maintain a slow speed.
- Crane operators are not to carry loads over the heads of employees.
- Compliance with all safety practices is required of all Quinn employees.
- Crane operators, riggers, and hookers, or other employees engaged in crane operation must have a valid safety permit.
- Do not pick up a load greater than the rated safe load capacity of your crane unless the overload has been approved by the safety engineer.

- Material must not be placed closer than 6 feet to railroad tracks unless otherwise covered by code.
- Hand signals are preferred. Use whistle signals only if hands cannot be seen.
- Lifts must be made vertically.
- Always be sure to take slack out of load swings gradually. When lift is made suddenly, slings or chains may weaken.
- Crane operators must see that loads are properly secured before making a lift.
- When carrying loads with a magnet, no people are to be allowed near the path of travel.
- Crane hook and sling must be high enough to clear all obstacles before traveling.
- Compressed gas cylinders or acid carboys are not to be lifted with a crane unless an authorized device for handling is available and its use approved by the supervisor.
- The operator must not take signals from more than one person at a time.
- The signals given by the rigger or hooker must be obeyed at all times.
- A distance of 15 feet must be maintained between cranes.
- The crane operator must not leave the crane while a load is suspended.
- Never allow anyone to ride on the crane hook, sling, or load.
- When going up or down crane-access ladder, do not carry anything under arms or in your hands.
- Allow only authorized personnel to ride in the crane cab.
- The crane operator will gather and dispose of all oily rags before operating his crane.

6. Write a set of procedures, using playscript organization, for a system involving several employees at your job. These procedures will be included in the new company procedures manual.

7. Write a process explanation of one of the following. Your reader is a foreign student who is studying American culture. Include a flowchart illustrating the process.

- playing a sport, e.g., baseball, softball
- performing a holiday activity, e.g., trimming a Christmas tree, decorating a wagon for the Fourth of July parade
- engaging in a social activity, e.g., holding a Superbowl party, organizing a bridal shower

8. Write a process explanation for a test or system you use in your major, *or* write a process explanation for a procedure used at your job. Identify a reader and purpose. Include one graphic aid.

CHAPTER 9

Formal Report Elements

SELECTING FORMAL REPORT ELEMENTS

Most in-house reports, whatever their purpose, are in memo format, as illustrated in Chapter 10. Long reports, however, whether internal or external, more often include the formal report elements discussed in this chapter.

Management or company policy usually dictates when formal report elements are appropriate. In some companies, certain report types, such as proposals or feasibility studies, always include formal report elements. In addition, long reports addressed to multiple readers often require formal report elements, such as glossaries and appendixes, to effectively serve all reader purposes.

The formal report is distinguished from the informal report by the inclusion of some or all of the special elements described in this chapter.

WRITING FRONT MATTER

Front matter includes all the elements that precede the text of a report. Front-matter elements help a reader (1) locate specific information and (2) become familiar with the general content and organization of the report.

Title Page

A *title page* records the report title, writer, reader, and date. It is usually the first page of a long formal report. In some companies, the format is standard. If it is not, include these items:

- Title of the report, centered in the top third of the page

- Name, title, and company of the primary reader or readers, centered in the middle of the page

- Name, title, and company of the writer, centered in the bottom third of the page

- Date of the report, centered directly below the writer's name

The title should accurately reflect the contents of the report. Use key words that identify the subject quickly and inform readers about the purpose of the report.

Title:	Parking
Revision:	Feasibility Study of Expanding Parking Facilities
Title:	Office Equipment
Revision:	Proposal for Computer Purchases

Transmittal Letter or Memo

A *transmittal letter* or *memo* sends the report to the reader. In addition to establishing the title and purpose of the report, the transmittal letter provides a place for the writer to add comments about procedures, recommendations, or other matters that do not fit easily into the report itself. Here, too, the writer may offer to do further work or credit others who assisted with the report. The transmittal letter is placed either immediately after the title page or immediately before it, as company custom dictates. In some companies, writers use a transmittal memo, but the content and placement are the same as for a transmittal letter. If the transmittal letter simply sends the report, it often is before the title page. However, if the transmittal letter contains supplementary information about the report or recommends more study or action, some writers place it immediately after the title page, where it functions as a part of the report. In your transmittal letter,

- State the report title, and indicate that the report is attached.

- Establish the purpose of the report.

- Explain why, when, and by whom the report was authorized.

- Summarize briefly the main subject of the report.

- Point out especially relevant facts or details.

- Explain any unusual features or organization.

- Acknowledge those who offered valuable assistance in gathering information, preparing appendixes, and so on.

- Mention any planned future reports.

- Thank readers for the opportunity to prepare the report, or offer to do more study on the subject.

- Recommend further action, if needed.

Table of Contents

The *table of contents* alerts the reader to (1) pages that contain specific topics, (2) the overall organization and content of the report, and (3) specific and supplemental materials, such as appendixes. The table of contents is placed directly after the transmittal letter or title page, if that is after the transmittal letter, and before all other elements. The title page is not listed in the table of contents, but it is counted as page i. All front matter for a report is numbered in small Roman numerals. The first page of the report proper is page 1 in Arabic numbers, and all pages after that have Arabic numbers. In your table of contents,

- List all major headings with the same wording used in the report.

- List subsections, indented under major headings, if the subheadings contain topics that readers are likely to need.

- List all formal report elements, such as the abstract and appendixes, except for the title page.

- Include the titles of appendixes, for example:

APPENDIX A: PROJECTED COSTS

- Do not underline headings in the table of contents even if they are underlined in the text.

List of Figures

Any graphic aid, such as a bar graph, map, or flowchart that is not a table with numbers or words in columns, is called a *figure*. The list of figures follows the table of contents. List each figure by both number and title, and indicate page numbers:

List of Tables

The list of tables appears directly after the list of figures. List each table by number and title, and indicate page numbers:

If your report contains only two or three figures and tables, you may combine them into one "List of Illustrations." In this case, list figures first and then tables.

Abstract and Executive Summary

An *abstract* is a synopsis of the most important points in a report and provides readers with a preview of the full contents. An abstract, which can be either descriptive or informative, is usually one paragraph of no more than 200 words. An *executive summary* is a longer synopsis of one to two pages that provides a more comprehensive overview than the abstract does. An executive summary covers a report's main points, conclusions, recommendations, and the impact of the subject on company planning. In some cases, readers may rely completely on such a synopsis, as, for instance, when a nonexpert reader must read a report written for experts. In other cases, readers use these synopses to orient themselves to the main topics in a report before reading it completely.

The abstract or executive summary in a formal report usually follows the list of tables, if there is one. In some companies, the style is to place an abstract on the title page or immediately after the title page. Whether you decide to include the longer executive summary or the shorter abstract depends on company custom and the expectations of your readers. In some companies, executives prefer to see both an abstract and an executive summary with long reports. If a report is very long, an executive summary allows a fuller synopsis and provides readers with a better understanding of the report contents and importance than an abstract will. Even though they are all synopses, the two types of abstracts and the executive summary provide readers with different emphases.

Descriptive Abstract

A *descriptive abstract* names the topics covered in a report without revealing details about those topics. Here is a descriptive abstract for a proposal to modify and redecorate a hotel restaurant:

> This proposal recommends a complete redesign of the Bronze Room in the Ambassador Hotel to increase our appeal to hotel guests and local customers. A description of the suggested changes, as well as costs, suggested contractors, and management reorganization, is included.

Because a descriptive abstract does not include details, readers must read the full report to learn about specifics, such as cost and planned decor. Descriptive abstracts have become less popular in recent years because they do not provide enough information for busy readers who do not want to read full reports.

Informative Abstract

An *informative abstract,* the one frequently used for formal reports and technical articles, describes the major subjects in a report and summarizes the conclusions and recommendations. This informative abstract is for the same report covered by the preceding descriptive abstract:

> This proposal discusses the 5-year decline in occupancy rates and local customer traffic at the Ambassador Hotel. The recommendation is to convert the Bronze Room into a turn-of-the-

century supper club. This motif has been successful in hotels in other markets, and research shows that it creates an upscale atmosphere for the entire hotel. The construction and decorating will take about 10 weeks and cost $206,000. Finishing the Bronze Room by the end of the year will allow the Ambassador to compete for the International Homebuilders Convention, which attracts more than 2000 members.

This informative abstract includes more details and gives a more complete synopsis of the report contents than the descriptive abstract does.

Executive Summary

An *executive summary* includes (1) background of the situation, (2) major topics, (3) significant details, (4) major conclusions or results, (5) recommendations, and (6) a discussion of how the subject can affect the company. Writers sometimes use headings in an executive summary to make it look like a miniature report. Here is an executive summary for the hotel proposal:

The Ambassador Hotel has experienced declining occupancy rates and declining local customer traffic for the past 5 years. During that period, three new hotels, all part of well-known chains, have opened in the downtown area. The Ambassador's image as an upscale, sophisticated place to visit has been eroded by the competition of the larger and more modern hotels. Beryl Whitman of the Whitman Design Studio, a consultant to the hotel, has recommended complete redecoration of the Bronze Room. The suggested changes will convert the present restaurant into a turn-of-the-century supper club.

Research indicates that the image of the main dining room in a hotel has a direct impact on the public perception of the hotel in general. A turn-of-the-century motif for the main dining room has been successful in hotels in Indianapolis, Milwaukee, and St. Louis. These markets are comparable to ours, and our survey, conducted in May by Hathaway Management Consultants, indicated that local customers would be interested in a dining atmosphere that reflects sophistication and elegance. Redesign of the Bronze Room has several advantages:

1. A turn-of-the-century atmosphere will create the sophisticated, upscale image we want to project.

2. By not copying the ultramodern look of the competing hotels, we will achieve distinction based on a perceived return to elegant and gracious hotel service in the past.

3. Other hotel facilities will not be disturbed, and construction can be completed by November 1, in time for the holiday season.

Renovation will take 10 weeks, and the total projected cost of $206,000 could be regained within 18 months or sooner if we can immediately attract conventions, such as the International Homebuilders Association. Even without such a convention, the Ambassador could expect an immediate 10% increase in occupancy rates and a 26% increase in local customers, based on the reports from Milwaukee, St. Louis, and Indianapolis. The recommendation is to redesign the Bronze Room with a target date of November 1.

Abstracts and executive summaries, important elements in formal reports, are difficult to write because they require summarizing in a few words what a report covers in many pages. Remember that an informative abstract or executive summary should stand alone for readers who do not intend to read the full report immediately. In preparing abstracts and executive summaries, follow these guidelines:

1. Write the abstract or executive summary after you complete the report.

2. Identify which topics are essential to a synopsis of the report by checking major headings and subheadings.

3. Rewrite the original sentences into a coherent summary. Simply linking sentences taken out of the original report will not produce a smooth style.

4. Write full sentences, and include articles *a, an,* and *the.*

5. Avoid overly technical language or complicated statistics, which should be in the data sections or an appendix.

6. Do not refer readers to tables or other sections of the original report.

7. If conclusions are tentative, indicate this clearly.

8. Do not add information or opinions not in the original report.

9. Edit the final draft for clarity and coherence.

WRITING BACK MATTER

Back matter includes supplemental elements that some readers need to understand the report information or that provide additional specialized information for some readers.

References

A *reference list* records the sources of information in the report and follows the final section of the report body. Preparation of a reference list is explained later in this chapter under "Documenting Sources."

Glossary/List of Symbols

A *glossary* defines technical terms, such as *volumetric efficiency,* and a *list of symbols* defines scientific symbols, such as *Au.* Include a glossary or list of symbols in a long report if your readers are not familiar with the terms and symbols you use in the report. Also include informal definitions of key terms or symbols in the text to aid readers who do not want to flip pages back and forth looking for definitions with every sentence. If you do use a glossary or list of symbols, say so in the introduction of the report to alert readers to them. The glossary or list of symbols usually follows immediately after the references. In some companies, however, custom may dictate that the two lists follow the table of contents. In either case, remember these guidelines:

- Arrange the glossary or list of symbols alphabetically.

- Do not number the terms or symbols.

- Include also any terms or symbols that you are using in a nonstandard or limited way.

- List the terms or symbols on the left side of the page, and put the definition on the right side on the same line:

  bugseed   an annual herb in northern temperate regions
  Pt   platinum

Appendixes

Appendixes are the final elements in formal reports. They contain supplemental information, information that is too detailed and technical to fit well into the body of the report, or information that some readers need and others do not. Appendixes can include documents, interviews, statistical results, case histories, lists of pertinent items, specifications, or lists of legal references. The recent trend in formal reports has been to place highly technical or statistical information in appendixes for those readers who are interested in such material. Remember these guidelines:

- Label appendixes with letters, such as "Appendix A" and "Appendix B," if you have more than one.

- Provide a title for each appendix, such as "Appendix A. Questionnaire Sample."

- Indicate in the body of the report that an appendix provides supplemental information on a particular topic, such as "See Appendix C for cost figures."

DOCUMENTING SOURCES

Documenting sources refers to the practice of citing original sources of information used in formal reports, journal articles, books, or any document that includes evidence from published works. Cite your information sources for the following reasons:

- Readers can locate the original sources and read them if they want.

- You are not personally responsible for every fact in the document.

- You will avoid charges of plagiarism. *Plagiarism* is the unacknowledged use of information discovered and reported by others or the use of their exact words, copied verbatim.

In writing a report that relies somewhat on material from other sources, remember to document information when you are doing either of the following:

- Using a direct quotation from another source

- Paraphrasing information from another source

If, however, the information you are presenting is generally known and readily available in general reference sources, such as dictionaries and encyclopedias, you need not document it. You would not have to document a statement that water is made up of two parts hydrogen and one part oxygen or that it boils at 212°F and freezes at 32°F. In addition, if your readers are experts in a particular field, you need not document basic facts or theories that all such specialists would know.

The documentation system frequently used in the natural sciences, social sciences, and technical fields is the *American Psychological Association (APA) system,* also called the *author/date system.* Another system often used in the sciences or technical fields is the *number-reference system.* Although all documentation systems are designed to help readers find original sources, the systems do vary slightly. For example, the APA system cites e-mail only in the text as "personal communication." The *Modern Language Association system,* used in the humanities, cites e-mail in the bibliography as "E-mail to the author." Always use the reference system that your instructor requires or, if you are writing for a technical journal, the editor requires. Following is a list of style guides for particular associations or fields.

> *American National Standard for Bibliographic References*
>
> *CBE Style Manual: A Guide for Authors, Editors, and Publishers in the Biological Sciences*
>
> *The Chicago Manual of Style*
>
> *Guide for Preparation of Air Force Publications*
>
> *Handbook for Authors of Papers in the Journals of the American Chemical Society*
>
> *A Manual for Authors of Mathematical Papers*
>
> *MLA Handbook for Writers of Research Papers*
>
> *NASA Publications Manual*
>
> *Publication Manual of the American Psychological Association*
>
> *Style Manual for Engineering Authors and Editors*
>
> *Uniform Requirements for Manuscripts Submitted to Biomedical Journals*

APA System: Citations in the Text

In the APA system, when you refer to a source in the text, include the author and the date of publication. This paragraph from a psychologist's report illustrates in-text citation:

> Television's portrayal of women has been called "the best of recent years" (Steenland, 1986, p. 17). Since reader-response theory (Allen, 1987) suggests that viewers interpret images individually, research is now focusing on testing viewer perceptions. Atwood, Zahn, and Webber (1986) used random telephone dialing to test viewer response to women on television and found no differences between male and female viewers. A British study (Gunter & Wober, 1982) found that heavy viewers of crime action shows had lowered perceptions of women as traditionally feminine. Durkin (1983) provides a comprehensive survey of all relevant studies of audience perception involving children. A recent study (Howard et al., 1992) reported significant differences in the ratings of female television characters based on the gender of the viewer. Howard et al. also provided comparisons within and among groups of male and female viewers.

Notice these conventions of the APA citation system:

1. If an author's name begins a sentence, place the date of the work in parentheses immediately after.

2. If an author is not referred to directly in a sentence, place both the author's last name and the year of publication, separated by a comma, in parentheses.

3. If there are multiple authors, cite all the names up to six. If there are more than six authors, cite only the first author and follow with et al.:

Jones et al. (1988) reported. . . .

4. If multiple authors are cited in parentheses, separate names with commas, and use an ampersand (&) between the last two names.

5. If an author is referred to more than once in a single paragraph, do not repeat the year in parentheses as long as the second reference clearly refers to the same author and date as in the first reference.

6. If you are using a direct quotation, state the page numbers immediately after the quotation:

". . . further research" (Jackson, 1995, p. 46).

Jackson (1995) found ". . . further research" (p. 46).

7. If you are citing two works by the same author, give the year of publication of both works:

Young (1979, 1984) disagrees. . . .

8. If you are citing two works by the same author, published in the same year, distinguish them by *a, b, c,* and so on:

Lucas (1987a, 1987b) refers to. . . .

9. If you are citing several works by different authors in the same parentheses, list the works alphabetically by first author:

Several studies tested for side effects but found no significant results (Bowman & Johnson, 1980; Mullins, 1979; Roberts & Allen, 1975; Townsend, 1988).

10. Use last names only unless two authors have the same surname; then include initials to avoid confusion:

W. S. Caldwell (1987) and R. D. Caldwell (1988) reported varied effects. . . .

Heightened effects were noted (W. S. Caldwell, 1987; R. D. Caldwell, 1988).

11. Use an *ellipsis* (three spaced periods) to indicate omissions from direct quotations:

Bagwell (1987) commented, "This handbook will not fulfill most needs of a statistician, but . . . model formulas are excellent."

12. If the omission in a quotation comes at the end of the sentence, use four periods to close the quotation:

    According to Martin (1984), "Researchers should inquire further into effects of repeated exposure. . . ."

13. Use brackets to enclose any information you insert into a quotation:

    Krueger (1988) cited "continued criticism from the NCWW [National Commission on Working Women] regarding salary differences between the sexes" (p. 12).

14. If you are citing personal communication, such as e-mail, telephone conversations, letters, or messages on an electronic bulletin board, state initials and last name of the sender and the date:

    K. J. Kohls said the sales reports were unavailable (personal communication, January 7, 1997).

    The sales reports were unavailable (K. J. Kohls, personal communication, January 7, 1997).

    Do not include personal communication in the reference list.

APA System: List of References

This list of references for a report on the job or college paper includes each source cited in the document. Follow these conventions for business reports and college papers:

1. Do not number the list.

2. Indent the second line of the reference three spaces.

3. List items alphabetically according to the last name of the first author.

4. If there is no author, alphabetize by the title, excluding *a, an,* and *the*.

5. Alphabetize letter by letter.

   Bach, J. K.
   Bachman, D. F.
   DeJong, R. T.
   DuVerme, S. C.
   MacArthur, K. O.
   Martin, M. R.
   McDouglas, T. P.
   Realm of the Incas
   Sebastian, J. K.
   St. John, D. R.
   Szartzar, P. Y.

6. Place single-author works ahead of multiple-author works if the first author is the same:

Fromming, W. R.

Fromming, W. R., Brown, P. K., & Smith, S. J.

7. Alphabetize by the last name of the second author if the first author is the same in several references:

Coles, T. L., James, R. E., & Wilson, R. P.

Coles, T. L., Wilson, R. P., & Allen, D. R.

8. List several works by one author according to the year of publication. Repeat the author's name in each reference. If two works have the same publication date, distinguish them by using *a, b, c,* and so on, and alphabetize by title:

Deland, M. W. (1978).

Deland, M. W. (1987a). Major differences . . .

Deland, M. W. (1987b). Separate testing . . .

Remember that each reference should include author, year of publication, title, and publication data. Here are some sample references for typical situations:

1. *Journal article—one author:*

Taylor, H. (1995). Vanishing wildlife. *Modern Science, 36,* 356–367.

Note:

- Use initials, not first names, for authors.
- Capitalize only the first word in a title, except for proper names.
- Underline journal names and volume numbers.

2. *Journal article—two authors:*

Hawkins, R. P., & Pingree, S. (1981). Uniform messages and habitual viewing: Unnecessary assumptions in social reality effects. *Human Communication Research, 7,* 291–301.

Note:

- Use a comma and ampersand between author names.
- Capitalize the first word after a colon in an article title.
- Capitalize all important words in journal names.

3. *Journal article—more than two authors:*

Geis, F. L., Brown, V., Jennings, J., & Corrado-Taylor, D. (1984). Sex vs. status in sex-associated stereotypes. *Sex Roles, 11,* 771–785.

Note:

- Use an ampersand between the names of the last two authors.
- List all authors even if *et al.* was used in text references.

4. *Journal article—issues separately paginated:*

   Battison, J. (1988). Using effective antenna height to determine coverage. *The LPTV Report, 3*(1), 11.

   Note:　If each issue begins on page 1, place the issue number in parentheses directly after the volume number without a space between them.

5. *Magazine article:*

   Lamana, D. (1995, August). Tossed at sea. *Cinescape, 1,* 18–23.

   Note:

   • Include the volume number.

   • Include day, month, and year for weekly publications.

6. *Newspaper article—no author:*

   Proposed diversion of Great Lakes. (1987, December 7). *Cleveland Plain Dealer,* pp. C14–15.

   Note:

   • If an article has no author, alphabetize by the first word of the title, excluding *a, an,* and *the.*

   • If a newspaper has several sections, include the section identification as well as page numbers.

   • Use pp. before page numbers for newspapers.

   • Capitalize all proper names in a title.

7. *Newspaper article—author:*

   Sydney, J. H. (1996, August 12). Microcomputer graphics for water pollution control data. *The Chicago Tribune,* pp. D6, 12.

   Note:　If an article appears on several pages, cite all page numbers, separated by commas.

8. *Article in an edited collection—one editor:*

   Allen, R. C. (1987). Reader-oriented criticism and television. In R. C. Allen (Ed.), *Channels of discourse* (pp. 74–112). Chapel Hill, NC: Univ. of North Carolina Press.

   Note:

   • Capitalize only the first word in a book title, except for proper names.

   • Underline book titles.

   • Use initials and the last name of the editor in standard order.

   • Use *pp.* with page numbers of the article in parentheses after the book title.

   • Use the Postal Service ZIP code abbreviations for states in the publication information.

9. *Article in an edited collection—two or more editors:*

Zappen, J. P. (1983). A rhetoric for research in sciences and technologies. In P. V. Anderson, R. J. Brockmann, & C. R. Miller (Eds.), *New essays in technical and scientific communications: Research theory, practice* (pp. 123–138). Farmingdale, NY: Baywood.

Note:

- List all editors' names in standard order.
- Use *Eds.* in parentheses if there is more than one editor.

10. *One book—one author:*

Sagan, C. (1980). *Cosmos.* New York: Random House.

Note: Do not include the state or country if the city of publication is well known for publishing, such as New York, Chicago, London, or Tokyo.

11. *Book—more than one author:*

Johanson, D. C., & Edey, M. A. (1981). *Lucy: The beginnings of humankind.* New York: Simon and Schuster.

Note: Capitalize the first word after a colon in a book title.

12. *Edited book:*

Hunt, J. D., & Willis, P. (Eds.). (1990). *The genius of the place: The English landscape garden 1620–1820.* Cambridge, MA: MIT Press.

Note:

- Place a period after *Eds.* in parentheses.
- Include the state if the city is not well known or could be confused with another city by the same name (e.g., Cambridge, England).

13. *Book edition after first edition:*

Mills, G. H., & Walter, J. A. (1986). *Technical writing* (5th ed.). New York: Holt, Rinehart and Winston.

Note: Do not place a period between the title and the edition in parentheses.

14. *Article in a proceedings:*

Pickett, S. J. (1995). Editing for an international audience. *Proceedings of the Midwest Conference on Multicultural Communication, 12,* 72–86.

Note: If the proceedings are published annually with a volume number, treat them the same as a journal.

15. *Unpublished conference paper:*

Dieken, D. S. (1994, May). *The legal aspects of writing job descriptions.* Paper presented at the meeting of the Southwest Association for Business Communication, San Antonio, TX.

Note: Include the month of the meeting if available.

16. Report in a document deposit service:

Cooper, J. F. (1995). *Clinical practice in nursing education* (Report No. CNC-95-6). Nashville, TN: Council for Nursing Curriculum. (ERIC Document Reproduction Service No. ED 262 116)

Note: Include document number at the end of reference in parentheses.

17. *Report—corporate author, author as publisher:*

American Association of Junior Colleges. (1992). *Extending campus resources: Guide to selecting clinical facilities for health technology programs* (Rep. No. 67). Washington, DC: Author.

Note:

• If the report has a number, insert it between the title of the report and the city of publication, in parentheses, followed by a period.

• If the report was written by a department staff, use that as the author, such as "Staff of Accounting Unit." Then give the corporation or association in full as the publisher.

18. *Dissertation—obtained on microfilm:*

Jones, D. J. (1986). Programming as theory foundation: Microprocessing and microprogramming. *Dissertation Abstracts International, 46,* 4785B–4786B. (University Microfilms No. 86-08, 134)

Note: Include the microfilm number in parentheses at the end of the reference.

19. *Dissertation—obtained from a university:*

Heintz, P. D. (1985). Television and psychology: Testing for frequency effects on children (Doctoral Dissertation, The University of Akron, 1985). *Dissertation Abstracts International, 45,* 4644A.

Note: When using the printed copy of a dissertation, include the degree-granting university and the year of dissertation in parentheses after the title.

20. *Review of Books, Films, and Television Programs:*

Kelves, D. J. (1995, July 30). The race to Armageddon [Review of the book *Dark sun*]. *The New York Times Book Review,* 9.

Jones, S. W. (1994, November 18). The big bite [Review of the film *Interview with the vampire*]. *Entertainment Weekly, 5,* 51–52.

Mason, S. B. (1995, August 12). [Review of television program *Justice Files*]. *Television Commentary, 16,* 36.

Note:

• Identify the book, film, or television program in brackets.

• When the review has no title, retain the brackets around the material identifying the book, film, or television program.

21. *Films and Television Programs:*

Reynolds, K. (Director). (1995). *Waterworld* [Film]. Los Angeles: Universal City Studios, Inc.

Golden, R. S. (Producer). (1995). *Sherlock Holmes mysteries*. New York: Arts & Entertainment Network.

O'Hara, S. C. (1995, June 4). The heist. (P. Corbett, Director). In W. Brown (Producer), *Matlock*. New York: American Broadcasting Corp.

Note:

- For a film, cite the director, considered the primary creative contributor.
- Identify the title as a film in brackets before the period.
- Cite the studio and the city where it has headquarters.
- For a small independent film or an industrial film, give the full address of the distributor or owner in parentheses.
- For a television series, cite the producer and the network that broadcast the series.
- For an individual television program, cite the writer first, the date of broadcast, with the title of the episode followed by the director in parentheses. Then cite the producer of the series and the series name.
- If the names of television writers, directors, or producers are not available, cite the title of the episode or the series name first as you would an article without an author.

22. *Computer Software or Program:*

Lippard, G. L. (1993). Torsion analysis and design of steel beams [Computer software]. Astoria, NY: Structural Design Software, Inc. (AX-P34-57)

Note:

- Identify the title as computer program or software in brackets following the title without any punctuation between the brackets and the title.
- Cite the city and producer of the software or program.
- If the item has an identification number, place that in parentheses following the name of the software producer.

23. *Information on CD-ROM:*

Mitchell, R. N. (1995, July 12). World mining trends [CD-ROM]. *Foreign economic projections*. U.S. Department of Commerce.

Brown, P. K. (1995). Investment banking in Norway [CD-ROM]. *Business Today, 23*(5), 16–18. Abstract from: ABI/INFORM: 12560.00

Note:

- Cite *CD-ROM* in brackets immediately after the title followed by a period.

- Give source and retrieval number if possible.
- Do not put a period after a retrieval number because it may appear to be part of the electronic address.

24. *On-line Data Bases:*

   Carew, M. S. (1995, October 3). Tennis profiles [On-line]. *Hard court facts.* Available: Internet: http://ESPENET.SportsZone.com

   Note:

- If the item is not dated, give the date you accessed it.
- Cite *On-line* in brackets after the title followed by a period.
- If there is no author, cite the title first and place *On-line* in brackets after the date.
- Identify the computer network and the electronic address.

Remember that information available on-line may change, and you cannot be sure it will be available or in the same form you saw it when someone else tries to access it. Standards for citing electronic material have not been completely developed, but specialized guides are being published and updated. Your library may have a style guide that covers the large variety of materials available electronically.

Number-Reference System

In the number-reference system, the references are written as shown above, but the reference list is numbered. The list may be organized in one of two ways:

1. List the items alphabetically by last name of author.

2. List the items in the order they are cited in the text.

The in-text citations use only the number of the reference in parentheses. Following is the same paragraph shown in APA style earlier to illustrate in-text citations. Here the number-reference system is used; the reference list is in the order the references appear in the text.

Television's portrayal of women has been called "the best of recent years" (1:17). Since reader-response theory (2) suggests that viewers interpret images individually, research is now focusing on testing viewer perceptions. Reference 3 used random telephone dialing to test viewer response to women on television and found no differences between male and female viewers. A British study (4) found that heavy viewers of crime action shows had lowered perceptions of women as traditionally feminine. A comprehensive survey (5) of all relevant studies of audience perception involving children was completed in 1985. A recent study (6) reported significant differences in the ratings of female television characters based on the gender of the viewer. The same study also provided comparisons within and among groups of male and female viewers.

Notice these conventions for the number-reference system:

1. Page numbers are included in the parentheses, separated from the reference number by a colon.

2. Sentences may begin with "Reference 6 states. . . ." However, for readability, rewrite as often as possible to include the reference later in the sentence.

For readers, the APA system is easier to use because it provides dates for information and the names of authors that readers may recognize as experts on the subject. The number-reference system requires readers to flip back and forth to the reference list to find dates and authors. Whichever system you use, be consistent throughout your report.

CHAPTER SUMMARY

This chapter explains how to prepare front and back matter for formal reports and how to document sources of information. Remember:

- Front matter consists of elements that help readers locate specific information and become familiar with report organization and content before reading the text. Included are the title page, transmittal letter or memo, table of contents, list of figures, list of tables, abstract, and executive summary.

- Back matter consists of elements that some readers need to understand the report information or that provide additional information for readers. Included are a glossary, list of symbols, and appendixes.

- Documenting sources is the practice of citing the original sources of information used in formal reports and other documents.

- Sources of information should be documented whenever a direct quotation is used or whenever information is paraphrased and used.

- The APA system of documentation is used frequently in the natural sciences, social sciences, and technical fields for citations in the text and for references.

- The number-reference system, similar to APA style, is also used in the sciences and technical fields.

SUPPLEMENTAL READINGS IN PART 2

Benson, P. J. "Writing Visually: Design Considerations in Technical Publications," *Technical Communication*, p. 451.

Bowman, J. P. "Electronic Conferencing," *Communication and Technology: Today and Tomorrow*, p. 474.

Tarutz, J. H. "Editing for an International Audience," *Technical Editing*, p. 572.

MODEL 9-1   Commentary

The following samples of front matter are from the same formal report—a feasibility study. The writer has evaluated three solutions to a problem and is presenting his findings along with his recommendation.

The title page reflects the contents and purpose of the report through a descriptive title.

The transmittal memo reminds the reader that she asked for the report, identifies the purpose and subject, and includes a recommendation. The writer also credits two people who assisted in his evaluation and offers to discuss the matter further. In using the memo format, the writer indicates that he regards the subject as an internal matter. If he thought the reader was likely to show the report to people outside the company, he would have written a transmittal letter.

The table of contents shows the main sections of the report. Notice that the writer uses all capitals for main headings and capitals and lowercase letters for subheadings. The pagination is in small Roman numerals for the front matter and Arabic numbers for the report and back matter. The writer appears to be using the ascending order of importance to describe the alternatives because the recommended solution—the Jackson Square building—comes last in the section discussing alternatives.

The list of illustrations includes both figures and tables. Notice that tables are listed second even though they appear in the report ahead of the figures.

The abstract for this report identifies the purpose, briefly explains the problem, names the alternatives and the basis for evaluation, and states the recommendation. Notice that the word abstract appears in all capitals centered above the underlined report title, and the pagination is centered at the bottom of the page.

Discussion

1. Compare this transmittal memo with the transmittal letter that appears in Model 10-7. Discuss which elements in each are meant to help the reader use the report.

2. Discuss the visual aspects of the table of contents. What features help the reader locate information quickly?

3. The table of contents lists the appendixes that contain figures and tables. Discuss whether a separate list of illustrations is of any value to the reader.

4. Identify the type of abstract—descriptive or informative—the writer uses for this report. Draft an abstract of the other type, using the information in this sample.

FEASIBILITY STUDY OF OFFICE EXPANSION
FOR UNITED COMPUTER TECHNOLOGIES, INC.

Prepared for
Joanne R. Galloway
Senior Vice President
United Computer Technologies, Inc.

By
William D. Santiago
Vice President
United Computer Technologies, Inc.

March 3, 1996

To: Joanne R. Galloway
             Senior Vice President

From: William S. Santiago
             Vice President

Date: March 3, 1996

Subject: Feasibility Study of Expansion Options

Here is the feasibility study you asked me to prepare. It concerns our options in expanding our physical space to accommodate our growing office staff and computer needs.

As we discussed in February, there appear to be three reasonable options—redesigning our current facilities, renovating the Wallhaven Complex and moving there, or leasing space in the Jackson Square Building. During the past month, I have researched these possibilities through discussions with Daniel Kaffee in Administrative Services and Paul Weinberger in Facility Planning. I also obtained data from the central New Orleans office of Administrative and Retail Facilities, Inc.

Although each alternative has merit, my conclusion is that leasing space in the Jackson Square Building is the best option for us at this time. The attached report reviews all three options.

If you have any questions or would like to discuss this material, I would be glad to meet with you. Please call me at Ext. 6113 if I can be of help.

WSS/sd

ii

TABLE OF CONTENTS

LIST OF ILLUSTRATIONS

Figures

Tables

iv

ABSTRACT

Feasibility Study of Office Expansion
for United Computer Technologies, Inc.

This report presents the evaluation of three options for expanding the office facilities of United Computer Technologies, Inc. Currently, there are 678 full-time employees, with 46 regular part-time employees. Also, the client traffic increased 13% in 1994 and 14% in 1995. The current floor space was designed to accommodate up to 600 at one time. Three possible solutions—redesigning the current facilities, renovating and moving to the Wallhaven Complex, and leasing space in Jackson Square Building—were evaluated on the basis of cost, timing constraints, capacity for computer equipment, location, and appropriateness for the client base. Of the three alternatives, the lease agreement with Jackson Square Building offers the most cost-effective and timely solution to the need for more space. Computer space would be adequate, and the location is readily accessible for clients. The recommendation is to lease space in Jackson Square Building immediately.

v

MODEL 9-2   Commentary

This model contains samples of back matter.

- The reference list is from a student research report on ancient Celtic weapons. The writer uses the APA documentation style. Notice the header at upper right includes the writer's name and the page number.

- The glossary is from a long technical report to multiple readers. The writer knows that at least half the readers are not experts in the technical subject and includes the glossary to help readers understand the information.

- The sample appendix is from a company reference manual and lists the specifications for a technical procedure. Notice that a brief description of the particular features or capacity of each component is included.

Discussion

1. Discuss the visual design of the glossary and the appendix. What features help readers who need this information?

2. As a self test, identify the type of source (i.e., article, book chapter, etc.) in each item of the reference list. Compare your results with a classmate. If you disagree about an item, compare it to the documentation samples in this chapter and identify the type of source.

Drake-16

REFERENCE LIST

Albers, G. T. (1994, March 3). Celtic chariots at Telemon. Historic trails, 12, 23–26, 87.

The Battersea shield. (1994, June 23). Boston Globe, p. B8.

Buford, J. G., & Longstreet, J. R. (1994). Celtic excavations in 1990. Journal of the ancient world, 42(3), 25–41.

Cunliffe, B. R. (1992). Pits, preconceptions and propitiation in the British Iron Age. Oxford Journal of Archaeology, 11, 69–83.

Dukes, J. T. (Director). (1994). Iron Age hillfort [Film]. (Available from History Cinema, 62 South Street, Chicago, IL 60610)

Hancock, G. H., Lee, R. T., & Berenger, T. N. (1995). The Celtic longboat. Proceedings of the Northeast Association of Historians, 16, 43–49.

Merriman, N. (1987). Value and motivation in prehistory: The evidence for Celtic spirit. In I. Hodder (Ed.), The archaeology of Celtic meanings (pp. 111–116). Cambridge, England: Cambridge Univ. Press.

Niblett, R. T. (1992). A chieftain's burial from St. Albans. Antiquity, 66, 917–929.

Pleiner, R. (1993). The Celtic sword. Oxford: Oxford Univ. Press.

Rigby, V. (1986). The iron age: Continuity or invasion? In P. Longworth & C. J. Cherry (Eds.), Archaeology in Britain since 1945 (pp. 52–72). London: British Museum.

GLOSSARY

Accelerometer ....An electrical device that measures vibration and converts the signal to electrical output.

Air/Fuel Mixture.........................A ratio of the amount of air mixed with fuel before it is burned in the combustion chamber.

Ammeter...................................An electric meter that measures current.

Amplitude ....The maximum rise or fall of a voltage signal from 0 volts.

Battery-Hot ....Circuit fed directly from the starter relay terminal. Voltage is available whenever the battery is charged.

Blown ....A melted fuse filament caused by overload.

Capacitor ....A device for holding or storing an electric charge.

DVOM
    (Digital Volt-Ohmmeter) ....A meter that measures voltage and resistance and displays it on a liquid crystal display.

ECA (Electronic Control
    Assembly) ....See Processor

Fuse...A device containing soft metal that melts and breaks the circuit when it is overloaded.

Induced Current ....The current generated in a conductor as a magnetic field moves across the conductor.

Oscillograph ....A device for recording the waveforms of changing currents or voltages.

APPENDIX D: ACS:180 SPECIFICATIONS

This section summarizes the ACS:180 specifications. The ACS:180 design meets the requirements of the following agencies:

- UL

- CSA

- IEC

- JIS

- FCC Class A

- VDE Class A

Component Specifications

Cuvette	disposable reaction vessel with a 1.0 mL maximum fill volume
Cuvette Loading Bin	holds 250 cuvettes and automatically feeds the cuvettes into the track
Cuvette Preheater	regulated at a temperature of 37.0°C (+/−0.5°C) to heat the cuvettes
Cuvette Track	aluminum track, thermostatically-controlled by four thermal electric devices (TEDs) to maintain the present temperature of 37.0°C (+/−0.5°C)
Cuvette Waste Bin	autoclavable collection bin fitted with a disposable, biohazard liner that holds up to 250 used cuvettes
Heating Bath	static fluid bath that contains a specially conditioned circulating fluid; fluid temperature is regulated at 37.5°C (+/−1.0°C)
Waste Bottle	removable container that holds approximately 2.8 liters (capacity of 200 tests) of waste fluid
Water Bottle	removable container that holds approximately 2.6 liters (capacity for 200 tests) of deionized water at temperatures between 15.0°C and 37.0°C

Chapter 9 Exercises

1. Christina Roberts, the vice president of your company, has been invited to speak to a management group on the subject of sexist language or gender bias in language. Your supervisor, Brian Arnold, asks you to find some background information for Ms. Roberts. In the library, find an article on the subject and write an informative abstract of it. Send the abstract with a transmittal memo to Ms. Roberts and explain who directed you to prepare the abstract for her and why you think the article would be helpful. Before going to the library, read the section on "sexist language" in Chapter 5.

2. Your supervisor, J. R. O'Keefe, is very nervous about a speech he is making in a week. Select one of the articles on oral presentation in Part 2 and write an informative abstract. Since Mr. O'Keefe did not ask you to do this, attach a transmittal memo in which you explain why you think he will find the article useful.

3. If you are writing a long report for one of your classes, write an appropriate transmittal memo to your instructor.

4. Here is a student's informative abstract of the article "Barriers to Effective Listening" by Hulbert in Part 2. Read the article, and then evaluate how well this abstract represents the content of the article. Write an improved informative abstract of the article.

ABSTRACT

People do not generally think listening is a skill even though they spend 45% of their time doing it. Poor listening causes many problems. Some people do not listen if they dislike the speaker. People also get distracted and daydream because the speaker talks too slowly. If listeners interrupt the speaker, they can confuse the speaker.

5. Assume you used the following sources for a report on the architecture of New Orleans' Garden District. Prepare a reference list in APA style as explained in this chapter.

  a. An article by John Archer in the Journal of the Society of Architectural Historians. The title was "country and city in the American romantic suburb." It appeared in the May 1983 issue on pages 139–156, Vol. 62.

  b. The Louisiana Historical Quarterly article by James A. Penshaw in January 1919. The title was "the lost city of Lafayette," and it appeared in volume 2 on pages 47–55.

  c. A book by Samantha Raymond called The Garden District, published in New Orleans in 1994 by Regis Press.

d. The article Mary Kramer and her husband Dudley Jakes published in the magazine New Orleans Weekly. The article, called "elegant homes," appeared on pages 20–32 in volume 16, published on April 12, 1996.

e. An article titled "the rediscovery of the Garden District" in the newspaper, New Orleans Beacon, published on November 6, 1995, appearing in section D on page 4.

f. An essay called "gothic villas in New Orleans" appearing in a collection of essays titled Views of New Orleans. The collection was edited by K. C. Browning and was published in New York in 1994 by Wiley Edwards Press. The author of the essay, which is on pages 24–39, is Michael Lee Karnes.

g. A report written and published by the New Orleans Historical Society titled "cornstalk fences and gaslight chandeliers." It was issued in 1994 and was report number nine in a series on historic architecture.

h. A book published in 1992 by Allyn & Bacon in Boston. Written by Joseph M. Fernandez, Rita Lou Carey, Corrine Calvet, and Manuel Vega, the book is titled A History of the New Orleans Garden District: Decay and Revival.

i. Vincent Note's book published in New Orleans by Crescent Publishing in 1995. Directory of Great New Orleans Architecture is in its third edition.

j. A film titled Grand Houses of New Orleans directed by Max Hunter and released in 1993 by Travelers, Inc. The company makes short films about local history and is located at 32 Sunset Boulevard in Nashville, Tennessee 37203.

6. Your supervisor, Michelle Klein, is planning a business trip that will include stops in two of the countries mentioned in the article, " 'Big Emerging Markets' Have Diverse Cultures, but Common Attributes," in Part 2. You select the two countries. Find another article on the customs in each country, and write an executive summary that covers the information in the two articles you find and the article in Part 2. Write a transmittal memo to accompany the summary. Offer to do more research. Ms. Klein did not ask you to find this information.

CHAPTER 10

Short and Long Reports

UNDERSTANDING REPORTS

Next to correspondence, reports are the most frequently written documents on the job. Reports usually have several purposes, most commonly these:

- To inform readers about company activities, problems, and plans so that readers are up to date on the current status and can make decisions—for example, a progress report on the construction of an office building or a report outlining mining costs.

- To record events for future reference in decision making—for example, a report about events that occurred during an inspection trip or a report on the agreements made at a conference.

- To recommend specific actions—for example, a report analyzing two production systems and recommending adoption of one of them, or a report suggesting a change in a procedure.

- To justify and persuade readers about the need for action in controversial situations—for example, a report arguing the need to sell off certain company holdings or a report analyzing company operations that are hazardous to the environment and urging corrective action.

Reports may vary in length from one page to several hundred, and they may be informal memos, formal bound manuscripts, rigidly defined form reports, such as an accident report at a particular company, or documents for which neither reader nor writer has any preconceived notion of format and organization. Reports may have only one reader or, more frequently, multiple readers with very different purposes.

Whether a report is short or long depends on how much information the reader needs for the specific purpose in the specific situation, not on the subject or the format of the report. The Kirtz and Reep article in Part 2 shows that people on the job tend to write more short reports (five pages or less) than long reports. Busy people on the job do not want to read reports any longer than necessary to meet their needs. Furthermore, for most company projects, writers supply several reports, or even a regular series of reports, to keep those concerned with the subject up to date rather than waiting to write one lengthy report at the end of a project. Long reports are usually necessary in these situations: (1) scientists reporting on the results of major investigations, (2) consulting firms providing clients with evaluations of their operations and recommendations for future actions, (3) company analysts predicting future trends and making forecasts on how well the company will perform in the future, and (4) writers reporting on any complex company situation with large amounts of data needed by multiple readers. These long reports usually include summaries for readers who do not need all the detailed information in the reports and are concerned only with conclusions and recommendations.

For all reports, analyze reader and purpose before writing, as discussed in Chapter 2, and organize your information, as outlined in Chapter 3. In addition, use the guidelines for planning, gathering information, taking notes, interpreting data, and drafting discussed later in this chapter. Reports for specific purposes are discussed in Chapter 11. The rest of this chapter focuses on the general structure of short and long reports and on ways to develop long reports that deal with complex subjects and require information from many sources.

DEVELOPING SHORT REPORTS

Most short reports within an organization are written as memos. Short reports written to people outside the organization may be formal reports, with the elements described in Chapter 9, or letters, as shown in Models 3-6 and 10-6. Because short reports provide so much of the information needed to conduct daily business, and because readers on the job are always pressed for time, most short reports, whatever their format, are organized in the opening-summary, or front-loaded, pattern. The delayed-summary pattern is used primarily when readers are expected to be hostile to the report's subject or conclusions.

Opening-summary Organization

The *opening-summary organization* is often called *front-loaded* because this pattern supplies the reader with the most important information—the conclusions or results—before the specific details that lead to those results or conclusions. The pattern has two or three main sections, depending on the writer's intent to emphasize certain points.

Opening Summary

The opening is a summary of the essential points covered in the report. Through this summary, the reader has an immediate overall grasp of the situation and understands the main point of the report. Include these elements:

- The subject or purpose of the report
- Special circumstances, such as deadlines or cost constraints
- Special sources of information, such as an expert in the subject
- Main issues central to the subject
- Conclusions, results, recommendations

Readers who are not directly involved in the subject often rely solely on the opening summary to keep them informed about the situation. Readers who are directly involved prefer the opening-summary pattern because it previews the report for them so that when they read the data sections, they already know how the information is related to the report conclusions. Here is an opening from a short report sent by a supervisor of a company testing laboratory to his boss:

> The D120 laboratory conducted a full temperature range test on the 972-K alternator. The test specifications came from the vendor and the Society of Automotive Engineers and are designed to check durability while the alternator is functioning normally. Results indicate that the alternator is acceptable, based on temperature ranges, response times, and pressure loads.

In this opening summary, the supervisor identifies the test he is reporting, cites the standards on which the test is based, and reports the general result—the alternator is acceptable. The reader who needs to know only whether the alternator passed the test does not have to read further.

Data Sections

The middle sections of a short report provide the specific facts relevant to the conclusions or recommendations announced in the opening. The data sections for the report about the alternator would provide figures and specific details about the three tested elements—temperature ranges, response times, and pressure loads—for readers who need this information.

Closing

Reports written in the opening-summary pattern often do not have closings because the reader knows the conclusions from the beginning and reads the data sections for details, making any further conclusions unnecessary. However, in some cases you may want to reemphasize results or recommendations by repeating them in a brief closing. Depending on the needs of your readers, your closing should:

- Repeat significant results/recommendations/conclusions
- Stress the importance of the matter
- Suggest future actions
- Offer assistance or ask for a decision

Here is the closing paragraph from the short report written by the supervisor in the testing laboratory:

> In conclusion, the 972-K alternator fits our needs and does not require a high initial cost. The quality meets our standards as well as those set by the Society of Automotive Engineers. Because we need to increase our production to meet end-of-the-year demands, we should make a purchase decision by November 10. May I order the 972-K for a production run starting November 20?

In this closing, the supervisor repeats the test results—that the alternator meets company standards. He also reminds his reader about production deadlines and asks for a decision about purchasing the alternators. Because of a pressing deadline, the supervisor believes he needs a closing that urges the reader to reach a quick decision.

Model 10-1 presents a short report in the opening-summary pattern. In this report situation, the writer was told to investigate a new scheduling system for working hours and report back with information. The opening summary reminds the reader of the previous discussions leading to the report. The writer also explains how he gathered information and states his general conclusion—the advantages outweigh the disadvantages in the new system. Although the reader of this opening summary does not know the details, he does have the answer to his original inquiry about the effectiveness of the new scheduling system.

The middle sections provide details about how the system works and about the advantages and disadvantages reported by those already using the system. The writer uses a conclusion section to emphasize how successful the system appears to be, and he offers further assistance. The organization of this short report gives the reader a quick overall understanding of the situation, followed by easy access to the details.

Delayed-summary Organization

The *delayed-summary organization,* as its name suggests, does not reveal the main point or result in the opening. This organizational pattern slows down rather than speeds up the reader's understanding of the situation and the details. Use the delayed-summary pattern when you believe that your reader is not likely to agree with your conclusions readily and that reading those conclusions at the start of the report will trigger resistance to the information rather than acceptance. In some cases, too, you may know that your reader usually prefers to read the data before the conclusions or recommendations or that your reader needs to understand the data in order to understand your conclusions or recommendations. The delayed-summary organization has three main sections.

To: Lee Eastland   Date: January 23, 1996

From: Aaron Berger

Subject: Flex-Time Advantages and Disadvantages

As you recall, at the last division meeting we discussed the possibility of instituting flex-time scheduling in all company departments, and I offered to check on the flex-time concept. Since Best Hospital Products and American Cabinetry in our city have operations similar to ours, I consulted with the personnel managers at both companies. In addition, I talked to the personnel director at our San Antonio branch, which uses flex-time scheduling now. Overall, the personnel managers report that the advantages appear to outweigh any disadvantages in the system.

Flex-Time Scheduling System

Flex-time scheduling is a system that allows individual employees to arrange their own work schedules, within defined limits. The work day usually extends 10 to 12 hours, five days a week, and certain hours are designated as core hours during which all employees must be on the job. Arrival and departure times are flexible for employees.

Best Hospital Products and American Cabinetry, for example, both use the same schedule. The companies open at 6:30 a.m. when one-third of the employees arrive. The core hours are between 9:00 a.m. and 3:30 p.m., and the closing hour is 6:00 p.m., with about one-third of the employees still on the job. Our San Antonio branch opens at 7:00 a.m., closes at 7:00 p.m., and the core hours are 9:30 to 4:30 p.m.

All three personnel managers reported that about 45% of the employees prefer to work the traditional hours of 8:00 a.m. to 5:00 p.m. Female employees with children in daycare centers and single, unmarried employees under age 35 were the most likely to arrange flex-time hours. No one reports any disputes among employees over scheduling.

Advantages of Flex-Time Scheduling

All three personnel managers cited significant advantages in the flex-time scheduling.

1. Employees have lower rates of absence and tardiness because they pick hours that complement their personal lives.

2. Employees have higher productivity when on the job because they take care of personal business outside the office.

MODEL 10-1   A Short Report Organized in an Opening-summary Pattern

L. Eastland   -2-   January 23, 1996

3. Employee morale is high because employees perceive the management as interested in their needs and problems.

4. Company customers have greater access to departments since business can begin earlier, accommodating customers on the East Coast, and end later, accommodating customers on the West Coast.

5. Use of office equipment, such as computers and copying machines, is more efficient because the use is spread over 12 hours instead of 8 hours.

With our nationwide network of dealers and customers, the convenience of expanded hours could contribute substantially to our growth.

Disadvantages of Flex-Time Scheduling

Personnel managers all cited the following disadvantages:

1. Key employees in one department may not be on hand when key employees in another department or customers need them.

2. Total utility bills are higher because the office is open longer hours and facilities are in use longer.

3. Cleaning services must accommodate the longer hours, and the San Antonio branch reports having to pay a premium rate because the service must start later than it does at other companies.

4. Direct employee supervision is not possible for a full day because supervisors will either start later than some employees or leave earlier.

Careful scheduling might compensate for the possible problems resulting if key employees are not on the job at the same time.

Conclusion

In spite of some disadvantages, the personnel managers report that there is general satisfaction with the flex-time scheduling system. Best Hospital Products conducted a formal survey after six months on flex-time, and results indicated employees were comfortable with the system and did not want to return to the traditional working hours. American Cabinetry and our San Antonio division did not formally survey employees, but both personnel managers reported employees appeared to be satisfied. If you would like to discuss this matter further, please let me know. I would be happy to give a presentation of my study of flex-time at the next division meeting.

AB:ss

MODEL 10-1 *continued*

Introductory Paragraph

The introductory paragraph provides the same information as the opening summary, except that it does not include conclusions, results, or recommendations.

Data Sections

The data sections cover details relative to the main subject just as the data sections in the opening-summary pattern do.

Closing Summary

Because the introductory paragraph does not include results, conclusions, or recommendations, a closing that summarizes the main points, results, general observations, and recommendations is essential. The closing also may include offers of assistance, reminders about deadlines or other constraints, and requests for meetings or decisions.

The short report in Model 10-2 shows the delayed-summary pattern. The writer is asking for expensive equipment, and he probably suspects the writer will be resistant to his recommendation. The writer uses the delayed-summary organization so that he can present his rationale, supported by data, before his request. In his closing, the writer stresses the need for the new equipment and suggests a meeting to discuss the matter. In this situation, the opening-summary organization could trigger immediate rejection by the reader, who might not even read the data. Also, depending on the relationship between writer and reader, the opening-summary might seem inappropriately demanding.

DEVELOPING LONG REPORTS

Long reports (over five pages) may be written as memos, but frequently they are written as formal documents with such elements as appendixes and a table of contents, as explained in Chapter 9. Long reports tend to deal with complex subjects that involve large amounts of data, such as an analysis of how well a company's 12 branch offices are performing with recommendations for shutting down or merging some offices. In addition to dealing with complicated information, a long report nearly always has multiple readers who are concerned with different aspects of the subject and have different purposes for using the information in the report.

TO: T. R. Lougani   January 16, 1996
          Vice President, Support Services

FROM: C. S. Chen   *CSC*
          Asst. Director of Radiology

SUBJECT: Ultrasound Equipment

Since ultrasound is a noninvasive procedure and presents no radiation
risk to the patient, it has become increasingly popular with most
physicians. In our department, ultrasound use over the past five years
has increased 32%. In 1992, we performed 1479 procedures, and last
year we performed 2186 procedures. We expect this increased demand
to continue. To prepare for the demand on our equipment (estimated
2297 this year), we need to consider ways to increase our capability.

Updating Current Equipment.   One possibility is to update the current
ultrasound unit with new software. Costs for updating the present
equipment are as follows:

Current unit update	$28,000
Maintenance contract	8,500
(first year)	
Total	$36,500

The maintenance contracts will increase slightly in each succeeding year.
The maintenance charge is rather high because as the equipment ages,
more replacement parts will be needed. The basic hardware is now
seven years old. Although updating the present equipment will improve
the performance of the equipment, it will only marginally increase the
number of procedures that can be performed over a 24-hour period. We
cannot reasonably expect to make up the cost of updating our equipment
because our volume will not increase significantly.

Purchasing New Equipment.   Purchasing new ultrasound equipment
will provide Columbia Hospital with the ability to keep up with the
expected growth in requests for the procedure. A new unit with
increased capability will allow us to expand by 15% in the first year. The
unit alone will enable this expansion; we will not need new staff or floor
space. Increased capability will also increase our patient referrals. At an
average cost of $120 per examination, an additional $41,000 will result

MODEL 10-2   A Short Report Organized in a Delayed-summary Pattern

T. R. Lougani   -2-   January 16, 1996

in the first year, and the full cost of equipment should be recovered within the first two years. Patients may also use other services at the hospital once they come here for ultrasound, resulting in further income. Cost of new equipment is as follows:

New unit $74,000
Maintenance contract   0
                          _____
Total $74,000

Conclusion

Updating old equipment is merely a holding technique, even though such a decision would save money initially. To increase our capability and provide the latest technology for our patients, I recommend that we purchase a new unit to coincide with the opening of the new community clinic on our ground floor, March 1. I would appreciate the opportunity to discuss this matter further. If you wish to see sales and service literature, I can supply it.

MODEL 10-2 *continued*

Planning Long Reports

Consider these questions when you begin planning a long report:

- *What is the central issue?* In clarifying the main subject of a long report, consider the questions your readers need answered: (1) Which choices are best? (2) What is the status of the situation, and how does it affect the company's future? (3) What changes must we make and why? (4) What results will various actions produce? (5) What are the solutions to certain problems? (6) How well or how badly does something work? Not all your readers are seeking answers to the same questions, so in planning a long report you should consider all possible aspects that might concern your readers.

- *Who are your readers, and what are their different purposes?* Because long reports tend to have multiple readers, such reports usually cover several aspects of a subject. You must consider your readers' purposes and how to effectively provide enough information for each purpose. Remember that long reports generally need to include more background information than short reports because (1) multiple readers rarely have an identical understanding of the subject and (2) long reports may remain in company files for years and serve as an information source to future employees dealing with a similar situation. Chapter 2 explains specific strategies for identifying readers' purposes.

- *How much information do I need to include in this report?* The relevant data for all readers and all purposes sometimes constitute masses of information. Determine what kinds of facts you need before you begin to gather information, so you are sure you are covering all areas.

Gathering Information

When you gather information for a long report, consult secondary and primary sources for relevant facts.

Secondary Sources

Secondary sources of information consist of documents or materials already prepared in print, on tape, or on film. For a long project, consult secondary sources first because they are readily available and easy to use. Also, the information in secondary sources reflects the work of others on the same subject and may help direct your plans for further research or trigger ideas about types of information your readers need to know. Major secondary sources are as follows.

Internal Company Documents.   Company records, reports, and correspondence contain information about past operations, trends in production and sales, decisions and their rationales, and agreements with people inside and outside the company. Most company projects have their beginnings in past decisions or events, and readers usually need to know background information about the main subject of a long report.

Government Agencies and Foundations.   Many government agencies, and private foundations support research in science and technology. The scientists conducting research must write a final project report on results, test methods, and conclusions. If the information is not classified, you can obtain copies of the final research reports from most agencies and foundations.

Library.   The library offers a rich collection of facts, figures, and research articles representing both historical and current information. Librarians are available to help you locate specific information. Here are the most frequently used sources in the library for science, technology, and business subjects:

1. *Library catalog.*   As either a computer catalog or file of bibliography cards, the library catalog of holdings lists all books, films, tapes, records, and any materials on microfilm or microfiche in the library. The catalog information will tell you the call number of each item, so you can send for it or find it on the shelf. The computer catalog also usually indicates whether the item is currently in the library or checked out and due back on a certain date.

2. *Periodical indexes.*   Published articles about science, technology, and business subjects are listed in periodical indexes, most of which are published monthly. The most useful for people in professional areas include *Engineering Index, Business Periodicals Index, Applied Science and Technology Index, Index Medicus, General Science Index, Biological and Agricultural Index,* and *Business Index.*

3. *Newspaper indexes.*   Newspaper indexes list the contents of a newspaper by subject, so you can find, for example, articles a newspaper may have run on toxic waste. The two indexes available in most college libraries are *The New York Times Index* and *The Wall Street Journal Index.*

4. *Abstract indexes.*   Abstract indexes provide summaries of published articles about science, technology, and business topics. Read the abstract to decide whether the article contains information you need for your report. If it does, look for the article in the journal listed in the abstract. Abstract indexes cover most fields and include such indexes as *Biology Digest, Chemical Abstracts, Electrical and Electronic Abstracts, Geological Abstracts, Mathematical Reviews, Microbiology Abstracts,*

Nuclear Science Abstracts, Water Resources Abstracts, and *Psychological Abstracts.*

5. *Annual reports.*   Libraries usually collect the annual reports of the Fortune 500 companies as well as those of local companies in the immediate geographic area. The reports provide financial information for the previous year.

6. *Government documents.*   The federal government publishes hundreds of scientific and technical reports, newsletters, and brochures every year. These documents are not listed in the periodical indexes, but the library should have available an index such as the *Monthly Catalog of United States Government Publications.*

7. *Encyclopedias, directories, business guides, and almanacs.*   Specialized encyclopedias on science and technology cover such subjects as computer science, space, energy, construction technology, and wildlife. Business guides and directories provide information about corporations, their officers, products, stock offerings, and sales trends. Almanacs give specific dates and facts about past events.

8. *CD-ROM data bases.*   Most libraries now have CD-ROM disks that contain the major periodical indexes, encyclopedias, and dictionaries. An advantage of the CD-ROMs is that the disks hold vast amounts of information (e.g., an entire encyclopedia), and you can search an entire text for key words. The opening screen of a CD-ROM will give you a menu of the data bases included. To search for a subject, you must select key words that accurately describe your topic without being too narrow or too broad. A librarian can help you use the CD-ROMs and select appropriate key words. The advantage of CD-ROMs is in the speed with which you can scan sources, and when you find the ones you can use, you can print out the information.

9. *Internet.*   The Internet is a network of connections linking thousands of computer information services and data bases throughout the world. Large libraries and research centers have made their extensive collections available on the Internet. In addition, corporations, nonprofit organizations, and government agencies provide information on the Internet. Because the system is changing and growing every day, ask the librarian to help you use the Internet if it is available at your school. There is often a cost involved in these searches, so you need to plan your search carefully.

Unless you have a specific author or title of an article in mind when you use these secondary sources, you must search for information by subject. For effective searches, check under other key topics as well as the main subject. If you are looking for information about diamonds, check under the key word *dia-*

mond, as well as under such topics as mining, precious gems, minerals, South Africa, and carbon.

Primary Sources

Primary sources of information involve research strategies to gather unpublished or unrecorded facts. Scientific research reports, for example, are usually based on original experiments, a primary source. A marketing research report may be based on a consumer survey, also a primary source. Secondary sources can provide background, but they cannot constitute a full research project. Only primary sources can provide new information to influence decision making and scientific advances. The major primary sources of information follow.

Personal Knowledge.   When you are assigned to a report project on the job, it is usually because you are already deeply involved in the subject. Therefore, much of the information needed for the report may be in your head. Do not rely on remembering everything you need, however—make notes. Writing down what you know about a subject will clarify in your own mind whether you know enough about a particular aspect of the subject or you need to gather more facts.

Observation.   Gathering information through personal observation is time-consuming, but it can be essential for some subjects. Experienced writers collect information from other sources before conducting observations so that they know which aspects they want to focus on in observation. Scientists use observation to check, for example, how bacteria are growing under certain controlled conditions. Social scientists may use observation to assess how people interact or respond to certain stimuli. Technology experts may use observation to check on how well machinery performs after certain adjustments. Do not interfere with or assist in any process you are observing. Observation is useful only when the observer remains on the sidelines, watching but not participating.

Interviews.   Interviews with experts in a subject can yield valuable information for long reports. Writers usually gather information from other sources first and then prepare themselves for an interview by listing the questions they need answered. Know exactly what you need from the person you are interviewing so that you can cover pertinent information without wasting time. Use the guidelines for conducting interviews in Chapter 2.

Tests.   Tests can be useful in yielding information about new theories, systems, or equipment. A scientist, for example, must test a new drug to see its effects. A market researcher may test consumer reaction to new products.

The tests themselves should be conducted by an expert to ensure a reliable study.

Surveys.   Surveys collect responses from individuals who represent groups of people. Results can be analyzed in various ways, based on demographic data and responses to specific questions. A social scientist who wants to find out about voting patterns for people in a specific geographic area may select a sample of the population that represents all voting age groups, men and women, income groups, and any other categories thought to be significant. Designing an effective questionnaire is complicated because questions must be tested for reliability. If you are not trained in survey research, consult survey research handbooks and ask the advice of experts before attempting even an informal survey on the job.

Taking Notes

Taking useful notes from the multiple sources you consult for a long report is necessary if you are to write a well-developed report. No one can remember all the facts gathered from multiple sources, so whenever you find relevant information, take notes.

Although putting notes in a spiral notebook may seem more convenient than shuffling note cards while you are gathering information, notes in a notebook will be more difficult to use when you start to write. Because such notes reflect the order in which you found the information and not necessarily the order relevant to the final report organization, the information will seem "fixed" and nearly impossible to rearrange easily, thus interfering with effective organization for the reader. You would have to flip pages back and forth, wasting time searching for particular facts as you try to organize and write. A more efficient way to record facts is to use note cards, because such cards are easy to rearrange in any order and are durable enough to stand up to frequent handling. Here are some guidelines for using note cards to keep track of the information you gather for a long report:

1. Fill out a separate note card for each source of information you use at the time you use it. Put complete bibliographic information on the card for a library source. For other sources, such as interviews, record the names of people, dates, subjects discussed, and any other identifying material. Model 10-3 shows a note card that contains a record of a source used for a long report. Notice that the authors, book title, publisher, city of publication, and date of publication are on the card. If any of this information is missing, you would have to return to the library to get it before citing this source in your report. Recording all the publishing information when you use the source will avoid delays later in the writing process. For convenience, also record the library call number. Many people now prefer to keep their bibliographies on

computers, adding items as they go along. If you do that, be sure to make a backup file every time you add to your bibliography.

2. Put only one item of information from only one source on each card. Putting multiple notes or multiple sources on one card will make it difficult to sort and reorder your notes when you begin to write. Many people now prefer to keep notes on their computers. If you do that, format your notes exactly like note cards, or you will end up with the same collection of unorganized information you would have if you had taken notes in a spiral notebook. Keep one note per page. Make a backup file every time you add notes.

3. Condense the information you find, but do not change the meaning. If the original source states, "The responses from consumers appear to indicate . . . ," do not write on your note card, "Consumer responses indicate. . . ." The original sentence implied some uncertainty by using the word *appears*. This meaning should be clear in your notes.

4. If you plan to quote directly from a source, use quotation marks, so you are certain later exactly which words are direct quotations.

5. Record precise figures and doublecheck your facts, so you do not write "1947" when you want to write "1974."

6. Record enough information so that you can recall the full meaning from the original. One or two key words are not usually enough to help you remember detailed information.

Model 10-4 shows notes taken for a student political science report from the following paragraph:

Even before Edison's incandescent-lamp system, telegraph linemen had organized in some assemblies of the Knights of Labor, particularly in the western part of the United States. During the 1880s the United Order of Linemen

NYE, D. E. (1990)

ELECTRIFYING AMERICA:

SOCIAL MEANINGS OF A NEW

TECHNOLOGY, 1880 — 1940

CAMBRIDGE, MA: MIT PRESS

HD9685. U 5 N 94   1990

Model 10-3   Sample Note Card Showing Source

formed in Denver, but it never became a truly national organization. Electrical fairs increasingly brought together employees of large companies from all over the country, and at a St. Louis trade fair in 1890 linemen and wiremen prepared to unionize under the aegis of the American Federation of Labor. The following year three hundred delegates established the National Brotherhood of Electrical Workers of America. The Steam Engineers organized next in 1896, followed by the Firemen and Oilers in 1898. All were American Federation of Labor craft unions, with the advantage that they each controlled a small class of workers, and the disadvantage that utility management was united while labor was splintered into groups often at war with each other.[1]

Note cards should contain three basic elements: (1) a brief statement of the information you need from the paragraph, (2) the authors' last names and the page number from which the information was taken in one upper corner, (3) a topic heading in the other upper corner for convenient sorting and organizing. Notice that the notes in Model 10-4 are not copies of the sentences in the original paragraph. Put notes in your own words to avoid inadvertently copying the original.

LABOR UNIONS FORMED   NYE
                                      p. 207

1880s — UNITED ORDER OF LINEMEN
           (FAILED)
1891 — Nat'L BROTHERHOOD OF ELECTRICAL
               WORKERS OF AMERICA
1896 — STEAM ENGINEERS
1898 — FIREMEN N OILERS
ALL WERE AM. FED. of LABOR

MANAGEMENT   NYE
                                      p. 207

ADVANTAGE MANAGEMENT
HAD WAS UNITY — LABOR
GROUPS OFTEN IN CONFLICT
w/EACH OTHER

Model 10-4   **Sample Notes for a Student Report**

Interpreting Data

Readers need the facts you present in a long report, but they also need help in interpreting those facts, particularly as to how the information affects their decision making and company projects. When you report information, tell readers what it means. Explain why the information is relevant to the central issue and how it supports, alters, or dismisses previous decisions or how it calls for new directions. Your objective in interpreting data for readers is to help them use the facts efficiently. Whatever your personal bias about the subject, be as objective as you can, and remember that several interpretations of any set of facts may be possible. Alert your readers to all major possibilities. Declining sales trends in a company's southwest sales region may indicate that the company's marketing efforts are inadequate in the region, but the trends also may indicate that consumers are dissatisfied with the products or that the products are not suitable for the geographic region because of some other factors. Give the readers all the options when you interpret facts. After you have gathered information for your report and before you write, ask yourself these questions:

- Which facts are most significant for which of my readers?
- How do these facts answer my readers' questions?
- What decisions do these facts support?
- What changes do these facts indicate are needed?
- What option seems the best, based on these facts?
- What trends that affect the company do these facts reveal?
- What solutions to problems do these facts support?
- What actions may be necessary because of these facts?
- What conditions do these facts reveal?
- What changes will be useful to the company, based on these facts?
- How does one set of facts affect another set?
- When facts have several interpretations, which interpretations are the most logical and most useful for the situation?
- Is any information needed to further clarify my understanding of these facts?

Presenting data is one step, and interpreting their meaning is the second step in helping readers. If you report to your readers that a certain drainage system has two-sided flow channels, tell them whether this fact makes the system appropriate or inappropriate for the company project. Your report should include the answers to questions relevant to your subject and to your readers' purposes.

Drafting Long Reports

Like short reports, long reports may be organized in either the opening-summary or delayed-summary pattern, depending on your analysis of your readers' probable attitudes toward the subject. Whatever the pattern, long reports generally have three major sections.

Introductory Section

The introductory section in a long report usually contains several types of information. If this information is lengthy, it may appear as subsections of the introduction or even as independent sections. Depending on your subject and your readers, these elements may be appropriate in your introduction:

Purpose.   Define the purpose of your report—for example, to analyze results of a marketing test of two colognes in Chicago. Include any secondary purposes—for example, to recommend marketing strategies for the colognes or to define the target consumer groups for each cologne. For a report on a scientific research project, tell your readers what questions the research was intended to answer. Also clarify in this section why you are writing the report. Did someone assign the writing task to you, or is the report subject your usual responsibility? Be sure to say if one person told you to write the report and address it to a third person.

Methods.   Explain the methods you used to obtain information for your report. In a research report, the methods section is essential for readers who may want to duplicate the research and for readers who need to understand the methods in order to understand the results. Include in this section specific types of tests used, who or what was tested, the length of time involved, and the test conditions. If appropriate, also describe how you conducted observations, interviews, or surveys to gather information and under what circumstances and with which people. You need not explain going to the library or searching through company files for information.

Background.   If the report is about a subject with a long history, summarize the background for your readers. The background may include past research on the same subject, previous decisions, or historical trends and developments. Some readers may know nothing about the history of the subject; others may know only one aspect of the situation. To effectively use the report information, readers need to know about previous discussions and decisions.

Report Limitations.   If the information in the report is limited by what was available from specific sources or by certain time frames or conditions, clarify this for your readers so that they understand the scope of the information and do not assume that you neglected some subject areas.

Report Contents.   For long reports, include a section telling readers the specific topics covered in the report. Some readers will be interested only in certain information and can look for that at once. Other readers will want to know what is ahead before they begin reading the data. Indicate also why these topics are included in the report and why they are presented in the way they are to help your readers anticipate information.

Recommendations/Results/Conclusions.   If you are using the opening-summary pattern of organization, include a section in which you provide an overview of the report conclusions, research results, or recommendations for action.

Data Sections

The data sections include the facts you have gathered and your interpretations of what they mean relative to your readers. Present the facts in ways best suited to helping your readers use the information. The patterns of organization explained in Chapter 3 will help you present information effectively. Chapter 11 explains data sections in specific types of reports. For a report of a research study, the data sections cover all the results obtained from the research.

Concluding Section

Long reports generally have a concluding section even if there is an opening summary because some readers prefer to rely on introductory and concluding sections. If the report is in the opening-summary pattern, the concluding section should summarize the facts presented in the report and the major conclusions stemming from those facts. Also explain recommendations based on the conclusions. Some readers prefer that recommendations always appear in a separate section, and if you have a number of recommendations, a separate section will help readers find and remember them.

If the report is in the delayed-summary pattern, the concluding section is very important because your readers need to understand how the facts lead to specific conclusions. Present conclusions first; then present any recommendations that stem from those conclusions. Include any suggestions for future studies of the subject or future consideration of the subject. Do not, however, as you may do in short reports, include specific requests for meetings or remind readers about deadlines. The multiple readers of a long report and the usual formal presentation of long reports make these remarks inappropriate. You may include such matters in the transmittal letter that accompanies your long report, as explained in Chapter 9.

CHAPTER SUMMARY

This chapter discusses the usual organization of short and long reports and provides guidelines for report planning, information gathering, note taking, data interpretation, and drafting. Remember:

- Reports generally have one or more of these purposes: to inform, to record, to recommend, to justify, and to persuade.

- Most short internal reports are written as memos, and most short external reports are written as letters or as formal documents.

- Most short reports are organized in the opening-summary pattern.

- Long reports may be in the opening-summary pattern or the delayed-summary pattern and are usually written as formal documents.

- Planning reports includes identifying the central issue, analyzing readers and purpose, and deciding how much information is necessary for your readers.

- Writers gather information for reports from both primary and secondary sources.

- Notes are best collected on note cards, one item per card.

- For effective reports, writers must interpret the data for their readers.

- Long reports usually have three major divisions: an introduction, information sections, and a concluding section.

SUPPLEMENTAL READINGS IN PART 2

Benson, P. J. "Writing Visually: Design Considerations in Technical Publications," *Technical Communication*, p. 451.

"Six Graphics Guidelines," *Simply Stated*, p. 562.

Tarutz, J. H. "Editing for an International Audience," *Technical Editing*, p. 572.

White, J. V. "Color: The Newest Tool for Technical Communicators," *Technical Communication*, p. 576.

ENDNOTE

1. From Nye, D. E., *Electrifying America: Social Meanings of a New Technology, 1880–1940* (Cambridge, MA: MIT Press, 1990), p. 207.

This short report is organized in the opening-summary pattern. The reader and writer have previously discussed the threat of competition from a new pet superstore. The writer has collected information and consulted with the marketing manager of a similar store in another city. After reviewing the development of superstore competition, the writer suggests ways to increase his store's competitive position. The closing repeats the recommendation and urges a meeting to discuss possible options. As a courtesy, the writer offers to arrange the meeting.

Discussion

1. Discuss the format for this report. How helpful are the headings the writers uses? Why did the writer use a list in one section? The writer and reader already have discussed the problem. Why does the writer include background information on superstore competition?

2. Discuss whether you think the reader needs more information about any topic. What types of information might be useful in future discussions?

3. In groups, identify a local store that is facing increased competition, such as a local supermarket with a new superstore built across the street, a drugstore with a new larger store built next door, or a video store with a larger video store in the same retail complex. Discuss strategies that the local store might use to resist competition from the larger store. Draft a memo to the store owner and suggest changes. Compare your drafts with those from other groups.

To: Margery King   April 6, 1996
        President

From: Kevin Darnell KD
        Manager

Re: Competition from SuperPet, Inc.

As we know, when the retail center on the north side of Talbot Road is
finished in mid-July, we will have competition from SuperPet, Inc.
directly across the street. Moreover, the retail center will include a
drugstore, supermarket, and video store. Consumers generally prefer to
park in one spot and shop for several items in one complex. Since our
last discussion, I have researched some background information and
consulted with Antonio Cordura, marketing manager of King Pet Shop in
River City. The King Pet Shop faced similar competition when Worldwide
Pet Supplies opened in 1994. Mr. Cordura told me that King Pet Shop
established a series of promotional and service programs and managed
to retain its position in the River City market. I believe we will need to
establish similar programs, and we should begin at once.

Superstore Competition

The pet superstore concept began in the late 1980s and has rapidly
grown in market share. Most superstores are about 25,000 sq. ft. and
offer a wide range of products as well as prices lower than nearby
independent pet stores. The superstore basic strategy is to lure
customers with the low prices on standard brands and then convert
customers to higher priced brands carried exclusively by the superstore.
Target customers are middle- and upper-class pet owners who shop for
pet supplies twice a week. These customers are also the people
independent pet stores rely on.

A second problem for independent pet stores is that superstores can
negotiate big discounts from the wholesale dealers. Also, a few premium
brands are dropping exclusive distribution clauses and supplying both
superstores and independents. Wilkins Dog Food announced this week
that it would not renew exclusive contracts when they run out. Our
contract with Wilkins expires August 1, and I am sure SuperPet, Inc.
will carry Wilkins immediately.

Marketing Strategies

Mr. Cordura at King Pet Shop explained several strategies that helped
them retain customers when Worldwide Pet Supplies opened. I believe we
need to consider all these options.

M. King   -2-   April 6, 1996

- Delivery service—Many of our customers are seniors; a delivery service would appeal to them, especially in the winter months.

- Extended store hours—The superstore will be open until midnight Monday through Saturday. We cannot continue our 6:00 p.m. closing and compete with the superstore.

- In-depth knowledge—We have an advantage in that all our clerks are carefully trained in products and care and are pet owners themselves. We need to stress this expertise in our advertising and printed materials. The superstore typically does not require specialized knowledge in its clerks.

- Pet care programs for elementary school children—King Pet Shop has been very successful in its Saturday morning programs for children. Often a child who owns a pet will bring a friend who develops an interest in pets during the program. New customers develop if the parents purchase a pet for the child on the spot along with pet supplies.

- Specialized products—We could add specialized feed for exotic pets. Because the market is small, superstores often don't carry specialized feed for pets, such as ferrets.

- Purchasing alliance—Mr. Cordura suggested we explore an alliance with other local independent pet stores to buy supplies in large volume from wholesalers. King Pet Shop has entered such an alliance and found price benefits.

Recommendation

I have copies of Mr. Cordura's marketing programs as well as research studies of market penetration by pet superstores. I recommend a meeting with senior staff to discuss our options in facing our new competition. I also believe we have no time to waste in developing a competitive strategy. I would be happy to set up a meeting if you wish.

MODEL 10-6 Commentary

This letter report was written in the delayed-summary organization. The president of the student senate chose to write her report as a letter because she felt uncomfortable sending a memo to the director of student services. Although both reader and writer are connected to the same organization, they are not both employees, and the writer preferred the slightly more formal letter format for her report. She begins by thanking the reader for his past assistance, then explains the survey she conducted, describes the results, and concludes by recommending the renovation (possibly costly) of a room in the student center.

Discussion

1. Discuss why the writer chose to present her report in the delayed-summary pattern. What kinds of difficulties might the opening-summary pattern have created in this situation?

2. Discuss the writer's opening paragraph. What impression is she trying to create?

3. How effectively does the writer present her results? How well do the details support her conclusions? Discuss whether she should have included cost figures for renovating the Hilltop.

4. In groups or alone, as your instructor prefers, draft a letter to the director of student services on your campus and ask for renovations of a specific room. Explain why the renovations are needed and discuss your proposed changes in detail.

South Central University
University Park, Georgia 30638

Office of Student Government
(912) 555–1100

April 21, 1996

Mr. Patrick R. Sheehan
Director, Student Services
South Central University
University Park, GA 30638

Dear Mr. Sheehan:

I appreciate your assistance in coordinating student organization events
this year and your efforts to expand services in Jacobs Student Center.
During our meeting in February, you suggested that I survey students
regarding the services in the Student Center and develop a five-year
agenda for issues and projects. I took your advice and conducted a
survey of students on several topics, and I can now report the results
and highlight the area of most interest.

Survey

With the assistance of my fellow officers, Carlos Vega, vice president,
and Marylee Knox, secretary, I surveyed 100 students in the Jacobs
Student Center, April 2–6, 1996. We interviewed only those students
who had at least two more semesters to complete at South Central. The
students surveyed were as follows: males 47% and females 53%;
freshmen 29%, sophomores 32%, juniors 39%.

Each student filled out a written questionnaire about number of hours
spent weekly in the Student Center, eating, and recreation time in the
Center, study time in the Center, and preferences in rooms. An open-
ended question asked students to suggest changes in the room they used
most often. We interviewed students at the main entrance to Jacobs
Student Center.

Results

Overall, students spend an average of 12 hours a week in the Center.
Study time averaged 5 hours, and eating/recreation time averaged 7

hours. There were wide variations in these figures from individual students. The student who spent the least amount of time reported only 1 hour, and the student who spent the most time reported 20 hours. Most students report both study time and eating/recreation time in the Center. Student responses included every public room in the Center—the first-floor food court, bowling alley, billiard room, Hilltop Cafeteria, lounge areas on every floor, and video game room. We were surprised to discover that the most frequently used room was the Hilltop Cafeteria. Students (73%) reported using the Hilltop Cafeteria for both study and eating/recreation at least 50% of the hours they were in the Student Center. Because 79% of the suggestions for changes focused on the Hilltop Cafeteria, I will concentrate on those in this report.

Proposed Changes for Hilltop Cafeteria

Students said they used Hilltop Cafeteria for studying, eating, and meeting with friends, and they had specific criticisms about the facility. As Hilltop also serves as a banquet hall and dance floor for special events, I believe the student concerns merit attention. Comments were primarily about the furniture, lighting, decor, temperature, and atmosphere.

Furniture: Students reported that many of the tables and chairs are in disrepair. Recently, a table collapsed while students were eating lunch, and chair backs often snap if leaned on. In addition, the tables and chairs are scarred, with chipped tabletops and cracks in the chair seats.

Lighting: The current lighting is both unattractive and too dim for efficient study. Part of the problem may be the wide spacing between light fixtures. Students requested more lights and higher power.

Decor: The dull green wall color was cited as making the room look "institutional." Also, the walls near the entrances are dirty from fingerprints, scrapes from chairs, and people brushing against them. Fresh paint in a soft color or muted white was suggested. Because the Hilltop has no windows, there is extensive wall space. Several students suggested wall decorations, such as photographs showing the university's history or student paintings.

Temperature: Students reported that Hilltop was frequently too warm for comfort. Stacks of cafeteria trays left over from lunch produce an

Mr. Patrick R. Sheehan   -3-   April 21, 1996

unpleasant aroma, making the room unappealing. One suggestion was to install several ceiling fans to circulate air more effectively. Also, the trays could be removed promptly at the end of the main lunch period.

Atmosphere: Students mentioned that the food court is usually noisy with heavy traffic and the lounge areas with couches are more suited for socializing than for studying. They prefer the Hilltop if they plan to eat and study. Several suggestions focused on providing classical music in the background, played at a low level. Rearrangement of tables and chairs could create study areas distinct from the eating areas while still allowing students the option of having soft drinks and snacks while studying.

Conclusions

Based on these student responses to our survey, I believe the first priority for the Office of Student Services should be improvements in the Jacobs Student Center, specifically renovation of the Hilltop Cafeteria. Renovation would include painting the room, installing improved lighting, installing ceiling fans, purchasing new tables and chairs, and installing a music system. I have not obtained any cost figures for these suggested improvements. Student suggestions for improving the Hilltop were so numerous I believe this issue should be discussed. I would be happy to meet with you and provide copies of the questionnaires used in our survey, so you can see the results in greater detail. The officers of the Student Senate are interested in working with you in evaluating student interests and needs on the South Central campus.

Sincerely,

Judith L. Piechowski

Judith L. Piechowski
President
Student Senate

JP:mk

MODEL 10-7   Commentary

This formal report is a feasibility study in which the writer compares two technical systems and recommends which is best for the company. The writer begins his report by explaining the expected benefits of installing this type of system and establishes the criteria he used in his evaluation. He then reviews in detail the qualities and cost of each system and concludes with his recommendation.

The report uses the opening-summary pattern because the reader has asked for the study and expects a recommendation. The writer discusses the features of each system in detail and includes a table showing cost comparisons.

The abstract for this report appears on the title page because that format is customary at this company. Although this is an internal report, the writer uses a transmittal letter rather than a memo.

Discussion

1. Discuss the headings in this report. How helpful are they for the reader who must make a decision based on this information?

2. The writer compares the two systems by topic. Discuss how helpful this organization is for the reader.

3. Discuss why the writer probably chose to write a transmittal letter rather than a memo.

4. In this chapter, Models 10-2, 10-5, 10-6, and 10-7 all make recommendations. Discuss the differences in reader, purpose, and writing situation that probably helped to determine the kinds of information included in the reports.

FEASIBILITY STUDY OF SYSTEMS FOR SLAG DETECTION
FOR THE CONTINUOUS CASTER AT
ALLIED STEEL WORKS

Prepared for
Edward P. Magnus
General Manager

Submitted by
Brian Fedor
Quality Manager

November 16, 1996

Abstract

Research conducted over a 30-day period determined the best slag detection system for the continuous caster at Allied Steel Works. The RVX Vibration and the Balid were compared for cost, installation, compatibility with current procedures, performance, reliability, and system maintenance. Although both systems exceeded our performance and minimum maintenance requirements, the RVX Vibration system is recommended because of its lower cost, ease of installation, fewer changes in operating procedure, and reliability.

ALLIED STEEL WORKS
1000 Industrial Parkway
Milwaukee, Wisconsin 53209

(414) 555–6000

November 16, 1996

Mr. Edward P. Magnus
General Manager
Allied Steel Works
1000 Industrial Parkway
Milwaukee, Wisconsin 53209

Dear Mr. Magnus:

Here is the feasibility study that you asked for concerning an effective slag detection system for Allied Steel Works. Over the last month, I have researched and compared slag detection systems. The only two systems used in the steel industry are the RVX Vibration and the Balid systems.

Even though both systems are capable of meeting the high performance and minimum maintenance requirements of the caster, I recommend the RVX Vibration system as the best one for Allied because of its lower cost, ease of installation, fewer changes in operating procedures, and reliability.

I'll be glad to discuss this research with you in detail before you present this report to the Executive Board.

Sincerely,

Brian Fedor

Brian Fedor
Quality Manager

BF:kk

Feasibility Study
of Systems for Slag Detection for
the Continuous Caster at Allied Steel Works

Introduction

This study compares two slag detection systems for use at Allied Steel Works. The two systems researched are the RVX Vibration and Balid. After reviewing the data sent by both companies as well as information from companies with continuous casters similar to ours, I recommend the RVX Vibration system.

Background

The need for a slag detection system has become necessary since the startup of the ladle metallurgical facility (LMF). Before the start-up of the LMF our quality index of 91% could not get better due to a lack of slag treatment at the basic oxygen furnace (BOF). Therefore, the present method of the ladleman closing the ladle when slag appears is sufficient. This reaction method can only allow us a maximum quality index of 94%. With the LMF now on line, we are supplied with 99.9% slag-free steel. This 99.9% slag-free steel means that our present 91% quality index reading can theoretically be raised to 99.9%. However, the only way we will obtain a quality index close to 99.9% is through the use of a slag detection system.

System Criteria

The system criteria were established by our operating staff. The two systems were judged on the following criteria in order of importance: cost, installation, compatibility with operating practices, performance, reliability, and maintenance.

Possible Alternatives

The RVX Vibration and the Balid systems are the only two systems on the market. Both are used throughout the steel industry. Even though they are used by several casters, I only considered data supplied by our sister casters at British Steel's Newcastle Works and Defasco's Erie Works. Like ours, the two casters listed are both built by Mannesmann-Demag and are rated at the same tonnage per year.

The two systems operate on different scientific principles. The RVX system uses an accelerometer to measure change in the vibration of the

2

ladle as the steel stream changes from liquid steel to liquid steel and slag.

The Balid system uses electromagnetic signals to detect a change in steel density as the steel stream changes from steel to a steel-slag mix.

Comparison of Systems

Cost

Cost was determined to be the most important criteria because of the decline in sales we have experienced in 1995. Due to the decline in sales, our capital improvements account has been limited to a balance of $170,000. If we spend over $170,000, the corporate finance office will deduct the excess from our general purchase fund. We cannot afford that because the general purchase fund is used to buy everyday operating supplies such as oil and grease.

The RVX system is considerably less expensive than the Balid system. The cost of each unit is as follows:

	RVX Vibration	Balid
Direct Labor*	$ 24,600	$ 33,628
Labor Overhead*	36,055	39,560
Initial Installation Parts	48,102	77,828
Spare Parts	17,480	22,000
Shipping	1,200	600
	$127,437	$173,616

*Direct labor is the cost of our mechanics installing the system, and labor overhead is the cost of training our staff and consultation fees.

The actual difference in cost between the two systems is $46,179. This difference makes the RVX system a better buy for the money.

Installation

Installation was considered the second most important aspect for three reasons. First, the slag detection system must be compact so that it does not crowd the limited work space on the ladle deck. Second, no extra down time can be used to install the system. This requirement means

3

that the system we choose must be installed during one repair turn. Finally, the installation must be done by our technicians. This requirement is in the union contract.

The RVX system is preferable in this category because it is the most compact unit of the two. The RVX unit is installed conveniently on the side of the ladle manipulator, and the signal cable runs under the tundish car floor to the ladle deck pulpit. The unit measures 1 foot in height, 2 feet in length and 6 inches in width. The RVX unit will fit under the fire protection shroud on the manipulator. Since the cable runs under the tundish car floor, there is no danger of tripping. This unit can be installed in a 12-hour repair turn.

The Balid system requires that the unit be mounted on the side of each ladle and a cable plugged into that unit on every ladle turnaround. This cable cannot be buried under the tundish car floor because the ladle sizes are different and the cable must be placed in different areas. This requirement means that the cable must be free to move, and the work area on the ladle deck would be decreased by 2 feet. Also, this unit would require a 16-hour repair turnaround for our technicians.

The RVX system best fills our needs because of its compact size and quick installation. Another added plus is the RVX system can be quickly installed by our technicians.

Compatibility with Operating Practices

This area is important for three reasons. First, the union contract does not allow this system to displace any workers. Second, the new system must not add a significant amount of time to ladle turnarounds because of possible breakouts while waiting for the ladle to open. Finally, the system must be able to operate on all grades of steel because of our vast product mix.

The RVX system will not displace any workers. Also, the RVX unit will save us time during ladle turnarounds due to its automatic ladle shutoff feature. This time-saving feature is a positive factor that will help make our process more efficient. Finally, the RVX system can be used on all grades of steel.

The Balid unit also will not eliminate any jobs. One drawback to the Balid system, however, is that it requires a ladleman to plug and unplug

4

the sensor. This activity adds an average of five seconds to a ladle turnaround. This extra five seconds would put us dangerously close to the maximum 40-second ladle turnaround time. Like the RVX unit, the Balid unit can be used on all grades of steel.

The RVX unit is the clear choice in this category not only because it can be used on all grades of steel and satisfies the union contract agreement, but also because it will speed up ladle turnarounds.

Performance

This category is important for a number of reasons. First, the use of a slag detection unit will improve our quality index. Second, our tonnage yield will increase. Third, tundish life will increase due to reduced tundish wear (a side effect of slag in the tundish). Finally, the potential for breakouts will lessen due to less slag in the tundish. The performance results were obtained from British Steel's Newcastle caster and Defasco's Erie Works caster, both of which are identical to our caster. We could not actually test the slag detection units in our plant without purchasing them.

The RVX system had an average response time of four seconds faster than the ladleman response method used at our caster. This faster response resulted in a reduction of slag in the tundish from 15% to 7.5%, which extended the tundish life one heat. Increased yield while the system was in use was an extra five tons a heat. This increase was due to fewer inclusion-rejected slabs. Tundish-to-mold yield also increased an average of five tons. Detected vortexing improved quality .01%, or one slab a heat. This vortex detection improvement would result in an extra 3000 slabs produced a year.

The Balid system had an average response time of two seconds faster than our ladleman reaction method. Slag in the tundish was reduced on average from 15% to 9.7%. This reduction in tundish slag extended the tundish life half a heat. Increased yield was five tons a heat. This increase was due to fewer inclusion-rejected steel slabs. Tundish-to-mold yield increased seven tons. However, this system cannot detect vortexing. Therefore, no extra slabs would be produced because of vortex detection.

Although both systems increase yield, the RVX unit performs the best because of its ability to detect vortexing and extend tundish life longer.

Reliability and Maintenance

Reliability and maintenance were combined as a topic by the operating staff because they are interdependent.

For example, the reliability will depend on routine maintenance procedures like calibration. Another factor that could affect the reliability of the units is the amount of maintenance that will have to be done on the units by departments other than ours.

The RVX unit needs to be calibrated twice a year by the RVX representative at a cost of $750 a visit. Routine maintenance must be performed every week to check for possible damage due to overheating or wire shorts due to steel splashing. The unit is self-contained on the ladle deck, so no other maintenance departments are involved in maintaining the system.

The Balid system needs to be calibrated once a year by a factory representative at a cost of $1000 a visit. Routine maintenance must be performed twice a week to check for wire and sensor damage. Since the plug and sensor are on the ladle, the BOF shop maintenance department must be relied upon to adequately maintain those delicate parts. Another area of concern with respect to reliability is that, with so many parts, the accuracy of the sensor will suffer as the ladle is used.

The advantages of selecting the RVX unit over the Balid are the fewer parts to maintain, and the RVX unit can be serviced by our technicians. With fewer parts to break down and all the maintenance work done by our staff, we will have a reliable, low maintenance slag detection unit.

Conclusions and Recommendation

A slag detection unit is necessary if Allied Steel Works is to remain a world-class quality supplier of steel slabs. Both the RVX system and the Balid system are quite capable of improving our quality with minimal maintenance well into the 21st century. However, the RVX Vibration system is considerably less expensive than the Balid while providing better performance, more reliability, and low maintenance. Therefore, I recommend the RVX Vibration system over the Balid.

Chapter 10   Exercises

1. You are assistant to President Justin Langford of Southwest Mutual Insurance, which employs 275 people. Mr. Langford wants to write a formal sexual harassment policy for the company and asks you to research what topics are usually included in such a policy. Use your campus written sexual harassment policy as one of your sources and find two articles that discuss appropriate content for such policies. Use the opening-summary pattern when you report to Mr. Langford.

2. Assume you are employed in your field. Austin Everitt Chancellor, the president of your company, plans to attend a high-level meeting of industry leaders. His assistant, Tiffini Mortenson, asks you to research one of the recent developments affecting your field and write a documented report that will bring Mr. Chancellor up to date on the subject. Topics such as new banking regulations, new technology, the impact of an emerging social or medical problem, foreign competition, mandatory drug testing, waste disposal, new government regulations, or public demands for safety, service, or conservation would be appropriate. You were told that Mr. Chancellor wants current information and is particularly interested in knowing how this subject is expected to affect your industry.

You plan to write a formal report with the appropriate elements—title page, letter of transmittal, abstract, reference list. Other elements may also be necessary, depending on your subject, and you may decide to include graphic aids. You will need to do library research to find recent information about the subject. Because Ms. Mortenson was so emphatic about Mr. Chancellor's desire for up-to-date information, you decide that your documented report will use at least three library sources, all written within the last three to four years. Review Chapter 9 for the appropriate formal report elements and for directions on documenting sources within the text and creating a reference list. Decide whether you will use the opening-summary or the delayed-summary organization. Your instructor may also want you to prepare a 5- or 10-minute oral presentation of your subject for your class. If so, review Chapter 13 and read the oral presentation articles in Part 2.

3. You are a summer intern for Investors Information, Inc. Your supervisor, Monica Quarles, has asked you to go to the library and look up the latest annual reports of three major manufacturing companies. She wants to know the latest sales figures, whether the company is doing better or worse than in previous years, how optimistic or pessimistic the tone of the president's letter is, and significant company developments in new products, plant expansion, or acquisitions. Ms. Quarles would like your opinion as to which of these three companies would be a good investment for her client J. Danforth Mitchell, who likes to invest in companies with good potential for growth. Ms. Quarles prefers the opening-summary report pattern.

CHAPTER 11

Types of Reports

UNDERSTANDING CONVENTIONAL REPORT TYPES

Over the years, in industry, government, and business, writers have developed conventional organizational patterns for the most frequently written types of reports. Just as tables of contents and glossaries have recognizable formats, so too have such common reports as progress reports and trip reports. Some companies, in fact, have strict guidelines about content, organization, and format for report types that are used frequently. Conventional organizational patterns for specific types of reports also represent what readers have found most useful over the years. For every report, you should analyze reader, purpose, and situation and plan your document to serve your readers' need for useful information. You will also want to be knowledgeable about the conventional structures writers use for common report types.

This chapter explains the purposes and organizational patterns of six of the most common reports. Depending on reader, purpose, situation, and company custom, these reports may be written as informal memos, letters, or formal documents that include all the elements discussed in Chapter 9.

WRITING A FEASIBILITY STUDY

A *feasibility study* provides information to decision makers about the practicality and potential success of several alternative solutions to a problem.

Purpose

Executives often ask for feasibility studies before they consider a proposal for a project because they want a thorough analysis of the situation and all the alternatives. The writer of a feasibility study identifies all reasonable options and prepares a report that evaluates them according to features important to the situation, such as cost, reliability, time constraints, and company or organization goals. Readers expect a feasibility study to provide the information necessary for them to make an informed choice among alternatives. The alternatives may represent choices among products or actions, such as the choice among four types of heating systems, or a choice between one action and doing nothing, such as the decision to merge with another company or not to merge. When you write a feasibility study, provide a full analysis of every alternative, even if one seems clearly more appropriate than the others.

Organization

Model 11-1 shows a feasibility study written by an executive to the president of the company. The company management has already discussed relocation to a new city and the need for this study. In her report, the writer presents information she has gathered about two possible sites, evaluates them both as to how well they match the company's requirements, and recommends one of them. Feasibility studies usually include four sections.

Introduction

The introduction of a feasibility study provides an overview of the situation. Readers may rely heavily on the introduction to orient them to the situation before they read the detailed analyses of the situation and the possible alternatives. Follow these guidelines:

- Describe the situation or problem.
- Establish the need for decision making.
- Identify those who participated in the study or the outside companies that provided information.
- Identify the alternatives the report will consider, and explain why you selected these alternatives, if you did.
- Explain any previous study of the situation or preliminary testing of alternatives.
- Explain any constraints on the study or on the selection of alternatives, such as time, cost, size, or capacity.
- Define terms or concepts essential to the study.
- Identify the key factors by which you evaluated the alternatives.

In Model 11-1, the writer opens with a short statement that includes the report purpose and her recommendation of which location is best.

Comparison of Alternatives

The comparison section focuses equally on presenting information about the alternatives and analyzing that information in terms of advantages and disadvantages for the company. Organize your comparison by topic or by complete subject. For feasibility reports, readers often prefer to read a comparison by key topics because they regard some topics as more important than others and they can study the details more easily if they do not have to move back and forth between major sections. Whether comparing by topic or by complete subject, discuss the alternatives in the same order under each topic, or discuss the topics in the same order under each alternative. Follow these guidelines:

- Describe the main features of each alternative.

- Rank the key topics for comparison by using either descending or ascending order of importance.

- Discuss the advantages of each alternative in terms of each key topic.

- Point out the significance of any differences among alternatives.

The writer in Model 11-1 compares the two possible sites by topic, using subheadings to help readers find specific types of information. The subheadings represent the established criteria for evaluating the locations.

Conclusions

The conclusions section summarizes the most important advantages and disadvantages of each alternative. If you recommend one alternative, do so in the conclusions section or in a separate section if you have several recommendations. State conclusions first, because they are the basis for any recommendations. If you believe some advantages or disadvantages are not important, explain why. Follow these guidelines:

- Separate conclusions adequately so that readers can digest one at a time.

- Explain the relative importance to the company of specific advantages or disadvantages.

- Include conclusions for each key factor presented in the comparison.

Recommendations

The recommendations section, if separate from the conclusions, focuses entirely on the choice of alternative. Your recommendations should follow logically from your conclusions. Any deviations will confuse readers and cast doubt on the thoroughness of your analysis. Follow these guidelines:

- Describe your recommendations fully.

- Provide enough details about implementing the recommendations so that your reader can visualize how they will be an effective solution to the problem.

- Indicate a possible schedule for implementation.

In Model 11-1, the writer combines her conclusions and recommendation. She reviews the company's decision to relocate, and she next explains that both sites are acceptable. Because Randolph Center involves less cost and will be ready for occupancy ahead of the company's deadline, she recommends that site.

WRITING AN INCIDENT REPORT

An *incident report* provides information about accidents, equipment breakdowns, or any disruptive occurrence.

Purpose

An incident report is an important record of an event because government agencies, insurance companies, and equipment manufacturers may use the report in legal actions if injury or damage has occurred. In addition, managers need such reports to help them determine how to prevent future accidents or disruptions. An incident report thoroughly describes the event, analyzes the probable causes, and recommends actions that will prevent repetition of such events. If you are responsible for an incident report, gather as many facts about the situation as possible and carefully distinguish between fact and speculation.

Organization

Model 11-2, written by a production supervisor at a manufacturing company, is an incident report about an industrial fire. Although the supervisor was not present during the fire, she is responsible for gathering the facts and writing the report.

Most large companies have standard forms for reporting incidents during working hours. If there is no standard form, an incident report should include the following sections.

Description of the Incident

The description of the incident includes all available details about events before, during, and immediately after the incident in chronological order. Since all interested parties will read this section of the report and may use it in legal action, be complete, use nonjudgmental language, and make note of any details that are not available. Follow these guidelines:

- State the exact times and dates of each stage of the incident.
- Describe the incident chronologically.
- Name the parties involved.

- State the exact location of the accident or the equipment that malfunctioned. If several locations are relevant, name each at the appropriate place in the chronological description.

- Identify the equipment, by model number, if possible, involved in a breakdown.

- Identify any continuing conditions resulting from the incident, such as the inability to use a piece of equipment.

- Identify anyone who received medical treatment after an accident.

- Name hospitals, ambulance services, and doctors who attended accident victims.

- Name any witnesses to the incident.

- Report witness statements with direct quotations or by paraphrasing statements and citing the source.

- Explain any follow-up actions taken, such as repairs or changes in scheduling.

- Note any details not yet available, such as the full extent of injuries.

The writer in Model 11-2 provides a chronological description of the events leading to the fire, including date and time. This section also identifies the employees involved and the unit leader who provided most of the details about the accident. The writer notes the estimated costs in damage and production time. For the record, she also notes that there were no injuries.

Causes

This section includes both direct and indirect causes for the incident. Be careful to indicate when you are speculating about causes without absolute proof. Follow these guidelines:

- Identify each separate cause leading to the incident under discussion.

- Analyze separately how each stage in the incident led to the next stage.

- If you are merely speculating about causes, use words such as *appears, probably,* and *seems.*

- Point out the clear relationship between the causes and the effects of the incident.

In analyzing the cause of the fire in Model 11-2, the writer states that she consulted with the unit leader. After assessing the information, she concludes that the two employees working on the same machine did not check to see what the other was doing. Unapproved lighting also was a factor in causing the fire.

Recommendations

This section offers specific suggestions keyed to the causes of the incident. Focus your recommendations on prevention measures rather than on punishing those connected with the incident. Follow these guidelines:

- Include a recommendation for each major cause of the incident.

- List recommendations if there are more than one or two.

- Describe each recommendation fully.

- Relate each recommendation to the specific cause it is designed to prevent.

- Suggest further investigation if warranted.

The supervisor's report in Model 11-2 recommends three actions: (1) Install more appropriate lighting, (2) improve employee communication, and (3) increase supervision when flammable liquids are in use.

WRITING AN INVESTIGATIVE REPORT

An *investigative report* analyzes data and seeks answers to why something happens, how it happens, or what would happen under certain conditions.

Purpose

An investigative report summarizes the relevant data, analyzes the meaning of the data, and assesses the potential impact that the results will have on the company or on specific research questions. The sources of the data for investigative reports can include field studies, surveys, observation, and tests of products, people, opinions, or events both inside and outside the laboratory. Investigations can include a variety of circumstances. An inspector at the site of an airplane crash, a laboratory technician testing blood samples, a chemist comparing paints, a mining engineer checking the effects of various sealants, and a researcher studying the effect of air pollution on children are all conducting investigations, and all will probably write reports on what they find. Remember that readers of an investigative report need to know not only what the data are, but also what the data mean in relation to what has been found earlier and what may occur in the future.

Organization

Model 11-3 is an investigative report based on the results of a survey. In such reports, the writer usually examines a research question or problem, discusses the need to find answers, describes the method of investigation, and then analyzes the results from that investigation. The conclusions often point out what questions remain unanswered and the kinds of future research needed. The report in Model 11-3 is an investigation of the percentage of U.S. homes that have lead-based paint. Results are based on a survey of a random sample of dwellings across the United States. Scientific investigation reports are often published in journals or by research centers and agencies. They generally include an abstract as the report in Model 11-3 does. Most investigative reports include the following sections.

Introduction

The introduction of an investigative report describes the problem or research question that is the focus of the report. Since investigative reports may be used as a form of evidence in future decision making, include a detailed description of the situation and explain why the investigation is needed. Readers will be interested in how the situation affects company operations or how the research will answer questions they have. Follow these guidelines:

- Describe specifically the research question or problem that is the focus of the investigation. Avoid vague generalities, such as "to check on operations" or "to gather employee reactions." State the purpose in terms of specific questions the investigation will answer.

- Provide background information on how long the situation has existed, previous studies of the subject by others or by you, or previous decisions concerning it. If a laboratory test is the focus of the report, provide information about previous tests involving the same subject.

- Explain your reasons if you are duplicating earlier investigations to see if results remain consistent.

- Point out any limits of the investigation in terms of time, cost, facilities, or personnel.

The report in Model 11-3 explains that past research on the incidence of lead-based paint has been inconclusive, and, therefore, a need for an accurate estimate exists. The introduction also discusses the hazard of lead-based paint. In some cases, specific objectives for a research study appear in a separate section, but, in this report, the writer includes a list of objectives in the introduction.

Method

This section should describe in detail how you gathered the information for your investigative report. Include the details your readers will be interested in. For original scientific research, your testing method is a significant factor in achieving meaningful results, and readers will want to know about every step of the research procedure. For field investigations, summarize your method of gathering information, but include enough specific details to show how, where, and under what conditions you collected data. Follow these guidelines where appropriate for your research method:

- Explain how and why you chose the test materials or specific tests.

- Describe any limits in the test materials, such as quantities, textures, types, or sizes, or in test conditions, such as length of time or options.

- List test procedures sequentially so that readers understand how the experiment progressed.

- Identify by category the people interviewed, such as employees, witnesses, and suppliers. If you quote an expert, identify the person by name.

- If appropriate, include demographic information, such as age, sex, race, physical qualities, and so on for the people you used in your study.

- Explain where and when observation took place.

- Identify what you observed, and why.

- Mention any special circumstances and what impact they had on results.

- Explain the questions people were asked or the tests they took. If you write the questions yourself, attach the full questionnaire as an appendix. If you use previously validated tests, cite the source of the tests.

The method section in Model 11-3 (1) identifies the type of housing surveyed for the study, (2) explains the coding system used in the survey, (3) describes how the sample of dwellings was chosen, and (4) explains the interview system used.

Results

This section presents the information gathered during the investigation and interprets the data for readers. Do not rely on the readers to see the same significance in statistics or other information that you do. Explain which facts are most significant for your investigation. Follow these guidelines:

- Group the data into subtopics, covering one aspect at a time.

- Explain in detail the full results from your investigation.

- Cite specific figures, test results, and statistical formulas, or use quotations from interviewees.

- Differentiate between fact and opinion when necessary. Use such words as *appears* and *probably* if the results indicate but do not prove a conclusion.

- If you are reporting statistical results, indicate (1) means or standard deviations, (2) statistical significance, (3) probability, (4) degrees of freedom, and (5) value.

- Point out highlights. Alert readers to important patterns, similarities to or differences from previous research, cause and effect, and expected and unexpected results.

The results section in Model 11-3 provides percentages of homes that have lead-based paint. In an appendix, the writer provides a table with results of the survey, but he also discusses the table in the results section and draws the reader's attention to specific figures. The results section also includes other survey results not shown on the table.

Discussion

This section interprets the results and their implications for readers. Explain how the results may affect company decisions or what changes may be needed because of your investigation. Show how the investigation answered your original research questions about the problem being investigated. If your results do not satisfactorily answer the original questions, clearly state this. Follow these guidelines where appropriate for your type of investigation:

- Explain what the overall results mean in relation to the problem or research question.

- Analyze how specific results answer specific questions or how they do not answer questions.

- Discuss the impact of the results on company plans or on research areas.

- Suggest specific topics for further study if needed.

- Recommend actions based on the results. Detailed recommendations, if included, usually appear in a separate recommendations section.

Conclusion

When a research investigation is highly technical, the conclusion summarizes the problem or research question, the overall results, and what they mean in relation to future decisions or research. Nontechnical readers usually rely on the conclusion for an overview of the study and results. Follow these guidelines:

- Summarize the original problem or research question.

- Summarize the major results.

- Identify the most significant research result or feature uncovered in the investigation.

- Explain the report's implications for future planning or research.

- Point out the need for any action.

In Model 11-3, the conclusion section summarizes the overall results. The writer also discusses the high cost of removing the lead-based paint and the need to evaluate available removal methods. Lastly, the writer calls for increased public awareness of the hazard and a comprehensive plan to deal with the problem.

WRITING A PROGRESS REPORT

A *progress report* (also called a *status report*) informs readers about a project that is not yet completed.

Purpose

The number of progress reports for any project usually is established at the outset, but more might be called for as the project continues. Progress reports are often required in construction or research projects so that decision makers can assess costs and the potential for successful completion by established deadlines. Although a progress report may contain recommendations, its main focus is to provide information, and it records the project events for readers who are not involved in day-to-day operations. The progress reports for a particular project make up a series, so keep your organization consistent from report to report to aid readers who are following one particular aspect of the project.

Organization

Model 11-4 is a progress report written by the on-site engineer in charge of a dam repair project. The report is one in a series of progress reports for management at the engineering company headquarters. The writer addresses the report to one vice president, but copies go to four other managers with varying interests in the project. The writer knows, therefore, that she is actually preparing a report that will be used by at least five readers. Progress reports include the following sections.

Introduction

The introduction reminds readers about progress to date. Explain the scope and purpose of the project, and identify it by specific title if there is one. Follow these guidelines:

- State the precise dates covered by this particular report.
- Define important technical terms for nonexpert readers.
- Identify the major stages of the project, if appropriate.
- Summarize the previous progress achieved (after the first report in the series) so that regular readers can recall the situation and new readers can become acquainted with the project.
- Review any changes in the scope of the project since it began.

The writer in Model 11-4 numbers her report and names the project in her subject line to help readers identify where this report fits in the series. In her introduction, she establishes the dates covered in this report and summarizes the dam repairs she discussed in previous reports. She also indicates that the project is close to schedule, but that the expected costs have risen because another subcontractor had to be hired.

Work Completed

This section describes the work completed since the preceding report and can be organized in two ways: You can organize your discussion by tasks and describe the progress of each chronologically, or you can organize the discussion entirely by chronology and describe events according to a succession of dates and times. Choose the organization that best fits what your readers will find useful, and use subheadings to guide them to specific topics. If your readers are interested primarily in certain segments of the project, task-oriented organization is appropriate. If your readers are interested only in the overall progress of the project, strict chronological organization is probably better. Follow these guidelines:

- Describe the tasks that have been completed in the time covered by the report.
- Give the dates relevant to each task.

- Describe any equipment changes.

- Explain special costs or personnel charges involved in the work completed.

- Explain any problems or delays.

- Explain why changes from the original plans were made.

- Indicate whether the schedule dates were met.

The engineer in Model 11-4 organizes her work-completed section according to the repair stages and then lists them in chronological order. She also includes the date on which each event occurred or each stage was completed.

Work Remaining

The section covering work remaining includes both the next immediate steps and those in the future. Place the most emphasis on the tasks that will be covered in your next progress report. Avoid overly optimistic promises. Follow these guidelines:

- Describe the major tasks that will be covered in the next report.

- State the expected dates of completion for each task.

- Mention briefly those tasks which are further in the future.

The work-remaining section in Model 11-4 describes the upcoming stage of the repair work and states the expected completion date.

Adjustments/Problems

This section covers issues that have changed the original plan or time frame of the project since the last progress report. If the project is proceeding on schedule with no changes, this section is not needed. If it is necessary, follow these guidelines:

- Describe major obstacles that have arisen since the last progress report. (Do not discuss minor daily irritations.)

- Explain needed changes in schedules.

- Explain needed changes in the scope of the project or in specific tasks.

- Explain problems in meeting original cost estimates.

The writer in Model 11-4 includes an adjustments section in her report to explain unexpected costs and a short delay because of the deteriorating condition of the dam area.

Conclusion

The conclusion of a progress report summarizes the status of the project and forecasts future progress. If your readers are not experts in the technical aspects of the project, they may rely heavily on the conclusion to provide them with an overall view of the project. Follow these guidelines:

- Report any progress on current stages.

- Report any lack of progress on current stages.

- Evaluate the overall progress so far.

- Recommend any needed changes in minor areas of scheduling or planning.

- State whether the project is worth continuing and is still expected to yield results.

The engineer's conclusion in Model 11-4 assures her readers that although she is three days behind schedule, she expects no further delays. She also identifies the final stage of the dam repairs and the expected completion date.

WRITING A TRIP REPORT

A *trip report* provides a record of a business trip or visit to the field.

Purpose

A trip report is a useful record both for the person who made the trip and for the decision makers who need information about the subjects discussed during the trip. The trip report records all significant information gathered either from meetings or from direct observation.

Organization

Model 11-5 is a trip report written in the opening-summary organization pattern described in Chapter 10. The writer has visited another company to learn about a training system for a new, complicated software package. The report covers a brief description of the training system and what she learned from the trainers at the other company. Trip reports should contain the following sections.

Introductory Section

Use the subject line of your trip report to identify the date and location of the trip. Begin your report with an opening summary that explains the purpose of the trip and any major agreements or observations you made. Identify all the major events and the people with whom you talked. Follow these guidelines:

- Describe the purpose of the trip.

- Mention special circumstances connected to the trip's purpose.

- If the trip location is not in the subject line, state the dates and locations you visited.

- State the overall results of the trip or any agreements you made.

- Name the important topics covered in the report.

The opening summary in Model 11-5 states the reason for the trip and includes the writer's recommendation that her company adopt the other company's training system.

Information Sections

The information sections of your trip report should highlight specific topics with informative headings. Consider which topics are important to your readers, and group the information accordingly. Follow these guidelines:

- State the names and titles of people you consulted for specific information.

- Indicate places and dates of specific meetings or site visits.

- Describe in detail any agreements made and with whom.

- Explain what you observed and your opinion of it.

- Give specific details about equipment, materials, or systems relevant to company interests.

The writer in Model 11-5 divides her information into two sections—one describing the training system and the other describing her talks with the company trainers.

Conclusions and Recommendations

In your final section, summarize the significant results of your trip, whether positive or negative, and state any recommendations you believe are appropriate. Follow these guidelines:

- Mention the most significant information resulting from the trip.

- State whether the trip was successful or worthwhile.

- Make recommendations based on information gathered during the trip.

- Mention any plans for another trip or further meetings.

In Model 11-5 the writer uses the final section to repeat her recommendation. She also mentions other materials she has from the trip and an offer of help from the trainer at the other company.

WRITING A PROPOSAL

Proposals suggest new ways to respond to specific company or organization situations, or they suggest specific solutions to identified problems. A proposal may be internal (written by an employee to readers within the company) or external (written from one company to another or from an individual to an organization).

Purpose

Proposals vary a great deal, and some, such as a bid for a highway construction job on a printed form designed by the state transportation department, do not look like reports at all. In addition, conventional format varies according to the type of proposal and the situation. Proposals usually are needed in these circumstances:

1. A writer, either inside or outside a company, suggests changes or new directions for company goals or practices in response to shifts in customer needs, company growth or decline, market developments, or needed organizational improvements.

2. A company solicits business through sales proposals that offer goods or services to potential customers. The sales proposal, sometimes called a *contract bid,* identifies specific goods or services the company will provide at set prices within set time frames.

3. Researchers request funds to pay for scientific studies. The research proposal may be internal (if an organization maintains its own research and development division) or external (if the researcher seeks funding from government agencies or private foundations).

Proposal content and organization usually vary depending on the purpose and reader-imposed requirements. External proposals, in particular, often must follow specific formats devised by the reader. This chapter discusses the conventional structure for a proposal that is written to suggest a solution to a company problem—the most common proposal type.

In general, this type of proposal persuades readers that the suggested plan is practical, efficient, and cost-effective and suits company or research goals. Readers are decision makers who will accept or reject the suggested plan. Therefore, a successful proposal must present adequate information for decision making and stress advantages in the plan as they relate to the established company needs. In a high-cost, complicated situation, a proposal usually has many readers, all of whom are involved with some aspect of the situation.

Proposals are either solicited or nonsolicited. If you have not been asked to submit a proposal for a specific problem, you must consider whether the reader is likely to agree with you that a problem exists. You may need to persuade the reader that the company has a problem requiring a solution before presenting your suggested plan.

Organization

Model 11-6 is an unsolicited proposal written by a manager of a city water treatment plant to his superior. The writer identifies a serious safety problem resulting from the current method of installing portable generators during rain storms. His proposal suggests changes that will eliminate the safety hazard. Most proposals that are not restricted by specific format requirements have the following organization.

Problem

The introductory section of a proposal focuses on a description of the central problem. Even if you know that the primary reader is aware of the situation, define and describe the extent of the problem for any secondary readers and for the record, and also explain why change is necessary. If the reader is not aware of the problem, you may need to convince him or her that the situation is serious enough to require changes. The first section of the proposal also briefly describes the recommended solution. Include these elements:

- A description of the problem in detail. Do not, for instance, simply mention "inadequate power." Explain in detail what is inadequate about the generator.

- An explanation of how the situation affects company operations or costs. Be specific.

- An explanation of why the problem requires a solution.

- The background of the situation. If a problem is an old one, point out when it began and mention any previous attempts to solve it.

- Deadlines for solving the problem if time is a crucial factor.

- An indication that the purpose of the proposal is to offer recommendations to solve the problem.

- Your sources of data—surveys, tests, interviews, and so on.

- A brief summary of the major proposed solution, for example, to build a new parking deck. Do not attempt to explain details, but alert the reader to the plan you will describe fully in the following sections.

- The types of information covered in the proposal—methods, costs, timetables, and so on.

The writer in Model 11-6 begins by stating that there is a safety problem in the current method of installing portable generators and then describes the method in detail, pointing out where the hazards occur. He also warns the reader that the department is in violation of the Occupational Safety and Health Administration regulations.

Proposed Solution

This section should explain your suggestions in detail. The reader must be able to understand and visualize your plan. If your proposal includes several distinct actions or changes, discuss each separately for clarity. Follow these guidelines:

- Describe new procedures or changes in systems sequentially, according to the way they would work if implemented.

- Explain any methods or special techniques that will be used in the suggested plan.

- Identify employees who will be involved in the proposal, either in implementing it or in working with new systems or new equipment.

- Describe changes in equipment by citing specific manufacturers, models, and options.

- Mention research that supports your suggestions.

- Identify other companies that have already used this plan or a similar one successfully.

- Explain the plan details under specific subheadings relating to schedules, new equipment or personnel, costs, and evaluation methods in an order appropriate to your proposal.

The writer in Model 11-6 proposes four new installations—all designed to simplify the current method of installing portable generators. He uses subheadings to direct the reader to specific information about the schedule, costs, and coordination of the project.

Needed Equipment/Personnel

Identify any necessary equipment purchases or new personnel required by your proposal. Follow these guidelines:

- Indicate specific pieces of equipment needed by model numbers and brand names.

- Identify new employee positions that will have to be filled. Describe the qualifications people will need in these positions.

- Describe how employee duties will change under the proposed plan and how these shifts will affect current and future employees.

Schedules

This section is especially important if your proposal depends on meeting certain deadlines. In addition, time may be an important element, if, for instance, your company must solve this problem in order to proceed with another scheduled project. Follow these guidelines if they are appropriate to your topic:

- Explain how the proposed plan will be phased in over time or on what date your plan should begin.

- Mention company deadlines for dealing with the problem or outside deadlines, such as those set by the IRS.

- Indicate when all the stages of the project will be completed.

The proposed changes in Model 11-6 will require the department to call for bids by contractors, obtain city permits, and review the design. Because of these requirements, the writer describes the necessary schedule in detail. For the reader's convenience, the writer separates the process into four stages.

Budget

The budget section of a proposal is highly important to a decision maker. If your plan is costly relative to the expected company benefits, the reader will need to see compelling reasons to accept your proposal despite its high cost. Provide as realistic and complete a budget projection as possible. Follow these guidelines:

- Break down costs by category, such as personnel, equipment, and travel.
- Provide a total cost.
- Mention indirect costs, such as training or overhead.
- Project costs for a typical cycle or time period, if appropriate.

In Model 11-6, the writer attaches a table to supplement the cost section. Because government units operate under budgets established by legislative bodies, the writer also explains how to cover the costs of this proposal under current budget allocations.

Evaluation System

You may want to suggest ways to measure progress toward the objectives stated in your proposal and for checking the results of individual parts of the plan. Evaluation methods can include progress reports, outside consultants, testing, statistical analyses, or feedback from employees. Follow these guidelines:

- Describe suggested evaluation systems, such as spot checks, surveys, or tests.
- Provide a timetable for evaluating the plan, including both periodic and final evaluations.
- Suggest who should analyze the progress of the plan.
- Assign responsibility for writing progress reports.

The writer in Model 11-6 offers to accept the responsibility of directing this project. As part of that responsibility, he will train employees in the new system, write monthly progress reports, obtain necessary permits, and monitor compliance with building regulations.

Expected Benefits

Sometimes writers highlight the expected benefits of a proposal in a separate section for emphasis. If you have such a section, mention both immediate and long-range benefits. Follow these guidelines:

- Describe one advantage at a time for emphasis.
- Show how each aspect of the problem will be solved by your proposal.
- Illustrate how the recommended solution will produce advantages for the company.
- Cite specific savings in costs or time.

Because this proposal involves a safety hazard, the writer in Model 11-6 uses the benefits section to emphasize how the proposed changes will solve the problem and bring the plant into compliance with existing safety regulations.

Summary/Conclusions

The final section of your proposal is one of the most important because readers tend to rely on the final section in most reports and, in a proposal, this section gives you a chance to emphasize the suitability of your plan as a solution to the company problem. Follow these guidelines:

- Summarize the seriousness of the problem.

- Restate your recommendations without the procedural details.

- Remind the reader of the important expected benefits.

- Mention any necessary deadlines.

The writer in Model 11-6 uses his conclusion to emphasize the safety hazard and stress the need for changes. He closes by urging prompt action and asks for authorization to begin arranging for the changes.

CHAPTER SUMMARY

This chapter discusses the conventional content and structure for the six types of reports most commonly written on the job. Remember:

- A feasibility study analyzes the alternatives available in a given situation.

- An incident report records information about accidents or other disruptive events.

- An investigative report explains how a particular question or problem was studied and the results of that study.

- A progress report provides information about an ongoing project.

- A trip report provides a record of events that occurred during a visit to another location.

- A proposal suggests solutions to a particular problem.

SUPPLEMENTAL READINGS IN PART 2

Benson, P. J. "Writing Visually: Design Considerations in Technical Publications," *Technical Communication*, p. 451.

Buehler, M. F. "Defining Terms in Technical Editing: The Levels of Edit as a Model," *Technical Communication,* p. 486.

"Six Graphics Guidelines," *Simply Stated,* p. 562.

Tarutz, J. H. "Editing for an International Audience," *Technical Editing,* p. 572.

White, J. V. "Color: The Newest Tool for Technical Communicators," *Technical Communication,* p. 576.

This feasibility study provides information to top executives who must select a site for the company headquarters in a new city. The report evaluates two available sites for their suitability for company operations and recommends one of them.

Discussion

1. The president of the company is the primary reader of this report, but other executives get copies. Officers of the company have already discussed moving to a new city, and the president is expecting this report. Review the "Introduction" section. What kinds of information would the writer have had to include if readers had never considered the possibility of moving the company to a new city?

2. Discuss the headings used in this report. How useful are they to a reader seeking specific information? What changes or additions might help the reader locate specific facts?

3. Discuss the overall organization in this report. How effective is it to discuss the Randolph Center ahead of the Lincoln Industrial Park in every section under the heading "Alternative Locations"?

4. Discuss how effectively the writer presents a case for choosing Randolph Center as the new location. Are there any points you would emphasize more than the writer does? What other kinds of information might support the writer's recommendation of Randolph Center?

To: Samuel P. Irving
           President

From: Isobel S. Archer
           Vice President—Administration

Date: April 16, 1996

Subject: Feasibility Study of Sites for Kansas City Offices

Introduction

This report assesses two available locations in greater Kansas City as possible sites for the new corporate offices of Sandrunne Enterprises. After reviewing the background, company needs, and features of the two available sites, my recommendation is to buy a building and lot in the Randolph Center.

Background

Sandrunne Enterprises has been considering moving the corporate headquarters to Kansas City from Springfield for about two years. Due to streamlining operations and expanding services, the current building in Springfield no longer fits the Company needs. Further, location in Kansas City will enhance our transportation connections and improve our ability to meet schedules. As you know, the Board of Directors has set strict parameters regarding the potential location for Sandrunne. The building/land must be large enough to accommodate our current requirements with enough room for reasonable expansion over the next five years, but overall acreage should not exceed two acres. The building/land must be in excellent condition, located in the greater Kansas City area in Missouri, and readily accessible to transportation carriers. Project cost should not exceed $600,000, and relocation should be completed by February 1997, when our current lease expires.

Possible Alternatives

I have surveyed the available building and land combinations with the assistance of Martin Realty Company, and the two locations that seem most appropriate are Randolph Center, a complex in North Kansas City, and Lincoln Industrial Park, also in North Kansas City. The two alternatives were chosen based on space suitability, condition of the

S. P. Irving   -2-   April 16, 1996

building/land, transportation accessibility, cost, and availability within
our time frame. Information for this study was obtained through
meetings with William Martin, president of Martin Realty, Tracey
Manchester, Director of Kansas City Regional Development Board, and
John Blackthorn, Real Estate Administrator for the Department of
Planning and Urban Development of Kansas City. I made two trips to
each site, accompanied by Rafael Mendez, from our transportation
planning division.

Alternative Locations

Space Suitability

The Randolph Center building is on 1.2 acres of land and fits the basic
corporate office/warehouse specifications required by the Board of
Directors. Although the acreage is less than two acres, the office
building, warehouse facility, and truck docks fit our exact requirements.
Only minor modifications to the office building and the warehouse would
be needed at Randolph Center. The warehouse space is actually 2,000
square feet over our current requirement and, therefore, allows for
future expansion.

The Lincoln Industrial Park site is 2.4 acres. Most industrial parks are
already plotted with specified acreage per plot, and the 2.4 plot available
was one of the smaller locations close to our two-acre ideal.

Condition of Building/Land

The Randolph Center location contains a brick building built in 1985 and
in excellent condition with well-landscaped grounds. We would need
inspections before purchase, but the current condition of the building
seems in good repair. The offices have oak paneling, new carpeting,
skylights in the reception area, windows and crown molding in every
office, six-panel doors, and tiled bathrooms. Overall, the offices have a
professional appearance in keeping with Sandrunne's image. The
warehouse is equally well-built with cement blocks throughout, and the
layout, including the two dock areas, would fit Sandrunne's activities
nicely.

The Lincoln Industrial Park location is newer (1990), and we would
have to landscape the area as well as build offices. The land is flat and

S. P. Irving   -3-   April 16, 1996

dry, making construction fairly straightforward. Paved roads to the site are complete, and other existing buildings are of high quality. Sandrunne would have to break ground for construction, but, of course, we could design the building exactly the way we want it.

Location and Transportation Accessibility

Since all of Sandrunne product is transported by truck, we must have access to a highway system and a layout and docking area in which the truckers can maneuver relatively easily. Both locations are within the general area we had chosen as appropriate. Both have adequate trucking access, and employees could reach either one via a four-lane highway system. Rafael Mendez assured me that the truckers would be pleased with the docking areas in Randolph Center. The basic docking areas at Lincoln Industrial Park are excellent too, and our new building could be constructed with the warehouse and docking facilities suitable for our operation.

Cost

Only minor modifications are needed at the Randolph Center location. At the Lincoln Industrial Park location, construction and landscaping will be required. Total estimated cost for the two locations is as follows:

Randolph Center

Office Modifications	$ 14,000
Warehouse Modifications	55,600
Total Improvements	$ 69,600
Purchase Price	$400,000
Total Randolph Center Cost	$469,600

Lincoln Industrial Park

Office Construction	$200,000
Warehouse Construction	400,000
Land Purchase	60,000
Total Lincoln Costs	$660,000

Note: Cost estimates are from Gramm, Weismann, and McCall, Associates, construction consultants

S. P. Irving   -4-   April 16, 1996

The Lincoln Industrial Park location would be $60,000 over the established limit. Both location costs are estimated, and construction overruns could add considerably to the total cost for the Lincoln location. Costs could also be higher at the Randolph Center, but the risk is less.

Feasible Relocation Date

According to the realtors, the Randolph Center building is currently used for storage by the owners and could be vacated quickly upon closing. The closing time would be about 60 days, and an additional 60 days would be needed for modifications and cleaning. Sandrunne could probably move into the Randolph Center offices by September 1, 1996, well ahead of our February 1997 deadline.

The Lincoln Industrial Park location has more variables. The timetable must include design plans, site preparation, general contractor bids, license permits, and landscaping; therefore, completion is harder to predict. John Blackthorn estimates that Sandrunne could move in by January 1, 1997, but the risk of not making that deadline is somewhat high.

Conclusion and Recommendations

Sandrunne Enterprises has reached the point of moving to Kansas City to solidify its corporate position and expand its operation further. Both the alternative sites I investigated in North Kansas City have long-range advantages and meet the Company criteria. However, Lincoln Industrial Park involves a greater risk that both cost and deadline limits will be exceeded. Considering our need to move without hindrance, I recommend Randolph Center as our best choice. The location is excellent, the project cost is under budget, and the deadline can be met easily.

I have reports from our consultants that I would like to discuss further with you. My secretary will make an appointment for a discussion time.

IA:sd
c: M.L. Wilding
   M.P. Todd
   E.T. Fishman
   R.D. Micelli
   J.J. Warner

This incident report, written by a supervisor in a manufacturing company, describes an accident resulting in a fire, property damage, and lost production. The writer includes information she got by consulting the unit leader who was present during the incident. In the description section, the writer gives a chronological account of events leading to the fire and concludes by stating the extent of the damage.

Discussion

1. Consider the "Recommendations" section of this report and assume that you want to write a memo to employees, establishing a communication system for employees who are working on the same machine. In groups, develop an appropriate communication system and write the memo announcing it.

2. Consider accidents or mishaps you may have experienced or seen at work or on campus. Draft an incident report based on that experience and compare your drafts with others in your class. If your instructor prefers, write a final incident report as if you were the supervisor or campus director investigating the accident.

To: David McGrath

From: Heather Weston   *HW*

Date: July 22, 1996

Re: Accident Report—Flash Fire in Machining Unit

Description of the Incident

On July 20, 1996, at 11:00 a.m., Joe Kelly began clearing a plugged oil coolant supply line at a Gearomatic machine. At 11:05 a.m., maintenance pipefitter Matt Arnold turned on the machine oil pump. The resulting pressure freed the plugged line and sent oil spraying upwards. The oil hit the light bulb overhead, causing the light to shatter and ignite the oil. According to Nico Alvarez, unit leader, the fire spread to the next machine at once. Fire brigade action by employees got the blaze under control, and 21 of the 24 sprinklers opened. The fire department was not called. There were no injuries. Damage was extensive, estimated at $19,000. Production loss was 24 hours because two machines were down, resulting in failure to produce 4800 gear blanks. Overtime will have to be scheduled on two shifts.

Causes

After consulting with Mr. Alvarez, I have determined two major causes for the fire. First, there was a lack of communication between the two workers who were both engaged on the same machine. Second, the light bulbs in use were not approved as fire- and explosion-resistant.

Recommendations

To prevent similar accidents in the Machining Unit, I recommend the following:

1. Install fire- and explosion-proof lighting on all automatic screw machines and throughout the unit.

2. Establish a standard communication system between workers on the same machine.

3. Supervise repair work involving flammable liquid.

This investigative report, adapted from a book-length report to Congress, gives the results of a survey to estimate the number of housing units with lead-based paint in the United States.

In research reports published in scientific journals or issued by research and government agencies, the abstract often appears on the first page between the title and the introduction, as shown here. A table showing partial results appears at the end of the report in an appendix.

Discussion

1. Discuss the "Method" section. How helpful is it for a reader who wants to know how the survey was conducted but does not intend to duplicate the survey? If the reader wants to duplicate the survey, what kinds of information about the method should be added?

2. Discuss the "Introduction." If a reader knows nothing about the lead-based paint hazard, how does the introduction help prepare the reader to understand the study?

3. Notice that the "Results" section contains some of the data available in the table at the end of the report. Discuss why the writer would repeat information from the table in the "Results" section.

4. The "Conclusion" section repeats the major results. As this information also appears in the "Results" section and in the appendix, why would a writer include it in the "Conclusion" section?

5. The investigative report format is designed for readers who are researchers particularly interested in the method of investigation. Such readers prefer to know results before conclusions. Discuss what format general readers probably prefer. In groups and using the information in this report, write a bulletin for general readers to alert them to the hazard of lead-based paint in homes.

SURVEY OF LEAD-BASED PAINT
IN U.S. HOUSING

Abstract

This report focuses on a 1989–90 survey conducted to estimate the number of housing units in the United States that contain lead-based paint. The survey centered on private single and multifamily dwelling units and public housing. In-person visits and interviews with a systematic random sample of houses were conducted. Overall results indicate that 74 percent of all homes built before 1980 have some lead-based paint, and 71 percent of the homes with lead-based paint have children under age seven in them. The survey also indicates that there is no difference in the incidence of lead-based paint based on income, home value, or rent. Methods for removing lead-based paint should be evaluated, and public awareness of the hazard should be increased.

Introduction

Medical research during the past decade has found that childhood lead poisoning is more widespread and has more serious consequences than previously thought. Published research has found strong connections between prenatal lead exposure and deficiencies in infant development. Such consequences indicate lead-based paint in houses poses a serious health hazard. Yet, the cost of removing lead-based paint is very high, and the removal process may increase the hazard by creating lead dust.

The 1987 amendments to the Lead-Based Paint Poisoning Prevention Act call for an estimate of the extent of lead-based paint hazard in the United States. Because there are no accurate estimates of the number of U.S. houses with lead-based paint, the Department of Housing and Urban Development sponsored the first national survey of lead-based paint in housing to provide estimates. The survey was conducted in 1989–90, and the objective was to obtain data for estimating the following:

- The number of housing units (private, single family, private multifamily, and public housing) with lead-based paint, by year of construction.

- The extent or surface area of lead-based paint in housing, to develop an estimate of national abatement costs.

-2-

- The condition of the paint.

- The incidence of lead in dust and in soil around the residential structure.

- The characteristics of housing with varying levels of potential hazard, to examine possible priorities for abatement.

Method

The study focused on housing constructed in the United States before 1980 and centered on private housing because data on public housing was too small to generalize. Newer houses were presumed to be lead-free because, in 1978, the Consumer Product Safety Commission banned the sale of lead-based paint to consumers and the use of such paint in residences. Housing excluded from the study included housing exclusively for the elderly, group quarters such as nursing homes and dormitories, homes in Alaska and Hawaii, and military housing.

Private housing was grouped into (1) private single family houses, defined as one to four dwelling units, and (2) private multifamily houses, defined as five or more dwelling units. Dates of houses were coded as (1) built before 1940, (2) built between 1940 and 1959, and (3) built between 1960 and 1979.

The objectives of the study required in-person visits to the dwelling units. A sample of 30 counties in the United States was selected, and within these counties, five geographic areas were chosen by random systematic selection. Samples of individual dwelling units were selected also by systematic random sampling. A field interviewer visited each unit and talked with an adult occupant to collect basic information. Inspection visits then were scheduled with residents who were willing to complete a full interview. Each resident who cooperated was paid a $50 incentive. Total sample size was 284 dwelling units. Because of disproportionate sampling of housing types, sampling weights were applied to each completed case, and initial weights were adjusted to balance differences in nonresponse and noncoverage.

Results

Table 1 (see Appendix) shows the results of coding homes for lead-based paint. An estimated 74 percent of all homes built before 1980

-3-

contain lead-based paint, and 71 percent of the homes with lead-based paint are occupied by children under age seven. Older homes are more likely to have lead-based paint than newer homes. An estimated 90 percent of homes built before 1940 have lead-based paint in the interior or on the exterior, while 62 percent of homes built between 1960 and 1970 have lead-based paint in the interior or on the exterior. The age of the home was the only distinguishing feature.

Based on the interviews, there are no significant differences in the incidence of lead-based paint relative to the income of the household, the value of the home, or the rent. There is also no significant difference between single family homes and multifamily homes. Lead-based paint is found in the South (58%) less often than in other regions because the South was significantly less urban than other regions until the 1970s, and its housing, on the average, was built more recently.

The survey also provides information about the location of lead-based paint in the home. While most public policy discussions have been concerned with lead-based paint on interior walls and in dust inside the dwelling unit, the survey shows that lead-based paint is more common on the outside of dwelling units. An estimated 23 percent of homes have lead-based paint only on the exterior; 14 percent have it only on the interior; 37 percent have it on both the interior and exterior.

Conclusions

This national survey tends to confirm earlier research about the incidence of lead-based paint: (1) housing built before 1940 is most likely to have lead-based paint; (2) about 74 percent of all housing built before 1980 has some lead-based paint; (3) about 71 percent of the housing with lead-based paint is occupied by children under age seven; (4) lead-based paint appears to contribute to lead in dust. This survey also provides new information about the problem of lead-based paint: (1) lead-based paint occurs as often in the homes of the wealthy as of the poor; (2) lead-based paint is more commonly found on the exterior than the interior; (3) lead dust is found more frequently around the windows than on the floors, and the dust comes from both the interior and the exterior.

The cost of lead-based paint abatement in American homes is potentially very large (from $2100 to $8900 per home, depending on the method), and the long-range effectiveness of any abatement method is

-4-

uncertain. The traditional abatement methods focus on peeling paint or interior paint to a height of five feet, and these methods contain a risk from the lead dust remaining after cleanup. Evaluation of possible alternative ways to clean up lead dust should be undertaken immediately. Except in cases of actual lead poisoning, little is being done to reduce the hazard in homes, even among the wealthy. Public awareness must increase. However, industry lacks the capacity to perform testing and abatement work. The nation requires a comprehensive plan to address the hazards of lead-based paint.

-5-

APPENDIX

Table 1
Estimated Number of Privately Owned
Housing Units with Lead-Based Paint

Characteristic	Housing w/Lead-Based Paint	No. of Units
Year:		
1960–1979	62%	120
1940–1959	80%	87
Before 1940	90%	77
Housing Type:		
Single Family	74%	227
Multifamily	73%	57
Children Under Age 7	71%	90
Region:		
Northeast	93%	53
Midwest	76%	69
South	58%	116
West	80%	46
Value of Owner-Occupied Home:		
Less than $40,000	79%	39
$40,000–$79,000	53%	46
$80,000–$149,000	65%	45
Over $150,000	87%	42
Rent:		
Less than $400	69%	59
Over $400	87%	40
Household Income:		
Less than $30,000	76%	156
Over $30,000	72%	107

This progress report, written by an on-site engineer, is one of a series of reports on a specific company project—dam repairs. The report will be added to the others in the series and kept in a three-ring binder at the company headquarters for future reference when the company has another contract for a similar job.

The writer addresses the report to a company vice president, but four other readers are listed as receiving copies.

Discussion

1. The writer knows that her readers are familiar with the technical terms she uses. If this report were needed by a nontechnical reader at the company, which terms would the writer have to define?

2. Discuss the information in the introduction and how effectively it supports the writer's assertion that work on the dam is progressing satisfactorily.

3. Discuss how the writer's organization and use of format devices support her report of satisfactory progress. Why did she list items under "Work Completed" but not under "Work Remaining"?

TO: Mark Zerelli   October 16,1996
           Vice President
           Balmer Company

FROM: Tracey Atkins   *TA*
           Project Manager

SUBJECT: Progress Report #3—Rockmont Canyon Dam

Introduction

This report covers the progress on the Rockmont Canyon Dam repairs
from September 15 to October 15 as reported previously. Repairs to the
damaged right and left spillways have been close to the original
schedule. Balmer engineers prepared hydraulic analyses and design
studies to size and locate the aeration slots. These slots allowed Balmer
to relax tolerances normally required for concrete surfaces subjected to
high-velocity flows. Phillips, Inc., the general contractor, demolished and
removed the damaged structures. To expedite repairs, construction
crews worked on both spillways simultaneously. Construction time was
further reduced by hiring another demolition company, Rigby, Inc. The
project costs rose during the first month when Phillips, Inc., had to build
batching facilities for the concrete because the dam site had no facilities.

Work Completed

Since the last progress report, three stages of work have been
completed:

1. On September 18, aggregate for the concrete mix was hauled
230 miles from Wadsworth, Oregon. The formwork for the tunnel linings
arrived from San Antonio, Texas, on September 20.

2. Phillips developed hoist-controlled work platforms and man-cars
to lower workers, equipment, and materials down the spillways.
Platforms and man-cars were completed on September 22.

3. Phillips drove two 20-foot-diameter modified-horseshoe-shaped
tunnels through the sandstone canyon walls to repair horizontal
portions of the tunnel spillways. A roadheader continuous-mining
machine with a rotary diamond-studded bit excavated the tunnels in
three weeks, half the time standard drill and blast techniques would
have taken. The tunnels were completed on October 15.

Mark Zerelli   -2-   October 16, 1996

Work Remaining

The next stage of the project is to control flowing water from gate leakage. Phillips will caulk the radial gates first. If that is not successful in controlling the flow, Phillips will try French drains and ditches. After tunnels are complete, both spillways will be checked for vibration tolerance, and the aeration slot design will be compared with Balmer's hydraulic model. Full completion of repairs is expected by November 15.

Adjustments

Some adjustments have been made since the last progress report. During construction work on both spillways, over 50 people and 200 pieces of equipment were on the site. Heavily traveled surfaces had to be covered with plywood sheets topped with a blanket of gravel. This procedure added $3500 to the construction costs and delayed work for half a day.

Conclusion

The current work is progressing as expected. The overall project has fallen three days behind estimated timetables, but no further delays should occur. The final stage of the project will require measurements at several areas within both spillways to be sure they can handle future flood increases with a peak inflow of at least 125,000 cfs. Balmer expects to make the final checks by November 25.

TA:ss
c: Robert Barr
   Mitchell Lawrence
   Mark Bailey
   Joseph Novak

This trip report describes a visit to another company to observe an in-house training system for new computer software. The writer addresses the vice president she reports to and recommends they adopt the training system.

Discussion

1. The writer of this report includes two information sections—one describing the training system and the other describing what the trainers at the other company told her about an alternative system. Discuss the headings for these sections. Why would the writer decide to emphasize her meeting with trainers in the heading rather than emphasize the alternative system? Her opening identifies Mr. Golden as the Bretton training coordinator. What is her purpose for identifying two more trainers later in the report?

2. Discuss how effective the opening summary is for the reader who needs to make a decision about training employees on the new software.

3. Discuss whether the report could—or should—be longer with additional information included. What kinds of information might be added?

To: Timothy O'Banyon, Vice President   Date: May 6, 1995
From: Melissa Thacker, Training Director
Re: Trip to Bretton Technology, Houston, Texas, May 1–2

Summary

To prepare for our conversion to the MIRA-32 integrated software package, I spent two days at Bretton Technology, observing the training system Bretton is using during its conversion to the software. Richard Golden, the training coordinator, met me and explained the training system, why it was chosen, and why it has proven effective. Based on my observation and the information from Mr. Golden, I recommend that we adopt the Bretton training system for our employees during our conversion to MIRA-32.

User Training

The Bretton system requires a minimum of 40 days of user practice in the company training room, using actual company records and dummy data files. Thus, employees learn the system while working with familiar files. Full implementation of the 15 modules in the MIRA-32 takes about 18 months, and training should begin on each module one week before it is implemented. This schedule allows employees to move smoothly from the dummy files to the real ones as the modules enter the system.

Meeting with Bretton Trainers

In addition to Mr. Golden, I met with Sara Wyman and Tyrone Parms, both experienced software trainers. Mr. Parms said Bretton had begun a "train the trainer" system for MIRA-32 with the idea of having the trainers monitor employees as they used the software on the job. However, immediate problems developed in coordinating training sessions with the vendor schedule for implementing the system. In addition, employees did not have time to practice on the software, and this training system did not create employee confidence about handling the MIRA-32. All three trainers at Bretton recommend the 40-day training schedule with hands-on practice.

Conclusion and Recommendation

I believe we should duplicate the training system used at Bretton Technology. Bretton's organization is similar to ours, and we can learn from the experience there. I have copies of the Bretton training outlines, and Mr. Golden has offered to consult with us via videoconference when we set up our training room and schedule.

This unsolicited proposal was written to identify a hazardous situation at a city water treatment plant. The writer describes the problem in detail and suggests a specific set of changes to eliminate the hazard to employees. In this case, the suggested changes are relatively uncomplicated, but the process of change contains specific stages. The writer describes those stages in detail.

Discussion

1. The reader of this proposal has not asked for it and may not be aware of any problem. Discuss how effectively the writer makes a case that a serious problem exists and needs to be solved.

2. The writer includes a timetable for the changes and a table of costs. Discuss whether these should have been placed in an appendix.

3. Discuss how effectively the writer presents the expected benefits.

4. Assume that the reader must pass on this report to other city administrators who are not familiar with the water treatment plant. In groups, write an abstract for this report that will help these readers understand the proposal easily.

TO: Richard T. Sutton

FROM: Michael J. Novachek, Water Department Manager

SUBJECT: STANDBY POWER IMPROVEMENTS AT WATER
           TREATMENT PLANT

DATE: November 16, 1996

Over the last five years, the city water treatment plant (WTP) has used two generators to operate high service pumps during electrical power failures. I believe that one of these generators creates an unsafe condition, which can be eliminated rather easily with a few minor improvements. This proposal recommends a solution and provides budget and time schedule figures.

Problem

The WTP uses four high-service pumps, which provide treated water to our customers. Three of the pumps have a rated capacity of 2 million gallons per day (MGD). The fourth pump has a rated capacity of 3 MGD. The average and peak daily demands at the WTP are 5 MGD and 7 MGD, respectively. Therefore, we typically run a combination of the pumps to meet our demand.

When an electrical failure occurs, we develop an unsafe situation for our electricians. The plant was originally designed and constructed to provide standby power only to the largest pump. The standby power came from the diesel-powered generator located alongside, and directly tied to, the 3 MGD pump. Therefore, when a power failure occurs, the power supply to the 3 MGD pump can be switched from the standard supply to the generator. Under normal conditions, the plant is required to operate a 2 MGD pump along with the 3 MGD pump to meet customer demand. During power failures, we temporarily connect a portable standby power generator to one of the 2 MGD pumps. This temporary generator installation creates an unsafe condition.

The portable standby generator is stored on a trailer at Pump Station No. 11. During power failures, two electricians transport the portable generator to the WTP. The portable generator is parked outside, next to the doors of the pump room. The electricians run power cables from the generator to the Motor Control Center (MCC) of the pump, which is located in the pump room. Since power failures usually result from a severe storm, the electricians often make the generator connections while standing in the rain. The doors to the pump room remain open to provide an opening for the power cables to run from the generator, along the pump room floor, to the MCC. This setup exposes plant personnel to a live power cable and wet floor conditions and is in violation of Occupational Safety and Health Administration (OSHA) regulations. These conditions could create an enormous liability to the City if they result in an accident to an electrician or plant operator.

Proposed Solution

To eliminate hazardous conditions connected with installing the portable generators, I recommend the following:

- install a male adapter plug to the portable standby generator

- install a female wall outlet at the exterior south wall of the pump room

- install an awning at the exterior south wall of the pump room

- install permanent wire and conduit from the outlet to the MCC of the pumps

During a power failure, plant personnel can transport the portable standby power generator to a covered area located at the south exterior wall of the pump room. Personnel can connect standby power to the pump by inserting the generator plug into the permanent outlet. The awning covers the generator and wall outlet and keeps this area relatively dry. The pump room doors could be kept closed. No live electrical connections are required. Finally, no power cables are strewn along the floor.

Schedule

In order to incorporate the recommended improvements, the project will require four phases.

The design phase will require the services of a consultant engineer. I have discussed the project with engineers at Raymond and Burnside

R. T. Sutton   -3-   November 16, 1996

Associates, the company that designed the plant 15 years ago. The
engineers assured me that the project is feasible and can be completed
within the budgetary and time constraints set herein. The consultant will
be responsible for the preparation of plans, specifications, and bid
documents, as well as permits required by the Environmental Protection
Agency. I recommend that Raymond and Burnside Associates handle the
design services for this project since we have an existing agreement and
they are familiar with the plant.

The bid phase will require the services of a consultant, as well as the
City law director, to review the bids and recommend a contractor.

The construction phase will require an electrical contractor to perform
the work. I recommend we use Raymond and Burnside Associates to
verify that the work is being performed in accordance with the design
plans and specifications.

The implementation phase comes after the improvements are completed.
Once the system is in place, the two electricians on standby duty will be
replaced by one on-duty plant maintenance worker.

I suggest the following schedule for the installation of the improvements:

Item	Completion Date
Service director approval to proceed	December 1, 1996
Procure agreement with engineer	December 14, 1996
Complete plans, specifications, and bid documents	January 3, 1997
City review of plans, specifications, and bid documents	January 17, 1997
Submit permits and plans to Ohio EPA	February 1, 1997
Ohio EPA review	April 1, 1997
Advertisement for bid	April 14, 1997
Bid opening	May 1, 1997
Award bid	June 1, 1997
Start construction	July 1, 1997
Complete construction	August 1, 1997

R. T. Sutton   -4-   November 16, 1996

Cost

The estimated project cost to install a new standby power system
improvement is $27,615. This cost includes engineering, construction,
and contingencies as shown in Table 1.

Table 1
Probable 1997 Project Cost

Engineering

Design	$ 8,000
Services During Construction	4,000
Total Engineering Cost	$12,000

Construction

Awning	$ 2,500
Electrical Adapter	500
Electrical Outlet	500
Wire and Conduit	7,000
MCC Switches	3,800
Total Construction Cost	$14,300
Total Project Cost	$26,300
With 5% Contingency	$27,615

The engineering fee includes design, preparation of plans, specifications
and bid documents, review of bid, and services during construction.
Construction costs include all labor and materials required to construct
the improvements. A contingency fee of 5 percent of the total
engineering and construction costs is included to cover costs not
foreseen at this time.

The expected 1997 annual operation costs with these improvements is
$400. Without the improvements, cost is $2500. This higher cost comes
from the additional employees required to provide the service necessary
to achieve the standby power.

R. T. Sutton   -5-   November 16, 1996

The project probably can be funded out of the water fund. We had $20,000 left from last year's budget. A line item of $7,000 could be allotted from this year's budget. The combination of funds will cover the total cost.

Coordination

The improvements will require the coordination and cooperation of City forces to construct and operate the system. As Manager of the Water Department, I will take full responsibility for the following:

1. Instruct the employees regarding the new operation procedures once the improvements are installed.

2. Provide monthly progress reports to the Mayor, and the Directors of Service, Law, and Finance.

3. Ensure that proper Ohio EPA and building permits are obtained.

4. Ensure that all City regulations involving capital improvements are followed.

5. Obtain proper approvals from the City Planning Commission and City Council.

Benefits

The main benefit of the proposed improvement is safety. As City leaders, we are responsible for the safety of our employees. The existing condition is unsafe and violates OSHA regulations. Also, the current permanent standby power system does not meet today's design standards. After improvements we will be in full compliance with all safety regulations. The expected initial cost is reasonable given the seriousness of the situation, and the proposed improvements will lower personnel costs in the future.

Conclusion

Currently, the City water treatment plant operates its standby power system in an unsafe manner, thereby risking the health and safety of plant electricians and operators. With the installations proposed, these unsafe conditions can be eliminated. In addition, these improvements will bring our operation up to current design standards.

R. T. Sutton   -6-   November 16, 1996

As manager of the WTP, I believe the proposed improvements are
urgently needed and request your authorization to proceed with the
project. If you would like to study the report from Raymond and
Burnside Associates, please call me at Ext. 7230, and I will send it to
your office.

MN:sd
Attachment

Chapter 11   Exercises

1. You have been hired as a management consultant to Mike Novello, who is starting a photo equipment store called Novello's Photography and Video Supply Center. Mr. Novello has been a successful free-lance photographer for 16 years and is well known in the community. He has obtained a small business loan and plans to open a store that offers a full range of equipment as well as a film-development section. Novello has leased space in Fairview Mall, a mall that attracts high-income shoppers, which Novello believes are his target customers. He has hired two full-time clerks and two-part time clerks. Initially, the film-developing business will be sent out to a large studio, but he hopes to set up an in-house development unit within a year. A part-time accountant will handle the payroll, tax reports, and invoicing, and will bill by the hour. Novello knows he needs a computer system, and he wants to start with a system that will handle any expansions or changes within the first 2 years. He asks you to prepare a feasibility study assessing two computer systems (hardware and software) for his new store. Prepare a formal feasibility study for Mr. Novello.

2. Assume you are the nursing director at Elmdale General Hospital. Yesterday an accident occurred on the hospital's seventh floor when Nurse Barbara Spencer slipped on a spilled liquid and fell. Nurse Spencer suffered a dislocated shoulder and a torn uniform. When you investigate the accident, you talk to people on the seventh floor. Dr. Mark Walton saw the accident and tells you that Nurse Spencer was "running to answer the telephone." Two patients also saw the accident. The patient in the wheelchair tried to help Nurse Spencer, but he knocked over his IV unit in the process and another spill resulted. The accident happened in front of the elevators at 11:00 a.m. when visiting hours were beginning. Gwen Palman, another nurse on duty, did not see the accident because she was assisting a doctor in room 706. The volunteer candy-stripper assigned to assist at the desk did not see the accident because she had gone to the lounge to straighten up before the visitors began coming. Dr. Walton recalls that just before the accident, he saw an orderly, Rich Gergen, pushing a cart filled with bottles of various solutions. Possibly something spilled from the cart. Dr. Monica Rodgers in Emergency treated Nurse Spencer's shoulder and sent her home for two days. An off-duty nurse, Nick Spanos, was called in to finish Nurse Spencer's shift. The next day's shifts were also reorganized. Write an incident report for this situation and address it to Ms. Sharon Ryder, Operations Director. Add any specific details you wish, but do not change the original incident.

3. This assignment requires a visual inspection of one public room on your campus. You select the room. Observation or inspection requires that you examine the area under *existing* conditions. Make no attempt to control or manipulate the situation. The purpose of your study is to investigate conditions in one room *after 10 a.m. or after the public has been using it for at least 2 hours.* Record what you see, smell, hear, and so on. You must interview at least one person, either someone using the room or someone responsible for maintenance, and include that person's comments in your report. You should inspect the following: light fixtures, doors/entrances, windows, walls/floors, and special features of the room, such as sinks, desks, blinds, and so on. Make notes on needed repair or replacement. *Also* observe how many people are using the room during your inspection and record any need for more supplies, more furniture, etc. You *will not* make any specific recommendations in this report, but you can conclude that the room needs attention in some ways. Address your report to Tom Ortega, director of physical facilities. Assume that you are a member of a team of students who have been hired to inspect campus facilities from the student perspective. If your instructor wants you to write a formal report, follow the guidelines in Chapter 9.

4. Based on the investigative report you wrote for Exercise 3, write a short informal proposal for one specific improvement in the room you observed. Address your proposal to Tom Ortega, director of physical facilities.

5. Assume that you are a member of the student government at your school and are writing a proposal on behalf of the officers. You want to establish a permanent student committee to investigate student inquiries or complaints about the *campus physical facilities* and to make recommendations for changes. You will have to consider such questions as the following: How will the committee members be selected? How big will the committee be? Will supplies or office space be needed? What are the costs involved? How will the committee process student complaints? Other questions must also be covered in your proposal. Remember, a proposal is a persuasive report. Convince the reader that this idea will be beneficial to your school. Address your report to the campus director of student services.

6. Study a problem at the company where you work. The problem should be a situation that requires a change in procedures or new equipment. Investigate at least two alternative solutions to this problem. Then write a feasibility study in which you evaluate all the solutions and recommend one of them. Address the report to the appropriate person at your company, and assume that that person asked you to write the report. If your instructor wants you to prepare a formal report, use the guidelines in Chapter 9.

7. Write a progress report for a project you are doing in a science or technology class. Report your progress as of the midpoint of your project. Address the report to the instructor of the science or technology class and say that you will submit another progress report when the project is nearly finished.

8. Write a proposal for a change at your job to your supervisor or the appropriate person. The change you propose may include equipment purchases, reorganizing work duties, a new system, new parking arrangements, and so on. If you do not have a current job, you may use a previous job or propose a change on campus, such as increased food services or reorganization in the bookstore.

Address the director of student services. Assume that your supervisor or the director of student services did not ask you for this proposal, so you need to make a persuasive case that a problem exists and needs to be solved. Include at least one graphic aid with your proposal. If your instructor wants you to write a formal proposal, use the guidelines in Chapter 9.

9. Prepare an investigative report on a subject that is a major concern in your community, on campus, or in your company. Consider a fairly complex problem that requires you to gather facts from printed sources and interview at least two people for opinions or information. Subjects for this report might be (a) rising crime rates on campus or in the community, (b) the need for day care on campus or in the community, (c) the need for computers, video equipment, or specific machinery in your company, (d) the need to restore an old building with historical significance in your community or on campus, (e) the need for a change in technology at your company, (f) inadequate recreation facilities for teenagers in your community, or (g) any currently important issue. In your investigative report, identify possible solutions to the problem. *Then* study two alternative solutions to the problem, write a feasibility study in which you identify the various factors that are important in each alternative, and recommend one of the alternatives. *Then* write a proposal for the option you have chosen as a solution to the original problem. You may assume that these reports have been solicited and address them to the appropriate person, such as the college provost, city mayor, or president of your company. These three reports should all be formal reports with appropriate front and back matter, as explained in Chapter 9. Your instructor will probably want you to submit the reports one at a time, so keep a copy of each for reference as you work on the next report.

CHAPTER 12

Letters and Memos

UNDERSTANDING LETTERS AND MEMOS

Correspondence includes both letters and memos. Although these frequently are addressed to one person, they often have multiple readers because the original reader passes along the correspondence to other parties or the writer sends copies to everyone involved. Letters and memos are versatile written documents and serve many purposes.

Letters

Letters are written primarily to people outside an organization and cover a variety of situations, such as (1) requests, (2) claims, (3) adjustments, (4) orders, (5) sales, (6) credit, (7) collections, (8) goodwill messages, (9) announcements, (10) records of agreements, (11) follow-ups to telephone conversations, (12) transmittals of other technical documents, and (13) job applications.

Memos

Memos are written primarily to people inside an organization. With the exception of job applications, memos cover the same topics as letters. In addition, many internal reports, such as trip reports, progress reports, and short proposals, may be in memo form.

Give the same careful attention to readers, purpose, and situation for letters and memos that you do in writing all technical documents. Because of its person-to-person style, however, correspondence may create emotional responses in readers that other technical documents do not. A reader may react positively to a set of new procedures in a company manual, but a memo from a superior announcing these same procedures may strike the reader as demanding and dictatorial. When you write letters and memos, consider tone and organizational strategy from the perspective of how your readers will respond emotionally as well as practically to the message.

E-Mail

E-mail (electronic mail) allows transmission of letters, memos, and other documents from one computer to another through a series of computer networks. Millions of people now use e-mail daily because of the speedy transmission and the convenience, especially for short messages between people who have an established subject or who are communicating about routine matters. E-mail has many clear advantages, such as the following:

- Managers can reach dozen of employees quickly.

- Team members working on projects can communicate easily on small points without meeting.

- People can avoid playing "telephone tag," which is frustrating and time-consuming.

- People can communicate over long distances without regard to time zone differences.

- Companies can save postage and paper costs.

E-mail, however, must be used with caution. Because e-mail does not pass through human hands and receivers use a password to access their e-mail, senders often assume it is private. E-mail is not private.

By pressing one button, a receiver can send your message to thousands of people. The consequences can be serious. Only hours after Air Force pilot Scott O'Grady, shot down in Bosnia, was rescued by other U.S. pilots, one of the pilots sent a long detailed message about the rescue to a few friends. The message included pilot code names, weapons loads, radio frequencies, and other classified information. Within minutes of reading the message, the pilot's friends forwarded it to other friends, who also passed it on. Finally the message was posted on bulletin boards available to millions of people. The classified information was now in the hands of anyone interested in U.S. military operations.[1]

There are other dangers in casual use of e-mail. Companies and individuals can be liable for messages sent on e-mail. Lawsuits for sexual harassment, age discrimination, product liability, and other matters have resulted from e-mail messages.[2] A receiver or a hacker can alter a message and send it under your name. Many people do not realize that employers have the right to monitor e-mail that is sent on a system paid for by the employer. Some computer systems save all e-mail even if the receiver deletes it, and computer experts can find files that were "deleted" months before. People have been fired as a result of information they have revealed in e-mail messages. Consider carefully the way you use e-mail, and do not send messages that could embarrass you, get you fired, cost you money, or send you to jail.

DEVELOPING EFFECTIVE TONE

Tone refers to the feelings created by the words in a message. Business letters and memos should have a tone that sounds natural and conveys cooperation, mutual respect, sincerity, and courtesy. Tone of this kind establishes open communication and reflects favorably on both the writer and the company. Because words on paper cannot be softened with a smile or a gesture, take special care in word choice to avoid sounding harsh or accusing. Remarks that were intended to be objective may strike your reader as overly strong commands or tactless insinuations, especially if the subject is at all controversial. Remember the following principles for creating a pleasant and cooperative tone in your letters and memos.

Natural Language

Write letters and memos in clear, natural language, and avoid falling into the habit of using old-fashioned phrases that sound artificial. A reader who has to struggle through a letter filled with out-of-date expressions probably will become annoyed with both you and your message, resulting in poor communication. This sentence is full of out-of-date language:

> Per yours of the tenth, please find enclosed the warranty.

No one really talks this way, and no one should write this way. Here is a revision in more natural language:

> I am enclosing the warranty you requested in your letter of March 10.

Keep your language simple and to the point. This list shows some stale business expressions that should be replaced by simpler, more natural phrases:

Old-Fashioned	*Natural*
Attached hereto . . .	Attached is . . .
We beg to advise . . .	We can say that . . .
Hoping for the favor of a reply . . .	I hope to hear from you . . .
As per your request . . .	As you requested . . .
It has come to my attention . . .	I understand that . . .
Prior to receipt of . . .	Before we received . . .
Pursuant to . . .	In regard to . . .
The undersigned will . . .	I will . . .

If you use such out-of-date expressions, your readers may believe you are as out of date in your information as you are in your language.

Positive Language

Keep the emphasis in your letters and memos on positive rather than negative images. Avoid writing letters or memos when you are angry, and never let anger creep into your writing. In addition, avoid using words that emphasize the negative aspects of a situation; emphasize the positive whenever you can, or at least choose neutral language. Shown below are sentences that contain words that emphasize a negative rather than a positive or neutral viewpoint. The revisions show how to eliminate the negative words.

Negative: When I received your complaint, I checked our records.

Positive: When I received your letter, I checked our records.

Negative: To avoid further misunderstanding and confusion, our sales representative will visit your office and try to straighten out your order.

Positive: To ensure that your order is handled properly, our sales representative will visit your office.

Negative: I am sending a replacement for the faulty coil.

Positive: I am sending a new coil that is guaranteed for one year.

Negative: The delay in your shipment because we lost your order should not be longer than four days.

Positive: Your complete order should reach you by September 20.

In these examples, a simple substitution of positive-sounding words for negative-sounding words improves the overall tone of each sentence, whereas the information in each sentence and its purpose remain the same.

No matter what your opinion of your reader, do not use language that implies that the reader is dishonest or stupid. Notice how the following revisions eliminate the accusing and insulting tone of the original sentences.

Insulting: Because you failed to connect the cable, the picture was blurred.

Neutral: The picture was blurred because the V-2 cable was not connected to the terminal.

Insulting: You claimed that the engine stalled.

Neutral: Your letter said that the engine stalled.

Insulting: Don't let carelessness cause accidents in the testing laboratory.

Neutral: Please be careful when handling explosive compounds.

Negative language, either about a situation or about your reader, will interfere with the cooperation you need from your reader. The emphasis in correspondence should be on solutions rather than on negative events.

You-Attitude

The *you-attitude* refers to the point of view a writer takes when looking at a situation as the reader would. In all correspondence, try to convey an appreciation of your reader's position. To do this, present information from the standpoint of how it will affect or interest your reader. In these sample sentences, the emphasis is shifted from the writer's point of view to the reader's by focusing on the benefits to the reader in the situation:

Writer emphasis:	We are shipping your order on Friday.
Reader emphasis:	You will receive your order by Monday, October 10.
Writer emphasis:	To reduce our costs, we are changing the billing system.
Reader emphasis:	To provide you with clear records, we are changing our billing system.
Writer emphasis:	I was pleased to hear that the project was completed.
Reader emphasis:	Congratulations on successfully completing the project!

By stressing your reader's point of view and the benefits to your reader in a situation, you can create a friendly, helpful tone in correspondence. Of course, readers will see through excessive praise or insincere compliments, but they will respond favorably to genuine concern about their opinions and needs. Here are guidelines for establishing the you-attitude in your correspondence:

1. Put yourself in your reader's place, and look at the situation from his or her point of view.

2. Emphasize your reader's actions or benefits in a situation.

3. Present information as pleasantly as possible.

4. Offer a helpful suggestion or appreciative comment when possible.

5. Choose words that do not insult or accuse your reader.

6. Choose words that are clear and natural, and avoid old-fashioned or legal-sounding phrases.

Tone is often a serious problem in e-mail messages. Because so much e-mail consists of short messages, senders often do not realize how abrupt or harsh they may sound. Check your messages carefully for appropriate tone and word choice before pushing the "send" button.

ORGANIZING LETTERS AND MEMOS

Most letters and memos are best organized in either a *direct* or an *indirect pattern,* depending on how the reader is likely to react emotionally to the message. If the news is good, or if the reader does not have an emotional stake in the subject, use the direct pattern with the main idea in the opening. If, however, the news is bad, the indirect pattern with the main idea after the explanation is often most effective because a reader may not read the explanation of the situation if the bad news appears in the opening. Most business correspondence uses the direct pattern. The indirect pattern, however, is an important strategy whenever a writer has to announce bad news in a sensitive situation and wants to retain as much goodwill from the reader as possible. A third letter pattern is the *persuasive pattern,* which also places the main idea in the middle portion or even the closing of a message. Writers use this pattern for sales messages and when the reader needs to be convinced about the importance of a situation before taking action.

Memos present a special writing challenge in that very often they have mixed purposes. A memo announcing the installation of new telephone equipment is a message to inform, but if the memo also contains instructions for using the equipment, the purpose is both to announce and to direct. Moreover, a memo can be either good or bad news, and if the memo is addressed to a group of employees, it can contain *both* good and bad news, depending on each individual's reaction to the topic. A memo announcing a plant relocation can be good news because of the expanded production area and more modern facility; however, it also can be bad news because employees will have to uproot their lives and move to the new location. You will have to judge each situation carefully to determine the most effective approach and pattern to use.

Direct Organization

Model 12-1 shows a letter that conveys good news and is written in the direct pattern. In this situation, a customer has complained about excessive wear on the tile installed in a hospital lobby. Because the tile was guaranteed by the company that sold and installed it, the customer wants the tile replaced. The company will stand behind its guarantee, so the direct pattern is appropriate in this letter because the message to the customer is good news. The direct pattern generally has three sections:

1. The opening establishes the reason for writing the letter and presents the main idea.

2. The middle paragraphs explain all relevant details about the situation.

3. The closing reminds the reader of deadlines, calls for an action, or looks to future interaction between the reader and the writer.

In Model 12-1, the opening contains the main point, that is, the good news that the company will grant the customer's request for new tile. The middle paragraph reaffirms the guarantee, describes the tile, and explains why the replacement tile should be satisfactory. In the closing, the manager tells the customer to expect a call from the sales representative and also thanks the

PRESCOTT TILE COMPANY
444 N. Main Street
Ottumwa, Iowa 52555–2773

April 13, 1996

Ms. Sonia Smithfield
General Manager
City Hospital
62 Prairie Road
Fort Madison, IA 52666–1356

Dear Ms. Smithfield:

We will be more than happy to replace the Durafinish tile in front of the elevators and in the lobby area of City Hospital as you requested in your letter of April 6.

When we installed the tile—model 672—in August 1994, we guaranteed the nonfade finish. The tile you selected is imported from Paloma Ceramic Products in Italy and is one of our bestselling tiles. Recently, the manufacturer added a special sealing compound to the tile, making it more durable. This extrahard finish should withstand even the busy traffic in a hospital lobby.

Our sales representative, Mary Atwood, will call on you in the next few days to inspect the tile and make arrangements for replacement at no cost to you. I appreciate your calling this situation to my attention because I always want to know how our products are performing. We guarantee our customers' satisfaction.

Sincerely yours,

Michael Allen

Michael Allen
Product Installation Manager

MA:tk

c: Mary Atwood

MODEL 12-1   A Sample Letter Using Direct Organization (in Semiblock Style)

customer for her information about the previous tile order. The writer uses a pleasant, cooperative tone and avoids repeating any negative words that may have appeared in the customer's original request; therefore, the letter establishes goodwill and helps maintain friendly relations with the reader.

Indirect Organization

The basic situation in the letter in Model 12-2 is the same as in Model 12-1 but in this case the letter is a refusal because the guarantee does not apply. Therefore, indirect organization is used.

The indirect pattern generally contains these elements:

1. The opening is a "buffer" paragraph that establishes a friendly, positive tone and introduces the general topic in a way that will later support the refusal or negative information and help the reader understand it. Use these strategies when appropriate:

   • Agree with the reader in some way:

     You are right when you say that. . . .

   • State appreciation for past efforts or business:

     Thank you for all your help in the recent. . . .

   • State good news if there is any:

     The photographs you asked for were shipped this morning under separate cover.

   • Assure the reader the situation has been considered carefully:

     When I received your letter, I immediately checked. . . .

   • Express a sincere compliment:

     Your work at the Curative Workshop for the Handicapped has been outstanding.

   • Indicate understanding of the reader's position:

     We understand your concern about the Barnet paint shipment.

   • Anticipate a pleasant future:

     The prospects for your new business venture in Center City look excellent.

   Do not use negative words in the buffer or remind your reader about the unpleasantness of the situation. Buffers should establish a pleasant tone and a spirit of cooperation, but do not give the reader the impression that the request will be granted or that the main point of the message is good news.

PRESCOTT TILE COMPANY
444 N. Main Street
Ottumwa, Iowa 52555–2773

April 13, 1996

Ms. Sonia Smithfield
General Manager
City Hospital
62 Prairie Road
Fort Madison, IA 52666–1356

Dear Ms. Smithfield:

You are certainly correct that we guarantee our tile for 20 years after installation. We always stand behind our products when they are used according to the manufacturer's recommendations and the recommendations of our design consultant.

When I received your letter, I immediately got out your sales contract and checked the reports of the design consultant. Our records indicate that the consultant did explain on March 6, 1994, that the Paloma tile—model 672—was not recommended for heavy traffic. Although another tile was suggested, you preferred to order the Paloma tile, and you signed a waiver of guarantee. For your information, I'm enclosing a copy of that page of the contract. Because our recommendation was to use another tile, our usual 20-year guarantee is not in force in this situation.

For your needs, we do recommend the Watermark tile, which is specially sealed to withstand heavy traffic. The Watermark tile is available in a design that would complement the Paloma tile already in place. Our design consultant, Trisha Lyndon, would be happy to visit City Hospital and recommend a floor pattern that could incorporate new Watermark tile without sacrificing the Paloma tile that does not show wear. Enclosed is a brochure showing the Watermark designs. Ms. Lyndon will call you for an appointment this week, and because you are a past customer, we will be happy to schedule rush service for you.

Sincerely,

Michael Allen
Product Installation Manager

MA/dc
Encs.: Watermark brochure
        contract page
cc: Ms. Trisha Lyndon

MODEL 12-2   A Sample Letter Using Indirect Organization (in Full Block Style)

2. The middle section carefully explains the background of the situation, reminding the reader of all the details that are important to the main point.

3. The bad news follows immediately after the explanation and in the same paragraph. Do not emphasize bad news by placing it in a separate paragraph.

4. The closing maintains a pleasant tone and, if appropriate, may suggest alternatives for the reader, resell the value of the product or service, or indicate that the situation can be reconsidered in the future.

The emphasis in an indirect pattern for bad news should be to assure the reader that the negative answer results from careful consideration of the issue and from facts that cannot be altered by the writer. As the writer of a bad news letter, you do not want to sound arbitrary and unreasonable.

In Model 12-2, the opening "buffer" paragraph does confirm the guarantee but mentions restrictions. In the next section the manager carefully explains the original order and reminds the customer that she did not follow the company's recommendation—thus the guarantee is not in effect. The manager encloses a copy of the waiver that the customer signed. The refusal sentence comes as a natural result of the events that the manager has already described. The final section represents a movement away from the bad news and suggests a possible solution—ordering different tile. The manager also suggests how some of the original tile can be saved. The final sentences look to the future by promising a call from the design consultant and noting the enclosure of a brochure that illustrates the suggested new tile. In this letter the manager does not use such phrases as "I deeply regret" or "We are sorry for the inconvenience" because these expressions may imply some fault on the company's part, where there is none. Instead, the manager emphasizes the facts and maintains a pleasant tone through his suggestion for a replacement tile and his offer to find a way to save some of the old tile.

Because you cannot give readers good news if there is none, use the indirect pattern of organization to help your readers understand the reasons behind bad news, and emphasize goodwill by suggesting possible alternatives.

Persuasive Organization

Model 12-3 shows a letter written in the persuasive pattern of sales messages. This letter was sent to company trainers who conduct seminars for employees on a variety of topics. The trainers are urged to give up traditional chalkboards and purchase porcelain marker boards for their training sessions.

SPEAKERS' SUPPLIES, INC.
1642 Ludlow Road
Portland, Oregon 97207-6123

Dear Trainer:

Would you like to eliminate irritating chalk dust and messy, hard-to-read chalkboards from your training sessions?

Let us introduce you to Magna Dry-Erase Boards. These heavy-duty, high quality marker boards use special dry-erase color markers that glide smoothly over the porcelain-on-steel boards. One wipe of the special eraser, and you have a spotless surface on which to write again. If you prefer to use washable crayons or water soluble markers, you can erase easily with a damp cloth. In addition, these versatile boards accommodate magnets, so you can easily display visuals, such as maps or charts, without extra equipment cluttering up your presentation area.

The Magna Dry-Erase Boards are suitable for a variety of training situations. Notice these special features:

- sizes from 2 ft × 3 ft to 4 ft × 12 ft
- beige, white, or silver-gray surface
- frames of natural oak or satin-anodized aluminum
- full-length tray to hold markers and eraser
- markers (red, blue, green, black) and eraser included
- hanging hardware included
- special board cleaner included

The enclosed brochure shows the beauty and usefulness of these durable boards—guaranteed for 20 years! Please call 1-800-555-3131 today and talk to one of our sales consultants, who will answer your questions and arrange for a local dealer to contact you. Or call one of the dealers in your area listed on the enclosed directory and ask about Magna Dry-Erase Boards. Get rid of that chalk dust forever!

Sincerely,

Nicole Fontaine

Nicole Fontaine
Sales Manager

NF:bp

P.S. Place an order for two 4 ft × 12 ft boards and get one any other size at half price.

MODEL 12-3   A Sample Letter Using Persuasion (in Semiblock Style)

The persuasive pattern generally includes these elements:

1. The opening in a persuasive letter catches the reader's attention through one of these strategies:

    - A startling or interesting fact:

        Every night, over 2000 children in our city go to bed hungry.

    - A solution to a problem:

        At last, a health insurance plan that fits your needs!

    - A story:

        Our company was founded 100 years ago when Mrs. Clementine Smith began baking. . . .

    - An intriguing question:

        Would you like to enjoy a ski weekend at a fabulous resort for only a few dollars?

    - A special product feature:

        Our whirlpool bath has a unique power jet system.

    - A sample:

        The sandpaper you are holding is our latest. . . .

2. The middle paragraphs of a persuasive letter build the reader's interest by describing the product, service, or situation. Use these strategies when appropriate:

    - Describe the physical details of the product or service to impress the reader with its usefulness and quality.

    - Explain why the reader needs this product or service both from a practical standpoint and from an enjoyment standpoint.

    - Explain why the situation is important to the reader.

    - Describe the benefits to the reader that will result from this product or service or from handling the situation or problem.

3. After arousing the reader's interest or concern, request action, such as purchasing the product, using the service, or responding favorably to the persuasive request.

4. The closing reminds the reader of the special benefits to be gained from responding as requested and urges action immediately or by a relevant deadline.

In Model 12-3, the first paragraph asks a question that probably will elicit a yes answer from the reader. The next paragraph describes the marker boards, pointing out how convenient and versatile they are. The list of special features highlights items that will appeal to the reader. The closing refers to the enclosed brochure and urges the reader to call a toll-free number and discuss a purchase. The final sentence returns to the topic in the first sentence and promises a solution to the chalk dust problems. Notice that a persuasive sales letter may differ from other letters in these ways:

- It may not be dated. Companies often use the same sales letters for several months, so the date of an individual sales letter is not significant.

- It may be a form letter without a personal salutation. The sales letter for marker boards is addressed to "Dear Trainer," identifying the job of the reader.

- It may include a P.S. In most letters, using a P.S. implies that the writer neglected to organize the information before writing. In persuasive sales letters, however, the P.S. is often used to urge the reader to immediate action or to offer a new incentive for action. The P.S. in the sales letter in Model 12-3 offers a special price on a third marker board if the reader buys two of the largest size.

- It may not include prices if other enclosed materials explain the costs. Sometimes the product cost is one of its exciting features and appears in the opening or in the product description. Usually, however, price is not a particularly strong selling feature. For example, the sales letter in Model 12-3 does not mention prices because they are listed in the enclosed brochure, and the writer wants the reader to see the color photographs before learning the cost. Most sales letters, such as those for industrial products, magazine subscriptions, or mail-order items, include supplemental materials that list the prices.

Persuasive memos rarely follow this persuasive sales pattern completely, but they often do begin with an opening designed to arouse reader interest, such as

With a little extra effort from all of us, South Atlantic Realty
will have the biggest sales quarter in the history of the company.

WRITING MEMOS AS A MANAGER

A mutually cooperative communication atmosphere is just as important between managers and employees as it is between employees and people outside a company. The tone and managerial attitude in a manager's memos often have a major impact on employee morale. Messages with a harsh, demanding tone that do little more than give orders and disregard the reader's emotional response will produce an atmosphere of distrust and hostility within a company. For this reason, as a manager, you need to remember these principles when writing memos:

1. *Provide adequate information.* Do not assume that everyone in your company has the same knowledge about a subject. Explain procedures fully, and be very specific about details.

2. *Explain the causes of problems or reasons for changes.* Readers want more than a bare-bones announcement. They want to know *why* something is happening, so be sure to include enough explanation to make the situation clear.

3. *Be clear.* Use natural language, and avoid loading a memo with jargon. Often employees in different divisions of the same company do not understand the same jargon. If your memo is going beyond your unit, be sure to fully identify people, equipment, products, and locations.

4. *Be pleasant.* Avoid blunt commands or implications of employee incompetence. A pleasant tone will go a long way toward creating a cooperative environment on the job.

5. *Motivate rather than order.* When writing to subordinates, remember to explain how a change in procedure will benefit them in their work, or discuss how an event will affect department goals. Employees are more likely to cooperate if they understand the expected benefits and implications of a situation.

6. *Ask for feedback.* Be sure to ask the reader for suggestions or responses to your memo. No one person has all the answers; other employees can often make valuable suggestions.

Here is a short memo sent by a supervisor in a testing laboratory. The memo violates nearly every principle of effective communication.

> Every Friday afternoon there will be a department cleanup beginning this Friday. <u>All</u> employees must participate. This means cleaning your own area and then cleaning the complete department. Thank you for your cooperation.

The tone of this memo indicates that the supervisor distrusts the employees, and the underlying implication is that the employees may try to get out of doing this new task. The final sentence seems to be an attempt to create a good working relationship, but the overall tone is already so negative that most employees will not respond positively. The final sentence is also a cliché closing because so many writers put it at the end of letters and memos whether it is appropriate or not. Although the memo's purpose is to inform readers about a new policy, the supervisor does not explain the reason for the policy and does not provide adequate instructions. Employees will not know exactly what to do on Friday afternoon. Finally, the memo does not ask for feedback, implying that the employees' opinions are not important. Here is a revision:

> As many of you know, we have had some minor accidents recently because the laboratory equipment was left out on the benches overnight and chemicals were not stored in sealed containers. Preventing such accidents is important to all of us, and, therefore, a few minutes every Friday afternoon will be set aside for cleanup and storage.
>
> Beginning on Friday, October 14, and every Friday thereafter, we'll take time at 4:00 p.m. to clean equipment, store chemicals, and straighten up the work areas. If we all pitch in and help each other, the department should be in good order within a half hour. Please let me know if you have any ideas about what needs special attention or how to handle the cleanup.

This memo, in the direct organizational pattern, explains the reason for the new policy, outlines specifically what the cleanup will include, mentions safety as a reader benefit, and concludes by asking for suggestions. The overall tone emphasizes mutual cooperation. This memo is more likely to get a positive response from employees than the first version is. Since a manager's success is closely linked to employee morale and cooperation, it is important to take the time to write memos that will promote a cooperative, tension-free environment.

SELECTING LETTER FORMAT

The two most common letter formats are illustrated in Model 12-1, the semi-block style, and Model 12-2, the full block style. In the *full block style,* every line—date, address, salutation, text, close, signature block, and notations—begins at the left margin. In the *semiblock style,* however, the date, close, and signature block start just to the right of the center of the page. Business letters have several conventions in format that most companies follow.

Date Line

Since most company stationery includes an address, or letterhead, the date line consists only of the date of the letter. Place the date two lines below the company letterhead. If company letterhead is not used, put your address directly above the date:

```
1612 W. Fairway Street
Dayton, OH 45444–2443
May 12, 1996
```

Spell out words such as *street, avenue,* and *boulevard* in addresses.

Inside Address

Place the reader's full name, title, company, and address two to eight lines below the date and flush with the left margin. Spell out the city name, but use the Postal Service two-letter abbreviations for states. Put one space between the state and the ZIP code. The number of lines between the date and the inside address varies so that the letter can be attractively centered on the page.

Salutation

The salutation, or greeting, appears two lines below the inside address and flush with the left margin. In business letters, the salutation is always followed by a colon. Address men as Mr. and women as Ms., unless a woman specifically indicates that she prefers Miss or Mrs. Professional titles, such as Dr., Judge, or Colonel, may be used as well. Here are some strategies to use if you are unsure exactly who your reader is.

Use Titles

When writing to a group or to a particular company position, use descriptive titles in the salutations:

```
Dear Members of Com-Action:

Dear Project Director:

Dear Customer:

Dear Contributor:
```

Use Attention Lines

When writing to a company department, use an attention line with no salutation. Begin the letter two lines below the attention line:

```
Standard Electric Corporation
Plaza Tower
Oshkosh, WI 54911–2855
```

Attention: Marketing Department

According to our records for 1996. . . .

Use an attention line also if the reader has not been identified as a man or a woman:

Standard Electric Corporation
Plaza Tower
Oshkosh, WI 54911–2855

Attention: J. Hunter

According to our records for 1996. . . .

Model 12-4 shows a letter that uses an attention line. The company is sending this form letter to all its suppliers; therefore, the attention line identifies the department or type of department that should respond to this inquiry.

Omit Salutations

When writing to a company without directing the letter to a particular person or position, omit the salutation and begin the letter three lines below the inside address:

Standard Electric Corporation
Plaza Tower
Oshkosh, WI 54911–2855

According to our records for 1996. . . .

General salutations, such as "Dear Sir" or "Gentlemen," are not used much anymore because they might imply an old-fashioned, sexist attitude.

Use Subject Lines

Some writers prefer to use subject lines in letters to identify the main topic immediately. A subject line may also include specific identification, such as an invoice number, date of previous correspondence, or a shipping code. The subject line may appear in several different places, depending on the preference of the writer or on company style. First, the subject line may appear in

YORK FOOD PRODUCTS, INC.
Harper Plaza
Windsor, Pennsylvania 15802-2600

January 23, 1996

Cabell Salt Company
400 Eastern Boulevard
Lexington, Kentucky 40503-1906

Attention: Product Control

As you know, the State of California has adopted the "Safe Drinking Water and Toxic Enforcement Act of 1986" also referred to as Proposition 65. The California Health and Welfare Agency, which administers Proposition 65, maintains a list of the chemical substances the State of California has declared cause cancer, birth defects, or other reproductive harm (see attached). The presence of any of these chemicals requires a warning on the label of the product.

Since the attached list is a revision, dated January 10, 1996, we are writing to ask if any of the chemicals listed are present in any products you supply to our company. If any are present, please (1) identify the specific chemical, (2) state its concentration level, and (3) state its form in the product. We are relying on your reports to us to determine whether warning labels are required on our products. Therefore, please respond within thirty days of the date of this letter.

When the Proposition 65 list is modified, we would also appreciate continuing information on whether any of the listed chemicals are present in any products supplied to our company.

Sincerely,

Ryan H. Grant

Ryan H. Grant
Vice President-Purchasing

RG/sd

Enc.

MODEL 12-4   A Sample Letter Using an Attention Line

the upper right-hand corner, spaced between the date line and the inside address:

September 24, 1996

Subject: Policy #66432–A6

Ms. Victoria Hudson
Marketing Analyst
Mutual Insurance Company
12 Main Street
Watertown, IL 60018–1658

Second, the subject line may appear flush with the left margin, two lines below the salutation and two lines above the first line of the letter:

Dear Ms. Valdez:

Subject: International Expo 1998

As you know, when the first contracts were. . . .

Third, some writers center the subject line between the salutation and the first line of the letter:

Dear Ms. Valdez:

Subject: International Expo 1998

As you know, when the first contracts were. . . .

The subject line may be underlined or typed in all capitals to help the reader see it quickly and to distinguish it from the first paragraph of the letter. Wherever you place a subject line, keep it brief, and use key terms or specific codes to help the reader easily identify the topic of the letter.

Body

The body of a letter is single-spaced, and double-spaced between paragraphs. The paragraphs may be indented five spaces, as shown in Model 12-3, or flush with the left margin, as shown in Models 12-1, 12-2, and 12-4. If the letter is very short, it can be double-spaced with the paragraphs indented five spaces. In this case, the semiblock style is more likely to look balanced on the page. Although word processors can justify (end the lines evenly) the right margins, most people are used to seeing correspondence with an uneven right margin. Justified margins imply a mass printing and mailing, while unjustified margins imply an individual message to a specific person.

Close

The close appears two lines below the last sentence of the body and consists of a standard expression of goodwill. In semiblock style, the close appears just to the right of the center of the page (see Model 12-1). In full block style, the close is at the left margin (see Model 12-2). The most common closing expressions are "Very truly yours," "Sincerely," and "Sincerely yours." As shown in Model 12-1, the first word of the close is capitalized, but the second word is not. The close is always followed by a comma.

Signature Block

The signature block begins four lines below the close and consists of the writer's name with any title directly underneath. The signature appears in the four-line space between the close and the signature block.

Notations

Notations begin two lines below the signature block and flush with the left margin. In Model 12-1, the capital initials "MA" represent the writer, and the lowercase initials "tk" represent the typist. A colon or slash always appears between the two sets of initials.

If materials are enclosed with the letter, indicate this with either the abbreviation *Enc.* or the word *Enclosure.* Some writers show only the number of enclosures as "Encs. (3)"; others list the items separately, as shown in Model 12-2.

If other people receive copies of the letter, be sure to indicate this. The notation *cc* means carbon copy, and although companies use photocopies now, *cc* is still the most popular way to indicate copies. Some companies now, however, use *c* alone or *copy* to signal the reader that other people received copies of this correspondence (see Models 12-1 and 12-2). For copy notations, use full names alone (see Model 12-1) or include courtesy titles (see Model 12-2). List people receiving copies according to company rank, the highest first. If space permits, type the copy notation two lines below any other notations, as shown in Model 12-1. If the letter is long, the copy notation should follow other notations without the extra line, as in Model 12-2.

Second Page

If your letter has a second page, type the name of the addressee, page number, and date across the top of the page:

Ms. Sonia Smithfield   2   April 13, 1996

This heading also may be typed in the upper left-hand corner:

Ms. Sonia Smithfield
page 2
April 13, 1996

Envelope

Post-office scanning equipment can process envelopes most rapidly when the address is typed (1) with a straight left margin, (2) in all capitals, (3) without punctuation, (4) with an extra space between all words or number groups:

DR RONALD BROWNING
1234 N SPRINGDALE LANE
AKRON OH 44313-1906

This format is not appropriate for the inside address of the letter.

SELECTING MEMO FORMAT

Many companies have printed memo forms so that all internal messages have a consistent format. If there is no printed form, the memo format shown in Model 12-9 is often used.

The subject line should be brief but clearly indicate a specific topic. Use key words so that readers can recognize the subject quickly and so that the memo can be filed easily. Capitalize the major words. The subject line in an e-mail message is especially critical because the entire message often does not appear on the computer screen. A reader can quickly glance over a full printed page and check for key words, but a full typed page on e-mail requires the reader to scroll through multiple screens. Often readers are reluctant to do that. Choose your key words for the subject line carefully.

Memos do not have a close, so you may initial your typed name in the opening or sign your name at the bottom of the page. The writer's initials and the typist's initials appear two lines below the last line of the memo, followed by enclosure or copy notations. If a second page is required, use the same heading as for a second page of a letter.

USING THE FAX

Most companies now have fax (facsimile) machines to receive and transmit copies of correspondence and graphics to readers inside and outside the organization. The fax uses telephone lines and, therefore, arrives much faster than correspondence sent through the mail or even through inter-office mail in large institutions, such as a university.

Standard cover sheets usually are available to use when you send a fax. Be sure to include your company name, address, telephone and fax numbers as well as your name, department, and telephone extension. Clearly write the name and title of the person receiving the correspondence along with the number of pages you are sending. Because the quality of fax machines varies and lines may experience interference, many people who fax correspondence in the interests of speed also send a printed copy through the mails, so the reader receives a high-quality document.

Be aware that using the fax machine prevents confidentiality. You rarely can be certain who is standing at the receiving fax machine when you send a letter or memo. Faxed correspondence arrives unsealed as loose sheets. Marking the cover sheet confidential will not necessarily create any privacy. Fax machines are usually in high-traffic areas, and many people have access to them. If your correspondence is confidential or potentially damaging to someone's interests, do not send a fax, or call the receiver and ask permission to send a confidential fax.

WRITING JOB-APPLICATION LETTERS

One of the most important letters you will write is a letter applying for a job. The application letter functions not only as a request for an interview, but also as the first demonstration to a potential employer of your communication skills. An application letter should do three things:

1. *Identify what you want.*   In the opening paragraph, identify specifically the position you are applying for and how you heard about it—through an advertisement or someone you know. In some cases, you may write an application letter without knowing if the company has an opening. Use the first paragraph to state what kind of position you are qualified for and why you are interested in that particular company.

2. *Explain why you are qualified for the position.*   Do not repeat your résumé line for line, but do summarize your work experience or education and point out the specific items especially relevant to the position you are applying for. In discussing your education, mention significant courses or special projects that have enhanced your preparation for the position you want. If you have extracurricular activities that show

leadership qualities or are related to your education, mention these in this section. Explain how your work experience is related to the position for which you are applying.

3. *Ask for an interview.*   Offer to come for an interview at the employer's convenience; however, you also may suggest a time that may be suitable. Tell the reader how to reach you easily by giving a telephone number or specifying what time of the day you are available.

In Model 12-11, the writer begins her application letter by explaining how she heard about the position, and she identifies her connection with the person who told her to apply for the job. In discussing her education, she points out her training in computers and mentions her laboratory duties that gave her relevant experience in product chemistry. Her work experience has been in research laboratories, so she explains the kind of testing she has done. In closing, she suggests a convenient time for an interview and includes a phone number for certain daytime hours. Overall, the letter emphasizes the writer's qualifications in chemistry and points out that the company could use her experience (reader benefits). An application letter should be more than a brief cover letter accompanying a résumé; it should be a fully developed message that provides enough information to help the reader make a decision about offering an interview.

WRITING RÉSUMÉS

The résumé for a new college graduate is usually one page long and summarizes the applicant's career objective, education, work experience, and activities. Model 12-12 shows the résumé that would accompany the application letter in Model 12-11. Remember that anyone reading a résumé wants to find information easily and quickly, so the headings that direct the reader to specific information should stand out clearly. Because the résumé in Model 12-12 is for a new college graduate, education has a prominent position. There are many résumé styles; this one is a basic chronological format:

Heading.   The heading should consist of name, address, and telephone number. A business telephone number also can be listed so that the reader can contact the applicant easily.

Objective.   List a specific position that matches your education and experience, because employers want to see a clear, practical objective. Avoid vague descriptions, such as, "I am looking for a challenging position where I can use my skills." Availability to travel is important in some companies, so the phrase "willing to travel" can be used under the objective. If you are not willing to travel, say nothing.

Education.   List education in reverse chronological order, your most recent degree first. Once you have a college degree, you can omit high school. Be sure to list any special certificates or short-term training done in addition to college work. Include courses or skills that are especially important to the type of position for which you are applying. List your grade-point average if it is significantly high, and indicate the grade-point scale. Some people list their grade-point average in their majors only, since this is likely to be higher than the overall average.

Work Experience.   List your past jobs in reverse chronological order. Include the job title, the name of the company, the city, and the state. Describe your responsibilities for each job, particularly those which provided practical experience connected with your career goals. In describing responsibilities, use action words, such as *coordinated, directed, prepared, supervised,* and *developed.* Dates of employment need not include month and day. Terms such as *vacation* or *summer* with the relevant years are sufficient.

Honors and Awards.   List scholarships, prizes, and awards received in college. Include any community honors or professional prizes as well. If there is only one honor, list it under "Activities."

Activities.   In this section list recent activities, primarily those in college. Be sure to indicate any leadership positions, such as president or chairperson of a group. Hobbies, if included, should indicate both group and individual interests. In Model 12-12, the applicant lists piano (an individual activity) and tennis (a group activity).

References.   Model 12-12 shows the most common way to mention references. If you do list references, include the person's business address and telephone number. Be sure to ask permission before listing someone as a reference.

It is best to omit personal information about age, height, weight, marital status, and religion. Employers are not allowed to consider such information in the employment process, and most prefer that it not appear on a résumé.

Model 12-14 shows a résumé for a job applicant who is more advanced in his chemistry career than the applicant in Model 12-12. This résumé lists experience first, in the most prominent position. Other significant differences from the résumé for the new college graduate include the following:

Major Qualifications.   Instead of an objective, this applicant wants to highlight his experience, so he uses the *capsule résumé* technique to call attention to his years of experience and his specialty. He can discuss his specific career goals in his application letter.

Professional Experience.   This applicant has had more than one position with the same employer because he has been promoted within the company. The applicant highlights his experience by stacking his responsibilities into impressive-looking lists.

Education.   This applicant includes his date of graduation but does not emphasize it, and he omits his grade-point average because his experience is now more important than his college work. He lists his computer knowledge because such knowledge is useful in his work.

Activities and Memberships.   After several years of full-time work, most people no longer list college activities. Instead, they stress community and professional service. This applicant lists his professional membership in the American Chemical Society to indicate that he is keeping current in his field.

Model 12-15 shows another résumé style. This job applicant is also advanced in his career, and he wants to emphasize the skills he has developed on the job as well as highlight his successes. His actual dates of employment or of college graduation are less important than the types of projects he has worked on. This résumé style is used most by experienced job applicants who want to change the focus of their careers or who have been out of the job market for a while and are now reentering it. New college graduates with activities and part-time work experience that developed skills relative to their career goals may also find this style useful. In addition, the job applicant using this résumé style may revise the lists of accomplishments and skills to emphasize different areas for different positions. This résumé does list employment and education but it differs from Models 12-12 and Model 12-14 in two important areas:

- *Accomplishments.*   Rather than beginning with his work record, the applicant lists significant achievements and honors to draw the reader's attention to a pattern of success. Many people are in sales. The applicant here emphasizes his out-of-the-ordinary performance.

- *Special Skills.*   The applicant identifies the types of skills he has developed and lists them under a specific heading. In this case, the applicant is interested in a management position, and he knows that communication and organization skills are crucial for effective managers. Other types of special skills might include researching, public speaking, writing, counselling, analyzing, managing, or designing. This applicant's record of employment supports his list of accomplishments and skills. Do not list skills so vague you cannot provide specific details to support your assertion. Saying that you are "good with people" without any specific accomplishments to demonstrate your claim will not strengthen your résumé.

Many large companies are now using computers to scan and store résumé information. In addition, many job seekers are filing their résumés with résumé data-base services that charge a fee to scan and store résumés for a set length of time. When employers want to interview prospective employees for a position, they use either their own electronic files or a service's files and screen every résumé in the files for key qualifications. For employers, the advantages of electronic screening are that it (1) eliminates the difficulty of fairly handling thousands of résumés, (2) quickly identifies candidates who have the primary job qualifications, and (3) processes more applications at less cost. For the job seeker, electronic résumé screening (1) makes a résumé available to all employers who use the data-base service, (2) reduces the need to send hundreds of résumés around the country, (3) ensures that a résumé will receive equal attention in the initial stage.

Electronic screening, however, does require a special résumé style. After writing your traditional résumé, you should rewrite it in appropriate electronic style, so you have both available. If you use a data-base service, the service usually will provide a format to follow. If you are applying to a company that uses electronic screening, you can inquire about a preferred format. If you cannot easily find out what the company prefers, send both a traditional résumé and an electronic-style résumé and state in your application letter that you are sending both as a convenience to the employer.

Following are guidelines for preparing a résumé suitable for scanning:

- *Name and address.*   Be sure your name is on the first line of your résumé. List your name, address, and telephone numbers in a stacked list.

- *Keywords.*   Immediately after your name, address, and telephone number, list key words that identify such items as your previous job titles, job-related tasks, skills or special knowledge, degrees, certifications, and colleges attended. Be sure to use the terms listed in a job advertisement because those are the terms the scanner is probably seeking. For example, if the advertisement asks for "public speaking," use that term rather than "business presentation." Some scanners only read a specific amount of text, so you want to be sure your key words appear early in your résumé.

- *Single columns.*   Scanners read across every line from left to right. Do not use double columns to list information, such as courses taken or activities. The information will look like gibberish in the data base.

- *Paper and typeface.*   Computers prefer clean and simple résumés. Use only smooth white paper with black ink. Use simple fonts such as 10- or 12-point Courier or Times Roman. Be sure that letters do not touch each other. Do not put boxes or parentheses around information or use graphics or unusual typefaces.

- *Abbreviations.*   Use abbreviations sparingly. Scanners can miss information if they are programmed to search for a whole word.

- *Folding and stapling.*   Do not staple or fold a résumé that will be scanned. The scanner may have trouble finding words that are in creases or that cover staple holes.

- *White space.*   Use plenty of white space so the scanner does not overlook key words.

Model 12-13 shows the electronic format for the résumé in Model 12-12. Notice that some information, such as activities and references, is omitted. For a comprehensive job search, you will need both the traditional résumé and the electronic version.

The purpose of the application letter and résumé is to present an interest-attracting package that will result in an interview. Because the letter and résumé are often the first contact a new college graduate has with a potential employer, the initial impression these documents make may have a decisive impact on career opportunities. Model 12-5 lists the 35 résumé items considered most important for new college graduates by personnel administrators at *Fortune* 500 companies.

WRITING OTHER JOB-SEARCH LETTERS

The article by Boe in Part 2 gives advice about preparing for the job interview. The first interview, however, may be only one step in the job application process. Many employers conduct several interviews with the top candidates before filling a position. The first interview may be brief, perhaps a half hour, allowing the interviewer to eliminate some candidates. Longer interviews then follow with the remaining candidates until the company offers the position to someone. If, after your first interview, you are very interested in the position, write a brief follow-up letter to remind the interviewer who you are and what special qualifications you have for the position. Because most job applicants do not take the time to write follow-up letters, you can make a stronger impression on the interviewer by doing so.

Write your follow-up letter within three to four days after your interview. The letter should be short but include the following:

1. Express appreciation for the opportunity to discuss the position.

2. Refer specifically to the date of the interview and the position you applied for.

3. Mention something that happened during the interview (e.g., a tour of the plant) or refer to a subject you discussed (e.g., a new product being developed).

4. Remind the interviewer about your qualifications or mention something you forgot to bring up in the interview.

5. Express your continuing interest in the company.

Résumé Content Items in Order of Importance	Percent Ranking Items Important (Fortune 500 Personnel Administrators)
1 Name	100.0
2 Telephone no.	100.0
3 Degree	100.0
4 Name of college	100.0
5 Jobs held (titles)	100.0
6 Address	99.3
7 Major	99.3
8 Employing company(s)	99.3
9 Dates of employment	99.3
10 Date of college graduation	95.3
11 Duties—work experience	94.7
12 Special aptitudes/skills	91.9
13 Job objective	91.7
14 Awards, honors—college achievements	91.4
15 Grade-point average	90.8
16 Willingness to relocate	89.4
17 Achievements—work experience (learning, contributions, accomplishments)	89.2
18 Professional organizations—college extracurricular activities	84.7
19 Scholarships—college achievements	84.1
20 Career objective	83.3
21 Years attended—college	83.0
22 Previous employers—references	81.8
23 Minor	80.8
24 Military experience	80.1
25 Student government activities—college	78.7
26 Publications	77.9
27 Combined job and career objective	76.6
28 References supplied only on request	75.5
29 Current organization memberships	75.5
30 Summary of qualifications	70.8
31 Community involvement	70.2
32 Yearbook editor, etc.—college	68.2
33 Professors/teachers—references	65.3
34 Athletic involvement—college	63.3
35 Social organizations—college	62.9

SOURCE: Adapted from Harcourt, J. and Krizan, A. C., "A Comparison of Résumé Content Preference of Fortune 500 Personnel Administrators and Business Communication Instructors," *Journal of Business Communication* 26 (2) (Spring 1989). Reprinted with permission of the authors.

MODEL 12-5   Résumé Content Ranked by Importance: The 35 Top-ranked Items

Here is a sample follow-up letter that covers these points:

Dear Mr. Price:

I appreciated the opportunity to talk to you on September 3 about the position in cost accounting. During my tour of your offices, Ms. McNamara gave me a thorough introduction to the accounting operation at HG Logan Associates, and I remain very interested in your company.

After hearing the details about the position, I believe my course work in cost accounting computer systems would be an asset in your organization.

Thank you for your consideration of my application, and I look forward to hearing from you soon.

Sincerely,

If you have another interview, write another follow-up letter to express your continuing interest.

If you receive a job offer and want to accept it, do so promptly and in writing. Use the letter to establish your eagerness to begin work and to confirm the details mentioned in the company's offer. Here is a sample acceptance letter:

Dear Mr. Strasser:

I am pleased to accept your offer of a position as financial analyst at Brady, Horton and Smythe at a salary of $31,000. As you suggested, I will stop in the Human Resources Office this week to get a packet of benefit enrollment forms.

I am eager to join the people I met during my visit to the Investment Sales Department and look forward to beginning work on June 15.

Sincerely,

If you receive a job offer, but you have decided not to accept it, write promptly and decline. Express your gratitude for the offer. You may or may not give a specific reason for your decision. Here is a sample letter declining a job offer:

Dear Ms. Turnbull:

Thank you for your offer of a position in the engineering division at Hughes Manufacturing. I was very impressed with the dynamic people I met during my visit, and I carefully considered your offer. Because of my interest in relocating to the Southwest, however, I have decided to accept a position with a company in New Mexico.

I appreciate your time and consideration.

Sincerely,

You may receive a job offer but be uncertain about whether you want to accept it because you have other interviews pending, and you want to complete those before making a decision. If so, write a letter asking for more time to respond to the company's offer. Express your interest in the position and explain that you need a short extension of their deadline in order to be sure of your decision. Here is a sample letter asking for a delay in responding to a job offer:

Dear Dr. Newman:

I appreciate your offer of a nursing position in your clinic. Your facilities and staff made a strong impression on me, and I know that working at Family Health Care would be an exciting challenge.

Because I do have two interviews scheduled at hospitals in the city, I would appreciate your giving me until March 1 to respond to your offer. The extra ten days will allow me the opportunity to evaluate my career options and make the decision that is right for me and for my employer.

If you need my answer immediately, I, of course, will give it. If you can allow me the extra time to make a decision, I would be grateful. Please let me know.

Sincerely,

All these letters may be part of your job-search process. Writing them carefully shows the company that you take the position seriously and you are professional in your approach to your career.

CHAPTER SUMMARY

This chapter discusses how to write effective letters, memos, job-application letters, and résumés. Remember:

- Letters are written primarily to people outside an organization, and memos are written primarily to people inside an organization.

- Effective tone in letters and memos requires natural language, positive language, and the you-attitude.

- E-mail transmits messages rapidly but lacks confidentiality.

- Letters and memos can be organized in the direct, indirect, or persuasive pattern.

- Direct organization presents the main idea in the opening.

- Indirect organization delays the main idea until details have been explained.

- Persuasive organization begins with an attention-getting opening.

- Managers need to create a cooperative atmosphere in their memos to employees.

- The fax machine transmits messages rapidly but is not confidential.

- The two most common letter formats are full block style and semiblock style.

- A job-application letter presents a writer's qualifications for a position and requests an interview.

- Résumés list a writer's most significant achievements relative to a position.

- A follow-up letter after a job interview will remind the interviewer about your qualifications.

SUPPLEMENTAL READINGS IN PART 2

Beswick, R. W. "Voicemail," *Communication and Technology: Today and Tomorrow,* p. 462.

Boe, E. "The Art of the Interview," *Microwaves and RF,* p. 470.

Bowman, J. P. "Electronic Conferencing," *Communication and Technology: Today and Tomorrow,* p. 474.

Humphries, A. C. "Business Manners for the '90s," *Business & Economic Review,* p. 520.

Kirtz, M. K., and Reep, D. C. "A Survey of the Frequency, Types and Importance of Writing Tasks in Four Career Areas," *The Bulletin of the Association for Business Communication,* p. 522.

Mascolini, M., and Supnick, R. "Preparing Students for the Behavioral Job Interview," *Journal of Business & Technical Communication,* p. 534.

Yates, J. "Electronic Mail," *Communication and Technology: Today and Tomorrow,* p. 588.

ENDNOTES

1. Brigid Schulte, "Pilot's Computer Note Reveals Military Secrets," *Akron Beacon Journal* (July 12, 1995): A2.

2. Stephanie Stahl, "Dangerous E-Mail," *Informationweek* (September 12, 1994): 12.

This model shows a claim letter for defective equipment and for costs incurred as a result. The writer addresses the reader by his first name because of the long business relationship the two have had. This long relationship also leads the writer to assume the reader will want to correct the situation promptly.

Discussion

1. Identify the organizational strategies used in this letter, and discuss why the writer would use this organization.

2. Why does the writer explain the problem in detail? Why not just state that the valves are defective?

3. Assume you are Howard Webster and write a response to this letter. Naturally, you will ship two new loader valves immediately, and you will send a check for the expenses listed in Harrison's letter. Your company has been supplying parts to Midwest Farming Implements, Inc. for 15 years, and you want to retain the company as a customer. You have alerted the quality control inspectors about checking settings on all valves, and you do not think the problem will occur again.

MIDWEST FARMING IMPLEMENTS, INC.
1622 Mandeville Road
St. Joseph, Missouri 64502-1206

October 15, 1996

Mr. Howard Webster
Vice President-Sales
Warfield Fluid Equipment
Mechanicsburg, PA 17056-4260

Dear Howard:

I appreciate your rushing our order of September 22, 1996, as we were behind in production and needed to make up inventory. We have had a problem with two of the loader valves in that shipment, and I would appreciate your taking care of the matter.

Apparently, the valve pressures were set in excess of 3000 psi. One of the valves (C21498) ruptured the outside shell of the orbit motor and damaged the holding valve. Unfortunately, we had to scrap both the motor and the holding valve along with four gallons of 10–40 oil. The second valve (C21487) also had the relief set too high, but we did not sustain damage to any additional pieces of equipment.

We need the two loader valves replaced, and we are requesting compensation for the orbit motor, holding valve, oil, and time lost as a result of the defective loader valves. The debit memo (D67–2) enclosed covers our costs as follows:

Orbit Motor	$187.55
Holding Valve	63.60
4 Gallons Oil	16.88
	$268.03
Labor (8 hours @ $20)	$160.00
Total	$428.03

Mr. Howard Webster   -2-   October 15, 1996

I am returning the defective valves by McGill Express, our usual carrier. Please ship two new loader valves immediately. In addition, I am sure you will want to take care of our damage expenses promptly. Although accidents do happen, Midwest Farming cannot be expected to absorb damage and lost time because of faulty settings.

Sincerely,

Kevin Harrison

Kevin Harrison
Product Supervisor

KH:sd

This model shows a form letter sent to all savings customers of a large bank. Although envelopes will be individually addressed and the letter is dated, there is no inside address. The writer is announcing a change that will affect all the bank's savings customers, so no references to specific accounts are included in the letter.

Discussion

1. Identify the specific organization pattern used in this letter and discuss why the writer chose that pattern.

2. In what ways does the writer imply the change is not a significant one?

3. In groups, draft a letter to all students at your school to announce a $50 increase in "special fees" beginning next term. This increase will cover the cost of periodical subscriptions in the library. Without the money from the special fee, the library will have to cancel over 200 subscriptions.

CONTINENTAL BANK AND TRUST COMPANY
1000 Central Plaza
San Antonio, Texas 78205-1104

January 6, 1996

Dear Savings Customer:

Thank you for choosing Continental as your full-service banking institution. We are committed to providing superior banking services that match today's needs and conditions.

As you no doubt are aware, today's economy is characterized by low inflation and declining interest rates. This low inflation rate has enabled our customers to experience a consistent return on their savings or even an increase in "real" returns compared to years of skyrocketing inflation. The lower interest rates have spurred economic growth and investment and allowed customers to purchase new homes and new cars. Both low inflation and lower interest rates have had an impact on all the financial plans available at our institution. Rates based on yesterday's economy do not reflect today's conditions. Therefore, effective January 15, 1996, the annual interest rate on the passbook savings account and the Money Market Deposit account will be reduced by 1 percent. No other features of your accounts will be affected.

Your personal banker will be happy to review the variety of services available for savings and investments to meet your financial needs. For example, our "supersaver" Certificate of Deposit offers an interest rate of 4.5% with a maturity of three years. All our savings plans, of course, are backed by the safety and security of FDIC insurance and Continental's 72 years of banking experience. Please call your personal banker at 555–7899 if you have any questions. We appreciate the opportunity to serve your financial needs now and in the future.

Sincerely,

LaShandra Perkins
Vice President

LP:sd

This persuasive letter is individually addressed but is actually a form letter that The Construction Specifications Institute sends to people who have contacted the Institute for technical information. The purpose of this letter is to persuade the reader to become a member.

Discussion

1. Discuss how this letter fits the persuasive organization pattern discussed in this chapter.

2. Identify the persuasive appeals used in this letter. How does the writer imply that membership in the Institute is essential for anyone in any area of construction?

3. Identify the format elements used in this letter. How do these elements serve the writer's purpose of persuading the reader to join the Institute?

4. In groups, draft a persuasive letter that could be sent to students on your campus to encourage them to join a particular campus group or activity. You may write a letter suitable for a specific group of students, such as freshmen or engineering majors.

THE CONSTRUCTION SPECIFICATIONS INSTITUTE
601 Madison Street
Alexandria, Virginia 22314
(703) 684–0300

August 3, 1996

Mr. Hunter Matthison
Randall Construction Company
1200 Union Drive
Memphis, TN 38104

Dear Mr. Matthison:

Thank you for your interest in The Construction Specifications Institute. I hope the information you received has served your purpose and that you will continue to consider CSI as a vital source of information in the future.

CSI has nearly 19,000 members who are dedicated to advancing construction technology through communication, education, research, and service. These members also enjoy:

- **Diverse membership**—CSI membership is open to everyone in the construction industry, including architects, engineers, specifiers, contractors, manufacturers' representatives, and product distributors, providing a diversity that makes networking with individuals from all phases of the construction process easy.

- **Subscriptions** to The Construction Specifier, the industry's leading monthly magazine, and Newsdigest, CSI's monthly newsletter, keep you informed about industry and association news.

- **Technical documents** standardizing the preparation of construction documents is the mainstay of CSI. Members receive substantial discounts.

- **Seminars** on timely and career-oriented topics are presented nationwide. Registration fees are discounted for members.

- **CSI's annual convention** is the largest exhibit of nonresidential construction products, materials, and services in the country, featuring more than 1,000 exhibit booths.

Mr. Hunter Matthison   -2-   August 3, 1996

- **Certification programs**—Certified Construction Specifier (CCS) and Construction Documents Technologist (CDT) programs elevate the skills and status of knowledgeable individuals.

Why not join the thousands of construction professionals who have found membership in CSI professionally rewarding? Simply fill out the enclosed application and return it with your dues payment to CSI. If you have any questions, call CSI's Membership Department at (703) 684–0300. Or fax your questions or requests to (703) 684–0465.

Sincerely,

Mary H. Bailey
Manager, Membership Programs

MHB/sd
Enclosure

MODEL 12-9   Commentary

This memo is from a supervisor to a division head, asking for maintenance support.

Discussion

1. Identify the organizational strategies the writer uses, and discuss why the writer probably chose these strategies.

2. Consider the tone of this memo. How does the writer place blame for the situation? How does the writer convey the seriousness of the problems?

3. In what ways does the writer show the reader that there are benefits in solving these problems? Is there any advantage to addressing the reader by name in the memo?

4. Write a brief memo to D. P. Paget from T. L. Coles announcing that R. Fleming, the maintenance supervisor, has been told to report on the problems within two days. Assure Paget that the problems are being taken seriously.

October 3, 1996

To: T. L. Coles, Division Chief

From: D. P. Paget, Supervisor   *DPP*

Subject: Problems in Cost Center 22, Paint Line

As I've discussed with Bill Martling, our department has had problems with proper maintenance for six weeks. Although the technicians in the Maintenance Department respond promptly to our calls, they do not seem to be able to solve the problems. As a result, our maintenance calls focus on the same three problems week after week. I've listed below the areas we need to deal with.

1. For the past two weeks, our heat control has not consistently reached the correct temperature for the different mixes. The Maintenance technician made six visits in an attempt to provide consistent temperature ranges. Supervisor R. Fleming investigated and decided that the gas mixture was not operating properly. He did not indicate when we might get complete repairs. In the last ten working days, we've experienced nearly five hours of total downtime.

2. The soap material we currently use in the water fall booth does not break up the paint mixtures, and as a result, the cleanup crew cannot remove all the excess paint. Without a complete cleanup every twenty-four hours, the booth malfunctions. Again, we have downtime. We need to investigate a different soap composition for the water fall booth.

3. The parking lever control has not been in full operation since January 14. Maintenance technicians manage to fix the lever for only short periods before it breaks down again. I asked for a complete replacement rather than continued repairs, but was told it wasn't malfunctioning enough to warrant being replaced. This lever is crucial to the operation because when it isn't functioning the specified range slips and a lot of paint literally goes down the drain. As a result, we use more paint than necessary and still some parts are not coated correctly.

I'd appreciate your help in getting these problems handled, Tom, because our cost overruns are threatening to become serious. Since all maintenance operations come under your jurisdiction, perhaps you could consider options and let me know what we can do. I'd be glad to discuss the problems with you in more detail.

This persuasive memo is from a supervisor in an insurance company to the district managers of the agents in the field. The supervisor asks the district managers to encourage the insurance agents to prepare routine proposals themselves rather than sending all proposals to the home office for preparation.

Discussion

1. Identify and discuss the persuasive strategies used in this memo. What are the advantages to using this organization in this situation?

2. Underline the places in the memo where the writer emphasizes the you-attitude and reader benefits. If you were the reader, how would you respond?

3. You are the owner of a small construction company. You have never had a smoking policy, and most of your engineers and drafters smoke at their desks. However, complaints are increasing from the nonsmokers in the office, and you noticed recently that some clients seem uncomfortable in the smoke-filled office when they visit. You decide to follow other companies in your community and limit smoking to the employee lounge and lunchroom. Write a memo to all employees and ask the smokers to stop smoking at their desks during working hours. You would like to avoid harsh rules and punishments, and you hope to persuade the smokers to cooperate out of consideration for others.

May 2, 1995

To: District Sales Directors

From: Julie Kelly
           Manager, Sales Proposal Division

Subject: Requests for Proposal Service

Thanks to the terrific job your agents are doing in the field, our division is experiencing a large increase in the number of proposal requests each week. Because we want to continue to offer high-quality service on complicated proposals, we need some assistance on the routine ones.

As you know, the company has an established format for Major Medical, Franchise, and Disability Income proposals. I'm enclosing sample forms as well as a checklist of items that must be included on each form. By using these checklists, agents can quickly prepare the simple proposals for presentation to clients. The usual 12 to 14 days our office needs to handle these requests can be eliminated, allowing agents to make follow-up calls as soon as they complete the proposals.

Please ask agents to use the samples and checklists to prepare the Major Medical, Franchise, and Disability Income proposals in their field offices. The complicated plans, such as those for company pension agreements, should be sent to this office. We will be able to prepare them within 4 to 6 days if the simpler plans are done in the field.

Can we have your help in asking agents to forward the complex proposals to us and to finish the easy-to-do proposals themselves?

JK:td
Enc.: Forms (3)
      Checklists (3)

cc: J. F. Cooper
    W. G. Simms

MODEL 12-11   Commentary

This job-application letter is from a recent college graduate inquiring about a specific company opening.

Discussion

1. Identify the organizational strategies the writer uses.

2. Read this letter in conjunction with the résumé in Model 12-12. Consider the specific details in the letter about education and experience. How do the letter and résumé together make a stronger case for the applicant than either would alone?

3. How does the writer manage to put the you-attitude into her letter?

1766 Wildwood Drive
Chicago, Illinois 60666
July 12, 1996

Mr. Eric Blackmore
Senior Vice President
Alden-Chandler Industries, Inc.
72 Plaza Drive
Milwaukee, WI 53211–2901

Dear Mr. Blackmore:

Professor Julia Hedwig suggested that I write to you about an opening for a product chemist in your chemical division. Professor Hedwig was my senior adviser this past year.

I have just completed my B.S. in chemistry at Midwest University with a 3.9 GPA in my major. In addition to chemistry courses, I took three courses in computer applications and developed a computer program on chemical compounds. As a laboratory assistant to Professor Hedwig, I entered and ran the analyses of her research data. My senior project, which I completed under Professor Hedwig's guidance, was an analysis of retardant film products. The project was given the Senior Chemistry Award, granted by a panel of chemistry faculty.

My work experience would be especially appropriate for Alden-Chandler Industries. My internship in my senior year was at Pickett Laboratory, which does extensive analyses for the Lake County Sheriff's office. My work involved writing laboratory reports daily. At both Ryan Laboratories and Century Concrete Corporation, I have worked extensively in compound analysis, and I am familiar with standard test procedures.

I would appreciate the opportunity to discuss my qualifications for the position of product chemist. I am available for an interview every afternoon after three o'clock, but I could arrange to drive to Milwaukee any time convenient to you. My telephone number during the day between 10:00 a.m. and 3:00 p.m. is (312) 555–1212.

Sincerely,

Kimberly J. Oliver

Kimberly J. Oliver

Enc.

These résumé models show a variety of styles:

- Model 12-12 is the résumé that accompanies the application letter in Model 12-11. The job applicant is a recent college graduate who uses the chronological format most recent graduates use.

- Model 12-13 shows the electronic-style résumé of the job applicant in Model 12-11. Notice the differences between this style and the traditional style in Model 12-12.

- Model 12-14 is the résumé of a job applicant who has significant professional experience. Notice he has had several positions with one employer, and the format stresses his experience rather than his education.

- Model 12-15 is a functional-style résumé, emphasizing the job applicant's special accomplishments and skills.

- Model 12-16 is the résumé of a job applicant who interrupted her education to marry and have children. Notice that she uses the functional style to emphasize the experience gained from both her jobs and her volunteer activities. She is now working full time and taking classes part time. Notice that she lists her degree as expected at a future date and uses the term "general studies" to describe her one year of college work in Texas.

Discussion

1. Compare these résumés and discuss the effectiveness of the differences in format.

2. Assume you were going to write an electronic-style résumé for Models 12-14 and 12-15. Identify key words you would use in each case.

3. In groups, write an application letter to accompany the résumé in Models 12-14 or 12-15. Assume the job applicant is writing to a company or institution that he thinks may have a suitable position.

Kimberly J. Oliver
1766 Wildwood Drive
Chicago, Illinois 60666
(312) 555–6644

Objective: Chemist with responsibility in product development and production. Willing to travel.

Education

Midwest University, Chicago, Illinois 1992–1996
B.S. in Chemistry; GPA: 3.6 (4.0 scale)

Computer Languages: FORTRAN, PASCAL, Lotus 1-2-3

Work Experience

Century Concrete Corp., Chicago, Illinois, 1994–present

Research Assistant: Set up chemical laboratories, including purchasing equipment and materials. Perform ingredient/compound analysis. Produce experimental samples according to quality standards. (part-time)

Pickett Laboratory, Chicago, Illinois, Summer 1995

Research Intern: Set up testing compounds. Wrote laboratory test reports for compound analysis.

Ryan Laboratories, Chicago, Illinois, Summers 1993–1994

Laboratory Assistant: Assisted in testing compounds. Prepared standard test solutions; recorded test data; operated standard laboratory equipment; wrote operating procedures.

Honors and Awards

Chemical Society of Illinois Four-Year Scholarship, 1992–1996
Senior Chemistry Award, Midwest University, 1995
Outstanding Chemistry Major, Midwest University, 1995

Activities

Member, American Chemistry Association, 1994–present
President, American Chemistry Association (student chapter), 1994–1995
Member, Toastmaster Association, 1993–1995
Council Member, Women in Science Student Association, 1994–1995
Hobbies: sailing, piano, tennis

References

Available on request.

MODEL 12-12

Kimberly J. Oliver
1766 Wildwood Drive
Chicago, Illinois 60666
(312) 555–6644

Key Words: Product chemistry. Bachelor's degree. Laboratory internship. Compound analysis. Laboratory test reports. Midwest University. Chemical Society of Illinois Scholarship. Written and oral communication skills. Lotus 1-2-3

Objective: Chemist in product development and testing.

Education

Midwest University, Chicago, Illinois 1992–1996
Bachelor's of Science in Chemistry; GPA: 3.6 on 4 point scale

Computer Languages: FORTRAN, PASCAL, Lotus 1-2-3

Work Experience

Century Concrete Corp., Chicago, Illinois, 1994–present

Research Assistant: Set up chemical laboratories, including purchasing equipment and materials. Perform ingredient/compound analysis. Produce experimental samples according to quality standards. (part-time)

Pickett Laboratory, Chicago, Illinois, Summer 1995

Research Intern: Set up testing compounds. Wrote laboratory test reports for compound analysis.

Ryan Laboratories, Chicago, Illinois, Summers 1993–1994

Laboratory Assistant: Assisted in testing compounds. Prepared standard test solutions; recorded test data; operated standard laboratory equipment; wrote operating procedures.

Honors and Awards

Chemical Society of Illinois Four-Year Scholarship, 1992–1996
Senior Chemistry Award, Midwest University, 1995
Outstanding Chemistry Major, Midwest University, 1995

Jack Montgomery
21 Camelot Court
Skokie, IL 60622
(312) 555-5620

Major Qualifications: Twelve years of experience in product development chemistry. Specialty: Adhesives

PROFESSIONAL EXPERIENCE

CDX TIRE AND RUBBER CORPORATION, Chicago, IL

Formulation Chemist, 1987–present
- Develop new hot-melt adhesives, hot-melt pressure sensitives, and hot-melt sealants
- Perform analysis of competitors' compounds
- Determine new product specification
- Calculate raw materials pricing
- Conduct laboratory programs for product improvement

Analytical Chemist, 1985–1987
- Performed ingredient/compound analysis
- Developed and tested compounds (cured/uncured)
- Wrote standard operating procedures
- Developed improved mixing design
- Supervised processing technicians

STERLING ANALYTICAL LABORATORIES, Pittsburgh, PA

Research Laboratory Assistant, 1983–1985 (part time)
- Prepared solutions
- Drafted laboratory reports
- Supervised students during testing procedures
- Inventoried laboratory equipment

EDUCATION

B.S. in Chemistry, Minor in Biology. University of Pittsburgh, Pittsburgh, May 1985

COMPUTER SKILLS

FORTRAN, PASCAL, Lotus 1-2-3

ACTIVITIES AND MEMBERSHIPS

District Chairman, United Way Campaign, 1992
Member, Illinois Consumer Protection Commission, 1987–1991
Member, American Chemical Society, 1985–present

References furnished on request.

MODEL 12-14

> **Jeffrey L. Hirsch**
> 1630 W. Lynd Drive
> Mount Troy, MI 448822
> (517) 555-2327

Objective: Marketing and Sales Management

Qualifications: Ten Years' Experience in retail marketing
MBA in Management

Accomplishments:
- Exceeded district objectives in 23 accounts, $2.6 million sales.
- Increased territory volume by 17%.
- Managed Sales Team of 12 people.
- Negotiated improved leases for retailers.
- Earned district, regional, and national awards for high performance including Market Development Award 1994, National R. B. Hall Award 1995, and Sales Development Professional of the Year 1995.
- Published marketing advice in *Sales World* and district newsletters.

Organizational and Communication Skills:
- Coordinated 1995 National Sales Meeting—Chicago.
- Developed regional sales programs and seminars.
- Presented district seminars for retailers.
- Conducted training seminars for new salespeople.
- Presented career seminars for high school programs.

Work History:
Hallmark Marketing Corporation, Hallmark Cards, Inc.
District Sales Representative, 1989–present.
Retail Sales Coordinator, 1986–1989.

Education:
MBA, emphasis in Management, University of Wisconsin, 1993.
BBA in Marketing, University of Wisconsin, 1986.

Professional Memberships:
Michigan Sales Associates, Program Coordinator, 1992–1994.
Metropolitan Business Association.
Retail Business Association High School Mentor Program.

Interests: Choral groups, hiking, theater.

References: Available on request.

Felicia Cummings
4236 N. Ryan Road
Port William, NY 10011
(216) 555-8457 (home)
(216) 555-1212 (business)

Objective: Museum Display/Historical Artifacts Displays

Qualifications: Six Years' Experience in Museum and Collectible Displays

Display Experience:
- Developed Southwest Artifacts Display for Museum
- Designed collectibles display for advertising photography
- Organized and directed display of historical weaponry for public exhibition
- Coordinated university displays of student art history research projects

Communication Skills:
- Wrote lectures and led museum tours for community groups
- Wrote brochures for museum fund-raising committee

Research Experience:
- Catalogued historical collectibles and replications for artifacts dealer
- Organized research notes and wrote reports for professor's archeology expedition to the Yucatan.

Work History:

Assistant Manager, Port William Collectibles, Port William, NY, 1992–present

Assistant to curator, Museum of Indian Art, El Paso, TX, Summers, 1988–1989

Education:

University of New York at Port William
B.A. in Art History (expected June 1998)

University of Texas-El Paso
General Studies 1988–1989

Activities:
Member, American Art History Association
Volunteer Guide, Port William Art Museum

References are available on request.

MODEL 12-16

Chapter 12   Exercises

1. The following memo is the first draft of Vance Schaffer, current chair of the office social committee. The committee is in charge of sending flowers to employees who are ill or who have had a death in the family. The fund collects $1 every payday from each employee. This amount is usually enough to cover expenses, but the fund has gone dry partly because several people had surgery recently. The members of the social committee have found it increasingly difficult to collect the money every payday. People make excuses to avoid paying immediately and promise to catch up later. You know at least fifteen people who have not paid any money into the fund for months. Vance asks you to look over the memo and make some suggestions. Rewrite this memo for you-attitude and persuasive appeal.

> Due to the unusual number of employee illnesses in the past two months, the Sunshine Fund is empty. We need to make a special collection of $2 on Friday to create a balance in case we need to spend money soon. Also, many of you have failed to contribute your fair share for months, and you seem to think no one cares if you shirk your duty. It is not fair to expect others to cover your obligation. Susan will pass out envelopes on Friday. PUT IN YOUR $2 WITHOUT FAIL!

2. As the security director of Knight Manufacturing, you have been struggling with security problems for several years. The manufacturing complex is located in a high crime area, and several employees have been mugged or assaulted in the parking lot. Two months ago, several intruders robbed workers in offices. At last the 12-foot chain-link fence has been completed. The fence surrounds the property but will have one opening at the east driveway. The north driveway will be closed with a locked gate. Nighthawk Patrol, a security company, has been hired as of next Monday to provide a security guard at the east entrance and to patrol the grounds between 8 p.m. and 6:30 a.m. when a company maintenance crew arrives. You must write the memo announcing the completion of the fence and the new security patrol. In addition, you believe you should add some general safety information. If employees see a suspicious car on the grounds or suspicious people lurking anywhere, you want them to call the security office or the personnel office immediately. Employees should not eat or sit in their cars during lunch or coffee breaks. Car doors and windows should always be locked. At regular closing times, you have arranged escort services for employees who park at the far edge of the parking lots, and employees can call the security guard if they intend to come to the offices at night or on the weekends. After thinking about the situation, you call your city's police department and make arrangements for an officer to present a personal safety seminar in the cafeteria next Thursday during the two lunch periods. Now you are ready to write the memo to all employees announcing the security changes and cautioning them to avoid safety risks. Add any details you wish as you write the memo.

3. You are the marketing director of HighTech Press, which is about to publish an electronics manual for consumers. The manual, *Guide to Electronics,* includes detailed descriptions of dozens of consumer electronics products, such as clock radios, television sets, VCRs, camcorders, and compact disk players. In addition, the book provides troubleshooting guides for diagnosing problems and instructions for repairing, rebuilding, and cleaning these products. You believe the guide will appeal to consumers who are frustrated with high repair bills and long service delays and who believe they can handle most repairs themselves if they had proper guidance. Also, some readers might be interested in developing a side career in part-time repairs or rebuilding and selling discarded electronics products. The book, which is published as a three-ring binder, includes over 600 photos and diagrams. You want to write a persuasive message that can go to some 3000 people on a mailing list. These people have purchased repair guides of various kinds in the past. Because the electronics industry changes so quickly, you are offering supplemental pages over a 2-year period to keep the guide up to date. The pages will be three-hole punched and will fit in the binder. Like all the books you publish, this guide comes with a 30-day trial period. The customer can return it if unsatisfied. Write the sales letter for this new book. Add any appropriate details you wish for a full, persuasive letter.

4. As the director of the Children's Services of the Monroe County Social Agencies Division, you have a problem. The social service departments are housed in several buildings on county grounds. The Children's Services building is a renovated Victorian mansion originally built in 1887. Over the last two months, safety concerns have developed. Raw sewage backs up nearly every night in the basement where records are kept. The air quality is suspect. One night the building filled with carbon monoxide, but, fortunately, no one was working there. Employees are concerned about water safety. Inspectors have come in and out without explaining exactly what they are doing, making everyone nervous. The south side of the building adjoins a parking lot, but apparently there was not adequate support at the foundation because the parking lot on that side caved in twice last month, and last week it caved in again. A car slipped under the building and had to be towed out of the hole. You feel the employees have to be assured by the county superintendent that there is a serious effort to take care of these problems. You believe the agency may be liable for a lawsuit if anyone becomes ill. Write a memo to the superintendent, reviewing the problems. Ask the superintendent to come to your department and tell the employees how the situation is being handled.

5. You and a partner have a thriving lawncare business. After two years, you have a list of loyal customers, and word-of-mouth keeps bringing you new ones. You decide to write a letter offering your services to all the homeowners in a wealthy suburb called Ocean Heights. The homes in this area all have big lawns and extensive shrubbery, and many have terraced hillsides. In your letter, you will introduce your company and offer your introductory plan for new customers—one month of lawn care at half price. Although the price is a good one, you know that these customers will be more interested in your experience handling various types of grass, soil conditions, and disease control. Both you and your partner (who has a bachelor's degree in botany) have been certified in lawn care from the National Association of Outdoor Growth and Maintenance, so you believe the two of you can handle anything these homeowners might want. Also, you have recently attended a seminar in classical garden design, and you believe a classical Italian garden would do well in this area. These gardens include a variety of trees and plants, such as winter jasmine, calla lilies, cornflowers, century plants, and cypress trees. The homeowner's favorite flowers and trees can be blended in with the others, and terra cotta pots and statues will be added to enhance the classical Italian accent. Write a sales letter to all the homeowners in Ocean Heights and interest them in trying your services. You do not want to address the letters individually, so you will write a form letter without a personal salutation.

6. As the director of the local "Be a Mentor" program, you must write a form letter to be sent to 130 local business executives. You need to convince them to participate in the program, which involves a high school senior spending a full business day with an executive so the student can observe typical business activities and decision making. In addition, the business executive agrees to act as a career adviser to the student for the rest of the year. The program has been a great success in other cities. Many of the students (who are all in the top 25% of their class) make career decisions based on their experiences and observations. Although your letter will be individually addressed, it will be a form letter suitable for male and female executives in a variety of businesses. Create any other specific details you want and write the letter, asking the executives to participate in this worthwhile program 2 months from now.

7. You are president of Lomax Athletic Gear, Inc. and have just received a letter from the "Be a Mentor" program as described in Exercise 6. You would like to cooperate with the program, but it is impossible. The annual sales representative meeting is scheduled for the same week in which the high school senior would be spending a full day in your office. The Lomax annual meeting attracts some 600 sales representatives including 200 to 300 spouses. Everyone in the company is involved in some way with a week of seminars, banquets, award ceremonies, and other activities. Write the director of "Be a Mentor" and express your regret at not participating this year.

8. As director of the County Environmental Services Office, you must write a form letter to all residents in and around Portage Lakes Township. You will not address the residents individually. The unusually heavy summer rains this year created widespread flooding, which resulted in sewer backups in this area.

Your office has set up two hot lines for residents. One line is a 24-hour emergency number for residents to report sewer backups or flooding. The other number for customer service will offer residents a chance to ask questions and discuss their problems with a technician. Along with announcing the new hot lines, you want to reassure residents that your office is concerned about their problems. The customer service line is open from 7 a.m. to 4 p.m., but an answering machine will take messages at other times. Create any other specific details you want and write the letter.

9. Select a "real world" memo or letter of at least one page. Make enough copies for class members. Present a critique of the memo or letter to the class, pointing out both effective and ineffective aspects of the sample. *In addition,* submit a revision of the sample. The revision should reflect your ideas about how to improve the original memo or letter for greatest effectiveness. Do not change the original situation in the writing sample. Your job is to improve and develop the message. You may add any logical material to your revision in order to improve it.

10. Prepare a résumé based on the formats discussed in class or using a sample from this chapter. Select a company in your area, and apply for a summer job (or a part-time job during the semester) in your career area. Graduating seniors should apply for a full-time job in their career area. Write an application letter that realistically discusses your interest in and qualifications for a position based on your *present* situation. Key your remarks to your résumé, and attach your résumé to the letter.

11. *Oral report project.* Your instructor will divide the class into groups, and each group will work on one of the topics listed below. Each group member will be responsible for gathering information from outside sources for one specific area of the panel topic. Consult Chapter 10 for a list of information sources. Read Chapter 13 and the article by Calabrese in Part 2 for guidance in organizing your oral presentation. Plan your oral report as a 10-minute presentation or for whatever length of time your instructor assigns, and practice it so you know it fits the required time. Remember that your audience consists of your classmates who are interested in information that will help them begin their careers. Tailor your oral report to this audience. After giving your oral report, submit an executive summary of your talk to your instructor. Write a transmittal memo to accompany the executive summary. Guidelines for executive summaries and transmittal memos are included in Chapter 9.

    a. *Women in careers*—Report on women in business and industry today—promotion chances, statistics on numbers of women in specific career areas, sexual harassment problems, and laws, mentors, and networks for career information.

    b. *Job prospects for this year's college graduate*—Report on the opportunities for new graduates in specific career areas that students in your class are studying, such as engineering, nursing, or marketing. Also cover types of entry jobs available in these fields, promotion possibilities, starting salaries, and how to find information about potential jobs.

c. *Body language and appearance as factors in the job search*—Report on body language (turn-ons and turn-offs), dressing for success (men and women), and effective body language in job interviews.

d. *Effective job interviewing*—Report on questions to expect during a job interview, difficult or hostile questions, and information sources for learning about the company with which you are interviewing. Also explain how to effectively present your experience and education.

e. *Business etiquette*—Report on how to evaluate your position in the company hierarchy, etiquette points the ambitious beginner must know, international business and culture/etiquette differences Americans need to be aware of, how to take part in a meeting, and symbols of status and power.

CHAPTER 13

Oral Presentations

UNDERSTANDING ORAL PRESENTATIONS

Although most people hate to speak in front of a group, you must be prepared to handle oral presentations gracefully. One recent study indicates that 30 million business presentations take place each day, and the 725 managers surveyed ranked the ability to communicate in front of an audience as the number one skill needed for career advancement.[1] Oral presentations can be internal, i.e., for management or staff, or external, i.e., for clients, prospective customers, or colleagues at scientific conferences. Most presentations are face to face, but videoconferencing, involving two or more groups at separate sites, is increasing in frequency and importance.

Purpose

Like written documents, oral presentations often have mixed purposes. A scientist speaking at a conference about a research study is informing listeners as well as persuading them that the results of the study are significant. Oral presentations generally serve these purposes, separately or in combination:

- *To inform.* The speaker presents facts and analyzes data to help listeners understand the information. Such presentations cover the status of a current project, results of research or investigations, company changes, or performance quality of new systems and equipment.

- *To persuade.* The speaker presents information and urges listeners to take a specific action or reach a specific conclusion. Persuasive presentations involve sales proposals to potential customers, internal company proposals, or external grant proposals.

- *To instruct.* The speaker describes how to do a specific task. Presentations that offer instruction include training sessions for groups of employees and demonstrations for procedures or proper handling of equipment.

Advantages

Oral presentations have these advantages over written documents:

- The speaker can explain a procedure and demonstrate it at the same time.

- The speaker controls what is emphasized in the presentation and can keep listeners focused on specific topics.

- A speaker's personality can create enthusiasm in listeners during sales presentations and inspire confidence during informative presentations.

- Speakers can get immediate feedback from listeners and answer questions on the spot.

- Listeners can raise new issues immediately.

- If most of the listeners become involved in the presentation—asking questions, nodding agreement—those who may have had negative attitudes may be swept up in the group energy and become less negative.

Disadvantages

Oral presentations are not adequate substitutes for written documents, however, because they have these distinct disadvantages:

- Oral presentations are expensive because listeners may be away from their jobs for a longer time than it would take them to read a written document.

- Listeners, unlike readers, cannot select the topic they are most interested in or proceed through the material at their own pace.

- Listeners can be easily distracted from an oral presentation by outside noises, coughing, uncomfortable seating, and their own wandering thoughts.

- A poor speaker will annoy listeners, who then may reject the information.

- Spoken words vanish as soon as they are said, and listeners remember only a few major points.

- Time limitations require speakers to condense and simplify material, possibly omitting important details.

- Listeners have difficulty following complicated statistical data in oral presentations, even with graphic aids.

- Audience size has to be limited for effective oral presentations unless expensive video/TV equipment is involved.

Types of Oral Presentations

An oral presentation on the job is usually in one of these four styles:

Memorized Speech.   Memorization is useful primarily for short remarks, such as introducing a main speaker at a conference. Unless it is a dramatic reading, a memorized speech has little audience appeal. A speaker reciting a memorized speech is likely to develop a monotone that will soon have the listeners glassy-eyed with boredom. In addition, in such presentations, if the speaker is interrupted by a question, the entire presentation may disappear from his or her memory.

Written Manuscript.   Speakers at large scientific and technical conferences often read from a written manuscript, particularly when reporting a research study or presenting complex technical data. The written manuscript enables the speaker to cover every detail and stay within a set time limit. Unfortunately, written manuscripts, like the memorized speeches, also may encourage speakers to develop a monotone. Usually, too, the speaker who reads from a manuscript has little eye contact or interaction with the audience. Listeners at scientific conferences frequently want copies of the full research report for reference later.

Impromptu Remarks.   Impromptu remarks occur when, without warning, a person is asked to explain something at a meeting. Although others in the meeting realize that the person has had no chance to prepare, they still expect to hear specific information presented in an organized manner. You should anticipate being called on at meetings about projects you are involved with in any way. Always come prepared to explain projects or answer questions about specific topics under your authority. Bring notes, current cost figures, and other information that others may ask you for.

Extemporaneous Talk.   Most oral presentations on the job are extemporaneous, that is, the speaker plans and rehearses the presentation and follows a written topic or sentence outline when speaking. Because this type of on-the-job oral presentation is the most common, the rest of this chapter focuses on preparing and delivering extemporaneous talks.

ORGANIZING ORAL PRESENTATIONS

As you do with written documents, analyze your audience and their need for information, as explained in Chapter 2. Consider who your listeners are and what they expect to get from your talk. The key to a successful presentation is knowing what facts your audience will be most interested in. Emphasize these points in your presentation. Oral presentations also must be as carefully organized as written documents are. Even though you are deeply involved in a project, do not rely on your memory alone to support your review of the information or your proposal. Instead, prepare an outline, as discussed in Chapter 3, that covers all the points you want to make. An outline also will be easier to work with than a marked copy of a written report you plan to distribute because you will not have to fumble with sheets of paper.

Use either a topic or a sentence outline—whichever you feel most comfortable with and whichever provides enough information to stir your memory. Remember that topic outlines contain only key words, whereas sentence outlines include more facts:

Topic: Venus—Earth's twin
Sentence: Venus is Earth's twin in size, mass, density, and gravity.

Some people prefer to put an outline on note cards, only one or two topics or sentences per card. Other speakers prefer to use an outline typed on sheets of paper because it is easier to glance ahead to see what is coming next. Oral presentations generally have three sections:

Introduction.   Your introduction should establish (1) the purpose of the oral presentation, (2) why it is relevant to listeners, and (3) the major topics that will be covered. Since listeners, unlike readers, cannot look ahead to check on what is coming, they need a preview of main points in the opening so that they can anticipate and listen for the information relevant to their own work. Your introduction also should define your terms. Even if your audience consists of experts in the topic, do not assume they understand everything you do. Explain the terms you use and check your audience's comprehension before continuing.

Data Sections.   The main sections of your presentation are those that deal with specific facts, arranged in one of the organizational patterns discussed in Chapter 3. Remember these tips when presenting data orally:

- Include specific examples to reinforce your main points.

- Number items as you talk so that listeners know where problem number 2 ends and problem number 3 begins.

- Refer to visual illustrations and explain the content to be sure people understand what they are looking at.

- Cite authorities or give sources for your information, particularly if people in the audience have contributed information for your presentation.

- Simplify statistics for the presentation, and provide the full tables or formulas in handouts.

Conclusion.   Your conclusion should summarize the main points and recommendations to fix them in listeners' minds. In addition, remind listeners about necessary future actions, upcoming deadlines, and other scheduled presentations on the subject. Also ask for questions so that listeners can clarify points immediately.

Model 13-1 is a sentence outline of an oral presentation by the communications manager at a large company. The manager is alerting company officers

VOICE MAIL SECURITY REPORT

I. Toll fraud is a growing problem in corporate telecommunications.
    A. Information in this report comes from the Society of Information Management seminar, New York, October 1–2, 1995.
    B. Toll fraud costs over one billion dollars annually.
       [SHOW SIM 5-YEAR TABLE]
       1. Long-distance carriers absorb most of the costs.
       2. All companies with a voice mail system are vulnerable.

II. Voice-mail systems have increased corporate risk of toll fraud.
    A. Hackers can browse through systems and use abandoned voice-mail boxes.
    B. Hackers can use voice mail to travel through corporate PBX systems and access a dial tone.
    C. Voice-mail fraud is difficult to trace.
       [SHOW FLOWCHART OF FRAUD ATTEMPT]

III. Voice-mail systems have two vulnerable elements.
    A. Most companies (including ours) have an 800 number for remote access.
    B. Employees overuse default passwords.
       1. Hackers can delete or alter messages.
       2. Hackers can access a remote dial tone.

IV. Companies must take steps to protect against voice-mail fraud.
    A. All default passwords must be changed.
    B. Passwords should be no shorter than six digits.
    C. Unused voice-mail boxes must be deleted.
    D. Ability to transfer from voice mail to a remote PBX should be disabled by the vendor.
    E. Billing for voice-mail 800 numbers should be monitored.

V. No company system can be 100% safe.
    [DISTRIBUTE TOLL FRAUD CHART AND ASK FOR QUESTIONS]

MODEL 13-1 Outline of Oral Presentation

to the dangers of voice-mail fraud based on information gathered at a seminar on communications security.

As the outline shows, the introduction (1) identifies the main topic—toll fraud and its costs and (2) identifies the source of the information. Sections II and III explain the risks of voice mail and the methods hackers use to enter the systems. Section IV provides strategies the company can use to protect itself, and the conclusion warns listeners that a company can never be completely safe. To help listeners understand the information, speakers often supplement oral presentations with handouts that highlight specific points or distribute full written reports on the subject of the presentation. Listeners then can check the report later for items they are most interested in, read sections not fully covered in the oral presentation, and confirm their memories of significant details. Notice that the speaker using the outline in Model 13–1 has inserted reminders of when to use graphic aids in Sections I and II, as well as a note to distribute handouts and ask for questions at the close. Such notes about when to use graphic aids or ask for questions are important reminders because, during a presentation, you may concentrate so much on the information involved that you forget to use the supplemental materials designed to aid listeners. Many speakers also put extra-wide margins in their outlines so that they can jot down more facts in the margins as reminders.

PREPARING FOR ORAL PRESENTATIONS

Because oral presentations usually have time restrictions, concentrate on the factors that your audience is most interested in, and prepare written materials covering other points that you do not have time to present orally. In addition, for oral presentations, you must check on these physical conditions, if possible:

- *Size of the group.* Is the group so large that you need a microphone to be heard in the back, and will those in the back be able to see your graphic aids? Remember that the larger the group, the more remote the listeners feel from the speaker and the less likely they are to interact and provide feedback.

- *Shape of the room.* Can all the listeners see the speaker, or is the room so narrow that those in the back are blocked from seeing either the speaker or the graphic aids? Does the speaker have to stand in front of a large glass wall through which listeners can watch other office activities? An inability to see or an opportunity to watch outside activities will prevent listeners from concentrating on the presentation.

- *Visual equipment.* Does the room contain built-in visual equipment, such as a movie screen or chalkboard, or will these have to be brought in, thus altering the shape of the speaking area? Will additional equipment in the room crowd the speaker or listeners? Are there enough electrical outlets, or will long extension cords be necessary, thereby creating walking obstacles for the speaker or those entering the room?

- *Seating arrangements.* Are the chairs bolted in place? Is there room for space between chairs, or will people be seated elbow-to-elbow in tight rows? If listeners want to take notes, is there room to write? People hate to be crowded into closely packed rows. An uncomfortable audience is an inattentive one.

- *Lighting.* Is there enough light so that listeners can see to take notes? Can the light be controlled to prevent the room from being so bright that people cannot see slides and transparencies clearly?

- *Temperature.* Is the room too hot or too cold? Heat is usually worse for an audience because it makes people sleepy, especially in the afternoon. If the temperature is too cold, people may concentrate on huddling in jackets and sweaters rather than listening to the presentation. A cool room, however, will heat up once people are seated because of body heat. Good air circulation also helps keep a room from being hot, stuffy, and uncomfortable.

You may not be able to control all these factors, but you can make some adjustments to enhance your presentation. You can adjust the temperature control or change the position of the lectern away from a distracting window, for example.

DELIVERING ORAL PRESENTATIONS

After planning your oral presentation to provide your listeners with the information they need and organizing your talk, you must deliver it. Fairly or unfairly, listeners tend to judge the usefulness of an oral presentation at least partly by the physical delivery of the speaker. Prepare your delivery as carefully as you do your outline.

Nerves

Everyone who speaks in front of a group is somewhat nervous. Fortunately, nerves create energy, and you need energy to deliver your talk. Prepare thoroughly so that you know you are giving your listeners the information they want. Picture yourself performing well beforehand, and remember that no one is there to "catch" you in a mistake. In fact, the audience usually does not know if you reverse the order of transparencies or discuss points out of order.

If you "go blank" during a presentation, pause and repeat your last point, using slightly different words. This repetition often puts a speaker back on track. Consider speaking in front of a group not as a dreadful ordeal that you must suffer through, but as an essential part of your job, and develop your ability to make an effective presentation.

Rehearsal

Rehearse your oral presentation aloud so that you know it thoroughly and it fits the allotted time. Rehearsing it will also help you find trouble spots where, for instance, you have not explained in enough detail or your chronology is out of order. If possible, practice in the room you intend to use so that you can check the speaking area, seating arrangements, and lighting.

Voice

If you are nervous, your voice may reveal it more than any mistakes you make. Do not race through your talk on one breath, forcing your audience to listen to an unintelligible monotone, but do not pause after every few words either, creating a stop-and-start style. Avoid a monotone by being interested in your own presentation. Speak clearly, and check the pronunciation of difficult terms or foreign words before your talk. Be sure also to pronounce words separately. For example, say "would have" instead of "wouldof."

Professional Image

When you speak in front of a group, you are in a sense "on stage." Dress conservatively but in the usual office style. Uncomfortable clothes that are too tight or that have unusual, eye-catching decorations are not appropriate for oral presentations. They will distract both you and your audience. Do not hang on the lectern, perch casually on the edge of a table, or sway back and forth on your feet. Be relaxed, but stand straight.

Gestures

Nervous gestures can distract your audience, and artificial "on purpose" gestures look awkward. If you feel clumsy, keep your hands still. Do not fiddle with your note cards, jewelry, tie, hair, or other objects.

Some gestures, however, can help focus the audience's attention on a specific point. If you suggest two solutions for a problem and hold up two fingers to emphasize the choice, the gesture will help your audience remember the number of alternatives you explained.

Eye Contact

Create the impression that you are speaking to the individuals in the room by establishing eye contact. Although you may not be able to look at each person individually, glance around the room frequently. Do not stare at two or three people to the exclusion of all others, but do not sweep back and forth across the room like a surveillance camera. Eye contact indicates that you are interested in the listener's response, and a smile indicates that you are pleased to be giving this presentation. You should project both attitudes.

Notes and Outlines

Have your notes organized before arriving in the room, and number each card or page in case you drop them and have to put them in order quickly. If a lectern is available, place your notes on that. In any case, avoid waving your notes around or making them obvious to your listeners. Your listeners want to concentrate on what you are telling them, not on a sheaf of white cards flapping in the air.

Visual Equipment

Practice using any visual equipment before your talk so that you know where the control buttons are and how the machine works. If you know you write slowly on chalkboards and flip charts, put your terms or lists on them before the presentation so that you can simply refer to them at the appropriate time. If you are using videotape machines or cassettes, set the tapes to the exact start spot and know which key word or image signals where you want to shut them off. If any equipment breaks during your presentation, simply continue without it. Trying to manage repairs in the middle of a presentation will result in chaos. No matter what kind of visual equipment you use, be sure that all members of the audience can see the visual part of your presentation adequately.

Questions

One of the advantages of oral presentations is that listeners can ask questions immediately. Answer as many questions as your time limitations permit. If you do not know the answer to a question, say so and promise to find the answer later. You may ask if anyone else in the audience knows the answer, but do not put someone on the spot by calling his or her name without warning. If there is a reason you cannot answer a question, such as the information being classified, simply say so. If you are not sure what the questioner means, rephrase the question before trying to answer it by saying, "Are you asking whether . . . ?" In all cases, answer a question completely before going on to another.

JOINING A TEAM PRESENTATION

In some instances, such as sales presentations to potential clients or training sessions, a team of people makes the oral presentation, with each person on the team responsible for a unit that reflects that person's speciality. Although each person must plan and deliver an individual talk, some coordination is needed to be sure the overall presentation goes smoothly. Remember these guidelines:

- One person should be in charge of introducing the overall presentation to provide continuity. That person also may present the conclusion, wrapping up the team effort.

- One person should be in charge of all visual equipment so that, for example, two people do not bring overhead projectors.

- If the question period is left to the end of the team presentation, then one person should be in charge of moderating the questions that the team members answer in order to maintain an orderly atmosphere.

- All members should pay close attention to time limits so that they do not infringe on other team members' allotted time.

- All team members should listen to the other speakers as a courtesy and because they may need to refer to each other's talks in answering questions.

FACING INTERNATIONAL AUDIENCES

As companies expand their operations into worldwide markets and become partners with companies in other countries, you may have to make an oral presentation to an international audience. If so, you must consider language barriers. First, determine whether your audience understands English or you will be using a translator. If a translator will be repeating your words in another language after every sentence, your presentation will take twice as long, and you must adjust the length accordingly.

Rather than speak from an outline, write out your speech in detail. You want to be sure that nothing in your speech will offend or confuse your audience. Ask someone who speaks your audience's language to review your speech carefully and cut out all confusing jargon, slang, acronyms, popular culture references, and humor. These elements do not translate well. When you give your speech, keep to the written script to avoid straying into comments that will present problems for the translator. As a courtesy, you might prepare visual aids in the language of your audience.

Even if your audience understands English, you will need to research the appropriate ways to open your presentation, how much time to allot for questions, and how to end without giving offense. For example, American presentation style is to begin by pointing out objectives. However, an Arab speaker may begin by expressing appreciation for hospitality and appealing for harmony. Germans typically do not interact with speakers, and the question session may be short, but Mexicans enjoy a long question-and-answer session. The American closing typically calls for action, but other cultures may close presentations by emphasizing future meetings or group harmony.[2]

It takes time and thought to prepare an appropriate oral presentation for an international audience. To be an effective speaker in such circumstances, you must develop techniques to ensure that your technical information is not changed in translation and your presentation style fulfills your audience's cultural expectations.

CHAPTER SUMMARY

This chapter discusses making oral presentations on the job. Remember:

- Oral presentations may have these purposes, separately or in combination: informing, persuading, instructing.

- Oral presentations have the advantages of allowing the speaker to create enthusiasm through a dynamic personality as well as allowing listeners to ask questions on the spot.

- Oral presentations have disadvantages in that listeners cannot study materials thoroughly and are easily distracted.

- Oral presentations may be (1) a memorized speech, (2) a written manuscript, (3) impromptu remarks, or (4) an extemporaneous talk.

- Speakers usually use topic or sentence outlines for oral presentations.

- If possible before a presentation, speakers should check the room layout, lighting, temperature, and visual equipment.

- Speakers should (1) control nerves by preparing thoroughly, (2) rehearse aloud, (3) speak clearly, (4) dress professionally (5) keep hand gestures to a minimum, (6) establish eye contact, (7) number notes and outline sheets, (8) practice with video equipment, and (9) answer audience questions fully.

- For a team presentation, one speaker should handle the general introduction and conclusion.

- For international audiences, prepare a written speech.

━━━━━━━ *SUPPLEMENTAL READINGS IN PART 2*

Beswick, R. W. "Voicemail," *Communication and Technology: Today and Tomorrow,* p. 462.

" 'Big Emerging Markets' Have Diverse Cultures, but Common Attributes," *Business America,* p. 466.

Bowman, J. P., and Okuda, T. "Japanese-American Communication: Mysteries, Enigmas, and Possibilities," *The Bulletin of the Association for Business Communication,* p. 480.

Calabrese, R. "Designing and Delivering Presentations and Workshops," *The Bulletin of the Association for Business Communication,* p. 496.

Holcombe, M. W., and Stein, J. K. "How to Deliver Dynamic Presentations: Use Visuals for Impact," *Business Marketing,* p. 509.

Hulbert, J. E. "Barriers to Effective Listening," *The Bulletin of the Association for Business Communication,* p. 515.

Martel, M. "Combating Speech Anxiety," *Public Relations Journal,* p. 531.

Sherblom, J. C. "Teleconferencing," *Communication and Technology: Today and Tomorrow,* p. 556.

Smith, T. C. "Listen Up—Tips from the Top on Talks," *Technical Communication,* p. 568.

━━━━━━━ *ENDNOTES*

1. "Critical Link between Presentation Skills, Upward Mobility," *American Salesman* 36.8 (August 1991): 16–20.

2. Elashmawl, Farid, "Multicultural Business Meeting and Presentations: Tips and Taboos," *Tokyo Business Today* 59.11 (November 1991): 66–68.

1. Read "Japanese-American Communication: Mysteries, Enigmas, and Possibilities" by Bowman and Okuda and " 'Big Emerging Markets' Have Diverse Cultures, but Common Attributes" in Part 2. Select one of the countries discussed in these articles. Research information on how to conduct meetings or how to make oral presentations in that culture. Consider such topics as setting the meeting agenda, seating arrangements, opening and closing the meeting or presentation, appropriate handouts or visual aids, appropriate presentation format. Prepare a 5-minute presentation of the information you find. *Or,* if your instructor prefers, join two classmates and conduct a panel discussion of tips for handling meetings and oral presentations in that culture.

2. Prepare a 3- or 4-minute oral presentation to give to your class based on one of your written assignments in this class. Prepare a sentence outline of your oral presentation to submit to your instructor.

3. Find a technical article about a topic in your field. Prepare a 2-minute oral presentation of the information in the article suitable for students in this class.

4. Using the evaluation sheet that appears in the article by Calabrese in Part 2, assess an oral presentation on your campus (e.g., outside speaker, student presentation in another class, chair of a campus meeting). Discuss the results. In groups, develop an evaluation sheet you would like to use for assessing oral presentations in this class.

Guidelines for Grammar, Punctuation, and Mechanics

These guidelines for grammar, punctuation, and mechanical matters, such as using numbers, will help you revise your writing according to generally accepted conventions for correctness. These guidelines cover the most frequent questions writers have when they edit their final drafts. Your instructor may tell you to read about specific topics before revising. In addition, use this Appendix to check your writing before you submit it to your instructor.

GRAMMAR

Dangling Modifiers

Dangling modifiers are verbal phrases, prepositional phrases, or dependent clauses that do not refer to a subject in the sentence in which they occur. These modifiers are most often at the beginning of a sentence, but they may also appear at the end. Correct by rewriting the sentence to include the subject of the modifier.

Incorrect:	Realizing the connections between neutron stars, pulsars, and supernovas, the explanation of the birth and death of stars is complete. (The writer does not indicate *who* realized the connections.)
Correct:	Realizing the connection between neutron stars, pulsars, and supernovas, many astronomers believe that the explanation of the birth and death of stars is complete.

Incorrect:	To obtain a slender blade, a cylindrical flint core was chipped into long slivers with a hammerstone. (The writer does not indicate *who* worked to obtain the blade.)
Correct:	To obtain a slender blade, Cro-Magnon man chipped a cylindrical flint core into slivers with a hammerstone.
Incorrect:	Born with cerebral palsy, only minimal mobility was possible. (The writer does not indicate *who* was born with cerebral palsy.)
Correct:	Born with cerebral palsy, the child had only minimal mobility.
Incorrect:	Their sensitivity to prostaglandins remained substantially lowered, hours after leaving a smoke-filled room. (The writer does not indicate *who* or *what* left the room.)
Correct:	Their sensitivity to prostaglandins remained substantially lowered, hours after the nonsmokers left a smoke-filled room.

Misplaced Modifiers

Misplaced modifiers are words, phrases, or clauses that do not refer logically to the nearest word in the sentence in which they appear. Correct by rewriting the sentence to place the modifier next to the word to which it refers.

| *Incorrect:* | The financial analysts presented statistics to their clients that showed net margins were twice the industry average. (The phrase about *net margins* does not modify *clients*.) |
| *Correct:* | The financial analysts presented their clients with statistics that showed net margins were twice the industry average. |

Squinting Modifiers

Squinting modifiers are words or phrases that could logically refer to either a preceding or a following word in the sentence in which they appear. Correct by rewriting the sentence so that the modifier refers to only one word in the sentence.

Incorrect:	Physicians who use a nuclear magnetic resonance machine frequently can identify stroke damage in older patients easily. (The word *frequently* could refer to *use* or *identify*.)
Correct:	Physicians who frequently use a nuclear magnetic resonance machine can identify stroke damage in older patients easily.
Correct:	Physicians who use a nuclear magnetic resonance machine can identify stroke damage in older patients frequently and easily.

Parallel Construction

Elements that are equal in a sentence should be expressed in the same grammatical form.

Incorrect:	With professional care, bulimia can be treated and is controllable. (The words *treated* and *controllable* are not parallel.)
Correct:	With professional care, bulimia can be treated and controlled.
Incorrect:	The existence of two types of Neanderthal tool kits indicates that one group was engaged in scraping hides, while the other group carved wood. (The verbal phrases after the word *group* are not parallel.)
Correct:	The existence of two types of Neanderthal tool kits indicates that one group scraped hides, while the other group carved wood.
Incorrect:	The social worker counseled the family about preparing meals, cleaning the house, and gave advice about childcare. (The list of actions should be in parallel phrases.)
Correct:	The social worker counseled the family about preparing meals, cleaning the house, and caring for children.

Elements linked by correlative conjunctions (*either . . . or, neither . . . nor, not only . . . but also*) also should be in parallel structure.

Incorrect:	Such symptoms as rocking and staring vacantly are seen not only in monkeys that are deprived of their children but also when something frightens mentally disturbed children. (The phrases following *not only* and *but also* are not parallel.)
Correct:	Such symptoms as rocking and staring vacantly are seen not only in monkeys that are deprived of their children but also in mentally disturbed children who are frightened.

Pronoun Agreement

A pronoun must agree in number, person, and gender with the noun or pronoun to which it refers.

Incorrect:	Each firefighter must record their use of equipment. (The noun *firefighter* is singular, and the pronoun *their* is plural.)
Correct:	Each firefighter must record his or her use of equipment.
Correct:	All firefighters must record their use of equipment.
Incorrect:	Everyone needs carbohydrates in their diet. (*Everyone* is singular, and *their* is plural.)

Correct:	Everyone needs carbohydrates in the diet.
Correct:	Everyone needs to eat carbohydrates.
Correct:	Everyone needs carbohydrates in his or her diet.
Incorrect:	The sales department explained their training methods to a group of college students. (*Sales department* is singular and requires an *it*. Correct by clarifying *who* did the explaining.)
Correct:	The sales manager explained the department training methods to a group of college students.
Correct:	The sales manager explained her training methods to a group of college students.
Incorrect:	The International Microbiologists Association met at their traditional site. (*Association* is singular and requires an *it*.)
Correct:	The International Microbiologists Association met at its traditional site.

Pronoun Reference

A pronoun must clearly refer to only one antecedent.

Incorrect:	Biologists have shown that all living organisms depend on two kinds of molecules—amino acids and nucleotides. They are the building blocks of life. (*They* could refer to either *amino acids, nucleotides,* or both.)
Correct:	Biologists have shown that all living organisms depend on two kinds of molecules—amino acids and nucleotides. Both are the building blocks of life.
Incorrect:	Present plans call for a new parking deck, a new entry area, and an addition to the parking garage. It will add $810,000 to the cost. (*It* could refer to any of the new items.)
Correct:	Present plans call for a new parking deck, a new entry area, and an addition to the parking garage. The parking deck will add $810,000 to the cost.

Reflexive Pronouns

A *reflexive pronoun* (ending in *-self* or *-selves*) must refer to the subject of the sentence when the subject also receives the action in the sentence. (Example: She cut herself when the camera lens cracked.) A reflexive pronoun cannot serve instead of *I* or *me* as a subject or an object in a sentence.

Incorrect:	The governor presented the science award to Dr. Yasmin Rashid and myself. (*Myself* cannot serve as the indirect object.)

Correct:	The governor presented the science award to Dr. Yasmin Rashid and me.
Incorrect:	Mark Burnwood, Christina Hayward, and myself conducted the experiment. (*Myself* cannot function as the subject of the sentence.)
Correct:	Mark Burnwood, Christina Hayward, and I conducted the experiment.

Reflexive pronouns are also used to make the antecedent more emphatic:

The patient himself asked for another medication.

Venus itself is covered by a heavy layer of carbon dioxide.

Sentence Faults

Comma Splices

A *comma splice* results when the writer incorrectly joins two independent clauses with a comma. Correct by (1) placing a semicolon between the clauses, (2) adding a coordinating conjunction after the comma, (3) rewriting the sentence, or (4) creating two sentences.

Incorrect:	The zinc coating on galvanized steel gums up a welding gun's electrode, resistance welding, therefore, is not ideal for the steel increasingly used in autos today.
Correct:	The zinc coating on galvanized steel gums up a welding gun's electrode; resistance welding, therefore, is not ideal for the steel increasingly used in autos today.
Correct:	The zinc coating on galvanized steel gums up a welding gun's electrode, so resistance welding, therefore, is not ideal for the steel increasingly used in autos today.
Correct:	Because the zinc coating on galvanized steel gums up a welding gun's electrode, resistance welding is not ideal for the steel increasingly used in autos today.
Correct:	The zinc coating on galvanized steel gums up a welding gun's electrode. Resistance welding, therefore, is not ideal for the steel increasingly used in autos today.

Fragments

A *sentence fragment* is an incomplete sentence because it lacks a subject or a verb or both. Correct by writing a full sentence or by adding the fragment to another sentence.

Incorrect:　　As the universe expands and the galaxies fly further apart, the force of gravity is decreasing everywhere. According to one imaginative theory. (The phrase beginning with *According* is a fragment.)

Correct:　　According to one imaginative theory, as the universe expands and the galaxies fly further apart, the force of gravity is decreasing everywhere.

Incorrect:　　Apes are afraid of water when they cannot see the stream bottom. Which prevents them from entering the water and crossing a stream more than 1 ft deep. (The phrase beginning with *which* is a fragment.)

Correct:　　Apes are afraid of water when they cannot see the stream bottom. This fear prevents them from entering the water and crossing a stream more than 1 ft deep.

Run-on Sentences

A *run-on sentence* occurs when a writer links two or more sentences together without punctuation between them. Correct by placing a semicolon between the sentences or by writing two separate sentences.

Incorrect:　　The galaxy is flattened by its rotating motion into the shape of a disk most of the stars in the galaxy are in this disk.

Correct:　　The galaxy is flattened by its rotating motion into the shape of a disk; most of the stars in the galaxy are in this disk.

Correct:　　The galaxy is flattened by its rotating motion into the shape of a disk. Most of the stars in the galaxy are in this disk.

Subject/Verb Agreement

The verb in a sentence must agree with its subject in person and number. Correct by rewriting.

Incorrect:　　The report of a joint team of Canadian and American geologists suggest that some dormant volcanos on the West Coast may be reawakening. (The subject is *report*, which requires a singular verb.)

Correct:　　The report of a joint team of Canadian and American geologists suggests that some dormant volcanos on the West Coast may be reawakening.

Incorrect:　　The high number of experiments that failed were disappointing. (The subject is *number,* which requires a singular verb.)

Correct:　　The high number of experiments that failed was disappointing.

> *Incorrect:*   Sixteen inches are the deepest we can drill. (The subject is a single unit and requires a singular verb.)
>
> *Correct:*   Sixteen inches is the deepest we can drill.

When compound subjects are joined by *and,* the verb is plural.

> Computer-security techniques and plans for evading hackers require large expenditures.

When one of the compound subjects is plural and one is singular, the verb agrees with the nearest subject.

> Neither the split casings nor the cracked layer of plywood was to blame.

When a compound subject is preceded by *each* or *every,* the verb is singular.

> Every case aide and social worker is scheduled for a training session.

When a compound subject is considered a single unit or person, the verb is singular.

> The vice president and guiding force of the company is meeting with the Nuclear Regulatory Commission.

PUNCTUATION

Apostrophe

An apostrophe shows possession or marks the omission of letters in a word or in dates.

> The engineer's analysis of the city's water system shows a high pollution danger from raw sewage.
>
> The extent of the outbreak of measles wasn't known until all area hospitals' medical records were coordinated with those of private physicians.
>
> Chemist Charles Frakes' experiments were funded by the National Institute of Health throughout the '70s.

Do not confuse *its* (possessive) with *it's* (contraction of *it is*).

> The animal pricked up its ears before feeding.
>
> Professors Jones, Higgins, and Carlton are examining the ancient terrain at Casper Mountain. It's located on a geologic fault, and the professors hope to study its changes over time.

Colon

The colon introduces explanations or lists. An independent clause must precede the colon.

The Olympic gymnastic team used three brands of equipment: Acme, Dakota, and Shelby.

Do not place a colon directly after a verb.

Incorrect: The environmentalists reported finding: decreased oxygen, pollution-tolerant sludgeworms, and high bacteria levels in the lake. (The colon does not have an independent clause preceding it.)

Correct: The environmentalists reported finding decreased oxygen, pollution-tolerant sludgeworms, and high bacteria levels in the lake.

Comma

To Link.   The comma links independent clauses joined by a coordinating conjunction (*and, but, or, for, so, yet,* and *nor*).

The supervisor stopped the production line, but the damage was done.

Rheumatic fever is controllable once it has been diagnosed, yet continued treatment is often needed for years.

To Enclose.   The comma encloses parenthetical information, simple definitions, or interrupting expressions in a sentence.

Gloria Anderson, our best technician, submitted the winning suggestion.

The research team, of course, will return to the site after the monsoon season.

The condition stems from the body's inability to produce enough hemoglobin, a component of red blood cells, to carry oxygen to all body tissues.

If the passage is essential to the sentence (restrictive), do not enclose it in commas.

Acme shipped the toys that have red tags to the African relief center. (The phrase *that have red tags* is essential for identifying which toys were shipped.)

To Separate.   The comma separates introductory phrases or clauses from the rest of the sentence and also separates items in a list.

Accurate to within 30 seconds a year, the electronic quartz watch is also water resistant.

> Because so many patients experienced side effects, the FDA refused to approve the drug.

> To calculate the three points, add the static head, friction losses, velocity head, and minor losses. (Retain the final comma in a list for clarity.)

The comma also separates elements in addresses and dates.

> The shipment went to Hong Kong on May 29, 1996, but the transfer forms went to Marjorie Howard, District Manager, Transworld Exports, 350 Michigan Avenue, Chicago, Illinois 60616.

Dash

The dash sets off words or phrases that interrupt a sentence or that indicate sharp emphasis. The dash also encloses simple definitions. The dash is a more emphatic punctuation mark than parentheses or commas.

> The foundation has only one problem—no funds.

> The majority of those surveyed—those who were willing to fill out the questionnaire—named television parents in nuclear families as ideal mother and father images.

Exclamation Point

The exclamation point indicates strong emotion or sharp commands. It is not often used in technical writing, except for warnings or cautions.

> Insert the cable into the double outlet.

> Warning! Do not allow water to touch the cable.

Hyphen

The hyphen divides a word at the end of a typed line and also forms compound words. If in doubt about where to divide a word or whether to use a hyphen in a compound word, consult a dictionary.

> Scientists at the state-sponsored research laboratory are using cross-pollination to produce hybrid grains.

Modifiers of two or three words require hyphens when they precede a noun.

> Tycho Brahe, sixteenth-century astronomer, measured the night sky with giant quadrants.

The microwave-antenna system records the differing temperatures coming from the Earth and the cooler sky.

Parentheses

Parentheses enclose (1) nonessential information in a sentence or (2) letters and figures that enumerate items in a list.

The striped lobsters (along with solid blue varieties) have been bred from rare red and blue lobsters that occur in nature.

Early television content analyses (from 1950 to 1980) reported that (1) men appeared more often than women, (2) men were more active problem solvers than women, (3) men were older than women, and (4) men were more violent than women.

Parentheses also enclose simple definitions.

The patient suffered from hereditary trichromatic deuteranomaly (red-green color blindness).

Quotation Marks

Quotation marks enclose (1) direct quotations and (2) titles of journal articles, book chapters, reports, songs, poems, and individual episodes of radio and television programs.

"Planets are similar to giant petri dishes," stated astrophysicist Miranda Caliban at the Gatewood Research Institute.

"Combat Readiness: Naval Air vs. Air Force" (journal article)

"Science and Politics of Human Differences" (book chapter)

"Feasibility Study of Intrastate Expansion" (report)

"Kariba: The Lake That Made a Dent" (television episode)

Place commas and periods inside quotation marks. Place colons and semi-colons outside quotation marks. See also "Italics" under "Mechanics" in this Appendix.

Question Mark

The question mark follows direct questions but not indirect questions.

The colonel asked, "Where are the orders for troop deployment?"

The colonel asked whether the orders for troop deployment had arrived.

Place a question mark inside quotation marks if the quotation is a question, as shown above. If the quotation is not a question but is included in a question, place the question mark outside the quotation marks.

Why did the chemist state "The research is unnecessary"?

Semicolon

The semicolon links two independent clauses without a coordinating conjunction or other punctuation.

The defense lawyer suggested the arsenic could have originated in the embalming fluid; Bateman dismissed this theory

All the cabinets are wood; however, the countertops are of artificial marble.

The semicolon also separates items in a series if the items contain internal commas.

The most desirable experts for the federal environmental task force are Sophia Timmons, Chief Biologist, Ohio Water Commission; Clinton Buchanan, Professor of Microbiology, Central Missouri State University; and Hugo Wysoki, Director of the California Wildlife Research Institute, San Jose.

Slash

The slash separates choices and parts of dates and numbers.

For information about the property tax deduction, call 555–6323/7697. (The reader can choose between two telephone numbers.)

The crew began digging on 9/28/96 and increased the drill pressure ¾ psi every hour.

MECHANICS

Acronyms and Initialisms

An *acronym* is an abbreviation formed from the first letters of the words in a name or phrase. The acronym is written in all capitals with no periods and is pronounced as a word.

The crew gathered in the NASA conference room and used the WATS line to call the engineering team.

Some acronyms eventually become words in themselves. For example, *radar* was once an acronym for *radio detecting and ranging*. Now the word *radar* is a noun meaning a system for sensing the presence of objects.

Initialisms are also abbreviations formed from the first letters of the words in a name or phrase; here each letter is pronounced separately. Some initialisms are written in all capital letters; others are written in capital and lowercase letters. Some are written with periods; some are not. If you are uncertain about the conventional form for an initialism, consult a dictionary.

The technician increased the heat by 4 Btu.

The C.P.A. took the tax returns to the IRS office.

When using acronyms or initialisms, spell out the full term the first time it appears in the text and place the acronym or initialism in parentheses immediately after to be sure your readers understand it. In subsequent references, use the acronym or initialism alone.

The Federal Communication Commission (FCC) has authorized several thousand licenses for low-power television (LPTV) stations.

In a few cases, the acronym or initialism may be so well known by your readers that you can use it without stating the full term first.

The experiment took place at 10:15 A.M. with the application of DDT at specified intervals.

Plurals of acronyms and initialisms are formed by adding an *s* without an apostrophe, such as YMCAs, MBAs, COLAs, and EKGs.

Brackets

Brackets enclose words that are inserted into quotations by writers or editors. The inserted words are intended to add information to the quoted material.

"Thank you for the splendid photographic service [to the Navy, 1976–1982] and the very comprehensive collection donated to the library," said Admiral Allen Sumner as he dedicated the new library wing.

Brackets also enclose a phrase or word inserted into a quotation to substitute for a longer, more complicated phrase or clause.

"The surgical procedure," explained Dr. Moreno, "allows [the kidneys] to cleanse the blood and maintain a healthy chemical balance."

Capital Letters

Capital letters mark the first word of a sentence and the first word of a quotation. A full sentence after a colon and full sentences in a numbered list may also begin with capital letters if the writer wishes to emphasize them.

> Many of the photographs were close-ups.
>
> Pilots are concerned about mountain wave turbulence and want a major change: Higher altitude clearance is essential.

Capital letters also mark proper names and initials of people and objects.

> Dr. Jonathan L. Hazzard
> Ford Taurus
> USS Fairfax

In addition, capital letters mark nationalities, religions, tribal affiliations, and linguistic groups.

> British (nationality)
> Lutheran (religion)
> Cherokee (tribal affiliation)
> Celtic (linguistic group)

Capital letters also mark (1) place names, (2) geographical and astronomical areas, (3) organizations, (4) events, (5) historical times, (6) software, and (7) some calendar designations.

> San Diego, California (place)
> Great Plains (geographic area)
> League of Women Voters (organization)
> Robinson Helicopter Company (company)
> World Series (event)
> Paleocene Epoch (historical time)
> WordPerfect (software)
> Tuesday, July 12 (calendar designations)

Capital letters also mark brand names but not generic names.

> Tylenol (acetaminophen)

Capital letters mark the first, last, and main words in the titles of (1) books, (2) articles, (3) films, (4) television and radio programs, (5) music, and (6) art objects. Do not capitalize short conjunctions, prepositions, or articles (*a, an, the*) unless they begin the title or follow a colon. *Note:* If you are preparing a reference list, see Chapter 9 for the correct format.

> *The Panda's Thumb* (book)
>
> "Information Base: On Line with CompuServe" (article)
>
> *Gunfight at Smokey Ridge* (film)
>
> "The Search for the Dinosaurs" (television program)
>
> *Concerto in D Major, Opus 77, for Violin and Orchestra* (music)
>
> *The Third of May* (art)

Companies and institutions often use capital letters in specific circumstances not covered in grammar handbooks. If in doubt, check the company or organization style guide.

Ellipsis

An *ellipsis* (three spaced periods) indicates an omission of one or more words in a quotation. When the omission is at the end of a sentence or includes an intervening sentence, the ellipsis follows the final period.

> General Donald Mills stated, "It is appalling that those remarks . . . by someone without technical, military, or intelligence credentials should be published."
>
> At the fund-raising banquet, Chief of Staff Audrey Spaulding commented, "All of the volunteers—more than 600—made this evening very special. . . ."

Italics

Italics set off or emphasize specific words or phrases. If italic type is not available, underline the words or phrases. Italics set off titles of (1) books, (2) periodicals, (3) plays, films, television and radio programs, (4) long musical works, (5) complete art objects, and (6) ships, planes, trains, and aircraft. The Bible and its books are not italicized.

> *The Cell in Development and Inheritance* (book)
>
> *Chicago Tribune* (newspaper)
>
> *Scientific American* (journal)
>
> *Inherit the Wind* (play)
>
> *Blade Runner* (film)
>
> *60 Minutes* (television program)
>
> *Carmen* (long musical work)

The Thinker (art object)

City of New Orleans (train)

Apollo III (spacecraft)

Italics also set off words and phrases discussed as words and words and phrases in foreign languages or Latin. Scientific terms for plants and animals also are italicized.

The term *mycobacterium* refers to any one of several rod-shaped aerobic bacteria.

These old fossils may be closer to the African *Australopithecus* than to *Homo.*

See also "Quotation Marks" under "Punctuation" in this Appendix.

Measurements

Measurements of physical quantities, sizes, and temperatures are expressed in figures. Use abbreviations for measurements only when also using figures and when your readers are certain to understand them. If the abbreviations are not common, identify them by spelling out the term on first use and placing the abbreviation in parentheses immediately after. Do not use periods with measurement abbreviations unless the abbreviation might be confused with a full word. For example, *inch* abbreviated needs a period to avoid confusion with the word *in.* Use a hyphen when a measurement functions as a compound adjective.

Workers used 14-in. pipes at the site.

The designer wanted a 4-oz decanter on the sideboard.

Ship 13 lb of feed. (Do not add *s* to make abbreviations plural.)

Ship several pounds of feed. (Do not use abbreviations if no numbers are involved.)

The pressure rose to 12 pounds per square inch (psi).

If the measurement involves two numbers, spell out the first or the shorter word.

The supervisor called for three 12-in. rods.

Here are some common abbreviations for measurements:

C	centigrade	kw	kilowatt
cc	cubic centimeter	l	liter
cm	centimeter	lb	pound

cps	cycles per second	m	meter
cu ft	cubic foot	mg	milligram
dm	decimeter	ml	milliliter
F	Fahrenheit	mm	millimeter
fl oz	fluid ounce	mph	miles per hour
fpm	feet per minute	oz	ounce
ft	foot	psf	pounds per square foot
g	gram	psi	pounds per square inch
gal	gallon	qt	quart
gpm	gallons per minute	rpm	revolutions per minute
hp	horsepower	rps	revolutions per second
in.	inch	sq	square
kg	kilogram	t	ton
km	kilometer	yd	yard

Numbers

Use figures for all numbers over ten. If a document contains many numbers, use figures for all amounts, even those under ten, so that readers do not overlook them.

The testing procedure required 27 test tubes, 2 covers, and 16 sets of gloves.

Do not begin a sentence with a figure. Rewrite to place the number later in the sentence.

Incorrect: 42 tests were scheduled.
Correct: We scheduled 42 tests.

Write very large numbers in figures and words.

2.3 billion people
$16.5 million

Use figures for references to (1) money, (2) temperatures, (3) decimals and fractions, (4) percentages, (5) addresses, and (6) book parts.

$4230
$.75
72° F
0° C

3.67

¾

12.4%

80%

2555 N. 12th Street

Chapter 7, page 178

Use figures for times of day. Because most people are never certain about P.M. and A.M. in connection with 12 o'clock, indicate noon or midnight in parentheses.

4:15 P.M.

12:00 (noon)

12:00 (midnight)

Add an *s* without an apostrophe to make numbers plural.

4s   1980s   33s

Symbols and Equations

Symbols should appear in parenthetical statistical information but not in the narrative.

Incorrect:	The *M* were 2.64 (Test 1) and 3.19 (Test 2).
Correct:	The means were 2.64 (Test 1) and 3.19 (Test 2).
Incorrect:	The sample population (Number = 450) was selected from children in the second grade.
Correct:	The sample population ($N = 450$) was selected from children in the second grade.
Incorrect:	We found a high % of error.
Correct:	We found a high percentage of error.

Do not try to create symbols on a typewriter or computer by combining overlapping characters. Write symbols not on the keyboard by hand in ink.

$$\chi^2 \, (N = 916) = 142.64 \qquad p < .001$$

Place simple or short equations in the text by including them in a sentence.

The equation for the required rectangle is $y = a + 2b - x$.

To display (set off on a separate line) equations, start them on a new line after the text and double space twice above and below the equation. Displayed equations must be numbered for reference. The reference number appears in parentheses flush with the right margin. In the text, use the reference number.

$$F(9,740) = 2.06 \qquad p < .05 \tag{1}$$

If the equation is too long for one line, break it before an operational sign. Place a space between the elements in an equation as if they were words.

$$3v - 5b + 66x$$
$$+ 2x - y = 11.5$$

Very difficult equations that require handwritten symbols should always be displayed for clarity. Highly technical symbols and long equations in documents intended for multiple readers are best placed in appendixes rather than in the main body of the document.

PART 2

Technical Writing: Advice from the Workplace

How to Avoid Costly Proofreading Errors

Carolyn Boccella Bagin and Jo Van Doren

Proofreading errors cost businesses money. This article tells you how to produce error-free copy. Try finding all the mistakes in the sample copy in the article, and check your results against the corrected version.

Are proofreading errors costing you money? Some organizations have sad stories to tell about the price of overlooked mistakes.

- One insurance firm reported that an employee mailed a check for $2,200 as a settlement for a dental claim. Payment of only $22.00 had been authorized.

- One executive wasted $3 million by not catching a hyphen error when proofreading a business letter. In originally dictating the letter to his secretary, the executive said, "We want 1,000-foot-long radium bars. Send three in cases." The order was typed, "We want 1,000 foot-long radium bars."

- A magazine accidentally ran a cake recipe in which "$\frac{3}{4}$ cup" was printed as "$\frac{1}{4}$ cup." Irate readers sent complaint letters and cancelled their subscriptions.

Your company's image could be marred by unfortunate mistakes that find their way into the documents you produce. Developing good proofreading techniques and systems can save time, money, and embarrassment.

HOW CAN YOU PRODUCE ERROR-FREE COPY?

- Never proofread your own copy by yourself. You'll tire of looking at the document in its different stages of development and you'll miss new errors. (If you must proof your own copy, make a line screen for yourself or roll the paper back in the typewriter so that you view only one line at a time. This will reduce your tendency to skim your material.)

- Read everything in the copy straight through from beginning to end: titles, subtitles, sentences, punctuation, capitalizations, indented items, and page numbers.

- Read your copy backward to catch spelling errors. Reading sentences out of sequence lets you concentrate on individual words.

- Consider having proofreaders initial the copy they check. You might find that your documents will have fewer errors.

- If you have a helper to proof numbers that are in columns, read the figures aloud to your partner, and have your partner mark the corrections and changes on the copy being proofread.

- If time allows, put your material aside for a short break. Proofreading can quickly turn into reading if your document is long. After a break, reread the last few lines to refresh your memory.

- Read the pages of a document out of order. Changing the sequence will help you to review each page as a unit.
- List the errors you spot over a month's time. You may find patterns that will catch your attention when you proofread your next document.
- If you can, alter your routine. Don't proofread at the same time every day. Varying your schedule will help you approach your task with a keener eye.
- Not everyone knows and uses traditional proofreading marks. But a simple marking system should be legible and understandable to you and to anyone else working on the copy.

WHERE DO ERRORS USUALLY HIDE?

- Mistakes tend to cluster. If you find one typo, look carefully for another one nearby.
- Inspect the beginning of pages, paragraphs, and sections. Some people tend to skim these crucial spots.
- Beware of changes in typeface—especially in headings or titles. If you change to all uppercase letters, italics, boldface, or underlined copy, read those sections again.
- Make sure your titles, subtitles, and page numbers match those in the table of contents.
- Read sequential material carefully. Look for duplications in page numbers or in lettered items in lists or outlines.
- Double-check references such as, "see the chart below." Several drafts later, the chart may be pages away from its original place.
- Examine numbers and totals. Recheck all calculations and look for misplaced commas and decimal points.
- Scrutinize features that come in sets, such as brackets, parentheses, quotation marks, and dashes.

TRY YOUR HAND (AND EYE) AT THIS TEST

Mark the mistakes and check your corrections with our marked copy on page 450.

It is improtant to look for certain item when proofing a report , letter, or othr document. Aside from spelling errors, the prooffer should check for deviations in format consitent use of punctuation, consistent use of capitol letters, undefined acronyms and correctpage numbers listed in the the Table of contents.

After checking a typed draft againts the original manuscript one should also read the draft for aukward phrasing, syntactical errors, and subject/verb agreement and grammatical mistakes. paralell structures should be used im listings headed by bullets or numbers: ie, if one item starts with the phrase "to understand the others should start with to plus a verb.

The final step in proofing involves review of the overall appearance on the document. Are the characrters all printed clearly Are all the pages there? Are the pages free of stray marks ? Is the graphics done? Are bullets filled in? All of the above items effect the appearance of the the document and determine whether the document has the desired effect on the reader.

HOW DID YOU DO?

Check your markup against ours. (We only show corrections in the copy and not the margin notes that most proofreaders typically use.)

It is important to look for certain items when proofing a report, letter, or othr document. Aside from spelling errors, the prooffer should check for deviations in format, consitent use of punctuation, consistent use of capital letters, undefined acronyms and correct page numbers listed in the the Table of contents.

After checking a typed draft against the original manuscript one should also read the draft for awkward phrasing, syntactical errors, and subject/verb agreement and grammatical mistakes. paralell structures should be used in listings headed by bullets or numbers; ie, if one item starts with the phrase "to understand, the others should start with "to" plus a verb.

The final step in proofing involves review of the overall appearance on the document. Are the characters all printed clearly? Are all the pages there? Are the pages free of stray marks ? Is the graphics done? Are bullets filled in? All of the above items effect the appearance of the the document and determine whether the document has the desired effect on the reader.

Writing Visually: Design Considerations in Technical Publications

Philippa J. Benson

Readers find documents most usable when the visual design guides them to the information they need. This article provides guidelines for using visual devices, such as typeface, headings, and graphics, to produce a document your readers can use easily.

Writers and graphic designers are working more closely together as each learns more about how the other approaches the task of planning and structuring a document. The field of document design has developed from this synthesis of the processes of writing and design: writers and designers have come to agree that the most effective documents are those that use both words and design to reveal and reinforce the structure of information in a text.

The synthesis of writing and design is supported not only by the developing bond between writers and designers, but also by the conclusions of applied research. Research in cognitive psychology, instructional design, reading, and graphic design indicates that documents are most usable when the information in them is apparent both visually and syntactically. In particular, the results of usability tests of documents are providing concrete evidence that readers find documents most usable when the visual aspects of a document support the hierarchy of the information in a text.[1-5]

The synthesis of writing and design has also been evolving because computers increasingly put control over typography and page format in the writer's domain. Although many text-formatting programs limit the design decisions that we can make, they do allow us to simultaneously write and design information.

The increasing use of computers has also led to the development of a new concern for document designers: online information. Designers of online documentation should be concerned with many of the same issues as page designers—that is, the legibility and accessibility of information.

UNDERSTANDING CONSTRAINTS ON DESIGNING A DOCUMENT

How effectively writers and designers can work together depends not only on how well they can communicate but also on the practical constraints of their working environment. Before you begin planning a document, find out about the limits of your schedule and budget, and the flexibility of the method you'll be using to produce the end product (printer, typesetter, printing process). Your schedule, budget, and method of printing may limit what you can do with the design of your document. Constraints may affect these aspects of your book:

- Page count, page size
- Packaging (binding, cover, separators, etc.)

451

- Typeface, type size
- Range of available fonts
- Use of color and graphics
- Number of heading levels available
- Kinds of graphics you can use (tables, flowcharts, illustrations)

If you find that the constraints depart from the principles of good document design, you should consider trying to change them. For example, you may be told you must use a type size of smaller than 8 or 9 points or set a sizable portion of text in uppercase. The research cited in this article provides evidence you can use to convince your managers to change the constraints that would make your document less usable. Once you know your constraints, you can choose design options that are compatible with them.

DESIGNING FOR YOUR AUDIENCE(S) AND THEIR TASKS

A primary step in planning a document is understanding the audience for the document and their purpose in reading it. For example, if you are writing a book about how to service a software product on a computer system, you may have several audiences. Some readers may simply want to know the procedures they need to follow to service the product, while other readers may want to know how these procedures affect the computer system as a whole.

Research indicates that document designers should consider how readers will use the document. In a document with multiple audiences, each with different purposes and tasks in mind, research suggests that you should design the document so that members of each audience can quickly find the specific information they need.[6-8]

Depending on the reading situation, readers come to a technical document with assumptions and expectations about its structure, in terms of both its language and its design. For example, readers of a tutorial manual may expect to see step-by-step procedural instructions, while readers of a reference manual may expect to see lots of definition lists. The tutorial or reference manual you design, however, may be very different from what the reader initially expects. The design options you use can affect the assumptions and expectations readers have when they begin using a book and, in doing so, can affect the way the readers understand and use it. To design a document well, you need to imagine what linguistic and visual organizers will help readers understand how the text is structured.[9,10]

Here are some guidelines you can use to help readers find, understand, use, and remember the information in a document:

Guideline: Provide Readers with Road Maps Through the Document

Think about how you can design the tables of contents, glossaries, indexes, appendixes, and other materials that support the body of text so that readers can quickly find the information they need. One type of road map is a separator between each section of a document, marked with icons, followed by text explaining the information that will be covered in that section.

add automatic reminders

One type of roadmap is a section heading with an icon.

Another type of road map is a table that directs readers to specific information. Here is an example of a table road map:

If you want to	*Go to*
Install product x	Section A
Use product x	Section B
Service product x	Section C

Guideline: Make Your Document Aesthetically Pleasing

Many readers are motivated to use a document that is aesthetically pleasing. Documents should be attractively bound and packaged, have well-balanced page layouts, contain some graphics and illustrations to break up the text, and be legible.

A good and a poor page layout.

Guideline: Be Consistent in the Visual Formats and Prose Styles You Use

Readers can use a document more effectively when it contains consistent visual patterns, such as use of boldface or italic type, and a consistent linguistic style, such as use of the active voice or direct address. Readers use these patterns and styles to help them structure, comprehend, and remember the relationships between different levels and types of information in a text.

DESIGNING THE VISUAL STRUCTURE OF YOUR DOCUMENT

You can think of the structure of a document on several levels: as a whole, as a set of interrelated parts (chapters/sections), as a series of pages, and as text. Because the audience, purpose, and information for each document are unique, the relationships between these levels are different for each document you produce. Your challenge as a document designer is to choose design options that will support the document on all levels.

Research on design options suggests guidelines on how to graphically reinforce the structure of a text and, therefore, how to improve its usability. These guidelines cover

- Serif vs. Sans-Serif Typeface
- Lowercase vs. Uppercase Type
- Type Weight and Font
- Type Size, Line Length, and Leading
- Justification of Lines, Size of Margins, Use of White Space
- Headings
- Graphs, Tables, Flowcharts, and Diagrams

Serif vs. Sans-Serif Typeface.   Guideline: Choose between a serif and sans-serif typeface according to the visual tone of the document you want. Note: Use a type size 10 points or larger, 2 or more points of leading between lines, and a moderate line length.

Serif typefaces have small strokes added to the edges of each letter. Serifs reinforce the horizontal flow of letters and make each letter distinct. Letters in sans-serif typefaces are less distinct from each other not only because they lack the extra, ornamental strokes of serif type, but also because the widths of the lines that constitute each sans-serif letter are often uniform. Sans-serif typefaces are generally thought to have a cleaner, more modern look than serif type.

Some studies indicate that readers can read text set in serif typefaces more quickly than text in sans-serif type. Readers also seem to prefer text set in serif type.

However, research also shows that the legibility of serif and sans-serif typefaces is approximately the same if the text follows general standards for type size and leading (10-point or larger type size with 2–4 points of leading). Because the legibility of serif and sans-serif print is so similar when properly designed, many researchers and typographers suggest that document designers choose a serif or sans-serif typeface according to what visual texture they want the text to have.[11–13]

Choose a serif or sans-serif typeface according to the visual texture you want your document to have.

Choose a serif or sans-serif typeface according to the visual texture you want your document to have.

Serif and sans-serif typefaces.

Lowercase vs. Uppercase Type.   Guideline: Avoid using all uppercase type. When you want to emphasize a word or portion of text, use boldface type or italics.

Research supports the conclusion that in printed text words set in lowercase are faster to read than words set in uppercase.[14–17] Text set in lowercase is easier to read than text in uppercase because

1. Lowercase letters take up less space and, therefore, allow readers to take in more words as they scan a line of text.
2. Each lowercase word has a distinct outline that aids recognition and recall of the word.

However, some research does indicate that in some situations, such as when readers are scanning text or reading short informational statements, words set in uppercase are easier for readers to locate and read.[18, 19] Therefore, you can put words in uppercase, like "WARNING!" when it is appropriate.

LOWERCASE WORDS TAKE UP LESS SPACE THAN UPPERCASE WORDS AND ALSO HAVE A DISTINCT OUTLINE.

Lowercase words take up less space than uppercase words and also have a distinct outline.

Text set in all uppercase and mixed upper- and lowercase.

Type Weight and Font.   Guidelines: Use a medium type weight. Use boldface type to emphasize words or short portions of text.

Research suggests that when a text has a logical structure, typographic distinctions such as changes in type weight or typeface may help readers understand the structure. Research specifically indicates that readers notice changes in type weight (heavy, medium, light) more readily than they notice changes in typeface and that readers find very light or very heavy type tiring and difficult to read.[20]

Readers may find large blocks of text set in very heavy or very light type difficult and tiring to read.

Readers may find large blocks of text set in very heavy or very light type difficult and tiring to read.

Text set in a very heavy type and a light type.

Type Size, Line Length, and Leading.   Guidelines: Use 9- to 11-point type for text. Use between 2 and 4 points of leading between lines of text. Use a moderate line length, approximately twice the length of the alphabet of the typeface you use.

Type size, line length, and leading all affect the legibility of print. The actual point size of a typeface does not necessarily reflect the perceived size of a letter. Words set in the same type size may appear larger or smaller because of variations in the height of the lowercase letters.

☐ ## And then there was light

☐ And then there was light

☐ And then there was light

Same typesize with different typestyles.

However, research supports a conclusion that type sizes larger than 9 points are easier to read than smaller type sizes—when they are set with an appropriate amount of leading, usually 2 to 4 points.[21, 22]

Although researchers have developed some rules of thumb for considering combinations of line length and leading, these rules are not hard and fast.[14, 16, 21, 23] For example, if a text is set in a typeface that appears small, reducing leading between lines may well have no effect on the legibility of the text.

When you consider options of type size, line length, and leading, remember:

- Sans-serif typefaces may be easier to read with slightly more leading.
- Long lines may be easier to read with more leading between them.
- As type size increases, the effect of leading on legibility decreases.

Justification of Lines, Size of Margins, Use of White Space.   Guidelines: Use ragged-right margins (unjustified text). Use white space in margins and between sections.

Unjustified text is less costly to produce and easier to correct than justified text. Also, many readers prefer unjustified text. However, many publications still set text with both left and right justified margins.

Unjustified text is less costly to produce and easier to correct than justified text. Also, many readers prefer unjustified text. However, many publications still set text with both left and right justified margins.

Unjustified and justified text.

Many researchers and typographers advocate the use of ragged-right margins both because research indicates that justified text is more difficult for poor readers to read and comprehend, and because many readers prefer text with ragged-right margins.[24–26] Unjustified text is also less costly to produce and easier to correct than justified text.

Headings.   Guidelines: Use informative headings. Make all headings consistent and parallel in structure.

Research suggests that readers understand and remember text preceded by titles and/or headings better than text with no headings or titles. Poor readers are significantly aided by headings that are full statements or questions.[27]

Clear, active, and specific headings can also alter how readers comprehend a text. Headings can affect both what sections of text readers choose to read and how readers remember the organization of the text.[28–32]

For example, which of the following headings do you find easier to understand and remember?

> Subpart B: Applications and Licensee
> 83.20 Authorization required.
> 83.22 General citizenship requirements.
> 83.24 Eligibility for license.

> or

> 2—How to get a license
> 2.1 Do I need a license?
> 2.2 How do I apply for a license?
> 2.3 May I operate my car while my
>   applications are being processed?

Graphs, Tables, Flowcharts, and Diagrams.   Guideline: When you are considering using graphics to convey quantitative or procedural information, you should consider

- The reader

- The amount and kinds of information the graphics must display

- How the reader will use the graphics

- What graphic forms you can use (tables, graphs, charts)

If you decide it is appropriate to use graphics, keep the following guidelines in mind:

1. Reinforce all graphics with supporting text.

2. Use typographic cues (changes in type weight and style) to distinguish between different types of information, such as headings or different kinds of data.

3. Use 8- to 12-point type and adequate spacing between printed items.

4. Include informative labels with all types of graphic devices.

5. Use only those lines, grid patterns, and other ink markings necessary to make the information clear.

6. Whenever possible, arrange items vertically so they can be easily scanned.

Because readers' skills in interpreting graphics vary so widely, and because graphic displays can be designed and used in so many different ways, a tremendous amount of research has been done to explore the most effective ways to present quantitative and procedural information.[33–40]

This research strongly suggests that many readers can understand and use complex information more quickly and accurately when it is presented in well-designed tables, graphs, flowcharts, or diagrams rather than solely in text. However, these graphic devices are even more effective when they are reinforced with explanatory text.[41–44]

Some research suggests that bar charts are easier to understand than line, pie, or surface charts; or text.[36, 45]

(A)

Range (in miles)		Payload (in lbs)
878	100	710
630	200	598
459	300	471
388	400	326

(B)

Range (in miles)	Payload (in lbs)	Payload (in lbs)	Range (in miles)
100	878	100	710
200	630	200	598
300	459	300	471
400	388	400	326

Table B is easier to use than Table A because the columns are explicitly labeled.

WHAT DOES THE RESEARCH SUGGEST TO THE PRACTITIONER?

Although the relationship between writers and designers is often a difficult one to develop, research in document design (and the practical experience of designers and writers) supports the conclusion that to produce good technical documentation, designers and writers must work together from the beginning of the document design process. As you begin to plan a document, you should not only consider who your audience is and how they will use the document, but also how you can use the visual presentation of the text to reinforce the structure of the information.

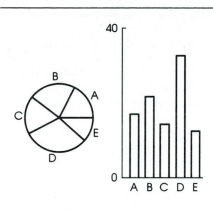

This bar chart reveals the difference in proportions more clearly than the pie chart.

To develop a sound working relationship, writers and designers should make conscious efforts to learn about how the other approaches planning and preparing a document so they can communicate effectively.

REFERENCES

1. J. Hartley, *Designing Instructional Text* (New York: Nichols Publishing Company, 1978).

2. D. H. Jonassen, ed., *The Technology of Text* (Englewood Cliffs, NJ: Educational Technology Publications, 1982).

3. P. Wright, "Usability: The Criterion for Designing Written Information," *Processing Visible Language, Vol. 2,* ed. Koler, Wrolstad, and Bouman (New York: Plenum Press, 1979), pp. 182–205.

4. L. T. Frase, "Reading Performances and Document Design," Bell Laboratories, paper given at Society for Applied Learning Technologies, Washington, DC, June, 1976.

5. R. Waller, "Typographic Access Structures for Educational Texts," *Processing Visible Language, Vol. 1,* ed. Koler, Wrolstad, and Bouman (New York: Plenum Press, 1979), pp. 175–187.

6. E. E. Miller, *Designing Printed Instructional Materials: Content and Format* (Alexandria, VA: Human Resources Research Organization, 1975).

7. W. Diehl and L. Mikulecky, "Making Written Information Fit Workers' Purposes," *IEEE Transactions on Professional Communication* PC-24 (1981).

8. J. Redish, R. Battison, and E. Gold, "Making Information Accessible to Readers," *Research in Non-Academic Settings,* ed. Odell and Goswami (Guilfor Press, in press).

9. P. Carpenter and M. Just, "Reading Comprehension as Eyes See It," *Cognitive Processes in Comprehension,* ed. Just and Carpenter (Hillsdale, NJ: Lawrence Erlbaum Assoc., 1977), pp. 109–139.

10. A. Marcus, "Icon Design Requires Clarity, Consistency," *Computer Graphics Today,* November 1984,

11. R. McLean, *The Thames and Hudson Manual of Typography* (London: Thames and Hudson, Ltd., 1980), pp. 42–48.

12. D. Robinson, M. Abbamonte, and S. Evans, "Why Serifs Are Important," *Visible Language* 4 (1971).

13. R. F. Rehe, *Typography: How to Make It Most Legible* (Carmel, IN: Design Research International, 1981), p. 32.

14. A. Seigel, *Designing Readable Documents: State of the Art* (New York: Scigel and Gale, 1978).

15. M. A. Tinker and D. G. Paterson, "Influence of Type Form on Speed of Reading," *Journal of Applied Psychology* 7 (1928).

16. J. Hartley, "Space and Structure in Instructional Text," paper given at the NATO Conference of the Visual Presentation of Information, Het Vennenbos, Netherlands, 1978.

17. E. C. Poulton and C. H. Brown, "Rate of Comprehension of Existing Teleprinter Output and Possible Alternatives," *Journal of Applied Psychology* 52 (1968).

18. E. C. Poulton, "Searching for Newspaper Headlines Printed in Capitals or Lower-case Letters," *Journal of Applied Psychology* 51 (1967).

19. A. G. Vartabedian, "The Effects of Letter Size, Case, and Generation Method in CRT Display Search Time," *Human Factors* 13 (1971).

20. H. Spencer, L. Reynolds, and B. Coe, *A Comparison of the Effectiveness of Selected Typographic Variations* (Readability of Print Research Unit, Royal College of Art, 1973).

21. M. A. Tinker, *Legibility of Print* (Ames, Iowa: Iowa State University Press, 1963), pp. 88–107.

22. D. Felker, *Document Design: A Review of the Relevant Research* (Washington, DC: American Institutes for Research, 1980), pp. 104–106.

23. M. Gray, "Questionnaire Typography and Production," *Applied Ergonomics* 6 (1975).

24. M. Gregory and E. C. Poulton, "Even versus Uneven Right-Hand Margins and the Rate of Comprehension in Reading," *Ergonomics* 13 (1970).

25. J. Hartley and P. Burnhill, "Experiments with Unjustified Text," *Visible Language* 3 (1971).

26. T. E. Pinelli, et al., "Preferences on Technical Report Format: Results of Survey," *Proceedings,* 31st International Technical Communication Conference (Society for Technical Communication, 1984).

27. J. Hartley, P. Morris, and M. Trueman, "Headings in Text," *Remedial Education* 16 (1981).

28. E. Kozminsky, "Altering Comprehension: The Effect of Biasing Titles on Text Comprehension," *Memory and Cognition* 5 (1977).

29. J. Hartley, J. Kenely, G. Owen, and M. Trueman, "The Effect of Headings on Children's Recall from Prose Text," *British Journal of Educational Psychology* 50 (1980).

30. H. Swartz, L. Flower, and J. Hayes, "How Headings in Documents Can Mislead Readers" (Pittsburgh, PA: Document Design Project, Carnegie-Mellon University, 1980).

31. P. Wright, "Presenting Technical Information: A Survey of Research Findings," *Instructional Science* 6 (1977), pp. 96–100.

32. L. T. Frase and F. Silbiger, "Some Adaptive Consequences of Searching for Information in a Text," *American Educational Research Journal* 7 (1970).

33. W. S. Cleveland and R. McGill, "Graphical Perception: Theory, Experimentation, and Application to the Development of Graphical Methods," *Journal of the American Statistician* 79 (1984).

34. W. S. Cleveland, "Graphical Methods for Data Presentation: Full Scale Breaks, Dot Charts, and Multibased Logging," *Journal of the American Statistician* 38 (1984).

35. A. S. C. Ehrenberg, "What We Can and Can't Get from Graphs, and Why," paper presented at American Statistical Association Meeting, Detroit, 1981.

36. M. MacDonald-Ross, "Graphics in Texts," in *Review of Research in Education,* Volume 5, ed. Shulman (Itasca, IL: RE. Peacock Publications, 1978).

37. P. Wright and K. Fox, "Presenting Information in Tables," *Applied Ergonomics,* September 1970.

38. P. Wright and K. Fox, "Explicit and Implicit Tabulation Formats," *Ergonomics* 15 (1972).

39. P. Wright, "Tables in Text: The Subskills Needed for Reading Formatted Information" (Cambridge, UK: MRC Applied Psychology Unit).

40. E. R. Tufte, *The Visual Display of Quantitative Information* (Chesire, CT: Graphics Press, 1983).

41. P Wright and F. Reid, "Written Information: Some Alternatives to Prose for Expressing the Outcomes of Complex Contingencies," *Journal of Applied Psychology* 57 (1973).

42. P Wright, "Writing To Be Understood: Why Use Sentences?" *Applied Ergonomics* 2 (1971).

43. R. Kammann, "The Comprehensibility of Printed Instructions and the Flowchart Alternative," *Human Factors* 17 (1975).

44. D. Felker, *Guidelines for Document Designers* (Washington, DC: American Institutes for Research, 1981).

45. D. D. Feliciano, R. D. Powers, and B. E. Keare, "The Presentation of Statistical Information," *Audio-Visual Communication Review* 11 (1963).

Voicemail

Raymond W. Beswick

Most companies now use voicemail as part of their office telephone systems. As a result, oral communication often consists of messages left by a caller on voicemail at one time and listened to by the receiver at another time. This article discusses guidelines for effective use of voicemail.

Voicemail is a computer-based oral communication system accessed by telephone. It works asynchronously, that is, the caller leaves a message that the recipient listens to later. Voicemail can resemble both text-based electronic mail and a telephone answering machine, depending on how it is used. Since it is available all the time, voicemail is time insensitive. Since it can be accessed from anywhere in the world, voicemail is distance insensitive.

INTERACTING WITH VOICEMAIL

Voicemail is a melding of telephone and computer technologies. Unlike electronic mail, there is no keyboard with which to type messages and no printer or video display from which to read messages. Voicemail systems interact with you by playing prerecorded messages, called prompts, over the telephone. The voicemail system asks you to select the function you want performed; you respond to the prompts by pressing the appropriate button on the telephone.

Answering Mode

When someone calling a voicemail user encounters voicemail in answering mode, instead of the person called, the caller decides whether or not to leave a message. On the voicemail system at Syncrude Canada Ltd., only one in three callers leaves a message when confronted by the voicemail system in answering mode. This is up from one in four when the feature was originally introduced.

On the Syncrude Canada, Ltd., voicemail system, 75% of the messages received by users are left in answering mode rather than in messaging mode. If a voicemail system is installed in conjunction with a text-based electronic mail system, it is very likely that the voicemail system will be used almost exclusively in answering mode.

An interesting sidelight of answering mode is that some people hide behind voicemail—just as they can hide behind telephone answering machines. Since they can forward their phones to voicemail and never have the phone on their desks ring, some people rarely deal over the telephone directly. Instead, they receive recorded messages and respond to them. If every phone in an area is forwarded to voicemail, then you cannot get through to anyone without physically going to the individual. For example, if everyone in the accounting department forwarded his or her phone to voicemail, someone who telephones to find out about the status of an invoice would not be able to talk to someone in accounting personally.

Messaging Mode

When people use voicemail as a messaging system, they deliberately choose to use voicemail as opposed to sending a memo or letter, telephoning, using text-based electronic mail (FAX or telex or TWX), or having a face-to-face conversation. The very nature of voicemail makes it a bad choice if you require documentation: storing voicemail messages takes up a lot of computer disk storage space (keeping them for long periods of time is discouraged by voicemail system administrators); finding a single message among many stored messages may not be an easy task; and, converting the voicemail message into written form cannot be done automatically (you would have to transcribe it). Voicemail cannot be used where synchronous communication is required. Also, voicemail cannot be used where an answer is required in a very short period of time—you can only guarantee instant delivery of the message to a mailbox; you cannot guarantee instant receipt by the addressee.

Voicemail users are often dismayed by people who do not regularly check their mailboxes. The message is delivered almost instantaneously, but the recipient causes a long delay by not checking frequently for messages.

Messages which are short, simple, and non-controversial are good candidates for voicemail. If there is a moderate or greater distance involved or if there is communication across chronological boundaries, e.g., work shifts, the likelihood of voicemail use increases.

People may choose to use voicemail rather than a memo when documentation is not required because voicemail takes less effort to create and send than a memo. In choosing to use voicemail for messaging rather than telephoning, a person may wish to avoid disturbing another person unnecessarily—since neither discussion nor an instant answer is required, why would you phone? Voicemail allows recipients to handle the message in their own time.

Voicemail is easy to use. Voicemail users find that they avoid telephone tag. "Time shifting' (completing communication tasks outside normal business hours and reducing business day interruptions) is often cited as a benefit. Some people may not agree that this is beneficial; they may see it as an intrusion of work life into their personal life.

Reasons proffered for not using voicemail are interesting. Infrequent users of voicemail sometimes report resistance to recording their voices, some resist because of 'old habits,' still some resist because of a need for transmitting large amounts of technical information, and some have a preference for typing. Some people will listen to voicemail messages but will respond via conventional channels because they find voicemail inappropriate.

Security of confidential messages is not seen as a problem. Voicemail system users are confident that private messages will not be listened to by unauthorized personnel. So, all manner of confidential information is exchanged.

Voicemail users prefer that all their usual contacts be on the voicemail system; otherwise, media other than voicemail, e.g., memos or telephone must be used to contact them. For example, dealing with a project team, some of whom are on voicemail and some not, means extra work: you leave a voicemail message for some of the team and write memos to others to give them exactly the same data.

Voicemail Uses

The following are examples of voicemail uses based on personal research where voicemail users gave their permission to have their voicemail calls monitored. These examples should give you a feel for the range of message types sent using voicemail.

Sustained Interaction

Voicemail was used for sustained interaction between a supervisor and a senior member of his staff who were on different shifts. Some problems had arisen with a contractor. Over the period of a week, the staff member not only kept his supervisor advised of the current status of the problem but also set out potential actions on the part of the contractor and suggested responses by the company. The supervisor queried the staff member on various aspects of the problem, responded to his suggestions, and made suggestions of his own for comment by the staff member. They had a sustained, asynchronous conversation.

Confidential Messages

The security of voicemail systems does not appear to worry people; therefore, confidential messages are sent frequently. If confidential matters reached those who did not have a need to know, considerable embarrassment (or even outright loss) could ensue. The discussion about contractor problems mentioned previously is one example. The company would not want the contractor to know how it proposed to deal with the potential actions which the contractor might take; if the contractor did know, the company might lose money. Messages from the human resources staff dealt with the deaths of retired employees and their survivors' benefits which are very personal matters. Poor employee performance was the subject of several messages between managers and supervisors. The matter of less than satisfactory performance is between the company and the employee and might prove embarrassing all around if it became general knowledge.

Reporting on Meetings

Numerous examples of people attending meetings and then reporting to their coworkers were found. Prior to voicemail, the information would have been put into a memorandum and mailed. With voicemail, the person attending the meeting sent a voice message immediately after the meeting. Information float, the time that information is available but has not been received by the people who need it, was greatly reduced.

Projects

Supervisors assigned work and checked on the status of projects. Staff members reported project status and requested direction. Supervisors gave "positive strokes" to their subordinates. Project team members requested information from one another and provided requested information.

Formal and Informal Information Exchanges

People requested all manner of information; people responded with the answers. Not all the information was work related; for example, there were queries about whether or not bridge partners were going to have dinner before playing cards, whether or not someone could come to lunch on Wednesday, and what time someone wanted to be picked up on Saturday morning to go shopping. Voicemail was used to facilitate both softball and volleyball leagues; mailing lists were used to broadcast messages to team members.

VOICEMAIL SKILLS

When you place a telephone call, you expect to have a person answer. With the proliferation of voicemail systems, however, chances are that you will encounter one of them. So, you should be prepared to leave a message. (Remember that you are in control of the voicemail system.) On the Syncrude Canada, Ltd., voicemail system, the etiquette is not to leave just a "call me back" message but, at the very least, to leave the subject to be discussed when synchronous contact is finally made. In some cases, a fair amount of detail is left when the caller re@es that asynchronous communication will suffice.

You must be prepared to leave a short, concise message whenever you make a telephone call. That messages should be short cannot be overstated; it is difficult for people to listen to long messages. Remember, receivers can do nothing but listen. You must guard against leaving a voicemail message if it forces the recipient to transcribe a lengthy or detailed message into writing. For example, leaving a voicemail message which contains detailed wording changes for a major project document would undoubtedly cause the recipient to write down what was said. Transcription is not a task for which voicemail systems were designed. Send a memo instead.

Dictation skills would appear to be universally applicable to voicemail. Remember, however, that the communication resulting from dictation is meant to be read while voicemail messages are meant to be heard. Most voicemail messages sound like one-sided telephone conversations.

Voicemail system etiquette is developing over time. The lack of "call me back" messages mentioned previously is one example. There are two others: the virtually universal greeting is "hi!" or "hi" followed by the addressee's name and messages sent to more than one person are invariably begun with a list of addressees. For example, "Hi. This message is going to John and Mary" or "Hi. This message is going to the Administration Team." This suggests that voicemail users must recognize and become familiar with the etiquette associated with their voicemail systems.

Getting maximum value from any communications tool requires education, training, and practice. Voicemail is no exception.

"Big Emerging, Markets" Have Diverse Cultures, but Common Attributes

Every year more companies become involved in world trade, and writers must learn to communicate effectively with international partners and customers. This excerpt from a publication by the Department of Commerce identifies some cultural differences that could affect business dealings in new important world markets.

Earlier this year the Commerce Department identified ten markets that hold great promise for large incremental gains in U.S. exports. These "Big Emerging Markets" are the Chinese Economic Area, Indonesia, India, South Korea, Mexico, Argentina, Brazil, South Africa, Turkey, and Poland.

These ten BEMs share a number of important attributes. They are all physically large. They have significant populations and represent considerable markets for a wide range of products. Virtually all have strong rates of growth, or clearly hold out the promise of economic expansion in the future. Virtually all have undertaken some significant program of economic reforms and seem likely to expand on those programs in the future. Virtually all are of major political importance within their regions; moreover, they are "regional economic drivers"—their growth will engender further expansion in neighboring markets.

CHINA, HONG KONG, TAIWAN

The customs of doing business in China, Hong Kong, and Taiwan are similar in many ways. Personal relationships are very important to business people in all three countries. There is usually little distinction made between business and personal relationships. To succeed in these countries, you must cultivate close personal ties with business associates and earn their respect and trust. A knowledge of and sensitivity for their cultures and way of doing things is essential to cultivating a sound relationship. Handshaking, imported from the West, is generally the appropriate form of salutation. The handshake is always followed by a ritualistic exchange of business cards. "Keeping face" is an old tradition in China that is still important today. It is reflected in sensitivity to status and title, and even in who sits down or enters a door first. Chinese are inveterate gift givers. Spend some time in choosing appropriate presents before visiting China. Gifts should not be expensive; the symbolic significance is more important than monetary value.

INDONESIA

Keep in mind that Indonesian society is based on respect for the individual. Business dealings in Indonesia can be long and frustrating. It is important to be punctual. While it is polite to take flowers to dinner at a private home, gifts are not generally expected; they should, however, be accepted graciously if offered. Bowing is not the accepted mode of greeting in Indonesia; rather, a handshake and nod of the head are the norm.

INDIA

India's long association with the British Empire and successor Commonwealth have minimized the cultural differences that might have distinguished the Indian business community from its Western counterparts. Nevertheless, religious beliefs play a major role in Indian dietary habits and can have a profound effect on social relationships stemming from business contacts. The Indian Hindu community's special reverence for bovine animals precludes both their slaughter and the consumption of beef by a community that makes up 83% of the population. While poultry and lamb are acceptable substitutes, a majority of Indians are vegetarians by choice or conviction. In India's Moslem community, which accounts for 11.4% of the population, pork products are proscribed from acceptance in the dietary habits of some 102 million people. While alcoholic beverages are similarly proscribed, the Indian majority favor their production and consumption, and the brewing industry is thriving.

KOREA

In Korea, men greet each other with a slight bow or by shaking hands. When presenting a business card, use both hands and position the card so that the recipient can read it. The data should be printed in Korean on the reverse side of the card. As in Japan, shoes should always be removed before entering a Korean home or restaurant. Bring a small gift or flowers when visiting a Korean home; the exchange of gifts is also expected in a business situation. Whether at a home or business, it is considered bad manners among Koreans to open a gift in the presence of the giver. Avoid using triangular shapes in Korea, as the triangle is considered a negative shape there.

MEXICO

In Mexico the length of the work day may vary, relative to the regional location and type of company you are doing business with. For example, in the Mexico City area, companies may open at 9 a.m. or 9:30 a.m. and close at 7 p.m. Federal Government offices in Mexico City typically open as late as 10 a.m. Two-hour lunches are normal, with federal employees taking longer and later lunches, and then returning to work for the evening, normally until about 9 p.m. Thus a 2 p.m. meeting time that is standard in the United States falls right at lunchtime in Mexico City, so be prepared for meetings at odd times from a U.S. perspective. As in the United States, shaking hands at the beginning and end of a meeting is customary. The use of professional titles (e.g., "doctor" or "professor") is extensive, and it is considered courteous to address your meeting hosts by their respective titles. The older and more senior members of your group can expect to be met with special courtesy and respect. Mexicans value courtesy, and the emphasis is on tactful and indirect phrasing. Mexicans make extensive use of business cards, so bring plenty with you. It is also considered to be a show of respect to have your cards printed in Spanish. It is common practice to conduct business over a meal, especially breakfast or lunch. It is customary to send a small gift at Christmas to key business contacts. Keeping to a precise schedule is less important to the Mexicans than bringing a meeting to a close at a comfortable and unrushed pace. You can expect meetings to start a little late and run a little longer than what is traditional in the United States.

ARGENTINA

In Argentina, business dress and appearance, as well as one's general approach to business relations, should be conservative. A prior appointment for a business call is usually necessary and considered a customary courtesy. The pace of negotiation is slower than in the United States and is based much more on personal contact. All business in Argentina is transacted in Spanish and all documents and records must be in Spanish to constitute valid evidence. Although most Argentines with a secondary school education understand English, a good working knowledge of Spanish is essential for anyone planning to work in Argentina for any length of time. While business hours are generally 8:00–8:30 a.m. to 5:00–5:30 p.m., executives usually begin work later in the morning and stay later in the evening. Other than business lunches, appointments with companies are generally not made between noon and 3:00 p.m. Banking hours vary slightly among provinces but are generally 10:00 a.m. to 4:00 p.m. Government offices are open Monday through Friday from noon to 7:00 p.m. during the winter and from 7:00 a.m. to 2:00 p.m. during the summer. Argentines take vacations in January and February, the summer season, so business travel to Argentina during that period could be unproductive unless prior arrangements have been made.

BRAZIL

A U.S. business-person is encouraged to learn as much about the Brazilian economic, political, and commercial environment as possible before doing business in Brazil. Compared to the United States, the pace of negotiations is slower and is based much more on personal contact. Letters and telephone calls are seldom used to close important business deals. A continuous and personal working relationship is valued. Many Brazilians who speak English may wish to conduct business in Portuguese. The non-Portuguese speaking U.S. executive may need an interpreter on more than 50 percent of business calls. Correspondence and product literature should be in Portuguese.

SOUTH AFRICA

Business customs in South Africa are generally similar to those in the United States and Western Europe. South African business leaders tend to dress conservatively. The uniform of the day for businessmen is a well-cut business suit of medium to heavyweight wool. Polyester fabrics, sport coats, and loud colors and patterns are not worn. Polished leather shoes and quiet socks are also part of the outfit. South African women are less visible in a substantive business setting in South Africa than in the United States. South African professional women wear business suits. Punctuality is routinely practiced regarding appointments. Appointments are scheduled in advance; "drop-in" meetings are not the norm. Letters of introduction from your local chamber of commerce or trade association are helpful in establishing your bona fides as a serious business person and are highly recommended. Form letters or faxes requesting appointments can be counter-productive. Personalize your introductory letter to the company and be specific about the purpose of your visit when you request your appointment. On arriving in your potential client's office, introduce yourself, shake hands, engage in minimal small talk, and then get down to business. Be alert to the kind of handshake you receive. South African blacks may engage in a more lingering grasp of your hand; reciprocate. If you are dealing with the white business community, price will play a leading role in the chemistry of the deal. If you are dealing with a member of the nonwhite business community, other factors will take the lead, particularly personal relations and quality; price will likely drop to third place.

TURKEY

When being introduced at any business meeting or social occasion in Turkey, shake hands with everyone present. Shake hands again when leaving. Use last names and appropriate titles until invited by your Turkish host or colleague to use first names. Allow the more senior person to initiate. Turks use first names when addressing each other, as described below. Turks are also quick with foreigners to go to first names. To address a man by his first name, use his first name + *bey* (bay), which means sir, e.g., *John Bey*. For a woman, use her first name + *hanim* (HAH-num), which means ma'am, e.g., *Alice Hanim*. It is not very important to use titles for professionals, e.g., doctor, Ph.D. Turkish people are very warm, friendly, and generous. If entertained in a home, bring a small token of appreciation, such as flowers, candy, etc. If you are someone's guest, that person will be insulted if you offer to pay. Do send a gift later. If you admire an object too much, it may be given to you. Do not show the soles of your feet. Do not point fingers at anyone. Never criticize or contradict someone. The thumbs up sign is disrespectful.

POLAND

Like most Europeans, Polish people are generally more formal than Americans and do not use first names when meeting someone for the first time. It is customary to greet by shaking hands. A businesswoman should not be surprised if a Polish man kisses her hand upon introduction, subsequent meetings, or saying goodbye. American men do not need to kiss a Polish woman's hand, but may simply shake hands. Business cards are the norm in Poland and are generally given to each person present in a meeting. As Polish businesspeople tend to bring more than one person to a meeting, U.S. visitors should bring plenty of business cards. It is not necessary that cards be printed in Polish. Business attire is generally formal, including a suit and tie for men, and a suit or dress for women. Casual wear, including jeans, is suitable for informal occasions, but more formal dress is usually customary for visiting or entertaining in the evening. Flowers, always in an odd number, are the most common gift among friends and acquaintances.

The Art of the Interview

Eivind Boe

A job interview is a sales presentation of your best features. This article explains how to prepare for a job interview by anticipating questions, practicing answers, and finding information about the company. Try preparing the answers to some of these standard questions before your next job interview.

The ad was found; the résumé was sent; the eagerly awaited phone call was received: You're to go for an interview. Unless you're unquestionably the best or absolutely the worst insofar as qualifications go, your performance at the interview is what makes you or breaks you as far as the job is concerned. There is no getting around this.

As with everything else in life, there is no way to ensure success at an interview. You can buy the fanciest clothes, but they will not buy you the job. The firm handshake is not an automatic in; nor is any connection or pull you might have. But aside from your qualifications and maturity, some fundamental concerns will greatly increase the percentages in your favor.

For one thing, study up on your résumé, your reasons for wanting a job at that particular company, and the points in your past that you want to talk about. The best way to be ready for an interview is to have something to say. Having nothing to say at your interview is about as self-defeating as can be.

Perhaps the greatest temptation for young people at an interview is to act, to try to adjust their personality for each interviewer. Aside from creating impossible problems, you're best off being you. Any company worth working for isn't looking for only exuberant people; nor do they want meek submission, nor frenzied aggressiveness, nor Laputan eggheadism. They want mature, capable human beings. *That* is the only category you have to fit into. The trick is to be the best *you* you can be.

Manners are those things mother taught you that you dispensed with in college. They are really codified courtesy, and courtesy is one of those deeper qualities that make people want to have you around. Things like standing when the interviewer stands and forgoing smoking if the interviewer doesn't offer it—and doing these things with an easy grace—are what interviewers notice. Remember it is the interviewer's prerogative to be irascible, abrupt, or prying: Maintain your courteous demeanor—even if you must demand courteous treatment, which sometimes happens.

SELLING YOURSELF

Remember your manners when you make that all important "sales call." For even if you never, EVER, wanted to go into sales, when you interview, you have something to sell: yourself. To sell effectively you need three things: a good presentation, a unique product, and an unshakable belief in that product.

A good presentation consists of simply this: as many reasons to hire you, and as few reasons not to hire you, as possible. The interviewer is mainly concerned

470

with if you *can* do the job, if you *will* do the job, and if you're going to *get along* with the rest of the company. Inspire the interviewer with confidence in you; handle every question with aplomb. If the interviewer points out that you haven't done such and such, which is an integral part of the job, you can say, "This is true, but I've done this and this, which are quite similar. In the past I've always been able to adapt this way to new situations." Consider every question the interviewer puts to you an opportunity to show how good you really are.

A product has to be distinct from other products, and for it to sell, it must be distinctly better. If you feel like everyone applying for a position has exactly what you have, say, a B.S.E.E. and 4 years of experience, don't worry: No one else has the unique background you have. Your work experience inevitably has had special projects, unusual situations, trying circumstances. Your education includes special courses and activities (even those unrelated to engineering). Everything else you've ever done defines your unique character, and can show some positive attribute in you: Your participation in team sports shows a willingness to work with others; your active involvement in town politics shows your willingness to get involved. An interest in trout fishing evinces patience, even strategy; an interest in music manifests a desire to organize, a penchant for system. Every positive aspect about you can be turned to account.

Believing in the product is paramount. Why apply for a job if you don't think you can do it well? You have already passed many tests in life: What is it about this job that, through perhaps some effort, you couldn't master? You do, of course, already know a lot; you can, of course, learn almost anything you care to. Nothing really stops you from succeeding—at anything.

Try bringing some of these attitudes with you to an interview. They are at least as true as any negative attitudes you may have, and are far more likely to get you the job. Yet the problem may not be one of lack of confidence, but nervousness due to pressure.

If you're nervous before an interview, that's *good*. The stampeding herd of butterflies in your stomach, the apple in your throat, and the 2-lb weight tied to your tongue indicate that your mind feels doubt and is telling your endocrine system to pump out loads of adrenaline. Naturally it won't do to let this unfocused energy mess up your interview. The trick is to channel the energy and make it work for you. Learn how to turn it to positive action, rather than negative reaction.

Awareness of interviewers' standard stock of questions is another way to beat nervousness and build confidence. Being prepared for these questions allows you to free your mind to concentrate on more challenging issues. Here are the questions and some suggestions on how to handle them.

1. *Tell me about yourself.* Actually not a question, of course. In answering this, stick to your life at work: This tack reinforces your interest in the job.

2. *What is it about the job that interests you most?* If you launch into extolling the benefits you'll accrue if you get the job, you will have lost. Make the interviewer believe that you are interested in performing the work, using your knowledge and energy to help the company.

3. *Where do you see yourself five years from now?* A classic question. Probably best handled by something like: "Doing more of the same, only better." Perhaps you can think of something more imaginative. Just leave the impression that you know what you want.

4. *What do you consider your major strengths/weaknesses?* You know your strengths, so tell them without sounding boastful. As for your weaknesses, make them sound like strengths: Sometimes you're just too much of a perfectionist, or you get impatient when coworkers don't work as hard as you do.

5. *Why do you want to leave your present job?* Avoid saying that you hate your boss, or that you don't get along with your coworkers. Such remarks leave a bad taste in the interviewer's mouth. Wanting more money or a higher position, and being able to do more at a higher level than your present company can reasonably give you, are good answers here.

Rest assured that these aren't the only questions you'll hear. Nor are the suggested answers the only ones you can give. But be prepared for these specific questions, and you'll have started off the interview right.

WARMING UP

How does one practice interviewing? Try this simple idea: Get yourself a tape recorder, tape yourself in an interview situation, and listen to yourself. Either ask some of the standard interview questions yourself (in a different voice if you choose) or have a friend ask the questions, and then answer them.

There are certain things to listen for in the recording. Are you answering the interviewer's questions directly, or do you sound too much like you're dodging? Are there some bad habits there that you can correct, such as an overuse of hems, ums, or y'knows? Do you have a ready answer for every question? Are you perhaps talking too fast?

Granted, this is not a realistic situation. After all, you already know the questions, whereas in an interview you don't. But in most interviews there are stock questions, which are really opportunities for you to glow. Using a tape recorder can allow you to practice the answers to those questions.

KNOW THY PROSPECTIVE COMPANY

Of inestimable value when you go into an interview is knowledge about that particular company. The more you know, the more you appear to be the perfect, ready-made employee. You'll inspire your interviewer with respect for you, and by having something to say, will simultaneously remove a great deal of the burden of the interview from his or her shoulders, a fact that will dispose the interviewer to liking you.

The next question is where to find this knowledge. First of all, a company library or even the local library is a good start. Simply ask the reference librarian to help you. Also, check out the Dun & Bradstreet reports, and the *Reader's Guide to Periodical Literature* for any articles that may have been written on the company. For the latter source, don't give up if you don't find anything under the first heading you look at; try several headings, as many as you can think of. At least look under the company name, electronics, electrical engineering, microwaves, and radio frequency. The second source to tap is the company's annual report. Get one of these by contacting the company. A third source of information is through friends and contacts: Grill them!

CALL THE COMPANY

Do not despair if next to no information can be located. If this is the case, try calling the company itself, explain that you have an interview with them, and that you'd like to find out more about the company. Many executives and personnel officers will often be pleased to send you brochures, pamphlets, and other information. They will, in addition, remember your name come interview time.

It's a good idea to keep in mind that this information search takes a little time. When preparing for the interview, allow for the time it takes for mail to travel, and remember that libraries are open only during certain hours.

Having gotten this information from your various sources, carefully examine it to determine company trends, policies, and concerns. Look for the company's strengths and weaknesses. Set the knowledge against the background of your general knowledge of the field. Express an interest in these concerns during the interview, and to a certain extent, identify with these concerns. Think of possible solutions to the company's problems—or better yet, how *you* could help the company improve, meet goals, achieve important successes in the market.

These are the weapons you gird yourself with for confronting the question, "Why are you interested in *our* company?" This is the way to show the interviewer, "This guy's no slouch—he's done his homework."

Electronic Conferencing

Joel P. Bowman

The rapid growth of electronic communication has changed many of the traditional methods of exchanging information. This article discusses how computers have replaced many face-to-face meetings and increased information-sharing worldwide.

What Is Electronic Conferencing?

In some ways, an electronic conference is the computer-based equivalent of a wall-mounted bulletin board. The earliest electronic conferences were, in fact, called bulletin board systems (BBSes) and served primarily as an electronic repository for public notices. The earliest of these systems simply collected and displayed the electronic notes posted by the users in the order in which they were received. Users who wished to read about specific topics had to search the postings for specific subject lines to find desired entries. As BBSes evolved, the abilities to respond to specific entries and to index entries and replies by topic were added, and BBSes began assuming many of the functions of face-to-face meetings and telephone conference calls. The terms electronic conference and electronic forum are usually reserved for the most sophisticated of the BBSes.

Unlike a face-to-face meeting or telephone conference call, however, communication on an electronic conference is asynchronous. The participants in the conference do not have to share the same time or place to hold their meeting. With the proper equipment and software, participants can join the conference at any time of day or night from virtually anywhere in the world. Conferences are usually organized around a specific topic or problem, and they are either open or closed depending on whether any interested person may participate or whether the conference is restricted to certain designated individuals.

Managed Communication

Unlike e-mail, communication on an electronic conference is managed. Although the degree of management may vary greatly from conference to conference, an individual or group of individuals will always have responsibility for the well-being of the conference. A systems operator (sysop) or conference organizer is responsible for ensuring that posted items and responses meet the criteria established for the conference. On closed conferences, the conference organizer also has the responsibility of reviewing requests for membership and for assigning passwords and any required access code. Open conferences allow anyone to join and post items and responses. The sysop may also be held legally responsible for information appearing on his or her conference should any of that information be considered illegal (such as pirated software or stolen credit card numbers) or obscene (whether graphic or textual). For this reason, some conferences are monitored, with the sysop reviewing the content of messages before they are posted. Messages found unsuitable for posting may be returned to the sender.

Advantages and Disadvantages of Electronic Conferencing

Over the past ten years or so, the use of electronic conferencing has been increasing at practically an exponential rate because of the advantages it offers as a means of distributing information throughout an organization or group of individuals sharing a special interest (often referred to as a Special Interest Group, or SIG). Businesses use electronic conferences to encourage improved communication between those involved in research and those concerned with production, to keep sales representatives current, to provide improved customer service, and to keep employees informed about benefits and other items of general interest. In general, organizations have benefitted both financially and in terms of increased productivity from their investment in conferencing hardware and software. CBS Records, for example, has been able to save more than $100,000 a year by using an electronic conference to facilitate the production of its catalog, and the Tax Technology Group of Price Waterhouse uses an electronic conference to answer tax questions posed by the company's 700 Fortune 1000 clients (Lockwood, 1990, March).

Electronic conferences do, of course, have disadvantages. An electronic conference, like the ubiquitous photocopy machine, is an easy medium to abuse, and abuse can be costly. While no one message on an electronic conference costs much in terms of the time spent to enter and read it or the computer resources used to process and store the message, the totals can be significant. Because participants usually consider electronic conferences an extension of the oral culture in the organization, conferences can become a substitute for an extended coffee break or hallway conversation, resulting in increased computer cost and loss of productivity (Zuboff, 1988, p. 365).

Another disadvantage of electronic conferences is flaring or flaming. For reasons not yet fully understood, messages posted on electronic conferences can be surprisingly hostile. Emotional responses, especially when they are hostile and accusatory, are known as flares or flames. Several researchers have postulated that the absence of nonverbal cues leads to misunderstanding and increasing levels of hostility. Memos, letters, and reports, however, also lack the same kind of nonverbal cues as do messages posted in an electronic conference, but flaming does not result. Perhaps the relative newness of this particular form of communication in combination with the immediacy of the communication and the reduced sense of audience increases users' tendencies to assume an egocentric point of view. Regardless of the causes of flaming, a particularly hostile flame can effectively kill further discussion on a conference for weeks or months; therefore, conference users need to be aware of this tendency and do their best to avoid it,

HOW ARE ELECTRONIC CONFERENCES USED IN BUSINESS?

In business and industry, electronic conferences are usually initiated to accomplish specific purposes. A division or work group, for example, might use a conference to communicate about a common problem, or an organization might use a conference to facilitate communication with employees, branch managers, or salespeople at remote locations. Some businesses provide electronic conferences for their customers, using the conference to answer product questions and to provide technical and other kinds of customer support. Businesses have discovered that the advantages of electronic conferences greatly outweigh their costs and other disadvantages. An electronic conference distributes information in a way that no other communication medium can and greatly amplifies each individual's access to the expertise of others. If an individual has a question about how to use a particular software package, for example, he or she could post the question on the appropriate conference and have an answer (or a variety of answers) within a few hours, whereas using the telephone could prove a hit-or-miss approach, depending on whether the individual was certain whom to call for the answer.

In face-to-face meetings, participants are aware, perhaps overly aware, of the titles and status of those present. Also, some people suffer from communication apprehension in group situations. As a result of these factors, the expertise of some individuals may be overlooked in solving a particular problem or reaching a decision. When individuals use an electronic conference for group communication, authority tends to depend more on expertise and communication skill than on title or personal charisma. Several years ago, a major Midwestern university established an experimental BBS to introduce faculty to this mode of communication and hired a 12-year-old, handicapped boy to manage the system. Because this young man had the authority of computer expertise and the communication skill required to convey that authority, faculty members who would have quickly dismissed him in person frequently requested and followed the advice he posted on the conference.

Another of the characteristics of electronic conferences is that communication styles are heavily influenced by the oral communication culture within the organization. Messages on most conferences tend to be informal, even when formal matters are being discussed. In general, users are less careful with spelling, grammar, and mechanics than they would be with the same (or similar) messages distributed through traditional, paper-based media. Users are also inclined to say things in an electronic conference that might be appropriate for a hallway conversation but are inappropriate for distribution on paper, such as questions about the competence of managers or executives within the organization. Postings on conferences can, of course, be redistributed electronically or printed and distributed as hard copy, often to the writer's embarrassment.

Business is now in a transitional phase. Some older managers, including some senior executives, continue to resist electronic conferencing because the wide distribution of knowledge deprives them of authority (see Zuboff, 1988, pp. 178–180). As the importance of knowledge to the long-term success of organizations increases, however, business and industry, and to a lesser extent nonprofit organizations as well, are being forced to rely on computer-based communication technologies for the speed and efficiency with which they disseminate information. Many senior executives who used to think that keyboarding was a secretarial skill are being forced to change their views. For most routine business communication, e-mail and electronic conferencing are simply more versatile and efficient than more traditional channels of communication.

WHAT SKILLS ARE REQUIRED FOR ELECTRONIC CONFERENCING?

Currently, most users of BBSes and electronic conferences learn by experimentation or on an impromptu basis, with a friend or coworker providing minimal orientation and instruction. A common assumption seems to be that if an individual has access to a computer and a passing acquaintance with the English language, he or she requires no special instruction to use an electronic conference effectively. This assumption is false, and it can be costly for the organization and certainly for the individual involved.

As each system, the combination of hardware and software configuration, is different, it is often argued that business and industry should assume the responsibility of training those in the organization who will be required to use an electronic conference. Effective communication on an electronic conference, however, should not be left to chance. Because the electronic conference substitutes for both oral and written communication channels simultaneously, it requires the successful adaptation of communication strategies from those media, in addition to new skills applicable only to electronic conferencing. Effective communication on an electronic conference requires the following specific skills:

1. An understanding of basic computer operations. Users need to be sufficiently familiar with computers to have lost their fear of experimentation and to have some conception of what they can do themselves and what will require specialized expertise. Selecting a file server or a multiplexor (for multiple telephone line access), installing and maintaining conferencing software, and solving terminal emulation problems are typically matters for those with special training and technical skills.

2. Relatively decent keyboarding skills. Even the kind of short messages common to e-mail and electronic conferences can be time-consuming for a hunt-and-peck typist. Inefficient keyboarding on the part of highly paid managers or executives costs the organization in terms of lost productivity and the individual in terms of lost time.

3. A knowledge of the system. In addition to a general knowledge of how electronic conferences work and of the features that most of them have in common, users will need to be familiar with the specific system (or systems) they will be using and the text editor(s) available to them. Lack of familiarity with the full range of capabilities of their text editors is a common failing of those using e-mail or electronic conferences.

4. Acceptable language skills. Although users of electronic conferences are generally more accepting of errors in spelling, grammar, and mechanics than readers of letters or reports would be, gross or numerous errors can damage a writer's credibility. This is especially true when items and responses are distributed as hard copy.

5. Sensitivity to the corporate culture. Users of electronic conferences need to be aware that postings on the conference may be read by a wide audience. In addition to the number of lurkers—those who read postings but rarely enter items or responses themselves—senior management may regularly review postings to determine whether the conferences are being used appropriately.

6. A basic knowledge of audience adaptation and communication strategies. In the absence of the nonverbal feedback typically available in face-to-face meetings, those using electronic conferences tend to forget that they are communicating with other human beings. In some cases, this is good: those

with communication apprehension may be more willing to share their ideas. In other cases, it is bad: users may be less polite and more abrupt than they would be in face-to-face or telephone communication. Users also need to remember that electronic conferences are public communication and that messages intended for one specific reader should be posted only when others will share the same concerns. Private messages should be sent by e-mail.

7. An understanding of the factors that influence readability. Reading text on a computer screen is not as easy as reading the same text on paper. Nevertheless, similar rules for readability apply. The single most common complaint about messages posted on electronic conferences is the tendency for new users to post messages using solid capital letters, which are difficult to read. In addition to using capital and lower-case letters appropriately, users may increase the readability of postings by keeping lines of text relatively short (about 60 to 65 characters, including spaces). Paragraphs are also more readable when they are short (no more than about eight lines). Even with paper-based text, long lines and long paragraphs can be difficult to read in single-spaced material. On a computer screen, long blocks of solid text are even more detrimental to reading ease.

8. A knowledge of the conference culture. Different conferences establish different communication conventions. Some conferences, for example, encourage the use of text-based graphical inserts to indicate humor, disappointment, and other emotions:

    Smile: :-)
    Frown: :-(
    Wink: ;-)

Other conferences consider such inserts childish and inappropriate.

Some of these skills will, most naturally, be learned on the impromptu basis currently employed in most business organizations; others will need to be specifically taught. As the use of computer-mediated communication continues to increase, e-mail and electronic conferencing will soon become dominant communication channels in modern organizations.

WHERE DO WE GO FROM HERE?

Electronic mail and electronic conferencing are both relatively new forms of communication. Their use is growing exponentially, both in business and industry and in colleges and universities. Already, if business and other professional people are not online, they are increasingly considered "out of the loop." Why call someone or send a letter when the same information is available more conveniently from someone else who is online? Because these new computer-based forms of communication offer both speed and convenience, they will increasingly be used as substitutes for telephone calls, conference calls, paper-based mail, and face-to-face meetings. Those who cannot or will not participate will be left to wonder what others are doing.

Along with increased use, standards of "electronic etiquette" will also evolve. As was true for print, the conventions of use will evolve as social relationships and technology change. Whether we will ever reach the kind of agreement once established for the appropriate formats for letters and memos, however, is another question. Electronic media are changing so quickly that new systems are coming online before most users have learned to take advantage of the features of the old.

While no one can predict the future for sure, what is evident is that e-mail and electronic conferencing are changing the way people communicate; and they will continue to do so at least until some new form comes along and proves itself to be faster, better, fancier, and more convenient

REFERENCES

Lockwood, R. (1990, March). The corporate bbs. *Personal Computing,* pp. 63–68.

Zuboff, S. (1988). *In the age of the smart machine: The future of work and power.* New York: Basic.

Japanese-American Communication: Mysteries, Enigmas, and Possibilities

Joel P. Bowman and Tsugihiro Okuda

As international business becomes more important, businesspeople have to learn about cultural differences in order to communicate effectively. This article explains some of the customs that differ between the Japanese and American cultures, such as proper greetings and eye contact.

Will the Japanese and American ever really understand one another? Sometimes it does seem as though "East is East and West is West and never the twain shall meet." In addition to overcoming the barriers caused by different languages, Japanese and American cultures are very different. This difference distorts the perceptions each has of the other and alters the standard rules of behavior for each, which causes even greater confusion than the differences in languages.

For a variety of reasons, it is imperative that individual Japanese and Americans learn to communicate with each other, and members of The Association for Business Communication and the Japanese Business English Association can play a pivotal role in this learning process. Because the authors recently have had the opportunity to work together at Western Michigan University and to correspond on a regular basis, we wanted to describe our experiences as we struggled to understand one another.

As a teacher of business English and English literature at Oita University, Professor Okuda was fluent in English before arriving in the United States, so we did not have to spend much time discussing the literal meanings of our words. Nevertheless, we did spend a great deal of time discussing semantics and checking dictionaries to see why each of us had a particular idea of what a word *should* mean. If the English language *per se* did not present a significant communication problem, cultural differences caused misunderstandings from first meeting through our last exchange of letters.

We thought that it might be interesting and useful for readers of *The Bulletin* of The ABC if we explained some of the differences between Americans and Japanese and showed how these differences influence perception and communication.

THE BOW AND THE HANDSHAKE

The nonverbal rituals of bowing and shaking hands are perhaps symbolic of the differences between the two cultures. Just as most Japanese have studied English and speak it at least fairly well, the Japanese have learned to shake hands, though they find it virtually impossible to shake hands without bowing at the same time. Americans, however, not only think that everyone should speak English, but also believe that bowing is at best a strange custom. Many Americans refuse to bow, believing it to be an unnatural act. Most who do try, do it badly.

When a Japanese and an American meet for the first time, their first misunderstanding is likely to result from failure of each to understand and properly execute the rituals of bowing and handshaking. What often happens is the Japanese is bowing while the American is extending his or her hand, and then the Japanese is extending his or her hand while the American is working at returning the bow. Both end up feeling awkward.

POLITENESS

The bow is an expression of Japanese politeness in relationships. The bow shows respect for the other person. The handshake is the American expression of the nature of relationships. The bow says, "I am willing to respect you," or "I acknowledge you with respect," whereas the handshake says, "I will meet you half way." One of the greatest hindrances to communication between Japanese and Americans is their differing perceptions about what is polite. To the average American, the average Japanese seems excessively polite—so polite as to be inscrutable. To the average Japanese, the average American seems impolite—so impolite as to be almost rude.

When asked a direct question, for example, a Japanese will often give an indirect answer if he believes that an honest, direct answer may offend. This tendency can drive Americans crazy. Discovering whether a Japanese would prefer coffee or tea following dinner, for example, can require twenty minutes of skillful questioning. Learning how to discover whether a Japanese guest is comfortable or whether he needs something may require a year's training in diplomacy. The Japanese are careful to avoid giving offense and causing inconvenience. A Japanese would probably starve to death before telling an American host that he can't stand hamburgers and French fries.

Americans, on the other hand, will frequently offer an honest, direct opinion when none is called for because they are so convinced that their opinions are right. An average American would not be shy about telling a Japanese host that the vegetables looked like sea weed and that the fish should have been cooked longer, never for a minute considering the possibility that the Japanese think that eating sea weed and raw fish is a perfectly normal thing to do. The American view often seems to be, if it doesn't happen in My Home Town, it either doesn't happen or (because Americans often take a moral position on cultural matters) it *shouldn't* happen.

Compounding this difficulty are the two cultures' differing attitudes toward eye contact. For Americans, eye contact ranks with Godliness and cleanliness as hallmarks of the trustworthy individual. Eye contact is not nearly so important for the Japanese. Too much eye contact, in fact, would be considered impolite. Historically, Japanese people used to show their respect for prominent people, such as Emperors, shoguns, and regional governors, by *not* looking them in the eye. The tradition of showing respect by avoiding eye contact remains.

For these reasons, a Japanese and an American may be suspicious of each other's motives. The Japanese may think that the American does not respect him or her, whereas the American may think that the Japanese is sneaky and untrustworthy.

THOUGHTFULNESS

The Japanese patterns of conversation also differ from those of Americans. The Japanese are much less afraid of silence than Americans are. In Japan, it's not uncommon for a bus to run for 20 minutes with none of the passengers talking. Americans, on the other hand, seem to have a compulsion to fill all silences with some kind of noise. Who but an American would desire music piped in to elevators to avoid even a few moments of silence? Japanese visitors to America are often shocked to hear an American crack a joke among a group of strangers to avoid the threat of silence during a single-floor elevator ascent. The Japanese are inclined to keep silent unless they have something significant to say.

Americans are frequently surprised to learn that a Japanese person will actually think about what someone has said before responding. Americans, eager to make a point, are much more likely to interrupt before the other person has had a chance to finish. But even when they aren't so eager as to interrupt, Americans have a pathological dread of silent periods in conversation. In a conversation between a Japanese and an American, it is possible for the American to do all the talking—guessing at what the Japanese is thinking, offering his or her own thoughts, and then filling in for the Japanese once again when an immediate response is not forthcoming.

If the matter is inconsequential, this pattern of conversation can be amusing. When Japanese and American business representatives are negotiating major contracts, however, the pattern can be extremely detrimental to the American negotiators. Assuming that the silent reflection on the part of the Japanese signals a rejection of the initial offer, Americans give away the store, making concessions left and right, before the Japanese have had a chance to reply. The Japanese end up with a much better deal than they expected, and the Americans go away thinking of the Japanese as "tough" negotiators.

FORMALITY

The average Japanese, especially those from a traditional background, are much more formal in their relationships than Americans. The Japanese, for example, call each other by their last (family) names and always use a courtesy or professional title (Mr., Mrs., Dr., Professor). Americans, on the other hand, prefer to use first (given) names, which seem more intimate. Japanese and Americans who work together frequently waste a great deal of energy trying to figure out what to call each other.

To the Japanese, using the professional or courtesy title and the last name seems perfectly natural. Americans, however, can't feel fully comfortable until they are on a first-name basis with their colleagues. In working with Japanese, Americans find not only that the Japanese strongly resist being called by their first names, but also that Americans can't pronounce most Japanese first names anyway.

Americans may attribute the Japanese reluctance to be on a "first-name basis" to unfriendliness, while the Japanese may attribute the American's desire to use a form of address other than the title and last name as a sign of lack of respect.

SOCIAL RELATIONSHIPS

Americans tend to be more casual in their social relationships than do the Japanese. In the United States, professors and students may even call each other by their first names, whereas in Japan only parents have the right to refer to their sons and daughters by their first names in either talking or writing.

American relationships are perhaps best illustrated by the variety and informality of greetings: "Hi," "Howdy," "How'r ya' doing'," "What's happenin',"

"How's everything," and so on. American professors have even been known to greet their students by saying, "Happy Monday," or "Happy Friday." Departures in America are also more casual than they are in Japan. Americans might say, "See you later," "Have a good weekend," or even "Have a good one."

The Japanese take greetings and departures much more seriously. Unlike Americans, who are inclined to greet practically anyone within sight, the Japanese do not greet strangers. Greetings are exchanged between friends and acquaintances in Japan. The circumstances in which greetings are exchanged are formal, and the phraseology is limited: "Good morning," "Good afternoon," "Good evening," or "Good night." There are few deviations from the standard expressions. The Japanese do not use each other's names as part of the greeting, but they may include some remarks about the weather.

Although the Japanese may be casual when leaving their friends, saying simply, "So long" or "Goodbye now," they are formal when departing from someone they don't know well. A Japanese might say, "I'm afraid I must excuse myself. Please give my regards to your wife (son or daughter)." Even when they know each other well, however, Japanese would not be so casual as to encourage a departing friend to "Enjoy the weather," especially when the weather is not especially enjoyable.

Even professional and social events are handled differently in Japan and the United States. In the U.S., a typical professional meeting begins with what is loosely called a "social hour," followed by dinner and a program, including a presentation by a guest speaker. The atmosphere is more formal in Japan than in the U.S. When socializing for business purposes, people bow and do not shake hands, and they are acknowledged in descending order of importance. During the process, people wait quietly for the proceedings to finish, and there would be no guest speakers. Should a presentation be required, that would be held in a different location or on a different occasion. When the Japanese have presentations, they have presentations only; when they socialize, they socialize.

SPECIFICNESS AND EXAGGERATION

Japanese people and Americans have different conceptions of when to be specific and when to exaggerate. Consider, for example, the Japanese who was told that the next town was "a stone's throw down the road," only to discover after walking five or six miles that this "stone's throw" happened to be 30 or 40 miles. Or think about the Japanese who was cautioned about the heat in parts of the U.S., where the temperatures "rise into the hundreds Fahrenheit."

American professors might tell their students that they have been "teaching for 100 years," even though they don't look nearly that old, or that a student has made "millions of mistakes," even though a Japanese observer can spot only ten. What is a Japanese to believe if told that there are 10,000 lakes in Minnesota? On the other hand, where a Japanese would say, "for about five minutes," when he or she wanted to indicate a relatively short time, an American might say, "3 minutes and 37 seconds," meaning an equally vague short time.

LANGUAGE

Very few Americans learn Japanese, seeming to believe that everyone can understand English when it is spoken loudly and slowly. The Japanese have, however, worked hard to learn English. Even so, many English metaphors are confusing to the Japanese. A university might be referred to as a "suit case" college if the students go home on the weekends, but think of how a Japanese might interpret that expression.

When a new American businessperson is "hanging out a shingle," a Japanese might wonder whether holding the nails would be of any help. Or if a real estate firm "puts some buildings on the block," the Japanese might wonder where they were before. Consider the television performer who said that he needed a *bomb* to wake up or the news commentator who had a *beef* with one football player but considered another a *recruiting plum*, and imagine what a Japanese might think.

Some of these confusing words and expressions can be clarified by consulting a dictionary. A Japanese who needs to understand *Pollyannaish* or a *Punch & Judy* act can look it up, but how is a Japanese ever to understand *party store*? A Japanese would logically conclude that a *party store* is either a store where one parties or where one may purchase parties. It would be hard for a Japanese to determine why somebody would want to rob one.

HOLIDAYS

Even holidays can cause problems. Because of the small area of Japan—about the size of Montana—the homogeneity of its population and the centralized system of government, the Japanese are characterized by "uniformity" and "regularity." Even the holidays are predictable in Japan, whereas in America, every person seems to observe a separate holiday system.

In Japan, schools, companies, and government offices all close on the 12 national holidays. Those holidays take place on a regular basis, and everything closes on a regular basis. It's difficult for a Japanese to understand why the post office is closed on the third Monday of February when classes are conducted at the local university. This would never happen in Japan. Both the post office and the university are state run, and both are closed on the same days to maintain the *synchronicity* of the social system.

The Japanese are born into and accustomed to a school system that observes a six-day week. The American admonition to "Enjoy the weekend," does not make much sense to the Japanese, who must plan weekends and holidays to take full advantage of the time available. An American might begin a three-week tour of the country by simply pointing his or her car in a direction and taking off, enjoying the unstructured time available. A Japanese, on the other hand, would plan the trip down to the last detail, ensuring that he or she would make the most effective use of precious vacation time.

POSSIBILITIES

Anyone who has read *Shogun* or seen the miniseries on TV knows that Japanese and American histories are very different. Japanese tradition is based on classification, rank, order, and harmony. American tradition is based on declassification, equality, exploration, and adventure. Both cultures, of course, contain elements of the opposite tendencies, but the Japanese place a much higher premium on the planned and the orderly than do Americans, who prefer spontaneous and unfettered energy to the restrictions of an imposed order. It is not by accident that the Japanese value the discipline of *haiku* poetry while Americans value free verse.

In spite of these differences in culture and language, the Japanese and Americans have made amazing progress in learning how to communicate with each other over the past 40 years. Because the cultures are so different, they have much that they can learn from each other, and the best way for this learning to take place is through individual representatives from the cultures who are willing to learn to communicate with and to understand one another. Although cultural differences can constitute communications barriers, problems will be minor and by no means insurmountable so long as good will is maintained along with a steady flow of communication, and as long as both parties have the attitude, "If you come 40 percent down the road, I'll travel the other 60."

People of good will can manage to reach agreements and to develop friendships in spite of difficulties encountered in the communication process. The willingness to accept differences, to suspend cultural prejudices, and to persevere in the face of misunderstandings can overcome even great differences in perceptions and expectations.

The Japanese need to understand that American casualness is a sign of friendliness and openness rather than a lack of respect, and Americans need to develop an appreciation for the Japanese conceptions of order and harmony. Both need to learn that difficulties in communicating are no one's *fault* but are the natural result of cultural and linguistic differences. Both also need to learn that these differences make communication between the Japanese and Americans richer and more interesting than it would be without them.

Defining Terms in Technical Editing:
The Levels of Edit as a Model

Mary Fran Buehler

The term editing *has been used to mean everything from reorganizing a document to correcting punctuation. This article discusses nine types of editing, grouped into five distinct levels of revision. These levels include* substantive editing, *which deals with the content of the report, and* integrity editing, *which checks to see that all the necessary parts of the document are in the final draft. Consider how you would apply these levels of editing to your own writing.*

> *We struggle all our days with misunderstandings, and no apology is required for any study which can prevent or remove them.* —I. A. Richards[1]

The goal of the technical editor is clear communication. But when we—as technical editors—try to communicate clearly about technical editing, we find that we have not yet agreed on standard meanings for our own terms. We may not even know whether we agree or not, because we may not know the meaning that someone else has attached to a given term. How can we know what we are talking and writing about if we do not have commonly understood meanings for the terms we use?

True, our field seems especially plagued with slippery terms. Take the word *copy,* for example. Or *style,* or *format,* or *composition.* (I remember telling an author that we would put his manuscript into composition. "Oh, no," he said. "It's already composed. I finished writing it last night.") But probably the slipperiest term of all is *editing*—which can mean anything from rearranging commas in a sentence to reorganizing a book-length treatise.

Clearly, publications people have recognized this difficulty; they have tried to solve it with such terms as *copy editing, manuscript editing, mechanical editing,* and so on. But these terms do not offer a general solution unless there is a common understanding of exactly what they mean. And, as we shall see, that has not been achieved.

Terminology and Misunderstanding

Take the term *copy editing.* The word *copy* seems a particularly unfortunate choice to restrict the meaning of *editing,* because all aspects of editing in which the editor works with a manuscript (or, more likely, a typescript) involve editing copy. But what other term was available? The range in meanings attached to the term *copy editing* can be illustrated with John B. Bennett's *Editing for Engineers*[2] and the venerable *Manual of Style* of the University of Chicago Press.[3]

Bennett divides the editorial process into three functions: styling, copy editing, and revising. Styling, he says, is the simplest and most mechanical, making sure that a manuscript will follow a prescribed format and style, and is "often the responsibility of an experienced secretary." Of copy editing, he says:

> *Copy editing* is more demanding but can also be carried out by an experienced secretary. Copy editing ensures that such conventions as grammar, spelling, and punctuation will be observed. Let us say, for example, that the organization asks its writers to avoid split infinitives. Determining that there are no split infinitives in a manuscript or correcting those that occur is copy editing. At a more demanding level copy editing ensures, for example, that the sequence of tenses is proper and that typographical errors have been found and corrected.[4]

We may ask why finding typographical errors (ordinarily a proofreading operation) is more demanding than ensuring correct grammar and punctuation, but we have a rather clear picture of the level of effort implied here by the term *copy editing*.

By contrast, the *Manual of Style* describes copy editing as follows:

> Copy editing . . . is the editor's most important and most time-consuming task. It requires close attention to every detail in a manuscript, a thorough knowledge of what to look for and of the style to be followed, and the ability to make quick, logical, and defensible decisions.[5]

The *Manual of Style* then goes on to detail the requirements of copy editing in slightly more than 11 pages, including instructions for editing text, footnotes, bibliographies, tables, illustrations, and front matter, as well as preparing indexes.

Still another aspect of copy editing is revealed in the Foreword of the *Prentice-Hall Author's Guide:*

> The duty of the "copy editor" is to go over your manuscript for errors or shortcomings in grammar, spelling, punctuation, sentence structure, organizational detail, inconsistency, redundancy, and like matters. The production editor assigns this work to a copy editor and corresponds with the author about the edited manuscript. The copy editor has no direct contact with the author and usually remains anonymous. We may often employ a professional freelance copy editor—a practice common in the industry.[6]

But not all editors who do "copy editing" are anonymous. Editors often work closely with other publications people, attend meetings, establish schedules, and deal in a variety of ways with authors. These functions may make up an enormously important part of an editor's working life. As Robert R. Rathbone tells us,

> Good editors are bound to spend a harassed existence. Their job requires more than an ability to recognize and to repair poorly constructed manuscripts. To do a good job, an editor must also be a salesman, a teacher, a diplomat, a psychologist, and at times even a chaplain.[7]

This description—which is only too true, as any experienced editor knows—carries another important implication: that editors work on other people's manuscripts. Editing, in other words, involves at least two people, the editor and the author. And, if the editor is doing a good job, the image of the reader is always hovering in the picture, too. This rhetorical situation, with the editor squarely in the middle between the author and the potential audience, has given rise to the useful metaphor of the editor as bridge-builder and bridge-tester, as envisioned by Lola M. Zook in her early, classic paper, "Training the Editor: Skills Are Not Enough":

> [The editor] must learn that he is now, basically, a bridge between two people—an author and a reader—and that he has responsibilities to both of them. These two people want to bring about a transfer of ideas or information from the first individual to the second, and the editor's place is to help them succeed.[8]

In this usage, the term *editing* becomes a subclass of the more general term *revision,* which refers to changes that are made in one's own material, as well as in other people's. I have generally tried to use the terms *revision* and *editing* in this sense—restricting editing to work with other people, and using *revision* as the more general term.[9] But this distinction is far from universal. To quote Rathbone again,

> All of us, whether we realize it or not, are editors. Perhaps not *good* editors, but editors nevertheless. Every time we read over something we have written we become editors; every time we change a word or add a phrase we are editing.[10]

And Bennett, as we have noted above, considers *revision* a subclass of *editing,* instead of the other way around.

So the questions remain: not only "What is copy editing?" but "What is any kind of editing?" and even "What is editing?"

The questions are not academic. Editing is not a theoretical exercise, though it may be based on theory. Editing is behavior, a series of actions. The actions an editor takes, in working on a manuscript or in communicating with other people, are specific, and they have specific results, for good or ill.

Moreover, the editor's behavior can be considered not only as a series of actions but as a series of responses to variables—variables that include the subject matter, the condition of the manuscript, the knowledge level of the audience, the purpose of the message, constraints of time and money, and so on. These variables are usually built in—they must be lived with, coped with, responded to.

How do definitions fit into this maze of editorial behavior? *The role of definitions is to stabilize responses to a term.*[11] As we have seen, the term *copy editing* can represent a variety of responses the editor may be expected to make. Unless *copy editing* (or any other term) is carefully spelled out by means of specific actions (i.e., unless it is carefully defined), the editor is unable to select the correct responses to the term with any confidence of success.

If, then, the editor's conception of the editorial function is also a variable—because there is no agreed-upon definition of just what the editor is supposed to do—the entire effort can become a mass of uncertainties. And chaos, which often lurks just out of sight in any sufficiently muddled situation, is invited to move in a little closer.

Because the notion of stabilizing responses may sound mechanical—while good editing, obviously, is not—a word of clarification is in order. Definitions set forth the *structure* of editing, *what* is to be done. This fact in no way disparages the *art* of editing, *how* it is to be done.

Indeed, sound structure would seem to make art more likely. The less time and energy the editor requires to determine what to do, the more can be spent on the art of doing it.

TERMINOLOGY AND THE LEVELS OF EDIT

I do not believe it is possible, or even desirable, to legislate standard terminology in technical communication. Still, in light of our obvious lack of commonly understood terminology—and in the interest of agreeing on some broad definitions—I offer in this article the concepts and terms worked out at the Jet Propulsion Laboratory (JPL) and reported in *The Levels of Edit*.[12] The levels-of-edit concept grew out of a study of technical editing that Robert Van Buren and I conducted at the Laboratory in the mid-1970s. We analyzed the editorial function into nine types of edit, which we combined into five levels. The types of edit we identified are Coordination, Policy, Integrity, Screening, Copy Clarification, Format, Mechanical Style, Language, and Substantive. Each type of edit covers a different domain of editorial activity and is set forth as a list of specific instructions to the editor.

In more than 5 years' experience with the levels-of-edit concept at JPL, we have found that the concept and the terminology work: the types of edit cover the field of what we do, without any obvious losses or overlaps. In fact, we have stabilized our definitions to the extent that we collect publications costs according to the level of edit performed on each document (that is, the aggregate of the types of edit), and we use the computer printouts of these historical costs in estimating new work.

And while we at JPL do not presume that the terminology of the levels-of-edit concept is the best that could be devised, we know that other people in technical publications organizations have found the concept useful, too. In addition, the levels-of-edit concept is being discussed in workshops on editing [13] and has been incorporated into a recently published textbook.[14] Since more acceptance seems to be building for the levels-of-edit terminology as time goes on, the types of edit may provide a foundation for some agreement on editorial definitions.

Although the levels-of-edit concept was formally developed at the Jet Propulsion Laboratory, it does not represent a unique achievement in technical communication; others have devised or suggested different levels of editorial effort to fit different needs. For example, Dr. Frank R. Smith, Corporate Manager of Technical Information at McDonnell Douglas Corporation, had derived a stratified scheme of editorial definitions several years before the levels-of-edit concept was formulated at JPL.[15] And Lola Zook, in the 1967 paper cited above, pointed out that

> *the editor needs to work, consciously, at many different levels.* The writer—though he will do well to keep in mind the audience he wishes to reach—is primarily concerned with getting onto paper the things that are in his mind. It is the editor who must make sure that the things the author wants to say are said in a way that will reach the reader—the particular readers of that particular item.[16]

Our effort at JPL was directed not toward defining terminology as such, but toward specifically identifying the domains of editorial activity and establishing the boundaries between them. In the process, we found we had also established the boundaries among the terms we used to identify the domains (or types of edit)—we had established a discrete, nonoverlapping terminology. A more complete discussion can be found in the article "Controlled Flexibility in Technical Editing: The Levels-of-edit Concept at JPL,"[17] or in *The Levels of Edit* itself. The types and their terminology are discussed below..

Coordination Edit.   The only type of edit that does not deal with copy or manuscripts, the Coordination Edit deals with people, budgets, schedules, paperwork, meetings, planning, liaison, monitoring, and other aspects of the publications process, as well as the explanation and interpretation of publications procedures.

By identifying the Coordination Edit as a discrete activity, we reveal the heavy administrative and communicative responsibilities inherent in producing publications, as well as the editor's need for skills in communicating effectively with *people*—an element that can be easily obscured by the somewhat common image of an editor as someone who spends the day bent quietly over a manuscript.

The free-lance copy editor who remains anonymous, as mentioned above, would presumably be concerned with fewer elements of the Coordination Edit, although schedules and budgets would seem to be universal. But for any editor who is not anonymous in relation to authors and others, the Coordination Edit is a crucially important activity—perhaps, in the last analysis, the most important activity of all.

Policy Edit.   The Policy Edit enforces those elements of institutional policy that are more important than simple "house rules" on format or mechanical style. Elements of Policy Edit can almost be defined by saying "These are the things we had better do or we will be in trouble." Because the authority for the Policy Edit comes from the individual institution or its parent organization, each set of Policy Edit rules may be different. At JPL, for example, one Policy rule dictates that distribution lists of (except in some cases) disclaimer statements may not be included in external technical reports. In other companies or institutions, exactly the opposite rules may apply—the point being that, in either case, the Policy Edit conforms to the requirements laid down by management.

Integrity Edit.   The Integrity Edit, primarily a matching function, makes sure, for example, that when the text of a report says "See Figure 1," there really is a Figure 1. The same matching activity is applied to tables, references, footnotes, appendixes, and the sections and subsections of the report. The Integrity Edit also ensures that there are no incorrectly identified sequences; that is, no two elements have the same alphanumeric designation and there are no gaps in the sequences (e.g., if there are 15 figures, Figure 13 is not missing) and no two figure captions or table titles are identical.

What the Integrity Edit does not do is to determine that the "Figure 1" mentioned in the text is *actually* the graph or diagram identified as "Figure 1." This is an important distinction; the Integrity Edit, as a simple matching activity, does not delve into the technical meaning of the report, which is the province of Substantive Edit. To determine whether the "Figure 1" included in the report is actually the "Figure 1" cited in the text, the editor may be required to have an extremely sophisticated knowledge of the scientific discipline being reported, particularly if a series of very similar graphs is grouped together, as can easily happen. In such a case, the author of the report may be the only person who can say with certainty that "Figure 1" is correctly cited.

Screening Edit.   The Screening Edit represents the minimum editorial standard that is acceptable in a JPL external report. Primarily, the Screening Edit is a minimal language edit, although it also requires the correction of certain other unacceptable items (e.g., hand-drawn graphs).

The Screening Edit allows the Laboratory to save time, money, and effort by accepting author-prepared text and artwork for publication (assuming it is sufficiently well executed) and by giving this input a minimal screening to take out any errors that fall below the level of acceptability.

The elements of the Screening Edit are specified: no misspelled words, no subject-verb disagreement, no incomplete sentences, no incomprehensible statements. (By *incomprehensible,* we mean sentences in which words have obviously been left out or garbled.) The Screening Edit could have been called a Minimal Edit—which is what it is—but that terminology could have been confusing, because *minimal* is also used generically: authors can ask for "just a minimal amount of editing," without knowing what, exactly, they will get in return. The Screening Edit lets both authors and editors know what to expect, thus stabilizing responses to the term on both sides.

Because the elements of the Screening Edit are institutionally imposed, it is possible that each publications organization could set up different standards for its Screening Edit, depending on how the institution defined minimal acceptable quality.

Copy Clarification Edit.   The Policy, Integrity, and Screening Edits can all be performed on publications that the author will prepare. When the manuscript must be more fully edited and composed, however, additional types of edit come into play. Copy Clarification and Format Edits are mandatory in order to convert manuscripts into publications. The Copy Clarification Edit provides clear, unambiguous instructions to the compositor or illustrator. Handwritten Greek letters are identified; subscript and superscript positions are clearly marked in mathematics; acceptable equation breaks are indicated; the tops of photographs are marked; and so on. The Copy Clarification Edit may seem mechanical, but it is not: it requires the editor to look at every aspect of the report from the point of view of other people (compositors, illustrators) who may not be familiar with the subject matter and who must never have to guess what a symbol or an instruction may mean.

Format Edit and Mechanical Style Edit.   Because so much confusion exists in technical communication between the terms *format* and *style,* the Format Edit and the Mechanical Style Edit are discussed together here, in order to emphasize the difference between the two. It will probably never be possible to dispel the style-format confusion completely, but enough progress has been made under the levels-of-edit concept to establish a working understanding of the differences.

The term *style* has the further disadvantage of many different, sometimes overlapping, shades of meaning: *style* can refer to literary production, "house style" as set forth in style guides, and typographic style, among others. To help stabilize our meaning, we chose the term Mechanical Style—no other use of the term *style* is made.

As types of edit, Format and Mechanical Style both refer to graphic and typographic treatment, but in different ways. The Format Edit is a macro approach concerned with the physical display of publications elements; it considers heading systems, type fonts, column widths, image areas, and similar matters. The essential questions answered by the Format Edit are "How does it look on the page?" and "Where is it placed in the book?' Some considerations in the Format Edit may be aesthetic and subjective—the choice of type font or column arrangement, for example—and some format decisions may be limited mechanically by what is available or by traditional usage. But whenever the Format Edit designates similarities and differences in content, it operates on *blocks of meaning* (e.g., sections, headings, paragraphs, listings, footnotes, appendixes) rather than on individual units of meaning (e.g., words or numbers).

The Format Edit, for example, may specify that all first-level heads are set in all-capitals, with second-level heads in caps and lowercase. Or the abstract of a report may be given a specified location and set in a different column width from that of the report body. These format instructions will apply regardless of the individual words in the headings or the text. But the format typography will signal to the reader the hierarchical organization of the material, the relation of subsections to larger sections, and so on, providing a typographical road map by which readers can quickly orient themselves in the terrain of an unfamiliar report.

The Mechanical Style Edit, by contrast, is a micro approach typographically and is applied to *individual units of meaning:* it answers the question "Are similar units of meaning treated consistently in graphic or typographic terms?"

For example, the Mechanical Style Edit makes sure that a publication does not randomly refer to "Reference 1," "reference 1," and "Ref. 1." Because the reference number citations represent similar units of meaning, they are treated consistently. A unit of meaning, in this sense, can be a single letter (W for *watts* rather than w), a numeral (4 rather than *four*), a word (*nonparallel* vs. *non-parallel*), or a group of words (*solid state device* vs. *solid-state device*).

As they are defined at JPL, the Format Edit and the Mechanical Style Edit can easily be performed separately, and, in fact, the addition of the Mechanical Style Edit (along with the Language Edit) raises the editorial effort from Level 3 to Level 2. Perhaps the most crucial difference between Format Edit and Mechanical Style Edit is that the Format Edit *must* be performed whenever material is to be composed or illustrated. The format instructions must be given to the compositor or the artist. The Mechanical Style Edit, however, is optional; it represents a desirable level of publications quality—typographic consistency on a micro scale.

Language Edit.   The Language Edit is a full treatment of grammar, punctuation, usage, parallelism, and similar components of what is often considered to be an editor's major—or even only—function. The Language Edit incorporates the Screening Edit but goes a great deal further. Because usage is variable and because editors—being only human—have different degrees of expertise in different aspects of language, the Language Edit is based on specific references: *Webster's Third*[18] for spelling, the *U.S. Government Printing Office Style Guide*[19] for punctuation, and Follett's *Modern American Usage*[20] for usage. Without specific references, we may find that some editors, for example, are meticulous about Fowler-style distinctions between *that* and *which,* while other editors may never have read Fowler[21] or may consider Fowler to be old-fashioned. Or some editors may be carefully concerned about dangling participles, while others adopt a permissive approach. Standardized references, like standardized definitions of terms, tend to stabilize these variables.

Substantive Edit.   The Substantive Edit deals with the content of the report, although not as review for technical accuracy. (If an organization specifies that the editor does review publications for technical accuracy, that review would be a component of the Substantive Edit.) As defined at JPL, the Substantive Edit emphasizes appropriate organization, ensuring that the material is grouped and subdivided in a rational manner, that apparent contradictions or inconsistencies are resolved, and that the presentation is complete and coherent. These requirements are set forth in a comprehensive list of actions concerning such elements as figures and tables, as well as the publication as a whole.

Interestingly, the University of Chicago Press *Manual of Style* identifies *substantive editing* as one of two elements making up the editorial function—the other being *mechanical editing,* which seems to combine the Mechanical Style Edit with elements of the Screening Edit. The *Manual* defines substantive editing to include "rewriting, reorganizing, or suggesting other ways to present material," and goes on to say that "The editor will know by instinct and learn from experience when and how much of this kind of editing to do on a particular manuscript." The *Manual* further states that "Since every manuscript is unique in the amount and kind of substantive editing desirable, no rules can be devised for the editor to follow."[22]

ANALYSIS, SYNTHESIS, AND DEFINITION

The terms of the levels-of-edit concept can be used straight—on a one-to-one basis—to denote the specific editorial domains. But the terms can also be used both analytically and synthetically to define other terms. Analytically, the terms can be used to break down fuzzy and ambiguous words into understandable, discrete units. Synthetically, the terms can be used to build up terminology that can be specified in detail. An example of each process is given below.

Analysis.   Consider the word style: a recent article, "Four Kinds of Style," in the compendium *Scientific Information Transfer: The Editor's Role,* stated that "Style may be the most common piece of jargon used by writers and editors; it may also be the most confusing,"[23] and asserted that the word style has four distinct meanings as used by authors and editors:

1. Editorial style (generally speaking, what is included in a Mechanical Style Edit)
2. Typographic style (included in a Format Edit)
3. Literary style (described as the author's distinctive mode of writing)
4. Usage style (defined as dealing with "grammar, syntax, idiom and shades of meaning," which would fall within a Language Edit).

The levels-of-edit terminology, as demonstrated above, can be used to differentiate these four types of "style," giving specific definitions to the three types that are of primary concern to the editor, and leaving the remaining type to be called Literary Style—the province of the author—which seems a useful and relatively unambiguous term.

Synthesis.   The terms can also be used to build up a definition (as we use them to build up levels of edit). If we wished to use the term *copy editing,* we could easily define the term by saying that copy editing includes, for example, the Integrity, Copy Clarification, and Format Edits. Or we could add Mechanical Style and Language Edits to *copy editing*. The various ways in which the term *copy editing* is used today suggest that even these possibilities may not exhaust the range of meanings currently attached to the words—but we could pin down the meanings if we wished to.

The Need for Definition.   And so we return to the question "What is editing?" As elements of the levels-of-edit concept, the types of edit specify what a technical editor does. Because these types indicate distinct domains of activity, they can be constituted with different specifics by different organizations and still carry a commonly understood meaning—Format Edit would still refer to blocks of meaning, for example, and Mechanical Style Edit would still operate on units of meaning. Language Edit and Substantive Edit could still play their individual roles.

Whether we in technical communication use the terminology of the types and levels of edit or not, we must find some commonly understood terms with which we can communicate, if we are to prevent or remove our misunderstandings—unless we are content to struggle with misunderstandings for all our days.

ACKNOWLEDGMENTS

I am grateful to Professor Walter R. Fisher, Department of Communication Arts and Sciences, and Professor Edward Finegan, Department of Linguistics, both of the University of Southern California, for their valued comments on this article. To Robert Van Buren, my colleague and the senior author of *The Levels of Edit,* go my thanks for his always perceptive criticism, especially on the distinctions between Format and Mechanical Style Edits.

The research described in this article was carried out in part by the Jet Propulsion Laboratory, California Institute of Technology, under contract with the National Aeronautics and Space Administration.

REFERENCES

1. I. A. Richards, *The Philosophy of Rhetoric* (New York: Oxford University Press, 1936, reprinted 1976), p. 3.

2. John B. Bennett, *Editing for Engineers* (New York: Wiley-Interscience, John Wiley & Sons, 1970).

3. *A Manual of Style,* 12th edition (Chicago: The University of Chicago Press, 1969).

4. Bennett, p. 2.

5. *A Manual of Style,* p. 40.

6. *Prentice-Hall Author's Guide* (Englewood Cliffs, NJ: Prentice-Hall, Inc., 1975), p. x.

7. Robert R. Rathbone, *Communicating Technical Information* (Reading, Massachusetts: Addison-Wesley Publishing Company, 1967), p. 88.

8. Lola M. Zook, "Training the Editor: Skills Are Not Enough," in *Technical Editing: Principles and Practices,* Anthology No. 4 (Society for Technical Communication, 1975), p. 13. (Originally presented at the 14th International Technical Communication Conference, Chicago, Illinois, May 1967.)

9. For example, in "Creative Revision: From Rough Draft to Published Paper," *IEEE Transactions on Professional Communication,* December 1976, pp. 26–32.

10. Rathbone, p. 84.

11. W. K. Wimsatt, Jr. and Monroe Beardsley, "The Affective Fallacy," in *The Verbal Icon* (University of Kentucky Press, 1967), p. 22.

12. Robert Van Buren and Mary Fran Buehler, *The Levels of Edit,* 2nd edition, Publication 80-1 (Pasadena, California: Jet Propulsion Laboratory, 1980), (available from the Government Printing Office).

13. For example, the 28th Technical Writers' Institute, Rensselaer Polytechnic Institute, Troy, New York, June 1980; and the Publications Editing Workshop, University of Illinois, Urbana, Illinois, February 1981.

14. Carolyn J. Mullins, *The Complete Writing Guide* (Englewood Cliffs, New Jersey: Prentice-Hall, Inc., 1980), pp. 217–235.

15. Frank R. Smith, McDonnell Douglas Corporation, St. Louis, Missouri, personal communication.

16. Zook, p. 14.

17. Mary Fran Buehler, "Controlled Flexibility in Technical Editing: The Levels-of-edit Concept at JPL," *Technical Communication,* Vol. 24, no. 1 (First Quarter 1977), pp. 1–4.

18. *Webster's Third New International Dictionary of the English Language, Unabridged* (Springfield, Massachusetts: G. & C. Merriam Company, 1965).

19. *U.S. Government Printing Office Style Manual,* Revised Edition (Washington, D.C.: Government Printing Office, 1973).

20. Follett, W., *Modern American Usage* (New York: Hill & Wang, Inc., 1966).

21. Fowler, H. W. *A Dictionary of Modern English Usage,* Second Edition (New York: Oxford University Press, 1965).

22. *A Manual of Style,* p. 40.

23. Wendell Cochran and Mary Hill, "Four Kinds of Style," in *Scientific Information Transfer: The Editor's Role,* Proceedings of the First International Conference of Scientific Editors, April 24–29, 1977, Jerusalem: edited by Miriam Balaban (Hingham, Massachusetts: D. Reidel Publishing Company, 1978), pp. 341–342.

Designing and Delivering Presentations and Workshops

Ric Calabrese

Many professional people have to make oral presentations or conduct workshops on the job. This article presents guidelines for planning and organizing a presentation, arranging the room, delivering the presentation, talking to listeners later, and conducting workshops. Use the preparation checklist to avoid last-minute problems before a presentation and the evaluation sheet to assess your own style after a presentation.

INTRODUCTION: KNOWLEDGE PLUS RISK EQUALS GROWTH

Today a significant responsibility included in the day-to-day life of many professionals includes making oral presentations and/or conducting workshops for groups of clients, customers, patients, other professionals, and the general public. Unfortunately, the skills needed to plan and deliver a message orally and articulately cannot be learned by reading alone; one must be prepared to digest the information and then have the courage to take risks.

While entire books are written on the broad and general subject of giving oral presentations, the purpose of this article is to develop and to discuss concisely the most salient principles occurring in the process of preparing and delivering oral presentations and workshops.

Following are suggestions for advance planning and organizing of a presentation, advance physical arrangements of the room, delivering the presentation, post-presentation actions, and conducting workshops.

ADVANCE PLANNING AND ORGANIZATION FOR THE PRESENTATION

Less is more when giving oral presentations. The key to holding an audience, particularly one with limited time to absorb the speaker's ideas, is to be coherent and to communicate simply; otherwise, their minds will wander. The secret of conciseness and simplicity is for the speaker to know his or her objectives prior to planning the talk. What does he or she want to accomplish? What changes in the attitude or behavior of the audience are desired? Does the speaker want them to perform a task or recall some information? A common mistake made among untrained presenters is to attempt to cover too much in the time allotted. Inexperienced speakers often feel the need to parade their expertise and thus they overload the audience with information.

Unlike reading, where one can go back and reconsider an idea, listening requires ongoing concentration. When the brain begins to feel overloaded and saturation sets in, it protects itself by shutting down. Has not everyone had the experience of pretending to be listening to an overly meticulous speaker while the imagination went elsewhere on holiday? Oral presentations need to be limited to a few major points that can be clearly explained and reinforced through details, examples, and a variety of media. Too much information and too many different points defeat the purpose. When listeners know where the presentation is going and are able to follow the presenter's reasoning, grasping examples with ease, they are much more likely to give their full attention.

Although presentations are often as brief as 10 minutes or as long as 90, presenters would do well to remember when adapting their goals to their group, what the Reverend William Sloane Coffin said about the length of an effective sermon: "No souls are saved after twenty minutes." Once the presenter has tailored the general and specific goals to a particular group, the next task is to organize them.

Introduction Critical to Speaker Credibility

Each of the three generally accepted divisions of a presentation (Introduction, Body, and Conclusion) requires its own internal organization and serves a specific function. The Introduction serves as the speaker's opportunity to establish credibility, to link himself or herself in some way with the audience, to let them know in what ways they will be better off as a result of having attended to the speaker, and to describe for them in some serial fashion what will be covered in the presentation.

Often when speakers are introduced, their credentials are presented in advance; however, there will be times when no one is present to introduce the speaker or, when "introducers" are available, they may neglect to mention important items related to the speaker's credibility. While self-serving comments delivered in a braggadocio manner may have a negative effect on audiences, audiences do, nevertheless, want to know that the person talking to them is worthy and knowledgeable. Presenters, therefore, should subtly let them know during the introduction that they are qualified. For example, one might say, "In an article I wrote last year for the journal XYZ . . . ," or "While I was completing my graduate work at . . . ," or "Of the several hundred accounts I have worked with in the past. . . . "

Audiences tend to be more attentive when they believe that the person speaking to them is able to relate to their circumstances. During the introduction, whenever it is possible, speakers would do well to underscore any connection they may have with a particular group. For example, the speaker might say, "I have lived in this community for fifteen years . . . " or "I see we are all baby boomers and share many of the same sentiments." If one gives it some thought, almost all audiences have some traits with which the speaker can identify.

During the introduction the speaker needs to let the audience know how the topic relates to their needs; in other words, *answer* the unasked question in everyone's mind, "What is in this for me?" Abraham Maslow has synthesized the basic human needs into five areas: physiological, safety and security, belonging and social activity, esteem and status, self-realization and fulfillment. When the presenter announces that after listening to the speech, the listeners will in some way be better able to control their health, be more secure, be in a position where others think better of them or respect them more, think more of themselves, or feel they have the knowledge to develop latent potential in themselves, the audience "perks up" and prepares itself to attend to the forthcoming message. Not every human need can be related to every topic, but as many as are possible and appropriate should be suggested during the introduction. During the "body" and "conclusions" of the speech as well, the speaker should remind the audience how what is being discussed can be related to fulfilling their own needs.

Finally, the last critical component to be included in the introduction is a list of topics that will be discussed. It might be presented something like this: "Today I intend to discuss three specific points. Number one, I will discuss the relationship of diet to heart disease; number two, I will illustrate the fat and cholesterol content of foods; and thirdly, I will model how to order at a restaurant." As mentioned above, not only does this help the audience to listen to the talk with an expectation of what is to come, but the organization itself adds to the "halo effect" and increases the audience's perception of the speaker's credibility.

Three Key Objectives of the "Body" of the Presentation

The Body of the presentation is the second major division and is where the points mentioned in the introduction are actually developed. Presenters need to have a rationale for the way they decide to organize this major section. The overall objectives generally are threefold: that the audience fully understand the message, that the audience believe, and that they be comfortable enough with the speaker to share their objections in the event that they are confused or wish to challenge the presenter.

To safeguard the first objective, understanding, speakers need not only to construct their messages clearly and concisely but also need to design visual aids, handouts, and/or participative experiences to enhance the audience's understanding. The second objective, audience belief, needs continuously to be reinforced throughout the presentation. Credibility or lack of credibility continues to be inferred from the presenter's style and the quality of all aids associated with the presentation. The third objective, to develop a rapport with the audience to the extent that they dare challenge or question, is critical. When objections are unexpressed, presenters may infer falsely that the audience agrees and understands, causing them to move too quickly from one point to another, leaving confused members behind.

A Presentation Can Be Concluded in More Ways than One

Like the first two, the third division of the presentation, the Conclusion, may be handled successfully in many different ways. The key is that all the ingredients be included somewhere. Ingredient one is for the audience to "feel" that the presentation is "winding down" and is about to end. This needs to be done gradually and smoothly. It sounds nonprofessional and haphazard to end with remarks like "any questions," "that's all folks," "thank you for your attention." Remember the presenter's credibility is influenced by the audience's perceptions of how well he or she is organized. Clues such as "In conclusion . . . ," "To summarize," "Before concluding, I want to leave you with one more thought," are helpful in letting the audience know that the presentation is about to terminate. If a summary is warranted, it should be given; if a final plea or pitch is warranted, that should be given; if a final quote, anecdote, or joke makes the point one more time, then that is appropriate.

One last word about conclusions is be proactive in asking if there are any questions. Of course there are, but people are often hesitant to ask. The speaker should prepare a few for the audience, and then call on a participant who has been paying close attention for a reaction. One might say, for example, "I noticed you looked confused when I was discussing the formula to determine appropriate profit levels. What is it you would like further discussion of?" After responding to that first question generated by the presenter, it is often much simpler to get others to respond when the question is asked: "Are there any *other* questions or comments?"

Correlation Exists between "Form" and Speaker "Credibility"

Although the discussion of the presentation's design is generally divided into three areas of introduction, body, and conclusion, there is no one perfect way to organize. Speakers with different styles can be equally successful. There are, however, several points to consider when deciding upon a presentation's format. A fact that most people are not aware of is that the presentation's organization is critical primarily because it relates to the presenter's credibility.

For example, if a speaker were to deliver a talk to two different audiences, giving one audience ten slices of information in an organized way and giving the second audience the same ten slices of information in a disorganized way, both audiences would retain about the same amount of information after hearing the talk. But only one audience would consider it seriously or possibly change their attitude toward the subject matter.

When an audience hears an organized speaker, one who gives the audience a sense that the presenter knows exactly where he or she is going, with a defined beginning, middle, and end, they are more likely to infer that the speaker is competent in the area being addressed. On the other hand, many brilliant and qualified professionals are not taken seriously when giving presentations because they sound too "loose," too unprepared, too disorganized.

Media credibility is related to inferences regarding presenter's credibility. All media, the way they are designed, presented, and utilized, are an extension of the speaker and, consequently, reflect directly the speaker's credibility. Media include such things as handouts, blackboard, flip chart, pad or easel, overhead projector, 35 mm slides, motion pictures, sound recording, videocassettes, samples of products, models or mock-ups, and so forth. "Excellence" tends to be inferred from those that are obviously carefully put together. For example, a presenter whose overhead transparencies are executed with large print that can easily be read (as opposed to ordinary typewriter print, which cannot easily be read from a transparency) allows for the inference of an experienced and considerate presenter. Other signs include using stenciled letters in bold colors on posters, rather than sloppy printing or cursive writing. The condition of the poster itself leads either to positive or negative impressions of the speaker. Those that are discolored, bent, and old looking suggest that the presenter doesn't care enough to add fresh aids for his or her group.

Even the quality and color of the paper used in handouts can add or detract from the overall impression. If it is possible, the presenter is wise to try and coordinate all aids in colors that may be symbolic or meaningful. For example, a presenter giving a talk to a group on Saint Patrick's Day could make use of green; a talk to an Italian-American Club could be done in red, white, and green. This may sound superfluous, but audiences do respond on an unconscious level to the extra care and preparation the speaker has made in tailoring a presentation on their behalf.

An unfortunate judgment is often made regarding presenters who do not carefully proofread all their materials, including handouts, overhead transparencies, flip charts, posters, and the like, prior to the audience's exposure to them. While it is not rational, audience members do tend to make negative inferences about how credible a presenter is in his or her area of expertise if he or she can't spell, count, or interpret statistics. PROOFREAD CAREFULLY.

Whenever presenters are going to be using audiovisual equipment with which they are unfamiliar, it is critical that they arrive early enough to study it beforehand. The most competent presenters may lose their credibility entirely by not knowing how to turn on a machine or advance a slide.

Language and Style of Oral Presentations Differ from Those of Written Presentations

The written text and the oral presentation are entirely different. There is no objection to a presenter writing out the entire talk, carefully organizing it according to topics, causes and effects, chronology, or whatever else seems appropriate. Once the talk is written, however, the speaker needs to recognize that the written manuscript represents the "science" of a presentation; the actual delivery represents the "art." Each time it is delivered, it should be somewhat different, using different words, different examples, different anecdotes, and so forth to suit each particular audience and situation.

The word "choice" in the spoken language tends to be different from the word "choice" used in the written language. Sentences in oral speech tend to be simpler, shorter, and sound more conversational, including common words and contractions, while the written manuscript may be more erudite and academic. The only way for speakers to develop the "art" of delivery is to rehearse from a simple outline and not from a manuscript, and to rehearse in front of real people who will react and comment, not mirrors, walls, or car windshields.

Oral presentations ought never to be read or memorized. There are good reasons for not rehearsing from a manuscript. The speech tends eventually to become memorized, and that can be deadly. Once a speech is memorized, speakers tend to become more "speaker-centered" than "audience-centered," which means that they tend to become more concerned about whether or not they can remember each line exactly as it is written on the manuscript and less concerned about whether or not the audience is enjoying, learning, listening, and understanding. Another problem that arises from manuscript speaking is that it is DULL! Because the facial expressions and vocal intonations are not spontaneous, the monologue tends to sound memorized and can easily become boring to listeners.

ADVANCE ARRANGEMENTS

Take control of seating the listeners before everyone settles down. It may be their boardroom, gymnasium, or meeting hall, but it is the presenter's "show." Conscious decisions should be made about whether to pull the group into a circle, half circle, rows, around tables, and so forth. When it is possible to know beforehand which persons are the most influential, their seats should be reserved and placed in the best position to see, hear, and appreciate any visual aids, as well as the speaker. A final checklist for presentations is found in Figure 1.

Attend to details and prepare a final checklist. Listed below are a few questions that the presenter might consider in order to avoid last-minute problems.

Do I have my presentation notes?

Do I have all my supporting materials?

Have I enough copies for each of the attendees?

Will the facility be unlocked and open?

Are the tables and chairs arranged to suit my design?

Do I understand how to operate the lighting system?

Do I understand how to operate the ventilation system?

Do I know the location and operational condition of the electrical circuits?

Do I know how to work the projector?

Do I have an extra bulb, cassette, video, extension cord, etc.?

Will the projection screen be in place and adequate for this size group?

Do I have the type of sound system I require? Is it working?

Have arrangements been made to handle messages during the presentation?

Are there arrangements for hats and coats?

Will there be a sign to announce the place of the presentation?

Will someone be introducing me, and have I given him or her all the information I want shared with the group?

Figure 1   Final Checklist

Creating positive impressions begins the moment the presenter enters the room. The presenter is being "sized-up" and adding to the presentation's ambience from the moment he or she enters the room. Therefore, the presenter should, whenever possible, arrive early and make an effort to meet people. The speaker's self-confidence, whether real or feigned, will relax the audience and increase their perceptions of his or her desire to share information. Presenters should never volunteer any negative information regarding their own stress or fear of speaking. The audience wants to learn and enjoy, and when they are aware of the speaker's fragility or stage fright, they tend to become nervous themselves in sympathy.

The presenter, waiting to be introduced, seated among the audience or on stage, should be aware that those people who know he or she is the guest speaker will be watching his or her every move. That means that even before beginning the presentation, speakers must be careful to smile, look confident, and extend themselves to others. Once introduced, the way the speaker walks up to the podium is critical. During those first moments an initial impression is being created. The speaker should consciously walk confidently, looking and smiling toward the audience. Prior to uttering the first words to the audience, it is a good technique to spend a long three seconds just looking out at the audience, smiling and establishing eye contact with several individuals. This allows them to infer poise, confidence, and the speaker's desire to "connect" with them.

DELIVERING THE PRESENTATION

Never share internal feelings of fright or anxiety. Speakers experience themselves in the situation from the inside out; the audience experiences them from the outside in. Simply, that means that if asked if he or she is nervous, the speaker should always answer "NO!" The audience is picking up the "tip of the iceberg" from their observations of the "outside" of the speaker; they do not actually feel the intensity of the speaker's anxiety and will probably be totally unaware of it, unless it is brought to their attention through one's own confession. One must act confident, even when one may not feel it internally.

One of the worst things presenters can do is to admit to an audience that they are scared, ill prepared, missing material, or have done the presentation better in the past for other groups. The audience does not know what it might be missing, and are generally much less critical of speakers than they are of themselves.

"Stage fright" is a vestige from our ancient past. The feelings commonly referred to as "stage fright" may date back to the dawn of the human race, a time when our prehistoric ancestors had to survive by living in caves and sharing the food supply with other beasts. Faced by a predator, our ancestors had a genuine use for a sudden jolt of energy, which gave them the power to do battle or run, fight or take flight. The vestiges of this power, stemming from the secretions of the adrenal gland, still manifest themselves today when people sense danger. Who has not felt that ice block in the stomach while being reprimanded by the boss, or experienced the sweaty palms and racing heart while walking into a room full of strangers?

Occasionally one still reads in the newspaper accounts of individuals under conditions of fear or danger exhibiting superhuman strength; the father, for example, who lifts the car off his child, who has been pinned under the wheels. This is an example of the power that comes with the adrenaline jolt; however, when one is unable to fight, run, or in some other way utilize this surge, he or she may become overwhelmed by the internal feelings themselves. It is this feeling prior to and during a presentation that is commonly labeled "stage fright."

The best safeguard against stage fright is adequate preparation and rehearsal. The more one practices in front of *live others,* the less nervousness one will have. Other ways of dealing with this feeling include being active during the presentation and "acting" calm and confident. If one knows one is going to be full of extra energy because of one's adrenaline flow, one could plan to engage in demonstrations during the presentation, distribute handouts, use a pointer, or any other activity that involves motion. Motion is a release for the tension and anxiety and allows the audience to infer enthusiasm from the speaker's movement rather than fright, nervousness, or tension. It may not work for everyone, but many people can learn to control their public behavior if they visualize themselves as acting. When one is "on" giving a presentation, one is acting. Regardless of how one may feel, one can *act* confident, calm, and poised.

Movement should be intentional and meaningful. All movement should be meaningful. Do not pace. Presenters ought to look for opportunities to break the invisible barrier between themselves and their audience. Walking toward the audience, walking around the audience, walking in and out of the audience, are all acceptable ways of delivering a presentation. What is not acceptable is pacing back and forth, particularly with eyes down, pulling thoughts together before uttering them.

Movement into an audience is a communication vehicle in itself. When the speaker penetrates that invisible barrier between speaker and audience, he or she tells the audience of a desire to connect, to be close, to better "sense" what they are feeling about him or her and the content. In fact, as one walks among the audience, one can begin to be seen from a different perspective and may gain new insights into how to better clarify the presentation's points from this experience.

Unnecessary barriers between the presenter and audience should be omitted. Presenters do best when they omit all barriers between themselves and their audience. Avoid using a podium or lectern, even when one is provided by the sponsoring organization. Of course, there may be times when, because of the quantity of material, a place to store things may be required. Even under this condition, using a table to set handouts and other materials on is preferred to a podium.

A lectern should only be used when the speaker does not intend to move about; intends to lecture and needs a stand to rest against and place notes upon. Adults generally do not learn optimally through the lecture method and unless the speaker is extraordinarily good, straight lecture behind a lectern should be avoided. When one delivers the message standing in front of the group, without a barrier, one is more disposed to stop the talk to respond to their verbal or nonverbal feedback. Gestures and movement too can be more expansive and visible without the lectern barrier.

Voice cadence, pitch, variation, and rate are communication vehicles. Vocal inflection and variation add interest and add to the impression of speaker enthusiasm. For some people controlling this variation is simple and natural, but for others it is a challenge. Nevertheless, the presenter needs to attend to voice modulation. The goal when speaking in front of a group is to sound natural and conversational; however, what sounds natural and conversational when one is standing in front of a large group is not the same as what sounds conversational in a small face-to-face group.

"Natural and conversational" from the presenter's point of view is exaggerated. The highs need to be a bit higher and the lows need to be a bit lower. What may sound to the presenter's ear as "phony" and "theatrical" generally sounds far less so to the listener. In any case, a delivery that is of narrow range or monotone is difficult to attend to for more than a few minutes. The good news is that this trait can be fairly easily and quickly developed, even in those who recognize a problem in this area. It requires risking sounding foolish and exaggerated in front of trusted others, until adequate reinforcement has convinced the presenter that the increase is really an advantage that allows him or her to be attended to more easily.

When talking in front of a group, generally the speaker should attempt to speak more slowly than in ordinary conversation. What is an appropriate rate in a small face-to-face discussion is probably too fast for a group presentation. For some reason, there seems to be a correlation between the speech rate of the speaker and the size of the audience. What might be easily grasped at a more rapid rate in face-to-face conversation, isn't understood as quickly in large groups. Also, the speaker's slower rate allows him or her to scan the audience to see if the presentation is being understood, to see if some people need an opportunity to disagree, to see if he or she needs to talk louder or increase variation because some look bored.

Nonverbal behavior, the silent language, can be meaningful and controlled. It is good practice to keep hands away from the body and from one another. Allow them to be free to gesture, and avoid holding anything in them while talking, unless it is a useful prop like a pointer or a visual aid. After twenty-five years of teaching presentational speaking to college undergraduates and corporate professionals, this writer knows empirically that once speakers allow their hands to mesh together or to grasp one another behind their backs, there is only a slight chance of their being released to gesture. Often people feel awkward with their hands hanging loosely at their sides. Perhaps if they could see themselves on videotape in this posture, they would realize that it is natural looking, but even more importantly, they would probably see that one tends not to stay in that position. If speakers talk with their hands hanging loosely at their sides, eventually their hands begin to rise and gesture spontaneously to emphasize important points.

It is very dangerous to begin a presentation holding a pen, paper clip, rubber band, or other instrument not directly related to the presentation. Unconsciously, the fingers begin to play with the instrument, and the audience becomes fascinated in watching to see what the speaker will do. A former student actually straightened out a paper clip and began to stab himself while talking. Needless to say, for the remainder of his presentation the class couldn't take their eyes off the mutilation scene, and missed the speaker's concluding points.

As one speaks so will one be judged. Professional speakers attend to their diction, particularly when pronouncing words like "for," "can," "with," "picture," "going to," and "want to." In ordinary conversation one isn't likely to judge negatively a speaker who mispronounces common words and engages in sloppy diction saying, for example, words like "fer," "ken," "wit," "pitcher," "gunna," and "wanna," for the words listed above. When that speaker is in front of an audience, however, these mispronounced words often stand out and lead to negative inferences regarding the speaker. If one thinks of well-known television anchor men and women, one will be unable to recall any who have faulty diction. Professionals who present themselves in front of groups must attend to their diction because they risk losing credibility if it is poor. Logical? No! True? Yes!

Once one has decided to become conscious of one's diction and decides to improve it, several steps are required. Step number one is for the speaker to inform trusted others who are often around him or her to listen critically, and to stop him or her each time a diction error occurs. Only after one is made aware of common errors, can one begin to train one's self to hear them. That is step two. Because the human mind operates generally at five times the rate of human speech, it is possible to listen critically to ourselves as we speak. So those who are attempting to rid themselves of poor diction or some other vocalized interference ("um," "an," "and a," etc.) can train themselves to listen for the errors and to correct them. Like learning to ride a bicycle or to use a computer, this learning and training task is uncomfortable at first, but improvement comes quickly. Working on one's diction is an ongoing task. Professional speakers never stop listening to the way their words are coming out and planning ahead to pronounce them correctly.

The visage itself is a communication vehicle. Presenters need to train themselves to keep their faces animated, using a variety of facial expressions. For many of the same reasons expressed above, it is important that speakers use all the communication vehicles available to maintain the audience's attention. One's facial expression is itself a communication vehicle. When it is lively, animated, expressive, and changing regularly while the speaker reacts to the feedback coming from the audience, it enhances the verbal message and allows the audience to go on unconsciously inferring the speaker's audience-centeredness. Because of a natural dispositional personality, ethnic background, life experience, and so forth, this is easier for some people to do than for others; however, everyone can improve! Because it isn't easy for one to "act" expressive does not mean that one can't grow considerably in the ability to look expressive. Indeed one can.

Eye contact is a vehicle of communication. It should be used to see the audience and respond to their nonverbal feedback. It is surprising how many people seem to remember having learned some rule about being able to fool the audience into thinking that the speaker is seeing them while he or she is actually looking over the heads of the people in the last row. The point is that when speakers have the opportunity to present themselves and their ideas to an audience, they want them to understand, to believe, and to follow their recommendations. Speakers have the best chance of being successful in achieving those goals when they are able to interpret the audience's ongoing reaction to what they are saying. Even though presentation speaking is generally considered a one-way communication situation, with the speaker talking at the audience as they listen, it is, in fact, a two-way situation with audience and speaker communicating with one another constantly and simultaneously.

Trained speakers see almost everything from their position in front of the room. If they are alert and looking, they see people who are beginning to fidget and interpret their feedback. They might decide from this observation to give the audience a short break; they might liven up their own movements to regain attention; they might engage in a new activity, one perhaps that involves audience participation, and so forth. The speaker might see some people coming in late, looking awkwardly for a seat. This provides the opportunity to publicly welcome them and ask others to move over to provide seating. The speaker might see people who look angry. This provides the opportunity to say, "You look angry. What have I said to offend you?" In other words, speakers who use their eyes to "connect" with the audience make them a part of the presentation. The audience knows it too, and will begin to send signals when they realize the speaker is sensitive to them.

Facial expressions are important. Smile, and look like you are having a good time. Smiling can be rehearsed and may feel phoney, but it needs to be built into the design of the presentation. One does not need to be constantly grinning, but one does need to maintain an expression of gentleness, approachableness, and nondefensiveness. The easiest way to convey these impressions is to smile often. Unfortunately, it isn't easy to smile when one is unsure of the material. All the principles above can only be worked at after the speaker has sufficiently mastered the content and consciously, through rehearsal, developed skills.

Although individual situations may make this difficult, a general rule to remember is that when speaking for an hour or less, always plan on at least ten minutes for some audience interaction. In talks of more than forty-five minutes, actual audience participation activities should be planned where possible and appropriate.

POSTPRESENTATION

Speakers should remember to bring business cards and to remain afterwards for people who may want to talk. If they have done a good job with eye contact, smiling, and prompting the inference of warmth, people will want to talk with them. This is frequently a source of repeat talks to other groups, and it is an opportunity for the best kind of public relations, face-to-face. When there is a long line of persons waiting to talk and time is limited, this writer passes out his business card and tells everyone they are entitled to one call for free consultation. It is amazing how many people follow up on the offer.

WORKSHOPS

Workshops differ from presentations. There are significant differences between a presentation and a workshop or training session. The differences are in the amount of time needed, the amount of audience participation recommended, and the goals of the leader. Presentations generally run no more than ninety minutes, while workshops may run from ninety minutes to several days. Audience participation and training are an integral part of workshop design, and the goals of workshops are generally to teach and train, while the goal of a presentation often is to persuade the audience to accept a specific proposal. The suggestions below are particularly appropriate when designing workshops.

Workshop leaders should plan to use techniques that involve all participants and encourage open communication between themselves and the participants and among the participants. Ways to encourage participation include: dividing the larger group into smaller groups, giving them time in their small group to get to know one another, and then giving them activities related to the workshop topic. These small group activities may include: case studies, either real or hypothetical; role playing; and questionnaire completion and discussion. Occasionally a group may be given a preworkshop assignment to complete a questionnaire, read material related to the workshop, or some other task. Reactions to these tasks can be processed among the participants in small groups.

Frequently, the most important point in determining the climate and direction of the workshop occurs during the first twenty minutes. Some suggestions for using the opening minutes to establish an open climate include using a group introductory activity to promote a relaxed and open atmosphere. When the group is small enough (generally twenty or less), spending time to allow each participant to identify major concerns and questions tends to encourage this involvement. Workshop leaders can relieve participant anxiety by introducing themselves, sharing both personal and professional information, giving a brief overview of the objectives for the workshop, the main topics to be covered, their sequence, and approximate time span. They should also reinforce often that they do have expectations in terms of participants' cooperation and participation. Even when such introductory activities take as long as an hour, they are justifiable, because of their importance in establishing a common frame of reference with shared goals in a relaxed and receptive setting.

Leaders should be aware of signals of fatigue or boredom from participants. Some techniques used to avoid these problems include: identifying two or three participants whose behavior provides some type of clue to group climate, providing a variety of activities to break-up the routine, and providing a change of pace. Most successful workshops are a blend of information-presenting activities with "hands-on," experiential types of activities.

Another way to safeguard understanding and attention is to summarize regularly what has occurred, especially before moving on to a new topic. Continuity of training is enhanced, if there are purposeful and periodic reviews and summaries during the workshop. Leaders should note that it is not essential that they do the summarizing; in fact, having the participants themselves do it provides feedback as to whether or not the group has grasped the important points.

Anticipate from among the alternatives the appropriate conclusion for the workshop. Just as the introductory period to the workshop should not be rushed, so too should closure be carefully attended to. This depends upon how much time is available for the entire workshop, of course. But in a day's workshop of from six to eight hours, allowing a full hour at the end for closure is appropriate. During this time loose ends are tied; the group's original expectations are reviewed and assessed as to how well these expectations have been met. Requiring the group to complete an evaluation of the workshop during the time provided for the workshop is the method most likely to get the largest return. These evaluations are most helpful to leaders who want to continue to grow. They will process the evaluations and make changes in subsequent workshops based on the responses. A sample evaluation sheet is available in the "Appendix." The emphasis in a workshop is always on quality not quantity. It isn't how much the audience has heard; it is how much they will learn, will remember, and will use in the future that is the final measure of the workshop's success.

APPENDIX

Evaluation Sheet

Presenter: _____

Date: _____

Presentation (Check your response)

	Excellent	Good	Satisfactory	Poor	Unsatisfactory
1. How would you describe the presenter's knowledge of the subject matter?	____	____	____	____	____
2. How did you find the presenter's style of delivery?	____	____	____	____	____
3. Did the presenter encourage individual participation?	____	____	____	____	____
4. Did the presenter hold your interest?	____	____	____	____	____
5. How did you find the organization of the content material?	____	____	____	____	____
6. How useful did you find the visual aids?	____	____	____	____	____
7. To what degree did you feel that the content and exercises were relevant to your job?	____	____	____	____	____
8. Comments:					

How to Deliver Dynamic Presentations: Use Visuals for Impact

Marya W. Holcombe and Judith K. Stein

Oral presentations are most effective when the speaker uses intriguing graphic aids. This article discusses how to choose graphics for certain audiences and purposes, how to prepare graphics, and how to use them effectively. Use the chart to select appropriate types of graphics for your oral presentations.

Presentations are more persuasive when supported by visuals. But audience members frequently walk out of a presentation wondering what the visuals were all about. Why? Because presenters often don't take the time to develop and learn how to use them. A little common sense and a few guidelines can help produce effective visuals.

People remember more when they see *and* hear a message. And they remember images better than words. But few people can read and listen at the same time. Thus, for visuals to be effective, the audience must be able to see the visual and grasp its message quickly. To meet these criteria:

- Select the best kind of visual support,

- Design visuals for the greatest clarity and impact, and

- Use visuals correctly.

CHOOSING PROPER SUPPORT

What types of visual aids are available?

Managers most often use transparencies, flip charts or 33 mm slides, usually in that order. Although some conference rooms contain blackboards, most managers regard "chalk talk" as too informal or too academic for anything but pure problem solving.

Audience size influences the choice of medium. So do the purpose of your presentation, industry and organizational norms and available resources.

Each audience member must be able to see the visuals clearly. If the group exceeds 20 people, flip charts are not effective. Overhead transparencies, on the other hand, can be used with groups containing up to about 100 people. But those transparencies should be shown on a large screen. Slides are necessary with audiences of several hundred people. Whatever visual you use, ensure that it is legible from a distance.

The purpose of your presentation also affects the type of visual you use. If you're trying to persuade your boss to approve your budget, you wouldn't put on a slide show in his or her office. Yet, if you're trying to persuade your company's board of directors that a major expansion program is vital, you wouldn't appear in the boardroom with rough, hand-lettered flip charts.

The type of visuals required to make a persuasive argument helps determine the appropriate medium. Only the simplest charts and graphs are appropriate for flip charts. For complex material, use transparencies, which are enlarged when projected onto a screen. If photographs are essential to your point, use slides. But remember: Copying a photograph onto a transparency generally is unsatisfactory because the reproduction will be poor.

Industry and organizational norms also influence selection of visuals. If your company has the attitude that "we're all in this together," you might prefer to use creative, informal visuals. Presentations usually follow a detailed format, sometimes preserved in a bound book, in organizations with rigid hierarchies. In that case, professionally produced slides may be in order.

Time, money and the availability of equipment also will guide your decision. Slides, for example, are expensive and take at least a day to produce.

You can make overheads on an office copier instantly and inexpensively by using a typed or hand-drawn original on letter-size paper. Although professionally made overheads are superior, do-it-yourselfers usually are acceptable if they are neat.

Flip charts are easy to make and are the least expensive form of visual. But when drawn professionally, time and cost factors increase.

How to Prepare Visuals

Visuals can consist of words or graphics, or both. They reinforce the presentation's main points and help the audience follow the flow of arguments.

Regardless of the type of visual used, two guiding principles surface. Keep it simple, and ensure that it focuses attention on your message.

Text visuals, consisting of only words, primarily are used as road maps. They preview or summarize information and remind the audience where you are in the presentation. Although text visuals also may emphasize main points, most presenters consider pictures more powerful than words.

Simple visuals, which allow the audience to grasp the concept easily, are best. Because the human eye can take in about 40 characters in one glance, lines should be limited to that number. Use phrases rather than full sentences, expanding on each phrase as you speak.

To ensure that the visual is easy to read, use upper- and lowercase letters. Choose a simple typeface. Use bullets or Arabic numerals to set off items in a list: They are easier to read than letters or Roman numerals.

Consistency and white space help the audience focus on your message. Start text at the same place on all visuals—about one-fifth down from the top. Leave a space about the height of a capital letter between each line. Then audience members will not have to search for a starting place each time a new visual appears.

Using color, boldface, or large-size type for important concepts helps distinguish them from supporting ideas. Reinforce your message by using the same feature each time you make a similar point. For example, you can use the same text visual several times to remind the audience of your place in the argument. Highlight your location each time with one of those features as you move through the presentation.

GRAPHIC VISUALS

People usually assimilate visual forms more quickly than words. Thus, use graphic visuals to emphasize important relationships. To create effective graphics, select the most appropriate chart form, follow the rules of good design and reinforce your message with headings.

Most management presentations include numerical data. For those presentations, line, bar and pie charts are the most frequently used graphic forms. Yet diagrams, maps and photographs also are valuable. Tables are appropriate only when the audience must have exact numbers.

Choose the form that best fits the point you are making:

- Line charts show changes over time of one or several variables.
- Bar charts, whether vertical or horizontal, show the relationship between two or more variables at one point in time or at several points in time. Although line and bar charts are used frequently for similar purposes, line charts are more effective in depicting change over time. Bar charts highlight differences between distinct time periods or compare components of a whole at different times.
- Pie charts show the relationship among parts of a unit at a given period. Although pie charts are round, other shapes, such as bars, also can be used to show parts of the whole.
- Diagrams, such as organization charts, process charts or flowcharts, help the audience visualize relationships and processes.
- Maps focus attention on one or several locations and indicate spatial relations and distances.
- Drawings show the details of a design. And cartoons can be used to make a point with humor.
- Tables provide data in a precise form. Complex tables, however, are inappropriate for presentations where the audience is expected to catch the visual message quickly. In addition, anyone seated behind the first row usually cannot see long columns of numbers. If you must show all the numbers, limit them to three or four columns and three rows. Or use handouts. Avoid using as an overhead or slide a full-page table copied from a written document.

DESIGN RULES

When preparing visuals, follow the rules of good design. Visuals are intended to be snapshots of your data, not detailed blueprints. Once you have selected an appropriate form for your chart, include only the data needed to get your message across.

If you want the audience to focus on declining sales, for example, leave out earnings and dividends. If you want to emphasize that two-thirds of corporate earnings went to pay the energy bill, a pie chart showing all other expenditures in detail will detract from your message.

Color, when used in moderation, is an effective way to focus the audience's attention. Shade a part of a graph, highlight a number, or use a colored arrow to point to details that specifically support your argument. Be consistent when using color so as not to confuse the audience. Remember these points when choosing colors for your visuals:

- Use colors in moderation;
- use bright colors to attract attention to your main point, but use red sparingly;
- use contrasting colors to contrast concepts or to signify a major change; and
- use two shades of the same color to point out minor changes.

Reinforce your message with headings. A good heading explains your visual explicitly. If an audience member is distracted while you are speaking, he or she still can determine significant points by looking at the heading. Even an attentive listener appreciates the reinforcement.

Useful headings contain a noun and a verb and tell the audience what is important. This heading, for example, makes a precise point that the audience will remember: "Earnings did not exceed 1972 levels until 1981." If the heading had been "Earnings: 1972 to 1983," audience members who had not heard the message would have been left to draw their own conclusions—possibly one the presenter didn't intend. Or, they might not bother to draw any conclusion at all.

The placement, size and kind of lettering also are important considerations. Headings always should be above the chart. And, in general, heading type should be twice as large as other type. Text identifying the mechanical proportions of the visual should be lightface, while text identifying the data lines, bars or parts in the graphic representation can be boldface. Again, for reasons of simplicity, run all lettering in the same typeface.

How to Use Visuals

Visual means "perceptible by sight; visible." Visuals are worthless if the audience can't see them because the speaker blocks their view, or the screen is out of place, or the focus is poor, or the projector is not working. Follow these simple rules when using slides, overhead projectors and flip charts:

Slides.   Effective slide presentations require careful orchestration; conscientious planning and rehearsing are important. Check that all slides in the carousel or tray are right side up and in the correct order. Use the slides as your notes; a lectern light is disconcerting to the audience. If the slide projector doesn't have a remote-control feature, rehearse the slide presentation with the projectionist. Saying "next slide, please" interrupts the flow of thought.

Use a pointer to focus attention. Some presenters use a "light" pointer, which allows them to point to the screen with a ray of light. However, the novelty of this tool may cause your audience to focus more on the pointer than on the point. Plus, your dependence on yet another battery and a bulb increases the chances of something going wrong. Unless you have a very large, high screen, use a conventional pointer.

Overheads.   When using overhead projectors professionally, your equipment must be in good working order. And you must know how to operate it properly.

Guidelines for Selecting Visuals

Considerations	Flip charts	Overheads	Slides
Audience size	Fewer than 20 people	About 100 people	Several hundred people
Degree of formality	Informal	Formal or informal	Formal
Design complexity	Simple	Simple; can be made on office copier	Anything that can be photographed
Equipment and room requirements	Easel and chart	Projector and screen; shades to block light	Projector and screen; dim lighting
Production time	Drawing time only	Drawing or typing time; may be copied instantly	Design and photographing time plus at least 24 hour production time
Cost	Inexpensive unless professionally drawn	Inexpensive unless professionally designed or typeset	Relatively inexpensive

Before anyone arrives, turn the projector on and off, check the focus and make sure you have an extra bulb. Also, know how to change the bulb, if necessary.

The visual on the screen should amplify the point you are making. If you finish the topic and do not have a visual for your next point, turn off the projector. A glowing, empty screen is a dreadful distraction, and a covered transparency with light leaking around the edges is almost as bad. Furthermore, by turning off the projector, you signal audience members to return their attention to you.

Where you position yourself throughout the presentation is important. Don't block anyone's view. When a transparency is projected on the screen, move to one side.

When you want to point to something on the screen, don't turn your back to the audience. Instead, point with your hand nearest the screen. Or use a pointer if the screen is large.

If you are near the projector, use a pencil, not a finger, to point to something on the transparency. Your finger would look enormous. Or, use a specially designed pen to circle the concept you want to emphasize.

Some presenters add information to a transparency while it's projected on the screen. Although writing on the transparency during the presentation adds action, it requires good handwriting and self-assurance. It is difficult to write on a transparency without having your hand shake (the projector will magnify the movement many times over) and without moving the transparency. If you do write on the transparency, always stand to one side of the machine as you write. Then move away so everyone in the audience can read what you have written.

Flip charts.   Because they require no electrical equipment, flip charts are easy to use. Easels should be anchored securely on the floor, and flip charts should be attached firmly to the easel. If using an adjustable floor stand, set the height so you can comfortably grasp the page in the middle and flip it over the pad. Moreover, ensure that the chart braces are fixed in advance so that your charts don't slide to the floor while you're speaking.

Before the audience arrives, open the chart to the first blank page. As you proceed from one visual to the next during the presentation, grasp and flip over the completed visual to the following blank page. Flip the visual with your hand nearest the chart as you face the audience. If you are not ambidextrous, stand on the side most convenient for you.

If you do not have a visual for the next section of your presentation, skip to a blank page, and move to another part of the room. And, as in any presentation, always face the audience.

Occasionally, for external presentations, managers use professionally made boards the size of flip charts. However, those are expensive and bulky to transport. Furthermore, they're unwieldy when showing and removing: Presenters usually need assistance to change the boards, which distracts the audience.

Making effective presentations is easy when you use a little common sense and follow these guidelines. Text and graphic visuals should be simple and should focus attention on your message. And remember: Review all visuals carefully. Ask an outsider or a disinterested co-worker to review them for typographical or conceptual errors, inconsistencies or points of confusion. Then set them aside until you are ready to rehearse the presentation.

Barriers to Effective Listening

Jack E. Hulbert

Many communication problems are caused by poor listening habits. This article discusses the major barriers to effective listening and gives advice on overcoming them.

INTRODUCTION

Although listening is our most frequently used communication skill, it is perhaps our least effective communication skill. Research indicates that people spend approximately 70 percent of their waking hours communicating (i.e., listening, speaking, reading, and writing) and that about 45 percent of that time is spent in listening while only about 30 percent is spent in speaking, 16 percent in reading, and 9 percent in writing. Studies also reveal that immediately after listening to a ten-minute presentation, the average person has heard, understood, properly evaluated, and retained only about half of what was said and that within 48 hours retention decreases to only about 25 percent.

In business, the list of problems caused by poor listening is endless. Because of ineffective listening, letters have to be retyped, appointments have to be rescheduled, orders have to be reprocessed, products have to be remanufactured, and shipments have to be rerouted. Because of poor listening, employees cannot understand and satisfy customers' and clients' desires; and managers cannot understand and satisfy employees' needs. As a result, customers and clients are alienated; and unnecessary employee-employer conflicts disrupt operations and decrease productivity. Although it is impossible to calculate the exact cost, it has been estimated that poor listening costs American business billions of dollars annually.

To improve listening comprehension, one must overcome many barriers which interfere with listening efficiency. Understanding these listening barriers can help listeners surmount these obstacles and establish a climate conducive to effective communication. Listening barriers may be classified under the following headings: content, speaker, medium, distractions, mind set, language, listening speed, and feedback.

CONTENT

An obvious barrier to effective listening is the content of the message. Some listeners may feel that their knowledge of the subject is so extensive that they have little to learn from the speaker. They, therefore, pay little attention to what the speaker says.

Other listeners may feel that their background is too limited to provide an adequate basis for interpreting the speaker's remarks. They "tune out" at the first sign that the discussion will involve difficult intellectual or emotional content. Still other listeners are inclined to accept only information which agrees with their own beliefs and automatically reject any information which disagrees with their personal views and opinions. In these situations, poor listeners usually just sit back and wait for the speaker to finish; but little real communication occurs.

Effective listeners know that they must do more than passively allow sounds to enter their ears. They participate actively in the communication process by attempting to develop a positive attitude toward the speaker's message and consciously anticipate the importance of the message content. They discipline themselves to seek areas of interest in any message and constantly remind themselves that something of value can be learned from every message.

SPEAKER

The speaker has a significant effect on the listener's ability and willingness to listen. Even the speaker's delivery—enunciation, organization, clarity, speed, volume, tone, inflections, emotions, and appearance—affects the listener's willingness and ability to interpret the message. Research indicates that listeners are influenced more strongly by their attitudes toward the speaker than by the information presented. If listeners like the speaker, they are much more likely to empathize with his or her viewpoint, and, therefore, agree with—or at least more fully comprehend—the speaker's message.

Good listeners are aware of these pitfalls to effective listening and attempt to elicit maximum message meaning by concentrating on the "what" of the message rather than on the "who" of the speaker or the "how" of his or her delivery.

MEDIUM

Another variable affecting listening is the medium through which the message is transmitted—because the distance between the listener and speaker has a strong impact on the amount of listening effort required. Contrary to what might be expected, least listening effort is required when the speaker is not visible—as with radio or recorded messages. Increasing amounts of effort are required as the speaker becomes visible—as with televised or filmed messages. And, maximum listening effort is necessary when the speaker is physically present and speaking directly to the listener. This phenomenon occurs in face-to-face communication because the amount and variety of input or stimuli is a potential source of confusion and disruption of message meaning. In face-to-face conversation, the listener receives rich—and sometimes conflicting—verbal and nonverbal stimuli about the subject matter, the speaker's emotional state, and the speaker's feelings about the listener. Although face-to-face communication provides the richest variety of stimuli and, therefore, offers potential for multiple levels of meaning and deeper understanding, good listeners realize that face-to-face communication increases the listening effort necessary for message comprehension.

DISTRACTIONS

It is well known that listeners are easily distracted by almost any extraneous stimuli—sounds, lights, odors, mannerisms, voice inflections, or moving objects. Psychological studies indicate that a listener's attention span is sometimes no more than two or three seconds. If listeners' already short attention spans are disrupted by distractions, they may miss part or all of the message meaning by the time they refocus on what the speaker is saying.

In the broad sense, any factor that interferes with the accurate transmission and reception of a message may be classified as a distraction. Distractions may be caused by environmental factors, such as noisy equipment, loud traffic, or other talking; or they may be linked to physical problems, such as impaired hearing or vision. However, distractions are most frequently related to psychological factors arising from differences between the speaker's and listener's frames of reference, emotions, values, understandings, experiences, or cultural backgrounds.

Good listeners constantly monitor the listening environment in an effort to identify and eradicate distractions. If environmental distractions cannot be eliminated, they attempt to overcome these obstacles with increased concentration. In addition, they consciously endeavor to eliminate psychological distractions by freeing themselves from preconceptions, prejudices, and negative emotions in order to develop open minds receptive to new ideas.

MIND SET

Because listening is an extremely subjective process, obstacles to effective listening can arise from the listeners' attitudes about themselves, others, and the environment. People perceive the world through their own personal "mind filters" structured by their unique physical, mental, and emotional characteristics. Therefore, each listener approaches a message with a unique mind set which influences message comprehension.

The listener's mind set about the speaker or the subject matter can either magnify or diminish certain stimuli and thereby distort message meaning. If a listener expects to hear certain things based upon preconceptions about the subject or the speaker's personality and background, information conflicting with the listener's mind set is frequently ignored. On the other hand, the listener may attach unintended importance to some of the speaker's statements since the portion of a message to which the listener assigns greatest importance is largely determined by his or her mind set.

Effective listeners realize that differences in the speaker's and listener's mind sets can pose a major barrier to understanding. They know that listeners can be immobilized by emotional static when listening to a speaker whose mind set differs from their own. Therefore, they continuously strive not to allow their personal biases to interfere with message comprehension.

Good listeners have the courage to be objective and flexible and are, therefore, willing to permit others the freedom to hold their personal values and beliefs. They realize that attempting to understand another's viewpoint does not necessitate agreeing with it. They respect the rights of speakers with whom they disagree and are intellectually capable of acknowledging the feasibility of more than one acceptable point of view.

LANGUAGE

Although the primary function of language is to facilitate understanding, at times language can be a barrier to effective comprehension because ambiguity is an innate characteristic of any language.

Listeners rarely hear every word spoken and frequently attach different meanings from those intended by the speaker to the words they do hear. Obviously, listeners are apt to misinterpret words which are not part of their vocabulary. They are also likely to misinterpret words which are imprecise, emotional, technical, or overly intellectual. However, the greatest cause of misunderstanding is probably the fact that listeners interpret words according to their own personal definitions determined by their background, education, and experience—which are likely to be quite different from those of the speaker.

Listening efficiency can be improved if listeners realize that the same words frequently have different meanings for different people. Good listeners understand that words are simply symbols with little or no intrinsic meaning. They realize that the meaning of a word is in the speaker's and listener's minds, not in the word. They know that the meaning of a word is strongly affected by the context in which it is used and that that context is at least two dimensional when viewed from the speaker's and listener's unique perspectives.

LISTENING SPEED

Another major barrier to effective listening arises from the difference between listening and speaking speeds. The average person speaks at a rate of between 125 and 150 words a minute while the average listener can comprehend information at about 500 words a minute. This difference in speaking and listening speeds affords the listener a great deal of excess thinking time.

Instead of using this excess time to concentrate on the speaker's message, poor listeners indulge in daydreaming. When they finally return from their mental tangents, they frequently find they have missed part of what the speaker said and the speaker's meaning is confused, if not totally lost.

In contrast, effective listeners use this excess thinking time to:

- Outline mentally the speaker's message.
- Identify the speaker's purpose and determine how the speaker's points support that purpose.
- Evaluate the soundness of the speaker's logic.
- Verify and integrate information presented with past knowledge and experience.
- Maintain eye contact in order to observe and interpret the speaker's nonverbal signals.
- Formulate questions to ask at appropriate moments in order to verify the accuracy of their understanding.
- Provide encouraging verbal and nonverbal feedback.

In other words, effective listeners use their excess thinking capacity to elicit as much meaning as possible from the speaker's message.

FEEDBACK

When listeners provide inappropriate feedback, they hinder the speaker's ability to provide complete and honest information. In general, people are far more driven to speak than to listen and, therefore, listeners often respond with premature comments or evaluations before fully understanding the speaker's viewpoint. This premature feedback can cause speakers to say things they do not mean or divert them to irrelevant tangents. In addition, if listeners respond with indifference or color their feedback with emotions of resentment, defensiveness, or suspicion, they greatly decrease the possibility for effective communication.

Good listeners provide appropriate supportive feedback by:

- Demonstrating interest in what the speaker says.
- Maintaining appropriate eye contact.
- Smiling and showing animation.
- Nodding occasionally in agreement.
- Leaning toward the speaker to demonstrate an attitude of interest and confidentiality.
- Using verbal reinforcers like "I see" and "yes."
- Phrasing interpretations of the speaker's comments to verify understanding.
- Consciously timing their verbal and nonverbal feedback to assist rather than hinder the speaker.

Good listeners know that by providing appropriate empathetic feedback they can create a supportive listening atmosphere in which speakers are encouraged to provide complete, honest disclosure.

SUMMARY

Listening is a highly selective, subjective process with many barriers to accurate comprehension. Because the average person has developed and reinforced careless listening habits through countless hours of social and recreational listening, it is difficult for many people to listen effectively in business or problem-solving situations. In fact, the message ultimately deciphered by the average listener frequently differs markedly from the speaker's original thought.

Awareness of the barriers to effective listening and how to combat these obstacles to accurate comprehension is vital to the development of efficient listening skills. Although research indicates that the average person listens at only about 25 percent efficiency, it is encouraging to note that in organizations that have instituted listening instruction employee comprehension has as much as doubled in just a few months.

Business Manners for the '90s

Ann Chadwell Humphries

Successful professionals must understand appropriate etiquette for typical business situations. Knowing proper business etiquette will instill confidence and help you respond effectively to others in the workplace. This article reviews common etiquette mistakes and gives advice on how to avoid making them.

COMMON ETIQUETTE BLUNDERS

1. **Being rude on the telephone.** This, the most common business etiquette blunder, includes not returning phone calls promptly, not identifying oneself, and screening calls arrogantly. Always return calls within 24 hours—and preferably the same day. Identify yourself and the nature of your business up front; anticipate resistance and be helpful. And help people get the information they need. Avoid overly protecting the boss with questions too directly asked, such as, "What is the nature of your call?"

2. **Interrupting.** Let people finish their sentences, and ask permission if you need to interrupt their work. Don't barge into conversations or offices without giving a signal.

3. **Introducing people incorrectly.** Say the most important person's name first, then the secondary person's. In the workplace today, the most important persons—regardless of sex or age—are outside guests, officially titled people, and superiors. "Outside visitor, this is our company President." "Mayor, this is our Vice-President of Marketing." "Boss, this is an employee of 35 years."

4. **Wimpy or vise grip handshakes.** Wimpy handshakes or overpowering grips are no-noes. Grab your handshake high, around the thumbs, and shake in kind. Don't swoop on delicate folks, or withdraw from an acrobatic handshaker. And women—get your hand out there! Men hesitate to initiate this action. They've been taught to wait for a lady to extend her hand first. Handshakes are expected in business life. So learn to shake hands well, and offer yours easily.

5. **Incorrect eye contact.** In the United States, looking people in the eye means you have nothing to hide, that you are listening, that you are interested. In certain other cultures, however, direct eye contact is considered confrontational and disrespectful. Vary eye contact from short glances to longer holds of 3–5 seconds, but don't stare to make yourself look good. You will be overbearing.

6. **Poorly managed business meetings.** Start and end them on time. Distribute agendas ahead of time so people can prepare. If you are the leader, control the action. Don't suppress confrontation, or it will emerge elsewhere. But you can defer it to a more appropriate time. Last, limit telephone calls to the leader, so the group will not be held up.

7. **Poor or inappropriate appearance.** To the business executive, appearance is important. It's not the only measure of a person, but it does give visual interest to

520

doing business and indicates your knowledge of, and respect for, the rules of the game. You must dress with understated distinction to be considered seriously in business. Invest in quality clothing, and be impeccably groomed.

8. **Forgetting names.** Ask anybody about his or her most uncomfortable business etiquette dilemma and forgetting names will emerge in the top five. To help you remember names, one positive strategy is to repeat the person's name as soon as you hear it, and to use the name at least once if you have a long conversation. Don't over-use a person's name, however.

But when you don't remember someone's name, there are several simple strategies to follow. Use your judgment about which is most appropriate for, and least embarrassing to, you and the other people involved.

a. **Introduce yourself first.** This is for the occassion—either in a one-on-one conversation or if you're part of a group—when you only vaguely remember the person. Introducing yourself helps take people off the spot.

b. **Stall for time.** When you know the person, but it takes a few minutes for your mind to compute the name, act friendly and don't withdraw. Don't sport the "Charlie Brown" nervous smile. Focus on them, not yourself.

c. **Introduce the people you do know.** Pause to let those whose names you don't remember introduce themselves. Or, say lightly, "I'm so sorry. I know who you are. I've just gone blank." Or, "I've just forgotten your name," with an implied, "Silly me." Keep the conversation going with what you do remember.

d. **Help out someone who looks as if he or she is struggling to remember *your* name.** This is not pompous or arrogant; it's considerate. Many people slur their names so they're unintelligible, or present themselves in an ordinary manner, so they aren't memorable. Take care when you introduce yourself.

A Survey of the Frequency, Types and Importance of Writing Tasks in Four Career Areas

Mary K. Kirtz and Diana C. Reep

Effective writing on the job is important for job performance and for promotion. This article reports the results of a survey of people working in four different career areas. Look for your career area in the three tables and check (1) the amount of time you are likely to spend writing on the job, (2) how important writing is for your career area, and (3) the kinds of documents you can expect to write on the job.

Results of a survey of people employed in four different career areas indicate that effective writing on the job is important both for job performance and for promotion. The survey, conducted in 1987 and 1988, asked 118 participants in writing seminars held in companies or on university campuses about the types of writing they did and how important writing was to their careers. Participants included 38 management people, 27 people in technical fields, 24 in clerical positions, and 29 in social service occupations.

Table 1 shows the percentage of time the participants said they spent writing while on the job. Although none of those surveyed was employed as a professional writer, writing clearly occupied a major part of the work day. Nearly 50% of managers said they spent from 21% to 60% of their day writing. In social services, 51% said they spent between 21% and 60% of their time writing. Over 40% of the technical people and 29% of the clerical people also wrote that much.

Table 2 reports the answers to questions about the importance of writing. Most said effective writing was either critically important or very important to job performance: 84% of the managers, 81% of the technical people, 86% of the clerical

Table 1   Percentage of Time Spent in Writing Tasks

	Management (N = 38)		Technical (N = 27)		Clerical (N = 24)		Social Services (N = 29)	
20% or less	17	(44.7%)	13	(48.1%)	10	(41.6%)	9	(31.0%)
21%–40%	15	(39.4%)	6	(22.2%)	5	(20.8%)	9	(31.0%)
41%–60%	4	(10.5%)	5	(18.5%)	2	(8.3%)	6	(20.6%)
61%–80%	2	(5.2%)	1	(3.7%)	4	(16.6%)	3	(10.3%)
81%–100%			1	(3.7%)				

Not all respondents answered, so totals may not be 100%.

people, and 89% of the social services people. For promotion, 70% of the technical people and 57% of the managers said writing well had an important effect on their opportunities for advancement.

Table 3 lists the kinds of documents written daily or often. Managers most frequently wrote letters, memos, short reports, and instructions or procedures. Technical people wrote fewer letters than other groups did, but they frequently wrote memos, short reports, and instructions or procedures. Clerical people wrote primarily letters and memos, while those in social services wrote primarily letters and short reports. In addition, individuals named a variety of documents that they wrote frequently in their work, such as policy statements, minutes, and proposals. Obviously, people on the job write often and they need to do it well to succeed.

Table 2   Importance of Communication to the Job

	Management (N = 38)		Technical (N = 27)		Clerical (N = 24)		Social Services (N = 29)	
How Important Is the Ability to Write Effectively in Your Present Job?								
Critically Important	11	(28.9%)	7	(25.6%)	6	(25%)	10	(34.4%)
Very Important	21	(55.2%)	15	(55.5%)	10	(41.6%)	16	(55.1%)
Somewhat Important	6	(15.7%)	5	(18.5%)	7	(29.1%)	3	(10.3%)
Unimportant								
Does the Ability to Write Effectively Have Any Effect on Promotion?								
Critical Effect	2	(5.2%)			4	(16.6%)	2	(6.8%)
Important Effect	22	(57.8%)	19	(70.3%)	8	(33.3%)	10	(34.4%)
Minor Effect	7	(18.4%)	5	(18.5%)	9	(37.5%)	11	(37.9%)
No Effect at All	5	(13.1%)	2	(7.4%)	1	(4.1%)	3	(10.3%)
Don't Know	2	(5.2%)	1	(3.7%)	1	(4.1%)	2	(6.8%)

Not all respondents answered, so totals may not be 100%.

Table 3   Kinds of Communication Written Daily or Often

	Management (N = 38)		Technical (N = 27)		Clerical (N = 24)		Social Services (N = 29)	
Letters	24	(63.1%)	5	(18.5%)	14	(58.3%)	16	(55.1%)
Memorandums	29	(76.3%)	13	(48.1%)	13	(54.1%)	5	(17.2%)
Short Reports (1–5 pages)	19	(50%)	9	(33.3%)	8	(33.3%)	22	(75.8%)
Long Reports (6+ pages)	4	(10.5%)	2	(7.4%)	1	(4.1%)	4	(13.7%)
Proposals (internal)	5	(13.1%)	3	(11.1%)	1	(4.1%)		
Proposals (external)	4	(10.5%)	3	(11.1%)	4	(16.6%)	2	(6.8%)
Instructions or Procedures	15	(39.4%)	11	(40.7%)	7	(29.1%)	3	(10.3%)
Policy Statement or Guidelines	13	(34.2%)	3	(11.1%)	3	(12.5%)	1	(3.4%)
Minutes	6	(15.7%)	5	(18.5%)	2	(8.3%)	1	(3.4%)
Journal Articles	2	(5.2%)	2	(7.4%)				
Speeches	4	(10.5%)	1	(3.7%)				
Advertising/ Promotion Material	4	(10.5%)			2	(8.3%)		
Other: Manuals	1	(2.6%)						
User Documentation			1	(3.7%)				
Patient Log			1	(3.7%)				
Case Log							7	(24.1%)

For Writers: Understanding the Art of Layout

James L. Marra

Writers and artists often have difficulty understanding each other's interests in designing manuals. This article explains the general principles of design and also describes how a group of technical writing interns designed a training manual. Notice the differences in visual-balance emphasis created by various cover designs.

Oftentimes, the difficulties encountered in the preparation of technical manuals are due to a lack of understanding between writers and artists. In effect, one hand doesn't know quite what the other hand is doing or why it's doing it. One reason for the problem is that the language of the two specialists is often full of esoteric, field-oriented jargon. For instance, the writer may well be mystified by the procedures involved in halftone or duotone reproduction. The artist, on the other hand, may be equally mystified by parallel or pyramidal sentence construction. And the danger, of course, is that such barriers hinder progress and strain work efforts and cooperation between two groups whose harmonious collaboration is a must if the "new look" in technical manuals is to be successful.

These barriers need not exist. If the writer understands the main principles of design, he or she will be better able to understand the artist's motivation and rationale. Conversely, such understanding will evoke an attentive ear from the artist when the writer enters the design field. All in all, more harmony between the two will become a distinct probability. And more effective manuals will result.

DESIGN PRINCIPLES

Virtually any good design book will elaborate upon a multitude of design principles which one should consider in creating layouts. Naturally, artists are schooled in such principles, which basically boil down to four fundamental concerns: unity, balance, sequence, and proportion.

Unity

The main principle, unity, is the relationship of all graphic elements, white or negative space included, on a page. It is the binding agent to the layout. In Gestalt thinking, the modes of perception patterns lead to the result that the whole of a visual image is greater than the sum of its parts. This is unity. It is the principle whereby type style and size, art (line or halftone), borders and frames, and colors all lend themselves harmoniously and efficiently to a unified presentation.

To achieve unity the layout artist develops axis points, or points around which the elements (type, art, etc.) revolve. As a result, the vibrating visual effect a reader experiences from widely spaced, random groupings is eliminated and a whole, unified image results. This idea of wholeness is unity. And in many ways it is the umbrella principle to balance, sequence, and proportion.

Balance

Balance is the distribution of optical weight represented in sizes of art and type, tones, and colors. It may be symmetrical (formal) or asymmetrical (informal). If symmetrical, the weight of the figures or elements on the ground of one-half of the layout page will be repeated on the ground of the other half. Thus, if one is working with balance left to right and places a mirror down the center of the page, one-half of the design will look like the other. The optical weights will be the same. In asymmetrical design, optical weight is still important, but the weight is not equally distributed. Rather, there is a shifting of its emphasis to one side or the other.

Sequence

Whereas balance involves weight, sequence involves rhythm. It is the guiding principle which emphasizes control of a reader's eye movement. Normally, the primary visual area of a page will be its top left. The eye will then move in a zigzag, or Z pattern, to the bottom right. Consequently, many layout artists are fond of placing the design elements within the path of the Z. However, eye movement can be created in any direction by the choice of position, size, or color of the elements.

Proportion

The final principle, proportion, is the relationship of sizes and tones. The layout artist who is considering how much width of an element to use compared to its depth is working in proportion. Likewise, when consideration is given to the amount of light area as opposed to the amount of dark area, proportion is the principle at work. The main idea to bear in mind when working with proportion is the need to employ the $\frac{3}{5}$ths rule. The $\frac{3}{5}$ths rule, or golden oblong as it is commonly referred to in design circles, simply says that a page layout is more dramatic, more appealing to the eye when the major element (photo, copy block, etc.) occupies $\frac{3}{5}$ths rather than half of the available space. In fact, any odd-fraction dimension is more suitable, avoiding the pitfall of humdrum which is a result of page layout in halves.

THE INTERN PROGRAM

And perhaps that is what layout design in action seeks to do—avoid the humdrum, the unevocative. In manuals the quest is under way. For instance, a select group of technical writing interns from the Redstone Arsenal in Huntsville, Alabama, recently underwent an intensive training program in technical communication at Texas Tech University in Lubbock, Texas. Organized by the Department of Mass Communications, the program was designed to bring the interns into contact with the layout possibilities of technical manuals. A key word here is "possibilities," for the instruction was geared to creative thinking in layout and design. First, the principles of design had to be understood. Then, by the actual employment of the principles, the interns were thrust into the hot seat of the layout artist. Possibilities emerged. Alternative methods of presentation were realized firsthand. And a number of workable, though rough, layouts were produced as alternatives to the training manual cover shown in Figure 1.

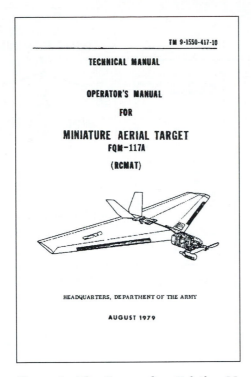

Figure 1   The Cover of an Existing Manual

The Procedures

Prior to these rough layouts, which originated with quick and plentiful thumbnail sketches (the crude, initial drafts of design possibilities), a critique of the existing manual cover was offered. For instance, as regards the design principles, the cover was found to be lacking axis points around which the elements of type and art should revolve. The lack of contrasting sizes for greater points of emphasis (proportion) was also noted, particularly in the typesize. In addition, there appeared to be no definitive attempt at balance, either symmetrical or asymmetrical. And overall, it was felt that the design gave the appearance of random selection and positioning.

Following the critique, the interns began thinking with their pencils in the form of thumbnails. Working with existing copy and art, they were encouraged to make size and position changes and to incorporate singly or in combination the four main design principles. A random selection of nine quick thumbnails, recreated for this article, is represented as Figure 2, A to I. At this stage the layout artist was simply attempting to imagine as many alternatives as possible, deferring judgment so as to allow the visual imagination free rein. Likewise, the writers, by entering into this initial phase of artistic production, experienced the problem as it would be attacked at an artist's drawing board.

Figure 2A–I   Thumbnail sketches of possible variations.

Figure 3   Symmetrical balance and tightening of the elements give the layout a dignified look.

Figure 4   A zigzag (Z) pattern of eye movement is created by the positioning of the elements.

Figure 5   Added weight is given to the illustration by its large size.

The Results

Following the thumbnail stage, the writers undertook execution of rough layouts. The second phase is generally the stepping stone to the comprehensive layout, which, in turn, evolves into the finished mechanical used in print production. In effect, the rough layout is that which the artist imagines to have the most promise of the many thumbnails produced. Consequently, it is given more detail and elaboration than the thumbnails and represents a more vivid picture of what the end product will be. Again recreated for reproduction here, a selection of rough layouts produced by the interns is represented by Figures 3, 4, and 5. These evolved from the thumbnails in Figure 2: A, B, and C, respectively (the remaining thumbnails are offered as alternative approaches). And in the rough layouts the design principles are well exemplified.

For example, in Figure 3 the intern sought to capture symmetrical balance in order to give the layout a dignified and formal look. The weight of the elements to the left equals the weight of the elements to the right. Also, the typesize has been altered to create contrast and thereby highlight the key parts of the message.

In Figure 4, the reader's eye is nicely directed through the principle of sequencing. By contrasting the weights of type and using reason in positioning the elements, the intern developed the zigzagging or Z pattern of eye flow. The reader's eye begins reading at the upper left because of the highlighting of "Miniature Aerial Target." It then moves down through the target to the propeller, which directs the eye back to the closing message, "Headquarters, Department of the Army."

In Figure 5, the abstracted view of the aerial target has been magnified, giving it a larger proportional weight and creating a dramatic effect as it becomes a dominant part of the layout. It is also consistent with the odd-fraction-dimension principle in that the line art now occupies the great percentage of the page. In addition, two more interesting visual effects are created. First, the lines of the art move off the page. This produces closure, a phenomenon which allows the reader's imagination to complete the drawing. More active involvement of the reader is the end result. Second, the terms "Operator's Manual For . . ." are placed in the wing span. From this device it is possible to create a dimensional effect which encourages the reader to move into the page, again creating more active involvement.

It is also interesting to note that in each of the figures represented there is a unified composition of the elements. The contrasting of weights establishes emphatic parts of the message. At the same time, the elements are tightly grouped in units and appear to flare out from various axis points while not giving the appearance of random scattering about the page. Consequently, the amount of vibrating space between the elements is diminished, and the reader's eye is able to fix on key parts of the message.

CONCLUSION

In conclusion, by employing one principle, then another, and by considering combinations of each, the interns were able to imagine a variety of possibilities. In addition, they were able to experience dilemmas which confront layout artists on a daily basis. And moreover, they were working with the language and processes of design which are the daily bread of those artists. The likely result in such a situation is that writers gain a better understanding of design and the people who create it. The language barrier is overcome. More harmony ensues. And the collaborative effort, relieved of the strain of communication problems, pursues a common direction toward more effective "new looks" in technical manuals.

Combating Speech Anxiety

Myles Martel

Most speakers suffer from anxiety before making an oral presentation. This article provides guidelines for controlling and deemphasizing fear of public speaking. Read the guidelines before making an oral presentation.

Call it stage fright, speech fright, speech or communicator anxiety or apprehension, its symptoms are unmistakable and its significance as a barrier to effective presentations cannot be overstressed.

A quaking voice, trembling knees, erratic pacing or rocking, stomach butterflies, pronounced monotone, a deadpan facial expression, and lack of eye contact are common cues that the speaker is experiencing the malady I prefer to call speech anxiety—a tension-laden self-consciousness which dominates the speaker's concern for communicating ideas.

Few speakers are immune from this phenomenon. Leaders in all professions in all ages have experienced speech anxiety, regardless of status, sex, intelligence, age or income. Sir Winston Churchill remarked that when he began to speak he felt as if there were a nine-inch block of ice in the pit of his stomach. And Cicero said, "I turn pale at the outset of a speech and quake in every limb and in all my soul."

Communication experts and psychologists are not certain about the precise causes of speech anxiety. The most popular explanation, however, calls it a form of approach-avoidance conflict. On the one hand, the speaker may feel impelled to represent the organization, while on the other, feel pulled in the opposite direction by another dominant force, often by some fear of failure.

Speech anxiety has no sure-fire cures, but it can be alleviated by a proper attitude toward (1) the anxiety, (2) the self, (3) the audience, (4) preparation and practice, and (5) delivery.

ATTITUDE TOWARD SPEECH ANXIETY

1. Recognize that most if not all speakers experience some form of normal nervous anxiety. If you feel a little anxious, don't panic. Say to yourself that you have normal nervous anxiety, which you can control—not eliminate.

2. Consider the normal nervous anxiety to be potentially helpful. Your anxiety may motivate you to speak with greater forcefulness, and result in a more animated presentation.

3. Realize that your anxiety state is often much more obvious to you than to your audience.

4. Don't be afraid to admit to your speech anxiety in discussions with friends or colleagues.

ATTITUDE TOWARD SELF

1. Think "expert." With few exceptions you would not be making an appearance if the host did not feel you had something of value to share with your audience.

2. Assume a 100 percent attitude regarding your engagement. Many speakers have a tendency to take on a "less than" attitude toward the engagement, often not realizing that this attitude may reflect their own fear of coping with the challenge to communicate. The ability to "wing it" is a talent presumed by many but possessed by all too few.

ATTITUDE TOWARD THE AUDIENCE

1. Regard the audience as being composed mainly of friendly listeners with whom you will be engaging in an enlarged conversation.

2. Don't overreact to hostility, disagreement, lack of interest or apparent confusion.

ATTITUDE TOWARD PREPARATION

1. Understand what a speech is, the specific means by which it can be prepared and practiced.

2. Avoid memorization. Fear of forgetting normally generates tension, self-consciousness and other unnatural delivery characteristics.

3. Learn how to speak extemporaneously from a carefully prepared outline consisting of key words and phrases. Conscientiously practice expressing each idea without "overscripting" yourself into memorized passages. Practicing with audio or videotapes while standing in front of one or more constructive critics can be especially helpful. Practicing in front of a mirror, despite the popularity of this advice, can be counterproductive; it can make you more concerned with your body than with your message.

4. Analyze the audience, occasion and setting well in advance. Learning about the demographic and attitudinal composition of your audience, the layout of the room and the specifics of the program can diminish your normal fear of the unknown.

5. Prepare a neat, well-spaced and well-selected set of notes with delivery advice and notations.

6. Devote extra efforts to creating within the speech itself an impactful introduction that captures the audience's attention, enhances your credibility and orients the audience toward your subject.

7. Do your best to be well-introduced. Send a suggested introduction to the host and always have a copy with you in case the host has lost the original.

8. Avoid major last-minute changes in your outline. The natural anxiety produced by the engagement may prevent you from handling such changes well.

9. Arrive early and mingle with the audience. This will help you to regard them as individuals with whom you can hold an enlarged conversation rather than as an unknown, fear-provoking mass of people.

10. Try relaxation exercises shortly before your appearance. Isometrics and deep-breathing exercises can be especially helpful.

11. To relieve your television or radio talk-show jitters it may help to have a friend ask you immediately before your appearance a few warm-up questions.

ATTITUDE TOWARD DELIVERY

1. Gesture and move around purposefully (when a lectern is not present) to reinforce the message physically, while you simultaneously create a natural outlet for your nervous anxiety.

2. Establish and maintain direct and distributed eye contact with the audience. The more you establish eye contact, the less you will be struck with fear of the unknown. Also, you will be better able to respond to their feedback with an enlarged-conversation frame of mind. The popular advice "pick a friendly face" may be helpful when you need visual reassurance, but don't concentrate on this person for too long.

3. Consider using visual aids. Flip charts in particular are effective means of inducing natural bodily movement.

Probably no one has ever conquered speech anxiety by just reading about it. Reading merely provides the insights to be applied in real speaking situations. The more you seek these situations and systematically prepare for them, the more confident—and compelling—you should become.

Preparing Students for the Behavioral Job Interview

Marcia Mascolini and Roberta Supnick

Along with questions about a job applicant's education and experience, many employers are using job interviews to test an applicant's ability to deal with work-related problems. For instance, instead of asking about long-term goals, an interviewer might ask an applicant to describe a recent goal and explain how it was achieved. This article gives tips on answering these kinds of interview questions.

For several years, a cornerstone of the task of preparing for the job interview has been to review the most frequently asked interview questions and to prepare appropriate responses to each. Several of the most popular business communication texts, in fact, contain lists of these questions and encourage students to prepare for the inevitable command, "Tell me about yourself."

Preparing formulaic responses to stock questions, however, may no longer be enough. Employers may be going beyond that generic approach. Because of the costs of recruiting, interviewing, and training, the interview has become much more deliberate. A critical issue is, of course, to avoid bad hires, that is, to avoid hiring applicants who prepare well for the standard interview and present themselves well but do not perform well on the job.

Companies extensively analyze positions that need to be filled and develop structured, tailored interviews. In the behavioral interview, applicants are asked to solve situational dilemmas that they are likely to encounter on the job. The critical difference, according to users of this approach, is the addition of behavioral questions. Applicants must recall and describe specific activities or behaviors. Rather than ask how an applicant might reprimand an employee, the interviewer would instead request a specific example illustrating the behavior. The applicant's description of the act of giving a reprimand would provide more meaningful information, reflecting concrete action rather than abstract prediction.

William S. Swan, an interview consultant writing for *Working Woman,* instructs managers to ask probing questions rather than rely on typical queries:

> Forget [stock questions]. Every candidate has a ready answer for them. . . . Start your questions with words like "what," "review," "tell me," "explain," and "describe." Follow it up with "How did you do it?" or "Why did you do it that way?" (96–97)

John LaFevre, director of human resources for Caradco, offers this advice to college seniors interviewing on campus: (a) State the strength you will prove, (b) describe an experience episode from your past that proves the strength, and (c) tell the interviewer what strength you have just proven (37–38). Using this behavioral method, students can demonstrate their skills more successfully than those who speak in more abstract terms. LaFevre further suggests that unless a job applicant can actually prove a strength or skill, no further contact will be made with the applicant (40).

REFERENCES

LaFevre, John A. "Interviewing: The Inside Story from a College Recruiter." *CPC Annual*. 32nd ed. 1988–1990: 37–40.

Swan, William S. "How to Hire Right." *Working Woman* 15.5 (1991): 96–97.

The Editor's Nightmare: Formatting Lists within the Text

Gene A. Plunka

Lists in technical writing emphasize specific information for readers. This article provides guidelines for preparing stacked lists and lists within sentences. The article includes samples of how to format lists effectively and tips on how to punctuate lists and when to use bullets. Take the quiz in the article to test your knowledge of how to format lists effectively.

Every experienced editor has been confronted with the task of editing lists within the text. Almost daily, editors encounter writers who do shoddy work and turn in sloppy copy. However, even quite capable writers often do not know how to handle large blocks of information that must be compiled in the form of a list. Because there are no standard rules for the preparation of lists, writers must invariably create their own system (or systems) of notation.

Such "creativity" causes major problems for the editor, especially when the writer is not even consistent in preparing the same type of list. In addition, the editor, who usually has only a vague notion of how to edit lists properly, must make arbitrary decisions based on personal preferences. Such capricious marking raises doubts about the validity of the editorial changes, especially when there are many lists to edit, as is often true of scientific or technical material.

In this article, I provide guidelines for editors and writers when preparing or editing either vertical lists or lists within a sentence.

MISCELLANEOUS ERRORS

As a former editor, I can recall some of the most common errors that made the editing of lists a tedious and frustrating task. First, many writers create their own notation system, using dashes, asterisks, daggers, or other artistic "designs" to introduce listed items. When preparing lists, writers could help the editor considerably if they used only the standard punctuation marks that will be discussed later in this article.

The second major headache-producer for the editor is the shoddy writer's insistence on using "For example" to introduce a list, thereby writing in phrases rather than sentences. I am not suggesting that "For example" must be eliminated from a writer's vocabulary; instead, just be sure that when "For example" begins a statement, the two words will be followed by a sentence and not by a colon.

The third major fault is the long list that is not grammatically parallel—e.g., participial phrases mixed with noun phrases, infinitive phrases with adverbial phrases, etc. The following example indicates why many editors cringe at the thought of editing technical manuscripts full of lists.

Our expenses included the following costs:

1. Mail—$500
2. Telephone—$230
3. Using the Printer—$200
4. Copier Fees—$75

Obviously, lines 3 and 4 need to be changed to "Printer" and "Copier" to maintain parallel structure. In short, when the editor has to worry about both formatting the lists for consistency and correcting for parallel structure, the editing of lists becomes that much more demanding, time consuming, and frustrating.

WHEN TO CREATE LISTS

First, try this quiz to test your knowledge of how to format lists. Choose the column number that represents the proper method for formatting the list in the following sentence:

The elements in the test included

I	II	III
1. zinc	(1) zinc	1) zinc
2. lead	(2) lead	2) lead
3. tin	(3) tin	3) tin

IV	V	VI
a) zinc	a. zinc	zinc
b) lead	b. lead	lead
c) tin	c. tin	tin

This example illustrates the types of decisions editors must make when correcting lists. The solution to the puzzle is that none of the six columns is the best choice. The writer should not have created a list at all. Instead, the sentence should read, "The elements in the test included zinc, lead, and tin." Most lists are superfluous. Scientists, engineers, and technicians frequently create lists when they could have otherwise saved space and avoided excessive formatting decisions. Thus, writers should first ask themselves whether there is a significant need for the vertical list that is being considered.

Lists within a sentence are often preceded by a colon. Most style manuals or grammar texts recite a rule that should be memorized by "list-happy" authors: **Do not use a colon between a verb or preposition and its direct object.** Often, however, writers assume that colons must automatically precede long lists, even when a verb introduces the list. To avoid violating the rule above, writers may merely add the words "as follows" or a similar variation after the verb. For example, instead of writing *The criteria were: (1) cost, (2) quality, (3) reputation, and (4) service*, the author should be consistent in applying the rule: *The criteria were the following factors: (1) cost, (2) quality, (3) reputation, and (4) service.*

Similarly, writers who use a colon after a preposition (e.g., *He supplied the scientists with: pipettes, bunsen burners, and ether*) should instead write *He supplied the scientists with the following materials: pipettes, bunsen burners, and ether,* or more simply, without the colon, *He supplied the scientists with pipettes, bunsen burners, and ether.*

Some writers insist on following the old rule that the first word after a colon is capitalized if a complete sentence follows the colon. Today, however, writers have the option of capitalizing or lowercasing the first word of a complete sentence following a colon; they must, of course, be consistent in following the chosen option throughout the text.

Elements in a list can be specifically enumerated to prevent misreading, to clarify a complex or lengthy series, or to highlight the listed items. Enumerations within a sentence should be introduced and identified only by numbers or lowercase letters, not by capital letters or roman numerals. In *A Manual for Writers of Term Papers, Theses, and Dissertations,* Kate L. Turabian notes that numbers or letters in a list stand out better when they are surrounded by parentheses rather than when they are followed by periods [1]. *The Chicago Manual of Style* concurs with Turabian's assessment and suggests double parentheses surrounding numbers or lowercase letters [2].

Following the colon that introduces the list, a comma or semicolon may be used to separate enumerated entries; again, the most important factor is consistency of style throughout the manuscript. Of course, when there are commas within the items of the list, semicolons must be used for clarification.

Thus, models to follow for enumerations within a sentence would be these four examples:

> The report consisted of four sections: (1) introduction, (2) discussion, (3) results, and (4) conclusion.
>
> The report consisted of four sections: (1) introduction; (2) discussion; (3) results; and (4) conclusion.
>
> The report consisted of four sections: (a) introduction, (b) discussion, (c) results, and (d) conclusion.
>
> The report consisted of four sections: (a) introduction; (b) discussion; (c) results; and (d) conclusion.

When writers use letters or numbers in a sentence list, they should keep in mind that a line that ends in (1) or (a) is considered a poor line break. Many editors will, by habit, mark such errors, even in draft copy, as carry-over lines to run over the letter or number to the rest of the list on the following line. By paying closer attention to inappropriate line breaks in the middle of lists, writers could simplify the editor's tedious and time-consuming job of correcting and marking errors concerning typography.

VERTICAL LISTS

Lists that contain four or more items in a series may be prepared vertically, set off from the sentence that introduces the list. Again, the rule to follow is that a short list should be incorporated into the sentence of which it is a part, not into a vertical list. Vertical lists are usually introduced by a colon; however, if the list is preceded by a complete sentence, a period may follow the sentence and thereby introduce the list. Dashes or other punctuation marks should not introduce vertical lists.

Introducing and Enumerating Vertical Lists

Writers who seek clarification with regard to the rules for enumerating vertical lists will discover a potpourri of contradictory information. *The Chicago Manual of Style* uses numbers and periods in its examples of such lists, yet no guidelines are provided. The *Publication Manual of the American Psychological Association* suggests the use of arabic numerals followed by a period but not enclosed or followed by parentheses [3]. The editors of *Words Into Type* also support the use of numerals with periods [4]. *The Council of Biology Editors Style Manual* states that lowercase roman numerals, arabic numerals, or lowercase letters in single or double parentheses may be used, or the writer may prepare the list "in accordance with the style of the journal" [5].

The other style manuals, including the *U.S. Government Printing Office Style Manual,* the *MLA Handbook, The Associated Press Stylebook and Libel Manual,* and *The New York Times Manual of Style,* offer no advice on the preparation of vertical lists. The consensus is that the format adopted for vertical lists should be arabic numerals or lowercase letters (be consistent as to which you use) followed by periods. The style therefore differs from the formatting of lists *within* sentences where double parentheses are suggested to make the items easier to differentiate for the reader.

Sometimes vertical lists may be introduced by phrases instead of sentences, or the items in the list may be needed to complete the sentence. In such instances, no colon is used to introduce the list items, thereby precipitating different rules to follow with regard to punctuation and numbering. The following sentence is an example of such a list:

> The hydroponic flooding system included
>
> > a sealed reservoir,
> > an aquarium vibrator air pump,
> > an automatic household timer, and
> > a plant container

Such lists cause numerous problems with regard to punctuation, numbering sequence, and capitalization. In addition, the editor must worry about whether or not the list's format is consistent with similar vertical lists displayed elsewhere in the text.

A good rule is to use the colon to introduce all lists (i.e., use complete sentences preceding vertical lists) so as to develop a degree of consistency in formatting vertical lists throughout the manuscript. When the colon is used to precede a list, rules can be followed. However, the lack of a colon usually leads to arbitrary rules with regard to style and formatting.

In vertical lists, numerals or lowercase letters are aligned by periods and can be set flush left or indented. Any run-over lines in the list should be aligned with the first word following the numeral, rather than aligned with the number, lowercase letter, or period. The writer has the option of either capitalizing or lowercasing the first word of each list item, provided that the style is adhered to consistently throughout the manuscript. An editor's work will be substantially increased when a writer capitalizes first-word list items in one sentence and then lowercases the next time around, and if the manuscript is of book length, obviously, errors of this sort will be more difficult for the editor to catch.

Punctuating Vertical Lists

Punctuating vertical lists is often a major source of contention among editors and writers. If the listed items are complete sentences, periods may follow each separate entry in the list. Otherwise, no punctuation marks should be included in the vertical list. The advantage of this simplified method of punctuation is that it eliminates semicolons or commas between entry items. The disadvantage is that no period ends the sentence, which is annoying to many writers and editors [*including this one, who ends lists with a firm period.-FRS*]. An example of the suggested format is found below.

Chapter Four includes the following information on flight dynamics:

1. Regional defenses against multiple ICBM attacks

2. Minimum energy and nonoptimum ICBM elliptic trajectories

3. Dynamic equations of interceptor rockets

4. Free-flight phases of ballistic missile trajectories

In this example, lowercase letters could be used to replace arabic numerals. In addition, each entry in the list could conceivably begin with a lowercase letter instead of a capital letter.

Using Bullets in Vertical Lists

During the past 25 or 30 years, bullets have been used increasingly to enumerate vertical lists. A bullet is a typographical mark, a solid dot, used to distinguish elements in a list. I have been unsuccessful in tracing the exact origin of the term, although I am fairly certain that it is not of British derivation. *The Oxford English Dictionary* does not refer to "bullet" in relationship to printing or proofreaders' marks. In addition, Judith Butcher, chief subeditor of Cambridge University Press and author of *Copy-Editing,* an important reference work for editors, does not mention "bullets" in her list of editorial marks.

In the United States, "bullet" did not appear as a typographical mark in *Webster's Second International Dictionary,* first printed in 1934 and reprinted in 1949. However, the first printing of *Webster's Third New International Dictionary* in 1961 defines the term as "a large solid dot so placed in printed matter as to call attention to a particular passage [6]." Thus, the term probably evolved in the United States sometime between 1949 and 1961.

The exact origin of the bullet is a mystery. In his humorous approach to the subject, Frederick P. Szydlik amused us with possible origins that he speculated upon in his 1986 article in *Technical Communication* [7]. In July 1983, the editors of *The Editorial Eye* suggested that bullets evolved from printers' center dots, but no specific date of origin was mentioned [8]. Robert Compton, writing in the October 1983 issue of *The Editorial Eye,* stated that representatives of the Burger writing course refer to bullets as "Burger dots" in honor of author/teacher Robert S. Burger, who claims to have invented them [9]. Burger has been teaching businessmen how to write since 1958, so he could be a likely candidate for authorship.

Style manuals and editing texts do not help much since most of them, including the *U.S. Government Printing Office Style Manual, The Chicago Manual of*

Style, and Karen Judd's *Copyediting: A Practical Guide,* do not even list the bullet as a typographical symbol. Even *The Associated Press Stylebook and Libel Manual* refers the reader to "Weapons" when one looks up "Bullets" in the body of the sourcebook.

Bullets are generally used as flagging devices, for they call attention to, and readily distinguish, items in a list. Writers choose bullets instead of numbers or letters when the items in the list have no special rank, sequence, or significance—in other words, when all of the elements in the list are equally important. In addition, bullets should be included when the listed information in each entry is composed of more than one line, e.g., one long sentence, two or more sentences, or a paragraph. In short, bullets are not used in lieu of numbers or letters; instead, they serve a distinct and different purpose in the enumeration process and should be used sparingly. As Szydlik wryly points out in his précis, poor writers are apt to substitute bullets for complete sentences, thereby turning some reports into long bulleted lists that put facts together in piecemeal fashion. In effect, what we are witnessing in private industry is that writers who have trouble constructing sentences are using bullets to convey ideas in the form of phrases.

Writers should take the time to format bulleted lists properly. There are essentially four ways to use bullets. First, bullets can be flush left with the margin, with the text also running over flush left. Second, bullets may be flush left, with the text running over only to the beginning of the first word in the copy (hanging style). Third, bullets may be indented from the left margin, yet when the copy runs over, it is flush left. In the last form, bullets start flush left, the copy extends flush left, but the bullets are run-on in such a way that they follow each sentence in the middle of the paragraph. The following examples differentiate the four methods of using bullets.

• XXXXXXXXXXX XXXXXXXXXXXXX XXXXXXXXXXXXX • XXXXXXXXXXX XXXXXXXXXXXXX Flush	• XXXXXXXXXXX XXXXXXXXXXX • XXXXXXXXXXX XXXXXXXXXXX • XXXXXXXXXXX Hanging
• XXXXXXXX XXXXXXXXXXX XXXXXXXXXXX • XXXXXXXX XXXXXXXXXXX Indented	• XXXXXXXXXXX XXXXXXXXXXX XXXXX • XXXXX XXXXXXXXXXX XX • XXXXXXXXX Run-On

Writers should decide which style is most appropriate to save space and make for easier reading; then they should avoid combining the various styles, thereby pleasing editors as well as attentive readers.

CONCLUDING REMARKS

As an increasing amount of our literature is becoming more scientific and technical, writers are including more lists in their manuscripts. Until there are standardized rules for the compilation of such lists, inconsistencies will increase in the formatting of scientific and technical articles and books. Writers could assist editors in reducing the number of formatting errors in lists by asking themselves these questions:

1. Is there a need for a vertical list, or will a list within a sentence be sufficient?
2. How should the list be punctuated?
3. Should numbers, letters, or bullets be used to format the list?
4. Have I been consistent in preparing all similar lists in the text the same way?
5. Are all of the items in the list parallel in structure?

Astute writers who pay attention to all five questions will improve the quality of their writing, develop an eye for detail, and spare their editors the extra antacid needed to get them through yet another manuscript.

REFERENCES

1. Kate L. Turabian, *A Manual for Writers of Term Papers, Theses, and Dissertations,* 4th ed. (Chicago: The University of Chicago Press, 1973), 28.

2. *The Chicago Manual of Style,* 13th ed. (Chicago: The University of Chicago Press, 1982), 245.

3. *Publication Manual of the American Psychological Association,* 3d ed. (Washington, D.C.: American Psychological Association, 1983), 68.

4. Marjorie E. Skillin and Robert M. Gay, *Words Into Type,* 3d ed. (Englewood Cliffs, NJ: Prentice-Hall, Inc., 1974), 175.

5. *Council of Biology Editors Style Manual,* 4th ed. (Arlington, VA: Council of Biology Editors, Inc., 1978), 111.

6. *Webster's Third New International Dictionary* (Springfield, MA: G. & C. Merriam Co., 1961), 294.

7. Frederick P. Szydlik, "The Bulleted List in Technical Communication: A High-Caliber Paradigm," *Technical Communication* 33, no. 2 (Second Quarter 1986): 93.

8. "Ask the Eye," *The Editorial Eye,* July 1983, 7.

9. Robert A. Compton, "About Those Bullets," *The Editorial Eye,* Late October 1983, 4.

Ideology and Collaboration in the Classroom and in the Corporation

James E. Porter

Collaboration among company departments is necessary to produce accurate product information. This article describes a problem in labeling that developed when a company's individual departments did not collaborate to ensure consistency.

In composing important, large-scale publications such as product information, packaging, and advertising, corporations usually rely on some kind of collaborative model—and it is the nature and effectiveness of these models that I have begun investigating in recent research.

We know that collaborative writing involves ideology because ideology is a component of all language practice, including classroom practice. Collaboration itself is ideological, John Trimbur (1989) argues, because it involves a group organizing itself to produce common work. Any such organization presupposes the existence of a political / ethical philosophy (or philosophies): that is, a set of beliefs about why the group exists, how it will function, and what it will do. Any collaboration adopts or determines an end, a goal, a purpose—whether that purpose is assigned by the teacher (or department supervisor) and whether the group agrees (tacitly or not) about that purpose.

Ideological issues are not matters of classroom interest only. Through policy or practice, corporations develop their own "mega-composing" processes—strategies for producing public documents (like product information) collaboratively—and ideology certainly influences this collaboration.

A recent lawsuit illustrates the influences of disciplinary ideology on corporate composing. Several fertilizer companies were sued by a competitor for mislabeling their bags of composted manure. One of these companies countersued, on the basis that the plaintiff's product was similarly mislabeled. Although the plaintiff's bags contained identical contents (7% sheep manure, 33% pig manure, and 60% cow manure), some bags were titled "sheep manure" and others "cattle manure." Is this a case of misleading labeling or simply harmless descriptive license?

The interesting thing about this case is that the law suit did not come from outraged customers. The dispute arose among competing fertilizer companies, which accused each other of unfair competitive practices. The case was settled out of court, but not before considerable legal expense and inconvenience to all parties involved. Several of the companies revised the information on their fertilizer bags.

What caused this problem in the first place? By what process were these "mislabeled" bags produced? It is easy to see how a labeling problem of this kind could arise in an organization with a compartmentalized notion of product responsibility. If the operations division (i.e., the technical people, such as agricultural chemists) sees itself as responsible only for the contents of the bag, and if marketing sees itself as responsible only for bag design (and not contents), then who takes responsibility for assuring referential accuracy?

The problem illustrates the tension that can exist between separate functions within the corporation. Collaboration in the corporation can, and often does, occur at the departmental or functional level. The operational function has responsibility for filling the bag with a salable product. The marketing function has responsibility for producing a bag labeled for consumers. The legal function has responsibility for assuring compliance with fair labeling standards. If these functions operate as separate political units and if they manufacture, promote, and distribute their product following a strictly linear, "division of labor" collaborative model (Killingsworth & Jones, 1989)—that is, operations makes fertilizer, marketing sells it, lawyers check the bag—problems are bound to result. Even if operations objects to the technical inaccuracies in labeling, in a strictly linear model of authority, marketing would have the final say on the label, and would not need to collaborate with operations. Legal collaboration is supposed to prevent these difficulties—and certainly packaging ought to be "edited" from a legal point of view, in light of state and federal regulatory restrictions on labeling. But an editing check of the label might not reveal the referential problem of a package not containing what it says it contains.

What might help the entire process is a more dynamic and interactive collaborative model, with opportunity for recursion built in, or a model that includes a coordinated holistic perspective. Such a perspective might be provided by a professional writer, with political allegiance neither to operations or marketing, who would track the product from design to manufacture to packaging and shipping, insuring that package labeling, package contents, and regulatory guidelines are all in mutual accord. A major computer software company, conscious of how a strictly departmentalized political outlook can threaten collaboration, has instituted strategies designed to counter such departmentalization. In the traditional, strictly linear model of composing, the computer specialist would design the software first; then the technical writer would take the completed software and write documentation for it. This company challenges that model by hiring writers who are capable of doing design and writing together (i.e., who have technical expertise as well as writing skills). The writer becomes an equal partner on the software development team and serves as an advocate for the user. This company is aware that a management ideology which supports a hierarchical and compartmentalized view of composing can block rather than promote effective collaborative writing.

REFERENCES

Killingsworth, M. J., & Jones, B. G. (1989). Division of labor or integrated teams: A crux in the management of technical communication? *Technical Communication, 36*(3), 210–221.

Trimbur, J. (1989). Consensus and difference in collaborative learning. *College English, 51*(6), 602–616.

The Practical Writer

Written documents often fail to achieve their purpose because they confuse or irritate readers. This article discusses how to achieve effective, clear style through careful word choice, using active voice instead of passive, and using concrete words instead of abstract ones whenever possible.

From time to time most educated people are called upon to act as writers. They might not think of themselves as such as they dash off a personal note or dictate a memo, but that is what they are. They are practising a difficult and demanding craft, and facing its inborn challenge. This is to find the right words and to put them in the right order so that the thoughts they represent can be understood.

Some writers deliberately muddy the meaning of their words, if indeed they meant anything to begin with. When most people write, however, it is to get a message across. This is especially so in business and institutions, where written words carry much of the load of communications. The written traffic of any well-ordered organization is thick and varied—letters, memos, reports, policy statements, manuals, sales literature, and what-have-you. The purpose of it all is to use words in a way that serves the organization's aims.

Unfortunately, written communications often fail to accomplish this purpose. Some organizational writing gives rise to confusion, inefficiency, and ill-will. This is almost always because the intended message did not get through to the receiving end. Why? Because the message was inadequately prepared.

An irresistible comparison arises between writing and another craft which most people have to practise sometimes, namely cooking. In both fields there is a wide range of competence, from the great chefs and authors to the occasional practitioners who must do the job whether they like it or not. In both, care in preparation is of the essence. Shakespeare wrote that it is an ill cook who does not lick his own fingers; it is an ill writer who does not work at it hard enough to be reasonably satisfied with the results.

Unlike bachelor cooks, however, casual writers are rarely the sole consumers of their own offerings. Reclusive philosophers and schoolgirls keeping diaries are about the only writers whose work is not intended for other eyes. If a piece of writing turns out to be an indigestible half-baked mess, those on the receiving end are usually the ones to suffer. This might be all right in literature, because the reader of a bad book can always toss it aside. But in organizations, where written communications command attention, it is up to the recipient of a sloppy writing job to figure out what it means.

The reader is thus put in the position of doing the thinking the writer failed to do. To make others do your work for you is, of course, an uncivil act. In a recent magazine advertisement on the printed word, one of a commendable series published by International Paper Company, novelist Kurt Vonnegut touched on the social aspect of writing: "Why should you examine your writing style with the idea of improving it? Do so as a mark of respect for your readers. If you scribble your thoughts any which way, your readers will surely feel that you care nothing for them."

In the working world, bad writing is not only bad manners, it is bad business. The victim of an incomprehensible letter will at best be annoyed and at worst decide that people who can't say what they mean aren't worth doing business with. Write a sloppy letter, and it might rebound on you when the recipient calls for clarification. Where one carefully worded letter would have sufficed, you might have to write two or more.

Muddled messages can cause havoc within an organization. Instructions that are misunderstood can set people off in the wrong directions or put them to work in vain. Written policies that are open to misinterpretation can throw sand in the gears of an entire operation. Ill-considered language in communications with employees can torpedo morale.

A CAREFUL WRITER MUST BE A CAREFUL THINKER

In the early 1950s the British Treasury grew so concerned with the inefficiency resulting from poor writing that it called in a noted man of letters, Sir Ernest Gowers, to work on the problem. Out of this Gowers wrote an invaluable book, *The Complete Plain Words,* for the benefit of British civil servants and anyone else who must put English to practical use. (Her Majesty's Stationery Office, London, 1954.)

Gowers took as his touchstone a quotation from Robert Louis Stevenson: "The difficulty is not to write, but to write what you mean, not to affect your reader, but to affect him precisely as you wish." To affect your reader precisely as you wish obviously calls for precision in the handling of language. And to achieve precision in anything takes time.

Gowers suggested that the time spent pursuing precision more than cancels out the time wasted by imprecision. People in administrative jobs might well protest that they were not hired as writers, and that their schedules are crammed enough without having to fuss over the niceties of grammar and the like. The answer to this is that it is an important part of their work to put words on paper. It should be done just as thoroughly and conscientiously as anything else for which they get paid.

No one should be led to believe writing is easy. As great a genius as Dr. Samuel Johnson described composition as "an effort of slow diligence and steady perseverance to which the mind is dragged by necessity or resolution." Writing is hard work because *thinking* is hard work; the two are inseparable. But there is some compensation for the effort invested in trying to write well.

The intellectual discipline required to make thoughts come through intelligibly on paper pays off in clarifying your thoughts in general. When you start writing about a subject, you will often find that your knowledge of it and your thinking about it leave something to be desired. The question that should be foremost in the writer's mind, "What am I really trying to say?" will raise the related questions, "What do I really know about this? What do I really think about it?" A careful writer has to be a careful thinker—and in the long run careful thinking saves time and trouble for the writer, the reader, and everybody else concerned.

The problem is that many people believe that they *have* thought out ideas and expressed them competently on paper when they actually haven't. This is because they use nebulous multi-purpose words that may mean one thing to them and something quite different to someone else. Gowers gave the example of the verb "involve," which is used variously to mean "entail," "include," "contain," "imply," "implicate," "influence," etc., etc. "It has . . . developed a vagueness that makes it the delight of those who dislike the effort of searching for the right word," he wrote. "It is consequently much used, generally where some more specific word would be better and sometimes where it is merely superfluous."

The Right Word Will Almost Tell You Where It Should Go

There are plenty of other lazy man's words lurking about, threatening to set the writer up beside Humpty Dumpty, who boasted: "When I use a word, it means just what I want it to mean." It is therefore wise to avoid words that can be taken in more than one way in a given context. This ties in with the first commandment of practical writing, which is: "Be Specific." "Specify, be accurate, give exact details—and forget about fine writing and original style," Rudolph Flesch says in his book, *How to Be Brief*.

Style tends to take care of itself if you select the right words and put them in the most logical order; so, to a large extent, do grammar and syntax. Find the right word, and it will almost tell you where in a sentence it should go.

This is not to say that grammar and syntax are not important. Words scattered on a page at the discretion of the writer simply would not be comprehensible. The rules of language usage also exert a degree of discipline over your thinking about a subject by forcing you to put your thoughts in logical order. Many grammatical conventions are intended to eliminate ambiguity, so that you don't start out saying one thing and end up saying something else.

Most literate people, however, have an instinctive grasp of grammar and syntax that is adequate for all ordinary purposes. The rules of usage (in English more so than in French) are in any case flexible, changeable, and debatable: new words are invented as the language lives and grows, and a solecism in one generation becomes respectable in the next. So while grammar and syntax have their roles to play in written communications, they must not be adhered to so slavishly that they interfere with intelligible expression. Gowers quoted Lord MacAulay with approval on this score: "After all, the first law of writing, that law to which all other laws are subordinate, is this: that the words employed should be such as to convey to the reader the meaning of the writer."

Vocabulary Is Usually the Least of a Writer's Problems

Since words come first, an ample vocabulary is an asset in conveying meaning. Oddly enough, though, people who have difficulty getting their written messages across rarely lack the vocabulary required. They know the apt words, but they don't use them. They go in for sonorous but more or less meaningless language instead.

People who are perfectly able to express themselves in plain spoken language somehow get the idea that the short, simple words they use in everyday conversation are unworthy to be committed to paper. Thus where they would say, "We have closed the deal," they will write, "We have finalized the transaction." In writing, they "utilize available non-rail ground mode transportation resources" instead of loading trucks. They get caught in "prevailing precipitant climatic conditions" instead of in the rain. They "utilize a manual earth removal implement" instead of digging with a shovel. When so many words with so many meanings are being slung about, nobody can be quite sure of just what is being said.

The guiding principle for the practical writer should be that common words should always be used unless more exact words are needed for definition. The reason for this is so plain that it is all but invisible. It is that if you use words that everybody knows, everybody can understand what you want to say.

A common touch with language has always distinguished great leaders. Winston Churchill comes immediately to mind; he "mobilized the English language and sent it into battle," as John F. Kennedy said. Churchill mobilized the language in more ways than in his inspiring speeches. As Prime Minister of Great Britain, he was that nation's chief administrator at a time when governmental efficiency was a matter of life and death for the democratic world. In August, 1940, while the Battle of Britain was at its peak, Churchill took the time to write a memo about excess verbiage in inter-departmental correspondence. It read:

> Let us have an end to such phrases as these: 'It is also of importance to bear in mind the following considerations . . .' or 'Consideration should be given to carrying into effect . . .' Most of these woolly phrases are mere padding, which can be left out altogether or replaced by a single word. Let us not shrink from the short expressive word even if it is conversational.

Churchill's own wartime letters and memos, reproduced in his memoirs, are models of effective English. It is interesting to speculate on how much his clarity of expression, and his insistence upon it in others, helped to win the war. He was, of course, a professional writer who had earned a living from his pen since he was in his early twenties. He was something of a literary genius. In the light of this, it may seem ridiculous to exhort modern white-collar workers to write like Winston Churchill. Nevertheless, the principles of writing which Churchill followed are not at all hard to grasp.

Churchill was an admirer of H. W. Fowler's *A Dictionary of English Usage,* to which he would direct his generals when he caught them mangling the language. Fowler set five criteria for good writing—that it be direct, simple, brief, vigorous and lucid. Any writer who tries to live up to these is on the right track.

By keeping in mind two basic techniques you can go some way towards meeting Fowler's requirements. These are:

Prefer the active voice to the passive.   It will make your writing more direct and vigorous. It's a matter of putting the verb in your sentence up front so that it pulls along the rest of the words. In the active voice you would say, "The carpenter built the house;" in the passive, "The house was built by the carpenter." Though it is not always possible to do so in the context of a sentence, use the active whenever you can.

Prefer the concrete to the abstract.   A concrete word stands for something tangible or particular; an abstract word is "separated from matter, practice, or particular example." Churchill used concrete terms: "We have not journeyed all this way, across the centuries, across the oceans, across the mountains, across the prairies, because we are made of sugar candy." If he had couched that in the abstract, he might have said: "We have not proved ourselves capable of traversing time spans and geographical phenomena due to a deficiency in fortitude." Again, there are times when abstractions are called for by the context because there are no better concrete words, but try not to use them unless you must.

Sticking to the concrete will tend to keep you clear of one of the great pitfalls of modern practical writing, the use of "buzz words." These are words and expressions that come into currency not because they mean anything in particular, but merely because they sound impressive. It is difficult to give examples of them because they have such short lives; the "buzz words" of today are the laughing stocks of tomorrow. They are mostly abstract terms (ending, in English, in *-ion, -ance, -osity, -ive, -ize, -al,* and *-ate*), but they sometimes take the form of concrete words that have been sapped of their original meaning. The reason for giving them a wide berth is that their meaning is seldom clear.

Jargon presents a similar pitfall. It has its place as the in-house language of occupational groups, and that is where it should be kept. It too consists mostly of abstract words, and by keeping to the concrete you can shut out much of it. But jargon is contagious, so it should be consciously avoided. Never use a word of it unless you are certain that it means the same to your reader as it does to you.

The combination of the active and the concrete will help to make your prose direct, simple, vigorous, and lucid. There is no special technique for making it brief; that is up to you.

The first step to conciseness is to scorn the notion that length is a measure of thoroughness. It isn't. Emulate Blaise Pascal, who wrote to a friend: "I have made this letter a little longer than usual because I lack the time to make it shorter."

Use your pen or pencil as a cutting tool. No piece of writing, no matter what its purpose or length, should leave your desk until you have examined it intensely with a view to taking the fat out of it. Strike out anything that does not add directly to your reader's understanding of the subject. While doing this, try to put yourself in his or her shoes.

Be hard on yourself; writing is not called a discipline for nothing. It is tough, wearing, brain-racking work. But when you finally get it right, you have done a service to others. And, like Shakespeare's cook, you can lick your metaphorical fingers and feel that it was all worthwhile.

The Writer as Market Researcher

Lee Ridgway

Writers who prepare instruction and reference manuals for products must be fully aware of the readers and their needs. This article explains how to interview product users and determine how they use the product in their work and what they need in manuals. Use the sample interview questions to generate your own set of appropriate questions for interviewing potential readers.

As technical writers, we have often defined our audience of readers. An article written for *Scientific American,* for example, is read by a well-defined audience with known characteristics and known variation. Any successful technical publication must know its readers, either through conventional market research techniques (such as reader surveys), association and contact (particularly for specialized trade or hobby magazines), or inspired guesswork by the editor (pretty risky). When we write for such a publication, therefore, we have a good audience description when we start.

But those of us who write instruction and reference manuals for manufacturers have been in a somewhat dangerous position. The people who bought the products (from can openers to software systems) received the information without any effort on their part. Furthermore, if they needed the information, they had to use the material, whether or not it was fun to read, whether or not it was useful, whether or not they understood it. In fact, the primary (buying) audience was the technical people who had built the product. If they didn't like the material, it didn't reach the customers. Everyone assumed that the users were just like the developers, and that developers' reviews were appropriate. So we wrote for an audience of developers.

For complex products, this approach often worked very well. Because only experts were expected to use the products, the developers were in fact very like the users of the products.

For simple products, people simply ignored the information. They used reference material as a last resort, when experimenting was not successful. Sometimes they drew inferences from pictures of the product. Frequently, such logic was enough.

But increasingly, ordinary people are being expected to master complex equipment and learn complex concepts. For many products, logic and past experience do not provide a basis for intuitive understanding. So we need to provide palatable information that ordinary people can cope with.

The Normal Writing Process

Normally, at the beginning of a project someone tells us who the buyers of the product will be. This identification is made by marketing and sales people and is based on some form of crystal-ball gazing. Somehow, given the predicted buyers, we deduce who the actual users will be. During the original writing, reviewing, and testing stages of the manuals, we assume that the identified audience is the real one.

550

We base our information design on that audience, and we use various techniques to see whether the design is acceptable.

Writers use their skills to write truthfully and in a way that is useful to the specified reader. We review for accuracy and completeness, we test for readability, we test for usability, and the test results help us present appropriate information in a helpful way for the assumed audience. When the information is complete, it has already been exposed to all sorts of checking. The information is fine for the audience as we or the product planners defined it.

But did we define it correctly?

INTERVIEWING THE AUDIENCE

When the products have actually become available and there are people actually using them, you have the opportunity and the duty to see whether the users are as you defined them and whether the tasks they perform are the ones that you supported. To do this, you must take on another role. You must become an interviewer, visiting customers and finding out how they do their work using the product.

Interview Techniques

Being a successful visitor requires a good deal of tact. Frequently visits are very structured, with you and your readers sitting in a conference room together. They are aware that they are criticizing your work and may be quite apologetic about their comments. You have to project genuine interest and acceptance and avoid defensiveness. If you argue, the users will stop volunteering opinions, or they will become angry and uncooperative. You may ask for clarification but must take care that the request doesn't sound challenging. ("I dare you to show me a place where that is true.")

When you ask questions, you should phrase them in such a way that the users do not know what answer you want (which may affect the reply). If it is quite obvious what the "right" answer would be, you may phrase a question in a way that invites another answer. ("I wasn't sure about the presentation of topic. How could it have been made clearer?" Or "I thought about putting in a diagram of the phlisbug. Do you think that would be a good idea?")

Especially during early use of the product, interviews give you the only feedback available, so you want to cover the right ground and talk to the right people. It often helps to have an outline or questionnaire to refer to. If you are asking about a specific manual, questions to ask are like these:

- How frequently do you use this manual?
- Under what circumstances do you use it?
- When did you last use it?
- What tasks are you doing when you use it?
- How do you use it? Do you sit down and read it, or do you refer to it while you are doing something else?
- How would you rate it (excellent, good, fair, poor, awful)?
- What do you like best about it?
- What would you change about it?

- Do you have marginal notations in it?
- Who else uses the manual?
- Do you know what they use it for?

When there is a set of manuals for a product, you may be interested in the library structure and the placement of information within manuals. You may ask questions like these:

- How easy was it to find the information you wanted? Did you
  1. always find the right manual right away
  2. sometimes try another manual before the right one
  3. almost always try the wrong manual first
  4. hunt through several manuals to find the information
  5. mostly not find it

- When you had the right manual, how easy was it to find information in it?
  1. very easy
  2. pretty easy
  3. took more than three tries
  4. had to leaf through looking
  5. never found it

- Were the titles of the manuals
  1. very descriptive
  2. descriptive
  3. all right
  4. not very descriptive
  5. not at all descriptive

If people admit to making marginal comments, and if you can persuade them to share them, you will find them invaluable. Information that people have added for themselves is obviously important to them. The way they organize the information and the level of detail that they add tell you how expert they are and how they want information to be presented. But people are often shy about their notes, because they are hastily or sloppily written. The notes often contain simple information that they feel they should not need, and they are embarrassed to show it to you.

Uses and Advantages of Interviews

During interviews, you are finding out something about the people who are using your material and about the tasks and responsibilities they have. But during these interviews, you see only a few of your readers and you must not generalize too much from the ones you meet and talk to. You can, however, learn about the mental set that at least a few readers have, and try to find out whether the writer and reader share the same assumptions.

Readers are usually not able to pinpoint what they dislike or would change. They know that they are dissatisfied with something, but they often do not know why they are dissatisfied. They are uncomfortable because their expectations (which may not have been conscious) have in some way not been met.

You have to listen carefully to deduce their unfulfilled expectations. Perhaps they thought that the product would be "like a typewriter," meaning that they could sit down and use it immediately. The 300-page user's guide makes them suspect that this is not true. They may then react by saying "The guide is too big," when what they mean is that the product requires too much information and it really isn't like a typewriter at all.

Often people have some analogy in their minds when they deal with something new ("It's a blender, really" or "It's an overgrown adding machine"). When the analogy fails in some crucial way, they feel that they have been misled. You need to understand what analogy they were making, whether you encouraged and supported it, and whether it failed or succeeded. If it failed, you need to discourage other readers from thinking along the same lines.

You are also trying to find out whether your understanding of the users' environment and duties is correct. If possible, you should observe users in their work setting, actually using information. You have to be very careful not to interfere with normal activities or to make people feel self-conscious by watching them too closely. But you might ask to see where the manuals are kept, or where the product is located, and see some of the environment that way. During a discussion, you might try to get a description of how things are done, establishing a scenario, as it were, of a day in the life of a terminal operator, or what the procedures are for running the payroll, to help you understand the real tasks.

To sum up, visits enable you to meet real readers, and to get a detailed picture of some readers and some work environments. You find out where your information fits and does not fit a few users. You may get new ideas from your reader sample. However, you have only seen a small sample of your readers. You must decide whether the sample is representative and whether it is complete enough to be useful.

SURVEYING THE AUDIENCE

Many products depend on mass markets, so that a few users may or may not be representative. What would suit one customer perfectly would suit only that one customer. To find out about the whole customer group, you have to prepare questionnaires and survey representative customers. You don't personally need all the skills of statisticians and market researchers, which include how to select samples and how to analyze the statistical significance of data. You do need to be advised by someone who has these skills, if you don't have them.

The selection of the sample is very important because it determines whether the results of the survey apply to the whole customer set. A sample can be the whole set, it can be customers chosen at random, or it can be representative customers. You need advice on sample selection to balance cost, time, and reliability. An appropriately chosen representative sample can yield more reliable results than a random sample of the same size, for example.

Surveys can be done by mail, by telephone, or in person. Mail is the most convenient but the least reliable and the least likely to get responses. You get few responses (sometimes only a few percent), and the people who reply are mostly people with very strong opinions (not necessarily representative). The sample is self-selecting, because every user chooses whether to respond and become a part of the sample. However, mail questionnaires can be longer and more detailed than telephone surveys, and may bring good results if used appropriately.

Telephone surveys have a much higher response rate, and the sample is chosen instead of choosing itself. The results are more reliable, but telephone survey questionnaires have to be written carefully, because the interview may be conducted by someone who does not know the topic at all. Questions have to be simple enough for answerers to understand them without explanation. Any list of choices must be short enough for the answerer to remember on one hearing.

However, you can be comforted by two facts about telephone surveys. First, people (surprisingly) are very cooperative about being interviewed over the telephone. Even so, they probably have an upper limit of about 20 minutes for question answering, except by special arrangement. (Many people do not like to talk on the telephone for long periods, so that their patience wears thin. They might also be very busy.) Second, there are professional market research companies that specialize in telephone surveys. They can help you with the questionnaire, do the actual telephone interviews, and gather and tabulate replies.

Personal-interview surveys are the most expensive and most difficult, but they can also be the most fruitful. The advantage is that a skillful interviewer can find out a great deal in a personal interview. The disadvantages are the cost and the need for a very skillful interviewer. The same considerations of personal interaction that affect visits also affect face-to-face surveys to a smaller degree. Interviewers are less likely than you to signal what they would like to hear. But sending trained interviewers to users can be very expensive, if a large sample is needed or users are spread thinly.

A variation of the face-to-face interview is the round-table discussion, where a number of customers discuss questions in the presence of an interviewer. The group interaction makes it easier for people to express opinions that they feel may not be flattering, but group pressure may give a false impression of unanimity. The interviewer tries to make sure that no one is dominating or dominated to a misleading degree.

USES AND ADVANTAGES OF SURVEYS

From surveys, you can get a broad picture of who the real users of the product are, what environment the product is used in, and how satisfied the users are with the product. Although you do not get an in-depth knowledge of any single user (unless the survey was done by personal interviews), you have a lot of sketches of users, and a high degree of confidence that the users sketched are a realistic picture of the various user types.

In addition, surveys can verify task definitions. Although you learn more about actual tasks in detail from visits and long interviews, you can check that those tasks are realistic by survey questions. As a result, task-oriented instructions can be refined if necessary to reflect the way tasks are really done.

Don't expect surveys to give you facts about how long it takes a user to do a task, or find a piece of information, or correct a mistake. People's perception of time depends on how anxious they are, how interested they are, how impatient, or worried, or tired. Their time sense is affected by how long they expected something to take. Five minutes can be a very long time or a very short time, and depending on circumstances will be seen by the user as much too long or very quick. Time estimates will be unreliable. People can tell you whether they were happy or unhappy with the time they spent doing a task. You can then deduce what tasks need to be redesigned so that they can be done more quickly.

At this point, you may go back to the testing lab to find the facts that users could not give you. You can compare how long a task takes in testing with the users' evaluation (too long, very short, etc.) to uncover problem areas and to provide a basis for measuring improved performance. This testing may not test the same tasks that were tested during development. Task descriptions may have been redefined as a result of customer visits and surveys.

You may change users' expectations by changing the description of the task. One description may make the task sound trivial, while a different description can make it seem reasonable that the task should take longer. You may break the task into two parts, describe checkpoints, or give the user a distraction. Tell the user that there will be 10 messages before the task is done, and the user may count the messages instead of being impatient.

In short, you use survey results to verify definitions of tasks and users and to gather user opinions about the information. These opinions, although highly subjective, can be shown to be valid if the sample is large and representative. By structuring the survey questions carefully, you or your statistics expert can find out what factors affected users' judgments and deduce what improvements will have most effect.

SUMMARY

Collection and analysis of feedback are new skills for the technical writer when they are undertaken in a systematic and formal manner. Technical writers working for manufacturers need to be very much aware of their audience and its needs. Since the usual indicators of acceptance do not apply very well to manufacturer supplied material, technical writers must depend on customer interviews and surveys to gauge their success. They therefore must develop interviewing skills and an understanding of statistical methods—another accomplishment of the Renaissance technical writer.

Teleconferencing

John C. Sherblom

Technology costs are decreasing, and travel costs are increasing. Companies that do business across long distances are using more audio and video conferences to hold meetings and make presentations to employees and clients in different locations. This article presents guidelines for participating in these oral conferences via technology.

TELECONFERENCING

In response to a financial crisis, the chancellor of a technical college system scheduled a teleconference with the five college campus presidents for ten o'clock in the morning. The presidents were separated by 500 miles. However, each participated in the lively discussion of the current budgetary problems and in the wording of their response statement to be released to the media that afternoon. By 11:30 a.m., they had reached consensus on their course of action and were able to speak through the press in a unified voice.

Teleconferencing is increasing in use and importance as a medium for business communication. As depicted in this scenario, teleconferencing can be an effective and efficient means of communication, particularly in a crisis or emergency situation when participants are geographically scattered, participant input is required, and decisions must be made in a timely fashion.

Definition

Teleconferencing is a broad generic term which identifies group communication through an electronic medium (Johansen, 1984). Rogers (1986) defines teleconferencing as a small group meeting of people at separate locations engaged in electronic communication. Olgren and Parker (1983) add that teleconferencing provides people at each location the opportunity to actively participate in the meeting. Tedesco (1990) concurs, describing teleconferencing as communicating through a telecommunications system "with two or more groups or with three or more individuals at separate locations (p. 464)." The key elements of these definitions show teleconferencing to be small group communication, typically in the form of a business or professional meeting, that is carried on through an electronic medium which facilitates interactive participation—although one-way broadcasts are sometimes also referred to as teleconferencing.

AUDIOCONFERENCING

An estimated 90% of the 2.5 million teleconferences made each year are audioconferences (Fielding & Hartley, 1987; Cowan, 1984). Audioconferencing relies on communication through the spoken word with only the voice to provide emphasis to the speaker's message or feedback from other participants. It is the form of tele-conferencing accessible to the largest number of businesses, organizations, and even private individuals.

Audioconferencing Facilities

Audioconferencing is done in one of three basic ways: through a dial-up conferenc-ing service, the purchase of speakerphones, or the installation of audioconferencing equipment. A dial-up conference call is coordinated by an operator or setup through a "meet-me" bridge provided by a telephone bridging service. For the "meet-me bridge," all participants call a central conferencing number provided by the bridging service for a specified time. Some bridges provide for the transmission of documents, graphics, and still video pictures as well. Even without the document transmission capability, this option is a good choice for the occasional user. A sec-ond type of audioconference is to use speakerphones at either end of a regular phone call. This can be adequate for two or three participants at two locations, but the audio quality deteriorates rapidly as the number of participants and locations increases. Speakerphones frequently generate a "barrel effect" created by echoes from the speaker's voice. This effect can be reduced by acoustically treating the meeting room and by reducing the distance between the speaker's mouth and the microphone. The third option, which is both the most sophisticated and expensive, is to purchase audio conferencing equipment for each site. This option provides for larger groups—15 to 25 participants—and for more frequent use. No matter which option is used, audioconferencing is more effective when the audio signal quality is enhanced through use in acoustically conditioned rooms.

Reasons to Audioconference

Audioconferences can usually be set up more quickly than face-to-face or video-conferences, they require only voice-grade telephone lines, they tend to be shorter and more organized, and they usually generate speedier decisions than face-to-face meetings. Audioconferencing is frequently the preferred way of meeting when (a) there is a physical distance between participants, (b) the message is short, (c) the message is not complex, (d) the message does not involve significant organizational resources or impact on personal relationships, (e) a low negative response is antici-pated from participants, (f) there will be little need for "face-saving" among partic-ipants, and (g) participants do not experience high levels of telephone apprehension. Finally, audioconferencing has been credited with improving time management, assisting managerial decision making, and facilitating responsiveness to market opportunities (Smeltzer & Vance, 1989).

Technical Concerns

Because the conference call is a relatively common medium for business communi-cation, audioconferencing is assumed to he easy. Yet, the most frequent complaint of participants in teleconferences is with the quality of the audio signal transmitted and received. A quality audio signal is important to the intelligibility and inter-pretability of multiple speakers' voices. Participants find audioconferencing demanding and tiring, and, if the audio quality is poor, they have a difficult time concentrating (Tedesco, 1990). Technical difficulties include audio echo, distortion, dropout, and participants not being heard equally well from all parts of the room. These difficulties are caused by inadequate audio conditioning of the conference rooms, unreliable audio equipment, and poor quality transmission lines. They can be taken care of through careful planning, equipment selection, and facilities installation. In general, audioconferencing works best when used in addition to regular face-to-face meetings and for coordinating future meetings of members who are geographically dispersed.

Pragmatic Impacts on Communication

Audioconferencing is susceptible to pragmatic conversational difficulties. These problems in conversational pragmatics may be more difficult to manage than the technical concerns. They include difficulty in determining a speaking order and awkward turn-taking caused by the lack of visual cues. Participants are sometimes unable to identify who is speaking, when someone is almost finished speaking, who is waiting to speak, and who should speak next. A frustration with these pragmatics of conversation can lead one or more participants to "drop out"—stop participating in the discussion though they remain physically connected through the medium. Participant drop-out is difficult for coordinators and other participants to identify and can be hard to prevent.

Audio-graphics

To enhance an audioconference, the audio signal may be supplemented with other mailed or electronically transmitted information in the form of a written meeting agenda; an outline of key points; computer printouts of data, charts, graphs, slides, and transparencies; and other similar materials. The availability of FAX (facsimile) machines makes the transmission of these materials easy. Freeze frame (still shot) video can also be transmitted to enhance the audio discussion.

Audioconferencing enhanced with computer graphics is becoming popular. It can be installed at sites for a reasonable expense, has low transmission costs, and is easy to use (Smeltzer & Vance, 1989). Multicolor, computer-generated graphics are easy to prepare and can be sent to multiple sites over long-distance telephone lines concurrent to the audio. The addition of these materials adds interest and substance to an audioconference.

VIDEOCONFERENCING

In videoconferencing, a television picture of each participant or group is transmitted to the other group along with the audio. Corporations currently operate more than 1,400 videoconferencing facilities connecting at least two locations. Videoconferencing works for many types of meetings and communication but is usually best limited to a small number of participants in each of two locations. As more locations and participants are added, videoconferencing becomes increasingly expensive and communication pragmatics more difficult.

For videoconferencing, the need for good quality audio remains imperative. In videoconferencing rooms, therefore, acoustical conditioning, as well as video equipment, is required. In addition, research has shown that room appearance and comfort have an impact on participants' impressions and use of teleconferencing facilities (Scott, 1990). For most videoconferences, fixed cameras showing all participants simplify the room controls. For larger teleconferences, having more than four to six participants at a site, a camera person may be required to ensure good eye contact and physical presence across the video link; otherwise, the chair of the meeting may be forced to become a camera operator. In larger cities, some videoconferencing services rent equipment and facilities for short-term use.

Reasons to Videoconference

Some of the reasons for videoconferencing are the same as those for audioconferencing: to improve time management and to communicate with employees or customers dispersed over a wide geographical area. In addition, videoconferencing has been credited with improving productivity, increasing problem-solving efficiency, facilitating employee training while cutting training costs, providing a timely way to announce new products and services, facilitating access to experts, and providing tighter control over meetings by structuring communication patterns and developing an increased awareness of limited meeting time.

Technical Concerns

When videoconferencing participants complain, it is about audio-sound quality and video-image size. Poor quality audio is distracting to participants and unsatisfactory to the purposes of a meeting. The audio components of a video teleconferencing system can suffer two types of technical difficulties: audio delay and audio clipping. Audio delay is introduced by the audio transmission medium, particularly when the teleconferencing sites are at a distance. Transmission of the audio signal from one site to another and back again across long distance land lines and satellite links can take from half a second to more than a second. While this does not sound like much time, it is sometimes enough to interfere with the flow of the meeting, to cause participants to become impatient, and to make those located at the distant site to feel ill at ease and intimidated. When this delay is not understood by participants to be a technical transmission issue, it can create a perception that the participants at the remote location are themselves slow and not well-prepared for the meeting. Audio clipping can occur in systems that only transmit audio in one direction at a time (half-duplex systems). These systems use push-to-talk microphones or voice-activated, electronically switched microphones. Neither design provides for the unconfined conversational interchange typical of informal meetings and working sessions. Single word responses may be completely lost, and participants interrupting each other may make it impossible to hear complete sentences of either person (Scott, 1990). Audio delay and clipping are best compensated for by a teleconferencing leader who conducts the meeting in a relaxed manner and who makes an effort to give each site and participant an explicit opportunity to comment on whatever is being discussed. These leadership responsibilities become particularly important when the matter under discussion is urgent and participants are excited.

Participants also complain that the video screen is too small or that the people appearing on the screen as a group are too small. When participants are shown individually as they speak, the video image changes too frequently. These difficulties can be partially overcome by having relatively small groups—no more than four participants—at each location. A group of six can be accommodated by using a video mixer which will input video images from two cameras. The six participants are divided into two groups of three in front of the cameras; and the video outputs from these two cameras are superimposed by the mixer, one on the top half of the screen the other on the bottom, and transmitted as a single picture. Alternately, the video image of the two groups can be transmitted as separate pictures to appear on two different monitors. Modular wall units and built-in installations provide an option for large screen projections. These large screen images are produced by either front-screen or rear-screen projectors. Front-screen projectors produce a brighter, sharper image but may not be ideal for teleconferencing facilities as equipment location can be obstructive and cooling fan noise can become noticeable. Rear-screen projectors have the advantage of remote equipment placement reducing both obstructiveness and noise, but the projected image must pass through the translucent screen reducing the image brightness and sharpness.

Pragmatic Impacts on Communication

Even when all participants remain constantly on the screen and are large enough to be seen, a spatial relationship may be felt to be missing, eye contact may be difficult, and facial expressions may be hard to interpret. When these nonverbal communication channels are critical to the purposes of the meeting or the groups, videoconferencing may not be the appropriate medium. A face-to-face meeting is a better choice.

Preparation and Participation are Keys to Success

Preparation and participation are keys to successful teleconferencing. Johnson (1983) spelled out what participants need to prepare for in his definition of a teleconference as a structured, private, interactive, electronic, and scheduled meeting. A teleconference coordinator and participant should prepare for a formal presentation, rather than an informal one; but participation should be relaxed. Organize the meeting with an agenda and use handouts or other materials distributed to all locations before the meeting begins. During the meeting, attention must be paid to the nonverbal aspects of communication. Reduce the formality imposed by the medium through the use of structured but informal communication. Be aware of participant nonverbals. Some participants may be intimidated by the camera and may need to be encouraged to speak. Others may appear unduly nervous, as nonverbal gestures and vocal intonations are enlarged and exaggerated by the video cameras. Repetitive and large gestures can become distracting and annoying to other participants. Attention to vocal loudness, articulate pronunciation, and speaking rate is essential. Some attention should also be paid to dress. Loudly patterned clothing may distract other participants while neutral colors and pastels help participants appear healthy.

REFERENCES

Cowan, R. A. (1984). *Teleconferencing: Maximizing human potential.* Reston, VA: Reston Publishing Co.

Fielding, G. & Hartley, P. (1987). The telephone: A neglected medium. In A. Cashdan, & M. Jordan (Eds.), *Studies in Communication,* 110–124. New York: Basil Blackwell.

Johansen, R. (1984). *Teleconferencing and beyond.* New York: McGraw-Hill.

Johnson, J. W. (1983). Some observations on teleconferencing. In E. A. Lazer, M. C. J. Elton, & J. W. Johnson (Eds.), *The Teleconferencing Handbook,* 1–12. White Plains, NY: Knowledge Industry.

Olgren, C. H. & Parker, C. H. (1983). *Teleconferencing technology and applications.* Dedham, MA: Artech House.

Rogers, E. (1986). *Communication technology.* New York: The Free Press.

Scott, D. L. (1990, November supplement). Video teleconferencing special report. *Video Systems,* 4–17.

Smeltzer, L. R. & Vance, C. M. (1989). An analysis of graphic use in audio-teleconferences. *The Journal of Business Communication,* 26(2) 123–141.

Tedesco, E. H. (1990) *Telecommunications for business.* Boston: PWS-Kent.

Six Graphics Guidelines

Typographic elements can help readers understand and use information efficiently. This article explains how to use specific typographic elements, such as type size, white space, and capital letters. Notice the samples of type style and size.

In the first part of this article, we present six graphics guidelines that the Document Design Center has developed to help writers and graphic artists produce documents that are both visually appealing and easy to read. Good graphics can help readers to overcome resistance to a text or even help them to understand the material more easily.

1. USE HIGHLIGHTING TECHNIQUES, BUT DON'T OVERUSE THEM.

Highlighting techniques are a way of emphasizing important aspects of your document by calling attention to them visually. Some highlighting techniques are: *boldface, italics, and white space.* The six guidelines are printed in boldface. The list of highlighting techniques in this paragraph is printed in italics. We have used all of those techniques in *Simply Stated.*

In addition to emphasizing a part of your document, highlighting techniques generally contribute to the attractiveness of your document by providing visual relief in what might otherwise be a uniform page of text.

You can use highlighting techniques to emphasize important points, set off examples from the rest of the text, or set off sections of text by calling attention to headings.

Be careful, however, not to overuse any highlighting technique. If too much of your text is highlighted, the purpose of highlighting will be defeated. For example, if a whole section is in italics, it will not stand out; in fact, it will be more difficult to read than text set in regular type. If too much is in boldface, your text will also become more difficult to read, because the page will look too black and heavy. Also be careful not to use too many different highlighting techniques in one document. This can make your text look cluttered and can lead to confusion. Finally, make sure you are consistent in the way you use a particular technique. For example, if you are going to use boldface for a certain level of heading, be sure always to use it for that level.

2. USE 8 TO 10 POINT TYPE FOR TEXT.

For most documents, 8 to 10 point type is the most readable size. If your type is too small, your document can look crowded and uninviting. Your readers may skip over text, or they may get eyestrain.

If your type is too large, your text will use more space than it needs to. If you have constraints on space, you may have to cut down on important information. If you choose to add pages to accommodate the large type, it can get expensive. Inappropriately large type can even make a text more difficult to read.

In addition to considering point size (see "Measuring Type"), you must consider the look of the type you choose. Some typefaces look larger than others of the same type size. For example:

This is an example of 10 point Souvenir type.

This is an example of 10 point Avant Garde type.

Simply Stated is set in 10 point Century Schoolbook. See how much more difficult it would be to read if it were set in 6 point type of the same style.

Simply Stated is set in 10 point Century Schoolbook. See how much more difficult it would be to read if it were set in 6 point type of the same style.

3. AVOID MAKING YOUR LINES OF TYPE TOO LONG OR TOO SHORT.

The best line length for most text is 50–70 characters. Experience has shown that this length is less tiring to the eye than either short lines, which make the eye jump back and forth, or long lines, which strain the eye as it tries to stay on course. With either extreme, the eye is likely to jump to another line.

The lines in *Simply Stated* average about 48 characters. If we were to keep the same type size but lay out *Simply Stated* in four columns, the line length would be too short. The short lines would make awkward breaks in the text and cause the eye to jerk back and forth. The change would make for uncomfortable reading.

If we were to keep the same type size and lay out *Simply Stated* all the way across the page, with no column breaks, the long lines would be difficult to follow, and the text would look too densely packed to make pleasant reading. It would even appear to have less leading between the lines. (See "Leading.")

4. USE WHITE SPACE IN MARGINS AND BETWEEN SECTIONS.

If you use white space well, you can make your document look better and easier to read. The term "white space" refers to any of the blank space on a document, such as the margins and the space between sections, or the space that sets off an example. A text with too little white space can look cramped.

Use white space as an integral element in designing your document, and use it functionally. For example, the white space between sections helps the reader to see how the document is organized. The white space surrounding a title or an example isolates it and emphasizes its importance.

In *Simply Stated* we use white space to isolate the masthead and the titles of the articles. We leave adequate margins and separate each paragraph from the next with white space. If the margins were narrower and there was no space between paragraphs, the text would look cramped and less inviting.

5. Use Ragged Right Margins.

When all the lines of text begin at a left margin but end at different points on the right, the right margin is "ragged." *Simply Stated* is set with a ragged right margin.

When the lines all end in the same place, the right margin is even. The text is "justified." This paragraph is justified, or set "flush left" and "flush right." To get the lines to come out even on the right, the typesetter had to put extra spaces between words and letters all along the line.

Many document designers today prefer ragged right margins, because they are less formal than justified text and create a more relaxed, contemporary look that many readers find inviting. Tastes do change, however, and ragged right margins may go out of fashion.

There are practical advantages to ragged right margins, however. Some printers have found that they reduce production costs, because it is easier to make corrections on unjustified type. It is not necessary to change every line in a paragraph in order to add or take out a word in one line. Some readers find that ragged right margins make a text easier to read. When lines end at different places, it is easier for readers to keep their place in the text. They are less likely to go back and reread the same line twice, because the right profile distinguishes one line from another. Also, the eye does not have to adjust to different spacing between letters, as it does with justified type.

6. Avoid Using All Capital Letters.

Some documents use ALL CAPS, or uppercase letters, for emphasis. But ALL CAPS interferes with the legibility of text. We recommend other highlighting techniques instead, such as boldface, italics, or color.

All caps make text harder to read because the shapes of the letters do not vary very much. One of the ways that readers differentiate among letters is by their shape. Lowercase letters have more distinctive shapes than uppercase. Compare the shape of these two sets of words:

FLASHLIGHT BATTERY

Flashlight battery

When a whole block of text is printed in ALL CAPS, it takes up more space and takes longer to read. Also, the highlighting effect of the uppercase letters is lost because it is overused. See how this paragraph would look in ALL CAPS.

WHEN A WHOLE BLOCK OF TEXT IS PRINTED IN ALL CAPS, IT TAKES UP MORE SPACE AND TAKES LONGER TO READ. ALSO, THE HIGH-LIGHTING EFFECT OF THE UPPERCASE LETTERS IS LOST BECAUSE IT IS OVERUSED. SEE HOW THIS PARAGRAPH WOULD LOOK IN ALL CAPS.

A Typography Primer

In this section, we describe the basic features used in typesetting.

Serif and Sans Serif Type

Type comes in many styles, but there are two basic ones: serif and sans serif. Serif type has short, horizontal strokes that project from the tops and bottoms of the letters. *Simply Stated* is printed in a serif typeface. Serifs enhance the horizontal flow of a line of type, making it easier to read across a line. Serifs also make the individual letters easier to distinguish. Ancient Roman stone cutters used serifs to make their hand cut lettering look more even and horizontal. Serif typefaces are generally considered to be formal and traditional.

Sans serif type is type without serifs. It has a clean, contemporary look, and is generally considered to give an informal feeling. The clean design of sans serif type makes it easy to read, but because it does not have serifs to enhance the horizontal flow, a sans serif typeface requires more space between lines of type than a serif typeface of the same size.

serif   Typography

sans serif   **Typography**

Families of Type

Most styles of type are available in six different versions. The *style* is the same, but the letters vary in thickness, width, or slant. For example, here are six versions of Helvetica, a sans serif typeface.

Light	typography
Regular	typography
Bold	**typography**
Condensed	typography
Extended	typography
Italic	*typography*

These six versions form a "family" of type. If you want to emphasize individual words or short passages, you can use bold or italic type of the same family as the rest of your text. Titles can be in a larger size of the same face. (See "Measuring Type.") You can mix light, regular, bold, and italic type, as long as they are in the same family. But do not mix condensed or extended type with regular type; the shapes of the letters differ too much to look good together. In addition, condensed and extended faces have their own families of light, bold, and italic.

Measuring Type

Graphic artists work with two basic measurements: picas and points. They use picas to measure the length of a line or the width of a column. There are six picas to an inch, twelve points to a pica, and 72 points to an inch.

Points are used to measure the size of the type itself—the individual letters. Typefaces are identified by *point size* and *style*; for example, *Simply Stated* is printed in 10 point Century Schoolbook. The point size measures the whole letter, including *ascenders* (the tops of the "T" and the "h") and *descenders* (the tails of the "y" and the "p").

Graphic artists also speak of the "x-height" of a letter. This is the height of the body of the letter *without* ascenders or descenders, or the height of a small letter like an "x." When you are choosing a type size, it is important to consider the "x" height of your typeface. Although two different styles of type may both be 9 point, one may have a smaller "x-height" than the other. If you choose that face, you might need to go up to a 10 point size to get as readable a text as you would with a 9 point size and a larger "x-height." "X-height" will also influence how much space or "leading" you need between lines of type. (See "Leading.")

Leading

The space between lines of type is called *leading*. This term derives from the practice of setting hot metal type. When the type is set, strips of lead are laid between the lines of type. Although phototypesetting is more common than hot metal today, graphic artists still use the term "leading" to describe the space between lines. The leading, like the type itself, is measured in points. A text set in 10 point type with 11 point leading is said to be set "10 on 11," or "10/11." *Simply Stated* is set 10/11.

The amount of leading you use can affect the legibility of your text. If your text is *set solid,* with no extra space between lines, it will look too heavy and difficult to read. If you put in too much leading, your lines of type will appear to drift apart, making it difficult for the reader to follow the text.

Features of the type will affect your leading. Very small type and bold type require extra leading to relieve the density of the text. Sans serif type requires more leading than serif type of the same size, because it does not have serifs to carry the horizontal flow of the line and establish a clean break between the lines. Long lines require more leading than short lines in the same typesize; the extra leading helps the reader to follow across the long lines.

Look how much easier it is to read this passage in 7 point type when it is set with 8 point leading, as opposed to 7 (set solid). But see how it floats apart when it is set 7/11. (This is set 7/8.)

Look how much easier it is to read this passage in 7 point type when it is set with 8 point leading, as opposed to 7 (set solid). But see how it floats apart when it is set 7/11. (This is set solid.)

Look how much easier it is to read this passage in 7 point type when it is set with 8 point leading, as opposed to 7 (set solid). But see how it floats apart when it is set 7/11. (This is set 7/11.)

Listen Up—Tips from the Top on Talks

Terry C. Smith

Most effective speakers "listen" to the audience by checking for comprehension and watching for restlessness. This article gives advice on responding to audience questions during an oral presentation and creating a decision-making atmosphere. Review the ten tips before giving an oral presentation.

Recently I interviewed several general managers from a large aerospace electronics corporation concerning advice they would give presenters. What better way to improve our speaking skills than to identify the likes and dislikes of one of our most important audiences? I wasn't disappointed.

One piece of advice that kept coming up in the interviews seemingly had little to do with speaking—but a lot to do with communication. It was LISTEN. In fact one GM's response was *"LISTEN, LISTEN, LISTEN!"* Another's went even further, pointing out that speakers should listen with their eyes (observing audience body language, etc.) as well as their ears. This particular GM suggested that speakers "measure their audience constantly to tell—

- Whether they are interested or bored
- Whether you're talking over or beneath the key players.

Then be willing to adapt on the fly, hitting key points, skipping details, asking if your points are making sense."

Listen as You Speak

Most of us have our hands full merely giving a presentation. Being a good listener while giving a talk will be a lot easier if you follow a few of the GMs' simple tips. First, keep your head up, maintaining eye contact rather than staying buried in a script. Better still, throw away the script by learning to extemporize. Put your key points and statistics on a single sheet, in large type, as a life preserver for use only if needed. (Practices, dry runs, and dress rehearsals will make this seem easy.) Secondly, work in a few pauses so the audience will have an opportunity to get a word in edgewise.

Before you start, let the audience know you welcome questions during your presentations. (Top management is unlikely to wait until the end anyway.)

Remember, your objective is to convey thoughts, issues, solutions—whatever, and a monologue may not do the trick. Delivery intermingled with questions and answers is far more likely to achieve your objective. For example, a key member of the audience engaging you in dialog and then reaching concurrence may have more *real* impact on others in the audience than your entire presentation delivered without interaction. (Of course, if that key person does not reach concurrence, or is perceived by the others not to have reached concurrence, you may have a problem. But it's better to know now than to find out later.) Whatever you do, never leave an issue hanging. Restate the situation and strive for concurrence that will be clearly evident to others, but be careful to do so without putting the person in an uncomfortable position.

Having *thoroughly* done your homework is a must for having things go smoothly. If you do run into difficulty and think you might be about to stumble, be willing to lateral to a team member. But do so advisedly. Establish eye contact to make sure your teammate looks like he or she knows the answer. Don't toss anyone the ball if the person's eyes are closed. A prearranged hand signal from a team member will tell you that your teammate is ready and allow you to control the lateral rather than be interrupted. (Particularly bad if the wrong person jumps in trying to be helpful because you waited too long or appeared too desperate.)

Once your team member has answered the question satisfactorily, regain control by expressing thanks and/or asking the questioner if his or her needs were satisfied. Then move on to your next point.

If both you and your team members are stumped, don't guess or speculate. Be willing to say you don't have the information, but you will get it. Then *always* follow up. And follow up with the entire audience, even if the information may only be relevant to one or two individuals. Credibility is your number one asset. Perhaps some easier questions asked earlier will have built up a credibility balance in your account that will carry you over the tough one you couldn't handle.

Even if a question is an easy one, don't cut the questioner off in a rush to show how smart you are. In addition to being rude, you may wind up giving an answer that's correct, but not the answer to the question that would have been asked had you allowed the person to finish. In many presentations you can't accomplish your objective until the audience starts talking. How foolish to cut off that flow with a snap answer.

One GM went so far as to say *never* give a one-way presentation. Find a way to make it two-way. Then there is much less risk of being accused of arrogance, talking down, or patronizing. "Polished speakers," he added, "know when to let it free wheel and when to control the interchange. Finally, they know when to stop talking: when they've convinced the audience and further talking may result in a step backwards."

This last point would seem a function of time as much as anything else. If you can present your ideas in 10 minutes, do so. If the audience wants more, they'll let you know by the questions. By all means avoid going beyond 20 minutes unless it's a training session or the subject matter is complicated. Even then, keep in mind that the purpose of most business presentations is to put forth ideas for consideration and not to provide step-by-step proof. The detailed proof can be provided in a handout or kept in reserve in the form of extra visuals to be used if needed. Having a few extra visuals set aside in case someone says "How do you explain . . ." or "Wait a minute" can have a great effect on an audience.

Don't get upset or lose your cool if you find yourself being challenged, particularly if your proposal involves big bucks. The people holding the purse strings have a right and a duty to probe deeply. As a minimum, you'd better be prepared to answer, "What is your confidence level in . . . ?"

So far this column has concentrated on the dialogue engaged in during a presentation. That's where the GMs I talked to placed the most emphasis and where there was the most agreement. Suggestions on other areas will be found in the accompanying checklist. Certainly these men and women practice what they preach.

Over the years I have watched each of them enter the ranks of management and progress upward. Anyone aspiring to move up the ladder of success would do well to follow their advice.

TEN MORE TIPS FOR SUCCESSFUL TALKS

1. Never be wishy washy about accepting an assignment to speak. Your acceptance should be an indication of the enthusiasm you will bring to the actual presentation. Consider it an opportunity to sell yourself and your ideas.

2. If there are other speakers, find out as much as you can about them and their talks in advance—particularly if they will precede you on the program. If you are in the same organization, sit in on their practice session. If they are outsiders, ask for a draft or at least a hard copy of their visuals. Offer yours in return.

3. KISS! Keep it short and simple. (No more than three main points.) Make it fun. Try to sell weddings instead of funerals.

4. Recipe for a talk . . .
   Add portions of Who, What, Why, Where, When, and How. Blend in the Problem, Approach, Results, Conclusions, and Recommendations. Concentrate on "What Happened?" and "So What?" Tell "What It Is," "What It Does," and "How It Does It." Drain complexities and discard. Sprinkle generously with Benefits. Finish with a Call to Action.

5. Still battling butterflies? If you've really done your homework, that fact should give you confidence. So should the fact that you have something worthwhile (benefits) to say. The practice/dry run/dress rehearsal approach means you've already given the talk at least three times. Get there early to check out *all* the mechanics and greet the audience as it arrives. Take a few deep breaths, pick out somebody who looks friendly, and start talking.

6. Watch out for slang, poor grammar, tasteless jokes (racist, ethnic, sexist, off color), and any appearance or dress factors that will make you appear less polished.

7. Give viewgraph projectors some room. After placing material, step away at least three feet to avoid blocking the image. Using a pointer will give you an opportunity to step away from the projector toward the side of the screen. But be sure to avoid the temptation to gaze lovingly at the screen with your back to the audience.

8. Avoid using the phrase, "As you can plainly see. . . ." while showing visuals that would send even a .300 hitter to the closest Pearle Vision Center. Remember that an illustration prepared for a report or a proposal will probably have too much detail and too small type to make a good visual for a presentation.

9. Use the end of your talk to cover all the bases. 1. Tell them what you told them (summarize). 2. Ask for the order (call to action or close). 3. Thank

them for their time and attention (and perhaps wish them good luck). 4. Ask for questions and then WAIT long enough to give them time to respond. If there are none, consider adding some of your own as a way to cover a few key points one last time.

10. After the presentation, follow up by sending extra information, or at least a thank-you note for their time. If you didn't get an answer to your call for action at the end of your presentation (quite likely), this may help jog them.

Editing for an International Audience

Judith H. Tarutz

Writers must be aware of pitfalls in writing for international audiences. This excerpt from a book about technical editing provides guidelines for preparing documents that will be used by international readers.

If you work for a multinational company or one that sells internationally, chances are the documentation you edit will either be used by foreign nationals or translated into other languages.

If internationalization is important where you work, you may even do a separate editing pass to ensure that the material is suitable for translation or use by a non-American audience.

Editing for an international audience requires a sensitivity to language, cultural, and technical differences.

LANGUAGE CONSIDERATIONS

Here are some ways you can make manuals easier to read and use for nonnative speakers of English:[1]

- Use simple, clear sentences.
- Use more illustrations.
- Provide an expanded glossary.
- Provide constant confirmation. For example, instructions for a call-forwarding service for a telephone could say, "When you press the # button, you hear a short beep. The beep confirms that the call-forwarding feature is activated."
- Use consistent terminology. Don't use more than one name for the same thing without a valid technical reason.

Here are some ways we inadvertently make manuals more difficult to read for our international audience:

- Changing voice within a paragraph.
- Using slang, idioms, colloquialisms: *stripped down version, jumping to conclusions, stop short, on the other hand.*
- Using industry jargon. (Be aware that readers outside the U.S. may be using the English of ten years ago; their technical dictionaries and glossaries—if they have them—may be out of date. For example, the term *unbundling* was being used in the U.S. to refer to a pricing and distribution practice for hardware and software long before the practice and the term became known in Europe and Asia.)

---

[1] These are good guidelines for material destined for domestic audiences, too.

- Using words that have more than one meaning, particularly verb forms with prepositions; for example, *make up* can mean *to compose* or *to reconcile; exhaust* can mean *to tire* or *to use up.*
- Using noun strings. Even if English is your native language, "logical operator precedence" and "DNA fingerprinting study results" are difficult to parse.
- Using nouns as verbs or using words that can be either nouns or verbs, such as *result* and *order.*
- Splitting infinitives, splitting verbs and adverbs. For example: "put down the telephone" is easier to read than "put the telephone down."
- Using abbreviations (even **Y** for *yes*) and acronyms, which are sometimes impossible to translate.

CULTURAL CONSIDERATIONS

Here are some ways we can be more sensitive to cultural differences:

- Avoid showing human figures, if possible, because of race, gender, and other stereotyping.
- Give metric measurements, followed by U.S. equivalents.
- Give the metric equivalent of the size of U.S.-based tools.
- Use culture-neutral examples, with respect to names, dates, numbers, and monetary systems. Tell what format (for dates and numbers) or system (monetary) you're using.
- Recognize that not all speakers of the same language are culturally the same. For example, there are cultural differences among French speakers in Canada, Switzerland, and France, just as there are cultural differences among English speakers in the United States, England, Australia, and the Philippines.
- Remember that humor doesn't travel easily.
- Use generic terms instead of trademarks, such as *photocopy* instead of *Xerox.* (Besides, you should not be using a trademark as a common noun or verb. A trademark is an adjective, as in Xerox copier.)
- As a matter of courtesy more than correctness, you might include non-Anglo-Saxon names in examples.
- Remember that not everybody knows U.S. geography. For example, the reference, "On the east coast" makes sense to a North American but probably doesn't to anyone else. If you need to refer to such a region, use a more definite reference, like, "On the east coast of North America."

TECHNICAL DIFFERENCES

Here are some production technicalities to consider:

- International paper sizes differ from "standard" American sizes, so you may need to adapt the page design to accommodate the different text image area.
- Many manuals in the U.S. are drilled with three holes. Binders in other countries vary in the number of holes.

- English is a concise language; when translated into other languages, text requires on average 30% more space. Ensure that illustrations have space for translated callouts and labels.

Here are some technical details to consider:

- Ordering is often culture-bound. For example, if the text says, "list the days of the week in order," an American would put Sunday first, but some Europeans would put Monday first. If it matters, make sure you spell out which day should be first.
- Americans would read the date 10/9/88 as October 9, 1988; Europeans would read it as September 10, 1988. The Japanese often format dates in year/month/day order. If you're editing a sample program that uses dates, make sure the text specifies the order expected for input or output.
- Time is culture-bound. Many countries use the 24-hour clock to express written times (although when speaking, people often still use the 12-hour clock). If you're using an American-style time, make sure you include AM or PM to avoid confusion.
- Be careful with time zones. Sometimes documentation refers to the time when daylight savings time begins but doesn't mention the specific date. The date can vary from country to country, and some countries don't go on daylight savings time at all. If the specific date is important, make sure you spell it out, rather than just imply it.
- If you give engineers feedback on the user interface, make sure there is enough room to display translated text in help screens, prompts, error messages, and menus. Editing instructions for a small screen—such as a copier—will be quite a challenge!
- When you organize information—such as reference pages—alphabetically, you may be giving the translator more work.
- Be aware that the American *billion* is 10^9; in the British system it is 10^{12}. The names of other high numbers (such as trillion, quadrillion) are likewise different in the two systems. Instead of using these terms, express the value as a power of 10.

Here are some technical details just for computer manuals:

- Make sure references to the ASCII character set are correct. In some cases, references to ASCII are justified; in others, they're holdovers from the days before companies supported larger character sets.
- Think about when you mean *byte* and when you mean *character*. The two terms are often used synonymously, but in an internationalized system, a character can consist of more than one byte. For example, you may be used to saying that a filename can have up to 256 characters, but that isn't correct if you're using a 16-bit character set.
- Watch for case conventions. Ideographic languages such as Japanese and Chinese have only one case—there are no separate uppercase and lowercase versions of characters. In addition, not all characters in alphabetical languages have uppercase and lowercase versions. Keep these differences in

mind if your text includes references to case conversion. The conversion may be impossible to do.

- If your products support European languages, common references such as "Identifiers can include any alphabetical character (A–Z)" may not be correct. Several European languages, Danish for one, have characters that occur *after* Z. Of course, A–Z as an all-inclusive range doesn't even begin to encompass all the possibilities in ideographic languages.

- Check references to sorting order. The text might read, "The utility sorts the names in alphabetical order." But "alphabetical order" differs from language to language—or doesn't exist at all for many Asian languages. For example, the Spanish alphabet begins *a, b, c, ch, d*. The correct wording differs according to what the software you're describing *actually* does. It might sort characters in code-set order, or in language order, or (for ideographic languages) in stroke order, or any number of different ways.

Color: The Newest Tool for Technical Communicators

Jan V. White

Appropriate colors in a technical document can direct readers to specific kinds of information, focus attention on particular elements, and establish consistency. This article excerpt discusses color as an editing device to help readers find useful information.

One of the myths of publishing is that readers are readers. Seldom is that true. Of course, there is a group of publications that are bought for the pleasure of reading (novels, whodunits, literary magazines), but they are a tiny segment of the total number of printed pages produced in a given time. Technical documentation uses much more paper, even if it does get less publicity.

Except for the true literati, readers are nothing of the sort: they are *searchers*. To do their searching, they start out as *viewers* or *lookers*. They flip pages, scan, hunt and peck, searching for the nuggets of information that they need and that might prove valuable to them.

CATCH YOUR READERS' ATTENTION

Overworked, in a hurry, saturated with "information," and perhaps a bit lazy, too, technical readers need to be lured into reading. Perhaps *persuaded* might be a better word than *lured,* because luring implies a little bit of bamboozling, and duplicity has no place in technical documentation. The least trace of cheating or trickery is self-defeating, because it destroys the potential reader's trust in the probity and seriousness of the document.

The only kind of persuasion that is credible must be based on the presentation of the values that are inherent in the message. Exposing those values and making them easily accessible does not destroy their dependability or credibility, for honest values are demonstrable. Making them easily accessible helps to make the document useful and liked. Combining accessibility (that is, making things easy to find) with speed makes the document a useful, dependable tool.

Where do people begin reading? Where do **you** begin? Observe your own reactions when you pick up a piece of printed matter, because you are typical. You probably don't always start at the beginning. In fact, you very seldom start at the beginning.

Like you, most people enter a document at a place where something catches their interest. If there is a picture, the first thing they look at is the image. But a caption, a word, a phrase, a concept, even a title can also catch their eye and fascinate them into paying attention. The trick is to find the valuable highlights that you know will be helpful to your audience, and deliberately display them. That is the way to make documents helpful and therefore irresistible.

Color Can Help or Hinder

Unfortunately, color is a material so beset with silly misunderstandings and imagined magic that it is the editor's worst temptation. It is perhaps even more difficult to exploit color simply and forthrightly than to use type simply and forthrightly. True, you can have a lot of fun with type . . . but you probably know simply from experience how far to go before making a fool of yourself. Everyone is more familiar with type because it has been around for so long as the fundamental black-and-white raw material.

But color is a material that has only lately become widely available. It is such an alluring material, it is so beautiful, so cheerful, so different, such a treat to work with. Look at all those magazines and posters and movies and videos bubbling with visual excitement. What an opportunity to be creative!

Please avoid that trap. Technical documentation is a serious product, and there is no place in it for amusement and evanescent trendiness.

Furthermore, today's audiences (those "readers") are so sated with visual excesses that whatever may be exciting to you and an innovation in the day-to-day techniques at your disposal is not nearly as exciting to them. Color may be new to you, since you have not had an opportunity to use it before, but it is old hat to them. It saturates whatever they look at all around. Therefore, color as plain, simple colorfulness carries little attraction any more.

A third depressing negative: However hard it may try, technical documentation is doomed to look like a poor cousin next to publications in which colorfulness is a functional and integral part of the product. Color is vital in *Vogue, Sports Illustrated,* and *National Geographic.* It is part and parcel of the message there. In some instances, color itself is the substance of the message. What fun it must be to work with material like that.

Alas, it is seldom fun to work with technical documents—unless you make it happen by clever and insightful analysis. You'll need a lot of thought and a lot of self-restraint, because color is such an amusing material to work with. If ever that cliché about "less being more" applied, here is that instance.

How cleverly you handle what you have to work with is the difference between mediocrity and greatness. There are no rules. There are only criteria by which to judge. Every communicator has to stand alone in his or her judgment as to the rightness or wrongness of a technique. Is red better than blue? It depends on what you are trying to do.

Should the background be in color and the foreground in black, or should the background be in black and the foreground picked out in color? It depends on what you are trying to do.

Everything always depends on what you are trying to do. That is what makes communication so exciting and challenging. That is also what makes it perfectly possible for a non-designer to be confident of making the right decisions about the daunting esoteric process of Design.

Color judgment should not be based on subjective, personal "liking." It must be used deliberately, fulfilling specific needs and purposes. It is not an artistic material but a communication material.

Here are some of the fundamental intellectual underpinnings for using color functionally—and appropriately—in the area of technical communication. You could think of them as criteria for judgment. Perhaps you could even use them as a mental checklist. If the way you intend using color fulfills one of these purposes, you are reasonably safe. At least you can rationalize its use. If it fulfills two of them, you can be confident that you are on the right road. If it fulfills three or more, you have nothing to worry about. Go!

Does the Color Focus Attention on an Element That Is Worthy of It?

Color is different from black. (Not a brilliant insight, but you would be amazed how often the most obvious is overlooked.) Since most of the surroundings are usually black and white and are expected by the viewer to be so, anything that departs from the norm is bound to attract attention to itself.

The question you have to ponder is whether that element is worthy of the attraction color gives it. Headings are often done in color. Why? They are already different from the body copy by virtue of their size and blackness. What quality does color add by making them even more different?

Perhaps it might add value, if you can honestly say yes to the next question.

Does the Color Establish Understanding Through Color-keyed Associations?

If some headings are in color because they belong to a subset of some sort (whether in ranking, quality, subject, or any other grouping), then their color is a mark of differentiation. They remain headings, but they become special. Color is a means of making them so.

But this recognition only works if you can say yes to the next question.

Does the Color Establish Identity Through Logical Consistency?

People are keenly aware of differences in color: red apples and yellow apples in a bowl are immediately sorted into Red Delicious and Golden Delicious, and a green Granny Smith obviously stands out as another variety. True, they are all apples, but they are sorted into kinds by color at first glance.

If you make some headlines red, some blue, and others green for no better reason than exuberance and because the colors are technically available, the viewer will not be able to sort them out. The result will be confusing. (Incidentally, black plus three other colors is the maximum that most people can easily remember as distinguishing characteristics for purposes of sorting, unless you provide a color key as a frequently repeated reminder.)

Does Color Rank Value by the Sequence in Which Elements Are Noticed?

Bold type screams and tiny type whispers. Those are qualities everyone understands, so they are used for fast communication by editors, writers, and designers; they rank information and attract attention.

Again, there is nothing startling about this concept. It has an exact parallel in color, where some hues jump off the page and others hide. Alas, however, the concept is a little more complicated than mere brightness ("chroma"). The **effect** of color depends on proportions and relationships to the surroundings. A huge area of very bright color is so loud that it repels, whereas a small spot of the identical hue may be just right. A tiny area of a pale, wan color may not be noticed at all, whereas a large area may be perfect as an identifying background for a box on the page.

It is impossible to generalize or make rules. But the principle is valid. Be aware of the comparative degrees of urgency your colors create, and apply them in such a way that the viewer is guided by them to understand the information in the appropriate sequence.

Does Color Facilitate Comprehension of the Document's Structure?

One of the most depressing characteristics of technical documentation is the apparent length of each volume. User manuals are especially daunting by their weight and the very number of their pages. If their enormousness is broken into segments, they become less terrifying, for even the longest journey starts with but a single step.

Color can be used to subdivide. Let's assume you print the glossary on blue, the index on green, and the introduction on yellow. Three units have been separated from the rest, making the residue appear shorter and more user friendly.

Now take your chapter openers, make them all a full spread and run red ink or toner full bleed all around. Such a strong organizational signal cannot be missed, especially when the document is held in the hand and examined—and the slivers of red are visible on the outer edge. (It is vital to have chapter starts use a full spread, so the color can appear on the edges of both left-hand and right-hand pages. That way it is noticeable in both directions).

Does the Color Imply the Right Connotations?

Colors carry cultural associations. Again, there are no general rules nor are the implications universal or standardized. They are based on common sense and knowing the culture of the demographic segment you are communicating with.

Take the case of bananas: They are yellow, but when flecked with brown they are ripening, yet an all-brown banana is over-ripe and a black one is rotten (especially if it has a few patches of green). A pale-green banana is unripe, and a blue one is frozen. A purple banana is a child's version of bananahood, and a striped banana is surprising (like a purple-and-green-striped zebra). A silver banana is inedible because it is a piece of sculpture, while a polkadotted one is a joke. And a red banana is not a banana at all but a plantain.

So which color do you use? The one that gets the right story across. Don't pick out dollar numbers in red: the company might be interpreted as being in the red. Beware of picking a color just because you like it. The color may skew the meaning in a given context. Green also means Go; amber, Caution; red, Stop.

Does the Color You Want to Use Fit Into the Corporate Idiom?

Your choice of hue may well be limited by the palette determined by the designers who produced the corporate style for the organization. As in most companies, it is very likely that these determinations were made for everything other than technical documentation. They were probably originally intended to create an identity in the marketing and advertising sphere, were then extended to include signage, the marking of vehicles, and then someone remembered, Oh yes! How about all that technical stuff? Oh well, let them figure that out for themselves, because it doesn't really matter.

Ah, but it does matter very much indeed. The way the techdocs look is a vital link in the total impression a company makes on the competitive world. Learn the rules, understand the need for discipline, and realize that the more restricted the variety of materials used, the stronger and more obvious the corporate image becomes. It is senseless to rail against the restrictions. It is far better to accept them and work with them.

Does Color Help to Give Order to Information Chaos?

- Does it explain relationships by the way segments relate to one another?
- Does it analyze data visually so they are obvious to the casual looker?
- Does it draw the looker into becoming interested, involved, and perhaps even into reading?
- Does it help that reader to understand the information?
- Does it enliven the atmosphere of the product, while making the information clearer?
- Does color add intellectual value?

If you can find a way to fulfill those purposes, you will have achieved something of inestimable value. The frustrating thing is that none of this is quantifiable. The first and most obvious reaction of everybody on looking at a page is whether it is pretty or not, irrespective of whether it works. Color is too often mistaken for cosmetics. Avoid that trap.

Use color to make the ideas on the pages clear, no matter whether the color adds deliberate prettiness or not. If you apply color functionally, you will discover to your amazement and delight that it also adds a degree of excellence that is in fact visually satisfying and perhaps even beautiful. However, that happens only if you do not pursue beauty as a goal. If you pursue clarity, you will find that beauty is an inevitable byproduct.

Having found the answer, standardize it. Repeat and repeat and repeat, because patterning creates clues for the viewer, who is taught how to react to the elements you are presenting on the pages. Besides, repetitive patterning also helps create personality for your product, a vital characteristic in the marketplace. So avoid the temptation to add, embroider, or make changes for the fun of it (or because you are afraid the viewers will get bored. They won't, even if you do, because they don't have to live with your product as long as you do.) Don't show off, don't be original for the sake of being original. On the contrary, guard your system carefully against erosion or dilution.

None of this is designing for Art's sake. That is why you need not be afraid of color. All it does is to exploit the capacity of design to help the user. As such, it is an integral part of editing for the reader. That is our profession.

Ethical Reasoning in Technical Communication: A Practical Framework

Mark R. Wicclair and David K. Farkas

Technical writers often confront ethical problems just as lawyers and other professionals do. This article discusses three types of ethical principles—goal-based, duty-based, and rights-based—and then describes and analyzes two cases in which a writer had to face an ethical dilemma. Notice that the third ethical case has no suggested solutions. Consider what you might do in these circumstances.

Professionals in technical communication confront ethical problems at times, just as in law, medicine, engineering, and other fields. In recent years STC has increased its effort to generate a greater awareness and understanding of the ethical dimension of the profession.[1] This article is intended to contribute to that effort.

To clarify the nature of ethical problems, we first distinguish between the ethical perspective and several other perspectives. We then discuss three types of ethical principles. Together these principles make up a conceptual framework that will help illuminate almost any ethical problem. Finally, we demonstrate the application of these principles using hypothetical case studies.

THE NATURE OF ETHICAL PROBLEMS

Typically, when faced with an ethical problem, we ask, "What should I do?" But it is important to recognize that this question can be asked from a number of perspectives. One perspective is an attempt to discover the course of action that will best promote a person's own interests. This is not, however, a question of ethics. Indeed, as most of us have discovered, there is often a conflict between ethical requirements and considerations of self-interest. Who hasn't had the experience of being tempted to do something enjoyable or profitable even while knowing it would be wrong?

A second non-ethical perspective is associated with the law. When someone asks, "What should I do?" he may want to know whether a course of action is required or prohibited by law or is subject to legal sanction. There is often a connection between the perspective of law and the perspective of self-interest, for the desire to discover what the law requires is often motivated by the desire to avoid punishment and other legal sanctions. But between the perspectives of law and ethics there are several significant differences.

First, although many laws correspond to moral rules (laws against murder, rape, and kidnapping, for instance), other laws do not (such as technicalities of corporate law and various provisions of the tax code). Furthermore, almost every legal system has at one time or another included some unjust laws—such as laws in this country that institutionalized racism or laws passed in Nazi Germany. Finally, unethical actions are not necessarily illegal. For example, though it is morally wrong to lie or break a promise, only certain instances of lying (e.g., lying under oath) or promise breaking (e.g., breach of contract) are punishable under law. For all these reasons, then, it is important to recognize that law and ethics represent significantly different perspectives.

One additional perspective should be mentioned: religion. Religious doctrines, like laws, often correspond to moral rules, and for many people religion is an important motive for ethical behavior. But religion is ultimately distinct from ethics. When a Catholic, Protestant, or Jew asks, "What should I do?" he or she may want to know how to act as a good Catholic, Protestant, or Jew. A question of this type is significantly different from the corresponding ethical question: "How do I behave as a good human being?" In answering this latter question, one cannot refer to principles that would be accepted by a member of one faith and rejected by a member of another or a non-believer. Consequently, unlike religiously based rules of conduct, ethical principles cannot be derived from or justified by the doctrines or teachings of a particular religious faith.

THREE TYPES OF ETHICAL PRINCIPLES

To resolve ethical problems, then, we must employ ethical principles. We discuss here three types of ethical principles: goal-based, duty-based, and rights-based. Although these do not provide a simple formula for instantly resolving ethical problems, they do offer a means to reason about ethical problems in a systematic and sophisticated manner.[2]

Goal-Based Principles

Public policies, corporate decisions, and the actions of individuals all produce certain changes in the world. Directly or indirectly they affect the lives of human beings. These effects can be good or bad or a combination of both. According to goal-based principles, the rightness or wrongness of an action is a function of the goodness or badness of its consequences.

Goal-based principles vary according to the particular standard of value that is used to evaluate consequences. But the most widely known goal-based principle is probably the principle of utility. Utilitarians claim that we should assess the rightness of an action according to the degree to which it promotes the general welfare. We should, in other words, select the course of action that produces the greatest amount of aggregate good (the greatest good for the greatest number of people) or the least amount of aggregate harm. Public-policy decisions are often evaluated on the basis of this principle.

Duty-Based Principles

In the case of duty-based principles, the focus shifts from the consequences of our actions to the actions themselves. Some actions are wrong, it is claimed, just for what they are and not because of their bad consequences. Many moral judgments about sexual behavior are in part duty-based. From this perspective, if patronizing a prostitute is wrong, it is not because of harm that might come to the patron, the prostitute, or society, but simply because a moral duty is violated. Likewise, an individual might make a duty-based assertion that it is inherently wrong to lie or break a promise even if no harm would result or even if these actions would produce good consequences.

Rights-Based Principles

A right is an entitlement that creates corresponding obligations. For example, the right to free speech—a right that is valued and protected in our society—entitles people to say what they want when they want to and imposes an obligation on others to let them speak. If what a person says would be likely to offend and upset people, there would be a goal-based reason for not permitting the speech. But from a rights-based perspective, the person is entitled to speak regardless of these negative consequences. In this respect, rights-based principles are like duty-based principles.

While many people believe strongly in the right to free speech, few would argue that this or other rights can never be overridden by considerations of likely consequences. To cite a classic example, the consequence of needless injury and death overrides anyone's right to stand up and cry "Fire!" in a crowded theater. Nevertheless, if there is a right to free speech, it is not permissible to impose restrictions on speech every time there is a goal-based reason for doing so.

APPLYING THESE ETHICAL PRINCIPLES

Together these three types of ethical principles provide technical communicators with a means of identifying and then resolving ethical problems associated with their work. We should begin by asking if a situation has an ethical dimension. To do this, we ask whether the situation involves any relevant goals, duties, or rights. Next, we should make sure that ethical considerations are not being confused with considerations of self-interest, law, or religion. If we choose to allow non-ethical considerations to affect our decisions, we should at least recognize that we are doing so. Finally, we should see what course, or courses, of action the relevant ethical principles point to. Sometimes, all point unequivocally to one course of action. However, in some cases these principles will conflict, some pointing in one direction, others in another. This is termed an "ethical dilemma." When faced with an ethical dilemma, we must assign priorities to the various conflicting ethical considerations—often a difficult and demanding process.

We now present and discuss two hypothetical case studies. In our discussion we refer to several goal-, duty-, and rights-based principles. We believe that the principles we cite are uncontroversial and generally accepted. In saying this, we do not mean to suggest that there are no significant disagreements in ethics. But it is important to recognize that disputes about specific moral issues often do not emanate from disagreements about ethical principles. For example, although there is much controversy about the morality of abortion, the disagreement is not over the acceptability of the ethical principle that all persons have a right to life; the disagreement is over the non-ethical question of whether fetuses are "persons."

We believe, then, that there is a broad consensus about many important ethical principles; and it is such uncontroversial principles that we cite in our discussion of the following two cases.

Case 1

Martin Yost is employed as a staff writer by Montgomery Kitchens, a highly reputable processed foods corporation. He works under Dr. Justin Zarkoff, a brilliant organic chemist who has had a series of major successes as Director of Section A of the New Products Division. Dr. Zarkoff is currently working on a formula for an improved salad dressing. The company is quite interested in this project and has requested that the lab work be completed by the end of the year.

It is time to write Section A's third-quarter progress report. However, for the first time in his career with Montgomery Kitchens, Zarkoff is having difficulty finishing a major project. Unexpectedly, the new dressing has turned out to have an inadequate shelf life.

When Yost receives Zarkoff's notes for the report, he sees that Zarkoff is claiming that the shelf-life problem was not discovered earlier because a group of cultures prepared by Section C was formulated improperly. Section C, Yost realizes, is a good target for Zarkoff, because it has a history of problems and because its most recent director, Dr. Rebecca Ross, is very new with the company and has not yet established any sort of "track record." It is no longer possible to establish whether the cultures were good or bad, but since Zarkoff's opinion will carry a great deal of weight, Dr. Ross and her subordinates will surely be held responsible.

Yost mentions Zarkoff's claim about the cultures to his very close and trustworthy friend Bob Smithson, Senior Chemist in Section A. Smithson tells Yost that he personally examined the cultures when they were brought in from Section C and that he is absolutely certain they were OK. Since he knows that Zarkoff also realizes that the cultures were OK, he strongly suspects that Zarkoff must have made some sort of miscalculation that he is now trying to cover up.

Yost tries to defuse the issue by talking to Zarkoff, suggesting to him that it is unprofessional and unwise to accuse Ross and Section C on the basis of mere speculation. Showing irritation, Zarkoff reminds Yost that his job is simply to write up the notes clearly and effectively. Yost leaves Zarkoff's office wondering whether he should write the report.

Analysis.   If Yost prepares the report, he will not suffer in any way. If he refuses, he will damage his relationship with Zarkoff, perhaps irreparably, and he may lose his job. But these are matters of self-interest rather than ethics. The relevant ethical question is this: "Would it be *morally wrong* to write the report?"

From the perspective of goal-based principles, one would want to know whether the report would give rise to any bad consequences. It is obvious that it would, for Dr. Ross and her subordinates would be wrongly blamed for the foulup. Thus, since there do not appear to be any overriding good consequences, one would conclude that writing the report would contribute to the violation of a goalbased ethical principle that prohibits actions that produce more bad than good.

Turning next to the duty-based perspective, we recognize that there is a duty not to harm people. A goal-based principle might permit writing the report if some good would follow that would outweigh the harm to Dr. Ross and her subordinates. But duty-based principles operate differently: Producing more good than bad wouldn't justify violating the duty not to harm individuals.

This duty would make it wrong to write the report unless some overriding duty could be identified. There may be a duty to obey one's boss, but neither this nor any other duty would be strong enough to override the duty not to harm others. In fact, there is another duty that favors not writing the report: the duty not to knowingly communicate false information.

Finally, there is the rights-based perspective. There appear to be two relevant rights: the right of Dr. Ross and her subordinates not to have their reputations wrongly tarnished and the company's right to know what is actually going on in its labs. Unless there is some overriding right, it would be morally wrong, from a rights-based perspective, to prepare the report.

In this case, then, goal-, duty-, and rights-based principles all support the same conclusion: Yost should not write the report. Since none of the principles furnishes a strong argument for writing the report, Yost is not faced with an ethical dilemma. But he is faced with another type of dilemma: Since refusing to write the report will anger Zarkoff and possibly bring about his own dismissal, Yost has to decide whether to act ethically or to protect his self-interest. If he writes the report, he will have to recognize that he is violating important goal-, duty-, and rights-based ethical principles.

Case 2

Susan Donovan works for Acme Power Equipment preparing manuals that instruct consumers on the safe operation and maintenance of power tools. For the first time in her career, one of her draft manuals has been returned with extensive changes: Numerous complex cautions and safety considerations have been added. The manual now stipulates an extensive list of conditions under which the piece of equipment should not be used and includes elaborate procedures for its use and maintenance. Because the manual is now much longer and more complex, the really important safety information is lost amid the expanded list of cautions. Moreover, after looking at all the overly elaborate procedures in the manual, the average consumer is apt to ignore the manual altogether. If it is prepared in this way, Donovan is convinced, the manual will actually lead to increased numbers of accidents and injuries.

Donovan expresses her concern in a meeting with her boss, Joe Hollingwood, Manager for Technical Information Services. Hollingwood responds that the revisions reflect a new policy initiated by the Legal Department in order to reduce the number of successful accident-related claims against the company. Almost any accident that could occur now would be in direct violation of stipulations and procedures described in the manual. Hollingwood acknowledges that the new style of manual will probably cause some people not to use the manuals at all, but he points out that most people can use the equipment safely without even looking at a manual. He adds that he too is concerned about the safety of consumers, but that the company needs to protect itself against costly lawsuits. Donovan responds that easily readable manuals lead to fewer accidents and, hence, fewer lawsuits. Hollingwood replies that in the expert opinion of the Legal Department the total cost to the company would be less if the manuals provided the extra legal protection they recommend. He then instructs Donovan to use the Legal Department's revisions as a model for all subsequent manuals. Troubled by Hollingwood's response, Donovan wants to know whether it is ethically permissible to follow his instructions.

Analysis.   From the perspective of goal-based principles, writing manuals that will lead to increased injuries is ethically wrong. A possible good consequence is that a reduction in the number of successful lawsuits could result in lower prices. But neither this nor any other evident good consequence can justify injuries that might have been easily prevented.

A similar conclusion is arrived at from a duty-based perspective. Preparing these manuals would violate the important duty to prevent unnecessary and easily avoidable harm. Moreover, there appear to be no overriding duties that would justify violating this duty.

Finally, from a rights-based perspective, it is apparent that important rights such as the right to life and the right to health are at stake. It might also be claimed that people have a right to manuals that are designed to maximize their safety. Thus, ethical principles of each of the three types indicate it would be morally wrong to prepare the manuals according to Hollingwood's instructions.

Because Case 2 involves moral wrongs that are quite a bit more serious than those in Case 1, we now go on to consider an additional question, one not raised in the first case: What course of action should the technical communicator follow?

An obvious first step is to go over Hollingwood's head and speak to higher-level people in the company. This entails some risk, but might enable Donovan to reverse the new policy.

But what if this step fails? Donovan could look for a position with a more ethically responsible company. On the other hand, there is a goal-based reason for not quitting: By staying, Donovan could attempt to prepare manuals that would be safer than those that might be prepared by a less ethically sensitive successor. But very often this argument is merely a rationalization that masks the real motive of self-interest. The company, after all, is still engaging in an unethical practice, and the writer is participating in that activity.

Would leaving the company be a fully adequate step? While this would end the writer's involvement, the company's manuals would still be prepared in an unethical manner. There may indeed be an obligation to take further steps to have the practice stopped. To this end, Donovan might approach the media, or a government agency, or a consumer group. The obvious problem is that successively stronger steps usually entail greater degrees of risk and sacrifice. Taking a complaint outside the organization for which one works can jeopardize a technical communicator's entire career, since many organizations are reluctant to hire "whistle blowers."

Just how much can be reasonably asked of an individual in response to an immoral situation? To this question there is no clear answer, except to say that the greater the moral wrong, the greater the obligation to take strong—and perhaps risky—action against it.

CONCLUSION

The analyses offered here may strike the reader as very demanding. Naturally, we are all very reluctant to refuse assigned work, quit our jobs, or make complaints outside the organizations that employ us. No one wishes to be confronted by circumstances that would call for these kinds of responses, and many people simply would not respond ethically if significant risk and sacrifice were called for. This article provides a means of identifying and analyzing ethical problems, but deciding to make the appropriate ethical response to a situation is still a matter of individual conscience and will. It appears to be a condition of human existence that to live a highly ethical life usually exacts from us a certain price.[3]

Case 3

This case is presented without analysis so that readers can resolve it for themselves using the conceptual framework described in this essay.

A technical writer works for a government agency preparing instructional materials on fighting fires in industrial settings. Technical inaccuracies in these materials could lead to serious injury or death. The technical writer is primarily updating and expanding older, unreliable material that was published 30 years ago. He is trying to incorporate recently published material into the older material, but much of the recent information is highly technical and some of it is contradictory.

The technical writer has developed some familiarity with firefighting through his work, but has no special training in this field or in such related fields as chemistry. He was hired with the understanding that firefighting specialists in the agency as well as paid outside consultants would review drafts of all the materials in order to catch and correct any technical inaccuracies. He has come to realize, however, that neither the agency specialists nor the outside consultants do more than skim the drafts. Moreover, when he calls attention to special problems in the drafts, he receives replies that are hasty and sometimes evasive. In effect, whatever he writes will be printed and distributed to municipal fire departments, safety departments of industrial corporations, and other groups throughout the United States.

Is there an ethical problem here? If so, what is it, what ethical principles are involved, and what kinds of responses are called for?

NOTES

1. Significant activities include the re-establishment of the STC Committee on Ethics, the preparation of the STC "Code for Communicators," the group of articles on ethics published in the third-quarter 1980 issue of *Technical Communication* (as well as several articles published in other places), and the continuing series of cases and reader responses that have appeared in *Intercom*.

2. The arguments justifying ethical principles as well as ethics itself are beyond the scope of this essay but can be examined in Richard B. Brandt, *Ethical Theory: The Problems of Normative and Critical Ethics* (Englewood Cliffs, NJ: Prentice-Hall, 1959) and William K. Frankena, *Ethics*, 2nd ed. (Englewood Cliffs, NJ: Prentice-Hall, 1973). Other informative books are Fred Feldman, *Introductory Ethics* (Englewood Cliffs, NJ: Prentice-Hall, 1978) and Paul W. Taylor, *Principles of Ethics: An Introduction* (Encino, CA: Dickenson Publishing Company, 1975). All of these books are addressed to the general reader.

3. STC might develop mechanisms designed to reduce the price that individual technical communicators have to pay for acting ethically. For their part, individuals may have an obligation to work for the development and implementation of such mechanisms.

Electronic Mail

JoAnne Yates

E-mail, used by millions of people daily, is rapidly replacing many memos and telephone calls. This article discusses the importance of e-mail and includes guidelines for writing effective e-mail messages.

At the beginning of the 1980s, electronic mail was a relatively rare and specialized communication medium, unfamiliar to most people in business and academia. By the early 1990s, electronic mail has become an important mode of communication for many people in firms and in universities. Its use continues to grow rapidly.

WHAT IS E-MAIL?

Electronic mail (or e-mail) refers to computer-based systems for creating, transmitting, and receiving text messages from one person to one or more specified individuals electronically and asynchronously (i.e., the sender and receiver are usually not both connected to the computer at the same time; messages sent at one time are received at some later point in time). System users send and receive messages from personal computers or terminals on a network using appropriate e-mail software (e.g., IBM Profs or America Online). Messages are routed by a network server (a computer, usually larger than others on the network with special software for managing the e-mail system and storing messages) from one electronic mailbox to another within the network where they wait to be picked up by the person assigned that mailbox. Users can often store electronic messages (those sent as well as those received) on the server or on their own computers. With an identification code and password issued by the network server, users can log onto the system and get access to their mailboxes and electronic files of stored-messages from any computer or terminal that is connected to the network.

E-mail systems may connect people within a single site, within a single but geographically dispersed organization, within connected organizations, or anywhere accessible by direct-dial telephones. Systems within a single site may be linked to the network server by a local area network (LAN) or by modem and telephone lines. Systems within a single but geographically dispersed organization have network servers at each site that are, in turn, linked to each other in a larger network.

Larger networks of servers may also connect different organizations with different e-mail systems. The Internet, for example, connects most universities and many firms and individuals. Such interconnected organizational networks provide links among members of all organizations on any of the connected networks. Public e-mail services such as CompuServe, America Online and Prodigy allow access to any subscriber.

588

How Does E-Mail Work?

While different e-mail systems offer different capabilities, the basic functions are fairly standard and tend to be used similarly. A person desiring to send a message first logs into the system using an official system identification code or ID and a secret password. In some systems, the ID is related to the user's real name (e.g., JYATES); in others, it is a system-designated sequence of letters and numbers (e.g., 10017cws or UX1). The sender then selects the option of sending a message and designates the ID(s) of intended recipient(s). If a recipient is on a different but connected network, the sender must provide additional addressing information, including the node name of the other network server (e.g., MIT or ASUCUAD) and sometimes a network designation (e.g., EDU for universities on the Internet). Just as you need a telephone number or address to call or write to someone, you need an e-mail address to send an e-mail message. The system itself generates the sender's ID and the date and gives the sender the option of designating a subject line. It formats this information into a memo-like heading for the message.

The sender then composes the message on the screen of a computer, using the editing and formatting capabilities of the e-mail system itself. Editing capabilities in most systems are less extensive than those in word processing programs and, in some cases, are minimal. Editing tasks such as moving and inserting sections of text may be very difficult or even impossible in some e-mail systems, and few e-mail systems allow boldface or underlining. Most systems allow the sender to compose a message in a word processing program then up-load it (more or less easily) for sending via e-mail. Once the message is complete, the sender can send it to the mailboxes of one or more recipients with the push of a button.

The message remains in the intended recipients electronic mailbox until that person logs onto the system and retrieves incoming mail. When the receiver logs onto the system, the system will usually indicate whether any messages are waiting. If so, the receiver can open the mail; at this point, he or she sees on the screen a list of the new messages with their senders, receivers, dates, and subject lines. The receiver can then open the messages and read them right on the screen or, less commonly, print them out for reading in hard copy (i.e., on paper). For each message, the recipient may typically take one or more of the following actions:

1. Reply to the sender (in which case the system automatically provides the addressing information and repeats the same subject line),

2. Forward it to another person on the network with or without an additional note,

3. Keep it in the mailbox (in which case it will still be listed next time the recipient retrieves mail),

4. Store it in a personal (electronic) file for later retrieval,

5. Discard it.

E-mail as a Communication Medium

The many avid users of e-mail find it a rapid and convenient medium for conducting business and for socializing. Although e-mail messages are written, they share characteristics with telephone calls as well as with correspondence; e-mail has a few advantages, as well as some disadvantages, in comparison with each alternative. While e-mail may be used to displace some telephone or paper-based communication, it is also used for some new types of communication that did not previously exist.

E-mail is often used for quick exchanges of news, information, and schedules that would otherwise occur over the telephone. While it lacks the added richness of vocal inflection and the immediate and interactive qualities of a telephone conversation, e-mail messages are often informal and conversational in style and tone. E-mail avoids, however, the annoyance of telephone tag, which can sometimes drag out for days. Moreover, both parties to an e-mail exchange can deal with the communication at times convenient for them, thus avoiding intrusive interruptions when they are involved with other business. E-mail messages arrive with little or no notice (some systems beep if the recipient is on-line to notify him or her that a message has arrived) and will wait indefinitely. Assuming that both parties check their electronic mail reasonably frequently each day, an exchange can usually be completed within a few hours and with minimum inconvenience.

Some users also argue that less time is wasted on polite chit-chat in this medium than on the telephone. When people visit someone's office or call someone on the telephone with a quick question, they often feel that they can't just blurt the question out as soon as they reach the other person and leave or hang up as soon as they get the answer. Social norms of politeness require some general conversation before or after the message or question itself. While some people see this social conversation as important to relationships and worth the time it consumes, others see it as a waste of time in many cases. Because e-mail does not have settled norms that require socializing, it is often used for brief questions and answers with no surrounding conversation. On the other hand, e-mail can also be the medium for much purely social, rather than task-oriented, communication. Some firms have been dismayed by such e-mail traffic, perceiving it as a waste of time. Researchers have suggested, however, that such communication is an important socializing force in an organization and, therefore, to be welcomed rather than discouraged.

Because e-mail messages are written rather than oral, they also share some characteristics with more traditional genres of written communication in organizations, such as memos, letters, and notes. Most obviously, because an e-mail message is recorded, it is not ephemeral like an (untapped) phone conversation. The fact that e-mail can be stored and retrieved for later use offers the advantages of paper documentation and filing, providing a reliable back-up to human memory. The relative permanence of e-mail messages has its disadvantages, as well. Once it is sent, an e-mail message, like a paper document, has a life of its own. Consequently, in some situations, users may be wary of sending highly confidential messages by e-mail, just as they may be of committing them to paper, for fear that the message might be forwarded to others, saved indefinitely by the system, and even read by system administrators or others gaining unauthorized access to the files.

The advent of rapid and inexpensive photocopying, with the introduction of the first Xerox machine in 1960, led to proliferation of paper copies; similarly, the even greater ease of sending or forwarding many copies of messages in e-mail often encourages proliferation of electronic documents. This proliferation may lead to electronic junk mail (unneeded or unwanted copies of messages or announcements) that clogs the system and wastes users' time. While storage of electronic messages takes up less space than storage of paper documents, even electronic storage has its limits. Of greater concern are the associated problems of information overload for message recipients. Individuals receiving a large amount of excess e-mail may be overwhelmed by it and may spend all their time dealing with it. Alternatively, they may learn to discard or ignore electronic junk mail, although, in doing so, they run the risk of accidentally discarding important messages.

In spite of these similarities between paper-based and electronic correspondence, there are also many differences. While local norms vary, e-mail messages are often informal and conversational in tone, less polished in format and style, and less correct in spelling and grammar than letters or memos. These differences derive, in part, from the fact that e-mail messages are generally created more quickly and with less human mediation than are most paper-based messages in organizations. Letters and memos are often written by one person but produced in final form by a secretary or member of a word-processing pool. Producing documents takes time, which slows the course of written exchanges but gives the originator of a message time to review and revise it. In e-mail, managers and professionals more frequently compose and send messages themselves. Rapid exchanges yield greater speed but often reduce the amount of time people think about their messages and the amount of revision the messages receive. While improvements in editing and formatting capabilities of systems are removing some of the barriers to revision, the future evolution of norms for use is less clear.

Another difference often noted between e-mail messages and traditional memos and letters is more extreme language and more emotional content, sometimes escalating into conflict that has to be resolved through other communication channels (e.g., face to face or over the telephone). Such conflicts probably arise in part from the rapidity and lack of mediation just noted. If a message irritates its receiver, that person may hit the reply key, compose an angry response, and hit the send key, all before having a chance to calm down and consider the implications of the response. Some researchers (Sproull and Kiesler, 1986; Siegal et al., 1986) have argued that this tendency towards extreme and uninhibited language—sometimes known as flaming (e.g., emotional outbursts, obscene language, and name-calling)—is widespread in electronic communication. They have suggested that e-mail and other forms of computer-mediated communication encourage this phenomenon by removing social context cues present in other modes of communication (e.g., the communicator neither sees nor hears the message recipient, and there is no paper letterhead to remind the communicator of the organizational context). Other researchers have argued that this phenomenon is less widespread than initially thought and emerges, in part, from the social norms of the computer-oriented groups that were initially e-mail's primary users. Research continues to explore both the extent of this phenomenon and the causes behind it.

E-mail has not just displaced some written documents and telephone calls; it is also used for certain types of communication that would probably not have occurred at all without the medium. E-mail provides a way to exchange information that would not have been worth a disruptive or lengthy telephone call, a formal written document, or even a walk down a hall. Users have found it particularly valuable in maintaining frequent contact between individuals over great geographical distances, especially when time differences and costs deter the use of telephone. While e-mail does not displace face-to-face communication, it may enrich face-to-face interactions by providing a channel through which minor details can be handled, thereby leaving more substantive issues for direct discussion.

Thus e-mail, like many new communication media before it, is probably more additive than substitutive. E-mail is not likely to replace the telephone or paper-based written correspondence, but it provides an additional channel that can enrich overall communication for individuals and groups.

Message Design

1. Because e-mail is usually read on the screen, not on paper, keep typical screen or window size in mind. For busy readers, get your main point (or your whole message) onto the first screen, as you would try to get the main point of a paper-based document onto the first page. And, don't let total length get excessive. Messages longer than a few screens demand a lot of your reader and should only be used when the content and your relationship with the recipient justifies the demand.

2. Keep lines and paragraphs short enough to allow for easy on-screen reading. Paragraphs should be significantly shorter than screen length (e.g., 8–12 lines) if they are to help the reader see subdivisions in the content. Lines that go to the edge of the screen are difficult to read. If your system does not allow you to set margins, use the line feed or carriage return command to end lines significantly short of the screen's right edge.

3. While e-mail generally does not allow for underlining and boldface, use subheads (designated by capital letters, a line of hyphens below the words, or other local conventions) and lists to format for effectiveness. When inserting pieces of a previous message into your message in order to reply to them, indent or otherwise set off the pieces so that formatting clearly differentiates them from your own message. Formatting helps the recipient read e-mail messages as well as paper documents.

4. Use capital letters only for emphasis. Sometimes individuals new to e-mail or unaccustomed to typing enter entire messages in capital letters. Such messages are hard to read and are often perceived as "shouting" at the reader.

5. Provide an appropriate subject line for most messages. Many systems list all received messages with sender, receiver, and subject line. A recipient who receives a lot of e-mail may decide whether or when to read a message based on the subject line. Moreover, the subject line (of your own stored messages as well as messages you receive and store) is an important aid in retrieving messages. Replying to a received message is easier than initiating a new one; however, it usually retains the subject line of the original message. As a result, the same subject line gets used again and again, losing any value as a scanning or retrieval device. Thus, you should initiate a new message when the subject changes significantly.

E-mail Style

1. While norms for formality and correctness vary, make sure that carelessness in matters such as typing and grammar do not interfere with your meaning. Reread your message to make sure it is clear and appropriate.

2. While e-mail messages are, on average, less formal than paper-based business documents, adjust your formality and tone to suit your purpose and

audience. Use your style to indicate to your reader how formal and serious you intend the message to be.

3. Be careful that your humor does not come across as sarcasm. Even with the sideways smiley face icon ":-)" or stage directions "she said with a chuckle" common in some systems, humor can be misread and resented. Choose your words, as well as symbols, with your audience in mind.

4. When you are angered or annoyed by a message, don't reply immediately. Give yourself time to consider the appropriateness of your response. You may regret a hasty and "flaming" response.

E-mail Etiquette

1. Avoid indiscriminate copying and forwarding of messages. Such behavior contributes to electronic junkmail. In replying to a message, you may insert the relevant pieces of that message, indented, into the message before your response, to avoid having to paraphrase the sender's question or comment. Avoid, however, just appending the entire previous message, especially if it is long.

2. If tensions have escalated in an e-mail exchange, switch to another medium (usually telephone or face to face) to address the issue and reduce tensions.

3. Never alter, then forward, another person's message without clearly labelling the alterations as your own. While some systems allow you to do this, it misrepresents the originator of the message.

4. Provide clear identification of yourself and the recipient, especially when communicating with individuals on different e-mail networks. In local systems which provide recognizable names (not just ambiguous or unintelligible IDs) for sender and receiver, further salutations and sign-offs such as "Hi, Bill—" and "Cheers, Mary" are not necessary and may not be customary, especially with those you know and exchange messages with frequently. When sending a message outside your local system, however, or within a system that does not provide adequate identifying information, you should generally use such devices to guarantee that the recipient knows who the message is from. Your ID may be recognizable to local users but not to remote recipients, and some receiving systems strip all information except the sender's official ID out of headers.

REFERENCES

Siegel, J., Dubrovsky, V., Kiesler, S., and McGuire, T. W. (1986). Group processes in computer-mediated communication. *Organizational Behavior and Human Decision Processes, 37*, 157–186.

Sproull, L. & Kiesler, S. (1986, November). Reducing social context cues: Electronic mail in Organizational Communication. *Management Science, 32*, 1492–1512.

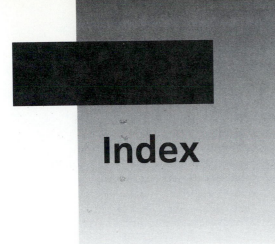

Index

CREDITS *(continued from copyright page)*

Pages 336–340. Based on information in *Comprehensive and Workable Plan for the Abatement of Lead-Based Paint in Privately Owned Housing.* Report to Congress, U.S. Dept. of Housing and Urban Development, December 7, 1990.

Pages 347–352. Revised and adapted from Novacheck, M. J. "Standby Power Improvement at Water Treatment Plant." Reprinted with permission of the author.

Pages 395–396. Letter reprinted with permission of The Construction Specifications Institute, 601 Madison Street, Alexandria, VA 22314.

Pages 448–450. Bagin, C. B. and Van Doren, J., "How to Avoid Costly Proofreading Errors," from *Simply Stated* 65 (April 1986). Reprinted with permission of Document Design Center, American Institutes for Research.

Pages 451–461. Benson, P. J., "Writing Visually: Design Considerations in Technical Publications," from *Technical Communication* 32(4) (1985). Reprinted with permission of Society for Technical Communication.

Pages 462–465. From Beswick, R. W. "Voicemail," in *Communication and Technology: Today and Tomorrow.* Ed. Al Williams. Denton, TX: Assoc. for Business Communication, 1994. Reprinted with permission of the author.

Pages 466–469. Adapted from " 'Big Emerging Markets' Have Diverse Cultures, but Common Attributes," *Business America* 115 (10) (October 1994). U.S. Dept. of Commerce, Washington, D.C.

Pages 471–473. Boe, E., "The Art of the Interview," *Microwaves and RF* 24 (December 1985). Reprinted with permission of Penton Publishing Co., Inc.

Pages 474–479. From Bowman, J. P. "Electronic Conferencing" in *Communication and Technology: Today and Tomorrow.* Ed. Al Williams. Denton, TX. Assoc. for Business Communication, 1994. Reprinted with permission of the author.

Pages 480–485. Bowman, J. P. and Okuda, T., "Japanese-American Communication: Mysteries, Enigmas, and Possibilities," *The Bulletin of the Association for Business Communication* 48 (December 1985). Reprinted with permission of the authors.

Pages 486–495. Buehler, M. F., "Defining Terms in Technical Editing: The Levels of Edit as a Model," *Technical Communication* 28(4) (1981). Reprinted with permission of the Society for Technical Communication.

Pages 496–508. Calabrese, R., "Designing and Delivering Presentations and Workshops," *The Bulletin of the Association for Business Communication* 52 (June 1989). Reprinted with permission of the author.

Pages 509–514. Holcombe, M. W. and Stein, J. K., "How to Deliver Dynamic Presentations: Use of Visuals for Impact," *Business Marketing* 71 (June 1986). Reprinted with permission from *Business Marketing.* Copyright Crain Communications Inc.

Pages 515–519. Hulbert, J. E. "Barriers to Effective Listening," *The Bulletin of the Association for Business Communication,* 52 (2) (June 1989). Reprinted with permission of the author.

Pages 520–521. From Humphries, A. C. "Business Manners for the '90s," *Business & Economic Review* 36(3) (April–June 1990). Reprinted with permission of *Business & Economic Review,* published by the University of South Carolina College of Business Administration, Division of Research.

Pages 522–524. Adapted from Kirtz, M. K. and Reep, D. C., "A Survey of the Frequency, Types and Importance of Writing Tasks in Four Career Areas," *The Bulletin of the Association for Business Communication* 53(4) (December 1996). Reprinted with permission of the authors.

Pages 525–530. Marra, J. L., "For Writers: Understanding the Art of Layout," *Technical Communication* 28 (3) (1981). Reprinted with permission of the Society for Technical Communication.

Pages 531–533. Martel, M., "Combating Speech Anxiety." Reprinted with permission from the July 1981 issue of *Public Relations Journal.* Copyright 1981 by the Public Relations Society of America.

Pages 534–535. From Mascolini, M. and Supnick, R. "Preparing Students for the Behavioral Job Interview," *Journal of Business and Technical Communication* 7(4) (October 1993), pp. 482–488. © 1993 by Sage Publications, Inc. Reprinted by permission of Sage Publications.

Pages 536–542. Plunka, G. A., "The Editor's Nightmare: Formatting Lists Within the Text," *Technical Communication* 35 (February 1988). Reprinted with permission of the Society for Technical Communication.

Pages 543–544. From Porter, J. "Ideology and Collaboration in the Classroom and in the Corporation." *The Bulletin of the Association for Business Communication* LIII(2) (June 1990). Reprinted with permission of the author.

Pages 545–549. "The Practical Writer," *The Royal Bank Letter* 62 (January/February 1981). Reprinted with permission of The Royal Bank of Canada.

Pages 550–555. Ridgway, L., "The Writer as Market Researcher," *Technical Communication* 32(1) (1985). Reprinted with permission of the Society for Technical Communication.

Pages 556–561. From Sherblom, J. C. "Teleconferencing," in *Communication and Technology: Today and Tomorrow.* Ed. Al Williams. Denton, TX: Assoc. for Business Communication, 1994. Reprinted with permission of the author.

Pages 562–567. "Six Graphics Guidelines," *Simply Stated* 30 (October 1982). Reprinted with permission of the Document Design Center, American Institutes for Research.

Pages 568–571. Smith, T. C. "Listen Up—Tips from the Top on Talks," *Technical Communication,* 38(4) (November 1991). Reprinted with permission from *Technical Communication,* published by the Society for Technical Communication, Arlington, VA.

Pages 572–575. Judith H. Tarutz, *Technical Editing: The Practical Guide for Editors and Writers* (pp. 120–123), © 1992 by Hewlett-Packard Company. Reprinted by permission of Addison-Wesley Publishing Company, Inc.

Pages 576–580. From White, J. V. "Color: The Newest Tool for Technical Communicators," *Technical Communication* 38(3) (August 1991). Reprinted with permission of the Society for Technical Communication, Arlington, VA.

Pages 581–587. Wicclair, M. R. and Farkas, D. K., "Ethical Reasoning in Technical Communication: A Practical Framework," *Technical Communication* 31(2) (1984). Reprinted with permission of the Society for Technical Communication.

Pages 588–593. Adapted from Yates, J. "Electronic Mail" in *Communication and Technology: Today and Tomorrow.* Ed. Al Williams. Denton, TX: Assoc. for Business Communication, 1994. Reprinted with permission of the author.